International Trade and Investment

Seventh Edition

Franklin R. Root

The Wharton School
University of Pennsylvania

COLLEGE DIVISION South-Western Publishing Co.

Cincinnati Ohio

Sponsoring Editor: James M. Keefe
Developmental Editor: Alice C. Denny
Production Editor: Shelley Brewer
Production House: WordCrafters Editorial Services, Inc.
Cover Designer: Lotus Witkopf
HV61GA
Copyright ©1994
by South-Western Publishing Co.
Cincinnati, Ohio

1 2 3 4 5 6 7 8 9 D 2 1 0 9 8 7 6 5 4 3
Printed in the United States of America

Library of Congress Cataloging-in-Publication Data

Root, Franklin R.
    International trade and investment / Franklin R. Root. -- 7th ed.
        p.   cm.
    Includes bibliographical references and index.
    ISBN 0-538-82286--4
    1. International trade.   2. International finance.
3. International economic relations.   4. International business
enterprises.   I. Title.
HF1411.R6345   1993
382--dc20   93-20445
                                                             CIP

IP

International Thompson Publishing

South-Western Publishing Co. is an ITP Company. The ITP trademark is used under license.

 This book is printed on acid-free paper that meets Environmental Protection Agency standards for recycled paper.

PREFACE

International Trade and Investment offers the reader an integrated treatment of theory, policy, and enterprise in international trade and investment. A knowledge and understanding of these interdependent subjects is vital for all those who plan to enter an international business career or work for governments and international organizations in activities that relate to international economic relations. Apart from career interest, persons who want to improve their understanding of the world in which they live are seriously handicapped without an awareness, if not comprehension, of the economic dynamics and policy issues of trade and investment flows among nations.

Theory refers to the body of knowledge that seeks to explain the causal factors that determine the size, composition, and direction of international economic transactions. A grasp of theory enables us to analyze events occurring in the world economy and to evaluate the wisdom of national policies.

Policy encompasses the role of governments in their efforts to regulate, restrict, promote, or otherwise influence the conduct of international trade and investment. A study of national policies brings us to an intersection of international economics and international politics, an amalgam traditionally designated as political economy. This book carries the description and analysis of national policies to a greater depth than is customary in a basic text, with emphasis on contemporary problems and issues.

Enterprise designates the multinational enterprise, which undertakes production in many countries in pursuit of a global business strategy transcending national jurisdictions. Study of the multinational enterprise brings us face to face with the business firms that are responsible for much of the trade and most of the direct foreign investment in the world economy today.

International economists have traditionally maintained a *macroscopic* perspective on international economic relations by considering trade and investment only at the national level. This macroscopic approach is necessary but no longer sufficient to explain the behavior of the world economy. Possessing vast resources, multinational companies enjoy a market power that makes them independent actors in the international economic system, forcing changes in national economies and provoking policy responses by governments. Hence, to understand the contemporary world economy we must combine the traditional, macroscopic perspective with a *microscopic* perspective of the multinational enterprise. This text offers a systematic presentation of the multinational enterprise as the dominant institution in international trade and investment.

This edition of *International Trade and Investment* is a major revision of the previous edition. I have revised every chapter and have almost completely rewritten some to account for recent developments in theory and policy. Chapter 21,

"Eastern Europe and China in the World Economy: The Transition from Centrally Planned to Market Economies," is entirely new.

I have tried in a period of rapid, often drastic, change to make this edition as up to date as possible without neglecting those conditions and forces that will shape our world a long time into the future.

In closing, let me express my thanks to readers and reviewers who cared enough about this text to make suggestions to improve it. In particular, I would like to thank the following colleagues for their observations and suggestions concerning the current edition:

Barbara J. Craig, Oberlin College

Norman J. Gharrity, Ohio Wesleyan University

Jannett Highfill, Bradley University

David D. Jaques, California State Polytechnic University-Pomona

David Kreutzer, James Madison University

Thomas Love, North Central College

Wendell H. McCulloch, Jr., California State University-Long Beach

William G. Moller, Jr., University of Michigan

Steve Steib, University of Tulsa

Howard Stein, Roosevelt University

Alexander Zamperion, Bentley College

George K. Zestos, Ball State University

Richard A. Zuber, University of North Carolina-Charlotte

I have worked hard to achieve a balance among theory, policy, and enterprise that I hope will please most of them without unduly annoying the rest.

Franklin R. Root
The Wharton School
University of Pennsylvania

CONTENTS

Chapter 1   The International Economy and the National Interest 1

The International Political System, 2. The International Economic System, 5. The Multinational Enterprise System, 6. Distinctive Features of International Trade and Investment, 7. The National Interest in International Trade, 11. The Goals and Instruments of Foreign Economic Policy, 18. Some Empirical Dimensions of International Trade, 27. What Lies Ahead, 32.

PART I   INTERNATIONAL TRADE

Chapter 2   Comparative Advantage and the Gains from Trade 38

Production Possibilities of National Economies, 39. Identical Production Possibilities with Dissimilar Tastes, 49. Offer Curves: The Determination of the Terms of Trade, 51.

Chapter 3   Comparative Advantage and Factor Endowments: The Heckscher-Ohlin Model 56

Dissimilar Factor Endowments and Trade: An Arithmetical Example, 56. Derivation of a Country's Production Possibilities Curve from Its Factor Endowments, 58. Heterogeneity and Change in Factor Endowments, 65. The Leontief Paradox, 73. Human-Skills Theory of Trade, 77.

Chapter 4   Comparative Advantage: Transfer Costs, Imperfect Competition, and Intra-Industry Trade 82

Transportation and Other Transfer Costs, 82. Imperfect Competition: Monopoly Profits, Increasing Returns, Product Differentiation, and Risk, 87. Overlapping Market Segments and Intra-Industry Trade, 100. Concluding Note on Imperfect Competition and International Trade, 106.

Chapter 5   Comparative Advantage: Technology, Factor Mobility, and Multinational Enterprise 110

Technology Theories of Trade, 110. Factor Mobility and Trade Theory, 123. Multinational Enterprise and Trade Theory, 128. Concluding Observations on Comparative Advantage, 129.

Chapter 6   Tariffs and Nontariff Trade Barriers 134

Economic Effects of Tariffs, 134. Nontariff Trade Barriers: Quantitative Restrictions, 147. Other Nontariff Trade Barriers, 151. Empirical Studies of the Costs of Protection, 157.

Chapter 7   Free Trade and Arguments for Protection 162

The Case for Free Trade, 162. The Case for Protection, 165. Fallacious Arguments for Protection, 166. Questionable Arguments for Protection, 169. Qualified Arguments for Protection, 174. Sophisticated Arguments for Protection, 178. Persistence of Protection, 184.

Chapter 8   Multilateral Trade Agreements Under GATT 187

The General Agreement on Tariffs and Trade (GATT), 188. The Tokyo Round of Multilateral Trade Negotiations (MTNs), 195. The Erosion of GATT, 199. The Uruguay Round of New Multilateral Trade Negotiations (MTNs), 203.

Chapter 9   U.S. Trade Policy in an Era of Global Competition 213

The Evolution of U.S. Trade Policy, 215. The Decline of U.S. Competitiveness in World Markets, 223. The New Protectionism, 236. Protection Through Trade Remedies, 237. Trade Disputes, 240. Whither U.S. Trade Policy?, 247.

Chapter 10   The Theory and Policy of Economic Integration: The European Community and NAFTA 252

The Theory of Economic Integration, 253. The European Community: The Creation of a Customs Union, 260. The European Community: Toward an Economic Union, 264. External Economic Relations of the Community, 274. The North American Free Trade Agreement, 277. A Closing Note, 281.

PART II   INTERNATIONAL PAYMENTS

Chapter 11   The Mechanism of International Payments and Foreign Exchange Markets 288

The Mechanism of International Payments, 288. The Foreign Exchange Market, 294. A Global Foreign Exchange Market: Exchange Arbitrage, 298. International Financial Centers, 299.

Chapter 12   Foreign Exchange Rates and Their Determination 305

The Rate of Exchange, 305. Freely Fluctuating Exchange Rates, 308. Stable Exchange Rates, 313. Controlled Exchange Rates, 317. Exchange Speculation and Capital Flight, 319. Some Additional Remarks on the Determination of Exchange Rates, 321.

Chapter 13   Forward Exchange Speculation and Hedging Against Exchange Risks 324

The Forward Rate of Exchange, 324. Interest Parity Theory, 325. The Modern Theory of Forward Exchange, 330. Forecasting Exchange Rates, 335. Hedging Against Foreign Exchange Risks, 339.

Chapter 14   The Balance of International Payments 350

The Compilation of the Balance of Payments, 351. Constructing the Balance of Payments, 353. Entering Transactions in the Balance of Payments, 355. Balance of Payments Analysis: Equilibrium and Disequilibrium, 359. The Need for Balance of Payments Adjustment, 364.

Chapter 15   International Payments Adjustment in a Fixed-Rate System 368

Determinants of the Current and Capital Accounts, 368. National Income, Foreign Trade, and Domestic Absorption, 369. Adjustment with No International Capital Mobility, 378. Adjustment with International Capital Mobility, 394. Balance of Payments Policy: Internal and External Balance, 397. The Monetary Approach to the Balance of Payments, 398. General Equilibrium in an Open Economy, 401.

Chapter 16   International Payments Adjustment in a Variable-Rate System 408

Variable Rates: Introduction, 409. Elasticities Approach to Exchange Rate Adjustment, 413. Absorption Approach to Exchange Rate Adjustment, 421. Monetary Approach to Exchange Rate Adjustment, 427. General Equilibrium in an Open Economy with Flexible Exchange Rates, 432.

Chapter 17   Nonmarket Suppression of External Payments Disequilibrium: Exchange Control 437

The Origins of Exchange Control, 437. The Objectives of Exchange Control, 439. Single-Rate Systems of Exchange Control, 442. Multiple-Rate Systems of Exchange Control, 446. The Effects of Exchange Control, 448. A Synoptic View of Contemporary Exchange Control Practices, 451.

Chapter 18   The Bretton Woods International Monetary System and its Collapse (1945–1971) 456

The International Monetary Fund (IMF), 456. The Central Reserve Role of the U.S. Dollar, 461. The U.S. Balance of Payments Deficit, 462. Monetary Crises in the Late 1960s, 470. The International Monetary Crisis of 1971, 471. The Smithsonian Agreement, 471. Weaknesses of the Bretton Woods System, 474.

Chapter 19   The Contemporary International Monetary System, The U.S. Balance of Payments, and Global Capital Markets 483

Foreign Exchange Arrangements, 483. Exchange Rate Behavior, 485. The Persistent Deficit in the U.S. Current Account, 490. Central Bank Intervention in Foreign Exchange Markets, 493. The Continuing Role of the International Monetary Fund, 497. Emergence of a Global Capital Market, 502. Performance of the Contemporary System, 506.

PART III INTERNATIONAL DEVELOPMENT

Chapter 20 The Developing Countries in the World Economy 514

The Economic Situation of the Developing Countries, 514. Capital Formation, Economic Growth, and Constraints on Domestic Investment, 523. Trade Policies of the Developing Countries, 528. External Financing and Debt of the Developing Countries, 539. Toward a Market-Friendly Approach to Economic Development, 547.

Chapter 21 Eastern Europe and China in the World Economy: The Transition from Centrally Planned to Market Economies 554

The Failure of the Centrally Planned Economies, 555. Transition from a Planned to a Market Economy: What Needs to Be Done?, 558. Economic Reform in Eastern Europe and China, 560. Some Closing Observations on the Role of Eastern Europe and China in the World Economy, 567.

PART IV INTERNATIONAL INVESTMENT/MULTINATIONAL ENTERPRISE

Chapter 22 The Nature and Scope of Multinational Enterprise 574

Some Definitions of the Multinational Enterprise, 575. The Multinational Enterprise System, 577. Transfers of Product, 580. Transfers of Capital, 583. Transfers of Technology, 587. Transfers of Entrepreneurial Skills, 590. The Contribution of the Multinational Enterprise to the World Economy, 592. Some Empirical Data on Multinational Firms, 594.

Chapter 23 Theories of Foreign Direct Investment and the Multinational Enterprise 600

Statistical Overview of Foreign Direct Investment, 600. Requirements for a Theory of Foreign Direct Investment, 607. The Theory of International Portfolio Investment, 608. The Monopolistic Advantage Theory of Foreign Direct Investment, 610. The Internalization Theory of Foreign Direct Investment, 618. The Eclectic Paradigm of Foreign Direct Investment, 620. The Choice Among Export, Licensing, and Foreign Direct Investment, 621. Toward a Synthesis of International Trade and Investment Theories, 623.

Chapter 24 Public Policy Toward the Multinational Enterprise 627

The Economic Benefits and Costs of Foreign Direct Investment to Host Countries, 628. The Challenge of the Multinational Enterprise to the National Sovereignty of Host Countries, 640. Policies and Actions of Host Governments to Minimize the Political Costs of Foreign Direct Investment, 644. Investment Incentives and Performance Requirements of Host Countries, 646. Toward an Accommodation Between Nation-States and the Multinational Enterprise, 647. U.S. Policy Toward Foreign Direct Investment and the Multinational Enterprise, 652. Closing Observations on U.S. Policy Toward the Multinational Enterprise, 663.

Glossary of Abbreviations and Acronyms 669   **Index 670**

chapter 1

THE INTERNATIONAL ECONOMY AND THE NATIONAL INTEREST

No nation inhabits an economic vacuum. Its industries, its commerce, its technology, its standard of living, and all the other facets of its economy are related to the economies of foreign nations by complex flows of goods, capital, technology, and enterprise. Every nation must come to terms with this interdependence, and every nation can enlarge the benefits and lessen the costs of interdependence through rational policies. But to do so, nations—individually and collectively—must base their policies on the objective analysis of international economic relations. It is the social function of international economists to develop the concepts and theories that make objective analysis possible.

From a broader perspective, every nation inhabits a global political and social environment as well as a global economic environment.[1] At the immediate, sensational level of perception, the international environment appears as a bewildering sequence of seemingly random events: A coup d'état occurs in country A, prices rise in country B, the government of country C devalues its exchange rate, the government of country D expropriates a foreign-owned company, and so on. When each event is perceived as a unique, isolated phenomenon unrelated to other phenomena, then it is impossible to understand *why* the event has occurred. To comprehend the international environment, therefore, we must simplify by classifying individual events into groups or categories of events and by tracing out the relationships among these aggregates. In other words, we must construct one or more abstract models that represent the international environment by identifying key variables and their functional relations. We are then able to interpret an event in the context of our model. If the model is a good approximation of the fundamental conditions and forces actually at work in the world, then we can also predict the consequences of an event with a reasonable degree of confidence. What we have

---

[1]Ecologists dramatically remind us that every nation also inhabits a global physical environment.

done is to build a model that enables us to comprehend a reality that defies comprehension in the raw.

In our exploration of international economic relations, we shall make use of many concepts (such as the nation-state, gross national product, the balance of payments, and multinational enterprise) that bring together diverse phenomena and order them in ways that facilitate analysis. We shall also employ theories that seek to explain *why* the international economy behaves as it does, or how it *should* behave to maximize certain values. However, before proceeding with our study of the international economy, some preliminary remarks are in order about the *international political system.*

THE INTERNATIONAL POLITICAL SYSTEM

The human race is organized in a society of nation-states. The elemental constituents of a nation-state are a people, a territory, an economy, and a sovereign government. The necessary constituent of statehood is *national sovereignty.*

National Sovereignty

International law recognizes the national government as having exclusive jurisdiction over the territory of the state and as being the only legal representative of the state vis-à-vis other states. The state is not subordinate to any legal authority, and it has the right to abrogate any agreements with other states or with their citizens. Furthermore, national states have a legal monopoly on physical force both at home and abroad. Since states control the entire land surface of the earth, every individual and organization is a legal resident of a particular state and is subject to its authority.[2] Among its other consequences, the principle of national sovereignty raises many problems for international economic relations and for multinational enterprises that operate on the territory of more than one nation.

Although *legally* a state can do as it pleases, its actual conduct in international affairs is constrained by the power of other states. For a very weak state, national sovereignty may become a legal fiction even within its own territory.

External Relations of States

Each state seeks to have relations with other states that will sustain or promote its own national interests as they are conceived by government leaders. Foremost among these interests is the continuing survival of the state itself; economic growth and development are also prominent interests of contemporary states.

To carry out its foreign policies a state must be able to influence the behavior of other states. In this sense, *power* is the essence of international political relations. The elements of state power include the armed forces, economy, population,

---

[2]This system of sovereign territorial states was formally established by the Peace Treaty of Westphalia in 1648. At first limited to Europe, it has since spread to encompass the globe. See Joseph Frankel, *International Relations* (New York: Oxford University Press, 1964), p. 7.

geography, government, morale, ideology, and other intangible factors. Because of the latter, precise measures of national power are illusory. Moreover, national power is a *relationship* between two or more states that depends, in part, on how each state perceives its own power compared with the power of others. History affords us many examples of misjudgments by states of their relative power positions.[3]

To say that international political relations are essentially power relations is not to say that they always involve conflict. National governments understand that the achievement of many, if not all, of their foreign policy goals depends on *cooperation* with other governments. States are willing, therefore, to take actions that benefit other states if those governments reciprocate in some measure. Cooperative arrangements among states are highly developed in economic and functional areas, such as trade, finance, communications, and transportation.

Antagonistic relations express a clash of interests between two or more states. When these interests are considered vital, they may limit or destroy cooperative arrangements. Before the "cold war" ended in the late 1980s, for instance, trade between the United States and the Soviet Union was restricted to very low levels.

Many international relations are *competitive* rather than cooperative or antagonistic. States exhibit various forms of rivalry that fall short of direct opposition to each other. They compete in economic performance, technological innovation, ideology, cultural achievements, and so on.

To conclude, the external relations of states are essentially power relations that are expressed in changing mixes of cooperation, competition, and antagonism. When account is taken of the existence of some 185 heterogeneous sovereign states, the pattern of international political relations becomes intricate indeed.

Nationalism

In the contemporary world, states are also nations. While the state is a political entity, the nation is an ethnic or social entity. When these two entities combine they form a *nation-state*.

The citizens of a nation experience a common identity stemming from a shared community, history, language, religion, race, or ideology. *Nationalism* is the emotional cement that binds a people together to make a nationality; it is marked by loyalty and devotion to a nation that exalt it above all other nations. At least since the French Revolution in the late eighteenth century, nationalism has been the driving force in the creation of new states. Born in Europe, nationalism was the primary force in the transformation of European colonies into independent states following World War II; it has now spread to all the world.

In the twentieth century it became a widely accepted principle that each national community merits its own government and political independence. Self-determination, however, has its practical limits. In recent years, several very small

---

[3]A recent example of such a misjudgment was the attempt by Iraq in 1990 to take over Kuwait by military force.

states have entered the United Nations, although their political and economic viability is highly questionable. At a time when sizable European states have begun a process of integration to overcome the liabilities of "smallness," the emergence of so many ministates in the past half century is a gross anomaly. The basic principle of self-determination also threatens the stability of older states that contain two or more ethnic groups, as witnessed by the separatist movements in Canada, Belgium, and Spain.[4] Ironically, many new states in Africa that owe their birth to the principle of national self-determination may eventually founder on divisive tribal loyalties that take precedence over national loyalties. The tragic civil war in Nigeria in the 1960s and the recent collapse of Somalia have emphasized the formidable obstacles to nation building in a multiethnic state.

However, for the most part the states of the world command the loyalties of their peoples and may be accurately depicted as nation-states, namely, a form of political organization whereby a relatively homogeneous people inhabits a sovereign state. Because the citizens of a modern state share a common national society and culture, national boundaries carry a sociocultural significance as well as a political one.

Nationalism injects an emotional energy into international relations, bedeviling cross-national communication and inciting governments to behavior that can undermine the achievement of their own political and economic goals. Encompassing a personal identification with, and a loyalty to, a particular state, nationalism often expresses negative attitudes toward other states. But nationalism is also a cultural phenomenon. Even before the emergence of nation-states, ethnic and tribal groups held attitudes toward other groups ranging from xenophobia (a hatred and fear of all foreigners) to, at times, cosmopolitanism (a sophisticated, open view of foreigners). Today, nationalistic attitudes toward economic relations with foreigners animate many government policies that restrict international trade and investment. When, for example, a business enterprise starts operations in a foreign country, its reception by the government and people will depend in substantial measure on the blend of nationalism that predominates there.

International Organizations

Cooperation among nation-states has led to the creation of many international organizations to serve both political and economic purposes. Although these organizations seldom have any explicit supranational powers, they may gain an institutional strength over time that enables them to influence the behavior of individual states to a significant degree. Hence, they may assume an autonomous international role that makes them "actors" in the international political and economic systems along with the nation-states. For example, the policies of the International Monetary Fund (IMF) and the International Bank for Reconstruction and Development (IBRD) are more than a simple consensus of the national

---

[4]In the case of Yugoslavia, self-determination has spawned a tragic war among ethnic groups. Another example of ethnic self-determination is the disintegration of the Soviet Union into separate nation-states.

policies of their member states. Even more impressive in this regard is the European Community.

Summing up, the international political system comprises some 185 sovereign nation-states and their mutual power relations, which may be characterized as cooperative, competitive, or antagonistic. Nationalism, which generally carries an antiforeign bias, adds an emotional tone to the foreign policies of nation-states, making them less cooperative than would otherwise be the case. On the other hand, some international organizations have emerged as autonomous (or quasi-autonomous) actors in the international political system along with the nation-states.

THE INTERNATIONAL ECONOMIC SYSTEM

Every nation-state has an economy, and the mutual relations among national economies constitute the *international economic system*. Just as the distinguishing feature of the political relations among states is power, the distinguishing feature of their economic relations is *market transactions*. With the rather modest exception of unilateral transfers ("gifts"), international economic relations result from the exchange of goods, services, and financial assets having market value. The sum of a nation's economic transactions with the rest of the world over a period of time is recorded in its balance of payments. Transactions give rise to flows of merchandise, services, money, capital, technology, and enterprise, thereby creating patterns of interdependence among national economies. Shifts in the size and direction of these flows that are initiated in one national economy will affect, directly or indirectly, the behavior of other national economies. The economic theory that explains *why* these flows occur and *how* national economies as a whole interact with the world economy is one of the three themes that animate this book.

Contemporary nation-states, however, are not willing to allow their international economic relations to be determined *only* by market forces. All national governments have foreign economic policies that are intended to regulate, restrict, promote, or otherwise influence international trade and investment. The description and evaluation of these policies comprise the second theme of this book.

The relative importance of noneconomic or political factors in the determination of foreign economic policies varies from one nation-state to another. However, we can loosely classify countries into two groups in that regard. International transactions of the *industrial countries* (mainly those in North America, Western Europe, and Japan) and of the *developing countries* (mainly nations in Africa, Asia, and Latin America) are predominantly undertaken by *private firms,* most notably in the form of multinational enterprises. Because the motivation behind these transactions is economic gain, the trade and investment flows among these countries are mainly explicable in economic terms. Nonetheless, government policies in these countries both constrain and stimulate international economic transactions so as to bring about a divergence from the pattern of interdependence that would result purely from market forces.

The second group comprises China and the countries of Eastern Europe and the former Soviet Union that until the 1990s were *centrally planned* (communist) economies in which all transactions were undertaken by state enterprises whose decisions were guided by a national planning authority rather than by market forces. Hence, the international economic relations of the communist countries were tightly controlled by state agencies. Now these countries are engaged in a historic transition to market economies. If this transition is successful, then all the world's countries will participate in a global economy by the end of the century.

It is fruitless to speculate in the abstract on whether international economic relations determine international political relations (as the Marxists contend) or whether international political relations determine international economic relations. International economic and political relations are interdependent; both the international economic system and the international political system are best regarded as subsystems of the same nation-state system. In some circumstances, political forces may dominate economic forces, while in other circumstances just the opposite occurs. One thing, however, is certain: Whenever a government considers the behavior of some or all of its country's international economic transactions as vital to national interests, the government will try to make that behavior conform to those interests.

THE MULTINATIONAL ENTERPRISE SYSTEM

International economists have traditionally taken a *macroscopic perspective* on international economic relations. By considering trade and investment only at the national level, they have implicitly regarded national economies as the *agents* of international transactions. Although we shall rely on the macroscopic (or national) perspective in Parts I, II, and III, we must recognize that this perspective is necessary but no longer sufficient to explain the behavior of the international economy. Multinational enterprises have become responsible for a sizable (and increasing) share of world trade and for most international investment. As big, oligopolistic companies, multinational enterprises possess a market power that makes them independent actors in the international economic system. Unlike firms in purely competitive markets, multinational enterprises enjoy managerial discretion in their decisions; they do not simply respond to market conditions and public policies in a predetermined way. Indeed, their actions force changes in national economies and compel governments to respond to them. Thus, to understand the contemporary international economy we must supplement a macroscopic perspective with a *microscopic* perspective that considers the role of the multinational enterprise. This is the third theme of this book, which is taken up in Part IV. Here we make only a few additional comments on this subject.

A firm becomes a multinational enterprise when it extends its production and organization into foreign countries.[5] The *multinational enterprise system,* therefore,

---

[5]For a fuller definition, see Chapter 22.

consists of a parent company; its producing and marketing affiliates in foreign countries; and the flows of products, services, capital, technology, management, and funds among them. These *intraenterprise transfers* (flows) cross national boundaries and therefore enter the balance of payments of nations in the same way as international transactions between independent buyers and sellers.

Although it has roots in the past, the multinational enterprise has become a dominant institution only since the late 1950s, when the political and economic systems of the industrial West began to favor the spread of international production by corporations in search of market opportunity and lower costs. As a consequence, the traditional *international* economy of traders has now given way to a *world* economy of international producers. Our comprehension of this world economy is modest indeed. Part IV will be an exploration of new terrain in international economic relations.

DISTINCTIVE FEATURES OF INTERNATIONAL TRADE AND INVESTMENT

The distinctive features of international trade and investment are traceable to the environment in which they occur—the nation-state system and its political, sociocultural, and economic subsystems. In particular, national sovereignty is the ultimate source of most of the differences that distinguish international trade and investment from their domestic counterparts. Since we have already indicated some of the implications of these environmental systems for international trade and investment, this section is partly a recapitulation of our earlier discussion.

Different Languages and Customs

Most nations have a distinctive linguistic and cultural identity in addition to a basic political identity. This is not always true; we can all call to mind nations that have more than one official language and more than one cultural group in their populations. Moreover, several nations may share a common language and a common cultural heritage. Nevertheless, it is true that people tend to be like each other in more ways when they belong to the same nation than when they belong to different nations. Hence, international trade and investment, unlike most interregional trade and investment within nations, involve persons of different languages, customs, attitudes, values, and other cultural traits. Although such differences do not affect the basic economic similarity between interregional and international trade and investment, they do complicate relations between governments and introduce many new elements into the conduct of international business enterprise. As noted earlier, nationalism intensifies the sociocultural differences among the world's peoples.

Separate National Economic Policies

National economic policies may be compatible with the free flow of goods, services, and enterprise between nations, or they may be responsible for the regulation and suppression of that flow. As we shall discover, national economic policies that are apparently wholly domestic in nature may have profound effects on international trade and investment. To maintain an equilibrium in its international payments without resort to controls, a nation must keep its economy adjusted to the world economy. This means, for example, that it must pursue fiscal and monetary policies that keep its prices and costs competitive with those of other nations. It also means that there is sometimes a conflict between the aims of domestic policy and international adjustment. Because of political pressures, this conflict is often resolved in favor of the former, while international maladjustment is frozen by the imposition of controls over foreign trade and payments.

When certain nations adopt domestic policies that are detrimental to their external stability, all trading nations suffer the consequences. For the international economy to function in an atmosphere of freedom, there must be agreement among nations as to the criteria of sound domestic and international economic policies. It too often happens, however, that nations follow policies that are conceived in purely domestic terms, and the resulting welter of policies causes international maladjustments that are met by a rash of restrictive measures.[6] Unlike domestic trade and investment, therefore, international trade and investment are often subject to the influence of many separate national economic policies that are in disharmony with each other.

One consequence of separate national policies is jurisdictional overlap. For instance, a multinational enterprise may be taxed on the same income by two governments (double taxation). More generally, the enterprise may be subjected to the conflicting demands of both home and host governments in any number of policy areas.

National Monetary Systems

Unlike their domestic counterparts, international trade and investment take place between economies that have different monetary systems. This gives rise to the need to exchange one currency for another. The purchase and sale of foreign currency are conducted in the foreign exchange market, and the exchange ratio between currencies is known as the *exchange rate*. Dealings in foreign exchange often appear mysterious to the average person, and perhaps more than anything else, except nationalism, they have convinced the average person that international trade and investment are entirely distinct from the familiar domestic trade and investment. Even domestic producers have been daunted by the prospect of dealings in foreign exchange until relieved by the calm advice and aid of bankers.

Actually, the presence of different monetary systems need not make the character of international trade and investment different from that of their domestic counterparts. When exchange rates are stable and currencies are freely convert-

---

[6]A current example (discussed in Chapter 9) is the enormous U.S. trade deficit that has spawned growing demands for U.S. import protection.

ible into each other, international payments are made just as easily as are domestic payments. In these circumstances the national monetary systems comprise one international monetary system, and for all practical purposes they are one and the same. Before World War I such an international monetary system did in fact exist. National currencies were linked to gold and were freely transferable into each other; an international payment differed from a domestic payment only in that it involved residents of different countries.

Today the situation is far different, and international trade and investment are sharply set off from domestic trade and investment by *variable* exchange rates and by *exchange restrictions* that render a currency inconvertible into other currencies. Although the currencies of the industrial countries (mainly in North America, Western Europe, and Japan) are freely convertible at variable rates, the currencies of many nonindustrial countries and former communist countries are inconvertible in one degree or another. Currency inconvertibility can have profound effects on the conduct of international trade and investment. An importer may not be able to buy merchandise from a given country because of the impossibility of buying the necessary foreign exchange from his or her government. The importer may be compelled, therefore, to import inferior or higher priced goods from a country to which he or she is permitted to make payments. When currencies are freely convertible but only at variable rates (as today), foreign traders and investors may suffer exchange losses unless they can hedge against them. We should remember, however, that the exercise of national sovereignty to restrict international payments or follow policies that cause volatile exchange rates is a more significant feature of international trade and investment than the mere presence of national monetary systems.

Government Regulation
of International Trade and Investment

Governments have interfered with international trade and investment ever since the beginnings of the nation-state system some five hundred years ago. Even during the last half of the nineteenth century, when the majority of governments followed a policy of laissez-faire with respect to domestic economic activities, the use of tariff protection was commonplace. Great Britain and the Netherlands were the only important trading nations that rid themselves of protective tariffs and adopted free trade in that period of liberal economic policies. Since World War I, all nations, without exception, have regulated their foreign trade and investment and have done so with many new control devices.

As noted previously, many contemporary governments restrict the convertibility of their currencies. This is known as *exchange control.* It allows a comprehensive regulation of the international movement not only of merchandise but of services and capital as well. Commodity trade is also regulated through quotas, licenses, tariffs, bilateral trading arrangements, commodity agreements, and other techniques. Restrictions are generally applied against imports, while exports may be stimulated by subsidies, exchange depreciation, bilateral agreements, and other methods. Mention should also be made of the fact that government regulation involves a great deal of red tape and bureaucratic delay, which are often potent deterrents to trade and to the entry of foreign firms.

The International Mobility of Factors of Production

In the nineteenth century, classical economists distinguished international trade from domestic trade by the criterion of factor mobility. It was assumed that the factors of production — capital, management, and labor — moved freely within a country but did not move between countries. For this reason international trade obeyed laws of economic behavior that differed from those of domestic trade.

As the nineteenth century progressed, these twin assumptions of perfect factor *mobility* within countries and perfect factor *immobility* between countries came more and more into conflict with the facts of economic life. Neoclassical economists observed that factors of production often did not move freely from one place to another inside the same country and, on the other hand, that a substantial migration of capital was proceeding from Europe to the other continents. Economists came to agree, therefore, that a sharp distinction between domestic interregional trade and international trade could not be drawn in terms of factor mobility. Rather, *both* kinds of trade were based on factor immobilities; that is, trade was a substitute for investment and other factor movements.

In the absence of political restrictions on the international movement of capital, enterprise, and persons, it is likely that factor mobility between countries would still be somewhat less than factor mobility within countries. International differences in customs and languages, distance, and the like would work in this direction. Under these circumstances no one would argue that factor movements between countries were essentially different from factor movements within countries. In actuality, as we all know, they *are* different, for nations throughout the world restrict immigration (and sometimes emigration) as well as the movement of capital and enterprise. Thus, the exercise of national sovereignty has greatly limited the international mobility of productive factors, and in so doing it has altered the scope and character of international trade and investment. At the same time, the multinational enterprise has remarkably *accelerated* the flow of factor services among countries since World War II.

To conclude, although the international mobility of factors tends to be less (and in the case of ordinary labor, much less) than their domestic mobility, the degree of factor mobility does not provide a *fundamental* distinction between domestic and international trade. It follows that international economic theory must encompass both trade flows and factor flows (mainly via the multinational enterprise) if it is to explain the behavior of the contemporary world economy.

THE NATIONAL INTEREST
IN INTERNATIONAL TRADE

What is the national interest in international trade? This question has colored many debates through the ages, and it will undoubtedly continue to do so in the future. In this introductory chapter we offer some preliminary remarks on the gains from trade at the levels of the nation, consumer, international business enterprise, and domestic import-competing enterprise.[7] We shall leave to Part IV a consideration of the national interest as it relates to international investment and to the multinational enterprise.

The National Gains from International Trade

Although conceivably a nation might have a sufficient variety of productive factors to produce every kind of good and service, it would not be able to produce each good and service with equal facility. The United States *could* produce handwoven rugs, but only at a high cost, since the production of such rugs requires great quantities of labor, which is expensive in this country. The production of handwoven rugs, however, would afford reasonable employment for the large supply of cheap labor in a country like India. It would be advantageous for the United States, therefore, to specialize in a commodity such as computers, whose production makes use of the abundant supply of technology in this country, and to export computers in exchange for handwoven rugs from India.

This example illustrates in a very simple way the gains that result from international specialization — each nation is able to utilize its productive factors in their most productive combinations. By raising the productivity of national economies, international specialization increases the output of goods and services. This is its economic justification and the principal justification of the international trade that makes possible such specialization.

The contribution of international trade is so immense that few countries could become self-sufficient even with the greatest effort. Contemporary economies have been shaped by the international trade and specialization of the past, and their continued viability is closely dependent on the world economy. For example, it is physically impossible for the United Kingdom or Japan to feed, clothe, and house their present populations at their current levels without imports from other countries. Economic self-sufficiency for these two nations would mean poverty standards of living unless emigration proved possible on a very large scale. The survival of these countries depends essentially on the export of manufactures that require little space to produce in exchange for foodstuffs and raw materials that require great space to produce or are found in only certain areas of the earth.

The United Kingdom and Japan are examples of high dependence on international trade. But even countries that are able to supply their own peoples with the

---

[7]The discussion of the basis and benefits of international trade in the following subsections is introductory to the detailed analysis of Chapters 2 through 7.

basic necessities of life out of domestic production would be faced with an unbearable decline in living standards if they were cut off from international trade.[8] New Zealand produces far more foodstuffs than are needed to nourish its sparse population, and it is able to trade this surplus for manufactures with industrial countries such as the United Kingdom and Japan. Hence, for New Zealand, economic self-sufficiency would not mean starvation but rather the deprivation of manufactured goods that are necessary to sustain its current standard of living. Of course, New Zealand could produce some manufactures to take the place of imports, but its efforts in that direction would be limited by its scarce supplies of labor, capital, and industrial raw materials. The New Zealand economy is itself the product of international specialization and trade, and a far different and poorer economy would have evolved in the absence of world markets.

The United States, with its continental sweep and immense resources, could afford economic self-sufficiency with the least cost of any nation, with the possible exception of Russia. Perhaps this explains why Americans, more than people of other countries, are inclined to underestimate the importance of international trade.

But even for this country, the cost of self-sufficiency would be formidable. American consumers would experience an immediate pinch in their standards of living. An entire range of foodstuffs would no longer be available or would be available only at exorbitant prices. That American institution, the cup of coffee, would become a luxury to all but a few, and most of us would be forced to do without our daily stimulant or to use inferior substitutes. Even then, the sugar for our beverage would be an expensive item.

Of basic foodstuffs, we would, of course, have a plentiful supply. In fact, we would become embarrassed by growing stockpiles of agricultural products as farmers lost export outlets for over one-half of their wheat crop, two-fifths of their cotton crop, and large fractions of many other crops. Eventually many farmers would be ruined, and the agricultural sector of our economy would become less important.

Manufacturing industries would also face many difficulties. Without imports, many raw materials would no longer be available and inferior substitutes would replace them. Domestic supplies of other raw materials would no longer be supplemented by imports, and their prices would rise to increase costs of production all along the line. The loss of export markets would also cause severe dislocations in many manufacturing industries. But the most dramatic and profound consequence of economic self-sufficiency in the United States would be a drastic decline in the availability of energy in the form of petroleum. Now dependent on imports for over one third of its petroleum supply, a self-sufficient United States would become a country that could no longer sustain its contemporary energy-intensive economy and consumer lifestyle.

---

[8]Much of the decline in living standards during a war is due to the cessation of international trade, as illustrated by the experience of neutral countries such as Sweden and Switzerland during World War II.

Thus, the outcome of economic self-sufficiency for the United States would be a fall in the American standard of living. Only those producers in direct competition with imports would benefit from self-sufficiency, but the improvement in their fortunes would be purchased at the cost of a general deterioration in the economic well-being of most Americans. Because of the rising dependence on imports of critical raw materials (particularly petroleum) and manufactures, the importance for the United States of foreign trade will grow in the future. More than at any time in the past, our economic prosperity in the years ahead rests upon an expanding world economy.

Domestic Specialization and Interregional Trade

The gains from specialization that are possible through international trade are fundamentally of the same nature as the gains from specialization achieved by interregional trade within a country. The distinctive features of international trade originate, for the most part, in the political fact of national sovereignty — not in economic conditions. Basically, trade within a country is identical with trade between countries. Both derive from the fact that individual regions and countries can gain through trade by specializing in the production of those goods and services that utilize the most productive combinations of their natural resources, labor, capital, management, and technology.

Over half of the foreign trade of Western European countries is with each other. If these countries should one day federate and become one nation, this trade would become interregional rather than international, but its virtues would be neither greater nor less by reason of that change alone.[9] International trade and interregional trade are substitutes for each other. Thus, the explanation of the *relatively* small foreign trade of the United States is found in the vast interregional trade within its borders.

We readily comprehend the great advantages of regional specialization within the domestic economy. Nationalism may blind us to the benefits of international trade, but it does not stand in the way of our appreciation of domestic trade. It is true that local producers and merchants may seek to turn consumers away from products "imported" from other domestic regions, but these efforts are largely wasted since localities and regions do not have the authority to impose restrictions on interregional trade.[10] Moreover, almost all of us consider the national economy to be a single economy rather than an agglomeration of regional economies, and we oppose any interference with trade in the domestic market.

---

[9]Undoubtedly trade among European countries would expand greatly if these nations merged into one political unit, since the restraints now imposed on this trade by individual governments would disappear. But this would not make interregional trade any "better" than international trade. See Chapter 10.

[10]Interstate trade barriers are forbidden by the United States Constitution. Despite this fact, individual states do restrain interstate trade in certain products (mostly agricultural) through a variety of devices ostensibly employed for other purposes, such as pest control and public safety. Arrangements between domestic producers to restrain interstate trade are forbidden by the antitrust laws.

To conclude, recognition of the basic similarity of interregional and international trade is essential to a proper understanding of the latter. That recognition will keep us from reaching the erroneous conclusion that, because of the many characteristics that distinguish international trade, it is a unique sort of trade and must be treated differently from domestic trade. Widespread awareness that the gains from international trade rest upon the same economic conditions as do the gains from domestic trade would eradicate much of the confusion and downright falsity that envelop public discussions of matters pertaining to our trade with other nations.

The Interest of Consumers

As consumers, all of us have an interest in international trade, although we are usually unaware of the influence of international trade on the prices, quality, and availability of goods. Goods are imported only because they are less expensive than domestic goods or are differentiated from them in one way or another. U.S. imports of watches from Hong Kong and cameras from Japan are examples of the first type of imports, while imports of perfumes from France, beer from Holland, and high-performance automobiles from West Germany are examples of the second type of imports. Without such imports the American consumer would pay a higher price for watches and cameras and would not have the opportunity to enjoy Chanel perfumes, Heineken beer, and Mercedes-Benz automobiles.

Imports of raw materials and other industrial goods likewise benefit the consumer by lowering domestic costs of production and in some instances enabling the production of goods that depend exclusively on foreign sources of supply. The consumer also has an interest in domestic exports, since they provide the means to pay for imports. Hence, as consumers, we all benefit from the greater abundance and variety of goods and the lower prices that international trade makes possible.

The contribution of international trade to the welfare of domestic consumers is the most basic of all. The end of economic activity is consumption; production is only a means to that end. A policy of production for the sake of production or of employment for the sake of employment ignores the fundamental reason for economic activity. Hence, economists have usually identified the national economic interest with the economic well-being of a nation's people. It follows that a sustainable policy or economic activity that adds to the supply of goods and services that people wish to consume is a policy or activity in the national interest. Conversely, a policy or economic activity that brings about a level of national consumption that is persistently below the level attainable by an alternative policy or activity is not in the national interest. This criterion of national interest may be modified to take into account illegal production, consumption harmful to health, the need to refrain from current domestic consumption to promote economic growth, and the like, but it differs from other criteria of national interest in its emphasis on consumer welfare. Of course, when a nation is at war, the aim of national survival takes precedence over consumer welfare or any other objective.

When we employ the criterion of consumer welfare to decide whether international trade is in the national interest, we find that permanently increasing the supply of goods and services available for domestic consumption benefits the nation. Moreover, all trading nations gain from international trade. This gain rests squarely on the specialization that arises from the opportunity to buy and sell in foreign markets.

The Interest of International Business Enterprises

The value of international trade to the manufacturers, extractive producers, intermediaries, transportation agencies, financial institutions, and other enterprises that engage in international trade is easily understood. Simply stated, international trade is a source of income and profits.

Domestic producers gain from international trade in many ways. They depend upon imports to meet their need for raw materials and productive equipment at a lower cost than if the same items were acquired from domestic sources of supply. Exports afford domestic producers a profit on sales, and they often make possible a larger scale of production with lower unit costs. Imports and exports, moreover, tend to moderate fluctuations in the supply, demand, and prices of individual goods. Sudden shifts in the availability of domestic raw materials may be offset by opposing shifts in raw material imports, and producers with substantial sales abroad are less sensitive to purely domestic economic conditions compared to producers in the same industries who dispose of their entire output at home.

A domestic concern may further find in export markets a means of additional growth that enables it to compete more effectively in the home market. Often the knowledge and experience gained from selling in foreign markets can be used to improve the efficiency and success of domestic marketing operations. In short, international trade allows domestic producers to escape the confines of the domestic market through imports that lower costs of production or improve the quality of the product and through exports that enhance sales and profits. For the multinational enterprise, international trade offers opportunities to link multicountry production bases with markets throughout the world.

International trade cannot be carried on by producers alone. Many specialized intermediaries and agencies are needed to conduct and facilitate its operations. This is particularly true of merchandise trade: The merchandise must be bought and sold; transportation services must be provided by railroads, ships, trucks, airplanes, and other agencies; international shipments must be insured, financed, and paid for; customs and other government requirements must be met; exports must be stimulated through advertising and other promotion devices; and so on. Specialized intermediaries and agencies are also needed in the field of international investment, in the tourist trade, and in other nonmerchandise transactions of an international character. All of the many business concerns involved in carrying out these functions have a direct stake in international trade. When international trade is booming, they experience expansion and profits. Conversely, when international trade enters a slump, these concerns are the first to suffer losses.

The Interest of Import-Competing Enterprises

The contribution of international trade to the many business enterprises involved cannot automatically be identified with the national interest, since other groups are also part of the national economy. Domestic producers who face close competition from imports may be injured by an expansion of international trade. Moreover, the labor used by such producers may suffer from unemployment or lower wages as a consequence of import competition. The adverse effects of import competition are particularly noticeable when import-competing industries are concentrated in specific localities. In measuring the national gain from international trade, therefore, the losses experienced by these groups must be set against the benefits received by other groups.

It must not be supposed, however, that the losses experienced by domestic producers and others hurt by import competition are permanent. In an expanding economy, labor, capital, and management are able to shift out of stagnant lines of production into more productive lines. Indeed, one of the virtues of a competitive economy lies in its flexibility in adjusting production to meet new technologies, new demands, and new competition—domestic or foreign.

Some Arguments Against International Trade

Despite the economic gain for the nation, many arguments have been voiced against international trade, including these:

1. A nation dependent on foreign sources of supply is in a particularly vulnerable position during a war.
2. International trade is a source of instability.
3. International trade creates losses for those domestic industries whose products are displaced by imports.

International specialization brings to a nation a higher standard of living, but it also implies dependence on foreign markets as sources of supply and as outlets for domestic production. Some persons contemplate this dependence with marked distaste and argue that the national interest demands that it be lessened to one degree or another. The aversion toward international specialization is rationalized in many ways, and it often camouflages the interests of private groups that stand to gain from the removal of import competition. The most important ally of attacks against international specialization and trade is nationalism—the ideology that holds the nation-state to be the *only* source of political and economic security.

National Defense It is argued that a nation dependent on foreign sources of supply is in a particularly vulnerable position during a war. The harrowing experience of the United Kingdom in both world wars is cited as proof of this assertion: Twice the German submarine blockade almost brought the country to its knees by cutting off imports of food and raw materials. This is, of course, a political or military argument rather than an economic one, but it has many economic implications. Its proper evaluation requires not only a careful forecast of the probable nature of a future war but a searching study of the relationships between economic strength and military capacity as well. For example, if another world war promises destruction of everyone's productive facilities within a few hours, then it is the existing military strength that counts, and the military argument for economic self-sufficiency falls by the wayside.

In conclusion, there is no assurance that greater economic self-sufficiency will enhance a nation's military power, and by the same token there is no justification to deny out of hand the compatibility of international specialization and a nation's ability to defend itself against armed aggression.

Instability International trade is also condemned as a source of economic instability. This attitude gained prominence in the 1930s when depression spread from one country to another by disrupting the international flow of goods, services, and capital. In particular, foreign observers were wont to protest the folly of close dependence on such a volatile economy as that of the United States. In our own day this argument against international trade has been reinforced by government policies directed toward high employment and economic development. This is not the place to evaluate the bearing of international trade and investment on domestic stability, employment, and economic development, but it may be pointed out that most nations are unable to achieve the objectives of high employment and economic development except as members of a world trading system.

Protectionism Traditionally, the attacks against foreign trade have been leveled against imports. Several arguments in addition to those already mentioned have been used to justify the protection of domestic industry against foreign competition. These arguments are described and analyzed in Chapter 7, and we shall say nothing about them here except to indicate that insofar as protectionism lowers a nation's imports, it also eventually lowers a nation's exports (unless the protectionist country loans or gives away its exports), since other nations must finance their imports through exports.

The roll call of arguments against international specialization and trade is indeed a formidable one — national security, economic stability, full employment, economic development, protectionism, and others of lesser note. All of these arguments pack a powerful emotional appeal to the person on the street. Nevertheless, international trade exhibits vitality and growth difficult to reconcile with its alleged disadvantages. It would appear that the economic advantages of international specialization and trade, when weighed against the economic costs of national self-sufficiency, cannot be denied by nationalistic fervor or the special pleading of private vested interests.

THE GOALS AND INSTRUMENTS
OF FOREIGN ECONOMIC POLICY

We have observed that pervasive government regulation is a distinctive feature of international trade and investment. The *ways* in which governments try to shape their external economic relations constitute the instruments of foreign economic policy. Here we offer some observations on the nature of foreign economic policy, its possible goals, and the instruments that may be used to achieve those goals.

The rationale of government economic policies throughout the world is that national economies, if left alone, would fail to achieve goals that are deemed to be in the national interest, such as full employment, a "satisfactory" rate of growth, price stability, an equitable distribution of income, and a "strong" balance of payments. Basically, therefore, national economic policies may be viewed as a rejection in whole or in part of the social virtues of an atomistic, laissez-faire economy, in which levels of economic activity and resource allocation are determined by impersonal market forces with only a minimal government presence.

Although governments have sought to influence the internal and external behavior of national economies since the birth of the nation-state in the sixteenth century, the goals and instruments of their policies have frequently shifted over time. Up to the middle of the nineteenth century, the major countries for the most part followed mercantilistic policies that sought to advance power-political interests through a variety of controls on international trade and factor movements. The subsequent period, which ended with World War I, was marked by the ascendancy of a belief in the blessings of free, unfettered markets. Governments relied on monetary policy to smooth the operation of the international gold standard and generally relaxed or abandoned restrictions on external trade, while at home they accepted with equanimity the ups and downs of the business cycle. The global depression of the 1930s ended this laissez-faire posture, as governments everywhere undertook a variety of policy measures to stimulate economic recovery at home and to insulate the domestic economy from external influences. In the 1930s economic nationalism ran rampant, international cooperation almost disappeared, and international trade was throttled by tariffs, quotas, exchange controls, and other devices. In our own day, national governments are committed to a broad range of economic goals that they try to achieve in a world of growing economic interdependence.

Because there is no clear-cut distinction between a government's foreign and domestic policies, we may conceive foreign economic policy either broadly or narrowly, depending on our purposes. Broadly conceived, foreign economic policy embraces all of the varied activities of national governments that bear, directly or indirectly, upon the composition, direction, magnitude, and growth of international trade and factor flows. This conception of foreign economic policy covers not only such obvious examples as tariff policy but also domestic governmental measures, such as monetary and fiscal policy, that have an impact upon foreign trade and investment. Since economic activity is characterized by mutual interdependence, there are few, if any, economic policies of government that have only domestic effects.

Because of the signal importance of the American economy in the world, the economic policies of the U.S. government, whether ostensibly domestic or foreign, are of particular significance to the well-being of the world economy. Probably the greatest single contribution that the U.S. government can make toward the promotion and development of world trade and investment is the pursuit of policies at home that ensure the stable, noninflationary growth of the American economy. In this sense the fiscal and monetary policies of the government are more basic to U.S. foreign economic policy than, for example, its much touted actions in the field of tariff negotiation. Just as policies undertaken to achieve domestic goals (such as high employment) will have repercussions on a country's external economic relations, so will policies undertaken with respect to foreign trade, foreign aid, foreign investment, and the balance of payments have repercussions on the level, composition, and growth of national output and income; on employment; on prices; and on other aspects of the domestic economy.

In terms of *effects*, therefore, it is impossible to classify government policies as exclusively domestic or exclusively foreign. Instead, they may be regarded as occupying different positions along a continuum that stretches between an "internal effects" pole and an "external effects" pole. Policies that have only insignificant effects on foreign trade and investment (such as government subsidies for housing) are close to the "internal effects" pole, while policies that have insignificant domestic effects (such as lowering a revenue duty on an imported good with no domestic substitute) are close to the "external effects" pole. Most government policies, however, fall between these two poles, and growing international interdependence is pushing more and more policies toward the center.

The interdependence of domestic and foreign economic policy (however defined) is a fact that must be kept in mind throughout our study of international trade and investment. Unfortunately for the peace of mind of those people who like to have everything in watertight compartments, the political boundary of a nation cannot serve to demarcate domestic and foreign interests. For reasons of space and analytical convenience, in this text we are compelled to limit foreign economic policy to the activities of government that are *intended* to regulate, restrict, promote, or otherwise influence the conduct of international trade and investment. While employing this narrower definition in our subsequent description and analysis of foreign economic policy, we do not propose to neglect its close relationship to domestic economic policy.

Foreign Economic Policy and Private Interests

The foreign economic policy of governments is pervasive; it affects all of us in a number of ways — as consumers, as producers, and as citizens of a nation that itself is a member of the community of nations. Restrictive government policy forces us as consumers to pay a higher price for many imported goods and, at times, to do without them. On the other hand, liberal government policy enables us to reap the advantages of international specialization. As domestic producers we may be benefited or hurt by specific aspects of foreign economic policy, depending upon our place in the economy. As international traders and producers we may be thwarted in our efforts to sell and produce in foreign countries by policies that keep us out or limit our opportunities. As international lenders or borrowers we may be encouraged or constrained by government policies at home or abroad. Finally, the foreign economic policy of our government may earn us the goodwill and support of other nations, or it may provoke mistrust and retaliation.

Although we cannot escape the impact of the foreign economic policy of our government and others upon our lives and fortunes, we are usually ignorant of its source. The bearing of this policy on our interests as consumers is ordinarily indirect and can be traced only by careful economic analysis. Certainly, the average person on the street is unaware of the relationship between foreign economic policy and the availability and prices of the goods and services that compose our standard of living — particularly in the United States. Consequently, most of us pay little attention to the foreign economic policy of our own government and few of us seek to change it.

The situation is far different for business enterprises that are directly engaged in international trade and investment or that face competition from imports. They know well that government actions in the world economy may spell the difference between profit and loss. Hence, they take steps to influence foreign economic policy in the direction that best accords with their interests. Because of the apathy of the general public, the individuals and groups that have an obvious financial stake in the foreign economic policy of their governments have been able to exert an extraordinary influence on policy formation. The effectiveness of protectionist lobbies in Washington and elsewhere is a good example.

The excessive weight given to private vested interests in the formulation and execution of foreign economic policy is not only undemocratic but also represents a yielding of the national interest to individual interests. Above our own individual welfare lies the welfare of the nation and the welfare of the community of nations, and, in the last analysis, they are inseparable. Enlightened self-interest demands, therefore, that we take full account of national and international interests in the formulation of foreign economic policy. To do so we must learn to evaluate foreign economic policy in light of these broad perspectives.

The Goals of Foreign Economic Policy

There are several ways to classify the goals that nations may strive to achieve in their foreign economic policy, and few classifications are apt to be exhaustive or mutually exclusive. We do not intend to catalog the many ends of foreign economic policy, but to illustrate their rich diversity we have chosen for discussion seven of the most fundamental goals. At this time we are not interested in an analysis of these goals; our purpose is simply one of identification.

Autarky At one extreme is the objective of *autarky* or national self-sufficiency. A full autarkic policy aims to rid the nation of all dependence on international trade and investment because this dependence is feared for economic, political, or military reasons. Autarky is clearly inconsistent with the continuance of economic relations with other countries; the political counterpart of autarky is isolationism. Of course, most nations do not possess the domestic resources required to practice any significant degree of autarky. More common is a qualified autarkic policy that seeks self-sufficiency in only certain articles of trade, generally of a strategic military value.

Economic Welfare At the opposite extreme to autarky lies the goal of *economic welfare,* which springs from a conception of international trade and investment as an opportunity to reap the benefits of international specialization. In Chapter 2 we present the cogent economic reasoning that underlies this conception of trade. Foreign economic policy in which the objective of economic welfare plays a leading role seeks to expand international trade and investment by lowering or eliminating tariffs and other barriers to the free exchange of goods, services, and factors. As noted earlier, this liberal philosophy of trade was dominant in the period preceding World War I, when the United Kingdom, the paramount trading nation at that time, espoused a policy of free trade and most other nations used only the tariff in controlling trade. After World War II, economic welfare emerged once again as a prominent goal in the foreign economic policies of the industrial countries of the West, led by the United States.

Protectionism Between the two extremes — autarky, which would regulate foreign trade out of existence, and free trade, which would impose no restrictions whatsoever — there are many other goals that serve to motivate foreign economic policy. Chief among them is *protectionism* — the protection of domestic producers against the free competition of imports by regulating their volume through tariffs, quotas, and the like. Identification of a specific foreign economic policy as protectionist is sometimes difficult, since any policy that restricts imports has protectionist effects regardless of its objective. Protectionism, therefore, has many guises, and it shows a remarkable ability to adjust to new circumstances by employing arguments and stratagems suited to the times. In the 1990s, protectionism continues to threaten the economic welfare of both industrial and nonindustrial countries.

Stable Levels of High Employment Since the 1930s, *stability of the economy at high employment levels* has been among the most important objectives of national economic policy. Contemporary governments try to restrain inflation while at the same time sustaining employment, although they are commonly frustrated by conflicts between the policies needed to achieve these goals. When the aim of high-employment stability dominates the foreign economic policy of a nation, international trade and capital movements are viewed as both a source of disturbances to the domestic economy and a means of compensating for disturbances originating within the economy. Whether foreign trade and capital movements are restricted or encouraged depends mostly upon current levels of domestic economic activity.

Balance of Payments   Sooner or later, all nations are compelled to remedy deficits in their *balance of payments,* whether through market adjustments or controls. When a country's balance of payments is weak, causing declining international reserves or a persistent depreciation in the external value (exchange rate) of its currency, the objective of payments equilibrium may come to dominate other objectives of its foreign economic policy and even of its domestic policy. In the decade following World War II, the elimination of the dollar shortage occupied first place among the foreign economic policy objectives of Western European countries. In the 1960s and again in the 1980s, the U.S. balance of payments problem overshadowed other foreign economic issues. As we shall observe, balance of payments policy may conflict with domestic policies of high employment and noninflationary growth.

Economic Development   Today the nonindustrial countries of Asia, Africa, and Latin America are striving to accelerate their economic growth and to raise the living standards of their peoples. The pressing concern of these nations with the mammoth problem of *economic development* has led their governments to regard international trade as an instrument to achieve such development to the exclusion of other ends. Thus, tariffs and other restrictive devices may be employed to protect "infant industries" or to keep out "nonessential" consumer goods. On the other hand, capital goods and other "essential" imports may be encouraged by subsidies or favorable exchange quotas. Exports may also be regulated in an attempt to promote economic development. As we shall observe in Chapter 20, the failure of controls to promote development led several developing countries in the 1980s to abandon controls in favor of market-oriented trade policies.

Economic Warfare   During periods of actual warfare the international economic policies of nations are directed toward the overriding objective of victory. Even in the absence of armed conflict, however, *economic warfare* is sometimes among the goals of international economic policy. Before the collapse of the Soviet Union, the United States and its allies imposed comprehensive strategic controls on trade with communist countries. At present, the United States maintains sanctions on trade with Cuba, Iraq, Vietnam, and Serbia.

The injection of political and military considerations into international economic policy is nothing new. After all, foreign economic policy is part of the foreign policy of the nation, and it is inevitably colored to some degree by national political aims. But the degree of coloring is important.

The Instruments of Foreign Economic Policy

Foreign economic policy involves instruments as well as goals. In accordance with our decision to use a narrower interpretation of the scope of foreign economic policy, we shall take policy instruments to signify the tools (market variables, such as exchange rates, and direct controls) that are employed by governments with the *intent* to influence the magnitude, composition, or direction of international trade and factor movements.

The instruments of foreign economic policy exhibit broad variety, and it will prove helpful to examine them in terms of four policy areas, three of which deal with different segments of the balance of payments and the other with the balance of payments as a whole.[11] Figure 1-1 lists these policy areas together with the principal policy instruments that are available to governments of countries with market economies. The dots indicate the policy instruments that are *primarily*

Figure 1-1

INSTRUMENTS / AREAS	Trade Policy	Investment Policy	Foreign Aid Policy	Balance of Payments Policy
Tariffs	●			
Nontariff trade barriers	●			
Export promotion	●			
Foreign investment restrictions		●		
Foreign investment inducements		●		
Official grants and loans			●	
Fiscal				●
Monetary				●
Exchange-rate adjustment				●
Exchange control				●

Areas and Instruments of Foreign Economic Policy.

---

[11]See Chapter 14 for a description of the balance of payments.

associated with each policy area. However, it would be a mistake to identify a policy area with a particular set of policy instruments, for many of them may be used to achieve different policy goals depending on the circumstances. In particular, balance of payments policy may utilize *all* of the policy instruments shown in Figure 1-1. Actually these policy instruments are more accurately defined as "policy instrument types," since each consists of several specific policy tools. For instance, nontariff trade barriers include quotas, border taxes, customs procedures, antidumping regulations, domestic subsidies, and others.

Agreements and Treaties   Much of the foreign economic policy of a nation is effected through agreements and treaties with other nations. For the most part, the legal rights that individuals and business enterprises enjoy in a foreign country are those spelled out in treaties and agreements previously negotiated by their own governments. Thus, international treaties and agreements determine the treatment to be accorded foreigners and foreign interests. Generally speaking, this treatment is either *national* or *most-favored-nation treatment.* Under national treatment, foreigners possess the same rights as nationals. National treatment extends chiefly to the protection of life and property; no Mexican policeman, for instance, would ask for a birth certificate before coming to the rescue of a person in trouble. Most-favored-nation treatment is based on a different concept of equity; it means that a nation treats a second nation as favorably as it treats any third nation. The main purpose of most-favored-nation treatment is to eliminate national discrimination. Its greatest application is in the field of tariffs and other measures of commercial policy.[12]

Trade and Investment Policies   *Trade policy* refers to all government actions that seek to alter current account transactions, especially trade in merchandise.[13] Historically, the main instrument of trade policy has been the import tariff, but today nontariff barriers and export promotion are often of equal or greater importance.

Investment policy covers government actions both with respect to international long-term lending and borrowing (portfolio investment) and with respect to the international movement of business enterprise, which involves not only capital but management and technology as well (direct investment). Ordinarily the governments of investing nations restrict investment outflows only for balance-of-payments reasons; indeed, they may promote direct investment outflows via inducements of one sort or another. On the other hand, although the governments of borrowing or host nations seldom deter inflows of portfolio investment, they frequently do so with certain forms of direct investment while at the same time encouraging other forms. Because of the rapid development of multinational companies that produce and sell throughout the world, foreign investment policy has assumed a critical importance for both home and host countries.[14]

---

[12]See Chapter 6.
[13]Current account transactions are exports and imports of physical goods and services. See Chapter 14.
[14]See Chapter 24.

Foreign Aid Policy *Foreign aid policy* includes all of the activities involved in the field of governmental loans and grants that are intended to aid in the reconstruction, economic development, or military defense of recipient countries. Compared with the other policies, foreign aid policy is a newcomer; it was born out of the vicissitudes of the early postwar period, when Europe lay economically prostrate. Later, a recognition of the obligation to help developing countries provided another stimulus to foreign aid policy. Simultaneously, the threat of the cold war gave rise to large-scale U.S. programs of military and economic aid that sought to buttress the free world against internal and external communist aggression. Today, assistance for economic development is the most pervasive rationale for foreign aid. All of the industrial countries and many international organizations have aid programs that transfer resources to the developing countries.[15]

Balance-of-Payments Policy *Balance-of-payments policy* embraces all of the actions of governments to maintain or restore equilibrium in their external accounts. In the face of an enduring, fundamental disequilibrium, governments generally respond to a deficit (surplus) by (1) deflating (inflating) the domestic economy with monetary and fiscal instruments, (2) devaluing (revaluing) the exchange rate, or (3) imposing exchange controls over some or all international transactions.[16] These basic instruments of adjustment may be used singly or in combination, and at times they may be rejected by governments in favor of policy instruments, such as tariffs and quantitative import restrictions, that are normally associated with other policy areas.

The Diversity and Conflict of Goals

The goals of foreign economic policies are diverse on two counts: (1) each nation ordinarily pursues several goals simultaneously in its own foreign economic policy, and (2) the mix of goals pursued by one nation does not necessarily correspond to the goal mixes of other nations over either the short or long run.[17] If these diverse goals could be successfully attained by each and every nation, there would be no need for our analysis of foreign economic policy. As is true of all human affairs, however, no single nation or group of nations can fully achieve the many objectives of its foreign economic policy. This failure stems from inconsistencies and conflicts among goals at both national and international levels and from inadequacies in policy instruments. Let us turn first to the question of goal conflict.

Except possibly during a war, when the issue of national survival is paramount, no nation seeks to achieve a single objective in its foreign economic policy; rather, it has several objectives that reflect the complex needs and demands of the

---

[15]See Chapter 20.

[16]Chapters 15 and 16 examine market adjustment to the balance of payments via changes in income, money, prices, and the exchange rate. Chapter 17 looks at exchange control.

[17]The mix of goals pursued by national governments changes over time. Hence, the diversity of goals is a dynamic phenomenon.

national society. A nation is made up of individuals and groups who occupy different positions in society, who do not equally benefit from the same economic events and government policies, and who have, therefore, diverse economic views and interests. It is to be expected that individuals and groups will try to direct government policies toward goals that they deem beneficial. This conflict of interests is not easily resolved, and often a government resolves it in a way that satisfies one or another vested interest while the national interest is sacrificed on the altar of political expediency.

Protectionism versus free trade is an age-old conflict in goals. Clearly a nation cannot pursue a policy of free trade and at the same time protect domestic industries against foreign competition. The justification of free trade is that it enables a nation to gain from international specialization, whereas protectionism precludes that possibility. And yet, nations are wont to subscribe to the principle of free trade and practice protectionism. Many other instances of an *internal* conflict of goals will be encountered in subsequent chapters, such as the conflict in many developing countries between autarky (economic nationalism) and economic development.

Some countries are extremely dependent upon international trade for their economic livelihood; other countries approach varying degrees of self-sufficiency. Some countries are industrialized and enjoy a high standard of living; other countries are in the early stages of economic development and many of their people live close to starvation. Some national economies are organized on a private enterprise basis; others have a feudalistic or socialistic basis of production. Some countries have strong balances of payments; others are hard pressed to meet their international obligations. These and the many other differences that distinguish one nation from another generate different and often conflicting attitudes and policies toward international trade and investment. One nation may seek to take advantage of the benefits of trade by lowering tariffs and other barriers while other nations are raising barriers to protect domestic industry or to meet a drain on international reserves. Such conflicts of national interest abound in the historical and contemporary economic policies of nations.

It is important to understand that the *external* conflict of economic goals does not arise out of diversity as such but rather out of the interdependence of national economies. If all nations were to adopt a policy of full autarky, there could be no external conflict of economic goals because there would be no flows of goods and factors linking their economies. By the same token, any increase in the degree of international economic interdependence (as is occurring today at a rapid pace) will heighten the probability of goal conflicts among economic policies that are determined at the national level. Interdependence calls into question the effectiveness of economic policies determined solely on the national level as opposed to the international level.

A great deal of international economic policy consists of efforts to alleviate both the internal and external conflict of goals. Persuasion and compromise are the hallmarks of these efforts. Today it is clear that the external conflict of goals will not be lessened except through understanding and compromise among nations, buttressed by formal treaties and agreements. If one accepts the belief that some lessening of this conflict is better than no lessening at all, the spirit of compromise that is necessary to achieve it must also be accepted. As an ongoing process, cooperation can point the way toward international economic policies that will benefit all nations, not simply the few who are strong.

Contemporary Issues of Foreign Economic Policy

Following is a list of ten contemporary issues of foreign economic policy. We shall encounter all of these issues in our study of international trade and investment. These issues reflect the tensions between the forces of global interdependence on the one hand and the forces of national autonomy on the other. Governments need somehow to reconcile the fact of global economic interdependence with responsibilities to their own peoples for jobs, stable prices, economic growth, an equitable distribution of real income, and security.

1. Maintenance of a global multilateral trading system.
2. U.S. international competitiveness.
3. Regional arrangements: the European Community (EC), the North American Free Trade Agreement (NAFTA), and others.
4. "New" protectionism.
5. The emergence of newly industrializing countries (NICs).
6. The transition of centrally planned to market economies.
7. The volatility of exchange rates.
8. The international debt burden of developing countries.
9. Environmental protection.
10. Control of multinational enterprise.

SOME EMPIRICAL DIMENSIONS OF INTERNATIONAL TRADE

In closing this introductory chapter, six tables are offered that indicate some of the quantitative dimensions of world and U.S. trade.

The Ten Leading Exporting and Importing Countries

Table 1-1 lists the ten leading exporting and importing countries in 1991. The following points may be drawn from an examination of the data.

1. Six of the major exporting countries and six of the major importing countries are located in Western Europe, showing the key role of that region in the world economy.
2. The order of countries is not always the same for both exports and imports. Canada ranks eighth as an exporter and seventh as an importer, indicating a negative trade balance.

Table 1-1   The Ten Leading Exporting and Importing Countries in 1991 (Billions of Dollars and Percentage Share)

Exporters	Value	Share	Importers	Value	Share
1. United States	422	12.0	1. United States	509	13.9
2. Germany	403	11.4	2. Germany	390	10.7
3. Japan	315	8.9	3. Japan	236	6.5
4. France	217	6.1	4. France	232	6.4
5. United Kingdom	185	5.3	5. United Kingdom	210	5.7
6. Italy	169	4.8	6. Italy	183	5.0
7. Netherlands	133	3.8	7. Canada	124	3.4
8. Canada	129	3.7	8. Netherlands	124	3.4
9. Belgium-Luxembourg	117	3.3	9. Belgium-Luxembourg	120	3.3
10. Hong Kong[a]	98	2.8	10. Hong Kong[b]	100	2.7
World[c]	3530	100.0	*World*	3660	100.0

[a]Includes re-exports of $69 billion.

[b]Includes substantial imports for reexport.

[c]The value of world exports is somewhat less than the value of world imports due to the fact that most nations value exports f.o.b. (free on board) at the point of exportation and imports c.i.f. (cost, insurance, freight) at the point of importation. Thus, the value of world imports exceeds the value of world exports by an amount of transportation and other costs incurred in the physical movement of merchandise between countries.

Source: Derived from *Focus,* GATT Newsletter no. 89, April 1992, p. 3.

3. Although the precise ordering may change from one year to the next, the principal trading countries were the same in 1980, with the exception of Belgium-Luxembourg, which was replaced by Saudi Arabia on the export side after the quadrupling of oil prices in 1974 and their doubling in 1979–1980. The sharp decline in oil prices in the 1980s knocked Saudi Arabia out of the ten top exporters. Since 1986, the United States and Germany have alternated as the number one merchandise exporter, depending on movements in each country's export volume and in the dollar/Deutsche mark exchange rate.

4. The total exports and imports of these ten countries were almost two-thirds of the respective world totals in 1991. Thus, the remaining 175 countries or so accounted for only about one-third of world trade.

The Origin and Destination of World Exports

Table 1-2 depicts the origin and destination of world exports during 1990. The dominance of high-income countries (mainly the Organization for Economic Cooperation and Development [OECD] industrial countries) is clearly evident. In 1990, they generated 82 percent of world exports and 80 percent of world imports. Furthermore, trade *between* the high-income countries accounted for 66.1 percent of world exports.

Table 1–2   Direction of International Trade in 1990 (Percentage of World Merchandise Exports)

Exports from \ Exports to	High-Income Countries	United States	Low- and Middle- Income Countries	All Countries
High-income countries[1]	66.1	*11.4*	15.9	82.0
United States	*8.6*		*3.4*	*12.0*
Low- and middle- income countries[2]	13.9	*3.5*	4.1	18.0
All countries	80.0	*14.9*	20.0	100.0

[1]High-income countries are mainly OECD countries plus Hong Kong, Singapore, Israel, Kuwait, Qatar, and the United Arab Emirates.
[2]All other countries.
Source: Adapted from *Global Economic Prospects and the Developing Countries,* (Washington, D.C.: World Bank, 1992), Table E8, p. 64.

U.S. exports (which are included in the figures for the high-income countries) were 12 percent of world exports, with about two-thirds of those exports going to other high-income countries.

The low- and middle-income countries—numbering three-quarters of *all* countries—originated only 18 percent of world exports and absorbed only 20 percent of world imports. Two-way trade between the low- and middle-income countries and the high-income countries was about three-tenths of world exports, but trade among the low- and middle-income countries themselves was only 4.1 percent of world exports in 1990.

The Tripolarization of World Trade

World trade is mostly generated by three poles or regions: OECD Europe, led by Germany; North America, led by the United States; and East Asia, led by Japan.[18] As shown in Table 1-3, in 1990 these poles accounted for over three-quarters (76.5 percent) of world imports, comprising intraregional imports (49.2 percent) and interregional imports (27.3 percent). The import share of the rest of the world was only 23.5 percent. The dominance of the three poles grew rapidly in the 1980s, moving from 59.4 percent of world imports to 76.5 percent.

*Inter*regional trade grew somewhat faster than *intra*regional trade during the decade, accounting for 35.7 percent of polar trade in 1990 compared to 32.7 percent in 1980. This higher interdependence among the poles reflects the progressive integration of the world economy. As we shall see in Chapter 10, OECD Europe has formed a regional integration arrangement (centered on the European

---

[18]The leaders—Germany, the United States, and Japan—are commonly referred to as the *Triad.*

Table 1–3 The Three Poles of World Trade (Percentage of World Merchandise Imports)

	1980	1990
Trade within each pole		
OECD Europe	28.0	33.2
North America[1]	5.9	6.5
East Asia[2]	6.1	9.5
Subtotal	*40.0*	*49.2*
Trade among the poles		
Europe-North America	7.7	8.0
East Asia-North America	7.1	10.5
Europe-East Asia	4.6	8.8
Subtotal	*19.4*	*27.3*
All other countries	40.6	23.5

[1]United States, Canada, and Mexico.
[2]Japan, South Korea, China, Taiwan, Hong Kong, and the ASEAN countries.
Source: Derived from *Changing Our Ways: America and the New World,* (New York: Carnegie Endowment for International Peace, 1992) p. 21.

Community) and North America is planning a North American Free Trade Area. Will these regional schemes promote *regional* integration at the expense of *global* integration? Will East Asia respond with its own integration scheme? These are important questions for trade policy in the 1990s.

Composition of U.S. Trade

Tables 1-4 and 1-5 indicate the percentage composition of U.S. exports and imports respectively by principal end-use categories since 1946.

Since World War II, U.S. *exports* of manufactures have steadily expanded their share of total exports, whereas exports of industrial supplies and materials and of food, feeds, and beverages have experienced a diminishing share. Capital goods have dominated the growth in exports of manufactures, accounting for two-thirds of them in 1991. After maintaining a fairly stable export share for most of the period, consumer goods showed a substantial growth in 1991. It is too soon to know whether this performance marks the start of a new trend. In sum, exports of manufactures now make up more than six-tenths of U.S. exports, and their share is almost certain to grow in the future.

Since 1946, the composition of U.S. *imports* has changed more drastically than the composition of U.S. exports. Imports of manufactures show an astounding increase in their share of total imports, rising from 10.7 percent in the 1946–1958 period to 64.2 percent in 1991.

Table 1-4   Composition of U.S. Exports by Principal End-Use Categories, 1946-1991 (Percent)

End-Use Category	Average 1946–1958	Average 1966–1970	Average 1978–1980	Average 1985–1987	1991
Manufactures	40.4	49.3	49.9	53.0	61.4
Capital goods[1]	25.1	33.0	33.4	35.4	40.5
Automotive[2]	7.4	9.4	9.4	11.0	9.7
Consumer goods[3]	7.9	6.9	7.1	6.6	11.2
Industrial supplies and materials	40.4	32.7	29.7	28.1	26.7
Food, feeds, beverages	16.5	15.0	17.2	10.4	7.7
All other[4]	2.7	3.0	3.2	8.5	4.2
Total exports[5]	100.0	100.0	100.0	100.0	100.0

[1]Excluding automotive products.
[2]Vehicles, parts, and engines.
[3]Excluding automotive and food products.
[4]Re-exports, low-value shipments, and miscellaneous special transactions.
[5]Excluding sales and transfers under military programs.
Source: Survey of Current Business, March 1971, June 1979, March 1981, June 1988, and September 1992.

The falling share of industrial supplies and materials was reversed in the 1970s owing to the quadrupling of oil prices by OPEC and the growing dependence of the United States on oil imports. But the drop in oil prices in the 1980s brought about a resumption of the long-term decline in relative imports of industrial supplies and materials. Their future share in U.S. imports will depend mainly on the volume and price of petroleum imports. The dominance of manufactures in U.S. imports rests on the continuing industrialization of other countries and the closing of technology gaps between them and the United States. To what extent this dominance indicates the United States is suffering from deteriorating international competitiveness is a subject for Chapter 9.

Top Ten U.S. Exporters

Our last table (Table 1-6) lists the top ten U.S. exporters in 1991. Observe that these exporters are all large industrial firms. As we shall discover in Chapter 22, they are also multinational enterprises that manufacture abroad as well as export from domestic plants. Observe again that the products of these firms are based for the most part on advanced technologies.

Together, these ten firms initiated three-tenths of all U.S. manufactured exports in 1991, which were $255.4 billion — the sum of capital goods, automotive products, and consumer goods.

Table 1-5 Composition of U.S. Imports by Principal End-Use Categories, 1946–1991 (Percent)

End-Use Category	Average 1946–1958	Average 1966–1970	Average 1978–1980	Average 1985–1987	1991
Manufactures	10.7	38.4	39.2	61.0	64.2
Capital goods[1]	2.1	8.8	11.8	19.6	24.7
Automotive[2]	1.1	12.4	12.5	20.4	17.4
Consumer goods[3]	7.5	17.1	14.9	21.0	22.1
Industrial supplies and materials	58.9	41.7	50.8	29.7	27.0
Food, feeds, beverages	27.8	15.9	8.2	6.4	5.4
All other[4]	2.6	4.0	1.8	2.9	3.5
Total imports[5]	100.0	100.0	100.0	100.0	100.0

[1]Excluding automotive products.
[2]Vehicles, parts, and engines.
[3]Excluding automotive and food products.
[4]Low-value shipments, U.S. goods returned, and miscellaneous special transactions.
[5]Excluding sales and transfers under military programs.

Note: Percentages may not add to 100.0 because of rounding.

Source: Survey of Current Business, March 1971, June 1979, March 1981, June 1988, and September 1992.

WHAT LIES AHEAD

It is not possible to study all aspects of the international economy at the same time. We have chosen, therefore, to organize our study in four major parts based on the principal economic flows among nations: International flows of goods and services (Part I, "International Trade"), international flows of money and payments (Part II, "International Payments"), international flows of development resources (Part III, "International Development"), and international flows of direct investment and enterprise (Part IV, "International Investment and Multinational Enterprise"). Each part investigates both the theory and policy aspects of its subject in search of answers to the questions, What is the nature of the flows? Why do they occur? How do actual government policies constrain them? What should government policies be toward these flows?

The reader should regard these part divisions as dimensions of international economic relations that are highly interdependent. Our purpose is to understand the *whole* of international economic relations, but we believe that the whole can be comprehended only through an understanding of its constituent elements. It behooves the reader, therefore, to exert a continuing effort to relate what is discussed in one part to what has been discussed in other parts. We have tried to facilitate this effort by making frequent cross-references among the four parts.

Table 1-6 The Top Ten U.S. Exporters in 1991 (Billions of Dollars)

Exporter	*Major Exports*	*Export Value*
1. Boeing	Commercial/military aircraft	17.9
2. General Motors	Motor vehicles, parts	11.3
3. General Electric	Jet engines, turbines, plastics, medical systems	8.6
4. IBM	Computers, related equipment	7.7
5. Ford Motor	Motor vehicles, parts	7.3
6. Chrysler	Motor vehicles, parts	6.2
7. McDonnell Douglas	Aerospace products, missiles	6.2
8. Du Pont	Specialty chemicals	3.8
9. Caterpillar	Heavy machinery, engines, turbines	3.7
10. United Technologies	Jet engines, helicopters, cooling equipment	3.6
All Ten		*76.3*

Source: Derived from "U.S. Exporters on a Global Roll," *Fortune,* June 29, 1992, p. 95.

SUMMARY

1. Every nation inhabits a global political and social environment as well as a global economic environment. To comprehend this international environment, we must simplify by classifying individual events into groups or categories of events and by tracing out the relationships among these aggregates. In other words, we must construct analytical models.

2. The human race is organized in a society of nation-states. The elemental constituents of a nation-state are a people, a territory, an economy, and a sovereign government. The principle of national sovereignty gives each national government exclusive jurisdiction over the national territory and makes it the only legal representative of the nation vis-à-vis other nations. The *external political relations* of nation-states are essentially *power* relations that are expressed in changing mixes of cooperation, competition, and antagonism. The *international political system* comprises some 185 sovereign nation-states and their mutual power relations. Nationalism makes nation-states less cooperative than would otherwise be the case.

3. Every nation-state has an economy, and the mutual relations among national economies constitute the *international economic system.* With the modest exception of gifts, international economic relations result from *transactions,* the exchange of assets having market value. The sum of a nation's economic

transactions with the rest of the world over a period of time is recorded in its balance of payments.

4. It is fruitless to speculate in the abstract on whether international economic relations determine international political relations or vice versa. International economic and political relations are interdependent; both the international economic system and the international political system are best regarded as subsystems of the same nation-state system.

5. Although we shall rely mainly on the macroscopic (or national) perspective in Parts I, II, and III, we must recognize that this perspective is necessary but no longer sufficient to explain the behavior of the international economy. Multinational enterprises have become responsible for a sizable (and increasing) share of world trade and for most international investment. The *multinational enterprise system* consists of a parent company; its producing and marketing affiliates in foreign countries; and the flows of products, services, capital, technology, management, and funds among them. Hence, *intraenterprise transfers* characterize this system.

6. The distinctive features of international trade and investment — different languages and customs, separate national economic policies, national monetary systems, government regulations, and the lower mobility of the factors of production — are traceable to the nation-state system and its subsystems.

7. The contribution of international trade is so immense that few countries could become self-sufficient even with the greatest effort. Even the United States would find the costs of self-sufficiency formidable. The benefits of international specialization are fundamentally of the same nature as the benefits of domestic interregional specialization. Thus, international trade and interregional trade are basically the same, and the distinctive features of international trade are largely owing to the political fact of national sovereignty.

8. Domestic consumers are benefited by international trade because it lowers the prices of goods and makes available goods that cannot be produced at home. If we agree that the proper end of economic activity is consumption, then we should agree that the interests of consumers in international trade are identical with the national interest. National welfare is enhanced by international trade because such trade permits international specialization that leads to a more productive use of the natural resources, capital, and labor of nations.

9. It is easy to understand the contribution of international trade to the business enterprises that are engaged in the export and import of merchandise, services, and capital. They are interested in international trade as a source of income and profits. On the other hand, management, labor, and capital employed in domestic industries in close competition with imports from abroad may be injured by an expansion of international trade. It must be noted, however, that such injury is one of the costs of a competitive economic system.

10. There are several arguments against international specialization and trade — national security, economic stability, full employment, economic develop-

ment, protection of domestic industries, and so on. Nevertheless, the advantages of international trade are so great that it exhibits vitality and growth.

11. For reasons of space and analytical convenience, we define foreign economic policy to include the activities of government that are *intended* to regulate, restrict, promote, or otherwise influence the conduct of international trade and investment. However, we do not propose to neglect the interdependence between foreign and domestic economic policies.

12. Enlightened self-interest demands that governments take full account of national and international interests as well as private interests in the formulation of foreign economic policy.

13. Seven fundamental goals that nations may pursue in their foreign economic policies are autarky, economic welfare, protectionism, high-employment stability, balance-of-payments equilibrium, economic development, and economic warfare.

14. It is helpful to examine the instruments of foreign economic policy in terms of four broad policy areas: trade policy, investment policy, foreign aid policy, and balance of payments policy.

15. The diversity of foreign economic policy goals engenders both internal and external conflicts. Interdependence among nations calls into question the effectiveness of economic policies determined solely on the national level as opposed to the international level. As an ongoing process, cooperation can point the way toward international economic policies that will benefit all nations, not simply the few who are strong.

16. The United States, Germany, and Japan lead the three poles (or regions), accounting for over three-quarters of world trade.

17. The composition of both U.S. exports and imports has shifted toward manufactured products and away from industrial supplies and materials and from food, feeds, and beverages.

18. The top ten U.S. exporters are large industrial firms whose products for the most part are based on advanced technologies.

QUESTIONS AND APPLICATIONS

1. What is a nation-state? What is the nation-state system? Compare the United States and four other nation-states of your own choosing in terms of territory, population, and gross national product.

2. Define the international political system. What is intended by the statement, "International political relations are essentially power relations"?

3. What is nationalism? Cite five cases of nationalism that have appeared in recent issues of *The New York Times* or other newspapers.

4. Define the international economic system. What is an economic transaction?

5. Why is a macroscopic or national perspective necessary but no longer sufficient to explain the behavior of the international economy? What is the multinational enterprise system?
6. What are the distinctive features of international trade and investment? Why are they distinctive?
7. What is the national interest in international trade? Why do we assert that the interest of consumers is identical to the national interest?
8. Which of the arguments against international trade presented in this chapter do you consider the most formidable? Why?
9. What is meant by the *instruments* of foreign economic policy?
10. Identify and discuss the goals of foreign economic policy.
11. Describe the four broad areas of foreign economic policy.
12. (a) Discuss the nature of the internal conflict of goals.
    (b) How does it differ from the external conflict of goals?
13. (a) Which are the principal trading countries?
    (b) What is the meaning of the "tripolarization of world trade"?
14. What have been the main shifts in the composition of U.S. exports and imports since World War II?

INTERNATIONAL
TRADE

To grasp the significance of everyday events occurring in the vast field of activity that we call international trade, we must first gain an understanding of fundamental causal relationships, institutions, and unifying concepts. Accordingly, we begin Part I by considering in four chapters the theories and models that have been created by economists to explain international trade phenomena. By their very nature, theories and models are abstract, leaving out much of reality to focus on essential relationships. But they are indispensable prerequisites to an understanding of the trade policies that are treated in the remaining chapters of Part I.

COMPARATIVE ADVANTAGE
AND THE GAINS FROM TRADE

Since the ending of the Middle Ages almost five centuries ago, two paradigms have dominated explanations of international trade: mercantilism (1500–1800) and comparative advantage (1800–   ). Both paradigms have had a profound effect on the trade policies of nations. The principle of comparative advantage remains today the single strongest intellectual influence on the trade policies of the United States and other industrial countries and is still accepted by the majority of economists. A natural starting point for an examination of international trade theory, therefore, is comparative advantage.

The principle of comparative advantage has an impressive lineage in economic thought. Its great progenitor was Adam Smith's *Wealth of Nations,* published in 1776.[1] Attacking the mercantilists, who argued for the regulation of trade to secure a "favorable balance of trade" (a surplus of exports over imports) that would bring in gold and silver in payment, Smith applied the doctrine of *laissez-faire* to international trade. All nations would benefit from unregulated, free trade that would allow individual countries to specialize in goods they were best suited to produce because of natural and acquired advantages. Smith's theory of trade has come to be known as the *theory of absolute advantage.*

The next and decisive step in the development of trade theory was the publication in 1817 of Ricardo's *On the Principles of Political Economy and Taxation,* which introduced the concept of *comparative advantage.*[2] Smith's theory of absolute advantage assumed that a country would export products that it produced more efficiently than foreign countries and import products that it produced less efficiently than foreign countries. But suppose a country did not produce *any* products more efficiently (and, consequently, at less cost) than foreign countries. What then? Ricardo answered that

---

[1]Adam Smith, *An Inquiry into the Nature and Causes of the Wealth of Nations* (New York: Random House, 1937). For the classic exposition of mercantilist doctrine, see Thomas Mun, *England's Treasure by Forraign Trade* (Oxford: Basil Blackwell & Mott, 1949), first published in 1664.

[2]David Ricardo, *On the Principles of Political Economy and Taxation* (New York: E. P. Dutton, 1948).

question with the theory of comparative advantage: Even if England were less efficient than Portugal in the production of both cloth and wine (as measured by labor hours), it would still be of benefit for England to specialize in cloth production and Portugal in wine production if England were *comparatively* more efficient (or less inefficient) in cloth than in wine production.[3]

In the century following Ricardo, many economists added refinements to the comparative advantage paradigm. As an example, John Stuart Mill (1806–1873) contributed the principle of reciprocal demand to explain the terms of trade. But the most significant new development came with the publication in 1933 of Ohlin's *Interregional and International Trade.*[4] Drawing on the pioneer work of Eli Heckscher, Ohlin further developed the proposition that a country exports those goods that use most intensively in their production the country's most abundant factors of production, and conversely. Ohlin replaced Ricardo's labor theory of value with a multiple-factor theory within a framework of mutually interdependent product and factor markets that determine trade. His theory is known as the Heckscher-Ohlin (H-O) model, and, together with subsequent refinements, it remains today the most widely accepted theory of international trade.

This chapter introduces the principle of comparative advantage by demonstrating how it answers three basic questions: (1) Why do countries export and import certain goods? (2) At which relative prices (terms of trade) do countries exchange goods? (3) What are the gains from international trade?

We start our review of comparative advantage by looking at the production possibilities of national economies. Chapters 3, 4, and 5 then examine particular theories that relate comparative advantage to certain attributes of trading countries, most notably, factor-of-production endowments, increasing returns, product differentiation, market structure, and technology.

PRODUCTION POSSIBILITIES
OF NATIONAL ECONOMIES

Production possibilities designate the capability of a country to produce goods when all of its factors of production are fully and efficiently employed. Using a two-country, two-commodity model, we examine production possibilities first with constant opportunity costs and then with increasing opportunity costs.

Production Possibilities: Constant Opportunity Costs

Assume there are only two countries in the world, the United States and France, and each produces only two commodities, beef and wine. Assume further that if each country uses *all* of its productive factors (land, labor, management, and capital) at a given level of technology, it can produce the alternative outputs of beef and wine shown in Table 2-1. Translating these output data into graphical form

---

[3]Ricardo adopted the "labor theory of value," which assumes that labor is the only factor of production and that workers in a country are all paid the same wage.

[4]Bertil Ohlin, *Interregional and International Trade* (Cambridge: Harvard University Press, 1952).

Chapter 2   Comparative Advantage and the Gains from Trade

Table 2-1 Alternative Outputs

	Units of Beef	Units of Wine
United States	100	50
France	50	150

gives us the production possibilities (or transformation) curves shown in Figures 2-1 and 2-2.

The U.S. production possibilities curve (Figure 2-1) indicates the various combinations of beef and wine that the U.S. productive factors can produce when they are fully employed and used efficiently. For example, one possible output combination shown by point *A* on the curve represents 45 units of beef and 27.5 units of wine. Point *B*, on the other hand, represents a beef-wine combination that is smaller than possible production because of factor unemployment or inefficient use. Point *C* to the right of the curve denotes a beef-wine combination that is beyond the physical production capacity of the United States. Similar remarks can be made about the French production possibilities curve (Figure 2-2).

Figure 2-1

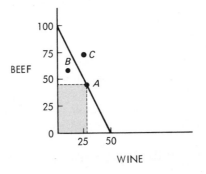

U.S. Production Possibilities: Constant Opportunity Costs. The U.S. production possibilities (or transformation) curve indicates the combination of beef and wine that U.S. factors of production can produce when they are fully employed and used efficiently at a given level of technology. Point *A* is one possible combination of beef and wine, but point *B* is a combination that is smaller than possible because of factor unemployment or inefficient factor use. Point *C* is a combination greater than the production capability of the United States at the given level of technology. In the absence of international trade, the United States can consume only beef-wine combinations that lie on or below its production possibilities curve.

Figure 2-2

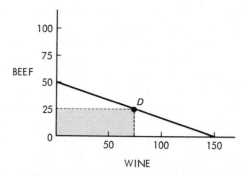

French Production Possibilities: Constant Opportunity Costs. The French production possibilities curve indicates the combinations of beef and wine that factors of production in France can produce when they are fully employed and used efficiently at a given level of technology. One possible combination is denoted by D. In the absence of international trade, France can only consume wine-beef combinations that lie on or below its production possibilities curve.

Both curves depict *constant* opportunity costs for beef and wine.[5] To increase the output of wine by 1 unit in the United States, factors must be taken away from the production of beef in such amount as to lower the output of beef by 2 units. Hence, the opportunity cost of 1 wine unit is 2 beef units, and this cost is not affected by the output levels of beef and wine. In France the opportunity cost of one wine unit is always one third of a beef unit. These constant opportunity costs are shown by the constant slopes of the curves, – 2 for the United States and – ⅓ for France. The rate at which the output of one product must be reduced to increase the output of the other product is the *marginal rate of transformation (MRT)*.

In the case of the United States, the *MRT* of beef into wine is 2, which (disregarding sign) equals the slope of the production possibilities curve. When opportunity costs are constant, the *MRT* is also constant. Under conditions of perfect competition, the *domestic terms of trade (DTT)* of beef for wine equal the *MRT* or slope of the production possibilities curve. In the United States 2 units of beef will exchange for 1 unit of wine while in France 1 unit of beef will exchange for 3 units of wine.

In the absence of trade, each country can elect to consume only a beef-wine combination that lies somewhere on its production possibilities curve, such as A in Figure 2-1 (45 beef units and 27.5 wine units) and D in Figure 2-2 (25 beef units and 75 wine units). The existence of different *MRTs,* however, offers both countries an opportunity to gain from mutual trade and to consume a beef-wine combination that lies beyond their production possibilities frontiers. This pleasant

---

[5]Constant opportunity costs imply that (1) the factors of production are perfect substitutes or are used in the same fixed proportions to produce both goods and (2) returns to scale are constant for both goods; that is to say, a doubling of all factor inputs will double output.

outcome will occur when beef and wine are traded at any *international terms of trade (ITT)* that fall between the two *DTTs*, which, in turn, are equal to the *MRTs*.

The gains from trade are depicted in Figures 2-3 and 2-4. Reciprocal demand determines an *ITT* (commodity terms of trade). This *ITT* is shown by the slope of the dashed lines, which is identical in both figures. At this *ITT* (1 beef unit = 1 wine unit), the United States will specialize completely in beef production, because it can obtain from France more wine for each unit of beef than it can at home. Conversely, France will specialize entirely in wine production, obtaining all its beef from the United States. If at this *ITT* the United States chooses to consume 40 units of wine, it will import them from France in exchange for 40 units of beef.[6] The converse is true for France. As a result of trade, then, the United States is able to consume a beef-wine combination, indicated by point *C* on the international terms-of-trade line in Figure 2-3, that is superior to any combination the United States can produce in isolation. For France, point *D* in Figure 2-4 represents a beef-wine combination that is superior to any combination producible at home. Both countries gain from trade; because of specialization their combined output of beef and wine is higher than before, and the production increment is shared by consumers in both countries. (It might be helpful to look at the arithmetic recapitulation of the before- and after-trade situations presented in Table 2-2.)

Table 2-2 Comparison of Before- and After-Trade Combinations

| | Before Trade | | | | | |
| | Production | | Consumption | | Gains from Trade | |
	Beef	Wine	Beef	Wine	Beef	Wine
United States	45	27.5	45	27.5	0	0
France	25	75	25	75	0	0
Combined	70	102.5	70	102.5	0	0

| | After Trade | | | | | |
| | Production | | Consumption | | Gains from Trade | |
	Beef	Wine	Beef	Wine	Beef	Wine
United States	100	0	60	40	15	12.5
France	0	150	40	110	15	35
Combined	100	150	100	150	30	47.5

[6]An explanation of consumption choices is offered in the next section.

Figure 2-3

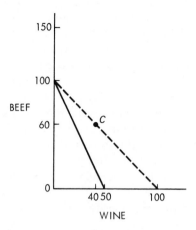

U.S. Gains from Trade: Constant Opportunity Costs. Reciprocal demand determines the international commodity terms of trade (*ITT*) depicted by the slope of the dashed line. At this *ITT*, the United States will specialize completely in beef production because it can obtain from France more wine for a unit of beef than at home. Here we assume that the United States decides to consume 40 units of wine, importing them from France in exchange for 40 units of beef. Hence the United States consumes a beef-wine combination denoted by *C*, a combination that is bigger than any combination the United States can produce (and consume) in the absence of trade.

Figure 2-4

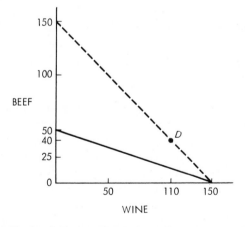

French Gains from Trade: Constant Opportunity Costs. At the *ITT* established by reciprocal demand, France decides to consume a beef-wine combination denoted by *D*, which is superior to any combination that France can consume (or produce) in isolation. At this *ITT*, France will specialize completely in wine production.

The *ITT* of 1 beef unit for 1 wine unit is an *equilibrium* rate because it clears the market; that is, exports equal imports. Any change in reciprocal demand, however, would establish a new equilibrium rate and thereby alter the division of gains. Gainful trade for both countries will occur at any *ITT* that falls between the two *DTTs*. At any rate beyond the range set by the two *DTTs*, only one country will gain, and trade will not occur because the other country will be better off without trade. When the *ITT* is the same as the *DTT* of one country, then that country will neither gain nor lose from trade and all the gain will go to the second country. This will happen when the trading economies differ so much in size that the bigger country cannot completely satisfy its demand for the product in which it has a comparative disadvantage through imports but must also rely on some domestic production. In that event, the bigger country will trade at its *DTT* and all the gain will go to the smaller country. Sometimes it pays to be small!

Production Possibilities: Increasing Opportunity Costs

The assumptions behind constant opportunity costs are highly unrealistic. In actuality, the factors of production are only partial substitutes for each other, and each good is produced with different factor combinations or intensities. With a given technology, good *A* will be generally more labor (and less capital) intensive in production than good *B*.[7] The existence of different factor intensities for two goods will make a country's production possibilities curve concave to the origin, indicating increasing opportunity costs.[8]

Such a curve is shown for the United States in Figure 2-5. Note that the *MRT* (the slope of curve *MN* at any point) is no longer constant. The meaning of increasing opportunity costs may be described as follows. Suppose the United States is producing only wine at *N*. Now it decides to produce 1 unit of beef. To do so, it must draw factors of production from wine, forcing a reduction in wine output. Note, however that this reduction is small (the slope of the production possibilities curve is steep near *N*), because the withdrawn factors of production are actually better suited to beef production than to wine production. But as the production of beef is progressively increased, greater and greater amounts of wine must be sacrificed to obtain 1 more unit of beef (the slope of the curve gets flatter and flatter). Why should the opportunity cost of beef increase? Because the factors of production drawn from wine production (such as land) are less and less suited to the production of beef. As the latter approaches *M,* very large quantities of wine must be given up to get 1 more unit of beef. Similarly, if the United States starts at *M* and then progressively transfers resources from beef to wine production, it will eventually encounter increasing opportunity costs.

---

[7]However, good *A* may not have the same labor intensity (1) at different prices of labor relative to other factor prices, or (2) at different scales of output. It is even conceivable that good *A* will switch from a labor-intensive to a capital-intensive good at some factor price relationship or scale of output, a phenomenon known as *factor reversibility.*

[8]Even if factor intensities were the same, decreasing returns to scale (a doubling of all factor inputs causes less than a doubling of output) for one good would create increasing opportunity costs for both goods.

Figure 2-5

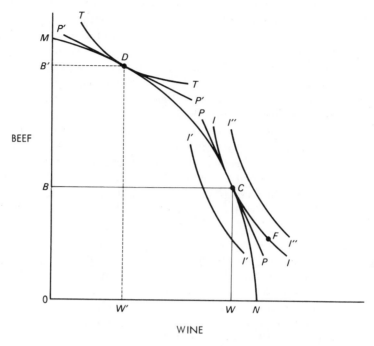

U.S. Production Possibilities: Increasing Opportunity Costs. With increasing opportunity costs, the production possibilities curve becomes concave to the origin so that its slope is no longer constant but varies from point to point. The *domestic terms of trade (DTT)* between beef and wine is determined by the demand preferences of consumers. These preferences are depicted by indifference curves *I-I*, *I'-I'*, and *I"-I"*. The slope of an indifference curve at any point is the *marginal rate of substitution (MRS)* between, in this instance, beef and wine. The highest *attainable* level of consumer satisfaction in the absence of international trade occurs at the point of tangency (point *C*) between the production possibilities curve and an indifference curve. At that point (and no other), *MRT* = *MRS* and the slope of this common tangent (indicated by the slope of *P-P*) is the *DTT*. Now suppose consumers experience a shift in preferences, preferring more beef and less wine. This shift generates a new indifference map indicated by *T-T*. Producers respond by moving out of wine into beef production until the *MRT* once again equals the *MRS* at point *D*, with a new *DTT* denoted by the slope of *P'-P'*. Hence, at point *D*, *MRT* = *MRS* = *DTT*.

What decides the *DTT* between beef and wine under conditions of increasing opportunity costs? The answer is the demand preferences or tastes of consumers — the combination of beef and wine that a nation's people want to consume. We can portray the demand preferences of U.S. consumers by an *indifference map* that consists of an infinite number of *indifference curves*. In Figure 2-5, *I*, *I'*, and *I"* represent indifference curves belonging to the same indifference map. *Each* indifference curve indicates all possible combinations of beef and wine that yield the same level of satisfaction; the nation's consumers are "indifferent" regarding the combinations lying on an individual indifference curve. Thus, the combination of beef and wine indicated by point F on indifference curve I-I provides the same satisfaction to consumers as the combination at C. The slope of an indifference curve at any point is the *marginal rate of substitution in consumption (MRS)*, in this instance, the amount of beef consumers are willing to give up to obtain another unit of wine. The shape of each indifference curve is determined by consumer tastes; a change in tastes will generate a new family of indifference curves.[9]

It follows from the definition of an indifference curve that different indifference curves offer different levels of satisfaction. Graphically, the further an indifference curve is from the origin, the higher its level of satisfaction. Thus, in Figure 2-5, I''-I'' represents a higher level of satisfaction than I-I, which in turn represents a higher level of satisfaction than I'-I'. Consumers, therefore, will maximize their satisfaction by consuming a combination of beef and wine that lies on the *highest* indifference curve attainable with their income. This occurs at point C, where the U.S. production possibilities curve is tangent to I-I. At that point consumers obtain the combination of beef and wine that gives them the most satisfaction of any combination the nation is able to produce. Indifference curve I''-I'' is not attainable in the absence of international trade because it lies beyond the production possibilities curve. At point C the MRT equals the MRS—any movement away from this equality would lower welfare. The slope of their common tangent, indicated by P-P, is the DTT between beef and wine. Hence, at point C, $MRT = MRS = DTT$.

Suppose there occurs a change in taste that generates a new indifference map. What happens? T-T is the new indifference curve that is tangent to the production possibilities curve at point D. Compared to point C, consumers now want more beef and less wine. Their demand, therefore, will push up the price of beef relative to the price of wine (in barter terms, *decrease* the MRS of beef for wine). Producers will respond by shifting out of wine into beef production until the MRT once again equals the MRS at point D. Here their common tangent, P'-P', becomes the new DTT.

Let us now consider the gains from trade under increasing opportunity costs of production. Figures 2-6 and 2-7 depict the production possibilities and indifference curves for the United States and France. Before trade the United States produces at C on its production possibilities curve, producing (and consuming) 0-B beef and 0-W wine (Figure 2-6). The U.S. DTT line $(P_s$-$P_s)$ is tangent to both the

---

[9]Indifference curves were devised to analyze the preferences of the *individual* consumer, who presumably is able to determine the different combinations of two goods that would yield the same satisfaction. Can we add up the indifference curves of individuals to get a *community* indifference curve for the entire nation? Strictly speaking, the answer is no. Different consumers have dissimilar indifference maps that are literally incomparable. One person may want a lot of beef and only a little wine; another may want the converse. Although it is not possible to make interpersonal comparisons of welfare (satisfaction), the community indifference curve is most useful in demonstrating the influence of demand preferences on international trade. In so using it, however, we must bear in mind that its welfare implications are ambiguous. For a discussion of trade and welfare, see Chapter 7.

production possibilities curve and the indifference curve *I–I* at point *C*. Hence, *C* is an equilibrium position. Similarly, France produces and consumes at *K* (0–*G* beef and 0–*F* wine), where its *DTT* line (P_f–P_f) is tangent to its production possibilities curve and the indifference curve *T–T* (Figure 2-7). Since the slopes of the two *DTT* lines differ, there is a basis for gainful trade.

When trade opens up, reciprocal demand determines an *ITT* line (*P–P*) that is the same for both countries. Since the international barter price of beef is higher than its U.S. domestic price, U.S. producers will shift out of wine into beef until the *MRT* is equal to *P–P* at *A*. Here the United States specializes in beef (0–*B'*) but continues to produce some wine (0–*W'*). At the *ITT*, U.S. consumers choose to

Figure 2-6

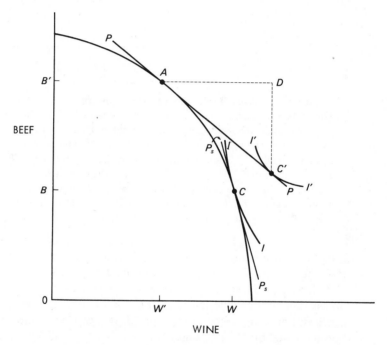

BEEF

WINE

U.S. Gains from Trade: Increasing Opportunity Costs.   Before trade with France, the United States produces and consumes a beef-wine combination denoted by point *C*, where *MRT* = *MRS* = *DTT*. When trade opens up, reciprocal demand determines an *ITT* denoted by the slope of line *P–P*. In response to this *ITT*, which offers a higher price for beef than the *DTT*, the United States shifts production from *C* to *A*. At the same time, U.S. consumers respond to the *ITT* by choosing to consume a beef-wine combination located at point *C'* on line *P–P*. At this point, a new equilibrium is established where *MRT* = *MRS* = *ITT*. The United States clearly gains from trade with France because it now consumes a beef-wine combination that lies on a higher indifference curve (*I'–I'*) than before trade (*I–I*). The United States exports *D–C'* beef in exchange for imports of *A–D* wine.

Figure 2-7

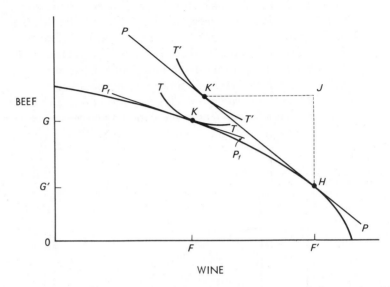

BEEF

WINE

French Gains from Trade: Increasing Opportunity Costs. Before trade with the United States, France produces and consumes a beef-wine combination denoted by point K. When trade opens up, reciprocal demand establishes an *ITT* denoted by the slope of the line P-P. (Line P-P, of course, has the same slope as line P-P in Figure 2-6.) In response to this *ITT*, France shifts production from K to H and shifts consumption from K to K'. At point K', $MRT = MRS = ITT$. France gains from trade because it now consumes a beef-wine combination that lies on a higher indifference curve (T'-T') than before trade (T-T). France exports K'-J wine (equal to A-D wine in Figure 2-6) and imports J-H beef (equal to D-C' beef in Figure 2-6).

consume a beef-wine combination denoted by C', the point of tangency between P-P and indifference curve I'-I' where $ITT = MRS$. The United States exports D-C' beef in exchange for A-D wine from France. After trade, U.S. beef consumption is domestic beef production (0-B') *minus* beef exports (D-C') and U.S. wine consumption is domestic production (0-W') *plus* wine imports (A-D), a combination indicated by C'. The United States clearly gains from trade because it is able to reach a higher indifference curve. It has chosen to consume more beef (0-C' > 0-B) and more wine (0-C' > 0-W) than before trade.[10] Observe that international trade allows the United States to *separate* the production of beef and wine (point A) from the consumption of beef and wine (point C').

In France, producers respond to P-P by shifting from beef to wine production until, at H, MRT equals ITT. France exports K'-J wine in exchange for J-H beef,

[10]Instead of more of both goods, the gains from trade might be a combination that has more of one good and less of another than the pretrade combination, but the former would lie outside the production possibilities curve. The precise combination will depend on demand preferences.

consuming a beef-wine combination denoted by K', where P-P is tangent to indifference curve T'-T' where $ITT = MRS$. This combination is superior to K because it lies on a higher indifference curve. France has chosen to consume more of both beef and wine than before trade.

Since U.S. exports of beef must equal French imports and vice versa, D-$C' = J$-H and A-$D = K'$-J. In after-trade equilibrium, the U.S. MRT is equal to the ITT, which in turn equals the MRS. Further, these rates are equal to the same marginal rates in France. Because of increasing opportunity costs, both countries continue to produce beef and wine.

IDENTICAL PRODUCTION POSSIBILITIES WITH DISSIMILAR TASTES

We have seen how dissimilar production possibilities curves of two countries afford a basis for gainful trade between them. But under conditions of increasing opportunity costs, dissimilar tastes in two countries can also provide a basis for gainful trade even when their production possibilities are the same.

Assume the United States and France have the same production possibilities curve F-F in Figure 2-8.[11] However, the Americans strongly prefer beef over wine, while French tastes run in the opposite direction, as shown by the indifference curves I-I and T-T, respectively. Consequently, before trade the United States chooses to produce and consume combination C of beef and wine with a domestic price line P_s-P_s. On the other hand, France chooses to produce and consume a great deal of wine and only a little beef, as shown by combination K, where its domestic price line P_f-P_f is tangent to its production possibilities curve and the indifference curve T-T. Since the $DTTs$ are different at C and K, there is a basis for gainful trade.

With the opening of trade, reciprocal demand establishes an international price line P-P. U.S. producers adjust to P-P by moving from C to G (cutting down on beef production, increasing wine production), while French producers do the opposite, moving from K to G. U.S. consumers adjust to P-P by consuming combination C' of beef and wine, where P-P is tangent to the indifference curve I'-I'. Hence, the United States exports C'-B wine in exchange for B-G beef. French consumers choose combination K', where P-P is tangent to indifference curve T'-T'. France exports H-K' ($= B$-G) beef in exchange for G-H ($= C'$-B) wine. Both countries gain from trade because their consumption now lies on higher indifference curves. The United States now consumes more beef and somewhat more wine as before trade, and France consumes more wine and slightly more beef. Where does this gain come from? Before trade the United States was highly specialized in beef production, using some factors of production that were much better suited to wine production. The converse was true for France. Trade permitted the United States to shift factors from beef to wine production

---

[11]Only the *shape* of the two curves has to be identical, not the absolute size.

Figure 2-8

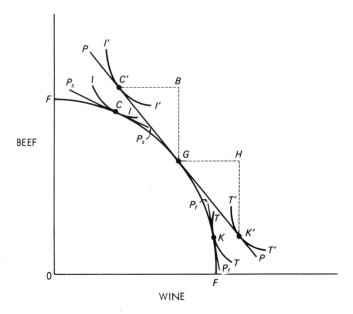

U.S. and French Gains from Trade: Dissimilar Tastes with Same Production Possibilities. The United States and France have the same production possibilities curve (*F-F*). However, American consumers prefer a lot of beef and not much wine, while French consumers prefer the converse. Hence, before trade opens up, the United States produces and consumes at *C*, with a domestic price line P_s-P_s (whose slope equals the *DTT*). France produces and consumes at *K*, with a domestic price line P_f-P_f. Because the *DTTs* of the two countries differ, there is a basis for gainful trade. When trade opens up, reciprocal demand establishes an international price line whose slope equals the *ITT*. In response to this *ITT*, both countries shift production to *G* (where *MRT = ITT*); U.S. consumers move from *C* to *C'* (where *MRS = ITT*) and French consumers move from *K* to *K'* (where *MRS = ITT*). The United States exports *C'-B* (= *G-H*) wine and imports *B-G* (= *H-K'*) beef.

and France to shift factors from wine to beef production. The gains from trade come from a lesser degree of specialization in production but a higher degree of specialization in consumption.

The assumption of similar production possibilities curves for two countries is, of course, unlikely to be matched in the real world. But can dissimilar tastes ever overwhelm dissimilar production possibilities so as to determine comparative advantage? Yes, theoretically. But the probability of such a situation may be regarded as very low. Actually, consumer tastes appear to be converging rather than diverging as "demonstration effects" penetrate all countries.[12] However,

---

[12]Demonstration effects are transmitted via communication of all kinds (including travel) as well as via trade and investment. But see the discussion of income gaps in Chapter 4.

demand preferences must be taken into account in any full statement of the theory of comparative advantage, because they undoubtedly influence *DTTs* (price ratios).

OFFER CURVES: THE DETERMINATION OF THE TERMS OF TRADE

In the preceding analysis we have assumed an *ITT* between the United States and France by attributing it to reciprocal demand. We now utilize offer curves to demonstrate the precise determination of the terms of trade between two countries. In doing so, we shall make use of our example in the discussion of trade under constant opportunity costs earlier in the chapter.

How is the dashed international price line (one beef equals one wine, or a ratio of 1:1) in Figures 2-3 and 2-4 determined? The answer is by the intersection of the U.S. and French *offer* curves. The U.S. offer curve indicates the amounts of beef (in which the United States has a comparative advantage) that the United States is willing to offer France for different amounts of wine (in which the United States has a comparative disadvantage). Similarly, the French offer curve indicates the amounts of wine that France is willing to offer the United States for different amounts of beef.

The U.S. offer curve is shown as 0–*A* in Figure 2-9.[13] The terms of trade for beef and wine at each point on the offer curve is the slope of the ray drawn from the origin through that point. Near the origin the U.S. offer curve has a terms of trade that matches the *DTT,* which is 2 units of beef for 1 unit of wine, as shown by the slope of the ray 0–*r* (2:1). At this terms of trade the United States is indifferent to trade with France but is willing to offer beef for small amounts of wine at its *DTT.* It should be obvious that the United States would not offer more than 2 units of beef for 1 unit of wine, because it could do better at home. For more and more wine imports, however, the United States is willing to offer only smaller and smaller amounts of beef for each additional unit of wine. The reason is that the marginal utility of wine decreases as the amount available to U.S. consumers increases relative to the amount of beef available to them. Hence, as the amount of wine increases, the U.S. offer curve bends further and further away from ray 0–*r*.[14]

At point *C* on the offer curve, the United States offers 0–b_1 beef for 0–w_1 wine at a terms of trade of 1:1, as shown by the slope of ray 0–*s*. At point *D* the United States is willing to export a larger amount of beef (0–b_2) but only at terms of trade of 2:3, which would obtain 0–w_2 imports of wine. Beyond point *D* the United States is unwilling to offer more beef for wine regardless of how favorable the terms of trade become, as shown by the horizontal slope of *D*–*A*.

---

[13] The offer curve may be derived from a country's production possibilities curve and indifference map.

[14] Under conditions of increasing opportunity cost the offer curve bends away also because the marginal opportunity cost of beef increases in the United States as more and more beef is produced.

Figure 2-9

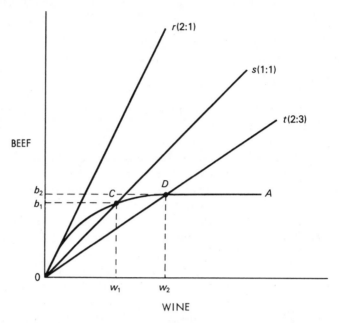

U.S. Offer Curve of Beef for Wine. The U.S. offer curve (0–A) indicates the amounts of beef (in which the United States has a comparative advantage) that the United States is willing to offer France for different amounts of wine. The terms of trade between beef and wine at each point on the offer curve is the slope of the ray drawn from the origin through that point. Near the origin, the U.S. offer curve has terms of trade that match its *DTT,* as is shown by the slope of ray 0–*r*. But as the amount of wine increases, the marginal utility of wine falls, so that the U.S. offer curve bends further and further away from 0–*r*. At point *C,* the United States offers 0–b_1, beef for 0–w_1, wine at a terms of trade of 1:1. Beyond point *D,* the United States is unwilling to offer more beef for wine regardless of the terms of trade.

The French offer curve of wine for beef shows an unwillingness to export more wine for beef except at progressively more favorable terms of trade for that country.

The U.S. and French offer curves are brought together in Figure 2-10. Again 0–*A* is the U.S. offer curve, while 0–*F* is the French offer curve. Given these two offer curves, the equilibrium terms of trade are given by the slope of ray 0–*t,* which passes from the origin through the point of intersection of the curves at *E.* Why? Because only this terms of trade clears the market so that U.S. exports of beef equal U.S. imports of wine, and conversely for France. Only at *E* is the amount of beef (0–*w*) that the United States offers for 0–*w* wine equal to the amount of beef (0–*b*) that France offers to take for 0–*w* wine.[15]

---

[15]In our earlier example, at *E* the United States would export 40 units of beef and import 40 units of wine.

Figure 2-10

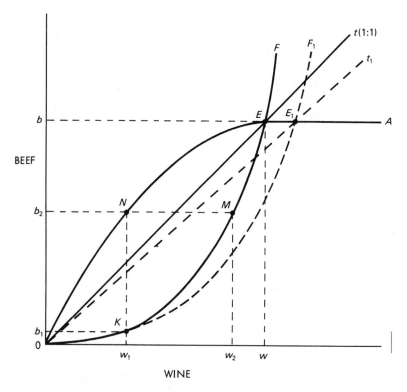

U.S. and French Offer Curves: Determination of the Terms of Trade. $0-A$ is the U.S. offer curve and $0-F$ is the French offer curve. The equilibrium terms of trade (ITT) are determined by the intersection of the two offer curves at point E, where the ITT equals the slope of ray $0-t$. Only this ITT (in this example, 1 unit of beef for 1 unit of wine) clears the market: At E, the amount of beef ($0-b$) that the United States offers for $0-w$ wine equals the amount of beef ($0-b$) that France is willing to take for $0-w$ wine. At any other point on either offer curve (such as K, N, or M), the ITT would fail to clear the market and would not last in a competitive market. If the French demand for beef increases while the U.S. demand for wine remains the same (as is shown by the shift of the French offer curve from $0-F$ to $0-f_1$, then the terms of trade worsen for France and improve for the United States at the new equilibrium point E_1. To conclude, the ITT is determined by the intersection of the offer curves of the trading countries.

At any other point on either offer curve the terms of trade would fail to clear the market and could not endure under pressure from competitive forces. Suppose, for example, that France offered to trade at point K on its offer curve by offering $0-w_1$ wine for $0-b_1$ beef. At the same time the United States would offer a large amount of beef ($0-b_2$) for $0-w_1$ wine, as shown by point N on its offer curve. But for $0-b_2$ beef, France would offer a larger amount of wine ($0-w_2$), as indicated by point M on its offer curve. The interaction of these offers would push the terms of trade to the point of intersection at E.

We can now make a precise statement of the principle of reciprocal demand. The terms of trade between two countries will be determined by the intersection of their respective offer curves.

We can also demonstrate the effects of a change in reciprocal demand with offer curves. Suppose that the French demand for beef increases while the U.S. demand for wine remains the same. This change in reciprocal demand is indicated by a shift to the right of the French offer curve from $0-F$ to $0-F_1$. Observe that this shift changes the intersection of the U.S. and French offer curves from E to E_1 and therefore results in new terms of trade, which is the slope of the ray $0-t_1$. The terms of trade are now worse for France than before the shift, and its gain from trade is also less. France now offers more wine for the same amount of beef (or takes less beef for the same amount of wine) than it did with its old offer curve $0-F$.

We have now completed our review of the principle of comparative advantage. We have seen how dissimilar production possibilities curves, together with demand preferences as expressed by indifference curves (which may or may not be similar across countries), determine different $DTTs$ and thereby create a basis for gainful trade. When trade opens up, reciprocal demand (as demonstrated by offer curves) determines the ITT. In equilibrium, the $MRTs$ in both countries equal the ITT, which in turn equals the $MRSs$ in both countries.

In the next three chapters, we investigate the principal explanations of comparative advantage: factor endowments, increasing returns, product differentiation, and technology gaps.

SUMMARY

1. This chapter introduces the principle of comparative advantage by demonstrating how it answers three basic questions: (1) Why do countries export and import certain goods? (2) At which relative prices (terms of trade) do countries exchange goods? (3) What are the gains from international trade?

2. A country's production possibilities curve shows the combination of goods that can be produced by its factors of production when they are fully employed and used efficiently at a given level of technology.

3. The slope of a country's production possibilities curve at any point is the *marginal rate of transformation (MRT)* at that point. The slope of a country's indifference curve at any point is the *marginal rate of substitution (MRS)* in consumption at that point. In the absence of international trade, equilibrium is achieved in both production and consumption at the point of tangency between the production possibilities curve and an indifference curve. The slope at this common tangency is the *domestic terms of trade (DTT)*. In equilibrium, therefore, $MRT = MRS = DTT$.

4. When the production possibilities curves of two countries have dissimilar shapes but their indifference curves have the same shape, then their pretrade

DTTs will differ, providing a basis for gainful trade. Under conditions of increasing opportunity cost, posttrade equilibrium is achieved when the *MRT* and *MRS* of each country equal the *international terms of trade (ITT)*. This is the optimal welfare position.

5. Although dissimilar tastes (indifference curves) afford a separate basis for gainful trade, they are not likely to overwhelm the influence of dissimilar opportunity costs in production on the direction of trade.

6. The equilibrium terms of trade for two countries is determined by the intersection of their respective offer curves.

QUESTIONS AND APPLICATIONS

1. Does trade under constant opportunity costs necessarily lead to complete international specialization in production in the absence of any restrictions?

2. Why are the assumptions behind constant opportunity costs in production "highly unrealistic"?

3. In the absence of international trade, what determines the domestic barter rate of exchange (*DTT*) between two goods under conditions of increasing opportunity cost?

4. After-trade equilibrium between two countries requires that *MRT* = *MRS* = *ITT* across both countries. Why is that so?

5. Why is international specialization incomplete under conditions of increasing opportunity cost?

6. Draw production possibilities curves, for two countries, that have the *same* shapes under conditions of increasing opportunity cost.
    (a) Assuming similar tastes (indifference curves), demonstrate graphically that no gainful trade is possible.
    (b) Assuming dissimilar tastes, demonstrate graphically that gainful trade is possible.

7. Construct offer curves for two countries. Show how a decrease in demand for imports in one country will cause an improvement in its terms of trade.

SELECTED READINGS

See the list of readings given at the end of Chapter 3.

COMPARATIVE ADVANTAGE AND FACTOR ENDOWMENTS: THE HECKSCHER-OHLIN MODEL

The Heckscher-Ohlin (H-O) model attributes comparative advantage to different proportions of national factor endowments of land, labor, and capital across countries.[1]

As is true of any theory, certain assumptions are made to *simplify* the H-O model to focus on those variables and their relationships that are viewed as critical to an explanation of international trade. These simplifying assumptions are (1) full employment of all factors of production, (2) the absence of transportation or other transfer costs in the international movement of physical goods, and (3) fixed supplies of homogeneous factors of production. Other assumptions of the H-O model are *critical* to the factor-proportions theory of trade. If these assumptions do not hold in the real world to a significant degree, then the theory is called into question as the *fundamental* explanation of international trade. These critical assumptions are (1) perfect competition, (2) the absence of technological innovation and the resulting sameness of production functions in different countries, and (3) perfect immobility of the factors of production among countries.

Before reviewing the H-O model, we offer some introductory remarks on the role of factors of production in the determination of comparative advantage.

DISSIMILAR FACTOR ENDOWMENTS AND TRADE: AN ARITHMETICAL EXAMPLE

Comparative advantage arises when *relative* price structures differ across countries. But why should they differ? The supply-side explanation is that dissimilar price structures reflect dissimilar *cost* structures. In a perfectly competitive market, the price of a good equals its marginal cost of production, which in turn reflects the prices of the marginal inputs of the factors of production—land, labor and capi-

---

[1]For that reason, the H-O model is also called the *factor-proportions theory of international trade*.

tal—used to produce the good. Further, different goods are produced with different combinations of factor inputs. Hence if *factor-price ratios* (the ratios among rent, wages, and interest) differ across countries, then *goods-price ratios* will also differ. In one country wages may be low relative to rent, whereas in another country wages may be high relative to rent. Thus, the first country can produce goods that require a great deal of labor and not much land more cheaply than goods that require a great deal of land but not much labor. In the second country, the opposite is true.

To summarize, it is because factors of production are not perfect substitutes for each other and must be used in different combinations to produce different goods that dissimilar factor price ratios in two countries give rise to dissimilar commodity cost and price ratios that provide a basis for gainful trade.

The role of factor prices in the determination of cost (price) ratios may be clarified by a simple illustration. Assume that in the United States the price of a marginal unit of land is $1 and the price of a marginal unit of labor is $2 and that in Japan the price of a marginal unit of land is Y800 and the price of a marginal unit of labor is Y200. Thus, land is relatively cheap in the United States (1:2 price ratio) and relatively expensive in Japan (4:1 price ratio), while the converse is true of labor. Assume further that to produce a unit of wheat in either country requires 5 units of land and 1 unit of labor and to produce a unit of textiles in either country requires 1 unit of land and 10 units of labor (see Table 3-1). These required inputs of land and labor are the *production functions* of wheat and textiles.[2]

The U.S. wheat-textile price ratio is 1:3 and the Japanese wheat-textile price ratio is 3:2. Clearly, the United States has a comparative advantage in the production of wheat and Japan has a comparative advantage in the production of textiles. This follows from the fact that wheat production is *land-intensive* and the United States can use its relatively cheap factor (land) to greatest advantage in that production. On the other hand, the United States has a comparative disadvantage

Table 3-1   Unit Costs of Wheat and Textiles Deriving from Unit Prices of Land and Labor in the United States and Japan

	United States (dollars)	Japan (yen)
Unit price of land	1.00	800.0
Unit price of labor	2.00	200.0
Unit cost (price) of wheat	7.00	4200.0
Unit cost (price) of textiles	21.00	2800.0

---

[2]The H-O model assumes that production functions are the *same* across countries. As we see in Chapter 5, when production functions are *dissimilar* across countries, then technology gaps can be a source of comparative advantage.

in textile production, which is *labor-intensive* and requires comparatively large amounts of its relatively expensive factor (labor). The converse situation holds in Japan.

But why should factor-price ratios differ across countries? The H-O model traces such differences to relative factor *endowments* (supplies) that are dissimilar across countries.[3] Countries differ greatly in their relative supplies of factors of production. A country like Canada has an abundant supply of natural resources (land) relative to its supplies of labor and capital. Therefore, rents in Canada are low relative to wages and interest. The Netherlands, on the other hand, has a relatively scarce supply of natural resources but relatively abundant supplies of labor and capital. In that country, rents are high relative to wages and interest. It is clear that such differences multiply when we consider that the individual factors of production are heterogeneous. Actually, there are several kinds of land factors and many varieties of labor and capital. For example, one country has a temperate climate, another has a tropical climate; one country has coal but lacks iron ore, another has iron ore but lacks coal; one country has large supplies of educated skilled workers, another has a predominantly illiterate, unskilled labor force; one country has steel plants, another has none; and so on. The number of specific factors is so large that any one country is certain to have factor-supply proportions that diverge in some respect from the proportions of other countries. Furthermore, as we shall see, national factor proportions change over time.

To conclude, the H-O model postulates that dissimilar commodity-price ratios (the immediate basis of gainful international trade) derive from dissimilar factor-price ratios and that these derive in turn from dissimilar factor proportions. A country has a comparative advantage in the production of goods that use relatively large amounts of its abundant factors of production and a comparative disadvantage in the production of goods that use relatively large amounts of its scarce factors of production. Indirectly, then, a country exports the services of its abundant factors of production and imports the services of its scarce factors of production.

DERIVATION OF A COUNTRY'S PRODUCTION POSSIBILITIES CURVE FROM ITS FACTOR ENDOWMENTS

In graphical language, the Heckscher-Ohlin model attributes the existence of dissimilar production possibilities curves among countries to dissimilar factor endowments. By using isoquant curves and the box diagram, we now offer a formal derivation of a country's production possibilities curve from its factor endowments.

---

[3]Factor prices are determined by both factor supply and the demand for factor use in production. Hence, dissimilar factor price ratios across countries imply dissimilar factor supply or factor demand ratios across countries. By assuming that factor demand ratios are the same across countries (reflecting similar demand preferences) and that production functions are also the same across countries, the H-O model focuses on factor supply (endowment) as the sole explanation of factor price differences.

Production Functions: Isoquant Curves

A production function expresses the physical relationship between the output of a good and the necessary factor inputs. It indicates the *maximum* output attainable with a given combination of factor inputs as determined by the technical conditions of production. A production function may be expressed most simply as follows: $P_i = f(a, b, c, \ldots, n)$ where P is the output of good i and $a, b, c, \ldots, n$ are factor inputs. Such a function may be depicted by an isoquant (equal-product) curve.

Assume that the United States has only two factors—land and labor—to produce beef or wine. The isoquant curve b–b in Figure 3-1 shows the combinations of labor and land inputs needed to produce a specified output of beef, and curve w–w does the same for wine. An isoquant curve is convex to the origin because the removal of 1 unit of a factor from production requires the addition of increasingly large amounts of the second factor to maintain the same level of production. That is to say, labor and land are not perfect substitutes in production; they can only be substituted for one another at increasing opportunity costs.

We also assume that the production functions of beef and wine are homogeneous in the first degree so that they show constant returns to scale. Hence a doubling of labor and land inputs causes a doubling of output. Constant returns to scale are indicated in Figure 3-1 by b_1–b_1, which is twice the distance from 0 as b–b and therefore represents twice the output of b–b. For the same reason, w_1–w_1 represents twice the output of w–w.

The *least-cost combination* of factor inputs to produce a good is determined by the relative prices (or price ratio) and marginal physical products of the two factor inputs.[4] Two *iso-cost* curves are drawn in Figure 3-1, E_1–E_2 and E'_1–E'_2; each iso-cost curve indicates the combination of labor and land that the producer can obtain at the same cost. E'_1–E'_2 represents twice the cost of E_1–E_2 because the former is twice the distance from the origin. The slope of an iso-cost curve is determined by the relative prices of labor and land. The producer can buy 0–E_1 of labor or 0–E_2 of land or any combination of labor and land that falls on E_1–E_2. The least-cost combination of factor inputs is at the point of tangency between the given iso-cost curve and an isoquant. For the iso-cost curve E_1–E_2, the point of tangency for wine (isoquant w–w) is at g. Hence the producer will use 0–m of labor and 0–n of land to produce wine. *Only at point g is the price ratio of the labor and land inputs equal to the ratio of their marginal physical products.* Putting the matter another way, w–w is the highest output of wine that can be obtained with the iso-cost curve E_1–E_2. For the same reason, h is the low-cost combination of factor inputs for beef.

Observe that the marginal rate of factor substitution in production is the same at points g and h because the slopes of the wine and beef isoquants are the same at those points. That is to say, the ratios of the marginal physical products of the two

---

[4]The least cost rule expressed algebraically is $MPP_w/P_w = MPP_c/P_c = \ldots$. That is to say, the least-cost combination of factors occurs when the ratio of the marginal physical product and price of each factor (MPP_i/P_i) is equalized across all the factors used in the production of a good.

Figure 3-1

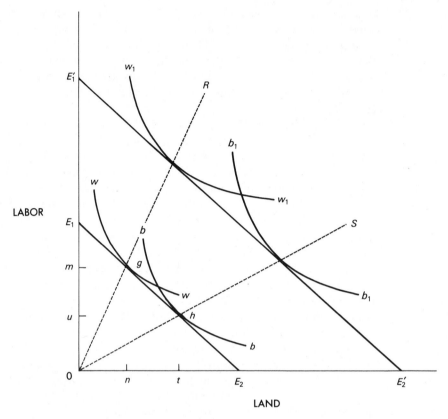

U.S. Production Functions for Wine and Beef: Determination of the Least-Cost Combination of Land and Labor. The b–b curve is the *isoquant* for beef, indicating the combination of labor and land needed to produce a specified output of beef. Curve w–w is the isoquant for wine. We are assuming constant returns to scale: A doubling of labor and land inputs causes a doubling of output. Hence, the beef isoquant b_1–b_1 represents twice the output of b–b because it is twice the distance from 0 as b–b. For the same reason, w_1–w_1 represents twice the output of w–w. Two *iso-cost* curves, E_1–E_2 and E'_1–E'_2, indicate combinations of labor and land that a producer can obtain at the same cost. The *least-cost combination* of factor inputs is at the point of tangency between the given iso-cost curve and an isoquant curve, such as point g on isoquant w–w. Only at point g is the price ratio of labor and land inputs equal to the ratio of their marginal physical products. For beef, the least-cost combination is indicated by point h. Observe that the ratio of marginal physical products of labor and land is the same at points g and h. The 0–R and 0–S rays cross the low-cost points on w–w and w'–w' and b–b and b'–b', respectively. Because 0–R has a steeper slope than 0–S, it is evident that the production of wine at g is more labor-intensive than the production of beef at h.

Part I   International Trade

factors are the same in wine and beef production, and these ratios, in turn, equal the factor-price ratio. If this were not so, it would pay producers to shift factor inputs between wine and beef production until it became true.

If outlays are doubled by moving to iso-cost curve E'_1-E'_2, the least-cost *proportions* of labor and land remain the same as long as the factor-price ratio does not change, which is true in this instance because the slopes of the two iso-cost curves are identical. We can show this by drawing ray 0-R from the origin to cross the least-cost points on w-w and w_1-w_1 and by drawing a second ray, 0-S, to cross the least-cost points on b-b and b_1-b_1. Since 0-R has a steeper slope than 0-S, it is evident that the production of wine at g is more labor-intensive than the production of beef at h (alternatively, beef is more land-intensive than wine). One of the assumptions of the H-O model is that wine will remain more labor-intensive and beef more land-intensive at all factor-price ratios, thereby ruling out factor reversibility.

It is evident without a graphic exercise that a change in the factor-price ratio (a change in the slope of the iso-cost curve) will bring about a new least-cost combination of factor inputs. We are now prepared to show how a country's relative factor prices depend on its total factor endowments.

Factor Endowments: Box Diagram

Each vertical side of the box diagram in Figure 3-2 measures the *total* labor endowment of the United States and each horizontal side measures its *total* land endowment. Hence the total labor endowment is 0-D or, alternatively, $0'$-R, and the total land endowment is 0-R or, alternatively, $0'$-D. The diagonal 0-$0'$, drawn as a dashed line, indicates the relative factor intensity of the U.S. economy.

Assume that the United States is once again producing only wine and beef and that it has not yet entered international trade. Beef output is measured from the origin at 0 toward the right, and wine output is measured from the origin at $0'$ toward the left. Although we can draw any number of isoquants indicating different output levels for wine and beef, we have drawn only two isoquants for each product to avoid cluttering the diagram, namely, b_1-b_1 and b_2-b_2 for beef and w_1-w_1 and w_2-w_2 for wine.

Any point inside the box represents a particular combination of wine and beef and also a particular combination of labor and land inputs at full employment. If we draw a line that connects the points of tangency between all the beef and wine isoquants (such as points A and F), we obtain a curve 0-$0'$, drawn as a continuous line, that represents all the *technologically efficient* combinations of product outputs and factor inputs. This line is called the *contract curve*. At any point on the contract curve, the ratio between the marginal physical products of labor and land inputs is the same in the production of both wine and beef. Consequently, it is impossible to produce more wine without producing less beef, and conversely. It follows that any point off the contract curve represents an *inefficient* combination of outputs and inputs that cannot endure under conditions of perfect competition.

Figure 3-2

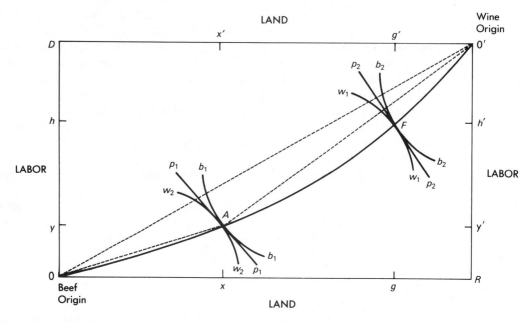

U.S. Factor Endowments: Determination of Beef and Wine Outputs.   Each vertical side of the box diagram measures the *total labor endowment* of the United States and each horizontal side, its *total land endowment*. The diagonal 0–0' (drawn as a dashed line) indicates the relative factor intensity of the U.S. economy. Assume that the United States produces both wine and beef and has not yet entered international trade. Any point inside the box represents a particular combination of wine and beef and also a particular combination of labor and land inputs at full employment. Although we can draw any number of isoquants indicating different output levels of wine and beef, we have drawn only two isoquants to avoid cluttering the diagram. The continuous line 0–0' connects the points of tangency between *all* the beef and wine isoquants (such as points *A* and *F*). This line is called the *contract curve;* it represents all the *technologically efficient* combinations of product outputs and factor inputs. Where the United States produces on its contract curve depends on the demand for wine and beef by U.S. consumers. Suppose consumers demand the combination denoted by point *A*. The ray 0–*A* (drawn as a dashed line) measures the factor intensity of beef output; the ray 0'–*A* does the same for wine. At point *A,* the United States uses 0–*y* labor and 0–*x* land to produce beef. How much labor and land is used to produce wine at point *A?* At that point, the factor-price line is p_1–p_1. An increase in demand for beef might cause production to move from point *A* to point *F.* How does the new factor-price line compare with the old one? The box diagram shows that with given isoquants (technology) the factor-price ratio is determined by the country's factor endowment and the relative demand for beef and wine.

Where will the United States produce on its contract curve? That depends on the demand for the two products by U.S. consumers. Suppose, for example, consumers demand the combination of wine and beef indicated by point *A*. By drawing ray 0–*A* (as a dashed line) we can measure the factor intensity of beef output, and we can do the same for wine output by drawing ray 0'–*A*. Thus to produce the amount of beef indicated by point A on the b_1–b_1 isoquant, the United States uses 0–x of land inputs and 0–y of labor inputs. The remaining land inputs $(0'$–$x')$ and the remaining labor inputs $(0'$–$y')$ are used to produce the amount of wine indicated by point A on the w_2–w_2 isoquant. Since the slope of ray 0–A is less than the slope of ray $0'$–A, it is evident that the production of beef at point A is more land-intensive (or less labor-intensive) than the production of wine at point A.

From our earlier discussion of isoquants, we know that the labor/land price ratio must equal the slope of the isoquant curves at their point of tangency (A) because only then does the factor-price ratio equal the ratio of the marginal physical products of labor and land in beef and wine production. This is shown in Figure 3-2 by the factor-price line p_1–p_1.

Now suppose an increase in demand for beef causes production to move from A to F. We know that the price of beef would rise relative to the price of wine, but what would happen to the factor-price ratio? Because beef is land-intensive, an increase in beef production would require more land inputs than labor inputs. This more intense demand for land inputs would cause the price of land to rise relative to the price of labor. This is shown by the steeper slope of the new factor-price line (p_2–p_2) as compared with the old factor-price line (p_1–p_1). To increase beef output from point A to point F, producers have drawn x–g land inputs and y–h labor inputs from the production of wine. As the reader can discover by drawing rays, the production of both beef and wine is more labor-intensive at point F than at point A. Why is this so? Because the price of labor has fallen relative to the price of land, producers of both beef and wine will achieve the least-cost combination of inputs by substituting labor for capital. The box diagram shows, then, that with given isoquants (technology) the factor-price ratio is determined by the country's factor endowment and the relative demand for beef and wine.

Derivation of the Production Possibilities Curve from the Box Diagram

The box diagram in Figure 3-2 contains all the information needed to construct the U.S. production possibilities curve. As we know, the slope of any point on the production possibilities curve is the marginal rate of transformation of beef for wine using the most efficient combination of factor inputs. Thus any point on the production possibilities curve corresponds uniquely with a point on the contract curve 0–$0'$. The production possibilities curve also indicates the quantities of beef and wine produced at each point on the curve. Similarly, each point on the contract curve indicates a particular quantity of beef and wine as measured by their isoquants, which are tangent at that point. All we need do, then, is to construct output scales for Figure 3-2 by measuring, say, beef along the bottom of the box (0–R) and wine along the left vertical side (0–D). The derivation of the production possibilities curve from the box diagram demonstrates that the *shape* of that curve is determined by the country's factor endowments at a given level of technology.

Chapter 3   The Heckscher-Ohlin Model

Dissimilar Factor Endowments
as the Basis of Trade

We are now prepared to show how dissimilar factor endowments serve as a basis of trade between two countries.

Let us assume that France has a higher endowment of labor relative to land than does the United States. Then it follows that the French box diagram has a different shape than the U.S. box diagram. We show this in Figure 3-3 by

Figure 3-3

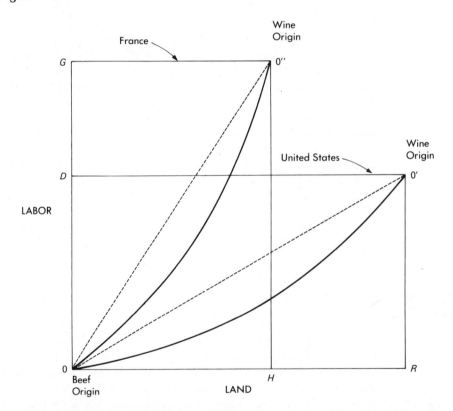

United States and France: Dissimilar Contract Curves. The diagonal (0–0″) in the French box diagram is steeper than the diagonal (0–0′) in the U.S. box diagram. The diagonals (shown as dashed lines) indicate that the French economy is more labor-intensive than the U.S. economy. Hence, the French contract curve (shown as a solid line from 0 to 0″) is steeper than the U.S. contract curve (shown as a solid line from 0 to 0′), as producers respond to a lower labor/land price ratio in France than in the United States. (Keep in mind that the H-O model assumes the same isoquants and demand preferences in both countries.) Because the French and U.S. contract curves are dissimilar, their production possibilities curves are also dissimilar. If wine is labor-intensive and beef is land-intensive, in which commodity does France have a comparative advantage? A comparative disadvantage?

superimposing the French box on the U.S. box. The diagonal in the French box (0–0″) is steeper than the diagonal in the U.S. box (0–0′), indicating that the French economy is more labor-intensive than the U.S. economy. Accordingly, the French contract curve (shown as a solid line from 0 to 0″) is steeper than the U.S. contract curve (shown as a solid line from 0 to 0′). Because French producers must combine more labor per unit of land than U.S. producers, the marginal physical product of labor is lower and the marginal physical product of land higher than in the United States. Therefore, the labor/land price ratio is lower in France than in the United States. (Keep in mind that the H-O model assumes isoquants are the same in both countries.) Hence, French producers will obtain their least-cost combinations of factor inputs in both wine and beef production by using more labor inputs relative to land inputs than U.S. producers.

Because the French and U.S. contract curves are dissimilar, we know that the French and U.S. production possibilities curves are dissimilar. *Hence, the different factor endowments of the two countries provide a basis for trade.* France has a comparative advantage in the labor-intensive good (wine) while the United States has a comparative advantage in the land-intensive good (beef). To arrive at this conclusion, however, we have assumed that consumer preferences for wine and beef in France and the United States are not so different as to offset the influence of factor endowments on factor prices.

HETEROGENEITY AND CHANGE IN FACTOR ENDOWMENTS

The H-O theory of trade assumes that the individual factors of production are homogeneous and fixed in supply. Actually, there are many subvarieties of land, human factors, and capital. Furthermore, factor endowments (however defined) are continually changing over time through the effects of technical advance, population growth, and investment. This section considers the implications of factor heterogeneity and change (mostly growth) for international trade.

Land Factors

Land factors, or natural resources, comprise the many elements of the natural environment that contribute to the production of goods and services useful to society. Whether a natural element can and does contribute to production at any given time depends upon the society's capacity and willingness to utilize it.

Contrary to popular understanding, natural resources are dynamic rather than fixed in supply. Elements of the natural environment *become* natural resources as society develops the need and ability to use them in production. Over the centuries more and more of the natural environment has been transformed into natural resources. Early civilizations made only modest use of the natural environment, as do the Australian bush people even today. The availability of coal had no effect on the economy of the American Indians because they had no productive use for coal; consequently, it was not a natural resource for them. In the 1930s, much the same could be said of uranium for our own contemporary economy. In the next century, the oceans will most likely become a much more important natural resource than they are at present. Fundamentally, therefore, what we call land factors, or natural resources, are dependent upon our technical knowledge and how we choose to use that knowledge. People must be aware of the existence of natural elements, must recognize their usefulness to them, and must want and know how to acquire them before they can become natural resources possessing an economic significance.

Natural resources are conventionally classified as agricultural land, forests, fisheries, and mineral deposits. Viewed broadly, natural resources also include topographical land features, solar radiation, water, winds, and any other natural elements that contribute directly or indirectly to economic activities. Each of these natural resource types has many variations. Agricultural lands differ in natural fertility, insolation, rainfall, latitude, height, and many other aspects. Mineral deposits are even more diverse. Not only are there hundreds of different minerals, but deposits of one mineral will vary in size, accessibility, and quality. The many kinds of natural resources and the wide variations in their quality and other attributes preclude any precise measurement of the *totality* of national resource endowments or their comparison. Even international comparisons of one resource type, such as agricultural land, can be approximate only. Because of this complexity, sweeping statements about a country's resource endowment can be misleading. For example, although Switzerland is often described as "resource poor," its topographical features (especially the Alps) are a prime tourist attraction and also provide an abundant supply of water power for electricity generation.

It should be evident that national resource endowments are dynamic. Technological innovations develop new natural resources from materials that had no previous economic use, and they also improve the accessibility of existing resources. New discoveries (also aided by technological advances) add to the known supply of resources. Offsetting this expansion is the exhaustion of natural resources through use and misuse. Oil wells run dry, iron mines peter out, forests sometimes disappear, fertile grasslands can become dust bowls, water tables sink, and so on. Because of this exhaustion process (as well as higher usage), the United States must now import many minerals, such as iron ore and petroleum, that were formerly supplied entirely from domestic sources or even exported in large quantities. The use (or misuse) of natural resources may also cause pollution and other environmental problems.

Human Factors

International variations in human factor endowments are both quantitative and qualitative. Aside from variations in overall size that derive mainly, although not exclusively, from variations in population, the *composition* of labor and management often differs markedly among nations. In poor, underdeveloped economies the bulk of the labor force is unskilled and occupied in traditional forms of agriculture, only a small fraction is skilled in industrial pursuits, and an even smaller fraction has technical and management training. In contrast, the labor force in highly developed economies, such as the United States or Japan, is mainly composed of semiskilled and skilled workers in industry, white collar workers engaged in service occupations, and a significant proportion of technical and management people.

International differences in the *quality* of human factors are difficult to measure but nonetheless important. Again, they are most striking between poorly developed and highly developed economies. Qualitative variations arise because humans are shaped by an economic, political, social, and cultural milieu that is not everywhere the same and is not ever likely to be. Thus, there is a diversity among peoples in ways that influence economic performance, such as physical vigor, motivation, attitudes toward work, technical skills, organizational and management capacities, and many other attributes. In addition to disparities among individuals living in different cultures, there are also dissimilarities in social conditions that bear directly on economic performance. Some societies are rigid, offering little opportunity for lower class individuals; other societies are open, allowing individuals to move upward to higher social levels (or fall to lower levels). In a rigid society, movement from one labor group to another is a slow, painful process that limits the capacity of the economy to make positive adaptations to change.[5]

Qualitative disparities among the human factors of different countries are so pervasive that skilled workers (or any other subtype of labor) in one country are never quite the same as in another country and may, in fact, be very dissimilar. Such qualitative disparities influence comparative costs in the same way as quantitative disparities. If workers in one country are generally twice as productive as workers in a second country because of quality differences (as distinguished from differences arising from the use of complementary factors, especially capital), then the effect on comparative costs is equivalent to doubling the size of the first country's labor force.

The gist of this discussion is that *at any time* the human factor endowment of a nation will be heterogeneous and will differ both in composition and quality from the human factor endowments of other nations. This, as we know, is a basis for profitable international trade. But this is not all. Each nation's human factor endowment changes *through time,* injecting a dynamic element into its comparative cost structure.

Transformations in the level, composition, and quality of the labor force introduce continuing changes in the relative factor endowments of a nation and hence in its foreign trade. First, the overall supply of labor is strongly affected by the rate of growth and the age distribution of the population. Second, the many

---

[5]Even in the mobile societies of advanced economies, the subtypes of labor tend to form "noncompeting" groups, with little movement of people among them over the short run. The persistence of structural unemployment in the United States is a case in point. Many of the American unemployed are workers whose services are no longer in demand because of technological innovations that require more education and new skills.

subtypes of labor—unskilled, semiskilled, technical, and so on—are subject to different rates of change. The radical expansion in the number of white collar workers and the simultaneous decline in the number of unskilled workers in the United States since the turn of the century are illustrative. Third, the quality of labor alters with changes in education, technology, and economic opportunity. An upgrading of labor has been particularly pronounced in this country—jobs once staffed by high school graduates are now staffed by college graduates. Because the formation of human skills requires saving and investment in education and training, economists regard human skills as *human capital*. As we shall see, the H-O model of trade has been extended to include the role of human skills in comparative advantage.

What we have said concerning labor is substantially true of another human agent of production—management. Changes in the size and the quality of the management force are largely determined by the freedom of economic opportunity, the rate of growth of the economy, and the rate of technological advance. When economic opportunity is impaired by a social caste system or by monopoly organization of the economy, when the economy is stagnant, or when the techniques of production are static, the management factor will initiate few changes in its supply relative to the supplies of other factors of production.

In an economy like the United States, however, management is a most dynamic factor of production. In this country, management adapted to the operation of large-scale business has grown at a faster pace than other types of management; and the rapid proliferation of business schools suggests the qualitative changes that have occurred, and are occurring, in this factor.

Capital

Along with human skills, capital is the most dynamic factor of production, and it exhibits most strongly the influence of changing technology. An economy becomes more productive by increasing the supply of its capital relative to other factor supplies and by improving the quality of its capital. Today the American factory worker produces more in less time than did workers of previous generations, primarily because the worker today has more (and better) machines and more horsepower to help in the productive process.

Growth in the quantity and quality of capital is spurred by technological improvements. An advancing economy produces not only more factories, utilities, machines, and other varieties of capital, but also more productive factories, utilities, and so on, to take the place of the old. The growth of capital may markedly alter the relative factor endowment of a country within a generation. An outstanding contemporary example is Japan, which was transformed from a labor-intensive to a capital- and skills-intensive economy in the space of thirty years, and in the process became the world's number two industrial power.

Drastic changes in a nation's capital supply cause substantial shifts in the nature of its foreign trade. The United States was once primarily an exporter of agricultural products and raw materials and an importer of manufactures. Now, with a relatively abundant supply of capital, this country is a major exporter of manufactures and a heavy importer of raw materials.

Nations differ widely both in their stocks of capital goods and in their capacity to add to capital stocks through investment. Capital stocks constitute *real capital,* which includes many varieties of equipment, buildings, and other instruments of production, as well as *social capital,* such as transportation, communications, education, and other infrastructural facilities. Basically, however, real capital must be financed out of savings representing the surplus of current production over current consumption. Unlike real capital, investment funds (*financial capital*) may be viewed as a homogeneous factor of production commanding a single price, which is the long-term interest rate adjusted for variations in risk.

Consumption exhausts most of the production of poor economies. Hence, the rates of investment of these poor economies tend to be low, perpetuating international differences in capital endowments. Because the supply of investment funds is low, long-term interest rates are high. Although investment funds flow from the more advanced economies, which have higher rates of saving, to underdeveloped economies to earn higher returns, international investment can do no more than supplement domestic investment, which must carry the main responsibility of financing additions to a country's capital stock.[6] As a result of persisting disparities in existing capital stocks and the rate of new capital investment among nations, capital endowments will continue to be an important factor in the determination of international differences in comparative costs.

Effects on Trade: Factor Heterogeneity

The heterogeneity of factors of production raises the possibility that a given subfactor may be *unique* to a nation with no counterparts in other nations. We can visualize this possibility most easily in the case of a mineral exploitable in only one country, but it could also happen with a labor or capital subfactor, at least in the short run. The possibility of subfactor uniqueness is heightened for labor and management when we take into account the many qualitative differences arising out of dissimilar sociocultural environments.

Unlike comparative advantage arising from dissimilar proportions of the *same* factors, a country's possession of a unique factor gives it an *absolute* advantage in those goods requiring that factor in production. However, absolute advantage based on a unique factor is probably not too important: Few subfactors are unique (without any substitutes), and even so, they are not likely to remain unique indefinitely in a world of rapid technological change. In this regard we can call to mind how Chile lost its sodium nitrate monopoly during World War I when chemists discovered an economical process for making nitrates out of nitrogen drawn from the air. As we shall see later, however, a nation may gain an absolute advantage in trade through product innovations that are not matched (at least for a time) in the rest of the world.

---

[6]Chapter 20 examines these and other aspects of underdeveloped economies.

More important, the existence of numerous subfactors indicates that national comparative cost structures are highly complex and that a broad similarity in the cost structures of two countries in terms of the three traditional factors most probably masks a rich diversity in their relative supplies of subfactors. For this reason, the possibility of identical comparative costs among nations is only theoretical. Nations can always find a basis to trade profitably with each other.

Effects on Trade: Factor Change

The effects of changes in a nation's factor endowments may be antitrade, neutral, or protrade. Figure 3-4 depicts these three possible outcomes.

Country X starts out with the production possibilities curve *A–B*. At the given terms of trade, it produces combination *C* of both goods and has a comparative advantage in the labor-intensive good that it exports in exchange for imports of the capital-intensive good. Now suppose that its supplies of labor and capital grow in the same degree so that factor proportions remain the same.[7] As a result, the *A–B* curve shifts outward to make a new production possibilities curve, *F–D*. Since the terms of trade are constant, country X now produces combination *K,* which represents more of both goods but in the same proportion as combination *C*. (Both *C* and *K* lie on the same straight line drawn from the origin.) The effect of these factor changes on trade is *neutral* because they do not alter the comparative cost advantage (or disadvantage) of the country: The *shape* of the production possibilities curve stays the same.

What happens if only the supply of capital grows with no change in the labor supply? This is shown by a shift of *A–B* to *A–B'*. Assuming once again that the relative prices of the two goods are constant, then country X uses the new capital to produce more of the capital-intensive (import-competing) good, at the same time drawing some labor away from the production of the labor-intensive good. The resulting production mix at *M* (where the terms of trade are the same as at *C*) has more of the import-competing good and less of the export good than the earlier mix at *C*. This increase in the country's relatively scarce factor (capital) is, therefore, *antitrade;* it has lessened the country's comparative advantage in the labor-intensive export good.[8]

Now take the converse situation: a growth in the labor endowment with no change in the capital endowment. *A–B* shifts to *A'–B,* with the country producing combination *N,* which has more of the labor-intensive, export good and less of the capital-intensive, import-competing good. Country X's comparative advantage in the labor-intensive good is now stronger than before and so, correspondingly, is its degree of specialization in that good. Hence, this increase in the country's relatively abundant factor is *protrade*.

---

[7]That is to say, the country's box diagram for capital and labor factors keeps the same shape, although it is now larger.

[8]If this capital growth continues, at some point country X will develop a comparative advantage in the capital-intensive good and start exporting it in exchange for labor-intensive imports.

Figure 3-4

LABOR–
INTENSIVE
EXPORT
GOOD

CAPITAL-INTENSIVE IMPORT GOOD

Production Effects of Factor Growth with Constant Terms of Trade. Country X starts out with the production-possibilities curve *A–B,* producing combination *C* of both goods at a given terms of trade (which remains constant throughout this example). The country has a comparative advantage in the labor-intensive good, which it exports in exchange for the capital-intensive good. Now suppose that country X's supplies of both labor and capital grow in the *same degree,* as depicted by the new production possibilities curve *F–D.* It now produces more of both goods but in the *same proportions* as at point *C.* Hence, the effect of these factor changes on trade is *neutral:* The shape of the production possibilities curve stays the same. But now suppose that the country's supply of capital grows while the supply of labor remains constant. This causes a shift from *A–B* to *A–B',* and the country now produces combination *M,* less of the labor-intensive (export) good and more of the capital-intensive (import) good. Because this unmatched growth in the country's relatively scarce factor lessens its comparative advantage, it is *antitrade:* There is less export of the labor-intensive good and less import of the capital-intensive good. When, however, the labor supply increases with no change in the capital supply, causing a shift from *A–B* to *A'–B,* then the effect is *protrade:* Combination *N* indicates more production of the labor-intensive commodity and less production of the capital-intensive good.

Suppose both factors are growing but at different rates. In that event the output of both goods will increase, but the resulting production mix will differ from the pregrowth mix. The effect will be antitrade if the scarce factor grows more than the abundant factor and protrade if the abundant factor grows more than the scarce factor.

We saw in Figure 3-4 that when the supply of capital increased, the production of the capital-intensive good rose while the production of the labor-intensive good fell, as shown by the shift from *C* to *M.* When the supply of labor increased, the converse happened: a shift from C to N. This biased effect of factor changes on production is known as the *Rybcznski effect*.[9] We can demonstrate this effect with a simple algebraic example. Let G_K and G_L represent the outputs of the capital-intensive good and the labor-intensive good, respectively. Assume that to produce a unit of G_K requires 2 units of capital and 2 units of labor, while to produce a unit of G_L requires 1 unit of capital and 6 units of labor. Assume further that the economy is endowed with 200 units of capital and 500 units of labor. Hence, for the full employment of both capital and labor, the following equations must be satisfied:

$$(1)\ 2G_K\ +\ G_L\ =\ 200\ \text{(full employment of capital), and}$$

$$(2)\ 2G_K\ +\ 6G_L\ =\ 500\ \text{(full employment of labor).}$$

The solution of these equations is $G_K = 70$ and $G_L = 60$. This is the only output combination that fully employs both capital and labor.

Now suppose the capital endowment rises to 300. This changes equation (1) to

$$(1a)\ 2G_K\ +\ G_L\ =\ 300.$$

The new combination at full employment of both capital and labor, therefore, becomes $G_K = 130$ and $G_L = 40$. To fully employ the new capital, G_K must be increased, but to do so, labor must be drawn from G_L because the labor endowment remains constant.

The *supply* effects of factor growth on trade may be intensified or weakened by the *consumption* effects of the higher real income (higher production) by country X. The consumption effect of a greater increase in the home demand for the import good than in the home demand for the export good is protrade, and vice versa. The *net* effects of factor growth on trade will depend, therefore, on both the production and consumption effects. A full analysis of factor growth effects on trade must also take into account any accompanying shifts in the terms of trade that were assumed to remain constant in the preceding analysis. Antitrade factor growth *improves* the terms of trade for country X when its import demand falls relative to the foreign export demand from combined production and consumption effects. On the other hand, protrade factor growth tends to *deteriorate* country X's terms of trade. If the production effects of growth strongly increase the supply of the export good while its consumption (income) effects strongly increase the demand for the import good, then the terms of trade may become so adverse as to lower country X's *pregrowth* gains from trade, a situation designated as *immiserizing growth*.[10]

---

[9]See T. M. Rybczynski, "Factor Endowments and Relative Commodity Prices," *Economica,* November 1955, pp. 336–41.

[10]Chapter 20 looks at the effect of international trade on growth rather than the effect of economic growth (factor change) on trade.

Part I   International Trade

This short appraisal of factor endowments has shown that each of the factors of production is subjected to many influences that alter its supply within a nation over time. Factor changes are a continuing phenomenon within nations, causing shifts in factor proportions and in comparative cost structures. Hence, a nation's trade is not stereotyped or static but frequently changing in magnitude, composition, and direction at a rate that varies from time to time and from country to country.[11] It follows that nations must adjust continuously to shifts in comparative advantage because they cannot reasonably expect their future trade to be a mere repetition of their present trade. In this dynamic world, nations that quickly adapt their trade and economies to change (regardless of its origin) have an obvious advantage over nations with sluggish responses.

THE LEONTIEF PARADOX

No empirical study has cast more doubt on the conventional (Heckscher-Ohlin) theory of international trade than the *Leontief paradox*.

The central proposition of the H-O model of trade is that a country will export products that use intensively its relatively abundant factors of production and will import products that use intensively its relatively scarce factors of production. Using input-output tables covering 200 industries and 1947 trade figures, Wassily Leontief tested this proposition for the United States by comparing the capital/labor ratios in U.S. export industries and in U.S. industries producing import-type goods (import-competing industries). Much to his surprise, he found that the capital/labor ratio in the export industries was *lower* than the ratio in the import-competing industries. His principal findings, shown in Table 3-2, indicate that a million dollars of import replacements requires more capital relative to labor to produce in the United States than a million dollars of U.S. exports.

Since the ratio of imports to exports in terms of capital per worker-year (18,184 ÷ 14,015) was 1.30, U.S. exports were *less* capital-intensive (or *more* labor-intensive) than U.S. import replacements, just the opposite of what would have been anticipated according to the H-O model for an "obviously" capital-abundant country such as the United States. Instead of capital-intensive exports and labor-intensive import replacements, Leontief showed that a representative bundle of U.S. import replacements required 30 percent more capital per worker-year to

---

[11]In a study of Japan's trade, Peter Heller concluded that the shift in Japan's factor endowments from a relative labor abundance to a relative capital/human skills abundance over the period 1956–1969 strongly altered its comparative advantage in favor of capital- and skill-intensive exports. See Peter S. Heller, "Factor Endowment Change and Comparative Advantage: The Case of Japan, 1956–1969," *Review of Economics and Statistics,* August 1976, pp. 283–92. In another study, Bela Balassa analyzed the changing pattern of comparative advantage in 184 categories of manufactured goods for 36 countries. His results show that intercountry differences in the structure of exports are in large measure attributable to differences in physical and human capital endowments. These results can also be used to forecast the direction in which a country's comparative advantage is moving by projecting the future values of its physical and human endowments. See Bela Balassa, "The Changing Pattern of Comparative Advantage in Manufactured Goods," *Review of Economics and Statistics,* May 1979, pp. 259–66.

produce than a representative bundle of U.S. exports. This unexpected result came to be called the *Leontief paradox*.

Leontief confirmed this empirical finding in a second investigation that applied the same input-output matrix to U.S. trade in 1951. In this instance the import/export ratio was 1.06.[12] Baldwin applied 1958 input-output data to U.S. trade in 1962 and got the same paradoxical result, an import/export ratio of 1.27.[13] Economists made similar studies for Japan, West Germany, India, and Canada with paradoxical results.[14]

The Leontief paradox has stimulated economists to search for explanations of the paradox and to test new trade hypotheses. The explanations fall into six major groups:

1. a *demand bias* in the United States in favor of capital-intensive goods
2. factor-intensity *reversal*
3. U.S. *import restrictions*
4. a scarcity of *natural resources* in the United States
5. the relative abundance of *skilled labor* in the United States
6. U.S. comparative advantage in *technology-intensive* industries

Table 3-2 Domestic Capital and Labor Requirements per Million Dollars of U.S. Exports and of Competitive Import Replacements of Average 1947 Composition

	Exports	*Import Replacements*
Capital (in 1947 dollars)	2,550,780	3,091,339
Labor (worker-years)	182	170
Capital per worker-year (dollars)	14,015	18,184

Source: Wassily Leontief, "Domestic Production and Foreign Trade; the American Capital Position Re-examined," in R. E. Caves and Harry G. Johnson (eds.), *Readings in International Economics* (Homewood, Ill.: Richard D. Irwin, 1968), pp. 503–27. This article was originally published in the *Proceedings of the American Philosophical Society* in September 1953.

---

[12]Wassily W. Leontief, "Factor Proportions and the Structure of American Trade: Further Theoretical and Empirical Analysis," *Review of Economics and Statistics,* November 1956, pp. 386–407.

[13]Robert E. Baldwin, "Determinants of the Commodity Structure of U.S. Trade," *The American Economic Review,* March 1971, pp. 126–46.

[14]The paradox was confirmed by Baldwin in a study of export/import capital intensities of some 30 countries. See Robert E. Baldwin, "Determinants of Trade and Foreign Investment: Further Evidence," *Review of Economics and Statistics,* February 1979, pp. 40–48. In opposition, Leamer argued that the paradox rests on a simple conceptual misunderstanding: When correct calculations are done, trade reveals the United States to be relatively abundant in capital compared with labor. See Edward E. Leamer, "The Leontief Paradox, Reconsidered," *Journal of Political Economy,* June 1980, pp. 495–503.

We shall briefly review the first four explanations in this section and then treat, at the end of this chapter and in Chapter 5, the skilled labor and technology explanations as new theories.

U.S. Demand Bias for Capital-Intensive Goods

In Chapter 2 we demonstrated that dissimilar tastes could afford a basis for gainful trade between two countries. We also answered "yes, theoretically" to the question, Can dissimilar tastes ever overwhelm dissimilar production possibilities so that a nation exports the product in which it has a comparative cost disadvantage while importing the product in which it has a comparative cost advantage? It follows that a *possible* explanation of the Leontief paradox consistent with the H-O model is that a U.S. demand bias in favor of capital-intensive goods is so strong that it reverses the U.S. comparative cost advantage in such goods. However, we must reject this explanation on the facts. The evidence indicates that U.S. consumers allocate about the *same* share of their expenditures to capital goods as consumers in the other industrial countries.

Factor-Intensity Reversal

The H-O model assumes that the relative factor intensity of two or more goods remains the same (or at least does not change its order) at different factor prices; that is, the production of good A stays, say, capital-intensive as compared to the production of good B over any likely range of factor prices (wages, interest, rent). But suppose this assumption does not hold? Then at one set of factor prices, good A would be capital-intensive compared to good B, but at another set of factor prices it would become labor-intensive compared to good B. In this way factor reversibility would break the link between factor endowments and comparative advantage. A labor-abundant country could conceivably have a comparative advantage in good A, exporting it to the capital-abundant country in exchange for good B.

A second possible explanation of the Leontief paradox, therefore, is that U.S. imports are produced abroad as labor-intensive and the same, or similar, goods are produced in the United States as capital-intensive. Is there evidence that factor reversibility actually occurs to a degree sufficient to support this explanation? Leontief himself has found little evidence of factor reversals.[15] Other investigations have come up with mixed results, but the weight of the evidence is against factor reversals on a significant scale. Although the agricultural sector is commonly cited as demonstrating factor reversal (e.g., capital-intensive rice production in the United States compared to labor-intensive production in Asia), it likely demonstrates dissimilar production functions rather than different positions on the same production function.[16] To conclude, factor-intensity reversal attributable to differ-

---

[15]Wassily Leontief, "International Factor Costs and Factor Use," *The American Economic Review,* June 1964, pp. 335–45.

[16]See Chapter 5 for a discussion of dissimilar production functions caused by technology gaps. Footnote 1 in Chapter 5 points out the empirical difficulty of distinguishing the use of the same production function with different factor coefficients from the use of different production functions based on different technology.

ent factor prices that reflect dissimilar factor endowments does not adequately explain the Leontief paradox.

U.S. Import Restrictions

In his original study, Leontief used the actual composition of U.S. imports in 1947 as the basis for the weights he assigned to the individual U.S. industries producing import-competing goods. But what if we suppose that U.S. tariffs and other restrictions were biased against the entry of labor-intensive imports to protect U.S. producers of similar products? In that event, Leontief's weights would result in a lower average labor intensity for U.S. import replacements than would occur in the absence of import restrictions. Under free trade the share of labor-intensive goods in U.S. imports would be higher than is actually the case.

In testing this explanation, Baldwin concluded that the capital/labor ratio of U.S. imports with no import restrictions would be about 5 percent lower than the ratio computed for actual imports.[17] This result offers a partial explanation of the Leontief paradox, but clearly it does not resolve the paradox.

Scarcity of Natural Resources

Leontief considered only capital and labor inputs, leaving out natural resource inputs. But if (1) the United States were heavily dependent on several natural resource imports, and (2) such imports required larger inputs of capital per worker-year to produce than imports that were not resource-intensive, then the link between natural resources and capital could explain the Leontief paradox. The United States would import domestically scarce imports of natural-resource products (in line with the H-O model) that were also capital-intensive.

This explanation was proposed by Vanek.[18] It was apparently supported by Leontief in his second article, which showed that the paradox disappeared when natural-resource industries were excluded from the calculations. When Baldwin did the same, the import/export ratio of capital per worker-year fell from 1.27 to 1.04, not quite eliminating the paradox. He also found that the Leontief paradox did *not* appear in U.S. trade with Western Europe and Japan but did hold in U.S. trade with Canada, the developing countries, and all other countries.[19] These results are consistent with the Vanek hypothesis, because the latter three areas are all relatively abundant in natural resources.[20]

---

[17]Baldwin, "Determinants of the Commodity Structure of U.S. Trade."

[18]Jaroslav Vanek, "The Natural Resource Content of Foreign Trade, 1870–1955, and the Relative Abundance of Natural Resources in the United States," *Review of Economics and Statistics,* May 1959, pp. 146–53.

[19]Baldwin, "Determinants of the Commodity Structure of U.S. Trade."

[20]The results are consistent but not fully supportive, because U.S. imports from these three regions are *more* capital-intensive than U.S. exports to them, even when natural-resource industries are excluded from the calculations. On the other side, the disappearance of the paradox in U.S. trade with Western Europe and Japan cannot be taken as supportive of the H-O model, because the capital/labor variable did not appear as statistically significant in multiple regression analysis with respect to those two areas. See Baldwin.

The evidence indicates that indeed there is a strong complementarity between certain raw materials, many of which are scarce in the United States, and capital. Hence, U.S. imports of natural-resource products make U.S. imports more capital-intensive than otherwise. At the same time, U.S. agricultural *exports*, which are capital-intensive, raise the average capital intensity of U.S. exports. The natural resource hypothesis, therefore, helps explain away the Leontief paradox on the import side, but it reinforces the paradox on the export side! As we have seen, the import effect more than offsets the export effect, so that the average import/export ratio becomes lower in the absence of natural-resource industries. In sum, natural resources offer a partial explanation of the Leontief paradox but not a resolution. Other factors are necessary for a more satisfactory explanation.

HUMAN-SKILLS THEORY OF TRADE

In our discussion of heterogeneity and change in factor endowments, we concluded that *at any point* the human factor endowment of a nation will be heterogeneous and will differ both in composition and quality from the human factor endowments of other nations. Although economists have long recognized these differences in human (labor) skills, the H-O theory of trade has nonetheless treated labor as a single homogeneous factor of production.

Would a separation of the labor factor into two or more labor-skill factors explain the Leontief paradox in U.S. trade? In his original article, Leontief himself thought that the labor factor would explain the paradox. Suppose that 1 worker-year of American labor were equivalent to 3 worker-years of foreign labor. Then the total number of American workers should be multiplied by 3 in calculating the U.S. capital/labor ratio, which would make it smaller than in many other countries. Hence, the United States would be relatively rich in labor and poor in capital, and it would trade labor-intensive goods for capital-intensive goods. But what would make the productivity of American labor superior to that of foreign labor? Rejecting the H-O assumption of technological parity among nations, Leontief mentioned entrepreneurship, superior organization, and education as possible sources of higher productivity. His explanation of the paradox would appear, therefore, to belong with the technology theories taken up in Chapter 5.

The human-skills theory of trade explains the Leontief paradox in terms of a U.S. comparative abundance of professional skills and other high-level human skills. Instead of adjusting the U.S. capital/labor ratio by multiplying the denominator (labor) by three or some other multiple, as suggested by Leontief, the human-skills theorists increase the numerator (capital) by adding the value of labor skills. The Leontief approach would make the United States labor-abundant; the human-skills approach would make the United States capital-abundant by redefining capital to include human skills.

It is well known that U.S. export industries pay higher wages than U.S.

import-competing industries.[21] Why should this be so? In answer, several empirical studies have shown that U.S. export industries employ higher proportions of highly skilled (and, therefore, highly paid) labor than do import-competing industries. As a consequence, the United States exports skill-intensive manufactures as compared with other countries.

Keesing applied U.S. skill coefficients involving eight categories of workers, based on the 1960 census of population, to the 1962 trade of the United States and thirteen foreign countries, which were all industrial except for India and Hong Kong.[22] He found that U.S. exports of *manufactures* embody a higher proportion of skilled labor (the first seven categories of workers) than U.S. import-competing goods (55 percent as compared with 43 percent) and a correspondingly lower proportion of unskilled and semiskilled workers (45 percent as compared with 57 percent). Also, of the fourteen countries in the study, the United States had the most skill-intensive exports, which reflected the greatest relative abundance of professional and other hard-to-acquire skills. Thus, the United States enjoys a persistent comparative advantage in products that require high labor skills.

Baldwin made other comparisons of skill requirements of U.S. import replacements and U.S. exports in 1962.[23] Excluding natural-resource industries, he calculated that the average years of education of labor in import-replacement industries was 10.3 as compared with 10.7 in export industries (an import/export ratio of .96), and the proportion of scientists and engineers was .0228 compared with .0369 (an import/export ratio of .62). Baldwin also found a significant positive relationship between the percentage of scientists and engineers employed in an industry and the industry's net exports to Western Europe and Japan.

Like physical capital, the creation of labor skills requires saving and investment. Labor skills may, therefore, be regarded as *human capital.* Does the combination of physical and human capital explain the Leontief paradox? When Baldwin added the average costs of education of labor (but not the costs of on-the-job training) to physical capital and then divided the sum by worker-years, the import/export ratio for all U.S. industries remained above unity but fell to .97 when natural resource industries were excluded from the calculation. Using a different approach, Kenen valued labor skills indirectly by capitalizing the incremental income such skills earn for workers over the income of unskilled workers. When this extra income was capitalized at less than 12.7 percent, the combination of physical and human capital reversed the Leontief paradox.[24]

The evidence indicates that the relative abundance of professional and other highly skilled labor in the United States is a major source of its comparative

---

[21]See the pioneer article by Irving B. Kravis, "Wages and Foreign Trade," *Review of Economic Statistics,* February 1956, pp. 14–30.

[22]Donald B. Keesing, "Labor Skills and Comparative Advantage," *The American Economic Review,* May 1966, pp. 249–58. Keesing's worker categories are (1) scientists and engineers; (2) technicians and draftspeople; (3) other professionals; (4) managers; (5) machinists, electricians, and tool and die makers; (6) other skilled manual workers; (7) clerical and sales workers; and (8) unskilled and semiskilled workers.

[23]Baldwin, "Determinants of the Commodity Structure of U.S. Trade."

[24]Peter B. Kenen, "Nature, Capital and Trade," *Journal of Political Economy,* October 1965, pp. 437–60.

advantage in manufactured products. The recognition of human skills as human capital also offers a partial explanation of the Leontief paradox. Rather than a separate theory, the human-skills approach may be regarded as a fruitful refinement of the conventional theory of trade. It adds a new factor of production (labor skills) to the H-O model and for that reason is sometimes called a "neofactor" theory. Against this view it can be argued that the human-skills theory is more properly regarded as a *technology* theory of trade because it rests on a country's possession of productive knowledge. When it is recalled that technological innovation undermines the critical assumptions of the H-O model (perfect competition, the sameness of production functions, and international factor immobility), the argument for treating human skills *directly* in a technology theory of trade appears most reasonable.[25] Efforts to rescue the H-O model by treating research and development (R & D) as a form of capital (along with physical capital and human capital) are even more questionable.

It is evident that national factor endowments (factor proportions) are *not* a complete explanation of comparative advantage. In Chapters 4 and 5 we examine imperfect competition and technological innovation (both assumed away by the H-O model) as other possible sources of comparative advantage.

SUMMARY

1. Because factors of production are *not* perfect substitutes for each other and must be used in different combinations to produce different goods, dissimilar factor-price ratios give rise to dissimilar commodity cost and price ratios, which provide a basis for gainful trade.

2. The Heckscher-Ohlin (H-O) model traces dissimilar factor-price ratios across countries to dissimilar factor endowments of land, labor, and capital.

3. The least-cost combination of factor inputs to produce a good is at the point of tangency between a given iso-cost line and an isoquant.

4. A country's production possibilities curve may be derived from its box diagram. This demonstrates that the *shape* of the production possibilities curve is determined by a country's factor endowment at a given level of technology. Hence, dissimilar factor endowments among countries are the basis of their mutual trade. This is the fundamental proposition of the H-O model of comparative advantage.

5. Although the H-O model assumes that the individual factors of production are homogeneous and fixed in supply, there are actually many subvarieties of

---

[25]The argument for treating technology as a distinctive determinant of trade (neotechnology approach) instead of as a form—or forms—of capital within the H-O model (neofactor approach) is supported empirically by Hirsch. See Seev Hirsch, "Capital or Technology? Confronting the Neo-Factor Proportions and Neo-Technology Accounts of International Trade," *Weltwirtschaftliches Archiv Review of World Economics,* no. 4 (1974), pp. 536–63.

land, human factors, and capital that are continually changing in supply over time through the effects of technical advance, population growth, and capital investment. The existence of numerous subfactors means that national comparative cost structures are highly complex, and the possibility of identical factor endowments among nations is only theoretical. The effects of changes in a nation's factor endowments may be antitrade, neutral, or protrade.

6. The central proposition of the H-O model of trade is that a country will export products that use intensively its relatively abundant factors of production and will import products that use intensively its relatively scarce factors of production. Much to his surprise, Leontief found in an empirical study that U.S. exports are labor-intensive and U.S. import replacements are capital-intensive, contrary to the H-O model.

7. The Leontief paradox has stimulated economists to find explanations for the paradox and to test new trade hypotheses. Explanations put forth to resolve the Leontief paradox include U.S. demand bias, factor-intensity reversal, U.S. import restrictions, and the scarcity of natural resources in the United States.

8. Two other approaches that help explain the Leontief paradox can be treated as new theories of trade: human skills and technology.

9. Supported by empirical evidence, the human-skills theory postulates that the United States has a relative abundance of professional and other highly skilled labor that is a major source of its comparative advantage in manufactured products.

QUESTIONS AND APPLICATIONS

1. (a) How does the H-O model explain dissimilar factor-price structures across countries?
   (b) According to the H-O model, in which commodities will a country have a comparative advantage?

2. (a) Demonstrate graphically how a change in a country's factor-price ratio will bring about a new least-cost combination of factor inputs to produce a good.
   (b) At their least-cost combination of factor inputs, the marginal rates of factor substitution in production are the same for two goods. Why?

3. (a) Why is the contract curve in a country's box diagram composed of the loci of all the efficient combinations of product outputs and factor inputs?
   (b) Assuming two countries share the same technology, how can they have dissimilar contract curves?

4. Construct a country's box diagram. Derive that country's production possibilities curve from the box diagram.

5. Explain how dissimilar factor endowments afford a basis for gainful trade.

6. What are the effects on international trade of factor heterogeneity? Of factor change?
7. What is the Leontief paradox? Evaluate the factor-intensity reversal and natural resource explanations of the Leontief paradox.
8. (a) What is the main proposition of the human-skills theory of trade?
    (b) What is the meaning of "human capital?"

SELECTED READINGS

Bhagwati, J. N. *International Trade: Selected Readings.* Cambridge: MIT Press, 1981. Part 1.

Caves, R. E., and H. G. Johnson, eds. *Readings in International Economics.* London: George Allen & Unwin, 1968. Parts 1 and 2.

Deardorff, Alan. "Testing Trade Theories and Predicting Trade Flows," in Ronald W. Jones and Peter B. Kenen, eds., *Handbook of International Economics,* vol. 1. Amsterdam: North-Holland Publishing Company, 1984.

Haberler, G. A. *Survey of International Trade Theory.* Special Papers in International Economics, no. 1. Princeton, N.J.: Princeton University Press, 1961. Chapters 2 and 3.

Heller, H. Robert. *International Trade: Theory and Empirical Evidence.* 2d ed. Englewood Cliffs, N.J.: Prentice-Hall, 1973.

Jones, Ronald W., and J. Peter Neary. "The Positive Theory of International Trade," in Ronald W. Jones and Peter B. Kenen, eds., *Handbook of International Economics,* vol. 1. Amsterdam: North-Holland Publishing Company, 1984.

Kindleberger, C. P. *Foreign Trade and the National Economy.* New Haven, Conn.: Yale University Press, 1962.

Ohlin, B. G. *Interregional and International Trade.* Cambridge: Harvard University Press, 1935. Part 2.

Ohlin, B. G. *Some Insufficiencies in the Theories of International Economic Relations.* Essays in International Finance, no. 134. Princeton, N.J.: Princeton University Press, 1979.

Ricardo, D. *Principles of Political Economy and Taxation.* New York: E. P. Dutton, 1912. Chapter 7.

COMPARATIVE ADVANTAGE: TRANSFER COSTS, IMPERFECT COMPETITION, AND INTRA-INDUSTRY TRADE

Chapter 4 continues our search for explanations of comparative advantage and gainful international trade. We look first at the influence on international trade of transportation and other transfer costs that constrain the movement of goods among countries. We look next at a general source of comparative advantage that was assumed away by the H-O model: imperfect competition.

TRANSPORTATION AND OTHER TRANSFER COSTS

The movement of tangible products from one country to another involves a number of transfer costs. They may be classified as (1) costs of physical transfer and (2) costs associated with government regulation of international trade. Costs of physical transfer include the costs incurred in packing, transporting, and handling merchandise. Such costs are omnipresent, and they affect the movement of goods both within and between nations. Transfer costs also arise out of government regulation of foreign trade, such as import duties, quotas, and exchange restrictions.[1] These transfer costs differ from physical transfer costs in that they pertain only to international trade. Their nature and individual effects on trade are described in Chapter 6; for the present we shall restrict our discussion to the significance of physical transfer costs.

Physical transfer costs influence international trade in two ways. First, transfer costs increase the prices of imports and thereby restrict the opportunity for gainful trade. Second, transfer costs affect international trade by their bearing on the location of industry and the geographical pattern of production.

---

[1]Trade restrictions that prohibit trade either entirely or beyond specified amounts, such as import quotas, have the same economic effects as infinite transfer costs. It should be noted that international trade in services (banking, insurance, tourism, law, education, construction, and others) does not incur physical transfer costs but is subject to government regulation.

The Effects of Transportation Costs on International Trade

Transportation is the main source of physical transfer costs; handling and packing facilitate transportation and are subsidiary to it. To simplify matters, we shall confine our analysis to the effects of transportation costs on international trade. The effects of handling and packing costs are the same, but usually of lesser importance.

We can show the restrictive effects of transportation costs on the volume of international trade with partial equilibrium analysis that focuses on trade in a single good in a two-country model. The right side of Figure 4-1 indicates the demand and supply schedules for wool in England, and the left side indicates those schedules in Australia. (To get both countries in the same figure, it is necessary to invert the Australian schedules, which should be read from right to left because the amount of wool increases in that direction.) It is evident that the equilibrium price of wool in Australia before trade is much lower than its equilibrium price in England, as shown by the intersection of their schedules. When trade opens up, therefore, Australia will export wool to England.

In the absence of transportation costs, the trade in wool will reach equilibrium when the excess supply of wool in Australia equals the excess demand for wool in England. This occurs at price P, where Australia exports $A–B$ wool while England imports $C–D$ wool. In equilibrium, the price of wool is the same in both countries and the volume of exports equals the volume of imports. ($A–B$ equals $C–D$).

The introduction of transportation costs breaks the common international price into two prices: The English price is now higher than the Australian price by the transport cost per pound of wool. Equilibrium is achieved at an Australian price of P_a and an English price of P_e. At those prices, Australia exports $A'–B'$ wool while England imports $C'–D'$ ($= A'–B'$) wool. Transportation costs, therefore, have lowered the volume of wool traded from $A–B$ (or $C–D$) to $A'–B'$ (or $C'–D'$). Observe also that the decline in the volume of Australia's exports lowers the Australian price from P to P_a; hence, the rise in the English price from P to P_e is less than unit transportation costs. In this example, Australia continues to export wool to England, but if transportation costs exceeded the difference between the pretrade prices of wool in the two countries, then Australia would cease to export any wool to England.

Actually commodities vary greatly in their capacity to absorb transportation costs. Commodities that are heavy, bulky, and hard to handle cannot absorb their transportation costs unless they command a high unit price. Bricks and sand are examples of this sort of commodity—to move them more than a short distance involves such high transportation costs that they cease to be competitive in price. On the other hand, commodities that take up little space or are easily handled may be economically transported over great distances even when their unit prices are low. The traditional staples of international trade, such as grains, wheat, cotton, and wool, are in the category of easy handling.

We may generalize this discussion of transportation costs in international trade by stating that the existence of transportation costs separates goods into two classes—*domestic* goods and *international* goods. Domestic goods do not enter international trade because transportation costs make it impossible to sell them at

Figure 4-1

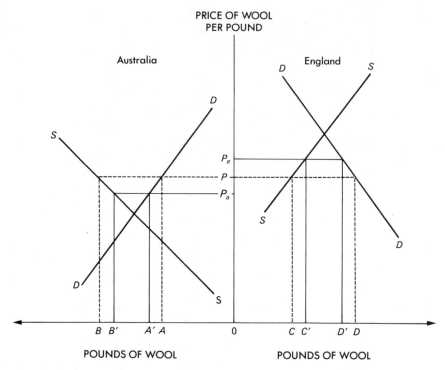

Effects of Transportation Costs on International Trade. The right side of Figure 4-1 shows the supply and demand schedules for wool in England; the left side shows those schedules for Australia. (The Australian schedules should be read from right to left.) Before trade opens up, the price of wool in England is higher than its price in Australia, as indicated by the intersections of their respective supply and demand schedules. *In the absence of transportation costs,* trade between the two countries would occur at price P, where Australia exports A–B pounds of wool, which is the excess of its amount supplied (0–B) over its amount demanded (0–A). At the same time, England imports C–D (= A–B) pounds of wool, which is the excess of its amount demanded (0–D) over its amount supplied from domestic production (0–C). *When transportation costs are introduced,* the English price of wool will exceed the Australian price by the transportation cost per pound of wool. Equilibrium is achieved at an Australian price of P_a and an English price of P_e. Transportation costs equal 0–P_e *minus* 0–P_a. Observe that transportation costs have lowered the volume of wool traded from A–B (or C–D) to A'–B' (or C'–D').

competitive prices in foreign markets.[2] International goods, however, are able to absorb transportation costs and still meet foreign competition.

---

[2]Perishable goods are likely to be domestic goods unless techniques of preservation or very rapid means of transportation permit their sale at competitive prices in foreign markets. This is also true of the interregional trade, as is testified by the local character of milk and bread production.

The existence of transportation costs, like increasing costs of production (increasing opportunity costs), means that international specialization will not be complete. When transportation costs are taken into account, there will be a number of goods that can be acquired more cheaply from domestic industries despite the fact that foreign industries can produce the same goods at a lower cost. Low-cost housing construction in one country will not benefit home buyers in another country. There is, however, no sharp dividing line between domestic and international goods. A higher foreign demand may make it economically feasible to export a good that has not entered foreign trade in the past. An improvement in transportation that greatly lowers cost will convert many domestic goods into international goods.

This last observation suggests the tremendous effects upon international trade of the "transportation revolution" that occurred in the nineteenth century, particularly in its last quarter. Before this revolution, the vast hinterlands of North and South America and the productive resources of such countries as Australia and New Zealand were unable to supply the world market, centered in Europe, because of prohibitive costs of transportation. Argentine beef was left to rot in the sun because only skins and horns could be exported to Europe. Australia was able to export wool but not mutton. North American wheat could not compete in European markets. Hence, the railroad, the steamship, refrigeration, and many other improvements in transportation that came thick and fast after 1870 completely altered the character of world trade. A worldwide system of multilateral trade evolved to bring an ever-widening exchange of goods, illustrating in reverse the restrictive effects of transportation costs.

The Effects of Transportation Costs on the Location of Industry

Transportation costs also influence international trade by affecting the *location* of production. In seeking to minimize costs of production, business firms must take full account of the transportation costs incurred in acquiring inputs of raw materials and intermediate components and in marketing final products. The best location for a plant is the location that minimizes total costs of production, including all transportation costs. This location may be near raw materials (*resource-oriented*), near the market or markets of the final product (*market-oriented*), or somewhere in between (*footloose*), depending upon the character of production processes.

When the cost of transporting raw materials used by an industry is substantially higher than the cost of shipping its finished products to markets, then the industry will usually locate closer to its raw material sources than to its markets. This situation exists when the industrial processes characterizing an industry use large quantities of bulky, low-value raw materials and fuels that do not enter into the final product. Such processes are described as *weight losing* because the final product is so much less bulky or weighty than the materials and fuels necessary for its production. Steel, basic chemicals, aluminum, and lumber are among the products that utilize weight-losing industrial processes for their manufacture.

When the cost of transporting finished products is substantially higher than the cost of transporting the raw materials and fuels that are used in their manufacture, industries locate close to their markets. This relationship develops when industrial processes add bulk or weight in production; that is, they are *weight gaining*. Then industries try to postpone manufacture of the final product until it is physically close to its market. Although U.S. automobile companies have concentrated basic manufacture in the Detroit area, they have established regional assembly centers within the United States and assembly centers in many foreign countries because it is much cheaper to ship unassembled auto parts than the whole vehicle.[3] Many other manufactured goods are shipped as parts to assembly plants located near markets for the same reason. A prominent example of weight gaining occurs in the construction of buildings, where the final product is so much bulkier than its components. Thus, building construction is mainly an assembly job at the construction site. Beverage manufacture offers another example of how weight-gaining processes push final manufacture toward the market. Coca Cola and Pepsi Cola ship syrup concentrate to plants all over the world, which in turn add water to the concentrate and bottle the mixture. Even some Scotch whiskey comes to the United States in concentrated form. Finally, mention should be made of the extreme market orientation shown by service industries, such as wholesaling and retailing firms and transportation agencies.

When transportation costs are not an important factor on either the resource or market side, or when they tend to neutralize each other, and when location close to the market is not particularly advantageous, then industries are highly mobile or footloose, locating where the availability and cost of labor and other factors of production give them the lowest manufacturing cost. Companies producing electronic components, shoes, garments, containers, and small housewares offer examples of high locational mobility. U.S. electronics manufacturers ship their components to foreign countries, such as Taiwan and South Korea, for assembly by low-cost, semiskilled workers. The assemblies are then brought back to the United States where they are "packaged" for the domestic market.

The economics of location is extremely complex. The fact that a firm may use several raw materials (including water, fuel, and power) drawn from different geographical areas and sell many products in several geographical markets can make it very difficult to determine the optimal location that minimizes transportation costs. This difficulty is compounded by the need to also consider the availability and cost of factors of production (land, labor, and capital) at different locations.[4] The availability and cost of unskilled and semiskilled labor is often decisive in location decisions, especially in market-oriented and footloose industries.

---

[3]Many countries also impose high duties on whole vehicles while imposing low or zero duties on vehicle parts to encourage assembly operations in their own territory.

[4]Local taxes are also a factor in location. Many governments seek to attract industry to less-developed regions within their countries by offering preferential tax treatment to domestic and foreign investors.

Part I International Trade

In effect, the influence of transportation costs on the location of industry is a supply-side determinant of a nation's comparative advantage, along with factor endowments and technology gaps in production. The cost of overcoming geographical distance for a given product may vary from one place to another, both within and among nations, because of the location of raw materials or markets. In resource-oriented industries, transportation inputs may be a stronger influence on location and international specialization than relative supplies of productive factors. They will also be significant in determining international specialization in many market-oriented industries. Only in the case of footloose industries can we safely ignore the independent effects of transportation costs on location and international specialization.

In broader terms, the influence of transportation costs on location suggests that countries that are distant from world markets for final goods and have no substantial domestic markets will tend to have a comparative disadvantage in market-oriented industries, whereas countries close to world markets or with large domestic markets will attract market-oriented industries. Thus, the location of a country may give it an advantage in export markets even though its factor costs of producing some export goods are no lower (or are even higher) than the factor costs of producing similar goods in a country distant from those markets.

IMPERFECT COMPETITION: MONOPOLY PROFITS, INCREASING RETURNS, PRODUCT DIFFERENTIATION, AND RISK

The H-O model of trade rests on the assumptions of perfect competition, which are as follows: (1) Many independent firms produce a homogeneous product (hence, the individual firm cannot influence price); (2) there are no legal, financial, technical, or other obstacles to entry into the industry; (3) there are many independent *buyers*, none of whom can influence price; and (4) each firm has full knowledge of cost and demand data for both the present and the future (economic risk and uncertainty are nonexistent and pure profits are zero in long-run equilibrium).

The first three assumptions are fairly representative of trade in basic foodstuffs and agricultural raw materials, although national farm programs and international commodity agreements have steadily introduced noncompetitive factors. However, international trade in minerals and manufactured goods departs in one way or another from the conditions of perfect competition. Although minerals are homogeneous commodities, their production and trade are usually dominated by a relatively small number of producers who can influence the market price and other conditions of sale. Much trade in manufactured goods and services also occurs under conditions of oligopoly (few sellers), and even when it does not, product differentiation is common. In brief, perfect competition is the exception rather than the rule in international trade.

The effects of this *imperfect* competition on international trade may be restrictive, neutral, or expansive, depending on the particular variety of imperfect competition in question and the policies of individual firms. In this section we sketch the principal types of imperfect competition and their most likely influence on the course of international trade. In particular, we wish to know whether international trade differs significantly from what it would be if all markets were perfectly competitive.

As shown in Table 4-1, three market structures differ in one way or another from perfect competition. Accordingly, they are designated *imperfect competition*. A critical distinction between perfect and imperfect competition is the role of the individual firm. Under perfect competition, the firm *cannot* affect market price because it is only one of many firms and its product is regarded by buyers as the same as the products offered by other firms in the industry. Also, the firm's *long-run* economic profit is zero because firms can freely enter or leave the industry.[5] Figure 4-2

Table 4-1   Key Features of Principal Market Structures

| | Perfect Competition | Imperfect Competition | | |
		Monopolistic Competition	Oligopoly	Monopoly
Number of firms	Many	Many	Few	One
Product	Homogeneous	Differentiated	Differentiated or homogeneous	No substitutes
Firm's demand schedule	Horizontal	Downward sloping	Downward sloping	Downward sloping
Information	Complete	Partial	Partial	Partial
Increasing returns	None	Possible	Possible	Possible
Entry/exit barriers	None	Modest	High	Very high
Marginal cost (*MC*) and price (*P*)	$MC = P$	$MC < P$	$MC < P$	$MC < P$
Long-run economic profit	Zero	Zero	Can be positive	Can be positive

[5]*Economic profit* is the difference between total revenues and total costs that include the full opportunity costs of all factors (including the *normal* profit of the entrepreneur). Economic profit (also called monopoly profit), then, is any profit above normal profit. Normal profit is the amount necessary to attract entrepreneurial services to the firm. A related term is *economic rent,* which is defined as the return to a factor of production above the amount required to keep the factor in its current occupation. For example, a baseball player earning $1 million annually whose next best employment would earn him only $50,000 enjoys an economic rent of $950,000. Monopoly profit or economic rent is possible only because the firm or factor of production possesses a skill or other asset that is impossible or difficult for others to emulate.

Figure 4-2

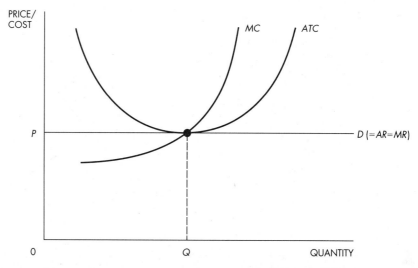

Long-Run Equilibrium Price and Output of the Individual Firm Under Perfect Competition. In a perfectly competitive market, the firm must take as given the market price determined by the intersection of the *industry* supply and demand schedules. It can sell an unlimited quantity of its product at that price (0–P) but cannot sell any quantity at a higher price. Hence, its demand curve (D)—also designated as the average revenue curve (AR)—is horizontal, indicating perfect elasticity of demand. Because average revenue is constant as the quantity sold by the firm changes, the marginal revenue curve (MR) is also constant and equal to AR. The firm produces and sells 0–Q where MC equals MR. At that output, the firm makes zero economic profit because average total cost (ATC) equals average revenues (AR). At any other output, the firm would incur a loss.

shows the determination under perfect competition of the firm's long-run equilibrium output at the industry's price.

In contrast to perfect competition, the firm faces a downward-sloping demand curve under imperfect competition. The firm, therefore, is able to influence price by altering the quantity of its product offered for sale. In other words, the firm enjoys some degree of *monopoly power* that derives from product differentiation (monopolistic competition), a small number of firms in an industry with high entry barriers (oligopoly), or a unique product with no substitutes protected by very high entry barriers (monopoly).

The most extreme divergence from perfect competition is monopoly. Figure 4-3 indicates the determination of the long-run equilibrium price and output in a monopoly market. The monopolistic firm can obtain long-run economic profits because entry barriers keep other firms out of the market. This can also happen for an oligopolistic firm but is less certain because declining entry barriers may allow new firms to enter the industry or rival firms may engage in price wars. The entry

Figure 4-3

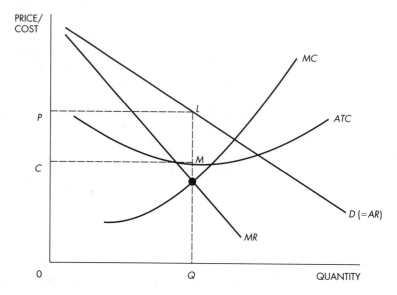

Long-Run Equilibrium Price and Output Under Monopoly. In monopoly, the firm faces a downward-sloping demand curve ($D = AR$). Hence, the MR curve lies below the AR curve. The monopolistic firm maximizes profit by producing $0-Q$ where $MC = MR$. At this output, price is $0-P$. Because total revenue ($0-P-L-Q$) exceeds total cost ($0-C-M-Q$), the firm enjoys an economic (monopoly) profit ($C-P-L-M$).

of new firms in a monopolistically competitive market prevents any long-run monopoly profits.[6]

Monopoly and oligopoly affect international trade through *monopoly profits, increasing returns,* and *technological innovation.* Monopolistic competition (and some oligopoly) also affect international trade through *product differentiation.*

Monopoly Profits

Traditionally, economists have extolled perfect competition and deplored imperfect competition. This attitude is based on the theoretical finding that, unlike the case of perfect competition, the allocation of factors of production under imperfect competition does not maximize consumer satisfaction. Under perfect competition the price of a good equals its lowest unit cost of production, and the cost of production includes only the profits necessary to attract and keep the management factor plus the other factor payments. Furthermore, the price of an individual factor in any employment is equal to the value of its marginal product in all employments. Thus, it is *not* possible to increase national output by reallocating

---

[6]For a thorough explanation of the different market structures, the reader is referred to any basic text in economics.

factor supplies among different lines of production. As observed in Chapter 3, this means that national price and cost ratios are the same, and cost ratios reflect relative factor supplies and demands. Under the equilibrium conditions of perfect competition, therefore, comparative cost advantages and disadvantages are fully expressed in international price differences.

Under monopoly and oligopoly, however, excess profits — profits not required to retain the management factor in production — may occur, although not necessarily. The existence of excess or *monopoly profits* makes the price of a good (or service) higher than its marginal cost of production and, for the nation as a whole, the price ratios between goods differ from their marginal cost ratios. In this way, the international allocation of production (international specialization) is not fully adjusted to opportunity costs; in other words, the gains from trade are less.

Figure 4-4 measures the social cost of monopoly power. The firm produces $0-Q$ at a price $0-P$ as determined by the intersection of its MC and MR curves. In a perfectly competitive market, the firm would produce $0-Q_1$ at a price $0-P_1$, as determined by the intersection of its MC and AR curves. (We assume that the firm

Figure 4-4

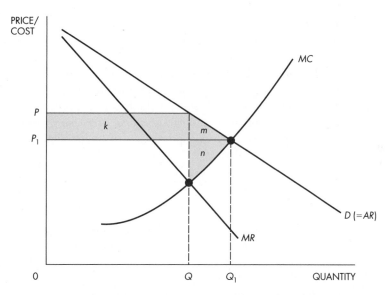

The Social Cost of Monopoly Power. The monopoly firm produces and sells $0-Q$ output at a price $0-P$ as determined by the intersection of its MC and MR curves. In contrast, a perfectly competitive firm produces $0-Q_1$ output at a price $0-P_1$ as determined by the intersection of its MC and AR curves. The shaded rectangle k and triangles m and n show the change in consumer and producer surpluses caused by monopoly power. Consumers lose surplus as measured by rectangle k and triangle m while the firm gains surplus measured by rectangle k but loses surplus indicated by triangle n. Hence, the deadweight loss or social cost of monopoly power is $n + m$.

would have the same cost curve in the monopoly and competitive markets.) We can measure the *social cost* of monopoly as compared to perfect competition by the net change in *consumer and producer surplus*. Consumer surplus is the difference between what consumers are willing to pay for a product and the market price. It is measured by the area between the equilibrium market price and the demand schedule. Producer surplus for the individual firm is the difference between the market price it receives and its marginal cost.

Because under monopoly consumers pay a higher price $(0-P)$ to buy $0-Q$ of the product than the competitive price $(0-P_1)$, they lose surplus indicated by the rectangle k. Consumers also lose surplus indicated by triangle m because they *would* have bought an additional amount of the product $(Q-Q_1)$ at the competitive price $(0-P_1)$. In contrast to consumers, the firm gains a surplus indicated by rectangle k because it charges for $0-Q$ a price higher than the competitive price. But it *loses* surplus indicated by triangle n because in a competitive market it would have sold an additional amount $Q-Q_1$ above its marginal cost curve. The net change in the combined consumer and producer surpluses, therefore, is $(k + m) - (k - n) = m + n$. This is the *deadweight loss* or social cost of monopoly power.

Increasing Returns

The H-O model denies increasing returns over the long run by assuming constant returns to scale and by ignoring economies of scope and *dynamic* increasing returns over time from learning curve effects.[7]

Increasing returns are defined as a proportionate increase in the output of a good that is greater than the proportionate increase in *all* the factor inputs that produced that output. Hence, a doubling of inputs would more than double the output of a good with a corresponding decrease in unit costs. The presence of increasing returns favors the creation of oligopolistic industries dominated by a small number of firms.

Increasing returns are associated with economies of scale, learning curve effects, and economies of scope.

Economies of Scale   Assume that two countries (A and B) have the same factor proportions, the same tastes, and the same level of technology. In terms of the H-O model discussed in Chapter 3, no gainful trade is possible under these conditions because cost and price structures are identical. But now suppose that country A has a big domestic market that allows it to achieve economies of scale in producing a manufactured product (say, automobiles), whereas country B has

---

[7]We are speaking here of *internal* increasing returns that accrue to the individual firm. In contrast, *external* increasing returns accrue to *all* firms in an industry as the industry grows in size, such as the benefits of a skilled labor force or a specialized parts industry. Silicon Valley in California is a good example of how external increasing returns benefit an entire industry (computers).

only a small domestic market that limits it to high-cost, small-scale production of automobiles. This is shown in Figure 4-5. Although the long-run average cost (*LRAC*) curve is the same in both countries, the representative producer in country A is producing 0–G automobiles at a unit cost of 0–C whereas the representative producer in country B is producing 0–F automobiles on a smaller scale at a unit cost of 0–K. Thus, country A has a comparative advantage in automobiles based on economies of scale. When trade opens up, country A will export automobiles to country B and, in return, import a product from country B in which country A has a comparative disadvantage. To eliminate country A's comparative advantage in automobiles, producers in country B would have to invest in new plant and equipment that would achieve the economies of scale enjoyed by producers in country A. But this would require both massive capital investment and time. And even if this investment were forthcoming, producers in country B would have to absorb losses until the new plants were actually in operation. Without government assistance, these obstacles might prove insurmountable, even over the long run.

Figure 4-5

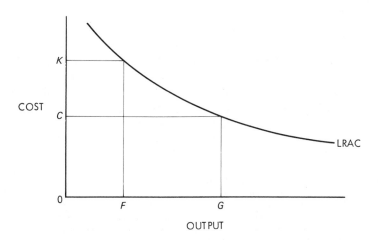

OUTPUT

Long-Run Average Costs with Economies of Scale. The declining long-run average cost (*LRAC*) curve reflects economies of scale in the manufacture of a product (say, an automobile). Assume that the *LRAC* curve for automobiles is the same in country A and in country B. However, the representative manufacturer in country A is producing 0–G automobiles at a cost of 0–C whereas the representative manufacturer in country B is producing 0–F automobiles at a cost of 0–K. Hence, manufacturers in country A produce at a lower cost than manufacturers in country B because of greater economies of scale. It follows that country A has a comparative advantage in automobiles and will export them to country B. This comparative advantage will endure as long as country B fails to match the economies of scale of country A.

The sources of internal economies of scale may be classified as specialization and technological innovation.[8]

Specialization can create economies of scale because a larger scale may enable a more productive use of specific factors of production. Giant machines, the assembly-line organization of production, high levels of labor and managerial specialization, extensive research and development, and mass marketing are economical only for firms that have reached a substantial size. Productivity increases at higher levels of output because indivisible factors of production can be more fully utilized, along with more specialized labor and management.

Technological innovation in capital goods commonly enhances economies of scale over the long run. Because increases in the scale of plants are so often associated with changes in technology, it is impossible to distinguish scale effects from technology effects in practice in any general way.[9] *Pure* scale effects occur only when the basic technology (production function) remains the same, as in oil tankers, for instance. On the other hand, technological innovations can change production functions without creating scale economies, as is true of mini-steel mills.[10] The effects of technological innovation on trade (apart from any scale effects) are treated in Chapter 5.

Learning Curve Effects   The *learning curve* traces a decrease in the average *total* costs of a product as a firm's *cumulative* volume of output grows over the long run. Substantial, if not conclusive, evidence regarding a wide range of products, including refrigerators, semiconductors, petrochemicals, paper, TV sets, beer, vacuum cleaners, primary aluminum, facial tissue, electric power, motorcycles, and aircraft, supports the proposition that total product costs decline by a constant percentage (typically 25 to 30 percent) each time volume doubles. That is to say, unit costs decline in constant proportion to cumulative volume. For instance in less than two decades, Du Pont cut the cost of rayon fiber from 53 cents a pound to 17 cents.[11]

---

[8]For a review of theory and research on economies of scale, see Bela Gold, "Changing Perspectives on Size, Scale and Returns: An Interpretive Survey," *Journal of Economic Literature,* March 1981, pp. 5–33. Another source of decreasing unit costs may be found in *external* economies of scale that arise outside the firm or industry. The individual firm or industry functions within a broad economic environment, and its costs of production are dependent upon the efficiency of the economy as a whole. As an economy develops, transportation and communication facilities, raw materials, capital equipment, supplies and parts, skilled labor, financing, and so on may become progressively more available and cheaper to the firm. The firm may also benefit from an expansion of its own industry. External economies—unlike internal economies—are compatible with perfect competition because they lower the costs curves of *all* firms.

[9]It may be done for very specific sectors. For example, differences between the basic oxygen and open hearth furnaces in steelmaking are attributable to technological differences and can be distinguished from scale differences within each category of furnace. See Gold, "Size, Scale, and Returns."

[10]Technological innovations are not always biased toward larger plants; they can also make smaller plants more economical. A case in point is the mini-steel mill, which is becoming more important in the United States. This mill depends solely on scrap metal, which is melted in electric furnaces and then poured into products. More generally, factory automation can overcome the diseconomies of short production runs through "flexible" manufacturing systems.

[11]William J. Abernathy and Kenneth Wayne, "Limits of the Learning Curve," *Harvard Business Review,* September–October 1974, p. 110.

Why should total unit costs fall with cumulative output? The explanation covers the entire firm, not only economies in the single plant. As the firm gains experience with a product over time, it can cut costs through a combination of effects, such as spreading overhead over a bigger volume; improving the performance of workers and managers through greater specialization, more effective work design and layouts, and a growing familiarity with the product and related processes; and reducing inventory costs as production and marketing become better organized. In sum, unit costs drop as experience leads to a smoother coordination of tasks and their performance.

The implication of the learning curve is obvious: The firm that achieves the greatest market share in a product will gain a cost advantage over firms with smaller market shares. Cost reductions, of course, will not go on forever. At some point, incremental learning effects will become inconsequential or market demand will limit further growth.

It is important to distinguish between economies of scale and the learning curve. The former depend on the *size* of output *at a given time.* In contrast, learning curve effects depend on cumulative output over a *period of time.* Because of economies of scale, the *big* firm has a cost advantage over the *small* firm. Because of learning curve effects, the *mature* firm has a cost advantage over the *young* firm. It follows that a small firm can benefit from the learning curve. The learning curve acts progressively over time to lower the *entire* long-run average cost curve deriving from economies of scale.

Economies of Scope   A third explanation of increasing returns is *economies of scope* that may occur in a firm producing two or more different products. Economies of scope appear when the unit costs of each of two or more products produced *jointly* by a firm are lower than the unit costs of the same products produced alone with the same level of inputs. The source of economies of scope is the common use of inputs, plant facilities, distribution channels, management, and other assets of the firm. Economies of scope can give a competitive advantage to the diversified firm.

The Effects of Monopoly and Oligopoly on Trade

The *net* effect of monopoly and oligopoly on international trade may be detrimental or beneficial. Monopoly profits are always detrimental, but they may be more than offset by increasing returns and rapid technological advance. The net effect of *pure* monopoly on trade is probably detrimental in most cases. Lacking the spur of competition, a monopoly firm may become stagnant or actually retard technological improvements to sustain high profits. Nor is a monopoly firm necessarily a large-scale producer enjoying decreasing unit costs. For these reasons a monopoly, particularly an old monopoly, is apt to restrict the opportunity for international specialization and trade by holding prices far above costs and charging "what the traffic will bear." Fortunately, pure monopoly is exceedingly rare in international trade. Its effects on trade, however, may be closely matched by cartels, commodity agreements and state trading.[12]

Oligopoly with differentiated products is the dominant market structure in international trade today. Multinational firms are oligopolists who compete in world markets against a few rival firms.[13] In practice, oligopoly differs from monopoly in that there may be effective competition among oligopolists unless they organize a cartel or reach a less formal agreement not to compete, both of which are forbidden by U.S. law but often permitted in foreign countries.[14] The possibility that the relatively small number of producers will "gang up" on buyers by agreeing to hold up prices, allocate markets, freeze technology, and the like is the greatest danger of oligopoly. When competition does exist in an oligopolistic industry, it will usually be *nonprice* competition in quality, style, or services rather than in prices. The heavy burden of fixed costs in the mass-production industries creates such a great risk of price wars that the firms within those industries tend to raise and lower prices together. We are all familiar with this sort of price behavior in cigarettes, automobiles, and gasoline — all products of oligopolistic industries.

When there is effective competition among oligopolistic firms, international trade will generally benefit from increasing returns and rapid improvements in technology. After all, the most dynamic industries are likely to be industries in which oligopoly is the market arrangement.[15] The aggressive competition of oligopolies in the United States and their willingness and ability to exploit foreign sources of supply and foreign market opportunities are mainly responsible for the expansion of U.S. trade in manufactured goods.[16]

International Price Discrimination by Oligopolists   A possible effect on international trade of oligopoly (or monopoly) is price discrimination among country markets, giving rise to the phenomenon of *dumping*. Economic analysis demonstrates that an oligopolist selling in two or more markets can maximize monopoly profit by treating the markets as separate and charging different prices when price elasticities of demand differ across those markets. This is shown in Figure 4-6.

Price discrimination works only when the oligopolist can keep its country markets segmented from each other. Otherwise, arbitragers will buy the product

---

[12]International cartels and commodity agreements involve restrictive arrangements among producers or national governments of several countries. State trading occurs when some or all of a country's foreign trade is conducted by government enterprises. With the collapse of the communist East European countries and the Soviet Union, state trading has diminished greatly in importance.

[13]See Chapter 22.

[14]The Webb-Pomerene Act, however, does allow U.S. producers to organize an *export* cartel.

[15]In 1991, the five hundred largest industrial companies in the world were all members of oligopolistic industries, ranging from aerospace to transportation equipment. See "Guide to the Global 500," *Fortune,* July 27, 1992, pp. 175 ff. This was also true of the world's five hundred largest *service* companies (finance transportation, retailing, utilities, and diversified services) in 1990. See "The Fortune Global Service 500," *Fortune,* August 26, 1991, pp. 165 ff.

[16]The fifty largest U.S. industrial exporters in 1991 belonged to oligopolistic industries. Their company sales ranged from $123.8 billion (General Motors) to $2.6 billion (Ethyl). Exports of these fifty companies totalled $130.4 billion, about two-fifths of U.S. nonagricultural exports. See "U.S. Exporters on a Global Roll," *Fortune,* June 29, 1992, p. 95.

Figure 4-6

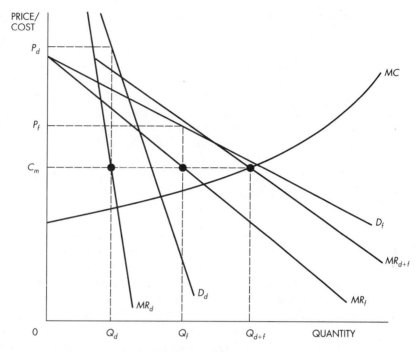

Price Discrimination Between Domestic and Foreign Markets: Dumping. In its pricing strategy, the price-discriminating oligopoly firm treats the foreign market as separate from the domestic market. The firm produces a total amount of its product $(0-Q_{d+f})$ as determined by the intersection of the MC curve and the MR_{d+f} curve, which is the horizontal summation of the MR_d and MR_f curves, that is, $MR_{d+f} = MR_d + MR_f$. Because MC at output $0-Q_{d+f}(0-C_m)$ must equal MR_d and MR_f if the firm is to maximize profits, it follows that $0-Q_d$ is sold in the domestic market at price $0-P_d$ and $0-Q_f$ is sold in the foreign market at price $0-P_f$. The foreign price is lower than the domestic price because D_f is more elastic than D_d. Consequently, the firm is *dumping*: selling at a lower price abroad than at home. Price discrimination enables the firm to capture more consumer surplus as monopoly profit than would be possible with the same price for both markets.

in the low-price country and simultaneously sell it in the high-price country, a practice known as "gray exports."

When the oligopolistic firm's profit-maximizing price in the foreign market is *lower* than the price for the same product in the domestic market, then it is practicing dumping. Dumping is viewed by governments as an unfair trade practice and we shall have more to say about it in chapters 6, 7, 8, and 9.

The defining feature of oligopoly is *strategic interdependence* among the small number of firms dominating the industry. In planning its pricing and other strategies, firm A must take into account the possible reactions of rivals to its strategic moves and, at the same time, those rivals must consider A's possible reaction to their own strategic moves. Because of this interdependence, it is impossible to know how an oligopolistic firm will behave in an ongoing "strategic game" with its rivals.

One consequence of a strategic game is *reciprocal dumping*. Assume an oligopolist industry comprising a Japanese and an American firm who directly compete with differentiated products. Both firms may charge high prices in their home markets (where entry barriers are strong) and, simultaneously, low prices to penetrate each other's home market. Hence, reciprocal dumping gives rise to *intra-industry* trade between Japan and the United States. Even though it increases transportation costs, this trade may be socially beneficial (gainful) because it stimulates competition in both countries.[17]

Nonprice Competition: Product Differentiation

Most manufactured goods and services entering international trade are sold in either oligopolistically or monopolistically competitive markets. In the latter variety of market, each good is produced by a large number of producers, but each producer has succeeded in differentiating the product from competitive products in some way. This differentiation is achieved through nonprice competition, which is the hallmark of monopolistic competition. Although price competition is close and competitors' prices can never be disregarded, it is nonprice competition in design, quality, style, and services that makes up the aggressive front of monopolistic competition.

American consumers encounter nonprice competition at every turn. Television, radio, and other advertising media daily assault our eyes and ears with clever appeals to buy this or that product. Price appeals are relatively rare, and they are usually drowned out by the host of selling points centered on nonprice factors. We are warned, cajoled, sweet-talked, entertained, and implored — all with the intent to make us rush out to buy brand X. American advertising has a pervasiveness and vigor that is seldom matched in other countries, but the use of advertising has risen sharply in all countries, much of it sponsored by international companies that market abroad.

Nonprice competition often employs appeals based on style factors. Not only is the style cycle of traditional style goods speeded up by this competition, but style is also created in goods that were formerly standardized. The evolution of the American automobile from the Model T to the contemporary stylized product is a case in point. Style introduces a rapid obsolescence of merchandise as each vogue has its day and then passes on; this raises problems of inventory, timing, and market information that are largely absent in the marketing of standardized merchandise. There is, however, another side of the coin — style obsolescence periodically renews demand by making buyers dissatisfied with their earlier acquisitions.

---

[17]Oligopoly may also lead to "reciprocal investment" in production facilities. In our example, the Japanese firm starts production in the United States while at the same time the U.S. firm starts production in Japan. The theory of foreign direct investment is covered in Chapter 23.

A great variety of services is also used to distinguish a product from its competitors — quick delivery, return guarantees, warranties, right of inspection before acceptance of merchandise, availability of repair parts, servicing of the product and instruction in its use, and so on. One reason for the establishment of overseas branches and subsidiaries by domestic concerns is to facilitate service competition.

The effect of nonprice competition on international trade is expansive. Nonprice competition stimulates demand by acquainting buyers with goods, transforming latent demand into active demand, introducing new products and new uses for old products, heightening the availability of products, adapting products to better match specific buyer needs and preferences, and in other ways. The dynamism of nonprice competition in creating new demand contrasts with the passivity of price competition — simply accepting demand and doing nothing to change it.

It is sometimes argued that nonprice competition restricts international trade because selling costs make prices higher than they would be under perfect competition. This accusation fails to note, however, that many goods do not sell themselves and that nonprice competition enlarges the sales of such goods beyond the levels attainable through perfect competition. Increasing returns may be possible only when production is bolstered through mass consumption that is induced by nonprice competition. The charge that nonprice competition is socially wasteful and costly is valid only when it does not enhance the demand for a product. This criticism is often leveled against cigarette advertising, which, it is alleged, does not raise the consumption of cigarettes but simply redistributes the existing demand among the individual producers.[18]

Over the long run, monopolistic competition forces an identity between costs and prices as products lose their differentiation through imitation by competitors. We may conclude, therefore, that nonprice competition brings a dynamic, expansive element to international trade without the distortion of chronic monopoly profits. This is not to deny the importance of price competition; nonprice competition does not take the place of price competition but rather supplements it. It does mean that the theory of comparative advantage must take into account nonprice competition as well as price competition if it is to explain international trade in manufactures and services.

Ignorance, Uncertainty, and Risk in International Trade

Ignorance and uncertainty are important sources of market imperfection in international trade that are assumed away in the H-O model. *Ignorance* refers to a

---

[18]Criticism of nonprice competition ultimately derives from welfare propositions, namely, that some things are better for society than others. The case for or against cigarette advertising is now complicated by the health issue. As for international advertising, a further point needs mention. International markets may differ greatly in the consumption levels and saturation percentages for the same product. Thus, the promotional elasticity of the same advertising may, and often does, vary widely among national markets. Finally, much criticism of nonprice competition either ignores product innovations and variety or denies their usefulness.

trader's incomplete knowledge about markets and costs in the present. This ignorance gap exists because information is not free; it is acquired only at a cost in time and money. For most business firms the acquisition of information about foreign markets is constrained by factors of distance, scarce or unreliable data, language and other cultural factors, and higher costs than for the acquisition of market information at home. Because of ignorance, traders do not fully utilize comparative advantage, and the gains from trade are correspondingly less. Thus, ignorance limits trade in much the same way as transfer costs. Conversely, improvements in market information widen the perceived opportunities for gainful trade among nations.

Uncertainty refers to a trader's incomplete knowledge about markets and costs in the future. Although the present is conceptually fully knowable (zero ignorance), only seers and astrologers claim to know the future with finality. For the rest of us (including the trader), the future offers an array of possible but uncertain events. In forecasting the future, therefore, the most that any trader can do is make probability judgments of possible future events and then relate those judgments to trading decisions. Although there are many forecasting techniques that may help the trader improve his or her judgments about the future, the trader must inevitably assume risks, because knowledge is never certain. Because of the greater number and variety of possible events in the world economy as compared to the domestic economy, firms tend to perceive risks in international trade (and investment) as higher than at home. Like ignorance, therefore, uncertainty also narrows the scope of international trade.

Another consequence of uncertainty is the appearance of windfall profits and losses and what may be called *entrepreneurial* profits and losses. *Windfall profits* accrue to the international trader when benefits from unexpected changes in the trading environment occur, such as an increase in market demand or a reduction in import duties. Windfall losses also come from unexpected events, such as the imposition of import barriers or the emergence of a strong competitor. *Entrepreneurial profits* are a reward for the *deliberate* assumption of risks by the trader. When, for example, a trader introduces a new product or enters a new market, risk is knowingly assumed in the expectation of a profit reward. Of course, the trader may be mistaken and end up with losses, but that is the meaning of risk. The presence of economic profit in international trade, therefore, is not necessarily a sign of monopoly; commonly, profits arise from unexpected events and from the deliberate assumption of risk by the trader. Entrepreneurial profits play a key role in the dynamics of international trade. We shall have more to say about risk and uncertainty in Part IV.

OVERLAPPING MARKET SEGMENTS AND INTRA-INDUSTRY TRADE

According to the factor-endowments theory, international trade is based on dissimilar cost structures that mainly derive from differences in factor endowments: The greater the differences, the broader the opportunity for gainful trade. One would expect, therefore, that the greatest share of trade occurs between industrial (capital-abundant) countries on the one hand and nonindustrial (land- and labor-abundant) countries on the other and that this trade involves the exchange of manufactured goods for primary goods. However, the factual evidence points to a contrary state of affairs. Statistical data reveal that (1) the industrial countries generate about three-fourths of total world exports; (2) two-thirds of these exports go to the industrial countries themselves, and this trade is primarily (although not exclusively) an exchange of manufactures for manufactures; (3) in turn, over half of this manufactures-for-manufactures trade is *intra-industry* trade, that is, the simultaneous export and import of products belonging to the *same* industry; (4) furthermore, a great deal of this intra-industry trade is also *intrafirm* trade between multinational enterprises and their own foreign subsidiaries; (5) trade between the industrial and nonindustrial countries is only about one-third of world trade, mainly consisting of an exchange of manufactures for primary products; and (6) the economic structures of the industrial countries are becoming more, not less, similar. At the same time, income gaps are widening between the industrial group of countries and the nonindustrial group (with the exception of the newly industrializing countries).[19]

Overlapping Market Segments: The Linder Model

Dissatisfied with the glaring discrepancy between the trade patterns predicted by the H-O theory and actual trade patterns, Linder has advanced the most heterodox theory in international trade.[20] Linder asserts that differences in factor endowments explain trade in natural resource-intensive products but not in manufactures. His basic proposition is that the range of a country's manufactured exports is determined by *internal* demand. Thus, it is necessary (but not sufficient) that a product be consumed or invested at home before it can become a potential export product. Comparative advantage in manufactures requires an earlier production for the domestic market. Linder supports this proposition by reference to the ignorance of entrepreneurs with regard to foreign markets as compared with domestic markets. He argues that an entrepreneur is not likely to think about satisfying a need that does not exist at home. Even if such a need were perceived, the entrepreneur might not conceive the product that would fill that need; and even if the right product were conceived and developed, it is still improbable that the product could be finally adapted to strange market conditions without prohibitive costs. Since internal demand also determines which products a country may import, the range of its potential exports is the same as, or included in, the range of its potential imports.

It follows that the more *similar* the demand preferences for manufactured

---

[19]See Chapter 20.
[20]Staffan Burenstam Linder, *An Essay on Trade and Transformation* (New York: John Wiley & Sons, 1961). Discussion in the text is drawn from Chapters 2 and 3 of Linder's book.

goods in two countries, the more *intensive* is the potential trade in manufactures between them.[21] If two countries have the same demand structures, then their consumers and investors will demand the same goods with the same degrees of quality and sophistication. But what determines the structure of demand?

The most important influence, says Linder, is average or per capita income.[22] Countries with high per capita incomes will demand high-quality, "luxury" consumer goods and sophisticated capital goods, whereas low-per-capita-income countries will demand lower-quality, "necessity" consumer goods and less sophisticated capital goods. Consequently, differences in per capita incomes are a potential obstacle to trade: A rich country that has a comparative advantage in the production of high-quality, advanced manufactures will find its big export markets in other rich countries where people demand such products, not in poor countries, where the demand will always be small. By the same token, manufactured exports of the poor countries should find their best markets in other poor countries with similar demand structures. Linder does not rule out all trade in manufactures between rich and poor countries, because there will always be some overlapping of demand structures due to an unequal distribution of income: Some of the people in rich countries are poor and some of the people in poor countries are rich. But when the degree of overlap in demand structures is small, the potential trade in manufactures will also be small.

Figure 4-7 depicts the Linder model. Line 0–P shows the *average* relationship between per capita income and the quality/sophistication of each product demanded. Consumers in country A, with a per capita income of 0–a, demand a *range* of product quality/sophistication indicated by line A–A. Demand is for a range rather than a single level (which would be shown as a point on 0–P), because consumers in country A fall into different income classes. Country B has a higher per capita income than country A, and so its consumers demand a higher *average* product quality/sophistication—but they also demand a range because of different income classes. Since the two country ranges overlap (m–n), there is a basis for trade between them. Although Linder does not use the term, each country's range may be viewed as an aggregation of different *market segments*. Rephrasing Linder's proposition, then, we can say that countries will trade in manufactures when they have market segments in common.[23]

The situation is different for primary products. Because they are land-intensive, relative factor proportions are the main determinant of their prices. Linder arrives, therefore, at two explanations for trade, one for manufactures, the other

---

[21] By "intensive" Linder does not mean the *absolute* size of trade between two countries, which is influenced by the absolute size of the trading economies, but rather the size of trade after adjustment for the size of the economies.

[22] The factor-endowments theory ignores the effects of per capita income differences on trade. It recognizes the influence of tastes (assumed to be marginal because of a similarity of tastes among countries), but tastes alone do not determine the structure of demand—they must be supported by purchasing power (income).

[23] Market segmentation is a key concept in modern marketing management. Marketing scholars have linked many factors in addition to income (such as age, occupation, and education) to market segments.

Figure 4-7

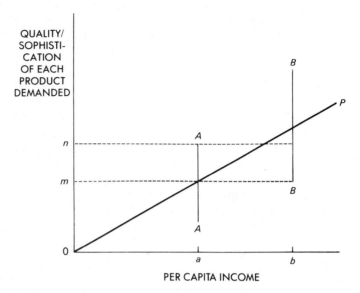

Overlapping Market Segments as a Determinant of Trade. 0–P shows the average relationship between per capita income and the quality/sophistication of each product demanded. Consumers in country A, with an *average* per capita income of 0–a, demand a *range* of product quality/sophistication, as indicated by A–A. Demand is for a range rather than a single level of quality/sophistication because consumers in country A fall into different income classes. It follows that consumers in country B, with a higher average per capita income (0–b), demand a higher range (B–B) of product quality/sophistication. Because the two ranges overlap (m–n), there is a basis for trade between them.

for primary products. Trade in the former is caused by the same forces that cause domestic trade: increasing returns, product differentiation, and technology gaps. Linder concludes that the effect of per capita income levels on trade in manufactures may be constrained or distorted by entrepreneurial ignorance, cultural and political differences, transportation costs, and legislative obstacles such as tariffs.

Linder's model is consistent with the observed pattern of trade in manufactured products. Furthermore, it is in agreement with studies of international marketing at the enterprise level and with the product life cycle model. Only with rare exceptions do manufacturers enter into exports (or foreign investment) before establishing firm market positions at home. Once they do venture into exports, manufacturers usually find their most attractive markets in other industrial countries where incomes, tastes, and demand patterns most closely resemble those at home. In estimating sales potentials for their products in foreign markets, entrepreneurs give more weight to per capita income (and related phenomena) than they do to any other single economic factor.

Further observations about Linder's model can be made. Although Linder distinguishes between manufactures and primary products, a finer distinction exists between differentiated products and nondifferentiated commodities. As we observe later in our discussion of the product life cycle, when manufactured products become mature, they compete on the basis of price and cost. Unless increasing returns are significant, therefore, the factor endowments underlying costs are the principal explanation of trade in commodities, whether they are manufactures or primary products. Thus, poor countries have a comparative advantage in labor-intensive commodity manufactures such as basic textiles.

A second observation concerns the bearing of factor mobility, particularly management, on Linder's major proposition that countries only export manufactures that are first produced for the home market. Although this proposition appears to be generally true today, it will probably be less true in the future. Multinational companies now establish manufacturing subsidiaries in poor countries as sources for products (mostly components rather than final products) that are exported to their operations in other countries. Because these arrangements are between a subsidiary and its parent, market separation is very low. Thus, the mobility of multinational companies may enable nonindustrial countries to export manufactured products that are not sold in their domestic markets.

A final observation is that the Linder model does not explain in a systematic fashion which *specific* manufactured goods a country will export and which it will import. More fundamentally, why should two countries that have the same factor endowments and that produce and consume the same types of products trade at all? The answer to this question must be found in a theory of intra-industry trade.

Intra-Industry Trade

Intra-industry trade is the exchange among countries of *similar* products belonging to the same industry. Economists have not yet worked out a theory of intra-industry trade, but their efforts so far have enhanced the importance of theories relating to overlapping market segments, product differentiation, increasing returns, and direct foreign investment.

In a pioneering study of intra-industry trade, Grubel and Lloyd used the following index to measure it:

$$B = 1.0 - \frac{|X - M|}{X + M},$$

where B represents the degree of intra-industry trade and X and M represent exports and imports, respectively, of products that belong to the *same* industry.[24] B has a maximum value of 1.0 when exports equal imports for a given industry ($X - M = 0$) and a minimum value of zero when an industry has exports but no imports

---

[24]Herbert G. Grubel and P. J. Lloyd, *Intra-Industry Trade: The Theory and Measurement of International Trade in Differentiated Products* (New York: John Wiley & Sons, 1975), pp. 20 ff.

or no exports but imports. Using the three-digit Standard Industrial Trade Classification (SITC) to represent industries, Grubel and Lloyd calculated weighted
averages of the index for ten industrial countries. The *combined* index for these
countries in 1967 was 0.48, indicating that almost half the trade among the
countries was in products belonging to the same industry. (For specific industries,
the index ranged from 0.30 for mineral fuels, lubricants, and related industries to
0.66 for chemicals.) The combined index was 0.36 in 1959, 0.42 in 1964, and 0.48
in 1967. The index for countries in the European Economic Community was 0.67
in 1967.

Some intra-industry trade is in *homogeneous* or *nondifferentiated* products, such as
raw materials and simple manufactures. The explanation of this trade is found in
transfer costs, seasonal or other periodic variations in supply, and entrepôts. The
production location of a homogeneous product (say, cement) in country A may be
closer to a market area in country B than any production location in that country,
and conversely. Hence, A exports cement to B while B exports cement to A.
Again, countries in different climatic zones may trade in the same agricultural
products, exporting them in one season and importing them in another, because
storage costs exceed transportation costs. Entrepôt countries such as Singapore,
Hong Kong, and the Netherlands collect homogeneous goods through imports,
sort and pack them, and then redistribute them through exports. Although intra-
industry trade in homogeneous products should not be ignored, the available data
indicate that most intra-industry trade is trade in *differentiated* products.

Linder's model of overlapping market segments offers a starting point to
explain intra-industry trade in differentiated products. For example, manufacturers in the United States continually strive to develop and maintain differentiated products to obtain a competitive advantage in *specific* segments of the domestic
market. When they are successful, differentiated products give manufacturers a
degree of monopoly power, because demand curves are downward sloping rather
than horizontal. The most prominent example of the pervasiveness of this strategy
is the multitude of brands in the same consumer goods, but the strategy is also
common for intermediate products.[25] A firm's products are distinguished from
similar products of other firms in several ways, most commonly through style and
design features, packaging, customer services, and promotion. Less commonly, a
firm makes a technological breakthrough with a new type of product that, for a
time, has no close substitutes.

When U.S. manufacturers look abroad for markets, they find them mainly in
foreign countries that have market segments matching the segments they are
currently exploiting in the U.S. market. According to the Linder model, these
overlapping segments are found in foreign countries whose per capita incomes
(level of economic development) are closest to that of the United States. Con-

---

[25]A recent study finds that intra-industry trade occurs primarily in *intermediate* products that are tailored
to meet the needs of manufacturers of particular final products. See Edward John Ray, "U.S. Protection and
Intra-Industry Trade: The Message to Developing Countries," *Economic Development and Cultural Change*,
1991, pp. 169–187.

versely, manufacturers in those countries export to the United States to exploit market segments similar to those at home.

Apart from marketing advantages, manufacturers may obtain *increasing returns* by specializing in differentiated products. In general, the fewer the number of differentiated products manufactured in a plant, the lower the unit costs; this is because of longer production runs and the experience curve. Thus a firm may gain a cost advantage over domestic and foreign competitors by specializing in a particular variant of a product while a firm in a second country gains a cost advantage by specializing in another variant of the same product. Increasing returns that are associated with product differentiation, therefore, also explain intra-industry trade.

It is evident that the explanation of intra-industry trade rests on factors that are *specific to the firm* (product differentiation and increasing returns) and on the existence of overlapping market segments. This firm-specific nature of intra-industry trade is highlighted when we recognize that much of that trade occurs between multinational enterprises and their foreign subsidiaries. Any theory of intra-industry trade, therefore, needs to be linked with a theory of foreign investment that explains the behavior of multinational enterprise.[26]

CONCLUDING NOTE ON IMPERFECT COMPETITION AND INTERNATIONAL TRADE

In recent years, international trade theorists have recognized in their models that trade among the advanced industrial countries is mainly based on imperfect competition. Taking account of increasing returns, oligopolistic strategies, and product differentiation, these models have stimulated new prescriptions for international trade policy, notably the argument for *strategic trade policy*. This policy would use trade restrictions to extract economic rent from oligopolistic foreign firms. For instance, it would use *import* restrictions to promote *exports* by enabling domestic oligopolists to expand production in the protected home market and thereby obtain economies of scale that would strengthen their export competitiveness. We shall examine this argument in Chapter 7 and its application to U.S. trade policy in Chapter 9.

The dominance of oligopoly in international trade means that the individual firm—the multinational enterprise—has a degree of monopoly power that provides the basis for an autonomous strategy, such as decisions on what to produce, how to produce, where to produce, and pricing. In designing its strategy and carrying it out, the firm must respond to market forces, but it decides how it will do so. It follows that international trade flows, particularly among advanced economies, *cannot* be explained without consideration of the strategy and performance of individual firms, a subject that has been mostly ignored by international economists. A recent attempt to remedy this neglect is Porter's model, which traces

---

[26]See Chapter 23.

the determinants of national competitive advantages to factor conditions; demand conditions; firm strategy, structure, and rivalry; and related and supporting industries.[27] Part IV examines the theory of multinational firms.

SUMMARY

1. Transfer costs may be divided into the costs of physical transfer and the costs associated with government regulation of foreign trade. The costs of physical transfer are mainly attributable to transportation. Transportation costs separate goods into two classes: domestic goods and international goods. Domestic goods do not enter international trade because transportation costs make it impossible to sell them at competitive prices in foreign markets. Hence, the existence of transportation costs narrows the opportunity for international trade.

2. Transportation costs also influence the location of industry and, thereby, the international specialization of production. In effect, transportation inputs must be viewed, along with the traditional factors of production, as a determinant of a nation's opportunity cost and comparative advantage.

3. International trade, especially in manufactured goods and services, departs in one way or another from the conditions of perfect competition.

4. The principal market structures of imperfect competition are monopoly, oligopoly, and monopolistic competition. At long-run equilibrium in a perfectly competitive market, $MC = AR = ATC$. Hence, the firm makes zero economic profit. But in imperfect markets, at the equilibrium output $MC < AR$. In the long run, monopolistic and oligopolistic firms can make economic profits because entry barriers are high, but such profits are wiped out in a monopolistically competitive market because new firms can enter the industry.

5. Economic profits result from *monopoly power*. Its social cost may be measured by the net change in consumer and producer surpluses when compared to such surpluses in perfect competition. By reducing the *combined* surpluses, monopoly power incurs a *social cost* (deadweight loss).

6. Increasing returns are associated with economies of scale, learning curve effects, and economies of scope. By lowering long-run unit costs, increasing returns enhance the opportunity for gainful trade. In sum, when the increasing returns (and technological innovation) of monopolistic and oligopolistic firms more than offset their monopoly profits, then the net effect of such firms on international trade is beneficial.

7. Oligopolists may practice price discrimination among country markets. To maximize profits, the oligopolist charges a lower price for the same product in

---

[27]Michael E. Porter, *The Competitive Advantage of Nations* (New York: The Free Press, 1990), p. 71. For a condensed presentation of this model, see Michael E. Porter, "The Competitive Advantage of Nations," *Harvard Business Review,* March–April 1990, pp. 73–93.

the more price-elastic of two markets. When price discrimination leads to a lower price in a foreign market than in the home market, the practice is called *dumping*. One consequence of the "strategic game" played by rival oligopolists is the phenomenon of *reciprocal dumping*.

8. Nonprice competition deriving from product differentiation brings a dynamic, expansive element to international trade; in the case of monopolistic competition, it does so without the distortion of monopoly profits.

9. Ignorance and uncertainty are important sources of market imperfection in international trade that are assumed away in the Heckscher-Ohlin model. One consequence of uncertainty is the appearance of windfall and entrepreneurial profits and losses. Entrepreneurial profits are a reward for the deliberate assumption of risk, and they play a key role in the dynamics of international trade. Hence, the presence of profits in international trade is not necessarily a sign of monopoly power.

10. The Linder model asserts that the more *similar* the demand for manufactured products in two countries, the more intensive is the potential trade in manufactures between them. The principal determinant of similarity is per capita income. The Linder concept of overlapping market segments, together with product differentiation and economies of scale, helps explain intra-industry trade.

QUESTIONS AND APPLICATIONS

1. How do transportation costs directly affect the volume of international trade?
2. What is meant by *weight-losing* and *weight-gaining* industrial processes? How do these processes influence location?
3. Why is the "economics of location" so complex?
4. (a) What are the three market structures of imperfect competition?
   (b) How do these structures differ with respect to number of firms in the industry, nature of the product, demand schedule, increasing returns, entry and exit barriers, and long-run economic profit?
5. (a) What is consumer surplus? Producer surplus?
   (b) Using graphical analysis, demonstrate the social cost of monopoly power.
6. (a) Identify the sources of increasing returns.
   (b) Distinguish between economies of scale and the learning curve.
   (c) What is the effect of increasing returns on international trade?
7. (a) Demonstrate graphically how price discrimination between the home country and a foreign country can maximize economic profit for the oligopolist.
   (b) What is dumping? Reciprocal dumping?
8. Why may the *net* effect of monopoly and oligopoly on international trade be detrimental or beneficial?

9. (a) What is nonprice competition?
   (b) Why is its effect on international trade likely to be expansive?
10. (a) Do you consider ignorance and uncertainty to be greater in international trade than in domestic trade? Explain.
   (b) Do ignorance and uncertainty constrain international trade? Why or why not?
11. (a) How does the Linder model explain trade in manufactures among the industrial countries?
   (b) Does the trade in manufactures between the United States and Western Europe support this model?
   (c) What are the implications of the model for the developing countries?
12. (a) Why should overlapping market segments provide a basis for intra-industry trade in differentiated products?
   (b) Explain how increasing returns may promote intra-industry trade in differentiated products.

SELECTED READINGS

See the list of readings given at the end of Chapter 5.

COMPARATIVE ADVANTAGE: TECHNOLOGY, FACTOR MOBILITY, AND MULTINATIONAL ENTERPRISE

We live in a world of continuing technological innovation. What are its implications for the comparative advantage of nations? This is the first subject addressed in this chapter. We also live in a world in which capital and advanced human skills move freely among nations. What are the implications of this international factor mobility for comparative advantage? Again, we live in a world of multinational enterprise. What are the features of multinational firms that need to be incorporated into a theory of international trade?

TECHNOLOGY THEORIES OF TRADE

The role that technology plays in shaping economic activities must be included in a theory of trade. In Chapter 3 we spoke of technological innovation as an agent of change in factor endowments. Here we take a closer look at the implications of technological innovation for a country's comparative advantage.

Technology is the accumulated knowledge, skills, and techniques that are applied to the production of goods and services. Inventions and discoveries are the source of technology, but they must be used in production to become innovations. Today, inventions and discoveries come mainly out of systematic research programs oriented toward technical innovations. The immense resources now devoted to research, along with the drive by management to apply its results to enterprise, have created an environment of explosive technological change, especially in advanced industrial economies. Technological innovations affect not only production and domestic and international trade but also the living styles of countless millions of people around the globe. One innovation alone—the automobile—has transformed societies throughout the world, and the computer is doing so today.

110

The Technological Innovation Process

Technological innovation is the *entire* process whereby research and invention are transformed by the firm into two basic forms: (1) new and more economical ways of producing existing products (new production functions) by innovations in producing specific products (such as a new way of making a chemical) or by general innovations affecting a broad range of production (such as automation), and (2) the production of wholly new products, both industrial and consumer (such as computers, televisions, plastics, and synthetic fibers to name only a few of the more prominent products introduced since the end of World War II), and improvements in existing products. These two forms are closely related; many new products, for example, are capital goods that make possible new production functions. Only when the whole innovation process is completed can the firm obtain a return on its R & D investment.[1] The firm creates economic value only through its sales to customers.

The completion of the innovation process is by no means certain. Many research discoveries are not developed into technology; technology may not be used to make new products or production functions; and new products may experience commercial failure. Mansfield indicates an average probability of only 12 percent that an R & D project will result in an economically successful product or process.[2] To innovate, therefore, firms need to manage the innovation process as a *system,* recognizing that technological innovation is (1) the outcome of many different activities undertaken by different groups of people, (2) dependent on coordinating linkages among the different activities and groups, and (3) most productive when its disparate elements are focused on a common set of goals. Figure 5-1 depicts the technological innovation process.

The circles in Figure 5-1 represent the activity sets of the process. Viewed dynamically, there are no beginning or end points. For the purpose of our exposition, however, let us start with *technical research.* This phase of the process features basic and applied laboratory research of which the output is ideas, discoveries, and inventions that hold technological promise. The *development* phase takes this research output and transforms it into technology, such as process and product designs, full-scale plans, and engineering specifications that can be translated into production. *Production start-up/improvements* includes engineering, tooling, and other activities needed to start commercial production of products using the new technology. This phase also includes later improvements in production as the innovation process extends into the future. Radical innovations go through many

---

[1]Ordinarily, the firm completes the process itself in order to capture all of the innovation's economic rent. But at times it may license its technology to another firm in return for royalties conditional on sales of the licensed product by that firm.

[2]This estimate is based on a study of two chemical firms and one drug firm. The probability of an R & D project's economic success is the product of (1) the probability of technical success, (2) the probability of commercialization given technical success, and (3) the probability of economic success given commercialization. See Edwin Mansfield, "How Economists See R & D," *Harvard Business Review,* November–December 1981, p. 100.

Figure 5-1

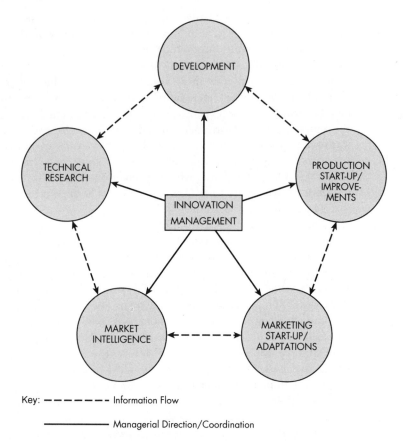

The Technological Innovation Process of the Firm. Technological innovation is the *entire* process whereby research and invention are transformed by the firm into new products or improvements of old products. The task of innovation managers is to plan, coordinate, and control the linkages between the different activities (indicated by circles) of the innovation process. Only upon completion of the full innovation process can the firm obtain a return on its R & D investment.

process and product improvements over time that cumulatively can have profound effects on competitive advantage. *Marketing start-up/adaptations* includes the design of marketing strategy and marketing plans for new products. This phase also covers later adaptations of the product to fit better consumer preferences in old and new markets and in market segments. *Market intelligence* acquires and evaluates information relating to actual and prospective market opportunities, competitive behavior, and any other developments that can help guide R & D.

The multi-fold task of innovation management is to plan, organize, direct, motivate, coordinate and control the innovation process as a single system. This can best be done in the context of a corporate-wide strategy that affords a framework for technology strategy. It is common to identify technological innovation with R & D. But R & D is an inadequate measure of innovation, and it usually bears only the smaller part of total innovation costs. Superior market forecasting and understanding of user requirements commonly distinguish successful innovations from failed innovations.

Because the influence of technological innovations on economic behavior is so pervasive, it has manifold effects on the volume, direction, and composition of international trade. Changing technology not only creates dissimilar production functions among countries at any given point of time but also transforms the trade of nations over time. We have already observed that technology determines what natural elements become land factors, making these factors dynamic rather than passive. Technology also vitally affects the training and education of labor, giving rise to qualitative differences among nations. Capital is directly influenced by technology because so much technology takes the form of capital equipment and, more basically, because technology contributes importantly to a nation's investment capacity by raising per capita productivity and real income.

The bearing of technology on international trade is not limited to the changes it provokes in the size and the quality of factor endowments. Technology also creates new production functions that raise the productivity of existing factors of production, and it profoundly affects the scope of international trade through innovations in transportation and communications. By fostering new products, technology has a direct impact on the composition and growth of international trade. The competitive strength of United States exports owes much to product innovations in capital and consumer goods—as older products, such as automobiles, are displaced by foreign competition, they are replaced by new products, such as computers, that for a time have no foreign counterparts. For this reason alone, a rapid rate of technological progress is a vital weapon in world markets.

The H-O model discussed in Chapter 3 made two implicit assumptions about technology: (1) the existence of a given state of technology, and (2) the same access to technology everywhere (that is, all countries use the same production functions). These assumptions do not hold in the real world. When we drop them, what happens to the factor proportions theory of trade?

Higher Factor Productivity via Innovation: Effects on Trade

When technological innovation takes the form of new ways to produce existing products, it pushes out a nation's production possibilities frontier. With new production functions the nation can now produce a greater output with the same endowment of productive factors. Indeed, technical advances in production are a major source of growth in contemporary economies. In effect, a new production function "saves" some or all the factors of production needed to produce a given level of output as compared with the old production function.

The effects of this saving may be neutral, protrade, or antitrade. Analytically, the situation is similar to the effects of factor growth on trade that were treated in

Chapter 3. A technological innovation that causes a rise in the productivity of, say, labor has a production effect similar to an increase in the supply of labor. When an innovation saves all factors to the same degree, its effect on trade is *neutral,* as in the case when all factors grow to the same degree. However, when an innovation saves a country's relatively abundant factors but does not save its relatively scarce factors (or saves them to a lesser extent), then the effect will be *protrade.* The country will now have a greater comparative advantage than before in the production of goods that require relatively large amounts of its abundant factors. Conversely, when an innovation saves a country's relatively scarce factors more than it saves the relatively abundant factors, the effect will be *antitrade,* since production will shift toward goods that replace imports.

International Technology Gaps: Dissimilar Production Functions

Technological innovations do not occur in all countries at the same pace. Neither do they spread instantaneously from one country to another. Ergas found three sets of factors that explain why the occurrence of innovations differs among countries: (1) the country's scientific base, education, and other *inputs* of the innovation process; (2) sophisticated consumers and industrial users who *demand* innovations; and (3) an *industrial structure* combining intense competition with some mechanism enabling firms to share the financing and diffusion of scientific research.[3] Clearly, these factors are found mainly in the advanced industrial countries that generate most of the new technology, which then spreads to other countries after varying time lags. The most prominent example of this diffusion process is the Industrial Revolution (a combination of technical innovations involving the steam engine, new kinds of machinery, the factory system of organization, and other developments adding up to a transformation of the entire economy). The Industrial Revolution started in England in the eighteenth century, then spread to Western Europe and North America during the following century, to Japan and Russia early in this century, and is still spreading to many parts of South America, Africa, and Asia. Because this process is not instantaneous, we can distinguish between nations that are technological leaders and those that are technological followers.

At any given time, therefore, countries may be using different technologies to produce the same products; that is, *dissimilar* production functions exist. Since most technological innovations in production take the form of capital, a technological leader usually employs a capital-intensive method to produce a good that is traditionally labor- or land-intensive. Dissimilar production functions are strikingly evident in agriculture. Over the past generation, a technical revolution has transformed U.S. agriculture, encompassing a high level of mechanization, improved soil care, pest control, new varieties of seed, and so on, as well as large-

---

[3]Henry Ergas, *Why Do Some Countries Innovate More Than Others?* (Brussels: Center for European Policy Studies, 1984).

114   **Part I   International Trade**

scale organization of production that is characteristic of manufacturing more than traditional farming. U.S. agriculture has become capital-intensive (there are less than three million farmers, and half of them produce almost all the commercial agricultural output), while in many countries it has remained labor-intensive. The employment of capital-intensive production functions (made possible by new technology) explains how the United States has retained, and probably increased, its comparative advantage in agriculture despite rising wage and land costs.

The point of this discussion is that a good cannot be uniquely defined as capital-intensive or labor-intensive (land-intensive), because it may be produced in *both* ways in countries using *different* production functions. Hence, the link between factor endowments and the *specific* kinds of products a country will export and import is now broken.[4] We can still say a nation will export those goods that use relatively large inputs of its abundant factors and import those goods that use relatively large inputs of its scarce factors, but we cannot say what those goods will be without knowing the production functions in question. In brief, by creating dissimilar production functions among nations, technological innovation can serve as a basis of international trade, along with dissimilar factor endowments, increasing returns, and product differentiation.

We can show this by means of a simple two-country (A and B), two-product (wheat and textiles), two-factor (labor and capital) model in which both countries have the same factor price structures (2:1) reflecting the same factor proportions (providing no basis for trade), but use different production functions to produce wheat. Specifically, both countries produce textiles with the same production function, which requires 3 units of labor and 2 units of capital to produce 1 unit of textiles. However, in producing 1 unit of wheat, country A uses 1 unit of labor and 4 units of capital (a capital-intensive process) whereas country B uses 5 units of labor and 1 unit of capital (the traditional labor-intensive process). Under these conditions, the two countries have different comparative costs: Country A has a comparative advantage in wheat and country B a comparative advantage in textiles, and both will gain from trade (see Table 5-1).

International technology gaps in production functions have a dynamic impact on trade among nations as innovations open up new gaps and technological diffusion closes old gaps. There is ample evidence that both the opening and closing of technology gaps now occur much more rapidly than at any time in the past. Diffusion occurs in several ways. Technical and other news media transmit knowledge of new discoveries from one country to another, as does trade in new products. Companies in advanced countries like the United States license technical know-how and assistance to foreign companies in return for royalty payments and

---

[4]This may also be true even when countries use the *same* production function for a specific product if there is a high degree of factor substitutability (that is, the technical coefficients of production can assume a broad range of values) such that at one set of factor prices the product is, say, capital-intensive whereas at another set of factor prices it becomes labor-intensive. Technically, this situation is called *factor reversal;* its frequency is a matter of dispute among economists. Part of the problem lies in the difficulty of distinguishing the use of the *same* production function with different coefficients of production on the one hand from the use of *different* production functions on the other in concrete situations where both differences may be operative.

**Table 5-1 Effect of Dissimilar Production Functions
on Comparative Advantage**

	Country A (dollars)	Country B (pesos)
Unit price of labor	2	4
Unit price of capital	1	2
Unit cost of textiles	8	16
Unit cost of wheat	6	22

fees or set up their own operations abroad using new technology.[5] Diffusion is especially swift among the industrial countries because they have the capacity to use the new technical knowledge immediately. An outstanding example of this rapidity is the transistor. Developed by the United States, it was Japan that first used the transistor to make small radios, which then found a big market in the United States. Technological leadership is constantly threatened, therefore, by innovations elsewhere; nations must run hard to avoid falling behind. In the nineteenth century, comparative advantages changed slowly over a generation or more; in our own time, a country may enjoy a comparative advantage in a product for only a few years before technical diffusion and imitation or new technical discoveries wipe it out. The life cycle of new products offers the most dramatic evidence of this process.

International Technology Gaps: New Products

Commonly, technological innovations assume the form of new products or product improvements rather than new production functions for old products. Such innovations may create entirely new industries. (In 1945, the television, jet travel, and digital computer industries were commercially nonexistent in the United States.) American manufacturers place thousands of new products on the home market every year, and sooner or later many of these products are exported to foreign markets. The technological leaders in American manufacturing are aerospace, electrical machinery (including communications), transportation equipment, chemicals (including pharmaceuticals), and nonelectrical machinery. It is hardly coincidental that these same industries are also the most aggressive competitors in world markets via direct exports and investment in foreign production.

There is abundant evidence that the United States has a comparative advantage in research-intensive, high-technology products. A pathbreaking study of nineteen U.S. industries found that the five industries with the strongest research effort (as measured both by total R & D expenditures as a percentage of sales and

---

[5]The role of international enterprise as a transfer agent for technology and technological innovation is examined in Chapter 22.

by the number of scientists and engineers in R & D as a percentage of total employment) accounted for 72.0 percent of U.S. exports of manufactures in 1962, although the same five industries were responsible for only 39.1 percent of U.S. total sales (domestic and export combined) of manufactured goods.[6]

These five high-technology sectors — transportation, electrical machinery, instruments, chemicals, and nonelectrical machinery — also performed 89 percent of total U.S. R & D. They represented, therefore, both "the heart of U.S. export strength in manufactured products and the heart of its industrial research effort."[7] These same sectors accounted for 88 percent of total U.S. company-sponsored R & D in 1991.[8] *All* of the top 50 U.S. exporting companies in that year belonged to these sectors, with the exception of three exporters of agricultural and forestry products.[9]

Technology theories postulate that certain countries have special advantages as innovators of new products. They also postulate that there is an "imitation lag" that prevents other countries from immediately duplicating in production the new products of the innovating country. These two conditions give rise to technology gaps in particular products that afford the innovating country an export monopoly during the period of imitation lag.

Posner has distinguished a *demand lag* and a *reaction lag* that together make up the imitation lag. The demand lag occurs because new foreign goods may not be regarded as perfect substitutes for old domestic goods. The reaction lag is the time between the production of a new product in the innovating country and the time when a potential producer in the local market views the new product as a competitive threat that should be met by local production.[10] The innovating country obtains an *export* advantage because the demand lag is ordinarily shorter than the reaction lag. The length of the reaction lag depends on increasing returns, tariffs, transportation costs, income elasticity of demand, and the income level and size of the foreign market.[11] Large economies of scale in production, low tariffs and transportation costs, a small income elasticity of demand, low income levels, and small market size act to favor a continuation of exports from the innovating country by delaying local production, and conversely. The innovating manufacturer enjoys an export monopoly advantage, but later imitators in other countries must depend on lower costs to justify local production.

---

[6]William H. Gruber, Dileep Mehta, and Raymond Vernon. "The R & D Factor in International Trade and International Investment of United States Industries," *Journal of Political Economy,* February 1967, pp. 20–37. Other studies have confirmed the key role of technology as a determinant of U.S. exports. See, for example, Thomas C. Lowinger, "Human Capital and Technological Determinants of U.S. Industries' Revealed Comparative Advantage," *The Quarterly Review of Economics and Business,* Winter 1977, pp. 91–102.

[7]Gruber, Mehta, and Vernon, "The R & D Factor," p. 26.

[8]"On a Clear Day You Can See Progress," *Business Week,* June 29, 1992, p. 104.

[9]"U.S. Exporters on a Global Roll," *Fortune,* June 29, 1992, p. 95.

[10]Michael Posner, "International Trade and Technical Change," *Oxford Economic Papers,* Vol. 13 (October, 1961), pp. 323–41.

[11]Louis T. Wells, Jr., "International Trade: The Product Life Cycle Approach," in *The Product Life Cycle and International Trade,* ed. Louis T. Wells, Jr. (Boston: Harvard Business School, Division of Research, 1972), pp. 3–33.

Trade in electronic calculators illustrates the importance of technology gaps during the period 1962–1976, when the United States and Japan switched back and forth in technological leadership. It also illustrates that the demand lag facing the Japanese in the U.S. market (where the product was first developed) was nonexistent and that the reaction lags were very short. The transistorized electronic calculator was first developed in the United States in 1962, but the Japanese had imitated the product by 1964.[12] In subsequent years, the United States and Japan become the major producers of electronic calculators, and their relative positions in the U.S. market showed dramatic reversals over time. Starting in 1967 with 17 percent of the U.S. market, the Japanese gained a market share of 80 percent by 1971. After that year, their market share began to fall until 1974, when it reached 25 percent. In 1975, the Japanese once again started to gain market share, attaining 40 percent in 1976 (when this account ends).

These shifts in competitive advantage can be explained by shifts in technological leadership. In the period 1962–1966 the United States led, but in 1967 Sharp Corporation, a Japanese firm, introduced integrated circuits (ICs) and the metal oxide/large scale integration (MOS/LSI) that reduced the number of components in the calculator from 5,000 to less than 1,000. In 1969, the Japanese replaced ICs with only four MOS/LSI chips, cutting the number of components to 57. The next important step was taken by Bowmar Instrument, a U.S. company, when it developed the first single-chip calculator in 1971. With this innovation, the Americans regained technological leadership and, as we have noted, the Japanese suffered a loss in their share of the U.S. market. But this competitive advantage did not last very long. In 1973, the Sharp Corporation replaced the conventional circuit board with a soda-glass substrate that cut the number of components to fewer than 40. With this innovation, the Japanese began to recapture more and more of the U.S. market.

Technology gap theories as such do not explain why certain countries are technological leaders and other countries are technological followers. Nor do they satisfactorily explain imitation lags. The product life cycle model helps make these phenomena understandable.

The Product Life Cycle Model

Although the significance of product innovations has been largely ignored by economic theorists until recently, marketing scholars had earlier introduced the concept of the *product life cycle.* One version of this concept involves four successive stages: product introduction, product growth, product maturity, and product decline. Briefly, the life cycle starts when a company introduces a product that is entirely or partially differentiated from old products. In the first stage, the product is a specialty and, for the time being, the manufacturer has a monopoly. However, most new products are soon imitated (or even improved upon) by competitors.[13]

---

[12]The following account is drawn from Badiul A. Majundar, "Innovations and International Trade: An Industry Study of Dynamic Competitive Advantage," *Kyklos,* no. 3 (1979), pp. 559–69.

[13]Patent protection may inhibit imitation (as in the case of Apple Computer), but it is seldom complete. Furthermore, many new products are not patentable.

Hence, the original product loses its specialty status and instead becomes a growth product that is manufactured and sold by several companies. In this second stage, some product differentiation is maintained by individual manufacturers through promotion, packaging, and services (nonprice competition), but as more companies enter the market and the different brands become more and more alike to consumers, the product may slip into the third stage as a mature product. Brand competition now gives way to price competition.

Vernon and others have used the concept of a product life cycle to explain the behavior of U.S. exports of manufactures.[14] A four-stage model is postulated: (1) The U.S. has an export monopoly in a new product, (2) foreign production begins, (3) foreign production becomes competitive in export markets, and (4) the U.S. imports the now-established product. Vernon asserts that U.S. producers are likely to be the first to exploit market opportunities for high-income and labor-saving new products, because such opportunities first appear in the affluent United States. Furthermore, they will first produce these new products in the United States, because close proximity to customers and suppliers is imperative for design and marketing flexibility. In this first stage, U.S. producers have a monopoly in export markets and they proceed to build up sales with no concern for local competition. However, during the second stage, producers in one or more industrial countries start to manufacture the product, whose design and production are now standardized.[15] Consequently, the overall rate of growth of U.S. exports declines and exports to the countries of foreign production become minimal. In the third stage, foreign producers displace U.S. exports in the remaining export markets. Finally, foreign producers achieve sufficient competitive strength (due to increasing returns and lower labor costs) to export the now-mature product to the United States itself. In short, the export effects of product innovation are undermined by technological diffusion and lower costs abroad.

Figures 5-2 and 5-3 depict the product cycle model of international trade for the innovating country and an imitating country, respectively. In Figure 5-2, the innovating country starts production of the new product at time 0, but it does not export that product until time A, when production exceeds domestic consumption. $0-A$, therefore, is Posner's demand lag. At time B foreign production begins to compete against the innovating country's exports, which in turn begin to fall as a share of its production. $0-B$ is thus Posner's reaction lag. Exports, indicated by the vertically lined area, come to an end at time C, and the innovating country becomes an importer (shown by the diagonally lined area) of the once-new product.

In Figure 5-3, an imitating country starts to import the new product from the innovating country at time A'. If an imitating country is a high-income advanced

---

[14]Raymond Vernon, "International Investment and International Trade in the Product Cycle," *The Quarterly Journal of Economics* (May 1966), pp. 190–207. Louis T. Wells, Jr., "A Product Life Cycle for International Trade?" *Journal of Marketing* (July 1968), pp. 1–6.

[15]Some of these foreign producers may be subsidiaries of American companies who anticipate later stages in the export life cycle. See Chapter 23.

Figure 5-2

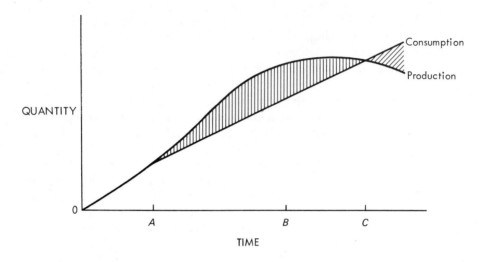

Product Cycle Model of International Trade: Innovating Country. The innovating country starts production of the new product at time 0 but does not export the product until time *A,* when production exceeds *domestic* consumption. At time *B,* foreign production starts to compete against the innovating country's exports, which then begin to lose their share of the foreign market. Ultimately, exports come to an end at time *C* and the innovating country becomes an importer, as shown by the diagonally lined area.

country, then time *A'* most likely coincides with time *A* in Figure 5-2. But if it is a low-income, developing country, then time *A'* will come later; that is, the demand lag will be longer. Local production begins at time *B',* when the local market grows to sufficient size and cost conditions favor production against imports. Once again, if the imitating country is an advanced country, then *B'* will coincide with *B* in Figure 5-2, whereas if it is a developing country, *B'* will come later, after a longer reaction lag. With a lower price and stronger marketing effort resulting from local production, consumption rises more quickly. At time *C',* when production begins to exceed consumption, the imitating country begins to export, at first to third countries and later to the innovating country. Thus, *C'* comes earlier in time than *C* in Figure 5-2.

An important feature of the product cycle model is the proposition that the factor proportions to produce a product will change in a systematic fashion as the product moves through its life cycle. The *new-product phase* (associated with the first production of the product in the innovating country and the early portion of the export monopoly stage) is characterized by unstable production functions, short production runs, and rapidly changing techniques that depend on scientists, engineers, and other highly skilled workers. Production, therefore, is skill-intensive rather than capital-intensive. In the *product-growth phase,* mass-production methods are introduced to exploit expanding markets, and consequently the factor inputs shift from skilled to semiskilled labor and from labor intensity to capital

Figure 5-3

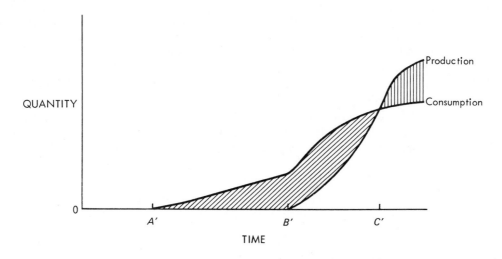

Product Cycle Model of International Trade: Imitating Country. The imitating country starts to import the new product from the innovating country at time A'. Local production begins at time B', when the local market grows to sufficient size and cost conditions favor local production against imports. At time C', when production first exceeds consumption, the imitating country starts to export, at first to third countries and later to the innovating country.

intensity overall. This growth phase is associated with the later portion of the export monopoly stage and the start of foreign production. The factor shifts continue in the *product-maturity phase,* which is characterized by long production runs with stable techniques; labor skills become relatively unimportant and production becomes more capital-intensive. This product phase is associated with the third stage of the product cycle model of international trade; the *product decline phase* is associated with the fourth stage.

These changes in factor requirements on the supply side are linked with systematic changes in market requirements on the demand side. In the new-product phase, the price elasticity of demand is relatively low, since there are no close substitute products and most potential consumers remain ignorant of the new product. Also, the number of firms is small. In the product-growth phase, however, the individual firm experiences a rising price elasticity of demand as the product moves into mass consumption and the number of competitive firms becomes large. Finally, in the product-maturity phase, the product becomes fully standardized and there is intense price competition even though individual firms may maintain some differentiation through advertising and sales promotion.

Product life cycles may be determined by product differentiation as well as technological innovation. Indeed, it may be argued that new products are related more closely to product differentiation than to technological innovation. Only when a product becomes differentiated in the perceptions of foreign industrial or household consumers can it obtain an export monopoly advantage. Differentiation may derive from technological innovation (as is most likely true of any *radically* new product), but it may also derive from changes in style, design, packaging, promotion, and product-related services. Furthermore, not all technological innovations are embodied in products; process innovations may simply improve the manufacture of *existing* products. It follows that the life cycle model can be used to explain trade in differentiated products whether or not they are associated with technological innovations.

Several empirical investigations have been stimulated by the product life cycle model. For U.S. trade, Hirsch has studied the electronics industry; Stobaugh, the petrochemicals industry; and Wells, the consumer durables industries. For the trade of other countries, Tsurumi has studied Japan; Mousouris, Greece; and De La Torre, Mexico, Colombia, and Nicaragua.[16] These studies affirm the importance of technology in international trade and the usefulness of the product life cycle model to explain patterns of trade in manufactured goods.

Unlike these earlier studies, a recent study casts doubt on the significance of the product life cycle for the explanation of international trade.[17] Using a four-digit Standard Industrial Trade Classification Index (SITC) of total U.S. and Japanese trade over the period 1962 through 1988, the researchers found that *most* U.S. and Japanese trade was accounted for by four-digit categories in *consistent* surplus or deficit as measured by the normalized difference between the exports and imports of a category. That is, if (say) product category A was in surplus (deficit) in U.S. or Japanese trade in 1962, then it was very likely to be in surplus (deficit) in 1988. This finding appears to contradict the product life cycle model because a new product *should* move from a trade surplus in early years to a trade deficit in later years. However, this study has limitations that are acknowledged by its authors. Most important, the four-digit categories (for example, television receivers) do not distinguish between the branded products of individual firms, failing therefore to capture product differentiation. Furthermore, the study ignores quality differences in the four-digit categories across producing countries and time. Instead, the authors assume that the quality of a given category remains constant over time. Hence, they view the product life cycle as starting with the discovery of a *new* good that is *never* again changed. This assumption is at variance with the actual conduct of innovating firms that make continuing changes in new products to defend monopoly profits. Thus an innovating firm is likely to shift over time from exporting the original version of its product to exporting higher-quality, more sophisticated versions while at the same time its home country is *importing* the

---

[16]The foregoing studies appear in Louis T. Wells, Jr., ed., *The Product Life Cycle and International Trade* (Boston: Harvard Business School, Division of Research, 1972). For a technology gap study, see Gary Hufbauer, *Synthetic Materials and the Theory of International Trade* (Cambridge: Harvard University Press, 1966). For a summary of empirical tests, see Rolando Polli and Victor Cook, "Validity of the Product Life Cycle," *The Journal of Business,* October 1969, pp. 385–400.

[17]Joseph E. Gagnon and Andrew K. Rose, *How Pervasive Is the Product Cycle? The Empirical Dynamics of American and Japanese Trade Flows,* Working Paper no. 3946 (Cambridge, MA: National Bureau of Economic Research, January 1992).

Part I   International Trade

lower-quality original version. This operation of the product life cycle would *not* be caught by this study.[18] To conclude, although this study does not disprove the product cycle model, it raises questions that should stimulate new empirical testing. This testing will need to define product at the level of the individual firm, where both innovation and product differentiation occur. Such testing will require field research because the available secondary data on international trade are limited to product categories at the industry level.

FACTOR MOBILITY AND TRADE THEORY

The H-O theory of international trade presented in Chapter 3 assumed the absence of *any* factor movements among nations. Given this assumption, national factor endowments are determined only by *internal* conditions that perpetuate international dissimilarities in endowment structures and thereby afford a basis for gainful trade. The significance of this assumption for the H-O model of trade may be understood by tracing the implications of the contrary assumption, namely, perfect international factor mobility.

International Mobility of Factors

If labor, capital, and other factors moved freely among nations in response to opportunities for economic gain, they would move until the supply of each factor was everywhere fully adapted to demand and the price of each factor was the same in every country and in every use. Under the assumptions of the H-O theory, therefore, perfect international factor mobility would destroy the basis for gainful trade; given identical production functions, the shapes of all national production possibilities curves would be similar and the opportunity cost of any good would be the same in all countries. In the H-O model, factor mobility acts as a perfect substitute for goods mobility (trade).[19]

However useful they may be for economic analysis, the assumptions of perfect international factor mobility or immobility are fictions; neither is found to exist in the real world. Instead we find different degrees of factor mobility that vary among factors, among nations, and over time. Even within a country, noncompeting labor groups and other conditions constrain the free movement of factors and thereby provide an opportunity for interregional trade. Although factor mobility among countries is usually (but not always) lower than domestic mobility because of physical, social, and political obstacles, it is by no means small. Indeed, a key development in the world economy in recent years has been an extraordinary

---

[18]Grossman and Helpman offer a rigorous model of the technology gap between rich and poor countries in which the rich countries produce and export higher-quality versions of a product and import lower-quality versions. See Gene M. Grossman and Elhanan Helpman, "Quality Ladders and Product Cycles," *The Quarterly Journal of Economics,* CVI-2, 1991, pp. 557–586.

[19]When we drop the assumptions of the H-O model, this statement is no longer valid. Even with perfect factor mobility, opportunities for gainful trade would continue to be generated by increasing returns, product differentiation, and technology gaps.

growth in international flows of management, capital, and technology, particularly among the advanced industrial countries. The principal agent in this factor transfer is the international enterprise (especially its most advanced form, the multinational corporation), which is the subject of Part IV. The emergence of customs unions and free trade areas, notably the European Community, has also encouraged the international movement of factors.

Resources *Natural resources* are completely immobile. It is not physically possible to move land area, climate, soil, forests, mines, land forms, and other "gifts of nature" from one place to another. Since the international distribution of natural resources is most haphazard, their immobility assures a permanent dissimilarity in the supplies of national land factors. This immobility is not a distinctive feature of international trade, however, because natural resources also cannot be moved among regions of the same country.

Labor *Ordinary workers* will not emigrate to a foreign country unless they are pressed by unhappy circumstances at home. Social inertia tends to keep people in their native countries. However, large masses of people have moved from one country to another, particularly during periods of widespread unrest brought on by natural disasters, revolution, or war at home.[20]

In our own day the absence of motivations to emigrate has been much less important than limited opportunities to emigrate in explaining the low international mobility of labor. All contemporary governments restrict immigration and some, such as China's government, also restrict emigration. Actually the international mobility of ordinary labor is so low that international differences in relative labor supplies are probably growing wider due to disparate rates of population growth and capital accumulation.

The international mobility of *professional workers,* such as engineers and scientists, is much higher than that of ordinary workers. At times, the mobility of professional workers may be so high that national governments become concerned about "brain drains." The developing countries annually lose hundreds of their brightest professionals to North America and Europe, many of them recent graduates who decide not to return home. Undoubtedly, this mobility would be far higher if governments did not impose entry restrictions.

The international mobility of *managers* is probably higher today than at any time in the past. The multinational company with production and marketing affiliates in several countries has become a powerful vehicle for the transfer of managerial skills such as innovating, planning, directing, organizing, and controlling. A new type of international executive is now coming to the fore, an individual who is able to move quickly from a management post in one country to a new post

---

[20]Many waves of migration to the United States have been associated with unrest in Europe and elsewhere. Recent examples of international migration are the movement of East Europeans to West European and other countries following the breakup of the Soviet Union, and the flight of Bosnians from war in the former Yugoslavia to neighboring countries.

in another country. Sophisticated, cosmopolitan, and highly educated, this new breed of international manager has the capacity to manage business operations effectively in a broad variety of national milieux. The movement of these managers has been enormously facilitated by jet travel.

Capital   The international mobility of *capital goods* (construction, capital equipment, and inventories) varies with the nature of the goods. It is important to realize that a nation does not necessarily transfer capital to another nation by exporting capital goods to it. Instead, capital is transferred by international loans and investments (and occasionally by gifts) that provide the purchasing power needed to finance either the construction of capital goods in the borrowing country or the importation of capital goods from abroad. Therefore, the criterion of the international mobility of capital is the ease of foreign investment.

Viewed in this way, the international mobility of capital itself may be very high. During the nineteenth century and up to the 1930s, most international investment took the form of private lending via subscriptions to foreign bond issues. Although in the 1970s private lending of this sort and by banks once again became substantial, much private foreign investment today is undertaken by international companies that make direct equity investments in foreign affiliates. The rapid expansion of foreign direct investment by U.S., European, and Japanese companies is a dominant force in the evolution of the contemporary world economy.[21] Much capital also moves from rich to poor nations through international institutions, such as the World Bank, and through bilateral government aid programs.[22]

International Trade and Factor Movements as Substitutes

Both trade and factor movements act to bring about a superior allocation of production among nations. As we have seen, trade achieves this result, according to the H-O model, through international specialization that allows nations to export products that require relatively abundant factors in their production in exchange for products that require relatively scarce factors. More generally, trade enables a country to export products with low opportunity costs and import products with high opportunity costs.

Factor movements achieve a superior allocation of productive agents directly. Relatively abundant factors in country A (such as management and capital) move to country B, where the same factors are relatively scarce; they are then combined in production with country B's relatively abundant factors. In terms of price theory, factors move from country A, where their marginal productivities are low (because they are relatively abundant), to country B, where their marginal productivities are higher (because they are relatively scarce). Under conditions of perfect competition, the flow of factors continues until their marginal productivities (and

---

[21]Chapter 23 treats the theory of foreign direct investment.
[22]See Chapter 20 for a discussion of official external assistance to the developing countries.

prices) are the same in all countries. When this occurs, the international allocation of factors is Pareto-optimal, because any further factor movement would lower production and consumer satisfaction for the world as a whole.[23] Because of many obstacles and continuous economic change, this ideal allocation can never be achieved, even among regions of the same country; it can only be approached in varying degrees. Thus, the higher the mobility of factors among countries, the better the global allocation of factors and production. At the same time, factor mobility will tend to equalize factor prices among countries.

Does international trade also tend to equalize factor prices? To answer that question, let us assume that the United States has a comparative advantage in wheat production and a comparative disadvantage in textile production, while the converse holds in the United Kingdom. The production of wheat is land-intensive, and the United States has a relatively abundant supply of land, which thus commands a relatively low rent. The production of textiles is labor-intensive, and the United States has a relatively scarce supply of labor, which thus commands a relatively high wage. The opposite is true in the United Kingdom.

When trade begins, the demand facing United States wheat rises as foreign demand is added to domestic demand. With increasing unit costs, this higher demand leads to higher wheat prices and feeds back to create a higher demand and higher prices for the factors of production—especially land—used to produce wheat. At the same time, imports of textiles from the United Kingdom are displacing the United States' production of textiles. The falling demand for textiles initiates a falling demand and falling prices for the factor of production—especially labor—used to produce textiles. As a consequence, land rent rises relative to wages in the United States. Simultaneously, wages rise relative to land rent in the United Kingdom. Thus, the abundant factors (land in the United States, labor in the United Kingdom) become relatively more expensive while the scarce factors (labor in the United States, land in the United Kingdom) become relatively less expensive. It follows that the gap between the factor prices of the two countries becomes narrower.

Will international trade ever achieve a full equalization of factor prices between the trading countries? Only under these limiting assumptions could it ever happen: National factor endowments are not too unequal, there are no transfer costs, technology is the same in all countries, and there is only partial specialization (each country continues to produce some import-type goods).[24] But only the last assumption holds in the real world.

The foregoing analysis points to a *substitutive* relation between trade and factor movements. In the preceding example, a flow of labor from the United Kingdom to the United States would increase the opportunity cost of textiles in the first country and lower it in the second country, thereby narrowing the gainful opportunity for trade. The question whether there is a substitutive relation between

---

[23]For a definition of Pareto optimality, see Chapter 7.

[24]The classic exposition of the factor-price equalization theorem is Paul A. Samuelson, "International Trade and the Equalization of Factor Prices," *Economic Journal*, June 1948, pp. 163–84.

foreign investment (capital outflow) and trade is a matter of controversy in the United States. Do restrictions on U.S. investment abroad raise or lower U.S. exports? What about U.S. imports? Labor unions assert that foreign investment causes a loss of jobs to American workers as U.S. companies transfer production to foreign locations. Some observations are made in the following section indicating that factor movements and trade may also be complementary.

International Trade and Factor Movements as Complements: Economic Integration

The conclusion that trade and factor movements are substitutes derives from the H-O factor endowments theory, which is concerned only with allocational efficiency under static conditions (perfect competition, fixed factor endowments, and no technology gaps). When these assumptions are dropped to allow for dynamic elements, it is no longer evident that international factor movements cause a general decrease in international trade. What the static analysis ignores are the effects of factor movements on economic growth and, particularly, economic integration.

As stated earlier, international factor flows are mainly initiated by multinational companies that transfer a mix of management, capital, and technology from one country to another. These factors are combined with local factors to manufacture products that, for the most part, are new to the host economy.[25] This process contributes both directly and indirectly to the growth of the economy.[26] By promoting economic growth, factor movements increase the capacity of nations to trade with one another; expansion occurs in both the size and diversity of production and markets. Although factor movements have displaced trade in some products, statistical data suggest that their growth effects on trade have been more powerful than their substitution effects. Trade and factor flows have expanded together for the world as a whole; in the European Community, factor transfers among the member countries have been accompanied by a growth in mutual trade that has exceeded the growth in trade with outside countries. At the enterprise level, it is also noteworthy that the principal exporters of manufactures from the United States are also the principal investors in production abroad.

Generally we are witnessing a process of economic integration on a global scale (particularly among the industrial countries) that is being carried forward by a complex mix of trade and factor flows. Economists generally agree that factor movements constitute a more powerful instrument for factor-price equalization than trade in products. Consequently, factor transfers can be expected to join national economies together to a higher degree than goods transfers alone. As local and regional markets earlier gave way to national markets, so national markets are now giving way to world markets. In the past, trade created an international economy; today, factor flows are creating a world economy.

---

[25]The term *host economy* refers to the country that receives the factor transfers.

[26]This is intended only as a general statement: Some factor transfers are more growth generating than others. For this and other qualifications, see Chapter 24.

MULTINATIONAL ENTERPRISE
AND TRADE THEORY

Part IV is devoted to the theory and performance of multinational enterprises that span the globe with their production, marketing, and financial operations. These firms are responsible for a large share of international trade and almost all foreign direct investment. Here we indicate only the principal features of multinational enterprises that need to be incorporated into a theory of trade in order to explain actual patterns of trade.

The multinational enterprise is the foremost agent in moving factors of production from one country to another. The intimate link between the trade and investment activities of multinational enterprises points to the need for a synthesis of trade and investment theories.

Multinational enterprises are large firms in oligopolistic industries. Furthermore, the manufacturing and service multinational enterprises are oligopolists producing and selling differentiated products. Strongly motivated by growth objectives and the maintenance of global market shares and sensitive to each other's behavior, multinational enterprises prefer to compete with new and differentiated products rather than with price. These firms are also characterized by increasing returns in production and organization that support their oligopolistic power. Competition among multinational enterprises occurs as a "strategic game" featured by a high degree of mutual interdependence played out in global markets.

Horizontally and vertically integrated across national boundaries, much of the international trade of multinational enterprises is among their national units. Indeed, one-third of U.S. exports of manufactures consists of transfers from U.S. parent companies to their foreign affiliates. The presence of intraenterprise trade raises the question of how sensitive such trade is to costs, prices, and other economic forces. By assuming exchanges between independent sellers and buyers, trade theory has ignored the phenomenon of *intrafirm* trade.

Multinational enterprises are more technologically intensive than their domestic counterparts. It is no coincidence that the five most R & D-intensive and export-intensive U.S. industries identified by Gruber, Mehta, and Vernon are also the industries most dominated by multinational enterprises. Such companies have the global capability to transfer technology through export goods, directly through licensing, or through production in foreign countries. They have speeded up the international flow of technology, and they are mainly responsible for both the creation and destruction of international technology gaps.

With their international information networks, multinational enterprises have a greater capability than other firms to reduce the ignorance and uncertainty gaps that constrain international trade. Furthermore, their size and the geographical diversification of their operations enables multinational enterprises to assume risks that would turn away other firms. One consequence of this "scanning ability" may be to speed up the product trade cycle: Anticipating foreign imitation of a new product, the multinational enterprise may itself start production in foreign markets. Moreover, it may "short-circuit" the trade cycle by locating capital-intensive production in a capital-poor country, bringing in the capital and other scarce factors such as technology.

By concentrating on trade only at the national level, economists until recently have left to marketing and management scholars the task of explaining the behavior of the international firm. As long as international trade was largely carried on by intermediaries and producers remained at home, this neglect was not serious. But today international firms have burst the confines of the individual nation-state to carry on their operations throughout the world. In the process, they bring to bear on international markets a mix of productive factors, technological innovation, and entrepreneurial drive. It is no longer possible to understand the trade of the industrial countries (notably the United States) unless full account is taken of the behavior of international firms. The theory of international trade must become part of a broader theory of *international economic integration* if we are to understand the forces now shaping the world economy.

CONCLUDING OBSERVATIONS ON COMPARATIVE ADVANTAGE

In this and in Chapters 3 and 4, we reviewed several theories that relate comparative advantage to certain attributes of trading countries: factor proportions, technology, increasing returns, product differentiation, and preference similarity. Each of these theories concentrates on a particular determinant that explains international trade under certain circumstances. Collectively, therefore, the theories offer a comprehensive understanding of international trade. In general, they provide complementary rather than conflicting explanations.

Table 5-2 indicates the *principal* explanations of comparative advantage depending on whether the product is (1) a primary or manufactured product, (2) a mineral or agricultural product (if a primary product), or (3) at an early, middle, or late stage of its life cycle (if a manufactured product).

Table 5-2 Principal Explanations of Comparative Advantage in International Trade

Explanations	Primary Goods			Manufactured Goods		
	Mineral	Agricultural		Early Phase	Middle Phase	Late Phase
Factor endowments	•	•				•
Technology gaps		•		•		
Increasing returns	•					•
Product differentiation					•	

Primary goods are nondifferentiated commodities whose prices are mainly set in commodity exchanges. Factor endowments are the main determinant of trade in such goods. However, a second-order distinction needs to be drawn between minerals and other (mostly agricultural) commodities. Big oligopolistic firms dominate the production and trade in minerals, such as petroleum, iron ore, bauxite, and copper ore. These firms exploit mineral deposits through large-scale, capital-intensive operations in mining, processing, transportation, and storage. Increasing returns, therefore, are an additional explanation of international trade in minerals. By and large, however, these firms share the same technology, and therefore technology gaps play only a modest role in minerals trade. In contrast, agricultural production is spread among many producers who have no marked increasing returns but who may be growing crops with dissimilar production functions, as pointed out earlier. For that reason technology gaps, along with factor endowments, are a determinant of trade in agricultural goods.

The principal source of comparative advantage in manufactured goods depends on the phase of their life cycles. In the early phase, when the product is new, comparative advantage mainly derives from technology gaps. In the middle phase, when the innovating manufacturer's product has some imitators, product differentiation, sometimes accompanied by increasing returns, becomes the principal explanation of comparative advantage. In the late phase, when the product loses differentiation, factor endowments and increasing returns emerge as the dominant influences on comparative advantage.

Only trade in agricultural commodities and commodity-like manufactures in the late phase of their life cycles takes place in markets that approach the economist's model of perfect competition. In perfectly competitive markets, we can ignore the behavior of individual firms because they have no market power. In contrast, technology gaps, increasing returns, and product differentiation give to the individual firm some degree of monopoly power in its market. It follows, therefore, that an explanation of trade in new and differentiated manufactured products and in minerals must pay attention to the market behavior of individual firms, particularly of multinational corporations.

In the remaining chapters of Part I, we describe and evaluate the international trade policies of the United States and other countries. Apart from its purely intellectual appeal to economists, the principal justification of international economic theory is to give government policymakers a related set of concepts, models, and analytical tools that will help them (1) understand what is happening in the world economy, and (2) design policies that will best achieve national and international objectives and goals. Can contemporary trade theory make these contributions to policymakers?

We conclude that the several trade theories focus on different aspects of international trade phenomena and that collectively they offer a much better understanding of those phenomena than any single theory. Indeed, the policymaker today is a notable beneficiary of the renewed activity of international trade theorists. This is not to deny the desirability of a single theory that would incorporate systematically the insights of the several theories of trade and, at the same time, explain the behavior of multinational enterprises.

SUMMARY

1. Technological innovation is the entire process whereby research and invention are transformed by the firm into new production functions and new products. The innovation process encompasses technical research, development, production start-up/improvements, marketing start-up/adaptations, and market intelligence.

2. Technological innovation influences trade through higher factor productivity, production functions, and new products. A new production function "saves" some or all of the factors of production needed to produce a given level of output as compared with the old production function. The effects of this saving may be neutral, protrade, or antitrade.

3. At any given time, countries may be using different technologies to produce the same products; that is, they have dissimilar production functions (technology gap). Hence, there is no fixed relationship between factor endowments and the *specific* kinds of products a country will export and import. Technological innovation also creates technology gaps in new products, giving rise to international trade cycles.

4. There is also abundant evidence that the United States has a comparative advantage in research-intensive, high-technology products. Technology theories postulate that the advanced industrial countries, such as the United States, Japan, and Germany, have special advantages as innovators of new products and that there is an "imitation lag" that prevents other countries from immediately duplicating in production the new products of the innovating country. The consequence is a technology gap that affords the innovating country an export monopoly during the period of imitation lag.

5. One of the technology theories postulates a product life cycle model of international trade. In the four-stage model an innovating country (the United States) moves from being the sole exporter of a new product to being an importer of the same product at a future time when the product is no longer new. The factor requirements of a product, as well as its market, change in a systematic fashion during the product life cycle (i.e., new product, product growth, product maturity, and product decline).

6. No matter how useful they may be for economic analysis, the assumptions of perfect international factor mobility or immobility are fictions; neither is found to exist in the real world. Instead we find different degrees of factor mobility that vary among factors, among nations, and over time.

7. A key development in the world economy in recent years has been an extraordinary growth in international flows of management, capital, and technology under the aegis of the multinational enterprise. Both international trade and factor mobility tend to equalize factor prices among nations, pointing to a substitute relationship between the two. But factor movements may also generate trade by stimulating economic growth.

8. Today we are witnessing a process of global economic integration that is being carried forward by a complex mix of trade and factor flows.

9. It is no longer possible to understand the trade of the industrial countries unless full account is taken of the behavior of multinational firms.

10. The several trade theories are more complementary than conflicting, and together they can offer substantial help to government policymakers.

QUESTIONS AND APPLICATIONS

1. Although the terms are frequently used interchangeably, can you draw a meaningful distinction between *technology* as such and *technological innovation?* Illustrate your answer with examples.

2. Explain why a firm can obtain a return on its R & D investment *only* after the entire innovation process is completed.

3. "The completion of the innovation process is by no means certain." Explain the meaning of this statement in terms of probabilities.

4. (a) What is the meaning of *imitation lag?*
   (b) Why should the United States have "special advantages" as an innovator of new products?

5. (a) What are the four stages of the product life cycle model of international trade?
   (b) How do factor requirements and market conditions change during the four product phases of the product life cycle?

6. Discuss the following statement: The human-skills and technology theories of trade are intimately related.

7. Explain how both trade and factor movements tend to equalize factor prices among nations. What conditions will prevent a full equalization of factor prices?

8. "The conclusion that trade and factor movements are substitutes derives from the factor endowments theory, which is concerned only with allocational efficiency under static conditions." Explain this statement.

9. Discuss four features of the multinational enterprise and their implications for international trade theory.

10. Do you agree that the different theories of trade are, for the most part, complementary rather than conflicting? Justify your answer.

SELECTED READINGS

Balassa, Bela. "The Determinants of Intra-Industry Specialization in United States Trade." *Oxford Economic Papers* 38 (1986), pp. 220–233.

Dosi, Giovanni. "Sources, Procedures and Microeconomic Effects of Innovation." *Journal of Economic Literature,* September 1988, pp. 1120–1171.

Dosi, Giovanni, and others. *The Economics of Technical Change and International Trade.* Brighton: Wheatsheaf, 1990.

Ethier, Wilfrid. "National and International Returns to Scale and the Modern Theory of Trade." *American Economic Review,* June 1982.

Giersch, Herbert, ed. *On the Economics of Intra-Industry Trade.* Tubingen: J.C.B. Mohr (Paul Siebeck), 1979.

Girifalco, Louis A. *Dynamics of Technological Change.* New York: Van Nostrand Reinhold, 1991.

Grossman, Gene M., ed. *Imperfect Competition and International Trade.* Cambridge: The MIT Press, 1992.

Helpman, Elhanan. *Monopolistic Competition in Trade Theory,* Special Papers in International Finance, no. 16. Princeton, N.J.: Princeton University, June 1990.

Helpman, Elhanan, and Paul R. Krugman. *Trade Policy and Market Structure.* Cambridge: The MIT Press, 1989.

Krugman, Paul. *Rethinking International Trade.* Cambridge: The MIT Press, 1990.

Linder, S. Burenstam. *An Essay on Trade and Transformation.* New York: John Wiley & Sons, 1961.

Porter, Michael E. *The Competitive Advantage of Nations.* New York: The Free Press, 1990.

Tharakan, P.K.M., and Jacob Kol, eds. *Intraindustry Trade: Theory, Evidence and Extensions.* New York: St. Martin's Press, 1989.

Vernon, Raymond. "The Product Cycle Hypothesis in a New International Environment." *Oxford Bulletin of Economics and Statistics* 41-1 (1979), pp. 255–267.

chapter 6

TARIFFS AND NONTARIFF
TRADE BARRIERS

This chapter begins our examination of international trade policies by describing the nature and economic effects of the policy instruments used by governments to influence the flows of goods and services in the world economy.

The traditional policy instrument is the import *tariff*. But governments also resort to a bewildering variety of measures to restrict imports or subsidize exports. These measures are collectively designated as *nontariff trade barriers*.

ECONOMIC EFFECTS OF TARIFFS

Simply stated, an import tariff (or customs duty) is a tax imposed by a government on physical goods as they move into a country. There are two basic kinds of tariff: ad valorem and specific. An *ad valorem* tariff is expressed as a percentage of the value of an import good, such as 10 or 20 percent ad valorem. A *specific* tariff is expressed as an amount of money for a physical unit of an import good, such as 20 cents per pound or per gallon. Ad valorem tariffs are more satisfactory for differentiated manufactured products, while specific tariffs are more adaptable to undifferentiated commodities. Specific tariffs have given way to ad valorem tariffs in response to inflation and the growing importance of trade in manufactures.

Tariffs may be designed to collect revenue for the government or to protect domestic industries against foreign competition.[1] To best perform their *revenue function,* tariff duties are applied to commodities of wide consumption and the rates of these duties are kept low enough to maximize customs collections. The same objective may also be attained by the imposition of a uniform low rate of duty on

---

[1]Revenue and protection are the principal functions of tariffs. At times, however, a government may raise tariff rates in response to a balance of payments deficit. In 1964, Great Britain imposed a 15 percent surcharge on all imports (roughly doubling the existing tariff level), which was then abandoned the following year. In 1971 both the United States and Denmark levied a 10 percent surcharge on most dutiable imports. Unlike tariffs for revenue or protection, such surcharges have an emergency, short-lived character.

all merchandise crossing the border either as exports, as imports, or in transit. The revenue function of a duty is a relative concept. A duty is always characterized by an element of protection, however small or unimportant, except, of course, when the taxed product is not domestically produced and the tariff serves a purely revenue function.

The *protection function* of the tariff depends upon a partial or complete restriction of imports. When complete protection is desired, a given duty must be high enough to cover the difference in the marginal cost of production between domestic and *all* foreign producers, including transportation and incidental expenses of importing. If the tariff is to be only partially protective, however, the duty must remain below this difference. When partial protection is desired, goods will continue to be imported, but they will be imported in smaller quantities and the government will collect customs duties. Therefore, the protection function—like the revenue function—will usually afford both protection and revenue, although its purpose is primarily one of protection.

The seeming incompatibility of the two functions in the same duty does not necessarily disqualify its adoption, since most countries generally desire both protection and revenue. In national tariff schedules, however, a tendency does exist to provide a certain number of generally low rates of duties designed essentially for revenue and other higher duty rates for protection.

The immediate effects of tariffs are those reflected in price changes and consequent adjustments in production and consumption. Because of the fact that tariffs for revenue have effects similar to but smaller than those of protective tariffs, our discussion shall be confined to protective tariffs, leaving it to the reader to make the appropriate application to revenue tariffs.

Price Effects of an Import Duty

The price effects of an import duty depend primarily on the elasticity of the supply schedule of the import good facing the duty-levying country.[2] Here we distinguish three price effects: (1) a rise in domestic price of less than the amount of the duty, (2) no change in domestic price, and (3) a rise in domestic price equal to the duty.

Price Rise of Less Than the Amount of the Duty   A large trading country, such as the United States, can influence world prices because its imports are a significant fraction of international markets. That is to say, it has some degree of *monopsonistic* power in international markets. Hence, the supply schedules of most foreign products entering the U.S. market are *price-inelastic* to some degree. In this situation, the imposition of an import duty on a product will cause foreign suppliers to lower the price, thereby absorbing some of the duty.[3] The postduty

---

[2]Price effects depend secondarily on the elasticity of the import demand schedule, which in turn depends on the elasticity of the domestic demand schedule and the elasticity of the supply schedule of the domestic import-competing good.

[3]As we shall discuss later, absorption of the entire duty by foreign suppliers will occur only when the import supply schedule is *perfectly* inelastic.

price for consumers in the tariff-levying country, therefore, will rise by less than the duty. Figure 6-1 demonstrates this price effect.

The diagram on the left shows the domestic demand schedule, D_d, and the domestic supply schedule, S_d, of product Y in country A. The diagram on the right shows the import demand schedule, D_m, and the import supply schedule, S_m, of product Y. The import demand schedule equals the excess of domestic demand over domestic supply at prices below the point of intersection of D_d and S_d. Before the imposition of an import duty, the domestic price of Y is $0-P_d$. At that price, country A imports $0-M$ of product Y, an amount that equals the excess of domestic demand over domestic supply (Q_1-Q_4). Because there is no duty on imports of Y, the domestic consumer price $(0-P_d)$ equals the import supply price $(0-P_s)$, which in turn equals the import consumer price $(0-P_m)$.

Now suppose country A imposes a duty. This causes the entire import supply schedule facing consumers in country A to shift upward by the amount of the duty

Figure 6-1

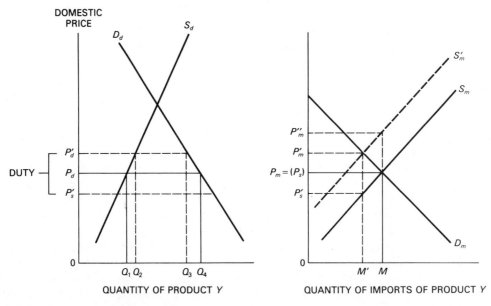

QUANTITY OF PRODUCT Y QUANTITY OF IMPORTS OF PRODUCT Y

Price Rise Less Than the Amount of the Duty. The diagram on the left shows the domestic demand schedule, D_d, and the domestic supply schedule, S_d, of product Y in country A. The diagram on the right shows country A's import demand schedule, D_m, and the import supply schedule, S_m, of product Y. The import demand schedule equals the excess of domestic demand over domestic supply at prices below the point of intersection of D_d and S_d. Before the imposition of an import duty, the domestic price of Y is $0-P_d$. Now suppose country A imposes a duty. This causes the entire import supply schedule facing consumers in country A to shift upwards by the amount of the duty and a new supply schedule, S'_m, is established. Because foreign suppliers absorb some of the duty, the increase in the domestic price of Y from $0-P_d$ to $0-P'_d$ is less than the duty, which equals the difference $P'_d-P'_s$. Imports fall from M to M', which equals Q_2-Q_3.

and a new supply schedule, S'_m, is established. At each quantity of imports, the new supply price for consumers is higher than the old supply price by the amount of the duty. At quantity $0-M$, for instance, the duty equals $P_s - P''_m$.[4] The new supply schedule creates excess demand at the preduty price of $0-P_m$. Hence, competition among consumers will raise the price to $0-P'_m$, where the amount demanded equals the amount supplied. At the same time, foreign suppliers lower the price from $0-P_s$ to $0-P'_s$, for which price they are willing to offer $0-M'$ imports.

The difference between the new import consumer price ($0-P'_m$) and the new import supply price ($0-P'_s$) is the tariff duty. Because foreign suppliers absorb some of the duty, the increase in the domestic price of Y from $0-P_d$ to $0-P'_d$ is less than the duty, which equals the difference $P'_d - P'_s$. Also, imports fall from M to M', which equals $Q_2 - Q_3$.

Foreign suppliers could shift the entire duty to country A's consumers only if the price rose to $0-P''_m$. But this price could not be sustained, because excess import supply would force it down to $0-P'_m$.

No Change in Price   When the duty-levying country is the sole buyer (monopsonist) of a good, then its import supply schedule is perfectly inelastic. Because foreign suppliers have no other market, they would lower price to absorb any import duty in order to maintain sales. Consequently, the price of the good for consumers in the duty-levying country would remain the same after imposition of the duty. This is shown in Figure 6-2.

The preduty domestic price of product Y ($0-P_d$) equals the import supply price ($0-P_s$), which in turn equals the import price for consumers of Y. Now suppose a duty is imposed equal to $P_s - P'_m$. If the duty is passed on fully to consumers of Y, then the import price rises to $0-P'_m$. But that price cannot endure, because there is an excess amount supplied: Competition among foreign suppliers forces down the price until the excess supply is wiped out at $0-P_m$. But to do this, suppliers need to absorb fully the duty by cutting their price by the amount of the duty from $0-P_s$ to $0-P'_s$. Consequently, the domestic price of Y remains $0-P_d$.

Foreign suppliers will continue to absorb the entire duty over the long run only if they can cover their unit costs at the supply price of $0-P'_s$. If the costs of some suppliers are *not* covered, then eventually they will eliminate or cut back production of Y. This cutback will appear as a leftward shift of the import supply schedule, bringing about a rise in the price of Y in country A. In sum, a perfectly inelastic import supply schedule is an extreme case that seldom exists in the real world, and even then the full absorption of an import duty will continue only if suppliers can cover all costs at their postduty price.

Price Rise Equal to the Amount of the Duty   When a country is too small to influence the world price of a product by altering its import demand, then the import supply schedule is *perfectly elastic*. In this situation, an import duty raises the domestic price by the full amount of the duty. This is demonstrated in Figure 6-3.

---

[4]Foreign suppliers view this postduty situation as a *downward* shift in the *demand* schedule facing their exports to country A: At each preduty price, they sell less than before.

Figure 6-2

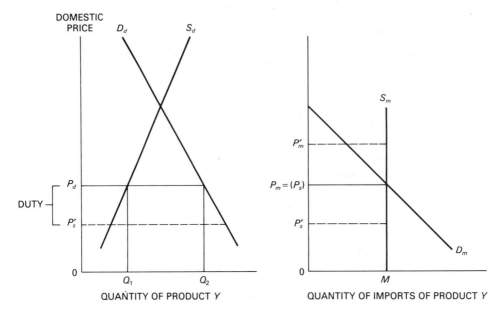

QUANTITY OF PRODUCT Y

QUANTITY OF IMPORTS OF PRODUCT Y

No Effect of Import Duty on Price. The preduty domestic price of product $Y (0-P_d)$ equals the import supply price $(0-P_s)$, which in turn equals the import price for consumers of Y. Now suppose a duty is imposed equal to $P_s-P'_m$. If the duty is passed on fully to consumers of Y, then the import price rises to $0-P'_m$. But that price cannot endure, because there is an excess amount supplied: Competition among foreign suppliers forces down the price until the excess supply is wiped out at $0-P_m$. Suppliers absorb fully the duty by cutting their price by the amount of the duty from $0-P_s$ to $0-P'_s$. Consequently, the domestic price of Y remains $0-P_d$. Foreign suppliers will continue to absorb the entire duty over the long run only if they can cover their costs at the supply price of $0-P'_s$.

Before the duty is imposed, country A imports $0-M$ of product Y at a price of $0-P_s$, which equals the domestic price of $0-P_d$. Now assume that country A imposes an import duty. This shifts the import supply schedule facing country A's consumers upward by the amount of the duty (which equals $P_s-P'_m$), and a new supply schedule, S'_m, is established. The new equilibrium import price is $0-P'_m$, as determined by the intersection of S'_m and D_m, and the new domestic price is $0-P'_d$. Observe that the fall in imports from $0-M$ to $0-M'$ does *not* cause foreign suppliers to lower their price, because country A's imports are an inconsequential fraction of the world demand for product Y. Hence, the entire duty is borne by consumers in country A as the price rises by the full amount of the duty.[5]

[5]An import duty may raise the price to the consumer by *more* than the amount of the duty when the domestic channel of distribution is lengthy and the different middlemen add individual markups (calculated as a percentage of their selling prices) at each step of the marketing process.

Figure 6-3

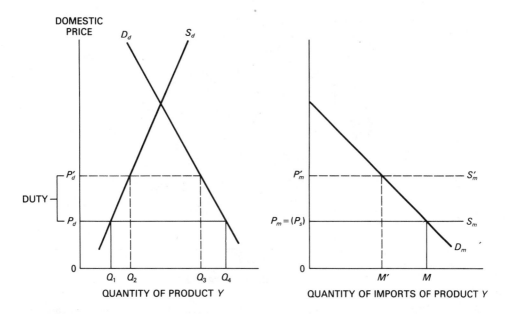

Price Rise Equal to Amount of Duty. Before the duty is imposed, country A imports $0-M$ of product Y at a price of $0-P_s$, which equals the domestic price of $0-P_d$. Now assume that country A imposes an import duty. This shifts the import supply schedule facing country A's consumers upward by the amount of the duty (which equals $P_s-P'_m$) and a new supply schedule, S'_m, is established. The new import price is $0-P'_m$, as determined by the intersection of S'_m and D_m, and the new domestic price is $0-P'_d$. The entire duty is borne by consumers as the price rises by the full amount of the duty.

The Social Cost (Deadweight Loss) of Tariffs

Although an import duty may induce many changes in both the importing and exporting countries, its *direct* effects in the importing country may be classified as price, revenue, trade, protection, consumption, and income-redistribution effects. Together these effects determine the *social cost* of a tariff for the tariff-levying country.

Figure 6-4 shows these effects under the simplifying assumption of a perfectly elastic foreign supply. At the prevailing price, $0-P_d$, the quantity demanded of a given product by country A is $0-Q$, determined by its domestic demand schedule, $D-D'$, of which the portion $0-Q_1$ is domestically produced (determined by the intersection of the price, $0-P_d$, and the domestic supply schedule, S_d), and the remaining part, Q_1-Q, is imported.

Upon the introduction of a tariff by country A, a customs duty of, say, $P_d-P'_d$ is levied, raising the cost to domestic users from $0-P_d$ to $0-P'_d$. At this higher cost, the quantities demanded of the protected product are reduced from $0-Q$ to $0-Q_2$,

Figure 6-4

Effects of an Import Duty with a Perfectly Elastic Foreign Supply. Before the duty, country A imports Q_1-Q at a price of 0-P_d. Because the import supply schedule (not shown here) is perfectly elastic, the imposition of the duty raises the *price* by the full amount of the duty—from 0-P_d to 0-P'_d. The *revenue* effect is the rectangle *d*, the *trade* effect is the drop in imports (Q_1-Q_3 + Q_2-Q), the *protection* effect is Q_1-Q_3, and the *consumption* effect is Q_2-Q. The *income-redistribution* effect is the quadrangle *r*. The *net cost* (deadweight loss) of the tariff for country A is the sum of the triangles *l* and *c*.

of which 0-Q_3 is domestically supplied and the remaining portion, Q_3-Q_2, is imported.

The *price* effect is the increase in price to domestic consumers because of the duty. In this instance, consumers bear the full incidence of the duty (price rises by the full amount of the duty, P_d-P'_d,) because the foreign supply price remains the same (foreign supply is perfectly elastic).

The *revenue* effect is the customs collections accruing to the government, represented by rectangle *d*. It is the product of the quantity of imports *times* the duty P_d-P'_d.

The *trade* effect is the decline in imports resulting from the duty. At the preduty price of 0-P_d, imports were Q_1-Q; after the duty was imposed, they fell to Q_3-Q_2. The negative trade effect, therefore, is Q_1-Q_3 + Q_2-Q.

The *protection* effect is the increase in domestic production that is induced by the import duty, namely, Q_1-Q_3. This represents the substitution of domestic production for foreign production.

The *consumption* effect is the decrease in consumption resulting from the tariff. Because of a higher price, consumers cut their consumption of the product from 0-Q

to 0-Q_2. Hence, the consumption effect is Q_2-Q. (Note that the trade effect is the sum of the protection and consumption effects.)

The *income-redistribution* effect is the shift in income from domestic consumers to domestic producers. It is shown by quadrangle r, which measures the *producer surplus* or extra revenue that is received by domestic producers above their supply cost (S_d) as a result of the duty.

In a perfectly competitive economy, the *net cost* (deadweight loss) of the tariff to the domestic country is the sum of triangles l and c. The reasoning behind this conclusion is as follows. Some consumers enjoy an economic gain or surplus because they are willing to pay a higher price than the market price that they actually pay for some of the product.[6] On the assumption that the prices consumers would be willing to pay for various quantities of the product measure the satisfactions they derive from the product, then the consumer surplus *before* the tariff is indicated by the area D-g-P_d in Figure 6-4. The higher price caused by the tariff, however, reduces the consumer surplus to D-h-P'_d, resulting in a net loss of P'_d-h-g-P_d, which is equal to the sum of r, l, d, and c. Since the net loss in consumer surplus is partly offset by the national gain of r and d, the net national loss is the sum of l and c. Specifically, l is the national loss attributable to the substitution of higher-priced domestic production for lower-priced foreign production, and c is the national loss in consumption due to the higher postduty price, which causes the substitution of other goods providing less satisfaction than the foregone imports. When the tariff-levying country faces a perfectly elastic import supply, it always experiences a net national loss because domestic consumers bear the full incidence of the duty. When import supply is less than perfectly elastic, however, a country can improve its terms of trade by imposing a tariff and it may even enjoy a net national gain, a subject that will be discussed in Chapter 7. If the duty is high enough to reach P''_d, there will be no imports—the entire quantity demanded, 0-Q_4, will be supplied by the domestic producers at price 0-P''_d.

With less-than-infinite foreign supply elasticity, the price effect would be less restrictive of imports and consumption, since the foreign price would drop, as established earlier in this chapter. In that case, the net cost of the tariff for the domestic country would be less than otherwise. This situation is likely if the importing country is a major consumer of the product.

Measurement of Tariff Systems

Several methods have been used to measure the trade and protection effects of national tariff systems.

Tariff Revenues The most naive approach, favored by protectionists, is to divide a country's customs revenue by the total value of its imports. This method implicitly assumes that the protection effect of a tariff system is directly related to

---

[6]A discussion of consumer and producer surplus in the context of the social cost of monopoly appears in Chapter 4.

the duties collected on imports: The lower the ratio of customs revenue to imports, the lower the degree of protection. This assumption is demonstrably false. Suppose a country's duties are so high that no dutiable goods are imported — the trade effect is equal to the preduty import volume. In that event, no revenue would be collected — the ratio of revenue to imports would be zero! To conclude that the protection and trade effects are also zero would be patently absurd.

Height of Duties   Another approach is to add up all the duties in a tariff system and then calculate the unweighted average. A more sophisticated version of this method is to calculate an average of all duties weighted by the country's imports of each dutiable product. Thus, a product with imports of, say, $2 million is given twice the weight of a product with imports of $1 million.[7]

This approach assumes that trade and protection effects are proportional to the height of a duty and they are the same for all products and all countries. The unweighted average ignores the varying importance of different products in trade. On the other hand, an average that is weighted by the tariff-levying country's imports of each dutiable product has a *downward* bias: Prohibitory duties are not counted (since they keep out all imports) and the more restrictive a duty, the less its weight. Despite this drawback, both the United States and the European Community have used such weighted averages to measure the heights of their own and the other's tariff system during negotiations.[8] The downward bias would be moderated, if not overcome, by using as weights the value of *world* trade in each product.[9]

Effective versus Nominal Rates   As we have seen, an import duty raises the domestic price of a good (unless the elasticity of its foreign supply is zero) and thereby encourages consumers to shift from the foreign good to a domestic substitute. Thus, the nominal duty, together with the relevant elasticities, determines the *consumption* effect.

But for domestic producers the *protection* effect of a nominal duty on their final product is *enhanced* by the fact that their own production activity is responsible for only a part of the final product's value. At the same time, the protection effect of a

---

[7]In mathematical form, the simple unweighted average is

$$\sum_{t=1}^{t=n} = d_t/\text{n},$$

where d represents the individual duty expressed as a percentage and n, the number of duties. The weighted average is

$$\sum_{t=1}^{t=n} = (d_t)i_v$$

where i is the weight defined as the fractional share of dutiable imports associated with the individual duty. The sum of all the weights is one.

[8]See Chapter 8.

[9]Due to lack of trade data, lack of comparability (different customs nomenclatures), and other statistical problems, weighting by world trade is generally considered impractical.

nominal duty is *lowered* for domestic producers by any import duties on raw materials and other inputs that they use in manufacturing the final product. The tariff rate that is relevant to the protection effect, therefore, is the *effective* rate that takes into account both of these factors. The effective rate measures the degree of protection that is afforded the *value added* to the final product by domestic producers.

The formula for the calculation of the effective rate is

$$r = \frac{n - \Sigma pi}{1 - \Sigma p},$$

where r is the effective rate, n is the nominal rate, p is the proportion of the final product represented by imported or importable inputs in the absence of any import restrictions, and i is the nominal rate of duty on raw materials and other intermediate goods. The expression $1 - \Sigma p$ is the value added to the final product by domestic producers as a proportion of the final value.

If no duties are imposed on imports of intermediate goods, then the formula becomes

$$r = \frac{n}{1 - \Sigma p}.$$

This gives the rate of protection against the value added by domestic producers (the final value of the product *minus* the value of importable inputs purchased from other producers, local or foreign).

Assume, for example, that a country places a 20 percent duty on imports of a final product but allows duty-free imports of intermediate goods that constitute one half of the final product's value. Then the effective rate is

$$\frac{.20}{1 - \frac{1}{2}},$$

or 40 percent. Assuming a price rise equal to the duty, this 20 percent duty enables domestic producers of the final product to increase their value added by 40 percent more than in a free trade situation with no duties.

Continuing with this example, let us now assume that a 10 percent rate is applied to imports of intermediate goods. (If more than one input is involved, then the rate is a weighted average.) The effective rate becomes

$$\frac{.20 - \frac{1}{2}(.10)}{1 - \frac{1}{2}},$$

or 30 percent. Note that the tariff on intermediate goods has lowered the effective rate although it remains higher than the nominal rate. When the nominal rates applied to the final product and to intermediate goods are the same, then the effective rate is *equal* to the nominal rate for the final product. When the intermediate duty rate exceeds the final-product rate, then the effective rate becomes *less* than the nominal rate and may even be negative. Because national governments generally admit raw materials and other intermediate goods either duty-free or at a lower rate than finished goods to encourage local manufacture, effective tariff rates are usually higher than nominal rates.

Elasticities and Market Share Any method that pretends to measure the protection effect of a duty by its height (even when the effective rate is substituted for the nominal rate) implicitly ignores the foreign and domestic elasticities of supply and demand that vary from product to product and from country to country. A duty of any given height may or may not be restrictive, depending on the relevant elasticities. But elasticities are difficult to determine empirically, even for a single product. It is no wonder, then, that efforts to measure entire tariff systems comprising thousands of product classifications have relied on weighted averages of nominal or effective duties. Although such averages may be useful for intercountry and intertemporal comparisons, they should be interpreted only as crude indicators of the degree of tariff protection.

The elasticity of import demand is influenced by the *share* of imports in domestic consumption and domestic production as well as by domestic supply and demand elasticities.[10] Other things being equal, the smaller the import shares, the greater the import elasticity. Given the domestic elasticities, therefore, a duty will restrict imports most when such imports are only marginal to domestic consumption and production, a situation that is probably more common in the United States than in most other countries.

General Equilibrium Analysis of Tariff Effects

Up to this point, our analysis of tariff effects has used a *partial equilibrium* approach that looks at a single market only, thereby ignoring possible effects on the rest of the economy. In this section we offer a *general equilibrium* analysis of tariff effects that looks at the entire economy.

Assume that a country produces two goods, high-technology manufactures (H-manufactures) and low-technology manufactures (L-manufactures), and that it exports the former and imports the latter. Assume further that the country is too small to influence the world prices of these goods, that is, it must accept the terms of trade as determined in world markets. Under this constraint, it sells H-manufactures at price P_h and buys L-manufactures at price P_l.

Figure 6-5 shows the general equilibrium conditions under both free trade and a tariff. Let us look first at free-trade equilibrium. The country produces $0-H_1$ of

---

[10]The formula is $e_m = e_d(C/M) + e_s(Q/M)$, where e_m is the import demand elasticity, e_d and e_s are the domestic elasticities of demand and supply, respectively, C is domestic consumption, Q is domestic production, and M is imports.

Figure 6-5

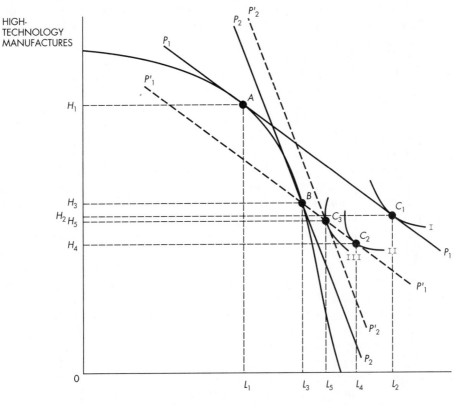

General Equilibrium Analysis of Tariff Effects in a Small Country. The tariff creates a domestic price line (P_2–P_2) that diverges from the international price line (P_1–P_1). In response, production shifts from A to B, causing a *production efficiency* loss, signified by a move from indifference curve I to II. The domestic price line also causes *consumption inefficiency,* signified by a move from indifference curve II to III.

H-manufactures and 0–L_1 of L-manufactures, as indicated by point A where the international price line P_1–P_1 (whose slope is the international terms of trade, namely, $-P_l/P_h$) is tangent to the country's production possibilities (transformation) curve. The country consumes 0–H_2 of H-manufactures and 0–L_2 of L-manufactures, as indicated by C_1 at the point of tangency between P_1–P_1 and the indifference curve I. The country exports H_1–H_2 H-manufactures and imports L_1–L_2 L-manufactures.[11]

Now suppose the country levies an ad valorem tariff on imports of L-manufactures at a rate of t. The price of the import good for domestic manufacturers and

---

[11]A fuller general equilibrium analysis of free trade is offered in Chapter 2.

consumers now rises from P_1 to $P_1(1 + t)$ and the new price line facing them, P_2-P_2, has a slope of $-Pl(1 + t)/P_h$, which is steeper than P_l-P_l, indicating that a unit of H-manufactures now exchanges for fewer L-manufactures than before. Manufacturers respond to the higher relative price of L-manufactures by expanding output of L-manufactures while contracting the output of H-manufactures. Production shifts from A to B.

What is the effect on consumption? Keep in mind that while consumers face a new domestic price line $(P_2$-$P_2)$, the international price line $(P_1$-$P_1)$ has not changed for the country as a whole. Out of the new domestic price of L-manufactures $(P_l(1 + t)$, only P_l is paid to foreign countries because t goes to the domestic government. The country continues to have available, therefore, all the consumption points on the dashed line $(P'_1$-$P'_1)$ running through B, which has the same slope as P_1-P_1, namely, $-P_l/P_h$. The country *must* trade along this international price line because only on this line do the consumption points involve an equal value of the country's exports and imports at *world prices*. The country could trade along the international price line, moving through B to the point tangent to the highest attainable indifference curve. This consumption point is indicated by C_2. The difference between the free-trade consumption point C_1 and C_2 demonstrates a welfare loss. At C_2 consumers enjoy less of both goods than at C_1: 0-H_4 compared to 0-H_3 of H-manufactures, and 0-L_4 compared to 0-L_2 of L-manufactures. This loss is due to *production inefficiency* at B. It is analogous to the deadweight loss in partial equilibrium analysis shown as triangle l in Figure 6-4.

C_2, however, is *not* the final equilibrium consumption point because consumers face the posttariff price line, P_2-P_2. The final equilibrium occurs in trading along the international price line to a point where the *domestic* price line is tangent to the highest attainable indifference curve. This point is shown by the intersection of P'_2-P'_2 (whose slope is $-P_l(1 + t)/P_h$) and P'_1-P'_1 (whose slope is P_l/P_h) at point C_3.[12] The welfare loss in moving from C_2 on indifference curve II to C_3 on the lower indifference curve III is due to *consumption inefficiency* as consumer choice is distorted by the tariff. This loss is analogous to triangle c in Figure 6-4 in the partial equilibrium analysis.

The general equilibrium effects of a tariff in a small country point to two general conclusions: (1) Consumer welfare is less with a tariff than with free trade (C_3 lies below C_1) because of production and consumption inefficiencies. Production at B has less value than production at A when measured in world prices. Hence, C_2 provides less consumer satisfaction than C_1. Consumption at C_3 offers less satisfaction than C_2 because consumers are prevented from making choices in

---

[12]The difference between P_2-P_2 and P_2'-P_2' is the tariff *revenue* that we assume is redistributed by the government to consumers. Therefore, consumers can spend the tariff revenue in addition to the income they receive at B from producing H- and L-manufactures. To understand this point, suppose *no* tariff revenue were collected by the government. This would mean that the tariff was prohibitory, keeping out all imports. In that case, the country would become *autarkic:* consumption would be confined to domestic production at B. In other words, with no international trade P_2'-P_2' would coincide with P_2-P_2. (We assumed that all tariff revenue was redistributed back to consumers to simplify our analysis, allowing us to use a single set of indifference curves representing consumer preferences.)

terms of world prices. (2) Trade is less with a tariff than with free trade. Posttariff imports of L-manufactures (L_3–L_5) are less than free-trade imports (L_1–L_2). Because the value of exports must equal the value of imports, posttariff exports (H_3–H_5) are also lower than free-trade exports (H_1–H_2). These conclusions agree with those reached through partial equilibrium analysis.

Suppose the country is big? Then when it imposes a tariff, the lower demand for imports can induce lower import prices. When this happens, the net welfare effects of the tariff are ambiguous because they depend on two opposing effects: the welfare loss of a tariff when the international terms of trade are constant (as in the small-country example) and the improvement in the country's terms of trade. We reached the same conclusion about the social cost of tariff with partial equilibrium analysis when import supply elasticities were less than infinite. The terms of trade argument for a tariff is taken up in Chapter 7.

NONTARIFF TRADE BARRIERS: QUANTITATIVE RESTRICTIONS

As the industrial countries have progressively cut tariff rates under the auspices of the General Agreement on Tariffs and Trade, nontariff trade barriers have become more and more prominent.[13] The lowering of tariffs has been compared to the draining of a swamp: The lower water level has revealed all sorts of stumps and snags (nontariff barriers) that still make the swamp difficult to cross. We look first at quantitative trade restrictions, the most visible kind of nontariff barrier, and then offer a brief review of the many other kinds of nontariff barriers to international trade in goods and services.

Quantitative measures of restriction, like tariffs, are tools of national economic policy designed to regulate the international trade of a nation. Unlike tariffs, however, they impose absolute limitations upon foreign trade and inhibit market responses; this makes them extremely effective. Quantitative restrictions ordinarily take the form of import quotas that are administered by the issuance of import licenses to individual traders.

Import Quotas

Three major types of import quotas are in use throughout the world: unilateral quotas, negotiated bilateral or multilateral quotas, and tariff quotas. All of them impose absolute limits in value or quantity on imports of a specific product or product group during a given period of time.

The *unilateral quota* is a fixed quota that is adopted without prior consultation or negotiation with other countries. It is imposed and administered solely by the importing country. Because of its unilateral aspect, this type of quota tends to create friction, antagonism, and retaliation abroad that undermines its ultimate success.

---

[13]The General Agreement on Tariffs and Trade (GATT) is discussed in Chapter 8.

A unilateral quota may be *global* or *allocated,* depending upon whether or not the fixed volume of imports is specifically assigned by shares to different exporting countries or to individual domestic importers or foreign exporters. A *global quota* restricts the total volume without reference to countries of origin or to established importers and exporters engaged in the trade. In practice, the global quota becomes unwieldy because of the rush of both importers and exporters to secure as large a share as possible before the quota is exhausted. The result is frequently an excess of shipments over the quota, and charges of favoritism may be raised against traders fortunate enough to be the first to seize a lion's share of the business. To avoid the difficulties of a global quota system, a quota may be allocated by countries and by private traders on the basis of a prior representative period. This type of import quota is known as an *allocated quota.*

The administration of quotas is fraught with difficulties. Foreign traders feel encouraged to misrepresent their products to exempt them from quota classification, resorting to methods ranging from simple persuasion to outright graft and corruption of government officials in charge of enforcement. To ease the administrative as well as political difficulties of unilateral quotas, many governments have turned to negotiated quotas.

Under the system of a *negotiated bilateral* or *multilateral quota,* the importing country negotiates with supplying countries, or with groups of exporters in those countries, before deciding the allotment of the quota by definite shares. Often the administration of licensing under a bilateral quota is left in the hands of the exporting countries.

A bilateral or multilateral quota tends to minimize pressure by domestic importers upon their own government and to increase cooperation by foreign exporters, thus enhancing the successful operation of the system. When licensing is entrusted to foreign firms, however, it often results in the bulk of trade falling into the hands of larger firms or of well-organized cartels that are able to squeeze out most of the monopoly profit induced by the restriction of supply relative to demand in the quota country. Hence, domestic importers are deprived of this source of income and their government is deprived of the opportunity to tax such income.

In recent years the United States has restricted certain imports through negotiated quotas administered by the governments of supplying countries, the so-called *voluntary export restrictions* (VERs). In 1981, for example, Japan agreed to impose "voluntary" quotas on exports of automobiles to the United States. Despite its name, a voluntary export quota is actually an import quota, since the initiative for its establishment comes from the importing country and the motivation is protection of domestic industry.

Under a *tariff quota* a specified quantity of a product is permitted to enter the country at a given rate of duty—or even duty-free. Any additional quantity that may be imported, however, must pay a higher duty. Thus, a tariff quota combines the features of both a tariff and a quota.

Export Quotas

Exports may also be subjected to quantitative restrictions by government action. Such export controls are intended to accomplish one or more of the following objectives:

1. to prevent strategic goods from reaching the hands of unfriendly powers
2. to assure all or a significant proportion of certain products in short supply for the home market
3. to permit the control of surpluses on a national or an international basis to achieve production and price stability

These objectives can be attained more easily with quotas than with tariffs. Like import quotas, export quotas may be unilateral when they are established without prior agreement with other nations and bilateral or multilateral when they are the result of agreements. They are administered chiefly by licensing. Export controls have featured many schemes to improve the market and the price of raw materials.

The Economic Effects of Quotas

This section examines the nature of quota effects and offers a short comparison of quotas and tariffs.

The Nature of Quota Effects   Figure 6-6 illustrates the effects of an import quota. Before the quota is imposed, country A imports $0-M$ of product Y at a price of $0-P_s$, which equals the domestic price of $0-P_d$. Now suppose A imposes a quota that restricts imports to $0-M'$. The price that consumers are willing to pay for $0-M'$ of product Y rises to $0-P'_m$, and at the same time foreign suppliers would be willing to supply $0-M'$ of product Y at price $0-P'_s$ in a competitive market.

This price differential gives rise to a monopoly rent or *quota profits,* as indicated by the rectangles d and e. Who gets these profits? That depends on the institutional arrangements to administer the quota. Here we distinguish four possible arrangements and their consequences. (1) When the quota is a *global* quota that is not allocated to individual importers or exporters, then domestic importers and foreign exporters compete on a first-come, first-serve basis to fill the quota. In this situation, importers and exporters share the quota profits. (2) When the quota is allocated among foreign exporters, then they obtain all of the quota profits. (3) Similarly, when the quota is allocated among domestic importers, they obtain all of the quota profits. (4) Finally, when country A's government auctions quota allocations to the highest bidder in a competitive market, then it gets the quota profits.

A comparison of Figures 6-4 and 6-6 indicates that the price, trade, protection, and consumption effects of an import quota are the same as those of a

Figure 6-6

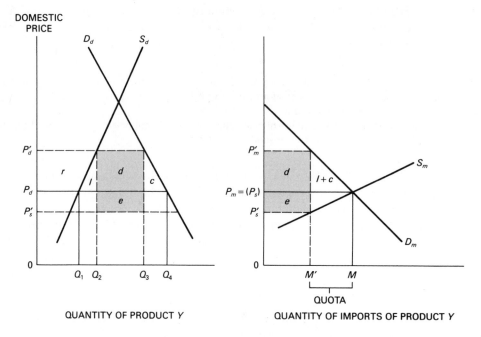

Effects of an Import Quota.   Before the quota is imposed, country A imports 0–M of product Y at a price of 0–P_s, which equals the domestic price of 0–P_d. Now country A imposes a quota that restricts imports to 0–M'. The price that consumers are willing to pay for 0–M' of product Y rises to 0–P'_m, and at the same time foreign suppliers would be willing to supply 0–M' of product Y at price 0–P'_s in a competitive market. This price differential gives rise to a monopoly rent or *quota profits*, as indicated by the rectangles d and e. Who gets these profits? That depends on the institutional arrangements for administering the quota. A comparison of Figures 6-4 and 6-6 indicates that the price, trade, protection, and consumption effects of an import quota are the same as those of a tariff.

tariff.[14] But the revenue effect of a quota is the same as that of a tariff only when the quota-levying government auctions quota allocations to the highest bidder in a competitive market. Otherwise, as we have noted, the revenue (quota profits) goes to domestic importers, foreign exporters, or both. When some or all quota profits go to foreign exporters, then the economic costs of the quota for the quota-levying country exceed the costs of a tariff duty that restricts trade in the same degree. Both the quota and the duty incur the same deadweight losses ($l + c$), but the

---

[14]This statement assumes there is competition in the protected industry. Otherwise, a quota allows noncompeting domestic producers to raise the price to whatever the market will bear; a tariff would allow those same producers to raise the price at most by the amount of the duty.

country also loses the revenue $(d + e)$ that now goes to foreign exporters who have the quota allocations.[15]

Quotas and Tariffs Compared   Quotas and tariffs are both tools of protection. Quotas, however, are absolute and inflexible, irrespective of prices and elasticities. In contrast, the degree of protection afforded by tariffs is relative, since it is subject to market responses. Quotas separate markets price-wise and raise domestic prices above world prices by freezing import supply relative to domestic demand. Quotas are not conducive to offering equal treatment to different countries; tariffs, on the other hand, are more amenable to such treatment under the most-favored-nation concept.[16]

Several other differences between quotas and tariffs are noteworthy:

1. Quotas are better suited for quick emergency application by administrative action. Tariffs often require statutory legislation, which is too slow for immediate action.
2. Quotas are a direct source of monopoly profits. Tariffs do not necessarily induce monopolistic practices, and they are ordinarily less burdensome to consumers.
3. Quotas invariably stifle import competition. Tariffs usually allow some import competition.
4. Quotas are simpler and easier to manage than tariffs, but they deprive the government of the revenues that accrue from customs duties (unless the state auctions import licenses).
5. Because quotas are a more effective tool of restriction than tariffs, they are also a more potent weapon for retaliation and bargaining.

In general, therefore, quotas are much more restrictive than tariffs.

OTHER NONTARIFF TRADE BARRIERS

Other nontariff trade barriers form a heterogeneous collection of government policies and administrative practices that in one way or another either discriminate against imports or discriminate in favor of exports. Some nontariff measures are protectionist in both intent and effect, such as discriminatory taxes and customs valuations that do not reflect actual costs. But some nontariff measures may be protectionist in effect rather than in intent, for example, border tax adjustments and health regulations. Their immense variety, their concealment in otherwise legitimate practices, and their difficult-to-measure trade and protection effects

---

[15]Rectangle e does not appear in Figure 6-4, which assumes a perfectly elastic import supply so that the import supply price remains the same after the duty. In contrast, Figure 6-6 assumes an inelastic import supply schedule; thus, if a tariff as restrictive as the quota were levied, the import supply price would fall to $0-P'_s$.

[16]For a definition of the most-favored-nation concept (or principle), see Chapter 8, footnote 4.

combine to make international efforts to eliminate other nontariff trade barriers an exceedingly difficult enterprise as compared with tariffs and quantitative restrictions. The following sections simply identify the major kinds of nontariff trade barriers and their implications for international trade.

Customs Classification and Valuation

When a tariff is ad valorem, the duty imposed on a particular import good depends on how it is classified in the tariff schedule and how it is valued by the customs authorities. Complicated and obscure tariff nomenclatures coupled with ambiguous rules of classification give customs authorities plenty of opportunity for arbitrary classifications. The resulting uncertainty (and the higher duties in many instances) can act as a strong deterrent to trade.

Much more attention has been given to customs valuations that depart from the actual market value of the imported good. The "American Selling Price" (ASP) was a prime example of a customs valuation that restricts imports. The United States values most import goods at their actual invoice value at the foreign point of export. For benzenoid chemicals and a few other products, however, the customs valuation was the selling price within the United States (ordinarily much higher than the invoice value) whenever it was determined that the import was "competitive" with or "like or similar to" a domestic product. Clearly both the intent and effect of the ASP was to afford the U.S. chemical industry higher protection than it would receive with the standard valuation. The United States agreed to eliminate the ASP in the Tokyo Round of multilateral trade negotiations.[17]

Antidumping Regulations

The disparaging term *dumping* describes the practice of selling a product in one national market at a lower price than that for which it is sold in another national market. Dumping, therefore, is price discrimination between national markets.[18]

Economists distinguish between sporadic, predatory, and persistent dumping. *Sporadic dumping* occurs when producers dispose of unexpected surpluses abroad at lower prices than at home. *Predatory dumping* occurs when a producer uses low prices to weaken or drive out competitors in a foreign market. After competition is eliminated, the victorious producer is able to charge high, monopolistic prices. *Persistent dumping,* as its name indicates, refers to the continuing sale of a product at lower prices abroad than at home. Such dumping may reflect the existence of a foreign demand that is more price-elastic than domestic demand. Persistent dumping may also arise when a producer prices exports so as to cover only variable costs while absorbing the fixed costs in domestic sales.

Although persistent dumping benefits the importing country by improving its terms of trade, governments consider all forms of dumping by foreign producers to be bad. Consequently, many governments have antidumping regulations that

---

[17]See Chapter 8.

[18]For an earlier discussion of dumping as price discrimination, see Chapter 4.

usually involve a remedial or punitive antidumping duty. This duty is intended to nullify the "harmful" effects of the lower dumping price on domestic producers. Article 6 of the General Agreement on Tariffs and Trade stipulates that two criteria must be met for the legitimate application of antidumping duties by member states: "sales at less than fair value" (sales abroad at prices lower than in the country of origin) and "material injury" to a domestic industry. It is widely recognized that antidumping regulations can easily be used for protection against foreign competition.

Subsidies

Many national governments, anxious to promote certain domestic industries, pay *subsidies* to domestic producers or exporters. Subsidies may be extended in the form of outright cash disbursements, tax exemptions, preferential exchange rates, governmental contracts with special privileges, or some other favorable treatment. The granting of subsidies results in a cost advantage to the recipient, so they are an indirect form of protection.

Subsidized products that move in international trade tend to nullify the protective effect of a tariff in the importing country. To reinstate the intended level of protection, the importing country may impose, in addition to the regular tariff duties, a special surtax or *countervailing duty,* which is generally equal to the amount of the foreign subsidy. In this manner, the landed cost to the domestic importer is raised by the amount of the subsidy granted to the foreign producer or exporter by the foreign government.

Direct export subsidies for manufactured goods are prohibited by the General Agreement on Tariffs and Trade.[19] However, most industrial countries provide special financing and insurance arrangements that enable exporters to extend easier credit terms to foreign buyers. Commonly exporters obtain credit at two or three percentage points below domestic market rates. This rate differential is a rough measure of the government subsidy. International efforts have been undertaken to harmonize national export credit policies, but many differences remain to distort the pattern of international trade.

Many *domestic* subsidies also influence imports, exports, or both. Agricultural support programs are notorious in this regard, as are subsidies for shipbuilding. Because domestic subsidies are justified as desirable *internal* policy measures, international negotiations to remove them are slow and seldom fully successful. The most prominent example of this situation is the agricultural support programs of industrial countries.

Technical Standards and Health Regulations

Governments apply many regulations to imports with respect to safety, health, marking, labeling, packaging, and technical standards. Although generally desir-

---

[19]Member states are also committed to "seek to avoid" export subsidies on primary (mainly agricultural) exports and in no event to use subsidies to exceed their "equitable share" of export trade.

able on social grounds, such regulations may discriminate against imports by imposing greater hardships on foreign than on domestic producers. At present, there is only a modest degree of international agreement on technical and health regulations. Products that may freely enter one country may be banned in another country, especially pharmaceuticals and foodstuffs. In illustration, U.S. producers cannot export pickles to Norway, because that country forbids the entry of food products containing alum, an ingredient of American pickle preservatives. In turn, the United States forbids the import of live animals or fresh meat products from a country in which there are cases of hoof-and-mouth disease, even though the livestock in question may be grown in a region of the country that is free from that disease, a common situation in Argentina. Despite some recent liberalization, the Japanese government still requires that some import goods be tested in Japan even when they have already been tested in the country of origin, a process that can take several years and result in substantial costs to foreign exporters.

Because of the increasing technical nature of products, rising living standards, and social pressures, we can expect a continuing proliferation of technical and health regulations. Foreign automobile producers, for instance, have complained that the unilateral U.S. safety regulations do not consider the special problems of the small car and hence discriminate against imports.

Government Procurement

The *procurement policies* of governments afford fertile soil for the discriminatory treatment of foreign products. The "Buy American" regulations of the U.S. government give domestic producers up to a 50 percent price spread advantage over foreign producers on Defense Department contracts and up to 12 percent on other government purchases. But the U.S. government procurement system relies mainly on competitive bidding open to all suppliers. This practice, coupled with the comparatively smaller role of the U.S. government in the economy, makes government procurement less discriminatory than in most other industrial countries. Generally, other countries practice procurement discrimination through administrative procedures (including closed bids) rather than through explicit laws or regulations. Discrimination, therefore, tends to be hidden and arbitrary.

The very large numbers of goods and services directly purchased by national governments and the enormous influence they can exert over the procurement policies of both public-sector and private domestic firms have made preferential government procurement one of the most prominent trade issues in the 1990s, particularly in high-technology products and services.

Taxes

Besides the basic customs duties prescribed in tariff schedules, certain imports may be subjected to excise taxes and processing taxes. *Excise taxes* are collectible upon the entry of the goods through customs, whereas *processing taxes* are payable upon the first domestic processing in the case of certain raw material and semifinished commodities. The purpose of these special import taxes is generally to compensate for similar taxation of domestic goods. Often, however, excise and processing taxes are levied exclusively on imports without corresponding levies on similar domestic products, or they may be levied when similar or competing products are not produced in the domestic market. When excise and processing taxes are assessed exclusively on imports, they become protective measures. They may be concealed behind a different rationale, but they are no less part of a protective tariff system.

Some internal taxes obviously discriminate against imports from some or all foreign countries, such as *road taxes* that are based on the cylinder capacity or horsepower of a vehicle rather than its value. Another illustration is the French practice of placing a surtax on grain spirits when all domestic liquors are distilled from fruits. To make matters worse, all advertising of grain liquors is prohibited in France. Actually, all governments are guilty of discriminatory taxation of one kind or another.

Border tax adjustments have received much attention in recent years because of their widespread use by the European Community. Under GATT rules, a country that imposes a domestic *indirect* tax (a sales, turnover, excise, or value-added tax) on a good is permitted to give a tax rebate on exports of the same good and to levy an equivalent tax on imports of a similar good. In France, the border tax is about 20 percent of the duty-paid value of most industrial products. However, GATT prohibits any border adjustment for *direct* taxes, such as income, profits, payroll, social security, and property taxes. This system of border tax adjustment would be neutral in its effects on trade only if indirect taxes were fully shifted forward into prices while direct taxes were not shifted at all. Insofar as these conventional assumptions do not hold, border tax adjustments offer a trading advantage to countries relying primarily on indirect taxes for their revenue over other countries that depend mainly on direct taxes. The U.S. government (which depends mostly on direct taxes) has argued that the border taxes levied by the countries of the European Community in the process of harmonizing their tax systems do, in fact, discriminate against American goods.

Local Content and Foreign Investment Performance Requirements

Many governments, particularly in the developing countries, promote import substitution by imposing local-content regulations on certain industries. These regulations specify that a certain percentage of a good's value or certain inputs used in the manufacture of a good must be produced inside the country.

Local-content laws not only restrain imports but also are among the *performance requirements* commonly imposed on foreign investors by host governments in developing countries. Another common performance requirement is the obligation of a foreign-investing firm to export a certain proportion of its output from the host country. Such performance requirements distort international trade and investment and constitute an important source of nontariff barriers.

Nontariff Trade Barriers in Services

About one-quarter of world trade is now in services: air and ocean transportation, banking, insurance, advertising, accounting, law, engineering, construction, franchising, tourism, education, health, business services, and others. Furthermore, service trade is growing more rapidly than merchandise trade. Despite its high growth rate, trade in services (commonly referred to as "invisible trade") is severely curtailed by nontariff trade barriers. The examples that follow indicate the nature of these barriers.

Many developing countries, having nationalized insurance companies, give their state insurance enterprises sole rights to domestic insurance business. Other countries refuse to license foreign-owned insurance companies. Norway, for instance, has not licensed a foreign insurance company in over fifty years.

National governments commonly discriminate against foreigners in their banking regulations. The United States is a major exception in this regard. For example, Canada limits foreign banks to a 25 percent interest in Canadian banks, and Japan makes it difficult for foreign banks to open branches and prohibits new foreign-owned banks from going into retail banking.

In shipping, many countries require that their own merchant fleets carry a certain fraction of their import and export cargoes. Generally, countries (including the United States) reserve intercoastal trade exclusively for domestic shipping companies.

Laws in many countries restrict the flow of data across their borders. For instance, Scandinavian governments require that most computer data be processed and stored within the country. West Germany prohibits the transmission of data outside the country unless some data processing is done within the country. Sweden does not permit the local offices of foreign companies to process payrolls abroad.

Many other restrictions on international trade in services distort the location of service activities and add to their costs. The U.S. government has compiled a list of two thousand instances of barriers that stultify the flow of services among countries.

Concluding Remarks on Nontariff Trade Barriers

Our description of nontariff trade barriers is far from exhaustive. For example, governments may stipulate the minimum prices for certain imports, known as *trigger prices*. In the 1970s, the United States imposed trigger prices on imports of low-cost steel products. Mention should also be made of the cumbersome red tape in the administration of trade restrictions, which generates uncertainties and costs for international traders. Enough has been said, however, to demonstrate that nontariff trade barriers are bewildering in their variety, frequently hidden in administrative practices, and, in many instances, exceedingly difficult to eliminate through international negotiations. Furthermore, new nontariff barriers are continually created as governments respond to changing circumstances.

In Chapter 8, we look at the progress that has been made in lessening tariff and nontariff trade barriers under the General Agreement on Tariffs and Trade. To round out our discussion of tariffs and nontariff trade barriers, we offer the results of some empirical studies of the costs of protection.

EMPIRICAL STUDIES OF THE COSTS OF PROTECTION

Several studies have estimated the costs of protection in the United States. Although these studies differ in estimation procedures and cover different time periods and industries, the results are consistent.

Tarr and Morkre estimated annual costs to the U.S. economy of $12.7 billion in 1983 from all tariffs and quotas on automobiles, textiles, steel, and sugar. This is a *net* measure of costs: losses to consumers offset by gains to domestic producers and the U.S. government.[20] Hickok estimated that U.S. trade restrictions on clothing, sugar, and automobiles caused increased consumer expenditures of $14 billion in 1984.[21]

Hufbauer looked at 31 cases in which the United States imposed trade restrictions on trade volumes exceeding $100 million.[22] In all but six cases, annual consumer losses were greater than $100 million; for all cases together, the costs to consumers exceeded $50 billion. The Hufbauer estimates for textiles and apparel, carbon steel, and automobiles are shown in Table 6-1.

In Phase I of protection for textiles and apparel, the cost to consumers was $9.4 billion (the extra amount paid due to the protection-induced rise in prices), gains to domestic producers totaled $8.7 billion (more sales at higher protection-induced prices), and tariff revenue was $1.2 billion. The *efficiency loss* was $1.1 billion.[23] Also, observe that the cost to save a single job in this industry through Phase I protection was $22,000. For all three industries, the highest cost to consumers was $27 billion for Phase III protection of textiles and apparel. The highest cost per job saved was an extraordinary $620,000 for Phase II protection of carbon steel.

Table 6-2 offers the results of nine empirical studies of U.S. protection in five industries. The first column indicates the *deadweight loss* ($l + c$ in Figure 6-6) of U.S. import restrictions, which are mostly quotas. Estimates are annual costs for the years between 1983 and 1987, centering on 1985. The estimates with ranges are based on two separate studies that differ in estimation procedures.

---

[20]David G. Tarr and Morris E. Morkre, *Aggregate Costs to the United States of Tariffs and Quotas on Automobiles, Steel, Sugar, and Textiles* (Washington, D.C.: Federal Trade Commission, December 1984).

[21]Susan Hickok, "The Consumer Cost of U.S. Trade Restraints," *Quarterly Review* (Federal Reserve Bank of New York), Summer 1985, pp. 1–12.

[22]Gary Hufbauer et al., *Trade Protection in the United States: 31 Case Studies* (Washington, D.C.: Institute for International Economics, 1986).

[23]Efficiency loss is the *deadweight* loss to the national economy traceable to the replacement of imports with less efficiently produced domestic output and the replacement by consumers of imports with substitute goods that offer less satisfaction. It is the sum of the triangles l and c in Figure 6-4.

Table 6-1 Distribution of Costs and Gains of Protection for the U.S. Textile and Apparel, Steel, and Automobile Industries (Millions of Dollars Except "Per Job Saved" in Thousands of Dollars)

Industry	Cost to Consumers		Gains to Producers	Tariff Revenue	Gains to Foreigners	Efficiency Loss
	Total	Per Job Saved				
Textiles and Apparel						
Phase I	9,400	22	8,700	1,158	—	1,100
Phase II	20,000	37	18,000	2,143	350	3,100
Phase III	27,000	42	22,000	2,535	1,800	4,850
Carbon Steel						
Phase I	1,970	240	1,330	290	330	50
Phase II	4,350	620	2,770	556	930	120
Automobiles	5,800	105	2,600	790	2,200	200

Note: The periods of protection for textiles and apparel are as follows: Phase I—January 1957–December 1973, Phase II—January 1974–December 1981, Phase III—January 1982–July 1986; for carbon steel: Phase I—January 1969–December 1974, Phase II—January 1978–February 1982; and for automobiles: April 1981–March 1985.

Source: Adapted from Gary Hufbauer, et al., *Trade Protection in the United States: 31 Case Studies* (Washington, D.C.: Institute for International Economics, 1986), Table 1.2 pp. 14–15.

Table 6-2 Annual Cost of U.S. Import Protection of Five Industries (Billions of Dollars Around 1985)

Industry	U.S. Deadweight Loss	Foreign Quota Rents	Foreign Deadweight Loss
Automobiles	0.2–1.2	2.2–7.9	0–3
Dairy	1.4	0.25	0.02
Steel	0.1–0.3	0.7–2.0	0.1
Sugar	0.1	0.4–1.3	0.2
Textiles and Apparel	4.9–5.9	4.0–6.1	4–15.5
Total	*7.9–12.3*	*7.3–17.3**	*4.3–18.8*

*Does not include quota rents of U.S. importers of dairy products.

Source: Adapted from Robert C. Feenstra, "How Costly is Protectionism?" *Journal of Economic Perspectives,* Summer 1992, p. 163.

Automobile imports are subject to a voluntary export restriction (VER) administered by the Japanese government, while dairy products (cheese, butter, and powdered milk) are protected with quotas administered by the U.S. government. Since 1985, steel has been protected by VERs, with almost all countries exporting steel to the United States. The United States determines an import quota for sugar based on its chosen domestic stabilization price and expected domestic supply and demand. The annual quota is allocated to sugar-exporting countries, who then allocate it to their own sugar-exporting firms. Textiles and apparel are protected by import quotas under the Multi-Fiber Arrangement. The total annual U.S. deadweight loss from the protection of these industries is between $7.9 and $12.3 billion.

The second column of Table 6-2 offers estimates of quota rents ($d + e$ in Figure 6-6). Except for dairy products, these rents are obtained by foreign firms with quotas allocated by their governments. Rents are obtained by U.S. importers only from dairy quotas that are administered by the U.S. government. Some studies measure only the quota rents causing U.S. losses (d in Figure 6-6). The total annual cost to the United States of quota rents accruing to foreigners is between $7.3 and $17.3 billion. The total annual cost of protection of these industries—deadweight loss plus quota rents obtained by foreigners—is between $15 and $30 billion.

The third column of Table 6-2 shows the *foreign* deadweight losses due to U.S. protection. Although foreign producers earn economic rent when the quotas are administered by their own governments ($d + e$ in Figure 6-6), they also suffer losses due to lower sales to the United States (shown by the triangle lying just below the $l + c$ triangle in the graph on the right side of Figure 6-6). In the case of textiles and apparel, this loss in producer surplus greatly exceeds quota rents because the quotas sharply restrict the volume of U.S. imports. Hence, the deadweight loss is estimated to fall between $4 and $15.5 billion a year. Total annual foreign losses are from $4 to $19 billion a year. Foreign losses from U.S. protection, therefore, can be significant and they need to be included in any estimate of the *global* losses resulting from protection by the United States (or any other country).

The foregoing estimates of the costs of protection are almost certainly too low, because they ignore the *dynamic* effects of protection, in particular, inefficient management and slower innovation bred by lower competition. The biggest cost of protection to a country over the longer run is the prolonged maladjustment of domestic industries to a changing world economy.

SUMMARY

1. Despite the theoretical support for free trade, governments, more often than not, have interfered with the international movement of goods. These

restrictive measures consist chiefly of (1) tariffs and (2) nontariff trade barriers.

2. Customs duties may be *ad valorem* or *specific*.
3. Tariffs may be designed to serve a revenue function or a protection function. The revenue and protection functions are contradictory: A tariff maximizes revenue when it does not restrict imports; it maximizes protection when it eliminates imports.
4. Depending primarily on import supply elasticities, an import duty may raise the price of an import good (a) not at all, (b) less than the amount of the duty, or (c) equal to the amount of the duty.
5. In addition to price effects, an import duty has revenue, trade, protection, consumption, and income-redistribution effects. Together, these effects determine the *social cost* of a tariff for the tariff-levying country.
6. Several methods have been used to measure the trade and protection effects of national tariff systems: (a) by tariff revenues, (b) by the height of duties (weighted or unweighted), (c) by effective rates rather than nominal rates, and (d) by elasticities and market share. Only the last method is fully justified by economic theory, but it is an enormous task to measure the elasticities of the thousands of products that make up a tariff system.
7. As the name implies, quantitative restrictions impose absolute limitations on foreign trade. Quantitative restrictions ordinarily take the form of import quotas administered by the issuance of import licenses to individual traders. Three major types of import quotas are in use throughout the world: unilateral quotas, negotiated quotas (bilateral or multilateral), and tariff quotas.
8. The economic effects of an import quota are similar to those of an import duty. Instead of generating government revenue, however, an import quota usually creates monopoly profits for the importers or exporters of the product in question.
9. Whereas quotas are absolute and inflexible regardless of prices and elasticities, the trade and protection effects of tariffs are dependent on the market conditions of production and consumption. In general, therefore, quotas are more restrictive than tariffs.
10. Besides quotas, nontariff barriers include a bewildering variety of government measures that in one way or another either discriminate against imports or discriminate in favor of exports. The major kinds of nontariff barriers include customs classification and valuation, antidumping regulations, subsidies, standards, government procurement, taxes, performance requirements, and restrictions on trade in services.
11. Empirical studies of U.S. protection find net deadweight and quota-rent losses for the United States. Foreign countries may also suffer net losses due to U.S. protection when their deadweight losses exceed any quota rents accruing to them.

QUESTIONS AND APPLICATIONS

1. What is a tariff?
2. Distinguish between ad valorem and specific duties.
3. "Tariffs provide revenue for the government and protection for domestic industries. Therefore, the higher the rate of duties, the greater the revenue and the greater the protection." Discuss the validity of this statement.
4. Utilizing supply-demand diagrams, indicate how the price effect of an import duty changes when the import supply schedule becomes less elastic.
5. If the duty on a final product import is 15 percent and the weighted average of duties on importable inputs that contribute one-fourth of the value of the final product is 10 percent, what is the *effective* rate of duty on the final product?
6. Distinguish between unilateral, negotiated, and tariff quotas.
7. Why and how do import quotas create economic rent? *Who* gets that rent?
8. With graphs show the *net social cost* of an import quota for the domestic country when (a) the import supply schedule is perfectly elastic, and (b) the import supply schedule is less than perfectly elastic.
9. "The general equilibrium effects of a tariff in a small country point to two general conclusions." Explain.
10. Compare quotas with tariffs, identifying their similarities and differences.
11. "Quotas are positive regulations of international trade, while the results of tariffs are uncertain. Since a country must know where it is heading, the use of quotas is therefore preferable to the use of tariffs." Evaluate this statement.
12. Discuss the meaning of the following statement: "Many nontariff measures are protectionist in effect rather than in intent."
13. Why are direct export subsidies considered a nontariff trade barrier?

SELECTED READINGS

See the list of readings given at the end of Chapters 7, 8, and 9.

chapter 7

FREE TRADE AND ARGUMENTS
FOR PROTECTION

International trade policy can be regarded as the result of the opposing forces of free trade and protection. Before examining the international trade policies of the United States and other countries, therefore, we need an understanding of the rationale for free trade and of the rival arguments for protection. As a policy, protection can use a broad variety of measures that restrict or otherwise distort flows of international trade. Our concern here is not with specific trade barriers, which were treated in Chapter 6, but with why governments are inclined to use them in general.

The issue of *free trade* versus *protection* has been in dispute since the eighteenth century; the literature on this controversy is one of the most extensive in the annals of political economy. The arguments are often complex and subtle, although the controversy itself is obvious.

THE CASE FOR FREE TRADE

The principle of comparative advantage demonstrates that for the world as a whole free trade leads to a higher level of output and income than no trade (autarky). Free trade also enables each nation to obtain a higher level of production and consumption than can be obtained in isolation. Under perfect competition, free trade achieves a worldwide allocation of resources that meets the requirements of Pareto optimality: It is impossible to make anyone better off (through reallocation) without making someone else worse off. In the language of Chapter 2, free trade achieves an equality between each country's marginal rate of transformation in production (MRT) and its marginal rate of substitution in consumption (MRS) and the international terms of trade (ITT). In contrast, trade barriers *prevent* this equilibrium condition by creating divergences between the domestic and international prices of tradable goods. Hence, under protection, $MRT = MRS \neq ITT$. It follows, therefore, that trade barriers cause a suboptimal allocation of the world's

162

factors of production and a lower world real income than would exist under free trade.

However, many contemporary economists (unlike their predecessors) are reluctant to support free trade without some reservations. Their qualifications of the free trade doctrine spring from two basic concerns: (1) the departure of actual markets from the conditions of perfect competition, and (2) the absence of any *necessary* correspondence between higher income and higher welfare at both national and international levels.

As we have discussed in earlier chapters, the most widely accepted theory of trade, the Heckscher-Ohlin (H-O) model, rests upon the assumptions of perfect competition: no monopoly or oligopoly; no product differentiation; no increasing returns; and no ignorance, uncertainty, or risk. Furthermore, the theory implicitly assumes that external economies and diseconomies do not cause a divergence between private and social benefits and costs, and that market prices truly indicate the full opportunity costs confronting a society.[1] Since these assumptions are only partially matched in actual markets, it follows that free trade will not achieve Pareto optimality and that more trade will not necessarily bring a higher allocative efficiency to national economies or to the world economy.

However, to say that the allocative efficiency of free trade may not be optimal is a poor argument for protection. Rather, it is an argument for direct measures to improve the functioning of competitive markets through antitrust policies that eliminate or restrain monopoly and oligopoly, through improvements in the flow of information to consumers and producers (to reduce ignorance and risk), through taxes and subsidies to remove any divergences between private and social benefits and costs, and through other measures that promote competition.

Actually protection is an ineffectual policy tool for overcoming the defects of imperfect competition as compared with more direct tools. Furthermore, there is little assurance that the trade restrictions actually imposed by a government will add to economic efficiency. When account is taken of protectionist politics, the probability is high that restrictions will *lower* economic efficiency — a policy of throwing out the baby with the bath water. The existence of market imperfections, therefore, has not turned economists into protectionists, although they may argue the desirability of selective restrictions in carefully defined circumstances, as in the "theory of the second best" and strategic trade theory, which are described later in this chapter. And, because of the possible existence of increasing returns as well as external economies, economists have also traditionally recognized (with qualifications) the legitimacy of the infant-industry argument for protection.

A second reason why most economists are reluctant to offer unqualified support of free trade is the question of economic welfare. Even if Pareto optimality

---

[1]External economies exist when a firm (or industry) creates values for society that it cannot sell in a market (such as training workers who subsequently leave the firm for other employment). This situation makes the private value of the firm's output less than its social value. External diseconomies refer to social costs of production (such as pollution) that are not borne by the producer, making private costs less than social costs. In the case of external economies, the firm is producing too little to maximize social value; in the case of external diseconomies, too much.

were achieved in the allocation of national and world resources, it would not *necessarily* follow that free trade would also optimize national and world *welfare*. One problem is that competitive markets determine not only the prices of goods but also factor prices (incomes). By altering relative prices, free trade also alters income distribution among individuals and groups, both within and between nations. If the last (marginal) dollar of income earned by recipients in all countries provided the same satisfaction (welfare), then free trade under perfect competition would indeed maximize national and world welfare. Unfortunately, there is no objective way to make interpersonal comparisons of welfare. The presumption is strong, of course, that the marginal dollar received by a poor person contributes more welfare than the marginal dollar received by a rich person and, by extension, that poor countries benefit more than rich countries from the marginal income dollar. But in the final analysis this is an ethical judgment, not a scientific one.

The welfare question is hardly a general argument against free trade. A priori, there is no reason to believe that free trade worsens income distribution compared to no or restricted trade. In view of the motivations and political factors that actually determine protectionist policies, one can also be justifiably dubious that governments will select only those restrictions that improve national welfare, to say nothing of world welfare. Protection, therefore, is a singularly inappropriate policy to achieve higher levels of welfare for a group or nation.[2] Protection would sacrifice the gains from economic efficiency to an uncertain (and at times, perverse) welfare effect. More to the point, direct measures to redistribute income are available to all governments in the form of subsidies and taxation.[3]

To sum up, economic theory *cannot* demonstrate that under all circumstances free trade will improve efficiency or enhance economic welfare. In practice, however, most Western economists remain firmly on the side of freer, if not free, trade. They remain skeptical of the capacity of governments to apply selective trade restrictions in such a way as to reach higher levels of economic efficiency or welfare. The history of protection is highly convincing on this score. At the same time, most economists would agree that free trade is not sufficient to achieve optimal world income and welfare but must be coupled with government policies that improve the efficiency of markets, achieve a better income distribution, and promote economic growth.

Strictly speaking, the argument for free trade (like all arguments for economic policies) is a conditional one. It states that *if* a nation wants to attain a higher level of economic efficiency, then it can do so by trading with other nations. But a

---

[2]What happens when governments seek to redistribute income by interfering with the market mechanism is clearly shown by agricultural programs that have promoted self-sufficiency at a cost of lower economic efficiency. A superior approach (granted the desirability of redistributing income to farmers) would be direct income subsidies financed out of general taxation, leaving markets free to allocate agricultural production both within and among nations.

[3]Mechanisms to redistribute income among countries are admittedly primitive compared to domestic mechanisms. There is no international authority to tax the rich and subsidize the poor. But attempts to achieve income redistribution between rich and poor countries via market restrictions (such as international commodity agreements) must reckon with the costs of lower economic efficiency. Direct income transfers avoid those costs.

nation can choose to reject economic efficiency for noneconomic values (such as the preservation of a social group or a way of life against foreign influences) and, in so doing, reject free trade in part or in whole.

Economists have long recognized the legitimacy of the national defense argument for trade protection. Commonly, however, nations have chosen trade protection in ignorance of its economic costs. Only the mythical economic person would argue that economic efficiency should be the exclusive goal of society, but only a fool would argue that economic efficiency does not matter at all.

One last comment is in order. No one, including the most ardent protectionist, opposes specialization and trade among the different regions of a country. And yet, the *economic* argument for free international trade is the same as the argument for unfettered interregional trade. The essential difference between external and internal trade is *political* only: One involves foreigners, the other does not. It is this difference that has nurtured protectionism through the ages; the principal ally of protectionism is economic nationalism.[4]

THE CASE FOR PROTECTION

Although in most circumstances the welfare of a country as a whole is reduced by import protection, the welfare of the specific factors of production associated with a protected industry will increase because of the income-redistribution effect.[5] In seeking protection, therefore, individual producers and labor unions are trying to improve their own well-being. Hence, any attempt to lower or eliminate existing protection is stubbornly resisted, and continuing pressure is applied to national governments to initiate new protection. Frank recognition of the fact that certain groups would lose with a free trade policy is essential to any understanding of the political strength of protectionism. Indeed, the conflict between particular interests and the national interest is the dominant feature of the persistent controversy over free trade and protection.

In presenting their case to the public and government, protectionists would not get far if they argued in terms of their own private gain. Thus, all their arguments assert that protection benefits the national interest. In so many words, protectionists maintain that "what is good for my industry is also good for my country."[6] In defending this proposition they are usually supported by the nationalistic attitudes of their fellow citizens.

The arguments against free trade try to show that (1) its advantages are outweighed by its shortcomings; (2) the interdependence of nations implicit in free

---

[4]As we shall observe in Chapter 24, economic nationalism also nurtures resistance to foreign enterprise — another form of protectionism.

[5]See Figure 6-4 in Chapter 6. In the longer run, when there is time for factors to move into the protected industry, marginal factor returns in that industry will tend to equal marginal factor returns in other (unprotected) industries. The ultimate beneficiary of protection is the factor (or factors) used intensively in the protected industry; other factors suffer a loss in welfare.

[6]For this reason, most protectionist arguments commit the *fallacy of composition:* What is true of the part is necessarily true of the whole.

trade subjects national economies to uncertainties inherent in sudden changes in the policies of other nations that often cause serious dislocations, if not losses, far greater than the benefits to be derived from a free trade policy; and (3) the price system and perfect competition underlying the theory of free trade are, at best, only partially true in the real world, where prices and production are subjected to controls and rigidities that contribute to what has been referred to as a *disequilibrium system* (i.e., a system in which restrictions on consumers or producers are the tools of adjustment rather than price).

In the course of time many ingenious pleas have been advanced in direct support of protection. The pleas have been based on a variety of arguments, none of which possesses unqualified economic validity. A few of these arguments rationalize short-term gains at the expense of long-term national benefits; others follow exactly the opposite approach; most of the remaining arguments have only partial economic validity or are completely fallacious, drawing their strength mainly from their engaging emotional mass appeal. The long series of arguments for protection may be classified into four categories: (1) fallacious arguments, (2) questionable arguments, (3) qualified arguments, and (4) sophisticated arguments.

FALLACIOUS ARGUMENTS FOR PROTECTION

Fallacious arguments for protection rely on plausibility or mass emotional appeal rather than economic logic.

Keep-Money-at-Home Argument

The proponents of this argument claim that when domestic residents buy imported goods, the country gets the goods and the foreigner gets the money. When, on the other hand, the residents buy domestic goods, it is argued that the country keeps both the goods and the money. Hence the country that prevents imports is richer for doing so.

The utter fallacy of this argument is rooted in the crudest form of mercantilistic theory, which maintained that money is wealth in itself. Money, as such, is a means of exchange. Money paid for imports must return sooner or later either in payment for exports or as investment, since it has no redemption value except in the country of its issue.

Home Market Argument

This argument claims that the domestic producer has a right to the domestic market and that by reducing or eliminating imports, more goods will be produced at home, more jobs will be created, and increased domestic activity will be the result. The fallacy of this argument stems from the fact that any shift from imports to domestic production is ultimately offset by a contraction of production for export. Unless a country is willing to give its goods away, it can only continue to export by continuing to import. Thus, the shift from foreign to domestic sources of supply does not in any way increase real purchasing power. In fact, the home market argument leads to a less efficient economy and a *decline* in real purchasing power.

Equalization-of-Costs Argument

Some protectionists have favored the so-called "scientific method of tariff making" that is intended to equalize the costs of production between foreign and domestic producers and to neutralize any advantage the foreigner may have over the domestic producer in lower taxes, cheaper labor, or other costs. This argument allegedly entails "fair competition," not the exclusion of imports. When, however, by reason of actual cost structure or artificial measures, costs of production become identical, the very basis of international trade disappears. The logical consequence of this pseudoscientific method is the elimination of trade between nations. Thus, the equalization-of-production-costs argument for protection is utterly fallacious and is one of the most deceitful ever advanced in support of protection.

A close examination of the equalization-of-costs argument reveals the presence of many problems. Producers in any country have different and constantly changing costs for the same products. Whose costs are to serve as a frame of reference?

If we aim for protection of *all* domestic producers against *all* foreign producers, we must equalize the lowest foreign costs with the highest costs of the least efficient domestic producers. To accomplish this, a very high duty is required to overcome the extreme cost differential. Domestic prices to the consumer must rise to the high level of the domestic marginal producer's cost. The efficient domestic producer will reap an extra monopoly profit, and the domestic consumer will be forced to subsidize the highest form of inefficiency.

In addition, the literal enforcement of such a policy entails considerable administrative difficulties in the collection of the necessary cost information for duty adjustments. This seems to be hardly worthwhile when the result can only be the prevention of imports, the ultimate elimination of trade, and the impairment of the country's standard of living—surely a misconception of the scientific approach, to say the least.

Despite these objections, a tariff provision to equalize the costs of production was actually incorporated in the United States Tariff Acts of 1922 and 1930. This provision, however, has been enforced in only a few instances.

In recent years, the equalization-of-cost argument has become the "fairness" argument. Its supporters allege that all they want is fair competition, that is, the equalization of wages and other factors affecting domestic and foreign costs. Then domestic firms would be able to compete against foreign firms on a "level playing field." Carried to an extreme, the fairness argument would block all international trade. It is nothing more than the old equalization-of-cost argument after a cosmetic facelift.

Low Wage Argument

Some protectionists claim that a high-wage country cannot afford to trade with low-wage or "pauper labor" countries without risking a reduction in its own wages through competition with the low foreign wage level and thereby jeopardizing its standard of living. They assert further that to protect its workers from the competition of low-paid foreign workers, a high-wage country must impose a tariff duty on cheap goods that are imported from the low-wage countries.

More fundamentally, it is alleged that a country can only *lose* from trade with a low-wage country, since that country can undersell it. This argument has several weaknesses. First, we may ask how any trade is possible if the domestic country is undersold in *all* products, for in that case it could neither export anything nor, therefore, import anything. If only *some* products are in question, then the argument is absurd, since trade obviously requires that one country undersell the other country in some goods, and vice versa. Second, it must be pointed out that wages may be low and unit costs high when productivity is low. Thus, there is no necessary connection between low wages and low costs. Third, the low wage argument must bow to the logic of comparative advantage. As long as cost structures are dissimilar, trade is profitable between countries regardless of absolute wage levels.

The proponents of the low wage argument are wrong when they suggest that high prices necessarily result from high wages and low prices from low wages. High wages in the United States are a consequence of the high productivity of American workers, who are aided in their tasks by the availability of raw materials; massive capital equipment; advanced technology; sophisticated management; and an elaborate infrastructure of communication, transportation, power, and other facilities. This high productivity explains both the high American standard of living and the ability of American exporters to compete effectively with foreign producers who pay far lower wages.[7] In light of the low-wage argument of U.S. protectionists, it is ironic that many producers in developing countries demand protection against U.S. products on the grounds that their (low-wage) industries cannot compete against the highly productive American industries!

It is true that domestic industries whose productivity is relatively low may find that high wages raise their costs above foreign costs. But such a situation is not a logical argument for protection. Rather, it is a signal for a reallocation of labor and capital to other lines of production that have a comparative advantage vis-à-vis foreign production. Such a reallocation occurs all the time as a result of domestic interregional competition, as witness, for example, the migration of the U.S. textile industry from New England to the South. It is the fear of a painful adjustment to import competition that really motivates the proponents of the low wage argument rather than the unlikely danger of a general deterioration of the

---

[7]Because of high worker productivity, the highest wages in the United States are generally found in the export industries, such as aerospace, electrical machinery, and chemicals. How, then, could anyone explain the existence of American exports if lower wages were the sole index of competitive advantage?

country's standard of living. Import restrictions, however, are neither the most desirable nor the only solution to this problem. What is needed is government assistance that will facilitate an orderly redeployment of capital and workers so as to minimize adjustment costs while at the same time preserving the benefits of international trade.

Prevention-of-Injury Argument

The prevention-of-injury argument is designed to safeguard the vulnerability of an economy to increased imports subsequent to contemplated tariff concessions or to concessions already granted under trade agreements. The advocates of this argument proclaim their willingness to reduce and maintain low tariffs, provided that in so doing no domestic industry or producer is threatened by excessive imports resulting from such low rates of duties. Any contemplated concession must not reduce an existing rate to a preestimated low point, or *peril point*, that would jeopardize domestic producers. In addition, when previously reduced rates begin to threaten domestic producers, there should be an escape mechanism, or *escape clause*, to permit the restoration of higher rates or the tightening of quota controls.

On the surface, this argument sounds reasonable and implies an attitude of moderation. What this argument means in actual practice, however, is the elimination of foreign competition when it threatens to take a share of the home market away from domestic producers. The prevention-of-injury argument is closely related to the home market and equalization-of-production-costs arguments. It is an argument that is likely to encourage the perpetuation of static and regressive industries.

QUESTIONABLE ARGUMENTS FOR PROTECTION

Certain arguments for protection, although not entirely fallacious, represent an inferior policy or easily lend themselves to abuse.

Employment Argument

The basis for this argument is that the imposition of a tariff or other form of import restriction in periods of unemployment will reduce imports and generate home production. Increased domestic production in turn will increase employment and national income. Furthermore, since imports (like savings) cause a leakage in the domestic income stream, a reduction of imports will generate an even greater amount of domestic expenditure via the income multiplier.[8]

Another version of the employment argument asserts that widespread unemployment justifies any sort of production, regardless of comparative advantage,

---

[8]See Chapter 15 for a discussion of the income multiplier.

since it will make a net addition to a country's national income. Thus, a country will benefit by restricting imports and using idle factors to produce similar goods at home—the opportunity cost of imports is the exports that must be exchanged for them, whereas the opportunity cost of new domestic production is zero. Hence, international specialization and trade must give way to self-sufficiency when unemployment arises in the domestic economy.

This argument was especially persuasive during the Great Depression of the 1930s, but it rests upon several questionable assumptions: (1) full employment is the overriding national economic objective; (2) international trade must be sacrificed to attain full employment; and (3) the international consequences of a domestic full-employment policy can be safely ignored. We now turn to a brief evaluation of these assumptions.

First, employment for the sake of employment cannot be a sound national objective. Full employment is most productive when the factors of production are allocated in accordance with comparative advantage. In that way each factor is engaged in production in which its productivity is highest. Full employment is a means to the higher objective of national welfare, and this is maximized only when productivity cannot be raised by shifting factors of production from one economic activity to another. When imports are curtailed to afford opportunities for domestic employment, the losses occasioned by a lesser degree of international specialization must be set against any gains in national production.

Second, even if the gains in national production are greater than the losses brought about by the decline in international specialization, the policy of sacrificing international trade to increase domestic employment is not in the national interest, for there are other ways of stimulating employment that do not require the restriction of trade. An anticyclical employment policy should place main reliance on government fiscal and monetary policies that feed the inadequate stream of purchasing power. Not only will such policies alleviate unemployment in the domestic economy, but by sustaining or increasing imports they will also benefit foreign countries.

Third, the policy of curtailing imports to stimulate domestic employment is never in the interest of the community of nations. Actually, that policy amounts to exporting unemployment to other nations, since the decline in imports will depress foreign economies. Moreover, foreign countries can retaliate by restricting their own imports. As a consequence, international relations become embittered, international trade spirals downward, and few countries are better off in terms of employment while many are much worse off in terms of economic welfare. This sequence took place to an unfortunate extent in the early 1930s.

While condemning the policy of exporting one's unemployment, we must also recognize the fact that few nations are capable of overcoming massive unemployment by the use of fiscal and monetary policies alone unless international economic cooperation is forthcoming. Such policies tend to increase imports, yet at the same time exports may be falling because of recession abroad. Few nations have the reserves to finance the resulting gap between their exports and imports until recovery sets in abroad.[9] When, however, nations — particularly the major trading nations — cooperate with each other by extending credit and by harmonizing their domestic recovery measures, it may be possible for them to restore employment without seriously curtailing trade.

The foregoing remarks apply to *cyclical* unemployment that results from a deflationary gap in effective demand that cuts across all sectors of the economy. When protection is advocated as a remedy for *structural* unemployment, then the employment argument becomes even more questionable.

Structural unemployment occurs when the composition of a nation's output or the quality and supply of its factors of production fail to adapt to new patterns of demand and competition. That is to say, the *structure* of the economy is no longer suited to changing markets. Declining industries and regions make their appearance, and workers gradually lose their jobs while the rest of the economy is growing. The basic disturbance causing structural unemployment may originate at home, abroad (as specific export markets dry up or foreign competitors enter domestic markets, or both at home and abroad.[10]

When import competition appears to be causing structural unemployment, workers and management in the affected industry are quick to demand that government curtail imports by higher tariffs, quotas, or other means. This protectionist solution attempts to preserve the status quo at the cost of losing the benefits of international specialization. If no other solution to the problem of structural unemployment were possible, protection would be justifiable as a way of utilizing labor and capital that would otherwise stand idle. But this is not the case. Basically, what is needed is a reallocation of productive factors, shifting the factors currently used in declining industries to expanding industries.

The capacity of an economy to adapt to change and thereby avoid or minimize structural imbalances is dependent primarily on the mobility of its factors of production and its overall rate of growth. When labor and capital move quickly out of declining industries into growing industries, then structural unemployment is transitional rather than prolonged. Mobility will be enhanced if the economy as a whole is growing, generating new opportunities for employment and capital investment. When, on the other hand, labor does not shift easily from one job to another or from one place to another, then structural unemployment may endure for a generation or more. Immobility is further intensified by a slowly growing economy.

---

[9]In a variable-rate system, expansive monetary and fiscal policies to restore employment during a worldwide recession cause a depreciation of a country's currency unless other countries are following similar policies. The example of France in 1981–1982 is instructive in this regard. Deliberate *overdevaluation* of a currency in a fixed-rate system to remedy unemployment is a beggar-my-neighbor policy of exporting unemployment, akin to import restrictions.

[10]Structural unemployment in the United States mainly results from changes *within* the economy, such as the automation of industry, the mechanization of agriculture, the migration of industry among regions, and the pervasive shift in demand toward services and away from physical goods. In the 1980s and continuing into the 1990s, however, structural unemployment in several industries has been intensified by a failure to compete effectively with foreign industries. The automotive and steel industries are leading examples. See Chapter 9 for a discussion of international competition in the contemporary world economy.

All economies suffer from factor immobility, but it is most pervasive in underdeveloped countries, where economic, social, and cultural conditions favor stability over change. For such countries import protection may be necessary to give them time to transform their economies, but the ultimate solution is to develop a capacity to grow and adjust to change. For developed countries, however, protection is not a reasonable alternative to measures that are aimed directly at increasing labor and capital mobility. In the last analysis, the cause of structural unemployment lies in a failure to adapt to technological and other changes. As we have stressed earlier, the world economy is dynamic and nations can obtain the full advantages of international specialization only by responding quickly to new market opportunities and competitive challenges.

Antidumping Argument

The dumping of goods in an importing country at prices below those prevailing in the exporting country may be beneficial or harmful, depending upon circumstances.[11] If dumping is persistent, buyers in the importing country reap a continuous benefit that results from lower prices for foreign goods. If the importing country has no domestic industry competing with the dumped product, there is, of course, no argument for protection. If, on the other hand, such an industry exists, domestic producers are in no different position than if the dumping price resulted from a normal cost advantage in the exporting country. The fact that there is some unfairness to domestic producers in the situation is not a valid reason for protection, since the nation as a whole is benefited.

When dumping is sporadic and is intended to harass a competing domestic industry or put it out of business in order to raise prices afterwards, dumping becomes undesirable. To prevent such *predatory dumping,* action is necessary. High protection that precludes the possibility of predatory dumping, however, inflicts upon the domestic economy a permanently higher cost that is totally unjustified. By administrative action or by antidumping duties, predatory dumping can be prevented if and when it occurs by making its practice costly and ineffective. Unfortunately, this *limited* use of antidumping measures is violated in practice: Governments do not distinguish between persistent and predatory dumping, and they frequently utilize devices in the name of antidumping that amount to sheer protection.

Bargaining-and-Retaliation Argument

It has been argued that a country with a protective tariff is in a better position to bargain with other countries for concessions on its exports than is a country that has nothing to offer in return. It follows, therefore, that a free trade (or low-tariff) country should adopt some form of protection to be in a bargaining position.

---

[11]For an analysis of dumping as a consequence of international price discrimination by an oligopolistic firm, see Chapter 4.

The logic of this argument is strong, and such a policy may work out in actual practice. It does not, however, necessarily follow that the argument has economic validity. A free trade country that resorts to protection for purposes of bargaining sacrifices the benefits of international specialization. Furthermore, once protection is introduced, domestic industries develop behind its shield and become entrenched, exerting pressures upon their government when the time comes to give up such protection. Experience proves that this kind of pressure is usually most successful in preventing the return to freer trade, and therefore the country will, in all probability, become permanently committed to protection. Similarly, a country adopting a tariff for retaliation purposes is, so to speak, adding insult to injury by depriving itself of the benefits from unhindered imports. More to the point, retaliation can easily breed counterretaliation and a general worsening of trade relations rather than an abandonment of the measure that provoked the retaliation. To conclude, the bargaining-and-retaliation argument involves a certain loss and an uncertain gain and presents ample opportunity for abuse.

Reciprocity Argument

Closely related to the bargaining-and-retaliation argument is the reciprocity argument, which has been advocated by some members of the U.S. Congress in recent years.[12] Whereas the former would impose higher tariffs (or other forms of protection) to gain bargaining leverage with other countries in negotiating reductions of their import barriers, the latter would have the United States impose *new* restrictions on imports from individual foreign countries unless those countries lowered their import barriers so as to give access to their markets "comparable" to their access to the U.S. market. The bargaining-and-retaliation argument holds out a carrot (lower import barriers) to get import concessions from other countries; the reciprocity argument waves a stick (higher import barriers) to get import concessions from other countries.

The reciprocity argument is beguiling because it appears to support freer trade. Starting from the premise that the U.S. market is more open to imports than foreign markets, it is alleged that the purpose of reciprocity is to gain access to foreign markets comparable to that afforded by the U.S. market. Only if a foreign country refused to grant this "reasonable" request for "equal access" by lowering its barriers against U.S. goods would the United States retaliate with higher protection against that country's goods. When the argument is closely examined, however, it becomes evident that its application would almost certainly lead to higher U.S. protection and counterretaliation by other countries. Indeed, this argument is more questionable than the bargaining-and-retaliation argument because it involves discrimination among countries as well as higher protection.

We shall encounter the reciprocity argument again in Chapter 9 when we examine U.S. trade policy. Here we merely point out three questionable aspects.

---

[12]It has also been advocated by some officials of the European Community. See Chapter 10.

First, what does "comparable access" mean? How would it be measured? The traditional measures are the general level of tariffs and the portion of a nation's market covered by nontariff trade barriers. By such measures, the United States is *not* more open than Japan and the European Community; access is about the same. What supporters of reciprocity appear to have in mind as *the* measure of comparable access is the size of any U.S. trade deficit with a foreign country, Japan being foremost in mind. But this measure is absurd, for a country experiences import trade balances with some countries at the same time as it experiences export balances with other countries. Does a U.S. export balance with EC countries indicate that the United States does not offer them equal access to the U.S. market?

Second, almost certainly some countries would not be able to make concessions to satisfy the requirements of equal opportunity. The consequent imposition of new U.S. import restrictions on those countries' goods would trigger counter-retaliation that would close off market opportunities for U.S. exports—a result directly opposite to that intended by the supporters of reciprocity.

Third, the unilateral imposition of higher U.S. import restrictions would incur all the costs of higher protection.

QUALIFIED ARGUMENTS FOR PROTECTION

Some arguments for protection find their justification either in noneconomic considerations, such as national defense, or in the expectation of long-term economic benefits that will more than compensate for the immediate cost of protection.

National Security Argument

Few would disagree with the need to maintain an "adequate" national defense. Even Adam Smith, the venerable father of free trade, wrote in 1776 that "defense is much more important than opulence."[13] The problem lies in defining the specific requirements of national defense and the proper way to meet those requirements. Otherwise the national security argument may be used to justify complete self-sufficiency or the protection of *any* industry. Since most producers consider their activities essential to the defense of their country, the national security argument is particularly subject to abuse. In the United States, manufacturers of peanuts, candles, thumbtacks, umbrella frames, gloves, and many other products of ordinary consumption have all asked for protection on grounds of national security.

Today military experts are inclined to view future wars in terms of "adequate strength in a constant state of readiness" rather than in terms of "potential production capacity." If this is the true situation, then the protection of "strategic" domestic industries can make no contribution to national security. Apart from this consideration, direct subsidies are better policy tools than import restrictions to

---

[13]Adam Smith, *The Wealth of Nations* (New York: Random House, 1937), p. 431.

maintain defense industries: They are more precise in their effects, more subject to review, and less costly to the nation.[14]

Infant Industry Argument

In its traditional form, the infant industry argument asserts that a new industry which has a potential comparative advantage may not get started in a country unless it is given temporary protection against foreign competition. Most often, the argument stresses the necessity of protected domestic markets that will offer an opportunity for economies of scale in production. Regarding the example presented in Figure 4-5 in Chapter 4, it would be argued that protection would enable local manufacturers to produce at least $0-G$ automobiles at a unit cost of $0-C$, thereby making them competitive with foreign manufacturers who already enjoy economies of scale. Aside from economies of scale, protection would also afford local producers the time to improve their skills in management, production, marketing, and the application of technology. Once competitive strength was built up, protection would be abandoned for free trade.

The infant industry argument is associated with Alexander Hamilton, the first Secretary of the Treasury of the United States, and Frederick List, a German economist who lived in this country as a political refugee. Alexander Hamilton published his famous *Report on Manufacturers* in 1791, urging the use of tariffs to foster the growth of manufacturing and to strengthen the American economy, which was then predominantly agricultural. He contended that the vast resources of the country could be advantageously developed to compete with foreign industries that held a vast lead due to a prior start; that even though time and ingenuity could ultimately bring about such a development, governmental aid and promotion would speed up the process; and that the provision of governmental assistance would constitute only a temporary departure from the free trade doctrine, since it would soon bring about a more secure and steady demand for the surplus produce of the soil.[15]

Frederick List's historical approach to the question of free trade versus protection led him to the general conclusion that free trade is a cosmopolitan concept that is not necessarily in the best interest of a country in an intermediate stage of economic development.[16] Such a developing country could not readily develop new industries without temporary protection.

Economists have long accepted the *theoretical* validity of the infant industry argument, recognizing that the H-O theory of trade is a static analysis that abstracts from increasing returns. On the other hand, they have raised many questions with regard to its practical application.

---

[14]Because subsidies do not raise the price of the product in question, they avoid the consumption loss of tariffs or import quotas; they do, however, involve a production loss. (See Chapter 6 for a discussion of consumption and production losses due to protection.) The United States subsidizes its merchant marine for reasons of national security.

[15]Isaac Asher, *International Trade, Tariff and Commercial Policies* (Homewood, Ill.: Richard D. Irwin, 1948), Chapter 4.

[16]Frederick List, *The National System of Political Economy* (London: Longmans, Green & Co., 1922). This book was first published in 1840.

First, it is not at all self-evident that an infant industry requires protection to get started. After all, many new enterprises are able to compete with well-entrenched older enterprises *within* a country under conditions of free trade. Some of these new ventures may even displace the less dynamic older ones through better management, product innovation, quick response to market opportunities, and the like. Why should international competition be any different? If the long-run outlook of a true infant industry is so good, why should domestic entrepreneurs need protection? After all, they can capitalize early losses as part of their initial investment, and as long as the eventual return will cover this investment at a satisfactory profit, they should go ahead. If the response to this line of reasoning is that a country lacks the necessary local entrepreneurs, then the remedy is not protection as such but rather state enterprise (assuming the government has the necessary entrepreneurial talents) or the attraction of foreign entrepreneurs.[17]

Second, it is most difficult for a government to identify an industry that deserves infant industry protection. The search for an industry that has a potential comparative advantage requires, in the words of one writer, "the skill of the engineer, the brain of the economist, and the audacity of the entrepreneur."[18] In light of historical experience, the probability of a mistake would certainly be very high. One illustration is the U.S. woolen-worsted industry. Started in the early years of this country as an infant industry, it must still be protected against import competition and shows no signs of being able to overcome its comparative disadvantage.

This last example indicates that a mistake tends to become irreversible. Once a new industry is protected, the pressure of vested interests prevents the removal of protection even (or especially) when it becomes evident that the industry will not be competitive. *Temporary* protection usually turns into *permanent* protection. The result is a misallocation of resources that thwarts rather than promotes economic development.

Third, even if the proper choice of an infant industry is made by a government, it does not necessarily follow that import protection is the best way to promote that industry. In particular, direct subsidies have several advantages over tariffs. For one thing, subsidies are less likely to end up as permanent protection, because they are dependent on annual appropriations. Protectionists oppose subsidies for this very reason, but manufacturers who honestly seek only infant industry protection should have no objection to them.

Although internal economies of scale are most often cited as the rationale for infant industry protection, a stronger case rests on *external* economies. Suppose the industry in question would powerfully stimulate the growth of other industries (and the economy in general) through its research and development activities, its training of managers and workers whose skills are transferable to other industries, its assistance to suppliers, and in other ways. Such an industry that generates

[17]Protection may be used to attract foreign entrepreneurs. See Chapter 24.

[18]John P. Powelson, *Latin America: Today's Economic and Social Revolution* (New York: McGraw-Hill, 1964), p. 198.

many backward and forward linkages with other industries (commonly termed "spillover effects") would have a social value greater than its private value. But since entrepreneurs could not retain this extra social value, they might not start the industry without protection of some sort. In this situation, protection would eliminate the disparity between private and social values and thereby improve the allocation of the country's resources. However, the practical application of protection to "strategic" industries encounters all of the difficulties already mentioned plus the added difficulty of identifying and measuring external benefits. The mistakes made by several developing countries in granting infant industry protection to supposedly strategic industries such as steel, chemicals, and automobiles testify to the perils of policy in this area.[19]

To conclude, the infant industry argument is theoretically sound, especially in regard to external economies. But the difficulties of practical application ensure that infant industry protection often becomes permanent protection, with all its attendant costs. It should also be evident that the infant industry argument does not apply to industrial countries such as the United States.

Diversification Argument

The diversification argument for protection is actually two arguments that commonly masquerade as one. One argument urges import protection as a means to bring about a diversification of *exports* so as to lessen instability in export income. The second argument proposes import protection as a means to achieve diversification in the *domestic economy* and thereby promote economic growth. Both arguments are put forth mainly by representatives of the nonindustrial, developing nations.

The *diversification-for-export-stability* argument proceeds from the dependence of many developing countries on one or two agricultural or mineral products for most of their export income. This "overspecialization" makes such countries highly sensitive to supply or demand shifts in a single export product. Furthermore, it is widely accepted that primary commodities experience wide cyclical fluctuations in price because of low price elasticities of supply and demand.[20] In this context, therefore, the export stability argument becomes an argument for the substitution of manufactured exports for primary exports via import protection that fosters the development of domestic industry.

Theoretically, the diversification-for-export-stability argument derives its validity from a possible divergence of private and social values in a world of change and uncertainty. When private costs do not fully reflect social costs, then the gains from higher economic efficiency may be more than offset by long-run losses due to economic disruptions caused by dependence on foreign markets. The policy application of this argument, however, is fraught with difficulties, notably the

---

[19]This external economies case has been incorporated in the new strategic trade theory taken up later in this chapter.

[20]The trade policies of the developing countries are explored in Chapter 20.

problem of choosing the proper diversification mix and the means to achieve it. These difficulties tend to make import protection an ineffective policy tool compared with export subsidies and other measures of direct export promotion. Indeed, protection has a qualified validity *only* when export diversification requires the prior development of new industries to produce goods that are presently being imported by the country in question. Thus, the diversification-for-export-stability argument for protection is really a version of the infant industry argument that emphasizes export stability rather than economies of scale.

The *diversification-for-domestic-growth* argument rests upon the doctrine of "balanced" economic growth, which asserts the necessity for a simultaneous or parallel development of all industries throughout the economy.[21] This argument, therefore, may be used to justify a policy of general import substitution that cuts across all categories of industrial products. Lacking the specific criteria of the traditional infant industry argument, the diversification-for-domestic-growth argument lends itself to easy abuse by protectionists. At its extreme, it closely resembles the argument for autarky in its real consequences.

Following World War II, many developing countries, especially in Latin America, adopted indiscriminate policies of import substitution under the banner of economic growth. Although these policies did achieve varying degrees of industrial diversification, they did so only in the form of many high-cost industries that made no contribution to the expansion of industrial exports. By discarding all considerations of comparative advantage in headlong pursuit of industrialization, these countries gratuitously forsook the gains from international specialization. In practice, therefore, the diversification-for-domestic-growth argument represents a highly questionable extension of the infant industry argument. Unless diversification is introduced with extreme care, the national loss in economic efficiency (to say nothing of the international loss) brought about by the sacrifice of international specialization will turn out to be greater than the realized gains of economic growth.[22]

SOPHISTICATED ARGUMENTS FOR PROTECTION

This section looks at three arguments that may justify import restrictions under certain conditions: the terms-of-trade argument (optimum tariff), the theory of the second best, and strategic trade policy. The first is an argument for the exploitation of a national monopsony (or monopoly) position; the second is an argument for the imposition of a tariff or other trade restriction as a second-best policy when

---

[21]In opposition, the doctrine of "unbalanced" economic growth emphasizes the need to concentrate on key or strategic industries that will stimulate general economic development. This doctrine is consistent with the traditional infant industry argument.

[22]The diversification-for-domestic-growth argument is now in disrepute in the developing countries because of the failure of protectionist policies to achieve economic growth. In the 1980s, the developing countries began to move toward freer trade by dismantling import restrictions. See Chapter 20.

the first-best policy (free trade) is not possible; the third is an argument for government assistance to domestic oligopolies to obtain a transfer of economic rent from foreign oligopolistic competitors. We call these arguments "sophisticated" because they derive from the models of international trade theorists rather than from the special pleading of industry spokesmen.

Terms-of-Trade Argument and the Optimum Tariff

The terms-of-trade argument rests upon the proposition that at least part of a duty is absorbed by foreign suppliers when the price elasticity of import supply is less than infinite and the price elasticity of import demand is greater than zero. Given these elasticity conditions, the imposition of a duty raises the domestic price of the import good by less than the amount of the duty as foreign suppliers lower their prices in an attempt to maintain sales in the tariff-levying country (see Figure 6-1 in Chapter 6). Hence, that country experiences an improvement in its terms of trade: The price it pays foreigners for the import good falls while the price it charges foreigners for its export goods remains the same.

The national gain from an improvement in the terms of trade, however, must be set against the national loss resulting from the trade effect of the tariff. In terms of Figure 6-4 in Chapter 6, the *net* national gain is the sum of the revenue effect (d) and the income-redistribution effect (r) *minus* the loss in consumers' surplus due to the negative trade effect (l and c). This analysis leads to the concept of the *optimum tariff* that maximizes the net national gain.

At one extreme, when the *entire* duty is absorbed by foreign suppliers (perfectly inelastic supply), the *net* national gain equals the revenue effect, which is fully traceable to an improvement in the terms of trade. Since the duty does not affect the price paid by domestic consumers, there is no change in consumers' surplus and the trade effect is zero. In this situation the optimal tariff rate is infinite; the tariff-levying country is a pure *monopsonist* that can continually improve its terms of trade by raising the duty while importing the same volume of the commodity in question.

At the other extreme, when import supply is perfectly elastic, the optimum tariff rate is zero. In this situation a country cannot improve its terms of trade by imposing a duty because the entire duty is absorbed by domestic consumers who pay a postduty price that is higher than the preduty price by the full amount of the duty. The outcome is depicted in Figure 6-4. Between the two extremes, the optimum tariff rate will depend on the price elasticities of import demand and import supply. In general, the more elastic the import demand and the more inelastic the import supply, the higher the optimum duty rate. However, this rate will be less than the rate that maximizes an improvement in the terms of trade because of the negative trade effect.

The terms-of-trade argument is not really an argument for protection, nor has it been used by protectionists. We have seen that the optimal tariff is highest when there is no protection effect, hardly a comforting thought to domestic producers who are anxious to keep out imports. When applied to imports, the terms-of-trade argument is rather an argument for the exploitation of monopsonistic power. It can be applied equally well to exports to justify an export tariff that improves the terms of trade by exploiting *monopolistic* power. The optimal tariff provides a gain to the tariff-levying country by causing the rest of the world to suffer a loss; and insofar as the optimal tariff lowers trade, it causes a net loss to the world economy.

Although the theoretical argument for an optimal tariff is valid (given its assumptions), its application in policy raises serious administrative, economic, and political questions. For one thing, the determination of the optimal tariff requires a knowledge of the relevant elasticities, which are likely to change over time. Their accurate measurement and the quick adjustment of the optimum rate to elasticity changes run far beyond the capabilities of economic analysts and tariff administrators. For another, an optimal tariff policy would transfer income from the poor to the rich countries that have monopsonistic power because of their huge markets.[23] This consequence would undercut the foreign aid programs of those same rich countries. Finally, an optimal tariff policy would probably effect its own failure by inciting retaliation by countries faced with a deterioration in their terms of trade. After a series of retaliations and counterretaliations, all trading nations would end up on lower indifference curves.

The Theory of the Second Best

The theory of the second best may be traced to the proposition that free trade will *not* necessarily achieve Pareto optimality in the worldwide allocation of production and consumption when private monopoly, government policies, and externalities create divergences between private and social costs and benefits. If policymakers cannot eliminate these divergences so as to pursue a first-best policy (free trade), then a second-best policy may require the introduction of new distortions (such as tariffs) that will neutralize or offset the existing distortions.[24]

The theory of the second best is applicable to all economic policy, not only trade policy. It recognizes that at any given time policymakers may confront many constraints that run beyond the constraints assumed by the theory of trade (factor supplies, tastes, technology, and foreign supply or demand conditions). Given the existence of constraints such as subsidies and taxes, the optimum values of other variables in the economy will differ from their values in perfectly competitive markets. That is to say, there will be a second-best optimum. The theory of the second best is pertinent to policymaking whenever market prices that guide the actions of producers and consumers fail to indicate the real opportunity costs of the economy and thereby cause discrepancies between private and social values.

---

[23]A poor country, or organized group of poor countries, might have *monopoly* power in the export of some primary products, such as coffee and petroleum. An exploitation of this power by export tariffs or other means would transfer income from the rich to the poor countries. In the 1970s, OPEC (Organization of Petroleum Exporting Countries) used monopoly power to force up the price of petroleum exports.

[24]The theory of the second best first appeared in J. E. Meade, *Theory of International Economic Policy,* vol. 2, *Trade and Welfare* (New York: Oxford University Press, 1955).

Part I   International Trade

The theory of the second best may justify *selective* import protection when price distortions make the private costs of particular domestic producers higher than the social costs to the country as a whole. Consider, for example, the cost effects of a selective excise tax imposed on a domestic producer. The tax makes the private costs (which include the tax) exceed the social costs (which do not include the tax, because it is an internal transfer from producers to the government of the same country). Hence, domestic production of the taxed product is less and imports of that product are greater than they would be in the absence of the tax. Since the country is obtaining additional imports at a higher social cost than if it were to obtain additional domestic output, the imposition of a "compensatory" import duty that would restrict imports and permit the expansion of domestic production would add to the nation's welfare up to the point where the marginal social costs of imports and domestic production became equal. Further restriction of imports beyond that point would lower the nation's welfare.

An important application of the theory of the second best is to customs unions and free trade areas, such as the European Community and the proposed North American Free Trade Agreement, which are examined in Chapter 10. To put the matter simply for the time being, it can be demonstrated that the elimination of import restrictions among members of a customs union or free trade area may cause a loss of welfare to the world as a whole. In other words, not every step toward free trade is necessarily a step toward greater economic efficiency and higher welfare.

In recent years, trade theorists have emphasized the presence of *knowledge externalities,* namely, the inability of firms, particularly in high-technology oligopolies, to *appropriate* all of the economic gain resulting from the creation of new knowledge through R & D. Consequently, such firms invest *less* in R & D than is socially desirable, justifying subsidies or other forms of government intervention to encourage them to invest more.[25]

It should be evident that the theory of second best is not a general argument for protection. Under certain conditions, a selective import restriction may improve welfare, but in other circumstances (for example, when private cost is *less* than social cost), the theory of the second best may entail the elimination or reduction of a specific import restriction. In a sense all arguments for protection (aside from the purely fallacious) may be regarded as calling for second-best policies, since they all argue that certain constraints justify protection. Correctly interpreted, the theory of the second best says that *any* policy that reduces divergences between marginal social costs and benefits will improve economic efficiency. This theory is not an argument for wholesale government intervention in the marketplace, especially when divergences are the result of previous intervention. The theory of the second best focuses attention first on the possible removal of distortion-causing constraints; only when their removal is deemed unfeasible

---

[25]The theory of *internalization* argues that firms invest abroad (rather than export) to appropriate more knowledge externalities. See Chapter 23.

does a second-best policy become appropriate. The first-best policy remains free trade.

Strategic Trade Policy Argument

In the 1980s, a group of young economists developed models of international trade based on the assumptions of increasing returns and imperfect competition.[26] Because traditional models of international trade assumed perfect competition, these models were collectively designated "new" trade theory. This theory has renewed interest in the infant industry, terms-of-trade, and second-best arguments for protection that we have already reviewed. Also, the new theory has engendered its own argument for protection, called *strategic trade policy*, by focusing attention on the behavior of domestic oligopolistic firms and their foreign rivals.

Strategic trade policy argues the case for protecting domestic firms in high-rent industries with subsidies, tariffs, or other forms of protection to strengthen those firms against their foreign rivals both at home and abroad. By thus enabling domestic oligopolists to capture economic rent from foreign oligopolists, it is asserted that strategic trade policy can increase national welfare. Undoubtedly, the emergence of strategic trade policy has been stimulated by events in the world economy over the past decade or so, notably the persistent U.S. trade deficit, the intensification of global competition, and the remarkable success of Japanese firms in penetrating markets in the United States and the European Community allegedly made possible by Japan's strategic trade policy.

Sectors of the economy that have, or will have, substantial economic rents are deemed "strategic." These sectors are high-technology industries dominated by a small number of domestic firms who compete with rival firms headquartered in other countries. Examples of such industries are telecommunications, computers, aerospace, and pharmaceuticals. The rationale for strategic trade policy is that government intervention will make possible the shift of excess oligopolistic profits from foreign to domestic firms, providing a net benefit to the home country. To illustrate, intervention might take the form of a *tariff* that raises entry barriers for foreign rival firms trying to enter the home market. With a bigger share of the home market, it is argued, domestic firms can obtain scale and learning economies that drive down their unit costs. Consequently, they may be able to export more than before. Somewhat paradoxically, higher import restrictions act to promote exports! Of course, intervention might take the form of an *export subsidy* to help domestic firms take away economic rent from their foreign rivals.

In sum, strategic trade policy is intended to shift excess returns from foreign to domestic oligopolists. To do so, it must change the strategic game played by oligopolists competing in world markets.

The new trade theorists agree that the effect on national welfare of strategic government intervention depends critically on the reaction of domestic and foreign

---

[26]Essays by several of these economists appear in Paul R. Krugman, ed., *Strategic Trade Policy and the New International Economics* (Cambridge: The MIT Press, 1986).

oligopolists in a particular industry. In modeling oligopolistic behavior, economists have usually assumed one of three forms of *duopolistic* behavior in a two-firm industry: Cournot, Stackelberg, or Bertrand. Briefly, with *Cournot* behavior, each firm treats the output of the other firm as fixed in deciding its own output level; with *Stackelberg* behavior, one firm sets its output first and then the other firm, after considering the first firm's output, makes its own output decision; and with *Bertrand* behavior, each firm takes the price of its rival as fixed in setting its own price, and the firm with the lower prices captures all the sales.

Because it is impossible to know a priori which of these three behaviors (if any) a given oligopolistic industry will follow, it is also impossible to know the effect on national welfare of a specific government intervention. Furthermore, these behavior forms are simplistic, and they by no means exhaust the behavior options that may be open to an oligopolist. For one thing, the three behaviors assume product *homogeneity.* If, instead, we assume product *differentiation,* which actually dominates in strategic industries, then the potential behavior patterns (firm strategies) multiply because firms compete not only in price but also in any of several kinds of nonprice competition, such as product innovations and services. Also, the duopoly assumption ignores the influence of the number of firms on their behavior. Again, when account is taken of the *dynamic* paths of possible interactions among rival firms, any forecasts of their specific responses over time to government interventions becomes hazardous indeed. Finally, we should bear in mind that the firms in strategic industries are mainly *multinational enterprises* with operations in several countries.[27] These firms may respond to government intervention not only with a change in trade flows but also with changes in the country location of their activities, ranging from R & D through production and marketing.

This empirical contingency of strategic trade policy is not the only consideration that makes it questionable in practice. There is also the question of *foreign retaliation.* After all, strategic trade policy is a zero-sum game: Economic rent taken from foreign firms is a welfare loss to their countries. For that reason, they are almost certain to retaliate with their own interventions. But if the leading industrial countries are all using strategic trade policies, then they are all likely to suffer a loss of national welfare as the ensuing trade war incurs the costs of protection with no offsetting redistribution of economic rent. Another question is the role of *special interests* in pushing for intervention even when the requirements for an effective strategic trade policy are not met by their industries.

There is no solid empirical evidence in support of strategic trade policy. Indeed, empirical studies of broad liberalizing changes indicate larger welfare gains when markets are imperfect than when markets are assumed to be perfectly competitive. The reason is the reduction of the markups of prices above marginal costs with greater competition and a reduction of costs as large firms replace small, inefficient firms.[28]

---

[27]For a description and analysis of multinational enterprise systems see Chapter 22.

[28]Robert E. Baldwin, "Are Economists' Trade Policy Views Still Valid?" *Journal of Economic Literature,* June 1992, pp. 822–823.

The difficulty in identifying strategic sectors, the uncertainty of oligopolistic reaction, the likelihood of foreign retaliation, and the role of special interests in deciding on government intervention have been recognized by the new trade theorists. Hence, they still support free trade as the best policy for countries to follow as a general rule. Indeed, a prominent new trade theorist concludes: "The economic cautions about the difficulty of formulating useful interventions and the political economy concerns that interventionism may go astray combine into a new case for free trade."[29]

Nonetheless, the strategic trade argument is very appealing to protectionists because it focuses on the individual firm and industry, unlike the terms-of-trade and second-best arguments, which are abstract and hard for the layman to understand. Protectionists can now hide their special pleading behind the facade of disinterested economic theory. Does there exist an oligopolistic firm that does *not* believe that its industry is strategic? As they pursue their own interests, we can be certain that protectionists will find it easy to ignore the contingencies, limiting assumptions, and caveats of the new trade theorists. As we shall observe in the remaining chapters of Part I, the strategic trade rationale will strongly influence the formulation of trade policies in the United States and the European Community in the 1990s.

PERSISTENCE OF PROTECTION

Our examination of arguments for protection has revealed their vulnerability to economic analysis. Aside from the purely fallacious arguments, we have found that arguments for protection have only a conditional validity when they are evaluated from the perspective of economic efficiency. In most instances, protection is an inferior policy instrument, because other policies can achieve the same result (or a better one) at a smaller cost. Even in those rare situations when protection brings a net gain to the protectionist country, it brings a net loss to the world economy. Because of their conditional validity, the arguments for protection are commonly abused in practice; the criterion of economic efficiency is overwhelmed by political factors. In light of historical experience, protection once established tends to become a permanent institution under the relentless pressure of the vested interests it benefits, even when it outgrows any original usefulness for the nation.

If so little can be said in its favor, why is protection so persistent? Why do all nations of the world continue to implement this restrictive policy to one degree or another? The answers to these perplexing questions are not to be found in the realm of logic or economics. The answers, deeply embedded in human behavior, are found in the same forces of narrow self-interest, fear, ignorance, and prejudice that afflict international relations in general. So long as groups who gain from protection are able to persuade policymakers that their private interests coincide with the national interest, protection will continue to stultify the flow of trade

---

[29]Paul R. Krugman, "Is Free Trade Passé?" *The Journal of Economic Perspectives,* Fall 1987, p. 143.

among nations who are otherwise committed to competitive market economies. By the same token, the struggle for free or freer trade is a never-ending chronology of victories and defeats with no final outcome.

SUMMARY

1. The theory of comparative advantage demonstrates that for the world as a whole free trade leads to a higher level of output and income than autarky. However, many contemporary economists are reluctant to support free trade unreservedly. Economic theory cannot demonstrate that *in all circumstances* free trade will improve economic efficiency or enhance economic welfare.
2. The essential difference between external and internal trade is political only; it is this difference that has nurtured protectionism through the ages. The long series of arguments for protection may be classified into four categories: (1) fallacious arguments, (2) questionable arguments, (3) qualified arguments, and (4) sophisticated arguments.
3. Fallacious arguments rely on plausibility or mass emotional appeal rather than economic logic. The keep-money-at-home, home market, equalization-of-production-costs, low wage, and prevention-of-injury arguments are traditional fallacious arguments.
4. Certain arguments for protection, although not entirely fallacious, represent an inferior policy or easily lend themselves to abuse. These include the employment, antidumping, bargaining-and-retaliation, and reciprocity arguments.
5. Other arguments for protection (the national security, infant industry, and diversification arguments) find their justification either in noneconomic considerations or in expectation of long-term economic benefits that will more than compensate for the immediate costs of protection.
6. Three arguments may justify protection under certain conditions: the terms-of-trade argument (optimum tariff), the theory of second best, and strategic trade policy. We call these arguments "sophisticated" because they derive from the models of international trade theorists rather than from the special pleading of industry spokesmen.

QUESTIONS AND APPLICATIONS

1. "Contemporary Western economists are reluctant to support the doctrine of free trade unreservedly but remain firmly on the side of a policy of freer, if not free, trade." What is the explanation of this seemingly contradictory statement?
2. Which is the strongest argument for protection? Why?

3. "Governments spend a great deal of effort promoting exports while, at the same time, they impose all kinds of restrictions on imports." Discuss.
4. Define a truly infant industry. On the basis of your definition, are there any infant industries in the United States?
5. Why is fiscal policy preferable to import restrictions as a response to cyclical unemployment?
6. In presenting its case for protection (import quotas), the American Textile Manufacturers Institute has made the following statement: "With very few exceptions, foreign-made textiles do not sell in the United States because they are better, more stylish, or made more efficiently. The basic reason foreign textiles sell in such volumes in this country is that they are produced at wages far below the legal minimum here." Assuming this statement is true, does the situation justify protection?
7. A spokesman for the U.S. steel industry concluded a plea for import quotas as follows: "Does America want and need a strong steel industry? Does it want to maintain the maximum number of jobs at high wage standards? Does it believe in fair play in the competition for its own markets? Does our nation's security demand all the strength in steel we can possibly achieve? If so, something has to be done. I believe the proposed legislation represents a realistic solution of this problem — fair to all — and that it is worthy of your sympathetic support." What arguments for protection are implied in these questions? Justify your own response to each question.
8. (a) What are "knowledge externalities"?
   (b) Do they justify government intervention? Why?
9. (a) What is the strategic trade argument for protection?
   (b) Identify and discuss three reasons why strategic trade policy may be ineffective or harmful to the national interest.
10. Why does protectionism persist despite the at-most conditional economic validity of arguments for protection?

SELECTED READINGS

Baldwin, Robert E. "Are Economists' Traditional Trade Policy Views Still Valid?" *The Journal of Economic Literature,* June 1992, pp. 804–29.

Baldwin, Robert E. "The Political Economy of Trade Policy." *The Journal of Economic Perspectives,* Fall 1989, pp. 119–136.

Bhagwati, Jagdish. *Protectionism.* Cambridge: The MIT Press, 1988.

Feenstra, Robert C. "How Costly is Protectionism?" *Journal of Economic Perspectives,* Summer 1992.

Krugman, Paul R., ed. *Strategic Trade Policy and the New International Economics.* Cambridge: The MIT Press, 1986.

Vousden, Neil. *The Economics of Trade Protection.* New York: Cambridge University Press, 1990.

chapter 8

MULTILATERAL TRADE AGREEMENTS UNDER GATT

As observed in Chapter 1, the rationale of government economic policies is that national economies, if left alone, would fail to achieve goals that are deemed to be in the national interest, such as full employment, price stability, a satisfactory rate of growth, an equitable distribution of income, and a strong balance of payments. Economic activity is characterized by a high degree of interdependence among the different nations of the world, and a policy in the best interests of a nation must take into account such interdependence, since it affects and, in turn, is affected by the policies of other nations. Consequently, a wise national economic policy must be conceived within a broad international frame of reference, especially when the nation involved holds a dominant position in world affairs and when its conduct is apt to have important repercussions abroad.

Unfortunately most nations, large and small, are inclined to disregard this dual aspect of their economic policies and to ignore the fact that by building roadblocks of interference on one side of the international highway of trade they block the other side as well. The United States, like other nations, has been guilty of this shortsighted approach to economic policy at various periods of its history.

Although its earlier position of dominance has been eroded by the remarkable resurgence of Western Europe and Japan and the emergence of newly industrializing countries, such as South Korea and Taiwan, the United States continues to exert a pervasive influence on the world economy. With only 5 percent of the world's population, this country produces about one-quarter of the world's goods and services and accounts for about 12 percent of all international trade. Thus, the economic behavior of the United States can do much harm or good, depending upon the growth and stability of its economy as well as the direction of its foreign economic policy. A liberal U.S. trade policy enhances the gains from international specialization and helps promote world economic growth. Conversely, a protectionist trade policy runs the risk of widespread retaliation by other countries and a return to the "beggar-my-neighbor" policies of the 1930s.

Since World War II, the trade policies of the United States and other industrial nations have been conducted mainly within the framework laid down by the *General Agreement on Tariffs and Trade,* known as GATT. In this chapter we describe GATT and note its achievements, including the last completed negotiations under its auspices, known as the Tokyo Round. We then discuss the erosion of GATT as industrial countries have increasingly circumvented its provisions in recent years. We conclude with a review of the key issues in the new round of multilateral trade negotiations now taking place — the Uruguay Round.

THE GENERAL AGREEMENT
ON TARIFFS AND TRADE (GATT)

After World War II, several international measures were undertaken to liberalize trade and payments between nations. Plans for the creation of a liberal, multilateral system of world trade were started while the war was still in progress. Initiated for the most part by the United States, these plans envisaged the close economic cooperation of all nations in the fields of international trade, payments, and investment. At the time, it was widely believed that such cooperation, formalized by agreements and implemented by international organizations, would avoid the mistakes of the past and lay the cornerstones for a progressive world economy. The two notable achievements of this wartime planning were the International Monetary Fund and the International Bank for Reconstruction and Development. The first institution was to ensure the free convertibility of currencies; the second was to supplement and stimulate the international flow of private capital.

Once the war had ended, it soon became apparent that the difficulties of postwar reconstruction in Europe and elsewhere had been greatly underestimated. Attention shifted from the now distant goal of a global system of multilateral trade to the immediate threat posed by Western Europe's economic distress and the spread of communism. The end of ambitious international planning was symbolized by the refusal of the United States Congress in 1950 to ratify the treaty establishing an International Trade Organization (ITO).[1]

The effects of the failure of the ITO on international cooperation in trade policy were considerably softened by the rise to prominence of the General Agreement on Tariffs and Trade. GATT was an almost casual offshoot of the international conference held at Geneva in 1947 to consider a draft charter for the ITO. There the United States initiated six months of continual negotiations with 22 other countries that led to commitments to bind or lower 45,000 tariff rates within the framework of principles and rules of procedure laid down by GATT.

---

[1]The ITO Charter was signed by representatives of 54 countries at Havana, Cuba, on March 24, 1948. The charter was an ambitious document, covering not only commercial policy but also such topics as employment, economic development, state trading, cartels, and intergovernmental commodity agreements. The charter has never been ratified by the signatory states. Late in 1950 the U.S. Department of State announced that it would no longer press for Congressional approval.

Part I   International Trade

GATT entered into force in 1948 with a membership of 23 industrial countries.[2] By 1992, its membership had risen to 103 countries that accounted for about nine-tenths of world trade. In addition, some 30 countries apply GATT rules de facto in their trade. All in all, therefore, over 130 countries subscribe to GATT's trading rules.[3]

Major Provisions of GATT

GATT contains numerous articles and annexes. The tariff schedules listing the thousands of concessions that have been negotiated by member countries are also part of the agreement. Despite its complexity, GATT comprises four basic elements:

1. the rule of nondiscrimination in trade relations among the participating countries
2. commitments to observe the negotiated tariff concessions
3. prohibitions against the use of quantitative restrictions (quotas) on exports and imports
4. special provisions to promote the trade of developing countries.

The remaining provisions of GATT are concerned with exceptions to these general principles, trade measures other than tariffs and quotas, and sundry procedural matters.

Tariffs   GATT obligates each member to accord nondiscriminatory, *most-favored-nation* (MFN) treatment to all other members with respect to import and export duties (including allied charges), customs regulations, and internal taxes and regulations.[4] An exception to the rule of nondiscrimination is made in the case of well-known tariff preferences, such as those between the countries of the British Commonwealth. No new preferences may be created, however, and existing preferences may not be increased. Frontier traffic, customs unions, free trade areas, and generalized systems of preferences extended by industrial countries to developing countries are exempted from the general rule of nondiscrimination.

GATT legalizes the schedules of tariff concessions negotiated by members and commits each member to their observance. An *escape clause,* however, allows any member to withdraw or modify a tariff concession (or other obligation) if, as a result of the tariff concession (or obligation), there is such an increase in imports as

---

[2]A signatory of GATT is known as a *contracting party,* since, legally, GATT is not an organization. For convenience of exposition, however, we shall use the term "member" to refer to participation in GATT.

[3]In 1992, six countries of Eastern Europe and the former Soviet Union gained *observer* status in GATT as a preliminary step toward eventual application for full membership. See *Focus,* GATT Newsletter, no. 91, July 1992, p. 2.

[4]Under the most-favored-nation principle, any tariff concession granted by one country to any other country is automatically extended to all other countries. GATT members are obligated to apply the MFN principle only to other GATT members, but they are free to apply it to nonmember countries as well.

to cause, or threaten to cause, serious injury to domestic producers of like or directly competitive products. When a member uses the escape clause, it must consult with other members as to remedies; if agreement is not reached, those countries may withdraw equivalent concessions.[5]

Quantitative Restrictions   GATT sets forth a general rule prohibiting the use of quantitative import and export restrictions. There are, however, several exceptions to this rule. The four most important exceptions pertain to agriculture, the balance of payments, economic development, and national security.

The agreement sanctions the use of import restrictions on any agricultural or fishery product where restrictions are necessary for the enforcement of government programs in marketing, production control, or the removal of surpluses. This exception is important to the United States, which has placed import quotas on several agricultural products.

GATT also permits a member to apply import restrictions to safeguard its balance of payments when there is an imminent threat, or actual occurrence, of a serious decline in its monetary reserves or when its monetary reserves are very low. The member must consult with GATT with respect to the continuation or intensification of such restrictions. GATT must also consult with the International Monetary Fund when dealing with problems of monetary reserves, the balance of payments, and foreign exchange practices. Members of GATT are not to frustrate the intent of GATT by exchange action nor the intent of the Fund agreement by trade restrictions. A country that adheres to GATT but is not a member of the Fund must conclude a special exchange agreement with the contracting parties.

GATT recognizes the special position of the developing countries and allows such countries to use nondiscriminatory import quotas to encourage infant industries. Prior approval, however, must be obtained from the collective GATT membership.

A member of GATT may use trade controls for purposes of national security. The strategic controls on United States exports come under this exception.

In addition to these four major exceptions, there are many of lesser importance. For example, members may use trade restrictions to protect public morals, to implement sanitation regulations, to prevent deceptive trade practices, and to protect patents and copyrights. All quantitative restrictions permitted by GATT are to be applied in accordance with the most-favored-nation principle. Import licenses may not specify that goods be imported from a certain country.

Special Provisions to Promote the Trade of Developing Countries   In 1965 the contracting parties added a new Part IV—Trade and Development—to the general agreement in recognition of the need for a rapid and sustained expansion of the export earnings of the less-developed member countries. Under the terms of the three articles composing Part IV, the developed countries agree to undertake

---

[5]The *escape clause* is now referred to as the *safeguard provision,* a terminological shift that reflects a shift from "freer" trade to "managed trade."

the following positive action "to the fullest extent possible": (1) give high priority to the reduction and elimination of barriers to products currently or potentially of particular export interest to less-developed contracting parties, (2) refrain from introducing or increasing customs duties or nontariff import barriers on such products, and (3) refrain from imposing new internal taxes that significantly hamper the consumption of primary products produced in the developing countries and accord high priority to the reduction or elimination of such taxes. In addition, the developed countries agree not to expect reciprocity for commitments made by them in trade negotiations to reduce or remove tariffs or other barriers to the trade of less-developed contracting parties. In return, the developing countries commit themselves to take "appropriate action" to implement the provisions of Part IV for the benefit of the trade of other less-developed contracting parties. A Committee on Trade and Development is charged with keeping under review the implementation of the provisions of Part IV.

Other Provisions   Many other substantive matters are covered by the provisions of GATT: national treatment of internal taxation and regulation, motion picture films, antidumping and countervailing duties, customs valuation, customs formalities, marks of origin, subsidies, state trading, and the publication and administration of trade regulations. The intention of most of these provisions is to eliminate concealed protection or discrimination in international trade.

Several articles of GATT deal with procedural matters. In meetings, each member is entitled to one vote and, unless otherwise specified, decisions are to be taken by majority vote. A two-thirds majority vote is required to waive any obligation imposed on a member by the general agreement.[6] Articles also cover consultation procedures and the settlement of disputes between members.

Activities of GATT

The members of GATT meet in regular annual sessions and special tariff conferences. A Council deals with matters between sessions and prepares the agenda for each session. In addition, intersessional working groups have been appointed at regular sessions to report on specific topics at subsequent sessions.

Adding further to the continuous influence of GATT has been the practice of member governments to consult with each other before the regular sessions. The membership has obtained a secretariat from the United Nations that, among other things, publishes an annual report. In these and other ways, GATT has behaved like an international organization and, as a matter of fact, has been more effective than some legitimate organizations.

The main activities of GATT fall into five categories: (1) tariff bargaining, (2) bargaining on nontariff trade barriers, (3) elimination of quantitative restrictions, (4) settlement of disputes, and (5) trade policy review.

---

[6]In practice, GATT decisions are generally arrived at by consensus rather than by vote.

Tariff Bargaining The parties to GATT have participated in eight tariff conferences to negotiate mutual tariff concessions, as indicated in Table 8-1. The initial conference at Geneva negotiated 45,000 different tariff rates, and today the schedules of GATT include products that make up more than half the world's trade. All of these rates have been either reduced or bound against any increase in the future.

The magnitude of this accomplishment is unprecedented in tariff history; it represents a new approach to the task of lowering tariff barriers. Before World War II the most successful attempt to reduce tariffs by reciprocal bargaining was the trade agreements program of the United States. That program was limited, however, by its bilateral nature. GATT has overcome this disability by applying multilaterally the underlying principles of the bilateral trade agreements of the 1930s.

The results of the round of tariff negotiations at each conference are not finalized until all of them are gathered into a single master agreement signed by the participating countries. The concessions in the master agreement then apply to trade among all members of GATT. In this way, each member receives the benefits of every tariff concession and becomes a party to every tariff agreement.

GATT has brilliantly overcome the difficulties of a purely bilateral trade agreements program: (1) the reluctance of nations to lower or bind tariff duties unless a large number of their trading partners are taking similar action, and (2) the time-consuming negotiation of individual trade agreements, each containing

Table 8-1   Multilateral Trade Negotiations under GATT

Date	Name	Outcome
1947	Geneva Round	45,000 tariff concessions representing half of world trade
1949	Annecy Round	Modest tariff reductions
1950–1951	Torquay Round	25 percent tariff reduction in relation to 1948 level
1955–1956	Geneva Round	Modest tariff reductions
1961–1962	Dillon Round	Modest tariff reductions
1963–1967	Kennedy Round	Average tariff reduction of 35 percent for industrial products; only modest reductions for agricultural products. Antidumping code
1973–1979	Tokyo Round	Average tariff reductions of 34 percent for industrial products. Nontariff trade barrier codes
1986–	Uruguay Round	To be decided in forthcoming negotiations

Source: Focus, GATT Newsletter, no. 44, March 1987, p. 5.

its own code of conduct and other provisions.[7] While it is negotiating, each member knows that other members are also negotiating and that the results of those negotiations will accrue to its benefit. Because the prospects of gain are greater, countries are apt to be more generous. Moreover, one set of rules applies to every tariff concession, and it is much more comprehensive in scope than would be possible in the case of individual bilateral agreements. GATT has also created an environment conducive to tariff bargaining, and it has often induced countries to bargain when they preferred to stand firm.

Bargaining on Nontariff Trade Barriers   The first six tariff conferences dealt only with tariffs, but it had become evident by the late 1960s that nontariff measures (apart from quantitative restrictions) were a more serious menace to international trade than were tariffs. Accordingly, the seventh conference (the Tokyo Round) undertook for the first time multilateral negotiations on several nontariff barriers. The outcome of this most recent conference is described later in this chapter.

Elimination of Quantitative Restrictions   Until 1959 GATT made only slow progress toward the elimination of import restrictions (quotas). The majority of GATT members took advantage of the balance of payments exception to the general prohibition of import quotas. The restoration of currency convertibility by Western European countries at the end of 1958 broke this logjam. The major trading countries then abandoned quantitative import restrictions that were previously justified on grounds of a weak balance of payments or low monetary reserves. However, the success of GATT in persuading industrial countries to eliminate import quotas on manufactured products in the 1960s is now being undermined by the reintroduction of such quotas through bilateral agreements known as voluntary export restrictions.

Settlement of Disputes   One of the most striking, but least publicized, of GATT's accomplishments is the settlement of trade disputes between members. Historically trade disputes have been matters strictly between the disputants; there was no third party to which they might appeal for a just solution. As a consequence, trade disputes often went unresolved for years, all the while embittering international relations. When disputes were settled in the past, it was usually a case of the weaker country giving way to the stronger. GATT has improved matters tremendously by adopting complaint procedures and by affording through its periodic meetings a world stage on which an aggrieved nation could voice its complaint.

---

[7]The superior effectiveness of the multilateral approach of GATT to the bilateral approach of the 1930s is clearly observable in the experience of the United States. Between 1934 and 1945 this country negotiated trade agreements with 29 countries, but in a single GATT conference at Geneva in 1947 it completed negotiations with 22 other countries. The experience of the 1930s showed that the abandonment of protective import quotas through bilateral bargaining was virtually impossible.

A large number of disputes have been resolved by bilateral consultations without ever coming before the collective membership. The mere presence of GATT was probably helpful in these instances. Thus, the British government repealed a requirement forbidding the manufacture of cigarettes of pure Virginia tobacco when the United States protested the requirement as a violation of GATT.

When a dispute is not settled bilaterally, it may be taken by the complainant country to the collective membership at the next regular meeting on the basis that the treatment accorded to the commerce of the complainant country by the other disputant is impairing or nullifying benefits received under the agreement. A panel on complaints hears the disputants, deliberates, and drafts a report. The report is then acted upon by the membership. For example, in 1990, on a complaint lodged by Japan, a panel ruled that the European Community's imposition of antidumping duties on "screwdriver assembly" products (products produced *in* the Community by Japanese-owned firms using imported components and parts) was contrary to GATT provisions.[8]

In the event that the GATT recommendation is not observed, the aggrieved party may be authorized to suspend the application of certain of its obligations to the trade of the other party. For instance, in 1992 the United States requested authorization from the Council to retaliate against alleged trade damages of $80.7 caused by Canada's discrimination against imports of U.S. beer.[9]

In recent years, member countries have turned to GATT to help resolve an unprecedented number of serious trade disputes. For instance, the European Economic Community (EEC) filed a complaint in GATT against Japanese trade practices, and the United States filed petitions against European subsidies on agricultural exports. The United States also started GATT proceedings against Canada on the performance requirements imposed on American investing companies (particularly the compulsory sourcing of Canadian products), which is the first time any country has asked GATT to deal with the trade aspects of foreign investment regulations. The number and importance of these disputes poses the greatest challenge ever faced by GATT's settlement machinery. To meet this challenge, the GATT Council adopted in 1989 a streamlined settlement procedure to speed up the resolution of disputes.

Trade Policy Review   In 1989 GATT established a trade policy review mechanism (TPRM) to encourage its member countries to live up to their multilateral commitments by providing in open discussion at Council meetings a greater transparency in, and understanding of, their trade policies and practices.[10] Under TPRM, the Council regularly reviews the international trade regime of each member country, requiring a report by each country according to a format that

---

[8]See *Focus,* GATT Newsletter, no. 70, April 1990, p. 2.
[9]See *Focus,* GATT Newsletter, no. 91, July 1992, p. 2.
[10]*Transparency* is the technical term used by GATT for the clarity, openness, and comprehensibility of a country's individual international trade regulations.

includes its trade policies and measures, wider economic and development needs, and statistical information.[11] The four biggest trading countries (currently the European Community, the United States, Japan, and Canada) are reviewed every *two* years; the next sixteen biggest trading countries every *four* years; and other GATT members every *six* years.[12]

THE TOKYO ROUND
OF MULTILATERAL TRADE NEGOTIATIONS (MTNs)

The Tokyo Round formally opened in Tokyo in September 1973, but bargaining did not start in earnest until January 1975, with the passage of the U.S. Trade Act of 1974. After five and a half years of acrimonious debates and tedious bargaining sessions, the Tokyo Round ended in April 1979 with the initialing of a comprehensive international trade pact.

What did the Tokyo Round accomplish? We offer the following summary descriptions of its major results.

Industrial Tariffs

Preceding the Tokyo Round, the sixth tariff conference (known as the Kennedy Round) had cut duties on industrial goods an average of 35 percent on some $40 billion of trade in 60,000 products. As a consequence of this reduction and reductions made in earlier conferences, the average tariff rates of the industrial countries were already very low by historical standards.

The Tokyo Round cut duties on industrial products an average of 30 percent on trade that amounted to more than $155 billion in 1977 dollars. The average tariff (weighted by actual trade flows) on manufactured products of the nine major industrial countries declined from 7.0 percent to 4.7 percent. The tariff cuts and resulting new tariffs on manufactures for the United States, the EC, and Japan are shown in Table 8-2. These tariff reductions were gradually applied over the seven-year period 1980–1987.

In addition to these MFN tariff reductions, several countries (including the United States) reached a *sectoral* agreement on trade in civil aircraft that eliminated all customs duties on civil aircraft, aircraft parts, and repairs on civil aircraft, effective January 1, 1980.

Agricultural Trade

The United States is vitally interested in reducing barriers to trade in agricultural products. As the world's most efficient agricultural producer, this country wants

---

[11]*Focus,* GATT Newsletter, no. 64, August–September 1989, pp. 1 and 12.

[12]With respect to the biggest trading countries, the Council completed its first review of the trade regimes of Japan and Canada in Spring 1990 and of the European Community in April 1991. It completed the second review of the U.S. trade regime in March 1992. See *Focus,* GATT Newsletter, no. 74 (September 1990), no. 81 (May–June 1991), and no. 90 (May–June 1992).

Table 8-2 Average Tariff Rates on Manufactures for the United States, the European Economic Community, and Japan before and after Implementation of the Tokyo Round

Country/Country Group	*Tariffs on Total Imports of Finished and Semifinished Manufactures*		
	Pre-Tokyo	*Post-Tokyo*	*Percentage Change*
United States	7.0%	4.9%	30%
European Community	8.3	6.0	28
Japan	10.0	5.4	46

Note: These averages were calculated in two steps: First, a simple (unweighted) arithmetic average for each heading in the Brussels Tariff Nomenclature (BTN) was calculated; second, these averages were weighted according to the imports of the United States, the EC, and eight other industrial countries to get a total weighted average. This method is superior to an unweighted average or an average weighted by the imports of the country in question. See the discussion of effective versus nominal tariff rates in Chapter 6 for an explanation of tariff rate measurement.

Source: The World Bank, *World Development Report, 1987* (New York: Oxford University Press, 1987), Table 8.1, p. 136.

freer access to EC and Japanese markets. In opposition to this U.S. interest, the EC insists on the maintenance of its highly protectionist agricultural policy, which is viewed as an integral part of the Common Market.[13] At the same time, Japan strongly resists pressures to moderate protection of its high-cost farmers, who possess substantial political strength. Not surprisingly, then, the most contentious differences between the United States and these two parties in the Tokyo Round were in agricultural trade. At one point, for instance, the Japanese refusal to liberalize its import quotas on oranges threatened to halt negotiations.[14]

In the face of these deep-seated differences, the Tokyo Round made little progress toward cutting barriers on agricultural trade, as was also true of the earlier Kennedy Round.[15] Pervasive regulation, protection, and subsidies continue to distort international trade in temperate agricultural products.

Nontariff Trade Barriers

The distinctive hallmark of the Tokyo Round was a series of agreements on nontariff trade barriers (NTBs). Earlier GATT conferences had paid little atten-

---

[13]See Chapter 10.

[14]"Japan's Tough Restrictions on Imported Oranges Endanger Settlement of U.S. Trade Agreements," *The Wall Street Journal,* November 1, 1978, p. 48.

[15]Early in the conference, the industrial countries offered concessions on tropical agricultural products, important to many developing countries.

tion to such restrictions. In preparation for the Tokyo Round, the GATT secretariat compiled a list of more than eight hundred specific nontariff distortions of international trade. These were grouped into five broad categories: (1) government participation in trade (export subsidies, procurement, countervailing duties, etc.), (2) customs and administrative entry procedures (classification, valuation, customs formalities, etc.), (3) standards and packaging regulations, (4) specific limitations on trade (quotas, export restraints, licensing, etc.), and (5) charges on imports (prior deposits, variable levies, etc.).

The Tokyo Round negotiated codes covering the first three categories, but it failed to reach agreement on the last two, with the exception of licensing. It also established standing committees to administer the individual codes that contain provisions for consultation and dispute settlement.

Subsidies and Countervailing Duty Code   American firms frequently complain that foreign firms benefit from government assistance that allows them to sell their products in the United States at "unfairly" low prices and to displace American products in third-country markets. This code is intended to ensure that the subsidies used by member countries do not injure the interests of another member country. It prohibits outright *export* subsidies for manufactures and primary mineral products, but for agricultural products subsidies are prohibited only when they displace the exports of other members or undercut prices in a particular market. Criteria are to be set up to determine injury resulting from *domestic* subsidies, and upon a showing of injury, countries would be allowed to take countervailing duty action to offset subsidies.

Technical Barriers to Trade (Standards) Code   This code seeks to ensure that product standards, product testing, and product certification systems that are adopted for reasons of safety, health, environmental protection, or other purposes do not create obstacles to trade. The code encourages the use of open procedures in the adoption of standards and the negotiation of international standards.

Government Procurement Code   This code is designed to inhibit discrimination against foreign goods at all stages of government procurement so as to encourage more international competition. It prescribes specific rules on drafting the specifications of goods to be procured, advertising prospective purchases, the time allowed for the submission of bids, the qualifications of suppliers, the opening and evaluation of bids, the award of contracts, and the hearing and review of protests.

The code applies to individual government contracts to purchase physical goods worth more than SDR 150,000. Services are not covered by the code except those incidental to the purchase of physical goods. Also, the code does not apply to the purchase of goods involving national security or agricultural support programs.

Customs Valuation Code   The method of valuation used by a country for imported goods can be as important as the rate of duty in determining the amount of duty. The code commits countries to base customs valuation on the actual price paid for a product, that is, its *invoice* value. Only when the invoice value of a product cannot be ascertained does the code allow countries to use other valuation bases in a manner stipulated by the code.

Import Licensing Code   Complicated procedures and bureaucratic red tape in the administration of import licenses can thwart or delay imports. Under this code, countries are obligated to simplify their import-licensing systems and apply them in a nondiscriminatory manner. Importers have to go to only one administrative body to secure licenses, and a license may not be refused for minor errors in documentation or minor variations in the value, quantity, or weight of a product under license.

Revised Antidumping Code   In addition to these five new codes, the Tokyo Round also revised the GATT Antidumping Code that had been in force for over 10 years. The revised code alters certain provisions to bring them into conformity with the code provisions on subsidies and countervailing duties. Both dumping (the action of a firm) and subsidies (the action of a government) can distort international competition in much the same way and may, in fact, occur together. The revised code redefines the determination of the cause and effects of dumping, clarifies the criterion of injury, and strengthens investigation procedures.

Safeguards Code   An outstanding failure of the Tokyo Round was the inability of negotiators to agree on a safeguards code. *Safeguards* are temporary emergency actions, such as higher duties, quotas, and voluntary export restrictions, intended to protect industries suddenly threatened by a large increase in imports. Agreement on a safeguards code is vital to the maintenance of open international markets because governments are strongly inclined to pacify protectionist interest groups with safeguards unwarranted by objective circumstances and to make them a permanent form of protection. Intense protectionist pressures in the industrial countries hardened their negotiating positions in the Tokyo Round, preventing any agreement.

Concluding Observations on the Tokyo Round

The Tokyo Round was a holding action against growing forces of protection that threaten to undermine the international trading system. But it was not a victory over those forces. Indeed, trade disputes and protectionist measures have multiplied since the end of the Tokyo Round.

The major achievement of the Tokyo Round was the negotiation of codes on nontariff trade barriers that for the first time subjected them to international agreement. Its signal failures were the inability to agree on a safeguards code and to lower significantly the heavy restrictions on trade in agricultural products. Although positive, the reduction of duties on industrial products will have only a marginal effect on trade, because such duties were already low.

THE EROSION OF GATT

As members of GATT, the United States and other industrial countries are committed to observe the principle of nondiscrimination (unconditional MFN treatment) in their trade policies. This means that a member country's tariffs and nontariff trade barriers are to be applied equally to all other member countries. In sum, no member country is to give a special trading advantage to another member country. The industrial countries are also committed to abstain from quantitative restrictions on imports.

Under the present GATT safeguards or escape clause (Article XIX), a member country can withdraw or modify concessions previously granted to other members if it can demonstrate that imports of a certain product have increased to such an extent as to cause or threaten to cause serious injury to domestic producers. Furthermore, a country needs to apply safeguards in a nondiscriminatory fashion and to consult with the supplying countries. If those consultations do not lead to an agreement, then the supplying countries can withdraw "equivalent" concessions previously granted to the safeguards country.

Article XIX has not worked well in recent years. Starting in the 1970s, industrial countries have increasingly circumvented it by negotiating *bilateral* agreements with particular exporting countries to allocate market shares in specific sectors, such as textiles, steel, and semiconductors. Usually these agreements take the form of *voluntary export restrictions* (VERs), whereby the first party, an exporting country, agrees to limit quantitatively its exports of specific products to the second party, an importing country. VERs enable the importing country to discriminate among supplying countries with no offsetting concessions. A supplying country agrees to limit its exports because it faces the threat of more restrictive measures by the importing country. The United States and the EC have negotiated VERs with Japan, South Korea, Hong Kong, and other countries that cover television sets, automobiles, footwear, ships, leather, steel, semiconductors, and other sectors.[16]

Bilateral agreements are *selective,* applying to a single exporting country (or country group in the case of the EC). They are, therefore, a clear violation of the principle of nondiscrimination. Because such agreements commonly use quotas (whether applied by the exporting or importing country), they also violate GATT's prohibition against quantitative restrictions. And, of course, they do not satisfy the safeguards criteria laid down in Article XIX.

Why have industrial countries applied import restrictions outside GATT? One reason that governments prefer bilateral agreements is that they appear less protectionist to consumers than import restrictions applied to *all* exporting countries. Also, the importing country can pretend that it supports free trade because the restrictions are imposed "voluntarily" by the exporting country. However, their main advantage is *selectivity.* By applying restrictions to imports of a product sector from a single country under a negotiated arrangement, bilateral agreements avoid

---

[16]VERs and other bilateral restrictive agreements used by the United States are discussed in the section on the new protectionism in Chapter 9.

giving other exporting countries the right to demand compensation or to retaliate under the dispute settlement provisions of GATT.

Clearly, a new safeguards agreement is needed to bring some order into a situation that is becoming anarchic. Without a new safeguards code, the industrial countries will continue to circumvent GATT with bilateral agreements that transform more and more of the international economy into *managed* trade, which is more responsive to political than to economic forces. A new code will have to allow selective restrictions. Otherwise, it will be ignored as Article XIX is today. The issues to be negotiated, therefore, are the rules, criteria, and surveillance arrangements that would govern selective safeguards. The failure to negotiate a new code in the Tokyo Round was a major setback for supporters of an open, multilateral trading system. In particular, it was a blow to the developing countries, whose exports of standard manufactured products, such as textiles, shoes, and steel, are frequently blocked by new import restrictions of the industrial countries.

Member countries have also weakened GATT by exploiting its provisions on antidumping and countervailing duties. Article VI permits countries to impose such duties in the event of unfair pricing and injury to producers in the importing country. But GATT has allowed a loose interpretation of Article VI. Dumping is now conceived as pricing imports at less than "full cost," which can be determined arbitrarily by trade officials, as is also true of actual or prospective injury to domestic producers. Consequently, countries have found it easy to justify import restrictions as antidumping or countervailing duties imposed in retaliation for unfair pricing or subsidization of the imports in question.

The reliance of the three major trading entities on nontariff trade barriers is shown in Table 8-3. Trade coverage ratios indicate that about one-quarter of their

Table 8-3   Trade Coverage of Nontariff Trade Barriers for the United States, the European Community, and Japan, 1986–1989 (Percentage)

Importer	1989	1986–1989 Change
United States	29.1	5.5
European Community[1]	22.5	− 0.2
Japan	23.6	− 0.1

Note: The trade coverage ratio measures the share of total imports by value subject to NTBs. This ratio does not indicate the restrictiveness of the NTBs. (A quantitative analysis of the *economic effects* of NTBs would require calculation of *ad valorem* equivalents for individual NTBs, import demand/supply elasticity estimates, and other information difficult to obtain.) The incidence of NTBs was evaluated using a constant 1986 import value; hence, changes over the 1986–1989 period are changes in NTB use only. This table includes trade in manufactures and agricultural products, but excludes petroleum and service trade.

[1]Excludes Spain and Portugal.

Source: Don P. Clark, "Recent Changes in Non-Tariff Measure Use by Industrial Countries," *The International Trade Journal,* Spring 1992, Table II, p. 317.

imports is restricted in some degree by NTBs. The ratios for the European Community and Japan show modest net declines over the period 1986–1989, but the ratio for the United States over that period rose by 5.5 percentage points, an increase of almost one-fourth over the 1986 level. Antidumping and countervailing-duty actions by the United States and, to a lesser extent, the EC were mainly responsible for the overall increase in NTBs.[17]

Table 8-4 provides more information on the use of antidumping and countervailing-duty restrictions by the United States and the European Community in the 1980s. The two trading entities were far more active than in previous years in using antidumping investigations to prosecute "unfair" trade. The United States also undertook far more investigations of alleged subsidization of imported products. Although not shown in Table 8-4, Canada and Australia also made intensive use of antidumping investigations in the 1980s, as did Brazil, Korea, Mexico, and several other developing countries.

Over the period 1980–1986, over half (195) of the U.S. antidumping investigations led to the imposition of a duty or other restriction, while in the EC three-fourths (213) did so. About two-thirds of the U.S. CVD investigations and nearly all the EC investigations ended in a restrictive action.[18]

Table 8-4   Antidumping (AD) and Countervailing-Duty (CVD) Investigations in the United States and the European Community, 1980–1988

	United States		European Community	
	AD	CVD	AD	CVD
1980	24	11	26	0
1981	15	22	47	1
1982	63	145	55	4
1983	47	22	43	3
1984	73	52	42	1
1985	65	38	35	0
1986	70	26	31	0
1987	14	5	34	2
1988	40	3	40	0
All years	411	324	353	11

Source: Derived from Richard Boltuck and Robert E. Litan, eds., Down in the Dumps (Washington, D.C.: The Brookings Institution), Table 1–4, p. 5.

---

[17]Don P. Clark, "Recent Changes in Non-Tariff Measure Use by Industrial Nations," The International Trade Journal, Spring 1992, p. 321.

[18]J. Michael Finger and Andrzej Olechowski, The Uruguay Round: A Handbook for Multilateral Trade Negotiations (Washington, D.C.: The World Bank, 1987), Tables A 8.1, pp. 258–59 and A 8.3, pp. 264–65.

The popularity of AD and CVD measures is attributable to their selectivity (focused on individual countries), flexibility, and GATT sanction.[19] Also, ordinary tariffs cannot be changed easily because they are bound by multilateral agreements. This intensive use of Article VI, which was never intended by the founders of GATT, is a gross violation of the spirit of GATT. One trade expert concludes: "Antidumping puts the fox in charge of the hen house: trade restrictions certified by GATT. . . . Antidumping is ordinary protection with a grand public relations record."[20]

The proliferation of NTBs may be viewed as a decline in trade policy liberalization. Table 8-5 measures the degree of trade liberalization by the *difference* between the growth rate of the world's export volume and the growth rate of its output volume. The rationale for this measure is that more liberalization will raise the growth rate of trade relative to that of production (output), and conversely. Table 8-5 reveals that this difference has steadily declined for manufactures over the period 1960–1988, and it has declined for agriculture in the 1980s.

This relative decline in the growth rate of international trade has also constrained the growth rate of output. A World Bank study estimates that the elimination of all tariffs and NTBs would add 2 percent to world gross domestic product.[21] This is *not* a small amount: 2 percent of world GDP in 1990 was $443 *billion.*

Table 8-5 Index of World Trade Policy Liberalization, 1960–1988 (Percent per Year)

	1960–1969	*1970–1979*	*1980–1988*
Manufactures			
Export volume growth	10.5	7.0	5.0
Output volume growth	7.5	4.5	3.5
Difference	3.0	2.5	1.5
Agriculture			
Export volume growth	4.0	4.5	2.0
Output volume growth	2.5	2.0	2.0
Difference	1.5	2.5	0.0

Source: GATT, *International Trade 1987/88* (Geneva: 1988), vol. 1, Table 1, and *International Trade 1988/89* (Geneva: 1989), vol. 1, Table 2.

---

[19]Between 1979 and 1988, antidumping procedures accounted for 77 percent of all trade actions monitored by GATT and CVD actions for 18 percent, or a total of 95 percent. See "Nothing to Lose But Its Chains," *The Economist,* September 22, 1990, p. 11.

[20]J. Michael Finger, "Dumping and Antidumping: The Rhetoric and the Reality of Protection in Industrial Countries," *The World Bank Research Observer,* July 1992, p. 141.

[21]Christian E. Petersen, "Trade Conflict and Resolution Methodologies," *The American Economic Review,* May 1992, p. 62.

THE URUGUAY ROUND
OF NEW MULTILATERAL TRADE NEGOTIATIONS
(MTNs)

A *declaration* adopted in September 1986 at Punta del Este, Uruguay, by GATT's member countries launched the Uruguay Round of trade negotiations.[22] The declaration was a victory for the United States, which had pressed hard for new trade talks that it hoped would stem the tide of protection both at home and abroad. Without a doubt, the Uruguay Round is the most ambitious and complex set of negotiations ever undertaken by GATT.

The *Trade Negotiations Committee* (TNC) oversees the conduct of the Uruguay Round. To carry out the negotiations, two groups were established: (1) the *Group on Negotiations on Goods* (GNG), whose purpose is to negotiate traditional trade issues and new issues relating to investment and intellectual property, and (2) the *Group on Negotiations on Services* (GNS), whose purpose is to negotiate trade in services. A third group, the *Surveillance Body on Standstill and Rollback,* was established at the insistence of the developing countries to get the industrial countries to dismantle existing trade restrictions inconsistent with GATT (rollback) and to avoid adopting new inconsistent restrictions (standstill). The complexity of the Uruguay Round is depicted in Figure 8-1.

Trade in Services

With modest exceptions, the GATT articles cover only merchandise trade. And yet the most dynamic segment of international trade in recent years has been trade in services. Clearly, it is time to bring the international trade in services under the same GATT regime as trade in merchandise.

The declaration of the Uruguay Round states that the aim of negotiations on trade in services is to establish a multilateral framework of principles and rules to achieve the progressive liberalization and expansion of such trade. This will not be easy to accomplish.

Three major issues need to be resolved in negotiations on services: (1) What *are* international service transactions? Services include financial services (such as banking, insurance, and accounting), professional services (such as legal, educational, and medical), business services (such as advertising, consulting, and design), communications, transportation, construction, retail and wholesale trade, and tourism. (2) Having decided on services to be covered in negotiations, what are the volume and direction of trade in those services, given the paucity of data that are comparable across countries? (3) What are the specific barriers to trade in services, for example, government procurement of services that favors domestic suppliers, outright exclusion of foreign service companies, and discriminatory restraints on the activities of foreign-owned service establishments (such as limit-

---

[22]GATT, "Launching of Uruguay Round," *Focus,* GATT Newsletter, October 1986, pp. 1 ff.

Figure 8-1 Structure of Uruguay Negotiations.

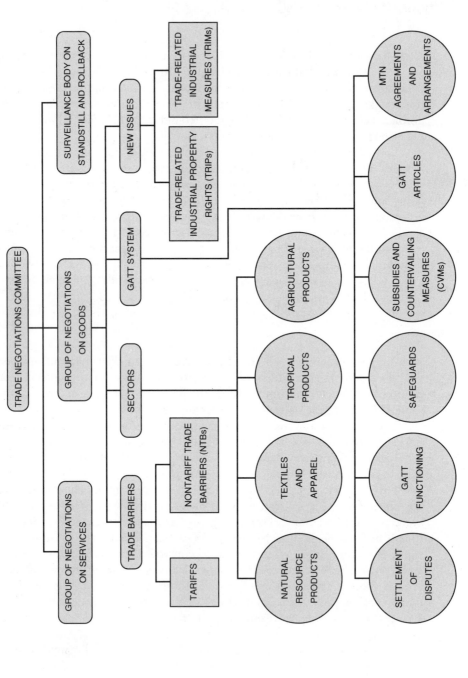

Source: Derived from Twentieth Century Fund, *The Free Trade Debate* (New York: Priority Press Publications, 1989), Figure 3.1, p. 183.

ing foreign insurance companies to the sale of certain policies or requiring foreign data-processing firms to process data locally).

The key challenge facing the GNS is to reach agreement on which government policies toward international trade in services are legitimate and which are illegitimate. There is no GATT experience to guide the group, and many policies on services are regarded by governments as domestic rather than international matters. The United States, the initiator of the service negotiations, believes that it has a comparative advantage in services that is all too often frustrated by barriers obstructing the sale of U.S. services in foreign countries. In contrast, several developing countries (notably Brazil and India) oppose the idea of service negotiations because they believe that restrictions are necessary to promote indigenous service firms.

It is evident that negotiations on services are moving in uncharted waters. Whether the negotiators can agree on a code (or codes) containing provisions for multilateral surveillance, complaint procedures, and dispute settlement remains to be seen. But at the very least, restrictions on the international trade in services are now recognized as a legitimate subject of GATT negotiations.

Trade in Goods

Fourteen *negotiation groups* have been set up under the GNG for the following subjects: tariffs, nontariff measures, tropical products, natural resource-based products, textiles and clothing, agriculture, GATT articles, safeguards, MFN agreements and arrangements, subsidies and countervailing measures, dispute settlement, trade-related industrial property rights (TRIPs), trade-related investment measures (TRIMs), and the functioning of the GATT system. We offer here comments on some of these subjects to indicate the scope of negotiation issues.

In general, the level of tariff protection of the industrial countries is now so low as to have only minor significance. However, there remain two issues on which tariff negotiations might be fruitful: (1) Tariffs are higher for manufactures than for primary products, and (2) tariff protection in the developing countries remains very restrictive.

Tariff escalation occurs when duties increase as the degree of processing of a product increases (as a result, the finished product pays a higher duty than the previous semifinished product, which in turn pays a higher duty than the primary, commodity form of the product). The elimination of tariff escalation is of special importance to the developing countries as they try to convert their commodity exports into exports of manufactures. These countries will be the main beneficiaries of negotiations on tropical and natural resource-based products.

Tariffs are not only high in the developing countries but also much less *bound* than tariffs in the industrial countries. Consequently, the developing countries can raise tariffs at will without negotiating with other GATT members for grants of compensation under Article XXVIII. This special treatment is granted developing countries by Chapter IV of GATT. But what treatment should developing countries be given in tariff negotiations in the Uruguay Round? Should the advanced developing countries, such as Brazil and South Korea, be "graduated" to assume the same obligations in tariffs (and other trade measures) as the industrial countries?

Trade negotiations are also aimed at reducing or eliminating nontariff trade barriers. To advance that purpose, negotiators will try to improve, clarify, or expand agreements reached in the Tokyo Round. For instance, the United States believes that the subsidies and countervailing duty code badly needs strengthening in three areas. In particular, there needs to be (1) a definition of subsidies that are *potentially* injurious to the interests of trading countries, whether such subsidies are granted to exporters or to domestic firms; (2) an agreement on criteria to be used to determine the "material injury" that is required to justify remedial action (notably countervailing duties) by the injured country; and (3) the design of procedures and remedies that would redress injury but not overcompensate for it. Negotiations on subsidies are impeded by different attitudes toward them. Some countries believe that *all* subsidies distort international trade and deserve retaliation regardless of material injury, whereas other countries believe that retaliation is justified only when there is indisputable, substantial injury.

Several *negotiating groups* are intended to strengthen the performance of GATT. The *Functioning of the GATT System Group* (FOGS) aims to enhance the surveillance by GATT of the trade policies and practices of member countries, improve decision-making, and strengthen GATT's relations with other international organizations, such as the IMF and the World Bank, so as to increase its contribution to global economic policymaking. The *GATT Articles Group* is reviewing existing GATT articles, provisions, and rules ("disciplines") as requested by member countries. Two sets of negotiations of particular importance are handled by the *Dispute Settlement Group* and the *Safeguards Group*.

It is widely agreed that prompt and effective settlement of trade disputes between member countries is essential to the GATT system. It is also widely agreed that dispute settlement needs to be improved by speeding up the settlement procedure and by strengthening the implementation of recommendations made by GATT panels. The United States is particularly unhappy with the present settlement provisions. For instance, in 1981 American pasta producers complained that European exporters of pasta were being subsidized by the EC in violation of GATT rules. It took two years to get a GATT panel ruling, which found in favor of the United States. The EC then refused to adopt the panel ruling (as it was entitled to do under the current GATT dispute provision), and it negotiated on and off with the United States over the next four years before the dispute was settled on terms less favorable to the United States than the panel recommendation.

The failure to negotiate a safeguards code is the most important unfinished business of the Tokyo Round. We have already discussed the main safeguard issues. The declaration on the Uruguay Round states that the agreement on safeguards shall be based on the GATT principles and, among other features, shall contain the following: transparency (that is, safeguards are public knowledge), objective criteria for action (including the concept of serious injury), temporariness of safeguard restrictions, structural adjustment, compensation and retaliation, multilateral surveillance and dispute settlement, and application to all member countries.[23] The outcome of safeguard negotiations in the Uruguay Round will determine the ability of GATT to bring under its authority the trade restrictions (particularly, bilateral market-sharing agreements) that have escaped its jurisdiction in recent years. Failure to negotiate an effective safeguards code will intensify the erosion of GATT, making it an agreement honored mainly in the breach.

Trade-related aspects of industrial property rights, and trade-related investment measures, are subjects that have never been negotiated in past GATT conferences. *Industrial property rights* refer to patents, trademarks, and copyrights that provide the owner with the right to exclusive use of the property in question (technology, products, printed materials). Industrial property rights are granted to individuals and business firms by national governments for designated periods of time. Their purpose is to encourage invention, discovery, and innovation. Negotiation issues include the adequacy of existing protection afforded industrial property rights; the enforcement of those rights by national governments, including action against counterfeit goods; and the abuse of industrial property rights to restrain legitimate trade.

Trade-related investment measures refer to restrictions imposed by host governments on the operations of subsidiaries owned by foreign firms when the restrictions have an impact on international trade. Such restrictions, which include local-content requirements and export requirements, are taken up in Chapter 24 in the discussion on host country policies toward multinational companies. The United States wants to bring trade-related investment measures under the same GATT regime that covers nontariff trade restrictions.

Trade in Agriculture

Negotiations in the Uruguay Round were due to end in December 1990, but this and successive deadlines have been thwarted by a bitter dispute between the United States and the European Community (EC) on agricultural subsidies. Previous GATT Rounds have failed to liberalize trade in temperate agricultural products, which remains greatly distorted by farm programs in the industrial countries.

The agricultural policies of the OECD countries cause annual transfers from consumers and taxpayers to farmers amounting to over $300 billion.[24] Import barriers prevent consumers from obtaining lower-priced agricultural products from foreign countries while, at the same time, they pay taxes to finance export subsidies (that get rid of excess production caused by high support prices) as well as other payments to farmers, such as low-cost credit. These policies markedly warp international trade in agricultural products, hurting low-cost producing countries.

---

[23]GATT, "Launching of Uruguay Round," p. 4.
[24]This estimate for 1990 appears in, "The Resistance to Agricultural Reform," *The OECD Observer*, August–September 1991, p. 5.

Table 8-6 shows the assistance to agriculture of individual OECD countries as measured by producer subsidy equivalents (PSEs). Looking first at 1990, we see that Australia and New Zealand have the lowest degrees of support, amounting to 5 percent and 11 percent respectively of their agricultural output. The only other country whose PSE is substantially below the OECD average of 44 percent is the United States. All other OECD countries have PSEs about the same as or higher than the OECD average. The European Community spends the most on agricultural support, amounting to $81.62 billion in 1990 or 48 percent of EC agricultural output.

A comparison of PSEs in 1990 with the average PSEs over the 1979–1986 period reveals a sharp jump: For the OECD as a whole, PSEs rose from $107.38 billion to $175.54 billion, and as a percentage of output from 37 to 44. Only Australia and New Zealand *reduced* percentage PSEs over the period, but the U.S. increase was modest, rising from 28 to 30 percent. In contrast, the EC percentage rose from 37 to 48.

Table 8-6   Producer Subsidy Equivalents (PSEs) of Agricultural Assistance by OECD Countries

	Billions of U.S. Dollars		*PSE as a Percentage of Agricultural Output*	
	1979–1986	*1990*	*1979–1986*	*1990*
Australia	1.07	1.30	12	11
Austria	1.07	2.37	32	46
Canada	4.19	6.46	32	41
European Community	39.87	81.62	37	48
Finland	2.25	5.32	58	72
Japan	21.56	30.86	66	68
New Zealand	0.74	0.17	25	5
Norway	1.71	3.13	72	77
Sweden	1.64	3.38	44	59
Switzerland	2.62	5.00	68	78
United States	30.66	35.93	28	30
OECD	*107.38*	*175.54*	*37*	*44*

Note: The *producer subsidy equivalent* (also called *public subsidy equivalent*) is a common measure of public support to agriculture that includes all programs and restrictions. The OECD also includes Turkey. The members of the European Community are Belgium, Denmark, France, Germany, Greece, Ireland, Italy, Luxembourg, Netherlands, Portugal, Spain, and the United Kingdom.

Source: Based on table in Gerard Viatte and Carmel Cahill, "The Resistance to Agricultural Reform," *The OECD Observer,* August–September 1991, p. 5.

The United States has demanded a drastic reform of the EC's common agricultural policy (CAP) with cuts of 70 percent in subsidies.[25] The Community, led by France, has rejected the U.S. position, offering instead a cut of 30 percent. Because of subsidies, the EC share of the world wheat market rose from 16 to 21 percent in the 1980s, while the U.S. share fell from 46 to 31 percent. In 1992 French grain growers sold wheat at a price of $163 a ton to dealers in France who then received an export subsidy to enable them to meet the world price of $99 a ton.[26] The United States also sets a target price for grain, and then pays an export subsidy to market it at the world price. But the U.S. program (unlike CAP) makes farmers take some land out of production in return for subsidies that are also limited in amount. The failure of the United States and the EC to resolve the subsidy dispute after six years of negotiation now threatens the success of the entire Uruguay Round.[27]

Concluding Observations on the Uruguay Round

The agricultural dispute has cast a pall over negotiations on other trade issues. Time is running out for the completion of the Uruguay Round. In the United States, the "fast-track" authority of the president (under which Congress must ratify or reject a Uruguay agreement as a whole without amendments) expires in mid-1993. After that time, fast-track authority would require a new trade act that could turn toward protection rather than freer trade.

It would be foolish for the United States and the EC to wreck the Uruguay Round. One study estimates that a "radical" outcome of the Round, including cuts of 70 percent in agriculture and 20 percent in the protection of services, would create annual gains of $262 billion. But such an outcome is not possible, as six years of negotiations have shown. Instead, a compromise deal that is possible (a 30 percent cut in agricultural support with modest progress in service and textiles trade) would create annual gains of $119 billion in which all countries would share.[28] This compromise outcome would give the United States cuts in EC farm subsidies, protection of intellectual property, and some liberalization of trade in services. Ultimately, only if the United States "cuts off its nose to spite its face" will the Uruguay Round end in failure and recriminations. Although it can no longer dominate international trade talks, the United States remains the only country able to lead the world toward a more open economy through the power of its own trade policy. It is from this perspective that we turn in the next chapter to an examination of U.S. trade policy and the powerful forces that threaten to undermine it.

---

[25]The common agricultural policy is discussed in Chapter 10.
[26]"Seven Nations Unable to Agree on Trade but See Progress, *The New York Times,* July 9, 1992, p. 1.
[27]Complicating the U.S.-EC dispute is Japan's refusal to allow any rice imports.
[28]"Poor Odds, High Stakes," *The Economist,* June 27, 1992, pp. 77–78.

SUMMARY

1. Since World War II, the trade policies of the United States and other industrial nations have been conducted within the framework laid down by the General Agreement on Tariffs and Trade (GATT).

2. GATT comprises four basic elements: (1) the rule of nondiscrimination in trade relations between the participating countries, (2) commitments to observe negotiated tariff concessions, (3) prohibitions against the use of quantitative restrictions on exports and imports, and (4) special provisions to promote the trade of developing countries.

3. The principal activities of GATT are tariff bargaining, bargaining on nontariff trade barriers, elimination of quantitative restrictions, settlement of disputes, and trade policy review.

4. The distinctive hallmark of the Tokyo Round was a series of agreements on nontariff trade barriers: subsidies and countervailing duties, standards, government procurement, customs valuations, and import licensing. The Tokyo Round also revised the antidumping code but failed to agree on a safeguards code.

5. The influence of GATT has eroded since the 1970s as the industrial countries have negotiated bilateral agreements (notably voluntary export restrictions [VERs]) outside the framework of GATT's safeguards provision (Article XIX), and have exploited GATT's provisions on antidumping and countervailing duties (Article VI). By the end of the 1980s, about one-quarter of the imports of all three major trading parties — the United States, the European Community, and Japan — was covered by nontariff trade barriers (NTBs).

6. A declaration adopted in September 1986 at Punta del Este, Uruguay, by GATT's member countries launched the Uruguay Round of trade negotiations. To carry out negotiations, two groups were established: (1) the *Group on Negotiations on Goods* (GNG), whose purpose is to negotiate traditional trade issues and new issues relating to investment and intellectual property, and (2) the *Group on Negotiations on Services* (GNS), whose purpose is to negotiate trade in services. A third group, *Surveillance Body on Standstill and Rollback,* was established to abolish existing restrictions (rollback) and to avoid adopting new ones (standstill) that are inconsistent with GATT.

7. Fourteen *negotiation groups* were set up under GNG covering the following subjects: tariffs, nontariff measures, tropical products, natural resource-based products, textiles and clothing, agriculture, GATT articles, safeguards, most-favored-nation (MFN) agreements and arrangements, subsidies and countervailing measures, dispute settlement, industrial property rights, trade-related investment measures, and the functioning of the GATT system.

8. The outcome of safeguard negotiations will determine the ability of GATT to bring under its authority the trade restrictions (particularly, bilateral market-sharing agreements) that have escaped its jurisdiction in recent years. Failure

to negotiate an effective safeguards code will intensify the erosion of GATT, making it an agreement honored mainly in the breach.

9. Trade-related aspects of industrial property rights (TRIPs) and trade-related investment measures (TRIMs) have never been negotiated in past GATT conferences.

10. The declaration of the Uruguay Round states that the aim of negotiations on trade in services is to establish a multilateral framework of principles and rules to achieve the progressive liberalization and expansion of such trade. This will not be easy to accomplish.

11. The failure of the United States and the European Community, after six years of negotiation, to resolve a bitter dispute on agricultural subsidies threatens the success of the entire Uruguay Round. The agricultural support policies of the OECD countries badly distort trade; annual transfers in those countries from consumers and taxpayers to farmers amount to over $300 billion.

12. The Uruguay Round will determine whether the trend toward managed international trade or the principles of comparative advantage and free trade will prevail in the next century.

13. Although it can no longer dominate trade talks, the United States remains the only country able to lead the world toward a more open economy through the power of its own trade policy.

QUESTIONS AND APPLICATIONS

1. What are the major provisions of GATT? Describe the mechanism for tariff negotiations under GATT.

2. What is the most-favored-nation principle? What is its purpose in international trade policy?

3. (a) What were the aims of the Tokyo Round?
   (b) What did the United States hope to get in the Tokyo Round?
   (c) What were the key negotiating issues in the Tokyo Round?
   (d) What were the actual results of the Tokyo Round?

4. Why has Article XIX of GATT not worked well in recent years?

5. (a) What is a voluntary export restriction (VER)?
   (b) In what ways does a VER violate the basic principles of GATT?

6. Design an international safeguards code. Be prepared to defend the specific provisions in it.

7. (a) What are antidumping (AD) and countervailing duties (CVDs)?
   (b) How have member countries been able to exploit Article VI to keep out imports?
   (c) Why have AD and CVD measures become so popular in the United States and the European Community?

8. Why are negotiations on service trade in the Uruguay Round more difficult than negotiations on merchandise trade?

9. (a) What is tariff escalation?

   (b) Why is tariff escalation important to developing countries?

10. "Some countries believe that *all* subsidies distort international trade and deserve retaliation regardless of material injury, whereas other countries believe that retaliation is justified only when there is indisputable, substantial injury." Discuss the merits of each position.

11. What are TRIPs? TRIMs?

12. Undertake your own study to answer the following question: What is the present status of the Uruguay Round?

13. On the basis of your own research, evaluate the role of GATT today.

SELECTED READINGS

Bhagwati, Jagdish. *The World Trading System at Risk*. Princeton, N.J.: Princeton University Press, 1991.

Finger, J. Michael. "Dumping and Antidumping: The Rhetoric and the Reality of Protection in Industrial Countries." *The World Bank Research Observer,* July 1992, pp. 121–144.

General Agreement on Tariffs and Trade. *Activities in [year]*. Geneva: General Agreement on Tariffs and Trade. Annual.

General Agreement on Tariffs and Trade. *Focus*. Monthly.

General Agreement on Tariffs and Trade. *What It Is, What It Does*. Geneva: General Agreement on Tariffs and Trade. Current edition.

Jackson, John. *Restructuring the GATT System*. New York: Council on Foreign Relations Press, 1990.

Schott, Jeffrey J. *The Global Trade Negotiations: What Can be Achieved?* Washington, D.C.: Institute for International Economics, September 1990.

Twentieth Century Fund. *The Free Trade Debate*. Task Force on the Future of American Trade Policy. New York: Priority Press Publications, 1989.

chapter 9

U.S. TRADE POLICY IN AN ERA
OF GLOBAL COMPETITION

Today, the United States faces formidable challenges in international trade and global competition. To cope with these challenges, this country needs to design a trade policy that will effectively promote its interests in an international economy that is undergoing deep-seated structural shifts.

Economic and technological forces are causing—and are almost certain to continue to cause—a migration of traditional industries, such as textiles and steel, from the industrial countries of the North to the developing countries of the South.[1] In particular, the closing of technology gaps, easier access to capital, and a supply of low-cost productive labor are transforming the economies of certain developing countries—the so-called newly industrializing countries (NICs)—as they actively compete in world markets with consumer electronics, light aircraft, automobiles, and other mature products. Undoubtedly, more NICs will appear in world markets in the next decade.[2] At the same time, economic and technological forces are causing a reallocation of resources in the North from capital-intensive traditional industries to knowledge-intensive or service-intensive emerging industries. In terms of trade theory, these changes represent systemic shifts in comparative advantage between the North and the South. In sum, economic and technological forces are fundamentally reshaping the world economy. In this new economy, the United States is no longer the dominant economic power it was in the three decades following World War II. Rather, it has become a "first among equals," a country that can lead through example but not dominate other countries.

Apart from shifts in comparative advantage between the North and South, the dependence of the United States and other industrial countries on international

---

[1]The world's countries are commonly classified into three groups: South, East, and North. The *South* designates the nonindustrial countries of Asia, Africa, the Middle East, and Latin America. The *East* mainly designates the Soviet Union, China, and East European countries that are now in transition from centrally planned to market economies. The *North* designates the industrial countries that belong to the Organization of Economic Cooperation and Development (OECD), mainly North American and Western European countries and Japan.

[2]Current NICs include Brazil, Hong Kong, India, Mexico, Taiwan, Singapore, and South Korea.

Figure 9-1

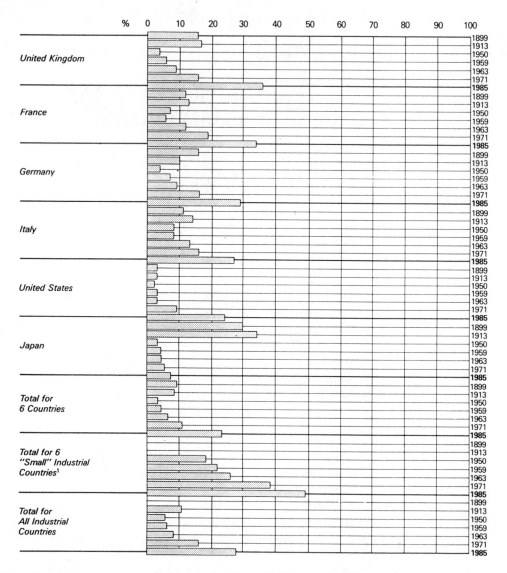

[1]Australia, Belgium-Luxembourg, Canada, Netherlands, Norway, and Sweden.

Source: The OECD Observer, no. 149, December 1987/January 1988, p. 16.

Import Content of Supplies of Finished Manufactures in the Industrial Countries, 1899–1985. The extraordinary growth of international economic interdependence over the period 1971–1985 is demonstrated by the leap in imports of finished manufactures as a percentage of total supplies of manufactures in the industrial countries. With the exception of Japan, all the industrial countries are far more dependent on imports of manufactures today than at any other time in the period 1899–1985. And Japan is more dependent today than at any time since World War II.

trade has dramatically intensified over the past decade. Figure 9-1 shows that the import content of supplies of finished manufactures (import penetration ratio) has surged upwards for all industrial countries in the 1971–1985 period, rising from 15 percent in 1971 to 28 percent in 1985. For the United States, the proportion has increased from 9 percent in 1971 to 22 percent in 1985.

In this chapter, we first trace the historical evolution of U.S. trade policy to give us a perspective on present and prospective policy. We then examine the issue of declining U.S. competitiveness in world markets. The enormous U.S. trade deficit in the 1980s (which is commonly, but falsely, viewed as an indicator of declining competitiveness) has sparked a "new protectionism" in the United States, which is the next subject of this chapter. We close the chapter with some reflections on the open question, Whither U.S. trade policy?

THE EVOLUTION OF U.S. TRADE POLICY

Contemporary U.S. trade policy was born with the passage of the Reciprocal Trade Agreements Program in 1934. Since that time, the main thrust of U.S. trade policy has been the achievement and maintenance of an open world economy through cooperation with other nations to lessen barriers that stifle trade among them. After World War II, the United States became the leader in the movement toward freer trade, mainly through GATT, which was designed and promoted by this country. Starting in the 1970s, however, U.S. trade policy has reacted to a decline in U.S. international competitiveness by shifting toward selective protection and managed trade and away from its traditional drive for freer trade, which it still professes to support.

Here we offer a description of the evolution of U.S. trade policy over the last half century and the contemporary expression of that policy.

Hawley-Smoot Act of 1930

Conceived at the beginning of an unprecedented world economic crisis, the Hawley-Smoot Tariff Act of 1930 was the crowning achievement of protectionism in this country. While the bill was still in the Senate, it brought protests from foreign nations and pleas from a group of American economists who opposed a policy fraught with disaster for the economy of this country and for the rest of the world. These economists pointed out that the contemplated action was unjustified either in principle or in practice and was sure to invite retaliation and threaten world peace. In spite of these warnings, the Act was passed by Congress and signed by President Hoover, unleashing a worldwide movement of retaliatory measures.[3]

---

[3]According to the League of Nations Economic Survey of 1932–1933, the Hawley-Smoot Tariff Act of 1930 was the signal for an outburst of tariff-making activity in other countries, partly, at least, by way of reprisal. Extensive increases in duties were made almost immediately by Canada, Cuba, Mexico, France, Italy, and Spain, followed by many other nations; and it was generally considered to be an unwarranted and unfriendly act of a creditor and powerful nation. See Asher Isaacs, *International Trade: Tariff and Commercial Policies* (Chicago: Richard D. Irwin, 1948), pp. 234–35.

Few actions of the United States have been more detrimental to the foreign relations of this country than the Hawley-Smoot Tariff of 1930. Almost none of the rates could be justified in terms of the infant-industries argument or on grounds of national security. Many of the items on which tariffs were imposed or the rates raised were not in direct competition with any American product. [4]

Such inordinate action could not long endure without giving rise to counter-vailing forces for redress. After two years of the Hawley-Smoot tariff, the shrinkage of trade and the deterioration of the American economy were instrumental in convincing influential groups of the mutual relationship between imports and exports and of the effects of the American tariff policy upon the level of world trade. Their voices found more sympathetic ears in the new administration that took the reins of the government in 1933. Under the stewardship of President Roosevelt and his Secretary of State, Cordell Hull, brighter horizons were in sight.

The Reciprocal Trade Agreements Program, 1934–1962

In 1934, Congress passed the Reciprocal Trade Agreements (RTA) Act as an amendment to the Hawley-Smoot Tariff Act of 1930. The act ushered in an era of commercial liberalism in this country and paved the way for similar trends abroad that culminated in GATT after World War II.

The RTA Act of 1934 recognized the relationship between imports and exports and authorized the reduction of tariff rates up to 50 percent by means of bilateral trade agreements with foreign countries. Each agreement was to contain an *unconditional most-favored-nation* (MFN) clause so that all concessions made by either party to third countries would freely and automatically apply to the trade of the other party to an agreement. Thus, the United States would always receive MFN treatment of its exports from every agreement country. The United States would grant the concessions it gave to *all* countries, whether parties to the agreement or not.

During the war years, the extension of the RTA Act evoked little concern or opposition. After World War II, however, Congressional attitudes toward the program were mixed and, at times, uncertain. Periodic renewals met with increased opposition. Although additional authority to reduce tariff rates was granted the president, other provisions were adopted to prevent actual or contemplated reductions from inflicting harm on domestic industries: (1) the *peril-point provision,* which required the Tariff Commission to set minimum rates for contemplated concessions below which domestic industries might be harmed by imports; (2) the *escape clause provision,* which permitted withdrawal of a tariff concession previously extended in an agreement; and (3) the *defense-essentiality amendment,*

---

[4]Raymond F. Mikesell, *United States Economic Policy and International Relations* (New York: McGraw-Hill, 1952), p. 62.

which called for the restriction of imports of a product whenever such imports threatened to impair the national security.[5]

The consequences of a general policy for an economy as complex as that of the United States defy any exact measurement. Hence, we cannot definitively measure the results of the RTA program. Nonetheless, the data on tariff rates do point out the long distance traveled from the highly protectionist Hawley-Smoot Act of 1930. As shown in Table 9-1, U.S. tariff rates fell from an average of 51.4 percent for dutiable imports in 1934 to 11.1 percent in 1962. Moreover, the percentage of dutiable imports to total imports rose from 37.6 percent to 61.6 percent over the same period.

Developments in the 1950s indicated a strong tendency in favor of moderation and even reversal of the country's liberal trade policy under the RTA program, as evidenced by (1) the stiffening attacks upon this program in general, (2) the opposition to specific rate reductions already effected, and (3) the implications of escape-clause and peril-point legislation. Moreover, the item-by-item approach to bargaining under the RTA procedures, coupled with the principal-supplier concept as the basis for negotiation, resulted in a proliferation of tariff subclassifications for many products in order to confine the benefits of the lower duties to the negotiating parties. Otherwise these benefits would have accrued to third countries producing similar but not identical products without reciprocal concessions be-

Table 9-1 Average Rates of Duty on Imports for Consumption under the U.S. Tariff Act of 1930, As Amended

Period	Dutiable Imports to Total Imports (Percent)	Duties Collected to Value of Dutiable Imports (Percent)
1931–1935	37.6	51.4
1936–1940	39.5	39.4
1941–1945	34.0	33.0
1946–1950	41.6	17.1
1951–1955	44.6	12.2
1956–1960	56.9	11.6
1961–1962	61.6	11.1

Source: Arranged from data in United States Department of Treasury, *Annual Reports of the Treasury on the State of the Finances* (Washington, D.C.: U.S. Government Printing Office, 1930–1964).

---

[5]The Tariff Commission was a nonpolitical government agency whose function was the investigation, study, and submission of recommendations to the president on tariffs and other matters pertaining to the foreign trade of the United States. It was replaced in 1975 with the International Trade Commission.

cause of the *unconditional* MFN principle.[6] After thirty years of tariff reductions under the RTA program, over four hundred U.S. industrial products remained unaffected by negotiations and subject to the high rates of the Hawley-Smoot Tariff of 1930—an inherent weakness of the item-by-item bargaining system.

In addition to domestic protectionist policies that weakened the original intent of the RTA Act, international developments (most notably, the abandonment by the European Community [EC] in 1960–1961 of the item-by-item approach to negotiations and the built-in preferential treatment within the EC and the European Free Trade Association [EFTA]) were creating a new situation and putting the United States at a distinct disadvantage.

The Trade Expansion Act of 1962

The Trade Expansion Act of 1962 was a direct response to the progressive establishment of a customs union by EC.[7] The provisions of this Act gave the president sweeping authority to reduce or eliminate U.S. import duties in return for similar concessions from the EC and third countries.

The key importance of EC markets to the United States and the threat that these markets would become limited by protectionist policies convinced the new Kennedy administration that the United States must make a strong effort to bargain down EC trade barriers and prevent, or mitigate, the trade diversion that menaced the export interests of countries outside the community. The persisting U.S. balance of payments deficit lent urgency to this decision.

During the five-year period from July 1, 1962, to June 30, 1967—the life of the new act—the president was authorized to do any of the following:

1. To reduce by as much as 50 percent the rates of duties existing as of July 1, 1962.
2. To reduce up to 100 percent the tariff rates on the products of industries where the United States and the EC combined represented 80 percent or more of the free-world trade.[8]
3. To reduce to zero tariff duties of 5 percent or less existing as of July 1962.
4. To eliminate tariffs on tropical products by agreement with the EC subject to its extending comparable treatment and without discrimination as to source of supply of these products, but only if such products were not produced in the United States in significant quantities.
5. To eliminate tariffs on certain farm products if in the opinion of the president such action would tend to ensure the maintenance or expansion of U.S. exports of like articles.

---

[6]Under the MFN policy any reduction in a nation's tariff is automatically extended to all nations, except, at times, to those considered politically or economically inimical. Item-by-item bargaining refers to tariff negotiations centered on specific products as opposed to across-the-board negotiations centered on linear percentage reductions in the entire tariff schedule for all products. In following the principal-supplier concept, the United States offered concessions in negotiations with another country only on products for which that country was the major supplier to the United States.

[7]See Chapter 10.

[8]The 80 percent authority was rendered almost useless by the failure of Britain to enter the EC.

Except for the tropical products authority, which might be applied when proclaimed, the act required that all other negotiable cuts be put into effect in at least five installments, a year apart (the first when concessions were proclaimed), to allow domestic producers time to adjust to foreign competition. Backed by the Trade Expansion Act, the United States called for a new GATT tariff conference, which became known as the Kennedy Round.

The Trade Act of 1974

Between the end of the Kennedy Round in 1967 and the end of 1974, protectionist forces in the United States prevented the passage of new liberal trade legislation. After pending in Congress for nearly two years, the Trade Act of 1974 became law on January 3, 1975. The act was a mixed bag of liberal and restrictive provisions that revised many elements of U.S. trade policy.

The Trade Act of 1974 gave the president the *negotiating authorities* that were necessary for U.S. participation in the Tokyo Round. The president could reduce by as much as 60 percent all tariff rates that were above 5 percent *ad valorem* and eliminate all tariff rates of 5 percent *ad valorem* or below. But any duty reductions had to be staged over ten years at a prescribed rate of decrease per year.

The president could also reduce, eliminate, or harmonize nontariff barriers under a "fast-track" procedure for Congressional approval. This procedure forbade amendments to an implementing bill and imposed time limits on its consideration by Congress.

The Trade Act of 1974 also made *adjustment assistance* for workers, firms, and communities injured by increased imports more accessible than they had been under the Trade Expansion Act of 1962.[9] The benefits could take the form of unemployment compensation and assistance in job search, training, and relocation for workers; loans and technical assistance for firms; and, for the first time, loans and grants to firms who would locate in communities adversely affected by import competition. Adjustment assistance explicitly recognizes that a policy of freer trade also demands a policy to facilitate the adaptation of workers and others to the new conditions of import competition.

The Trade Act of 1974 made it much easier for a domestic industry to get safeguard protection against import competition. Under the previous escape-clause law, to get protection an industry had to demonstrate that higher imports were caused by an earlier tariff concession and that these higher imports were the "major" cause (greater than all other causes) of injury or threat of injury. The 1974 Act eliminated the causal link between increased imports and concessions and required that imports be only a "substantial" cause (not less than any other cause) of injury or threat of injury.

Upon a determination of injury by the International Trade Commission (ITC), the president had to impose a higher duty or quota or negotiate an orderly

---

[9]Under the Trade Expansion Act of 1962, the rules for trade adjustment assistance were so stringent that not a single firm or worker qualified for assistance in the 1960s. In 1975 the Labor Department made 18,000 Chrysler workers eligible for benefits under the new Act.

marketing agreement with foreign suppliers unless any of these actions would hurt the U.S. economic interest. However, if the president took no action or an action different from the ITC recommendation, then Congress could overrule by a concurrent resolution. Import protection would be granted for a five-year period, with a single extension of three years. These restrictive provisions could be softened in practice by the right of the ITC to recommend adjustment assistance as an alternative to import protection.

The Trade Act of 1974 also gave the president more authority to retaliate against "unfair trade practices." The president could retaliate on a nondiscriminatory or a selective basis by withdrawing tariff concessions or by imposing import restrictions. The act tightened provisions of existing laws against dumping, export subsidies, and unfair practices.

The issue of Soviet emigration restrictions delayed passage for over a year, despite the fact that the central purpose of the Act was to allow negotiations with the noncommunist industrial countries. The Trade Act authorized the president to extend nondiscriminatory MFN treatment to imports from non-market economy (communist) countries, but only if the president found that such countries were not denying their citizens freedom of emigration. The extension of U.S. government credits and investment guarantees to communist countries would also depend on the same finding. Furthermore, any granting of MFN treatment to imports from a communist country had to be done under a bilateral commercial agreement requiring approval by Congress.

Another provision authorized the president to extend preferential duty-free treatment to a broad range of manufactured products imported directly from developing countries for a period up to ten years.

The Trade Act of 1979

Although Congress had delegated tariff-cutting authority to the president in the Trade Act of 1974, Congressional approval was needed for the nontariff agreements negotiated in the Tokyo Round. Accordingly, President Carter submitted to Congress in June 1979 a text of the nontariff agreements, a draft of an implementing bill, and a statement of administrative action. The implementing bill became law as the Trade Act of 1979. It revised the law and rules governing antidumping, countervailing duties, customs valuation (including the abandonment of the American Selling Price), government procurement, and standards to make them conform with the new GATT codes. The Act did not grant the president any new authority to lower trade barriers. Provisions of the Trade Act of 1974 relating to adjustment assistance, safeguard protection, unfair trade practices, trade with communist countries, and preferential treatment of imports from developing countries continued to remain in force.

The Trade Act of 1974 and the Trade Act of 1979 provided the legislative framework for U.S. trade policy in the 1980s. Not until 1988 were these acts superseded by the Omnibus Trade and Competitiveness Act, which responded to concerns about the decline of U.S. competitiveness in world markets and to the influence of protectionist interests.

The Omnibus Trade and Competitiveness Act of 1988

The huge, persistent U.S. trade deficits, together with intense lobbying by protectionist interests, led to the passage of the Omnibus Trade and Competitiveness Act of 1988, which runs for one thousand pages and contains a variety of provisions. We note here only the most significant ones.

Unfair Trade Practices   The Act raises the probability that the United States will retaliate in the future against what it regards as the unfair trade practices of foreign countries.[10] The Act instructs the Administration to identify countries that have persistent trade surpluses and that also maintain pervasive trade practices that are "unjustifiable" or "unreasonable." If negotiations fail to remove these practices, then the United States could retaliate by restricting an offending country's access to U.S. markets. Hence, the Act stresses *reciprocity:* obtaining from other countries the kind of access to their markets that the United States offers them.

The Act gives the president specific authority to deny foreign companies access to the U.S. telecommunications market to the degree that foreign countries deny American companies access to their own telecommunications markets. (The main targets of this provision are Japan and West Germany.) Also, the Act prevents foreign companies from serving as primary dealers in U.S. government securities unless their own governments allow American firms to compete on an equal basis with local primary dealers. (Japan is the chief target here.)

Although the Act transfers from the president to the U.S. Trade Representative the authority to initiate investigations of unfair trade practices and to order sanctions, the president ultimately retains control over the timing and method of any retaliatory measures. The president can choose to act or not to act under this provision as his or her own judgment dictates. For instance, the president can deny an industry import protection on grounds that such protection would hurt the poor, national security, or American companies that depend on the import in question. In sum, the new trade legislation opens the door to major changes in U.S. trade policy, but it does not force the president to walk through the door.

Trade Relief   Under the Act, industries seriously injured by imports could receive some protection if they are willing to make a "positive adjustment" to foreign competition. Firms obtaining such relief would have to agree to a five-year plan to restore their competitiveness.

Worker Assistance   The Act creates a $1 billion retraining program (financed by an import fee) to help workers displaced by imports. Also, as noted above, worker

---

[10]The act defines unfair practices to include workers' rights and the violation of intellectual property rights as well as tariff and nontariff trade barriers.

rights in foreign countries are one of the factors in determining unfair trade practices.

Intellectual Property   The Act has measures to enhance the protection afforded by U.S. patents, copyrights, and other intellectual (industrial) property rights. It strengthens the ability of U.S. companies to block imports — without the need to prove damages — if patents are violated.

Use of the Metric System   Under the Act, the government is required to use the metric system of measurement in its procurement, grants, and other business-related activities. The government and business firms are also required to use the metric system in the documentation of exports and imports as mandated by the International Convention on the Harmonized System, the classification of international goods that has been adopted by all major trading countries. However, private firms remain free to decide whether or not to convert to the metric system. The United States, Burma, and Brunei are the only countries in the world that have *not* gone metric. The lack of metric product designs and labeling constrains U.S. exports, amounting to a self-imposed nontariff trade barrier.

Negotiating Authority   The Act grants to the president authority to continue negotiations under the Uruguay Round sponsored by GATT. As observed in Chapter 8, the United States intends to use these negotiations to open foreign markets for banking, insurance, and other services; to gain protection for patents, trademarks, copyrights, and other intellectual property rights; to liberalize rules pertaining to foreign direct investment; and to cut tariffs by up to 50 percent. Further, the Act establishes a procedure — voting up or down without any amendments — to expedite the ratification by Congress of Uruguay Round agreements submitted by June 1, 1991.[11]

Competitiveness   The Act makes mention of education reforms to increase the language and technical skills of American workers and managers, but it provides only modest funding for that purpose. It calls on the National Bureau of Standards (renamed the National Institute of Standards and Technology) and other government agencies to allocate more resources to the transfer of government technology to private companies.

Closing Observations   Japan and the European Community strongly criticized the Omnibus Trade and Competitiveness Act of 1988 as protectionist legislation that allows the U.S. government to act unilaterally in settling trade disputes.[12] In rebuttal, supporters of the Act argued that it would open up markets rather than close them, because of the U.S. threat to retaliate against unfair trade barriers.

---

[11]This deadline has been extended to June 1, 1993.

[12]It is estimated that lobbyists for foreign governments spent more than $100 million in trying to stop the trade bill in Congress. See "Major Trade Bill Sent to President by Senate, 85-11," *The New York Times,* August 4, 1988, p. 1.

The original language of the Act was much more protectionist, with provisions that would have *compelled* the president to take restrictive or retaliatory actions. Instead, the Act gives discretionary authority to the president. How, in fact, the president has used that authority is discussed later in this chapter.

THE DECLINE OF U.S. COMPETITIVENESS IN WORLD MARKETS

National competitiveness is a country-level concept that cannot be expressed in income or balance sheet statements, as can the competitiveness of individual firms or industries. The President's Commission on Industrial Competitiveness adopted the following definition: *National competitiveness is the degree to which a nation can, under free and fair market conditions, produce goods and services that meet the test of international markets while simultaneously expanding the real incomes of its citizens.*[13] National competitiveness, therefore, means the ability to compete in free and open markets (1) without resort to protectionist restrictions and (2) while maintaining and improving real incomes (which rules out competing in ways that lower real incomes, such as a continuing depreciation of the country's currency in foreign exchange markets).[14] We shall use this definition in our treatment of international competitiveness.

It is common to view a growing external trade deficit as a symptom of declining national competitiveness. But the trade balance is a misleading measure of competitiveness because it is sensitive to temporary shifts in real exchange rates and to the business cycle. Changes in the share of a country's exports in international markets and changes in imports as a fraction of domestic production (import penetration ratio) are also defective measures of competitiveness, although less so when measured over a period of time long enough to eliminate transitory influences (say, five years). Much more reliable indicators of national competitiveness measure changes in the stock and use of a country's human and physical capital, such as the amount of capital per worker, the proportion of scientists and engineers in the work force, and productivity.

The long-term trend in a country's productivity (usually expressed as output per man-hour) relative to those of other countries is the single most important indicator of changing competitiveness. If a country's productivity rises at a lower rate than the productivity of other countries, then its costs per unit of output will increase over time relative to foreign unit costs when measured at a constant rate of exchange. Consequently, the country cannot compete in world markets while expanding the real income of its people. Furthermore, a country can raise its real

---

[13]*Global Competition: The New Reality,* Report of the President's Commission on Industrial Competitiveness, vol. 3 (Washington, D.C.: U.S. Government Printing Office, 1985). This definition has been adopted (with a change in wording but not meaning) by the Competitiveness Policy Council. See its First Annual Report to the President and Congress, *Building a Competitive America,* March 1, 1992, p. 1.

[14]For an explanation of depreciation and its effects, see Chapter 16. *Real* income is nominal income adjusted for changes in the price level in order to measure its power to purchase goods and services, that is, to obtain a given standard of living.

standard of living only when its productivity gains are greater than its population gains.

Is the United States losing its international competitiveness? Although this remains a controversial question in the national debate over U.S. economic policy, a comparison of U.S. and foreign productivity trends points to a persistent deterioration in the *relative* strength of the United States in the world economy. But before examining these trends, we will look first at the U.S. trade balance and the U.S. export share in manufactures.

The U.S. Trade Deficit

The astounding rise — without precedent — of the U.S. merchandise trade deficit in the 1980s is shown in Table 9-2. The popular press has pointed to this deficit as

Table 9-2   U.S. Merchandise Trade Balance, 1970–1991 (Billions of Dollars)

Year	Exports	Imports	Balance
1970	43.2	42.4	0.8
1971	44.1	48.3	− 4.2
1972	49.8	58.9	− 9.1
1973	71.3	73.6	− 2.3
1974	98.7	110.9	− 12.2
1975	108.1	105.9	2.2
1976	115.4	132.5	− 17.1
1977	121.3	160.4	− 39.1
1978	143.8	186.0	− 42.2
1979	182.0	222.2	− 40.2
1980	220.8	257.0	− 36.2
1981	233.6	273.4	− 39.8
1982	212.3	254.9	− 42.6
1983	200.5	269.9	− 69.4
1984	224.0	346.4	− 122.4
1985	218.8	352.5	− 133.7
1986	223.3	368.4	− 145.1
1987	250.2	409.8	− 159.6
1988	320.2	447.2	− 127.0
1989	361.7	477.4	− 115.7
1990	388.7	497.6	− 108.9
1991	416.0	489.4	− 73.4

Source: U.S. Department of Commerce, *United States Trade, Performance and Outlook* (Washington, D.C.: U.S. Government Printing Office, October 1986), Table 1, p. 111 and "U.S. International Transactions," *Survey of Current Business,* June 1992, Table 1, p. 79.

proof of a declining U.S. competitiveness, and spokespersons for industries facing import competition have used it as an argument for protection.

Table 9-2 reveals a volatile trade balance over the period 1970–1991. That balance was slightly positive in 1970, turned negative in 1971, and then became positive again in 1975. In 1976, the trade balance turned negative, but it showed improvement in the 1978–1980 period. Starting in 1981, however, the gap widened, exhibiting explosive growth after 1982. A jump in exports after 1987 cut the deficit to $73.4 billion by the end of 1991.

Why these shifts? As we shall learn in Part II, (1) the trade balance (like the balance of payments as a whole) is determined mainly by changes in *macroeconomic* variables such as a country's real income, price level, interest rate, and rate of exchange; (2) over the long run, the trade balance plus the balance on trade in services (the net balance on current account) *must* net out to zero, because the rest of the world will not indefinitely finance a country's deficit on merchandise and service trade; and (3) a persistent current account deficit eventually will be eliminated through a decrease in the deficit country's real income relative to that of its trading partners, usually brought about by a depreciation of its currency.

And so, it is simply wrong to argue that the U.S. trade deficit is an unequivocal sign that the United States is losing its international competitiveness.[15] Indeed, the shifts in the U.S. trade balance over the period 1977–1991 make a mockery of that argument. Does anyone believe that U.S. international competitiveness started out well in 1970, then worsened in 1971–1972, got better in 1973, then worsened again in 1974, and so on? Although the trade deficit is *not* an indicator of declining U.S. competitiveness, it has nonetheless greatly intensified the demand for protection by U.S. industries.

The U.S. Share in World Exports of Manufactures

Figure 9-2 depicts the export shares of the United States, West Germany, and Japan for 1977, 1982, 1987, and 1992. The shares of all three countries show volatility. In particular, the U.S. share *increased* between 1977 and 1982, *decreased* between 1982 and 1987, and then *increased* again between 1987 and 1992. Consequently, the United States started and ended the entire period with the biggest export share, slightly ahead of West Germany's.

Export shares are a faulty measure of competitiveness for several reasons. Movements in exchange rates—unrelated to long-run competitiveness—can radically alter the real volume of trade flows over the short run. Further, as other countries industrialize, the U.S. share of manufactured exports is certain to fall, but, at the same time, the *absolute* value of U.S. manufactured exports may *increase* in a growing world economy. Export market shares are also sensitive to the business cycle. If, for example, the U.S. economy is growing more rapidly than the world economy, then exports to the United States will grow more rapidly than U.S. exports to the rest of the world.

---

[15]The macroeconomic causes of the U.S. trade deficit are discussed in Chapter 19.

Figure 9-2

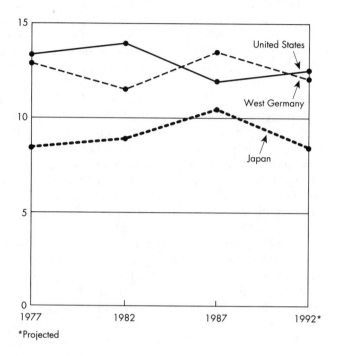

Source: Derived from "The World Economy in Charts," *Fortune,* July 27, 1992.

Merchandise Exports of the United States, West Germany, and Japan as a percentage of World Merchandise Exports, 1977, 1982, 1987, and 1992. The export shares of all three leading countries in the world economy changed direction once or twice over the period 1977–1992. Because they are affected by exchange rates, the business cycle, and random factors in the short run, export shares are unreliable indicators of international competitiveness.

Enough has been said to explain why a shift in export market shares *alone* is an unreliable indicator of national competitiveness. However, if other leading industrial countries are maintaining their export shares while the United States is losing its share *over the long run* (a decade or more), this shift points to a loss of U.S. competitiveness even though it does not prove it.

Import penetration ratios (imports as a share of domestic production) are also poor indicators of national competitiveness. Like export market shares, they are also sensitive to exchange rates and the business cycle. More fundamentally, import penetration ratios are bound to increase as the world economy becomes more integrated, as shown in Figure 9-1.

The Deterioration of U.S. Productivity

A country's economy can grow either through an increase in its factor inputs (land, labor, and capital) or through higher productivity (more efficient use of those inputs). The first way is called *extensive* growth; the second, *intensive* growth.

Productivity is usually expressed as *labor* productivity, namely, the output per hour of labor. Changes in a country's labor productivity come from (1) changes in the amounts of other factors of production used with labor, particularly changes in the capital/labor ratio (the land/labor ratio is comparatively stable); (2) changes in the mix of sectors with different labor productivities that make up the national output, notably a shift from the manufacturing sector (relatively high productivity) to the service and government sectors (relatively low productivity); and (3) changes in *total* factor productivity.[16]

We shall use *labor productivity in manufacturing* to compare productivity performance across countries because there are no reliable comparative data on total factor productivity and on productivity in the service and government sectors. Another reason is that a country's standard of living is closely tied to its labor productivity. By focusing on manufactures, we eliminate change in the sector mix as an explanatory variable. But the variables indicated in (1) and (3) remain as sources of changes in labor productivity. It is evident, therefore, that labor productivity reflects not only changes in the efficiency of labor but also changes in other factors, particularly capital, that are combined with labor in production. Although emphasizing manufacturing productivity, we also offer a broad measure of productivity — gross domestic product per employed person — to show convergence between the United States and other OECD countries since World War II.

A country can sustain its competitiveness in world markets only if its productivity performance keeps pace with that of other countries. As observed earlier, if a country's growth in productivity remains persistently below that of other countries, then its unit costs of production will become *relatively* higher than those of its competitors in world markets. Symptoms of this relative productivity decline are likely to appear initially as falling export market shares in *individual* industries and related trade deficits. Subsequently, in adjusting to persistent balance of payments deficits, the country's currency will lose value and its standard of living will stagnate or even decline (a weaker currency means that the country will receive less for its exports and pay more for its imports). In sum, by competing with relatively low wages and profits, the country would *not* be competitive in a way that would help to increase the real incomes of its people. Thus the key to long-run competitiveness (accompanied by rises in real per capita income) is a country's ability to achieve productivity gains that match those of other countries.

---

[16] *Total factor productivity* attempts to measure changes in the more efficient use of *all* factors of production. It is commonly derived as a residual after subtracting the contributions of additional amounts of land, labor, and capital to the growth of the gross domestic product. Because land grows slowly if at all, a good approximation of this residual is obtained by subtracting the additional contributions of labor and capital.

Figure 9-3 demonstrates that productivity growth in the United States over the period 1960–1990 has lagged behind that of the other two leading industrial countries. As a result of this lag, Japan and West Germany now have productivity levels in manufacturing that match or even exceed the U.S. level. Because of the relatively slow productivity growth of the United States, a remarkable convergence

Figure 9-3

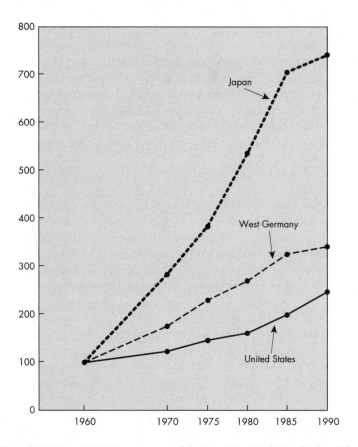

Source: Compiled from U.S. Department of Labor, *Monthly Labor Review,* May 1988, Table 47, p. 105, and December 1991, Table 2, p. 29.

Indexed Labor-Productivity Growth Rates for Manufacturing Industries of the United States, Japan, and West Germany, 1960–1990 (1960 = 100). Labor productivity in the manufacturing sector has grown more rapidly in Japan and West Germany — the other major industrial countries — than in the United States. This means that the U.S. manufacturing sector as a whole has become less competitive in international markets. Also, real income in the United States has grown less rapidly than in Japan and West Germany.

Part I   International Trade

Figure 9-4

Note: Figures are based on purchasing power parity exchange rates. The eleven OECD countries are Belgium, Canada, Denmark, France, Italy, Japan, the Netherlands, Norway, Sweden, the United Kingdom, and West Germany.
Source: Derived from Table 2 in John W. Kendrick, "International Comparisons of Productivity Trends and Levels," *Atlantic Economic Journal,* September 1990, p. 44.

Convergence of Real Gross Domestic Product Per Employed Person Between the United States and OECD Countries, 1950–1988 (United States = 100). Higher rates of productivity gain since 1950 have enabled other industrial countries (OECD) to approach the U.S. level of gross domestic product per employed person by 1988. If these trends continue, Germany and Japan will match the U.S. level by the year 2000.

has taken place between U.S. output per employed person and that of West Germany, Japan, and other OECD countries. This is shown in Figure 9-4 for the period 1950–1988.

What explains the poor productivity performance of the United States over the last quarter century? Many variables can affect productivity, including changes in plant and capital equipment, technology, skill levels of workers and managers, organization of the workplace, labor-management relations, and the scale of operations. The relative importance of these variables varies across countries and in a single country over time. Economists would agree, however, that changes in plant and equipment and in technology are *always* major sources of productivity gains.[17] We need, therefore, to say something about those two factors.

Comparative Investment Figure 9-5 compares the gross private investment of the United States, Germany, and Japan over the period 1960–1990. When mea-

Figure 9-5

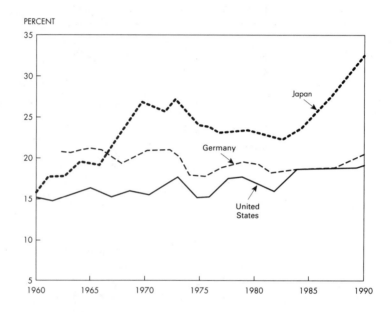

Source: Derived from Figure 15 in Competitiveness Policy Council, *Building a Competitive America,* First Annual Report to the President and Congress (Washington, D.C.: U.S. Government Printing Office, March 1, 1992), p. 19.

Gross Private Investment of the United States, Germany and Japan, 1960–1990 (Percentage of Gross Domestic Product). During the last 30 years, Japan's gross private investment as measured by the percentage of GDP has exceeded U.S. investment by a growing margin. In most of those years, Germany's investment was also higher than U.S. investment. Since investment is a major source of productivity gains, it is not surprising that U.S. productivity growth has been outpaced by these two countries.

---

[17]Many empirical studies support this agreement. Mohr, for example, in comparing the slowdown in growth of output per hour in the United States in the period 1973–1978 with the period 1948–1966, attributed 25 to 30 percent of the slowdown to lower capital formation and a decline in capital quality and 20 to 50 percent in residual productivity (mainly attributable to advances in knowledge). See Martin N. Baily and Alok K. Chakrabarti, *Innovation and the Productivity Crisis* (Washington, D.C.: Brookings Institution, 1988), Table 2-2, p. 32. For the results of other studies, see Committee for Economic Development, *Productivity Policy: Key to the Nation's Economic Future* (New York: Committee for Economic Development, 1983), Chapter 4.

sured as a percentage of gross domestic product (GDP), Japan's investment was significantly higher than U.S. investment starting in the second half of the 1960s. In most years, Germany's investment was also higher than U.S. investment. In 1990, U.S. investment was about half of Japan's as a percentage of GDP. Indeed, in that year Japan was investing more capital in *absolute* amount than the United States.[18] Although it is not shown in the figure, the United States has the lowest rate of investment of any industrial country.

The level of gross private investment is critically dependent on the level of *national* saving.[19] Although a nation can borrow funds from the rest of the world to finance domestic investment, it cannot do so indefinitely. At some point, it will need to repay those funds. As Figure 9-6 shows, Japan's rate of national saving as a

Figure 9-6

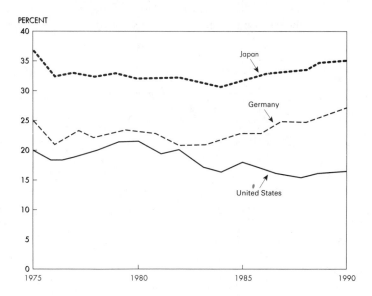

Source: Derived from Figure 14 in Competitiveness Policy Council, *Building a Competitive America,* First Annual Report to the President and Congress (Washington, D.C.: U.S. Government Printing Office, March 1, 1992), p. 18.

National Saving Rates of the United States, Germany, and Japan, 1975–1990 (Percentage of Gross Domestic Product). Since 1975, the U.S. national saving rate has declined from 20 percent of GDP to 15 percent in 1990. But even the higher rate of 1975 was markedly below the Japanese and German rates. The low and generally declining U.S. saving rate has constrained domestic investment, which, in turn, has hurt productivity growth and the international competitiveness of the U.S. economy.

---

[18]Competitiveness Policy Council, *Building a Competitive America,* pp. 2–3.

[19]National saving is the sum of household saving; corporate retained earnings; and federal, state, and local government budget surpluses. Government budget deficits reduce this sum.

percentage of GDP is now more than twice, and Germany's rate is almost twice the U.S. rate.

The decline in the 1980s of the already comparatively low rate of U.S. national saving was caused primarily by the explosive growth in the U.S. government budget deficit (which is *dissaving*) and secondarily by a decline in household saving as a percentage of disposable income. The extraordinary growth of the U.S. budget deficit is depicted in Figure 9-7. In 1992, the *national debt* was approaching $4 *trillion,* about $50,000 for every American family.

In the 1980s, national saving was insufficient to finance desired national investment. Hence, the United States borrowed heavily from abroad, about $1 *trillion.*[20] Despite this huge inflow of capital, the U.S. investment level in the 1980s was about the same as in the 1970s. In effect, much of this capital inflow was used to finance the U.S. budget deficit, adding to consumption but not investment. The deficit "crowded out" private investment, depriving the country of the productive assets needed for higher productivity and long-term growth.[21]

Figure 9-7

Source: Adapted from Competitiveness Policy Council, *Building a Competitive America,* First Annual Report to the President and Congress (Washington, D.C.: U.S. Government Printing Office, March 1, 1992), Figure 12, p. 13.

U.S. Government Budget Deficit, 1962–1992 (Percentage of Gross Domestic Product). The U.S. federal budget deficit exploded in the 1980s and reached almost 8 percent of GDP in 1992. By lowering the national saving rate, the budget deficit "crowds out" U.S. investment.

---

[20]The net amount borrowed from abroad equals the deficit on current account in the U.S. balance of payments. For the relationship between national income accounts and the balance of payments, see Chapter 15.

[21]*Net* private investment (gross investment *minus* depreciation) was lower in 1990 than in 1980 as a percentage of GDP. See Competitiveness Policy Council, *Building a Competitive America,* Figure 16, p. 19.

Part I   International Trade

The United States cannot depend on foreign countries to support domestic consumption in one of the richest countries in the world. Continued borrowing would make the debt service burden so large as to stultify U.S. economic growth and threaten financial collapse. The United States entered the 1980s as the world's largest *creditor* nation, but it left that decade as the world's largest *debtor* nation. As shown in Table 9-3, in 1991 this country owed a net amount of $361.5 billion to the rest of the world. Until the negative U.S. saving/investment balance is eliminated, this external debt will become ever larger.

Technology Innovation   The second major source of productivity gains is the application of new knowledge to the creation and commercialization of products.[22] Measured as a percentage of GDP, Germany and Japan have outspent the United States in civilian (nondefense) R & D over the last two decades (Figure 9-8). If current trends continue, this country will become progressively a technological follower rather than a technological leader as it has been in the past. The end of the cold war offers the United States an opportunity to shift scientists and engineers from defense to civilian industries.

Profile of U.S. Competitiveness

The President's Commission on Industrial Competitiveness drew up a profile of U.S. competitive advantages as of the beginning of 1985. This is depicted in Figure 9-9.

Table 9-3   U.S. International Investment Position at Year End 1980, 1985, and 1991 (Billions of Dollars)

Type of Investment	1980	1985	1991
U.S. assets abroad	*936.3*	*1,252.6*	*1,960.3*
U.S. official reserve assets	171.4	117.9	159.2
Other U.S government assets	63.9	87.8	78.7
U.S. private assets	701.0	1,046.9	1,722.3
Foreign assets in the United States	*543.8*	*1,113.6*	*2,321.8*
Foreign official assets	176.1	202.5	396.6
Other foreign assets	367.7	911.1	1,925.2
Net U.S. international investment position	*392.5*	*139.0*	*– 361.5*

Note: Totals may not add precisely because of rounding.

Source: "The International Investment Position of the United States in 1991," *Survey of Current Business,* June 1992, Table 3, p. 49.

---

[22]See Chapter 5 for a discussion of technology theories of international trade.

Figure 9-8

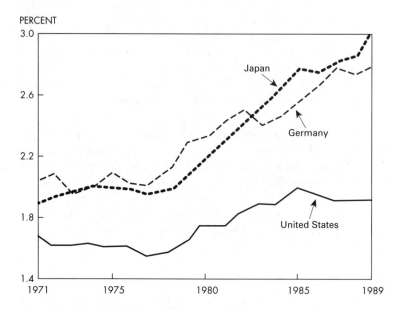

Source: Competitiveness Policy Council, *Building a Competitive America,* First Annual Report to the President and Congress (Washington, D.C.: U.S. Government Printing Office, March 1, 1992), p. 3.

Total Civilian (Nondefense) R & D as a Percentage of Gross Domestic Product for the United States, Germany, and Japan, 1971–1989. U.S. civilian R & D has not kept pace with that of Germany and Japan over the last two decades. Consequently, the United States has fallen behind in the creation and commercialization of new products that are at the cutting edge of international competition.

Major *disadvantages* were high capital costs (real interest rates), a strong dollar exchange rate, and high labor costs. Minor disadvantages were U.S. trade policy and international trade laws. The single current major *advantage* was product technology; process technology (new production functions) and labor quality were cited as minor advantages.

The commission made several recommendations to shift the disadvantages toward parity (except labor costs, which reflect the high living standard of American workers) and to transform minor advantages into major ones, including incentives for private-sector R & D, more investment in new manufacturing technologies, more protection of industrial property rights (patents, trademarks, and copyrights), a cut in the federal budget deficit to increase the supply of capital available to private investment at lower real interest rates, more worker training, and the establishment of a department of international trade to make trade a national priority.

Figure 9-9

	Disadvantage		Parity	Advantage	
	Major	Minor		Minor	Major
Product Technology					●→○
Process Technology				●	→○
Capital Cost	●		→○		
Exchange Rate	●	→○			
Labor Cost	●				
Labor Quality				●	→○
U.S. Trade Policy		●	→○		
International Trade Laws		●	→○		

● 1985   ○ Potential

Source: President's Commission on Industrial Competitiveness, 1985.

Competitive Advantages of the United States in 1985. In 1985, the United States suffered from the major competitive disadvantages of high capital costs, a strong dollar, and high labor costs. In contrast, product technology was its only major *advantage*. Since 1985, depreciation has eliminated the strong dollar as a competitive disadvantage, but the United States has not yet gained parity with other countries (notably Japan and West Germany) in long-term capital costs. Nor has it made process technology and labor quality major competitive advantages.

So far the most evident improvement in competitive advantage has come from the sharp depreciation of the dollar that started in 1985. But as we have stated earlier, depreciation will not by itself improve U.S. competitiveness when defined in terms of expanding real incomes for Americans.

Improvements in other areas have been modest or nonexistent. As we have observed, U.S. investment and saving rates remain below those of competitor countries, the budget deficit continues to crowd out investment even as the United States continues to borrow from the rest of the world, and U.S. R & D expenditures fail to match those of Japan and Germany. In its 1992 Report to the President and Congress, the Competitiveness Policy Council identifies six issues deserving prompt attention: (1) saving and investment, (2) education and training (American elementary and high school students rank near the bottom of all recent international comparisons), (3) technology, (4) corporate governance and financial markets (American managers have shorter time horizons than their counterparts abroad), (5) health care costs, and (6) trade policy.[23]

In sum, the outlook for U.S. international competitiveness is cloudy. The steps needed to restore high productivity and growth in the U.S. economy remain to be taken. Failure to take these steps has been costly to American business and the American family.[24] The restoration of U.S. competitiveness will remain, therefore, a major challenge for this country throughout the 1990s and probably into the next century. How this challenge is met will profoundly shape U.S. trade policy, as it has already done.

THE NEW PROTECTIONISM

The progressive liberalization of international trade initiated by the United States after World War II came to a halt in the mid-1970s, when a resurging protectionism in new forms swamped further efforts to lower trade barriers in the industrial world. As we observed in Chapter 8, the Tokyo Round of 1974–1979 was at best a holding action against protectionist forces, and it failed to reach agreement on a new safeguards code.

The proliferation of protection since the mid-1970s is a consequence of both short-run cyclical developments and long-run structural shifts, notably the sharp recessions precipitated by the two OPEC oil crises (1973–1974 and 1979–1980), which were accompanied by high levels of unemployment; the strong U.S. dollar of 1980–1985, coupled with enormous trade deficits; the decline in U.S. competitiveness; and the explosive rise in the economic interdependence of the industrial countries. Slower growth, unemployment, and intense import competition have created a political environment favorable to protectionist interests, particularly in the United States.

Old arguments for protection examined in Chapter 7 — the employment, low-wage, fairness, antidumping, bargaining-and-retaliation, reciprocity, and national security arguments — have been dressed in new clothing to suit the times. Also, the new argument for strategic trade policy has been eagerly adopted by protectionist interests. The advocates of a particular trade restriction usually claim to be against protectionism in general. The rhetoric of freer trade is still voiced: Each act of protection is viewed as an exception to the rule or as a means to open up export markets by pressuring foreign countries to eliminate import restrictions. Despite these pretensions, the resurgence of protectionism has inspired manifold trade disputes among the three giants of world trade: the United States, the EC, and Japan.

---

[23]Competitiveness Policy Council, *Building a Competitive America,* p. 16.

[24]If the United States had maintained its productivity growth at the 1948–1973 average of 2.5 percent annually from 1973 through 1990 (instead of letting it fall to 0.8 percent), the median family income in 1990 would have been $47,000 instead of $35,000. Ibid., p. 10.

The revival of protectionism since the mid-1970s is called the "new protectionism" because it relies heavily on new forms of nontariff trade barriers (NTBs), notably voluntary export restraints (VERs) and orderly marketing agreements (OMAs), and on trade-remedy laws.[25]

A second feature of the new protectionism is its focus on a comparatively small number of sectors: steel, automobiles, textiles and apparel, televisions, machine tools, footware, VCRs, semiconductors, and ships.

A third feature of the new protectionism is its bilateral application, which violates GATT's principle of nondiscrimination (most-favored-nation policy). VERs, OMAs, and subsidies are initiated by the United States and other industrial countries outside Article XIX of GATT, the safeguards article. Hence, countries hurt by these restrictions seldom invoke Article XIX, which provides for compensatory or retaliatory actions when authorized by GATT. This, of course, is viewed as an advantage by the country imposing such restrictions.

A fourth feature of the new protectionism is its lack of "transparency." The new protectionist devices allow for a great deal of administrative discretion, which can be used to hide their effects from outsiders. Again, this is an advantage to the restricting country, for it can then claim that a device is *not* protectionist.

PROTECTION THROUGH TRADE REMEDIES

Starting in the mid-1970s, the United States has increasingly resorted to trade-remedy laws to (1) protect domestic industries against dumping and foreign export subsidies and (2) open up foreign markets to U.S. exports by threatening retaliation. The principal provisions of these laws are described in Table 9-4.

The U.S. trade-remedy laws are aimed at alleviating the hardships of U.S. firms resulting from the policies and actions of foreign firms and governments. Their supporters argue that the laws create a "fair and free" trading environment. But what is *fair trade?* Two different interpretations of fair trade are based on two different concepts of reciprocity. The concept of *first-difference* reciprocity postulates that fair trade is the outcome of reciprocal cuts in trade barriers of equal value to the trading countries. This is the concept underlying GATT negotiations. In contrast, the concept of *full* reciprocity asserts that fair trade requires that countries offer each other *identical* access to their respective markets. This concept, which implies that countries have identical trade restrictions in each economic sector, animates the administration of U.S. trade-remedy laws.[26]

The escape clause (Section 201) allows the use of import duties to limit rising imports that injure or threaten to injure a domestic industry. (Prior to 1974, the escape clause remedy required that rising imports be due to a prior reduction in a trade barrier; this remains the GATT interpretation in Article XIX.) Unlike the

---

[25]For a definition of VERs, see "The Erosion of GATT" in Chapter 8. Unlike VERs, OMAs rely on restrictions imposed by the importing country. Both VERs and OMAs are negotiated bilaterally between the importing and exporting countries.

[26]The concept of full reciprocity is often called the "level playing field."

Table 9-4   Principal Provisions of U.S. Trade-Remedy Laws

Statute	Criteria for Action	Policy Instruments	Administration
Section 201: Fair Trade (escape clause)	Increasing imports are substantial cause of injury	Duties, quotas, tariff quotas, orderly market arrangements, adjustment assistance	President (ITC recommendation)
Section 301: Unfair Trade	Unjustifiable, unreasonable, or discriminatory practices harmful to U.S. commerce	All appropriate and feasible action	U.S. trade representative subject to direction by the president
Section 701: Subsidized imports	Material injury or threat of material injury	Duties	Injury determination by ITC; subsidy determination by ITA
Section 731: Dumped imports	Material injury or its threat from imports sold below cost or below foreign market price	Duties	Injury determination by ITC; dumping determination by ITA

Note: The origins of these provisions are the Tariff Act of 1930 (as amended), the Trade Act of 1974 (as amended), the Trade Agreements Act of 1979 (as amended), the Trade and Tariff Act of 1984, and the Omnibus Trade and Competitiveness Act of 1988. ITC is the International Trade Commission, a six-member appointed body. ITA is the International Trade Administration of the U.S. Department of Commerce.

Source: Based on Table 1 in Cletus C. Coughlin, "U.S. Trade-Remedy Laws: Do They Facilitate or Hinder Free Trade?" *Review,* The Federal Reserve Bank of St. Louis, July–August 1991, p. 5.

other remedy laws, the escape clause does not depend on the existence of unfair trade. Such action occurs within the GATT and requires compensation to trading countries hurt by the action; otherwise, they are allowed to retaliate to a degree determined by a GATT panel.

In Chapter 8, we discussed the growing use by the United States and the European Community of antidumping (AD) and countervailing duties (CVD). U.S. AD and CVD law requires a finding of actual or threatened *material injury,* which is defined negatively by the Trade Act of 1930 as "harm which is not inconsequential, immaterial, or unimportant." To determine material injury in AD and CVD cases, the International Trade Commission is required to consider the volume of imports and the impact on the petitioning industry. The AD provision (Section 731) aims to prevent sales of products by foreign firms in the United States (1) at prices below the prices they charge in the exporting country or (2) at prices below their total cost of production.

Unlike the other remedies, Section 301 (the unfair trade statute) is focused on removing "unjustifiable, unreasonable, or discriminatory" foreign practices that hinder U.S. exports. This provision is mainly a response by the U.S. Congress to the alleged ineffectiveness of GATT in resolving trade disputes.[27] *Unreasonable* is broadly defined in the Trade and Tariff Act of 1984 to include any act, policy or practice that denies either national or MFN treatment of U.S. exporting firms.[28] If the U.S. trade representative (USTR) does not reach a negotiated settlement with a country it accuses of unfair trade practices denying market access to U.S. firms, then it can suspend any benefits of a trade agreement with the offending country or impose import restrictions on products coming from that country.

Table 9-5 indicates the number of petitions under the U.S. trade-remedy laws in the first and second halves of the 1980s. Observe that AD and CVD actions account for about nine-tenths of the petitions in both periods, while the escape clause was hardly used. The percentage share of Section 301 petitions doubled between the two periods. The total number of petitions fell from 594 in the first period to 290 in the second, but it would be wrong to interpret this decline as a weakening of protectionist forces. Over 200 cases in the first period were initiated by the steel industry prior to the voluntary export agreement of October 1984.

Table 9-5 U.S. Trade-Remedy Petitions, 1981–85 and 1986–1990

Type of Petition	1981–1985		1986–1990	
	Number	Percent	Number	Percent
Escape clause	21	3.5	8	2.8
Antidumping	263	44.3	190	65.5
Countervailing duty	279	47.0	61	21.0
Section 301	31	5.2	31	10.7
Total	*594*	*100.0*	*290*	*100.0*

Source: Based on Table 2 in Cletus C. Coughlin, "U.S. Trade Remedy Laws: Do They Facilitate or Hinder Free Trade?" *Review,* The Federal Reserve Bank of St. Louis, July–August 1991, p. 11.

---

[27]GATT has no authority to enforce its decisions or impose sanctions on members found guilty of unfair trade practices.

[28]In traditional international law, national treatment means that a country does not discriminate against foreign firms. But in the administration of Section 301, national treatment is taken to mean that a country treats all firms as favorably as they are treated in the United States.

Chapter 9   U.S. Trade Policy in an Era of Global Competition

Moreover, because AD and CV duties can last a long time, many industries that got relief in the early 1980s were still protected in the late 1980s.[29]

None of the trade-remedy laws requires consideration of losses to U.S. consumers or to other U.S. industries in deciding on import protection for the petitioning industry. Although their self-described purpose is to create "fair trade," the laws and their administration are biased in favor of protection. Seventy percent of the U.S. CV and AD duty actions completed between 1980 and 1988 restricted imports in some way. One analyst of the trade-remedy laws concludes that they hinder free trade and are more accurately described as a bedrock for protectionism than a bedrock for free trade, as their protagonists claim.[30] Another analyst asserts that "fair trade is a system for the redistribution of income based on the capture of political power."[31]

TRADE DISPUTES

We do not have the space to describe the many trade disputes that the United States has had with Japan, the EC, and other countries in recent years. For the most part, these disputes have revolved around U.S. allegations of unfair trade practices (dumping and government subsidies) and high nontariff barriers that keep out U.S. goods and services, especially in Japan. We offer below a short review of the issues involved in the more prominent disputes — steel, automobiles, textiles, and semiconductors. But first we list some representative headlines that appeared in *The New York Times* over the period March 1990 to October 1992. These headlines eloquently express the "flavor" of recent trade disputes:

"U.S. Lists Barriers to Trade" (March 3, 1990, p. 31)

"Tougher Stance Is Taken by U.S. on Japan Trade" (January 7, 1991, p. 1)

"Japan Shuts U.S. Rice Exhibition" (March 18, 1991, p. D1)

"Washington Presses Japan to Open Construction Jobs" (April 27, 1991, p. 38)

"Duty to Rise for Japanese Processors" (August 9, 1991, p. D1)

"U.S. Rebuffs Japan Concern on Complaint About Trade" (September 27, 1991, p. D1)

"U.S. Tariffs Imposed on Hondas" (March 3, 1992, p. D1)

"U.S. Tariffs on Honda Roil Japanese" (March 4, 1992, p. D6)

"U.S. Adds 7 Countries to Trade Barriers List" (March 31, 1992, p. D2)

"Unfair Pricing Is Found on Japanese Mini-Vans" (May 20, 1992, p. D1)

"Turning Tables, Japan Says U.S. Trades Unfairly" (June 8, 1992, p. 1)

"Big U.S. Steelmakers to Seek Billions in Tariffs" (June 27, 1992, p. 37)

"U.S. Warning to Japan Over Chip Agreement" (August 5, 1992, p. D2)

---

[29]At the end of 1990, 171 CVD orders were in effect, exceeding the 61 petitions occurring between 1986 and 1990.

[30]Cletus C. Coughlin, "U.S. Trade-Remedy Laws: Do They Facilitate or Hinder Free Trade?" *Review,* The Federal Reserve Bank of St. Louis, July–August 1991, p. 17.

[31]James Boward, *The Fair Trade Fraud* (New York: St. Martin's Press, 1991), p. 321.

"U.S. Presses for an End to European Trade Rift" (October 1, 1992, p. D2)

"U.S. and Europe to Try Again on Trade Disputes" (October 10, 1992, p. 35)

"Japan and U.S. in Dispute on Cray Supercomputers" (October 10, 1992, p. 35)

Steel The U.S. steel industry has steadily declined in international competitiveness since World War II. The reasons for this decline are manifold, but two stand out: a failure to innovate in production processes and high wage costs. Starting in the 1950s, U.S. steel companies ignored new production technology (notably, the basic oxygen process) and the threat of import competition. By the 1970s, Japan had become the leader in steel technology, and today American steel firms obtain technical assistance from Japanese firms. In the 1970s, the output per worker-hour in Japanese steel plants was more than 50 percent higher than in U.S. plants. Low productivity was compounded by high wages paid to American steel workers, some 80 percent above the average wages in U.S. manufacturing and more than twice the wages paid in the Japanese steel industry. In the first half of the 1980s, the international competitive disadvantages of the U.S. steel were intensified by a strong U.S. dollar. By the mid-1980s, imports of steel from Japan and other countries had captured one-quarter of the U.S. market.

The American steel industry reacted to import competition primarily by getting import protection. In the late 1960s and early 1970s, imports from Japan and Europe were restricted through voluntary export quotas. Foreign producers responded by shifting their exports from basic steel products to specialty steel, which in turn caused problems for U.S. specialty steel producers. In 1978, import protection took a new form — the *trigger-pricing mechanism* (TPM). The TPM established reference prices pegged to the lowest-cost international producer, namely, Japan. Any steel imports below their reference prices were subject to antidumping duties imposed within sixty to ninety days. The U.S. steel industry had become disenchanted with the TPM by 1980, alleging that the trigger prices were too low and their enforcement by the U.S. Treasury Department too lax.

The U.S. government ended the TPM in January 1982, when the major U.S. steel producers filed petitions with the International Trade Commission (ITC) and the Department of Commerce for relief from injury caused by the sale of steel in the United States at below-fair-market prices by subsidized foreign producers, mainly located in Western Europe. These petitions then underwent a long legal process that ended in October 1982 when the International Trade Commission ruled that several European steel firms illegally dumped steel in the United States by selling at prices below "fair value." Rather than face higher duties (ranging up to 26 percent) European steel producers agreed to limit their shipments during 1983–1986 to 5.5 percent of the U.S. market, down from 6.4 percent.

In response to a petition filed by the United Steelworkers of America and the Bethlehem Steel Corporation under Section 201 (the "escape clause") of the Trade Act of 1974, the ITC ruled in 1984 that certain carbon and alloy steel products (amounting to 70 percent of *all* steel imports) were being imported into the United States in such quantities as to be a substantial cause or threat of serious injury to the domestic industry. The ITC recommended that the president impose a combination of tariffs and quotas on these imports. However, such action by the United States would have allowed foreign steel-exporting countries to demand compensation under the rules of GATT for lost exports to the United States (possibly amounting to several billion dollars). Compensation would take the form of lower restrictions on U.S. imports of other products. In the event compensation could not be agreed to, the injured countries could retaliate by eliminating an equal amount of imports from the United States — again under GATT rules. To avert this compensation-retaliation procedure, the president negotiated VERs with 29 countries limiting their steel exports to the United States. These agreements, which were intended to hold steel imports to about 20 percent of U.S. domestic consumption, expired in March 1992.

By 1992, there were several signs that the U.S. steel industry had become more competitive: The average man-hours per ton of steel fell from over 10 in 1980 to less than 5 in 1991, steel exports were up, and steel imports had a smaller share of the U.S. markets.[32] Although protection probably gave the steel industry more time to restructure, two other factors were more important in restoring competitiveness: the dollar depreciation starting in 1985 and the competition coming from domestic low-cost, nonunion minimills.

The competitive revival of the steel industry has not quenched its desire for protection. After multilateral negotiations to limit government subsidies to steel companies collapsed in April 1992, U.S. steel companies filed over 100 AD and CVD petitions amounting to billions of dollars in duties on imports from Japan, the EC, and several developing countries. Because AD penalties are retroactive, AD petitions immediately cut purchases of foreign steel as buyers face uncertainty about the ultimate cost.

Further protection is unlikely to benefit the U.S. steel industry beyond providing *temporary* relief from import competition. In the long run, the U.S. steel industry — as well as the European and even Japanese steel industries — will be forced out of bulk steel manufacture by new low-cost producers in developing countries. To survive in the long run, the industry must turn to technology-intensive specialty steel manufacture, in which it will continue to have a comparative advantage. By delaying this inevitable adjustment, import protection injures not only the national interest but the U.S. steel industry itself.[33]

Automobiles By 1980, automobiles — imported mostly from Japan — had captured more than 25 percent of the U.S. market. The competitive advantage of

---

[32]"An Industrial Comeback Story: U.S. Is Competing Again in Steel," *The New York Times,* March 31, 1992, p. 1.

[33]The national costs and gains of steel protection are shown in Tables 6-1 and 6-2 in Chapter 6. (These tables also show the costs and gains for textiles, autos, and other industries.) A study by the Institute for International Economics estimates that the cost to consumers of steel protection from 1982 to 1986 (Phase III) was $750,000 per job saved in the steel industry. See Gary C. Hufbauer and others, *Trade Protection in the United States: 31 Case Studies* (Washington, D.C.: Institute for International Economics, 1986), Table 1.2, p. 14.

Japanese manufacturers over their American counterparts was based on lower costs and higher quality. Several studies indicated that the Japanese, at the 1980 dollar/yen exchange rate, could build a car and ship it to the United States for $1,300 to $1,700 less than it cost the Americans to build a comparable vehicle. This cost advantage was traceable to both higher productivity and lower wages. On the average, Japanese companies could manufacture an automobile in 30.8 hours compared to the 59.9 hours it took U.S. companies. Toyota, for instance, built cars with about one-third the worker-hours needed in the United States and paid its workers about half the U.S. wages.

Unlike the steel producers, the U.S. automobile companies conceded that the decline in their competitiveness was largely of their own doing: sloppy management, poor quality control, a failure to anticipate the shift toward smaller cars, poor employee relations, and so on. Nonetheless, the Ford Motor Company asked the U.S. government in 1980 to restrict imports of Japanese vehicles. The government responded by getting the Japanese to agree in March 1981 to limit their exports of automobiles to the United States for two, possibly three, years.

The automobile VER was intended to be a *temporary* crutch for the U.S. industry, which was facing international competition and a domestic recession. But despite record profits earned by the American auto companies in the mid-1980s, the VER remains in existence to this day. The U.S. government stopped asking Japan for export restraints in 1985. However, the Japanese government voluntarily decided to keep them because they feared that an abandonment would trigger new protectionist demands in the United States and also because the Japanese auto industry was a beneficiary of the VER. The quota was 1.68 million cars per year for 1981–1983 and 1.85 million for 1984; it was then set at 2.3 million by the Japanese government for 1985 and later years.

The Japanese auto industry has responded to the VER in several ways. First, because the quota is expressed in physical units, the Japanese exports moved from low-priced compact cars to high-priced luxury cars. Second, the Japanese auto companies invested in manufacturing facilities in the United States. Third, by curtailing the supply of cars to the American market, the VER enabled the Japanese to charge high prices and make big monopoly profits.[34] In effect, the VER created a Japanese export cartel that rationed automobiles to the United States at monopoly prices—all with the approval of the U.S. government!

Has the VER enabled the U.S. auto industry to become competitive with the Japanese industry? Undoubtedly, American automobile companies have greatly improved their productivity and quality through a massive restructuring involving sharp cuts in employment and large-scale investments in automation. But they are still running behind their Japanese competitors. A study sponsored by MIT's

---

[34] A study by the Federal Trade Commission calculated that the VER transferred $750 million a year from American consumers to Japanese auto firms. (At the same time, American consumers subsidized the U.S. auto firms at an annual rate of $100 million.) For this reason, the Japanese government has been content to maintain the VER since 1985. See "A Victory for Car Buyers," *The Economist,* March 9, 1985, p. 69.

International Motor Vehicle Program measured productivity and quality in thirty-eight auto plants around the world in 1987. It found that the average Japanese plant was 39 percent more productive than the average U.S. plant and that Japanese cars sold in the United States averaged forty-four assembly defects per one hundred cars while American cars averaged eighty-seven.[35] In sum, the VER has been an ineffective instrument to restore competitiveness in the U.S. auto industry. Indeed, it can be argued that the VER has slowed the adjustment of American auto firms while it has enhanced the adjustment of Japanese auto firms. By accelerating the establishment of U.S. plants and causing a shift to luxury cars, the VER has made the Japanese stronger competitors in the U.S. market and much more able to cope with a weak dollar.

Unhappy with the results of the VER, U.S. auto manufacturers are seeking other forms of protection—not always successfully. In 1991, they initiated an antidumping petition alleging that Mazda and Toyota were dumping minivans in the United States. However, in June 1992 the ITC ruled that minivan shipments by the two Japanese companies had *not* inflicted "material injury" on the American auto companies, which have 88 percent of the U.S. minivan market.[36] The companies are now trying to get protection against minivan imports through congressional action.

The debate over protection has become confusing because it is more and more difficult to distinguish between "American" manufacturers' cars and "foreign" manufacturers' cars now that many companies sell a mixture of imported and U.S.-made cars. In the first five months of 1992, 9.5 percent of all cars sold by Chrysler (a U.S. firm) in the United States were *foreign-made* while 72.1 percent of all cars sold by Honda (a Japanese firm) in the United States were *U.S.-made*. In the same period, seven Japanese companies (Honda, Mazda, Mitsubishi, Nissan, Toyota, Subaru, and Suzuki) imported 763,698 cars into the United States but also manufactured 4,451,572 cars *in* the United States.[37]

The question of identity becomes even more puzzling when it is recognized that domestic-made autos may be assembled with parts coming from abroad. For example, the domestic content of the 1992 models of the Ford Crown Victoria and Mercury Grand Marquis is 73 percent. At the same time, the domestic content of the Honda Accord manufactured in the United States is 75 percent.[38] Which car, then, is more "American"?

Finally, the U.S. auto manufacturers have alliances with several Japanese and other foreign manufacturers. To illustrate, the Dodge Stealth sold by Chrysler in the United States is made by Mitsubishi in Japan; a Ford minivan is produced in Ohio by a joint venture between Ford and Nissan; the Ford Festiva is designed by Mazda and assembled by Kia in Korea for shipment to the United States; General

---

[35]See "Japan's Carmakers Take on the World," *Fortune,* June 20, 1988, p. 69.

[36]Earlier, the ITA of the U.S. Department of Commerce had ruled that Mazda and Toyota were selling minivans below "fair value" despite the fact that their U.S. prices were *not* below their prices in Japan.

[37]"Return of an Issue: Protectionism," *The New York Times,* June 16, 1992, p. D1.

[38]"Do You Know Where Your Car Was Made?, *Fortune,* June 17, 1991, pp. 52–56.

Motors' Geo Metro is built by Suzuki in Japan. Also, Chrysler has an equity stake in Mitsubishi; Ford, in Mazda; and General Motors, in Isuzu.

Textiles Unlike steel and automobiles, the textile trade dispute is between the industrial and developing countries. Largely because of pressure from the United States and the EC, the International Cotton Textiles Arrangement was entered into by some thirty countries in 1962 under the auspices of GATT. The arrangement allowed a country suffering from "disruptive imports" of cotton textiles to request the exporting country to restrict its exports to a specified level. If agreement was not reached, then the importing country could impose a quota related to past imports. But the importing country was committed to increase regularly permitted levels of imports and to enlarge existing quotas.

The present regime is the Multifiber Arrangement (MFA), which covers textiles made from both natural and manufactured products. The most recent renegotiation of the MFA occurred in 1991. It provides a legal framework within which importing and exporting countries can negotiate bilateral pacts on levels of trade. The MFA allows the United States to restrict textile imports without violating its GATT obligations. This country is currently party to textile agreements with over forty countries, and the EC has about the same number. In effect, the MFA amounts to a cartelization of world trade in textiles and apparel.[39]

The prospects for any liberalization of the MFA depend critically on the outcome of the Uruguay Round. But even under the most optimistic assumptions, the pace of liberalization will be slow. U.S. and E.C. textile firms still plead for more protection. Also, the MFA is supported by the weaker textile exporters, such as Colombia and Kenya, who are fearful of open competition from stronger exporters, such as Taiwan and Hong Kong. The latter, however, are not terribly upset by the MFA because efficient producers earn high quota rents from quota rights.[40] In sum, the MFA is deeply entrenched in many developing countries as well as in the industrial countries. The unsung victims of the MFA are consumers in the industrial countries, as is indicated for U.S. consumers in Table 6-1.

Semiconductors By 1985, U.S. semiconductor manufacturers had lost a key sector of their industry—dynamic-random-access memory (DRAM) chips—to Japanese manufacturers. DRAM chips are standard memory chips that store data in all sorts of electronic products, such as computers and videocassette recorders. The Japanese were able to dominate the DRAM chip market by drastic cuts in prices and continual improvements in quality. By 1985, only three U.S. companies still sold DRAM chips on the commercial market.

---

[39]Together, textiles and apparel account for about 9 percent of world exports of manufactures. It is estimated that textile and apparel imports by the industrial countries could easily increase by $50 billion a year with free trade. See William R. Cline, *The Future of World Trade in Textiles and Apparel* (Washington, D.C.: Institute for International Economics, 1987), Table 8.1.

[40]Quota rents resulting from U.S. textile import quotas were estimated to be about $3 billion and from OECD (including the United States) import quotas, at least $10 billion in 1986. Ibid., pp. 276–77.

In 1984, the Semiconductor Industry Association filed an unfair trade complaint with the U.S. government against Japanese semiconductor producers under Section 301 of the Trade Act of 1974. This was followed in 1985 by petitions of American semiconductor manufacturers asking the government to impose antidumping duties on imports from Japan of 64K DRAM chips and other memory chips. At the end of that year, the U.S. government itself filed an antidumping case against Japanese semiconductor manufacturers of 256K DRAM chips and, significantly, of future generations of chips. By then, only two U.S. companies still remained in the market for DRAM chips: Texas Instruments and Micro Technology. In 1986, the government ruled that Japanese producers were selling DRAM and other chips in the U.S. market for less than production costs and were subject to antidumping duties of up to 35 percent.

The U.S. Department of Commerce and the Semiconductor Industry Association wanted to stop alleged Japanese dumping (denied by the Japanese) without going through cumbersome antidumping procedures that could take two years between the time of petition and the time of ruling. Accordingly, the U.S. and Japanese governments reached a semiconductor agreement in July 1986 in which the United States agreed not to retaliate for the dumping of Japanese chips in the American market in return for Japan's commitment to establish a price-monitoring system and to obtain greater access to the Japanese market for U.S. semiconductor producers. The Japanese agreed not to sell their chips below a "fair market value" (assigned by the U.S. Department of Commerce) to the United States and other countries.

In the following year, the United States contended that Japan failed to comply with the semiconductor agreement: It had not improved U.S. access to the Japanese market and it continued to dump semiconductors in third-country markets. In retaliation, in April 1987 the president imposed 100 percent duties on imports of Japanese computers, TV sets, and power tools worth $300 million. (These duties were removed some months later.)

The semiconductor agreement, renewed in 1991, commits Japan to help foreign manufacturers get 20 percent of its microchip market. Even though Japan has no tariffs or quantitative restrictions on semiconductor imports, by mid-1992 the market share of foreign suppliers was only about 15 percent. Ironically, American and European chipmakers were finding it hard to sell in Japan because Japanese computer firms (the biggest users of chips) were being hurt by U.S. competitors, notably IBM, Compaq, and Del.[41]

Has the semiconductor agreement been successful? The Japanese government argues that it has improved access to their market (the U.S. share rose from 8.5 percent in 1985 to 12.5 percent in 1991) and has fostered cooperative agreements between Japanese and foreign microchip firms. The U.S. government disagrees, pointing to the failure of the foreign-held market share to reach 20 percent. From a broader perspective, the effectiveness of the agreement is dubious. Artificially high

---

[41]"Japan's Chip Market, Difficult to Rig," *The Economist,* October 3, 1992, p. 72.

prices have generated monopoly profits for Japanese producers and at times have caused a shortage of DRAM chips in the United States. U.S. semiconductor firms have failed to reenter the DRAM chip business because of the expense and risk. Also, the American consumer has paid higher computer prices. On the other hand, the U.S. share of the world market in microchips has stabilized at about 40 percent, the quality of U.S.-made chips has greatly improved, and U.S. producers lead the world in specialized chips, such as microprocessors. However, this improvement is mainly attributable to the innovation and responsiveness of American firms to international competitive forces.

The semiconductor agreement is now threatened by the globalization of the industry as multinational corporate strategies replace national strategies. This is most clearly demonstrated by alliances between American microchip firms and their counterparts in Japan and Europe. Already in the 1990s alliances have been formed between IBM, Toshiba, and Siemens; Advanced Micro Devices and Fujitsu; Micron Semiconductor and NEL; Intel and Sharp; Texas Instruments and Hitachi; Advanced Micro Devices and Sony; and Motorola and Toshiba. These alliances are transforming the semiconductor industry, and they should alleviate trade tensions by making them obsolete. For example, in 1985 Advanced Micro Devices charged Japanese companies with dumping chips in the United States, but now it is making those same chips with a Japanese company.

WHITHER U.S. TRADE POLICY?

We have now completed our review of U.S. trade policy.[42] As background, we analysed specific tariffs and nontariff trade barriers in Chapter 6, evaluated arguments for free trade and protection in Chapter 7, and examined multilateral trade agreements under GATT.

Table 9-6 identifies the U.S. trade policy options for the 1990s. After World War II and up to the mid-1970s, the United States followed a policy of *reciprocal liberalization* (Option II). Then policy shifted to a reliance on trade-remedy laws, notably Section 301, with its emphasis on *threats to gain foreign market access* (Option III). Will policy now shift toward *managed trade* (Options IV or V)?

Basically, managed trade is an agreement between countries that goes beyond setting *trade rules* (such as GATT agreements on tariffs) to determining *trade outcomes*. The semiconductor agreement is an example of managed trade because it establishes a goal of 20 percent penetration of the Japanese market by foreign producers at a certain date. In effect, managed trade attempts to replace market forces with government edicts to determine trade outcomes. Managed trade may employ any of the rationales for protection that were discussed in Chapter 7, including strategic trade policy.

---

[42]U.S. trade policy relating to the European community, the U.S.-Canada Free Trade Area, and the North American Free Trade Area is discussed in Chapter 10; trade policy relating to the developing countries, in Chapter 20; and trade policy relating to China, East Europe and the former Soviet Union, in Chapter 21. TRIMs are taken up in Chapter 24.

Chapter 9   U.S. Trade Policy in an Era of Global Competition   247

Table 9-6 U.S. Trade Policy Options for the 1990s

Option	*Description*
I. Unilateral liberalization	Liberalization is good policy even if it is *not* reciprocated by foreign countries. (Exception: industries that must be kept for national security reasons.)
II. Reciprocal liberalization	Liberalization is good policy only if reciprocated by foreign countries. (Offsetting concessions can be in different economic sectors.)
III. Threats to gain foreign market access	Threats of new U.S. trade restrictions are sometimes needed to open up protected foreign markets even at the risk of higher worldwide barriers.
IV. Retaliatory managed trade	The U.S. government needs to manage trade in important (strategic) sectors because the governments of other major trading countries do so.
V. Unilateral managed trade	Trade restrictions to protect strategic sectors are desirable regardless of what other governments do.

Source: Based on Twentieth Century Fund, *The Free Trade Debate* (New York: Priority Press Publications, 1989), p. 7.

From the perspective of the early 1990s, the most probable direction of U.S. trade policy is a gradual shift toward Option IV—*retaliatory managed trade*. Undoubtedly, this would provoke a similar shift by other industrial countries. It would also mark a failure of the Uruguay Round, which is intended to return trade policy to *reciprocal liberalization*. A shift toward managed trade would sacrifice the gains from free trade on the altar of special-interest protection. It would also risk the breakdown of the multilateral trading system created by U.S. leadership after World War II. That breakdown would have profound effects on all trading countries.

SUMMARY

1. Today, the United States faces formidable challenges in international trade and global competition. To cope with these challenges, this country needs to design and carry out a trade policy that will effectively promote its interests in an international economy undergoing deep-seated structural shifts.

2. Apart from shifts in comparative advantage between the North and South, the dependence of the United States and the other industrial countries on international trade has dramatically intensified over the past decade.

3. Modern U.S. trade policy was born with the passage of the Reciprocal Trade Agreements Act of 1934. After World War II, the United States became the leader in the movement toward freer trade. The Trade Act of 1974 and the Trade Act of 1979 provided the legislative framework for U.S. trade policy in the 1980s.

4. The emphasis of the Omnibus Trade and Competitiveness Act of 1988 is on foreign "unfair practices" that restrain market access for U.S. exports. The Act gives the president authority to act unilaterally in the settlement of trade disputes.

5. National competitiveness is the degree to which a nation can, under free and fair market conditions, produce goods and services that meet the test of international markets while simultaneously expanding the real incomes of its citizens.

6. The U.S. trade deficit in the 1980s rose to an astounding degree. However, this deficit is not a sign of declining U.S. competitiveness, because the trade balance is determined by macroeconomic variables such as real income, the price level, the interest rate, and the rate of exchange. Export shares and import penetration ratios of manufactures are also inadequate indicators of competitiveness.

7. A country can sustain its competitiveness in world markets only if its productivity performance keeps pace with that of other countries. Labor productivity in the manufacturing sector has grown much more rapidly in Japan and West Germany than in the United States. As a result, Japan and West Germany now have productivity levels in manufacturing that match or even exceed the U.S. level.

8. In large measure, the poor productivity record of the United States is due to low levels of investment and nondefense R & D. This country has the lowest rates of investment and saving in the industrial world. (Much of the low saving rate is traceable to the enormous U.S. budget deficit.) By the end of 1991, the United States owed the rest of the world a net amount of $361.5 billion. Also, U.S. civilian R & D has fallen behind that of Germany and Japan in the last two decades.

9. The achievement and maintenance of national competitiveness will remain a major challenge for the American people throughout the 1990s and beyond.

10. The revival of protectionism since the mid-1970s is called the "new protectionism" because it relies heavily on new forms of nontariff trade barriers, notably voluntary export restraints (VERs), orderly marketing agreements (OMAs) and trade-remedy laws. Other features of the new protectionism are its focus on a comparatively small number of industries, its bilateral application (which violates GATT's principle of nondiscrimination), and its lack of transparency.

11. Starting in the mid-1970s, the United States has increasingly resorted to trade-remedy laws to (1) protect domestic industries against dumping and foreign export subsidies and (2) open up foreign markets to U.S. exports by threatening retaliation.

12. In recent years, the United States has experienced numerous trade disputes with the European Community, Japan, and other countries. For the most part, these disputes revolve around American allegations of unfair trade practices (dumping and government subsidies) relating to U.S. imports and allegations of high nontariff trade barriers that keep U.S. goods out of foreign markets.

13. A review of U.S. protection for steel, automobiles, textiles, and semiconductors indicates that import restrictions have offered only short-term benefits to these industries at a very heavy cost to the American consumer.

14. From the perspective of the early 1990s, the most probable direction of U.S. trade policy is a gradual shift toward retaliatory managed trade.

QUESTIONS AND APPLICATIONS

1. Why is the Reciprocal Trade Agreements Program described as a "watershed" in U.S. trade policy?

2. Identify and be prepared to discuss the major provisions of the Omnibus Trade and Competitiveness Act of 1988.

3. Define *national competitiveness*.

4. "A growing external trade deficit is commonly viewed as a symptom of declining national competitiveness." Comment on this statement.

5. What is the single most important indicator of changes in national competitiveness? Why?

6. What is the relationship between investment and productivity?

7. (a) Why did the U.S. national saving rate decline in the 1980s?
   (b) What can be done to increase the saving rate in the 1990s?

8. (a) What happened to the U.S. international investment position in the 1980s?
   (b) Why did it happen?

9. (a) Is the United States losing its international competitiveness? Be prepared to defend your position.
   (b) Prepare a report on the international competitiveness of a particular U.S. industry.

10. (a) What is the "new protectionism"?
    (b) Explain the resurgence of protectionism in the United States since the mid-1970s.

11. (a) What are the principal provisions of U.S. trade-remedy laws?
    (b) What are the criteria for action under these laws?

12. Undertake research to identify and describe the major protectionist interests in the United States.
13. Undertake research on new developments relating to international trade disputes in steel, autos, textiles, and semiconductors.
14. Be prepared to engage in a debate on "Protectionism versus Free Trade in the 1990s."

SELECTED READINGS

Baumol, William J., and others. *Productivity and American Leadership: The Long View.* Cambridge: The MIT Press, 1989.

Bovard, James. *The Fair Trade Fraud.* New York: St. Martin's Press, 1991.

Bhagwati, Jagdish, and Hugh T. Patrick, eds. *Aggressive Unilateralism, America's 301 Trade Policy and the World Trading System.* Ann Arbor: University of Michigan Press, 1990.

Boltuck, Richard, and Robert E. Litan, eds. *Down in the Dumps.* Washington, D.C.: The Brookings Institution, 1991.

Brock, William, and Robert Hormats, eds. *The Global Economy.* New York: W. W. Norton & Company, 1990.

Committee for Economic Development. *Breaking New Ground in U.S. Trade Policy.* Boulder, CO: Westview Press, 1991.

Krugman, Paul. *The Age of Diminished Expectations.* Cambridge: The MIT Press, 1990.

Lawrence, Robert Z., and Charles L. Schultze, eds. *An American Trade Strategy, Options for the 1990s.* Washington, D.C.: The Brookings Institution, 1990.

Lincoln, Edward J. *Japan's Unequal Trade.* Washington, D.C.: The Brookings Institution, 1990.

Reich, Robert B. *The Work of Nations.* New York: Vintage Books, 1992.

Spence, A. Michael, and Heather A. Hazard, eds. *International Competitiveness.* Cambridge: Ballinger Publishing, 1988.

Stern, Robert M., ed. *U.S. Trade Policy in a Changing World Economy.* Cambridge: The MIT Press, 1989.

Thurow, Lester. *Head to Head: The Coming Economic Battle Among Japan, Europe and America.* New York: William Morrow and Company, 1992.

U.S. Trade Representative. *Annual Report of the President of the United States on the Trade Agreements Program.* Washington, D.C.: U.S. Government Printing Office, Annual.

Williamson, Jeffrey G. "Productivity and American Leadership: A Review Article." *Journal of Economic Literature,* March 1991, pp. 51–68.

Womack, James P., and others. *The Machine That Changed the World: The Story of Lean Production.* New York: Harper Perennial, 1991.

chapter 10

THE THEORY AND POLICY OF ECONOMIC INTEGRATION: THE EUROPEAN COMMUNITY AND NAFTA

Economic integration occurs when two or more countries join together to form a larger economic space. Countries enter integration arrangements in the expectation of economic gain, although they may pursue political and other interests as well. This chapter evaluates economic integration from the perspective of economic theory that focuses on the welfare gains and losses from economic integration. After reviewing integration theory, we look at the most successful integration effort, the European Community (EC) and the newest effort, the North American Free Trade Agreement (NAFTA). We end the chapter by examining the implications of regional integration schemes for the world trading system.

Before moving to integration theory, it is instructive to outline the form and stages of economic integration (Table 10-1).

Table 10-1 Stages of International Economic Integration

Stage of Integration	Abolition of Tariffs and Quotas among Members	Common Tariff and Quota System	Abolition of Restrictions on Factor Movements	Harmonization and Unification of Economic Policies and Institutions
1. Industrial free trade area	Yes[1]	No	No	No
2. Full free trade area	Yes	No	No	No
3. Customs union	Yes	Yes	No	No
4. Common market	Yes	Yes	Yes	No
5. Economic union	Yes	Yes	Yes	Yes

[1]Industrial goods only.

A *free trade area* is established when a group of countries abolishes restrictions on mutual trade but each member country retains its own tariff and quota system on trade with third countries. An *industrial free trade area* covers only trade in industrial products, whereas a *full free trade area* includes all products. As an industrial free trade area, the European Free Trade Association represents only a modest form of economic integration.

A *customs union* is created when a group of countries removes all restrictions on mutual trade and also sets up a common system of tariffs and quotas with respect to third countries. A customs union becomes a *common market* with the removal of all restrictions on the movement of productive factors—labor, capital, and enterprise. The EC is now in this stage of evolution but is attempting to become an economic union.

The completion of the final stage of *economic union* involves a full integration of the member economies with supranational authorities responsible for economic policymaking. In particular, an economic union requires a single monetary system and central bank, a unified fiscal system, and a common foreign economic policy. The task of creating an economic union differs significantly from the steps necessary to establish the less ambitious forms of economic integration. A free trade area, a customs union, or a common market mainly results from the abolition of restrictions, whereas an economic union demands a positive agreement to transfer economic sovereignty to new supranational institutions.

THE THEORY OF ECONOMIC INTEGRATION

The theory of economic integration identifies two types of gains and losses: (1) *static* gains and losses that result from a reallocation of the existing capital, labor, and other resources of the member economies, and (2) *dynamic* effects that affect the productive capacity, productivity, and growth of the member economies. In explaining these effects, we shall restrict our attention to customs unions.

Static Effects of a Customs Union

The theory of customs unions, a relatively new branch of economics, represents an extension of tariff theory to multinational discriminatory systems.[1] This theory analyzes the static, one-for-all changes in trade and welfare induced by the formation of a customs union or a free trade area.

Trade Effects Because a customs union involves both free trade among its member countries (liberalization) and, at the same time, restrictions on imports

---

[1]The pioneer work in this field is Viner's. See J. Viner, *The Customs Union Issue* (New York: Carnegie Endowment for International Peace, 1950). The theoretical effects of a tariff are discussed in Chapter 6.

from nonmember or third countries (protection), it has both positive and negative effects on trade. A positive effect occurs when the elimination of internal tariffs and other barriers stimulates *new* trade among the member countries that does not displace third-country imports. That is to say, the customs union induces a shift from a high-cost producer inside the union to a lower-cost producer also inside the union. This positive effect is called *trade creation*. On the other hand, a negative trade effect occurs when member countries now buy from each other what they formerly bought from third countries. Known as *trade diversion*, this negative effect results from a shift from a low-cost producer outside the union to a higher-cost producer inside the union.

A simple model will clarify the meaning of trade creation and trade diversion. Let us assume three countries (A, B, and C) that are each capable of producing wheat and automobiles. Country A is the high-cost producer of both products, country B is the low-cost producer of automobiles, and country C is the low-cost producer of wheat. In the absence of restrictions, therefore, country A would import automobiles from country B and wheat from country C. Actually, however, country A keeps out automobile imports with a tariff and imports wheat despite a tariff. Now suppose country A and country B form a customs union, leaving country C outside the union as a third country. The trade effects on automobiles and wheat are shown in Tables 10-2 and 10-3 respectively.

Table 10-2   Positive Trade Effect of a Customs Union: Trade Creation (Dollars)

	Country A	Country B	Country C
Unit cost (price) of automobile production	1,500	1,300	1,400
Cost plus country A's duty (20%)	1,500	1,560	1,680
Cost plus common duty (10%) after formation of customs union	1,500	1,300	1,540

Table 10-3   Negative Trade Effect of a Customs Union: Trade Diversion (Dollars)

	Country A	Country B	Country C
Unit cost (price) of wheat production	5.00	4.20	3.80
Cost plus country A's duty (25%)	5.00	5.25	4.75
Cost plus common duty (20%) after formation of customs union	5.00	4.20	4.56

After the formation of the customs union, buyers in country A shift from high-cost domestic automobiles to country B's automobiles, which can now be purchased at country B's domestic cost because country A's 20 percent duty is abolished within the union. These imports represent trade creation because they do not displace automobile imports from country C, which are nonexistent. However, this is not true in the case of wheat. Buyers in country A shift from country C's wheat to country B's wheat, which they can obtain free of duty after the formation of the customs union. Although country C is the low-cost producer, it must pay a 20 percent duty to sell in country A, making its wheat noncompetitive with country B's.

Under what circumstances is a customs union likely to create trade rather than divert it? First, trade creation is enhanced when the economies of the member countries are very *competitive* and have overlapping patterns of production. Then there are plenty of opportunities for specialization and trade among them. Conversely, when the pre-union economies are complementary, then the opportunities for new trade are limited, because the economies are already specialized with respect to each other. Second, trade creation is positively related to the size of the customs union (as measured by its share of world trade and production), because the larger the size, the greater the probability the lowest-cost producers will be located inside the union. Conversely, a customs union of small economic size is more likely to induce trade diversion. Third, the higher the pre-union duties of the member countries, the greater the likelihood of trade creation in products that were formerly protected against imports. Finally, the smaller the distances among member countries, the greater the scope for trade creation (because of low physical transfer costs).

Welfare Effects What are the welfare effects of trade creation and trade diversion? Let us first analyze the welfare effects for a member country.

Assume two countries, A and B, form a customs union. Assume, further, that prior to the union both countries manufacture product Y. Figure 10-1 demonstrates the welfare effects of the union for country A.[2]

D_a-D_a and S_a-S_a are the demand and supply schedules of country A, respectively. P_f-$S_{b,f}$ is the supply schedule of imports from country B under free trade. (To simplify the analysis, we are assuming a perfectly elastic import supply schedule.) But before formation of the customs union, country A imposes a duty of P_f-P_t that raises the import supply schedule to P_t-$S_{b,t}$. Hence, before the union the price of product Y in country A is 0-P_t, as determined by the intersection of P_t-$S_{b,t}$ with D_a-D_a at point k. At this price, country A consumes 0-Q_3, producing 0-Q_2 at home and importing Q_2-Q_3 from country B.

The customs union wipes out country A's duty on product Y so that the import supply schedule falls to the free-trade schedule, P_f-$S_{b,f}$. The price of product Y drops from 0-P_t to 0-P_f. At that price, country A consumes 0-Q_4, producing 0-Q_1

---

[2]Figure 10-1 is similar to Figure 6-4 in Chapter 6, which demonstrates the social cost of an import duty.

Figure 10-1

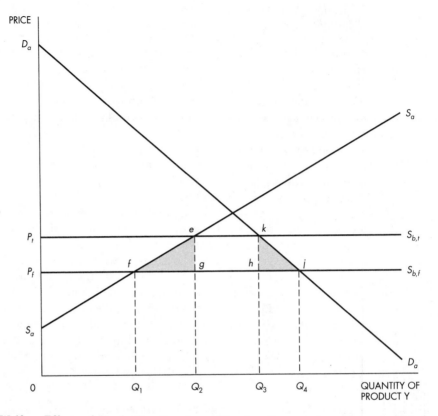

Welfare Effects of Trade Creation for a Member Country in a Customs Union.
Before formation of the customs union, country A imposes a duty on product Y coming
from country B or any other countries. Because country B is the lowest-cost producer,
country A gets all its imports of Y from country B. The duty raises country B's import
supply schedule from P_f-$S_{b,f}$ to P_t-$S_{b,t}$. At the resulting price of 0-P_t, country A consumes
0-Q_3, producing 0-Q_2, and importing Q_2-Q_3. After country A enters a customs union
with country B, imports of product Y from country B come in duty-free at a price 0-P_f. At
this price, country A consumes 0-Q_4, produces 0-Q_1, and imports Q_1-Q_4. Its net welfare
gain is shown by the two shaded triangles. This is a case of trade creation because lower-
cost imports from country B are replacing higher-cost production in country A.

and importing from country B, Q_1-Q_4. This shift in trade is *trade creation* because
higher-cost production in country A has been replaced by lower-cost production in
country B. The gain in consumer surplus for country A is indicated by the area P_f-
P_t-k-j. But some of this gain is offset by the elimination of domestic producer
surplus (P_f-P_t-e-f) and by the elimination of tariff revenue (g-e-k-h). Consequently, the net gain to country A is shown by the two shaded triangles, f-e-g and
h-k-j.

Part I   International Trade

The preceding analysis assumes that country B is the lowest-cost manufacturer of product Y. But suppose that a country outside the union is the lowest-cost manufacturer. Then the customs union will cause *trade diversion,* as depicted in Figure 10-2, which is the same as Figure 10-1 except that we have added free trade and post duty import supply schedules for the rest of the world (ROW), which is not party to the customs union.

Figure 10-2

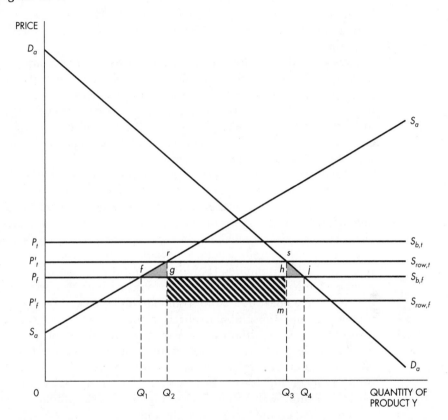

Welfare Effects of Trade Diversion for a Member Country in a Customs Union. Before formation of a customs union between countries A and B, country A imports product Y from the rest of the world (ROW) at a price lower than it would pay for imports from country B (0–P'_t compared to 0–P_t.) But after the formation of the union, imports from country B no longer pay duty and the import price drops to the free trade level (0–P_f), which is lower than the postduty price of imports from ROW (0–P'_t). Hence, country A now imports product Y from country B. This is a case of trade diversion because higher-cost exports from country B have replaced lower-cost exports from ROW. Country A has a welfare gain, as measured by the two shaded triangles, but this gain is offset by a welfare loss, as measured by the cross-hatched rectangle. Country A's net gain (or loss) depends on the relative size of the sum of the triangles versus the size of the rectangle.

Before formation of the union, country A imposes the same duty on imports from country B and ROW ($P_f - P_t = P'_f - P'_t$). Because its postduty price is lower than country B's, ROW supplies all of country A's imports at price $0-P'_t$ where A consumes $0-Q_3$ as determined by the point of intersection of D_a-D_a and ROW's after-duty supply schedule. Country A produces $0-Q_2$ and imports Q_2-Q_3 from ROW.

The customs union removes the duty on imports from country B, but not from ROW. Hence, country B now offers the lower import price, $0-P_f$ compared to $0-P'_t$. At the former price, country A consumes $0-Q_4$ of product Y, produces $0-Q_1$ at home, and imports Q_1-Q_4 from country B. This is a case of trade diversion because the union has replaced ROW's lower-cost exports with country B's higher-cost exports.

What are the welfare effects of trade diversion? Following the same reasoning used for Figure 10-1, the net gain to country A appears to be the two shaded triangles, $f-r-g$ and $h-s-j$.[3] But this is not the whole story: country A is now paying a higher price for imports that it formerly imported from ROW, as indicated by the cross-hatched rectangle ($l-g-h-m$). If the sum of the two triangles (the welfare effect of more trade) is less than the rectangle (the welfare effect of trade diversion), then the *net* welfare effect for country A is negative.

What of the welfare effects of a customs union for the *world?*

Customs union theory has been mainly concerned with the static effects of a customs union on *world* welfare rather than on the welfare of individual member or nonmember countries. From this perspective, the customs union "problem" is viewed as a special case of the theory of the second best.[4] Starting from the premise that universal free trade would achieve the most efficient allocation of the world's resources and consumption (Paretian optimum), it does not follow that free trade among a limited number of countries would *necessarily* raise world welfare. Rather, the *net* welfare effect of a customs union would depend on the net balance of the production and consumption effects associated with trade creation and trade diversion, together with any changes in income distribution.

As to the production effects, trade creation improves the world's economic efficiency (and thereby raises its potential welfare) by substituting lower-cost production for higher-cost production. Conversely, trade diversion lowers the world's potential welfare by substituting higher-cost production within the union for lower-cost production outside the union.

As we have seen, trade restrictions also have *consumption* effects because they introduce discrepancies between the relative prices at which goods can be purchased (the international terms of trade) and their relative costs of production (the marginal rate of transformation).[5] By reducing this discrepancy, trade liberaliza-

---

[3]These triangles are smaller than those in Figure 10-1 because A was obtaining its imports from ROW at a lower pre-union price than it was obtaining them from B in Figure 10-1. Hence, the formation of the union caused a smaller drop in import price in Figure 10-2 than in Figure 10-1.

[4]See Chapter 7 for an explanation of the theory of the second best.

[5]For a review of these terms, see Chapter 2.

tion allows consumers to move to a higher level of satisfaction (higher indifference curve). It follows that trade creation has a positive consumption effect on welfare, because it brings the production possibilities and the consumer preferences of the union into conformity. Conversely, trade diversion has a negative consumption effect, because it widens the gap between the preferences of consumers in the union on one hand and the world's production possibilities on the other. Trade creation enhances consumer choice; trade diversion constricts it.

To sum up, a customs union will improve world economic efficiency and potential welfare when trade creation outweighs trade diversion. However, *potential* welfare is not the same as *actual* welfare. Actual welfare depends not only on economic efficiency (the size of the pie) but also on income distribution (the sharing of the pie). In particular, income redistribution between the customs union and outsiders must be taken into account in any thorough evaluation of its welfare effects.

Dynamic Effects of a Customs Union

The static theory of a customs union ignores the many dynamic effects of customs unions (and other forms of economic integration) on *economic growth*. A customs union can promote economic welfare not only by inducing higher allocative efficiency (a movement *along* the production possibilities frontier) but also by stimulating growth (an *outward* movement of the production possibilities frontier). Indeed, the impact of its dynamic effects on world welfare may well overwhelm any negative static effects. Here only brief mention will be made of the many ways a customs union may promote economic growth.

The most obvious consequence of a customs union is *market extension:* Producers (and consumers) enjoy free access to the national markets of all member countries, whereas formerly their access was hindered or blocked by import restrictions. Market extension sets in motion many forces. It makes possible *economies of scale* in many industries that could not be achieved in narrow national markets. A broader market also intensifies *competition*, forcing producers to cut costs, sell more aggressively, and look for new products. The combination of economies of scale and heightened competition is also apt to foster an increase in *enterprise size*, whether through internal growth, merger, or acquisition. Bigger firms, in turn, have more capacity to finance research and development and thereby compete more effectively in *product innovation*.

To take advantage of new market opportunities and withstand the pressures of new competition, firms are compelled to make *investments* in plant and equipment that directly create new employment and income. Furthermore, the quality of investment will improve because investment decisions are made in light of cost and market conditions throughout the union. By forcing the development of industrial centers that serve the enlarged market, a customs union also creates external economies; interactions among the many specialized firms in those centers bring costs down for all of them. Moreover, a bigger market induces new investment in infrastructure (such as transportation, power, and communications), which in turn promotes general economic efficiency and growth. Mention should also be made of the reduction in risk and uncertainty for entrepreneurs. With assured access to the markets of the member countries, a customs union's internal trade more closely resembles domestic interregional trade than international trade. Faced with less uncertainty, therefore, entrepreneurs within the union are encouraged to make investments in plants and research to exploit the extended market over the long run.

It is to be expected that the greater the degree of economic integration, the greater the impact of these dynamic effects on growth. The liberalization of factor movements (common market) is especially noteworthy in this regard. It is not too much to say that the presence or absence of dynamic effects spell the success or failure of a customs union and more advanced forms of economic integration.

THE EUROPEAN COMMUNITY: THE CREATION OF A CUSTOMS UNION

Postwar European economic cooperation began with the establishment of the Organization for European Economic Cooperation (OEEC) in 1948 to allocate Marshall Plan aid and accelerate the recovery of Western Europe. In the 1950s, quotas and payments restrictions on intra-OEEC trade were rapidly dismantled, and European countries grew accustomed to close cooperation on trade and other economic matters. However, many Europeans, as well as Americans, considered economic cooperation under the auspices of the OEEC inadequate to cope with Europe's problems. They argued that only economic integration transcending national boundaries would enable Europe to match the continental economies of the United States and the Soviet Union. Economic integration would create the large competitive markets that are the necessary counterparts of mass production and economies of scale, and it would stimulate a more efficient allocation of labor, materials, and capital.

Supported by the United States, the drive toward European economic unity gained strength in the 1950s despite widespread doubts as to its ultimate success. Its first notable success was the establishment of the European Coal and Steel Community (ECSC) in 1952 to create a common market in coal, steel, and iron ore that encompassed the six nations of France, West Germany, Italy, Belgium, the Netherlands, and Luxembourg. The second big step toward economic unity was the negotiation and approval by these same countries of a treaty establishing the European Economic Community (EEC) in 1957.[6] (It has now become standard practice to use the designation *European Community* [EC] in place of *European Economic Community*.)

---

[6]The treaty was signed in Rome on March 25, 1957, and was then ratified by the six countries. A separate treaty setting up a European Atomic Energy Community (Euratom) was signed and ratified at the same time. Both the EEC and Euratom treaties went into effect on January 1, 1958. Fusion of the three communities (EEC, ECSC, and Euratom) into a single European Community was substantively accomplished in 1967.

The failure of negotiations for an OEEC-wide free trade area led to the formation of the European Free Trade Association (EFTA) in 1960 by Great Britain, the three Scandinavian countries, Switzerland, Austria, and Portugal. During the 1960s Western Europe remained "at sixes and sevens," but the split between the EC and the EFTA is now minimal. Great Britain, Denmark, and Ireland entered the Community at the beginning of 1973, and the other EFTA countries made free trade arrangements with the Community short of full membership.[7]

The main feature of the European Community is the creation of a customs union for both industrial and agricultural goods, involving the abolition of all restrictions on trade among member countries and the erection of a common external tariff. But the EC goes much further than this. A second objective is the establishment of a *common market* with free movement of labor, capital, and other factors of production as well as products. A third objective is a full *economic union,* with free movement of products, persons, services, and capital, and the harmonization and unification of social, fiscal, and monetary policies. The ultimate objective is a *political union* of the member countries.

The formation of the EC introduced a new force to world trade and has provoked major attempts by the United States to negotiate with the EC to lower tariffs and other trade barriers. In this section, we describe the creation of a customs union involving free trade in industrial and agricultural products inside a common external tariff. In the following section, we examine the drive to complete the common market, a process that came to be called "Europe 1992" because of its target date for implementation at the end of that year. Next, we review the ambitious effort to form an economic union centered on the creation of a European Monetary System (EMS) with a single central bank. Finally, in a new section, we discuss EC policies toward the outside world, particularly toward EFTA and the United States.

Institutions of the European Community

The basic institutions, or organs, of the EC are five in number: European Commission, Council of Ministers, European Parliament, Court of Justice, and European Council. The *Commission* is the executive body of the EC and has two main functions. First, it administers the treaty and other EC policies. Second, it initiates new policies by making proposals to the Council. The Commission represents the Community rather than the member states, and it is the driving force in the EC.

All members of the *Council of Ministers* represent their own national governments. For the most part, the Council makes final policy decisions, but it can do so only on proposals by the Commission. At first, Council decisions required a unanimous vote, but they now require only a majority vote. It is through the

----

[7]With the entry of Greece in 1981 and Spain and Portugal in 1986, the EC now has twelve members.

Council that national governments influence and control the evolution of the EC by approving, amending, or rejecting Commission proposals.

The *European Parliament* draws its members from general elections in the member countries. However, the Parliament does not pass laws and is not a true legislature, since this function is performed jointly by the Commission and the Council. The Commission must report to the Parliament annually, and the Parliament must be consulted before certain specific decisions are made. But the only important power of the Parliament is the right to remove the Commission by a motion of censure voted by a two-thirds majority.

The *Court of Justice* has the sole power to decide on the constitutionality of acts performed by the Commission and the Council. The Court's judgments have the force of law throughout the EC, and they are binding on all parties, whether individuals, business firms, national governments, or other Community institutions.

The *European Council* is composed of the twelve heads of state of the member countries and the EC Commission president. It holds summit meetings three times a year. The Council provides the main political guidance of the EC.

Free Trade in Industrial Products

The European Community became a full customs union in July 1968, when tariffs and quantitative restrictions were removed on all trade among its original member countries and a common tariff system was established vis-à-vis nonmember countries. Behind this signal achievement lay a decade of commitment that was tested by a series of hard-fought negotiations, especially in agricultural policy.

Although trade in industrial products within the EC is no longer obstructed by tariffs and quotas, it is not yet as free as trade within a single country. Many nontariff barriers continue to clog the arteries of commerce, such as differences in customs classification, varying taxation systems, border restrictions (for security, health, and technical reasons), and state monopolies. The Commission is working steadily on measures to harmonize customs legislation and eliminate licenses, visas, permits, and other export-import formalities so that the common market will have the same characteristics as a domestic market. However, certain barriers (for example, "tax frontiers" resulting from different tax systems) cannot be eliminated until the member countries agree to transfer more sovereignty to the EC.

Free Trade in Agricultural Products

Each of the original six countries came into the EC with its own domestic farm program involving price supports and import restrictions. This situation called for a different approach to free trade in agricultural products, namely, the establishment of a common agricultural policy that would not only free intra-EC trade but, at the same time, improve the economic position of EC farmers.

Although the farm problems in the EC and the United States have common features, their impact on international trade is very different.[8] The EC is still the largest importer of farm products in the world, whereas the United States is the world's largest exporter. Hence, U.S. agricultural policy is aimed at opening up (and keeping open) foreign markets to American farm products, with import restrictions playing only a modest role except in the case of dairy products. In contrast, agricultural policy in the EC — a net importer of farm products — is based primarily on the restriction of imports. In this way the EC hopes to avoid production controls and surpluses by placing the burden of adjustment on third-country suppliers, notably the United States.

The structure of the common agricultural policy (CAP) in the EC is illustrated by the common grain policy. First, there is a *target price*. This is the base price for grains and is to be established annually at the market of the region in the Community with the least adequate supplies. Farmers receive subsidies to sell their crops at prices as close as possible to the target price.

Second, there is an *intervention price*. This is the price (determined annually) at which the Community will buy from producers. It is the guaranteed minimum selling price.

Third, there is a *threshold price*. This is the price used to calculate the variable levy on imported grains. The threshold price is fixed at a level that will bring the selling price of imported grains up to the level of the target price in the region of the Community with the least adequate supplies.

Fourth, the *variable import levy* is a tariff imposed on grain imports from countries outside the group. It is determined daily and is equal to the difference between the world price for grain imports and the Community threshold price, taking any quality differences into account.

A hypothetical illustration involving common wheat may help to clarify the price structure of the common grain policy and the determination of the variable import levy:

		Per Metric Ton
1. Target price		$290
2. Intervention price		$200
3. Threshold price		
Target price	$290	
Less transportation and marketing costs	5	$285
4. Variable import levy		
Threshold price	$285	
Less adjusted world price	$125	$160

---

[8]The U.S. and EC producer subsidy equivalents of their agricultural assistance are shown in Table 8-6 in Chapter 8.

In conclusion, two points need stressing. First, there are no production controls: The EC must buy any quantity of a commodity offered at the intervention price. Second, variable import levies make third countries *residual* suppliers of farm products; imports are allowed only when EC producers fail to meet the EC's market demand. Consequently, the target prices are a key concern of the United States and other outside suppliers. High target prices encourage EC production and cut down on imports; low target prices greatly mitigate this effect.

In the 1970s, the common agricultural policy was plagued by food surpluses and a continuing deterioration of farm income relative to other sectors. High support prices encouraged overproduction in butter, sugar, wine, beef, grains, and other products.

In the 1980s, the EC "solved" the problem of surpluses: It stepped up agricultural exports through massive subsidies made necessary by high domestic prices. It became the world's largest exporter of dairy products, sugar, barley, wheat flour, and poultry. It also became the second largest exporter of beef, although per capita beef consumption is comparatively low in the EC, held down by high prices. Only a few years before, the EC was a net importer of most of these products. Subsidized exports cut deeply into the agricultural exports of the United States and other countries to their traditional markets outside the EC.

In the early 1990s, the common agricultural policy was caught in a vicious spiral of ever-rising costs with no end in sight: Ever-higher support prices caused more surpluses, which in turn required ever-higher export subsidies to eliminate them. The cost of protecting agriculture was absorbing over two-thirds of the EC's budget. Moreover, protection had failed to halt the slippage of farm income. EC target prices remain far above world prices, thereby stimulating excess production that is exported via subsidies to the rest of the world.

Because the common agricultural policy is viewed as a vital element of economic integration and because the farm lobbies in the EC are strong, any fundamental reform of the policy may prove to be impossible. As discussed in Chapter 8, the agricultural trade dispute between the EC and the United States threatens to wreck the Uruguay Round, raising the specter of retaliation and trade wars.

THE EUROPEAN COMMUNITY: TOWARD AN ECONOMIC UNION

The EC is much more than a customs union; it seeks to integrate all facets of the national member economies. The result would be an *economic union* — a single economic system embracing the entire EC. It was recognized from the start that a truly successful customs union would not be possible if each member country were free to choose its own policies without regard to the others.

Harmonization is a key word in the evolution of the economic union. Harmonization calls for the gradual elimination of differences in national legislation and administrative practices and policies and their eventual integration to form a

Community-wide policy carried out by common institutions. Since economic integration involves all aspects of the national economies, harmonization must proceed simultaneously on many fronts: antitrust policy, transportation and energy policy, trade policy, monetary and fiscal policy, wage and social policy, and so on.

Europe 1992: Completing the Common Market

To establish a common market that will match the freedom of national markets, the EC must go far beyond the traditional dimensions of a customs union. To enhance the gains from a superior allocation of resources, factors of production must be free to move among the member countries and thereby equalize factor returns for all the members. Furthermore, many nontariff measures that restrict trade or confer artificial competitive advantages on the producers of only one of the member countries must be eliminated if the pattern of EC production and trade is to reflect fully the forces of competition, costs, and markets.

The drive for a common market and economic union faltered badly in the 1970s and first half of the 1980s as two oil crises and a slowdown in economic growth accompanied by high unemployment caused member countries to turn inward and institute policies that prevented any further progress toward integration. The twenty-fifth anniversary of the EC was celebrated amidst a general pessimism about its future. By the mid-1980s, it had become evident that the Community would stagnate and possibly break up unless the remaining barriers on trade and factor movements among the member countries were abolished. It had also become evident that the EC was losing ground to the United States and Japan in the global competition of high-technology industries.

The 1985 White Paper and the Single European Act of 1987 Faced with these gloomy prospects, the EC Commission in 1985 made a dramatic effort to relaunch the drive toward economic union by issuing a White Paper titled *Completing the Internal Market.*[9] The White Paper listed 300 proposals (later reduced to 279 directives) to wipe out existing barriers, which it classified in three categories, as shown in Table 10-4.

The Single European Act (SEA) of 1987 paved the way for implementation of the White Paper.[10] The SEA committed the EC to establish a *single market* by the end of 1992. It defined a single market as an area without internal frontiers that ensures the free movement of goods, persons, services, and capital By sweeping away frontiers, the EC would create the largest single market in the world with 345 million people. The SEA raised the probability of doing so by replacing unanimous voting in the Council of Ministers with qualified majority voting for many of the decisions needed to complete the single market.

---

[9]An EC White Paper announces policies; an EC Green Paper sets out technical requirements for policy implementation.

[10]The SEA, which revised the Treaty of Rome, was signed by all member states in February 1986.

Table 10-4   Trade Barriers within the European Community Identified by the EC Commission in its 1985 White Paper

1. Physical
    Frontier controls
    Veterinary and plant health controls
    Control of individuals including customs posts
2. Technical
    Standards and regulations
    Discretionary public procurement
    Restrictions on the movement of individuals and the professions
    Restrictions on financial services
    Restrictions on transportation services
    Restrictions on new technologies
    Capital controls
    Differences in company law, intellectual and industrial property law, and
        taxation law
3. Fiscal
    Differences in value-added tax (VAT) rates and the goods to which they
        apply
    Differences in rates of excise duties and the goods to which they apply

Source: EC Commission, *Completing the Internal Market* (Brussels: 1985).

Another important step to smooth the unifying process was a new approach to harmonization adopted by the Council. Instead of trying to create detailed EC-wide technical standards and regulations for every product and service, each member country is required to accept the products and services of an EC firm that satisfy its home country's standards and regulations. This is the principle of *mutual recognition.* For example, following this principle banks in one EC country would be able to operate in all EC countries under the regulations of the home country. Common EC standards will remain, however, for measures involving environmental, health, and safety areas.

Micro- and Macroeconomic Effects of Europe 1992   To demonstrate the positive economic effects of Europe 1992, the Commission sponsored a study published in 1988.[11] This study, known as the *Cecchini Report* from the name of its principal author, used two complementary approaches to estimate the effects of Europe 1992: microeconomic and macroeconomic. The *microeconomic* approach is depicted in Figure 10-3.

---

[11]EC Commission, *Cecchini Report,* 1988.

Figure 10-3

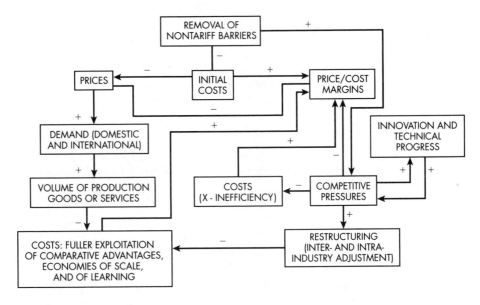

Note: + = increase, − = decrease.
Source: EC Commission, *Cecchini Report,* 1988.

Flow Chart of Microeconomic Effects Triggered by EC Market Integration.

The microeconomic approach takes as its starting point the removal of non-tariff barriers identified in Table 10-4. This removal generates a "supply-side" shock that causes gains and/or losses for consumers and companies. By cutting initial costs, the removal of barriers lowers prices and induces an increase in the amount demanded (both domestic and international) and in the volume of production of goods and services. A higher volume of output enables firms to exploit more fully comparative advantages, economies of scale, and learning effects. At the same time, the removal of barriers intensifies competitive pressures that force firms to cut price/cost margins. However, when competitive pressures reduce the costs of X-inefficiency (due to slack management in firms formerly protected against competition), firms are able to increase price/cost margins. Further, competitive rivalry induces more innovation and technical progress and compels firms to restructure to cut costs and raise productivity.

The report concludes that net effect of the microeconomic effects is positive. Consumers gain substantially from lower prices, higher quality, and more product choice. Producers incur both losses and gains: in the short run, their profits may be cut, but in the longer run, they benefit from economies of scale, learning curves, improved management, and higher levels of innovation as they respond to the single market. Overall, the report estimates total one-time gains that average

$270 billion, or 5.3 percent of the EC gross domestic product. The steps leading to these total gains are indicated in Table 10-5.

The *macroeconomic* approach of the *Cecchini Report* traces the effects of the removal of barriers on the main indicators of the Community economy: GDP, inflation, employment, public budgets, and the trade balance. This approach is depicted in Figure 10-4.

The macroeconomic model starts with four major features of market integration: (1) opening procurement by government agencies in public sectors (such as

Table 10-5   Microeconomic Estimates of Potential One-Time Gains for the European Community Resulting from Completion of the Internal Market

	Billions of Dollars	Percentage of GDP
Step 1		
Gains from removal of barriers affecting trade	10.0–11.0	0.2–0.3
Step 2		
Gains from removal of barriers affecting overall production	71.0–89.0	2.0–2.4
Gains from removing barriers (subtotal)	*81.0–100.0*	*2.2–2.7*
Step 3		
Gains from exploiting economies of scale more fully	76.0	2.1
Step 4		
Gains from intensified competition, reducing business inefficiencies, and monopoly profits	58.0	1.6
Gains from market integration (subtotal)	*76.0–134.0[a]*	*2.1–3.7[a]*
Total gains		
For 7 member states at 1985 prices	*157.0–234.0*	*4.3–6.4*
For 12 member states at 1988 prices	*218.0–323.0*	*4.3–6.4*
Midpoint of above	*270.5*	*5.3*

Note: ECU values have been converted to U.S. dollars at the following rate: 1 ECU = $1.25 on March 31, 1988. The ranges for certain lines represent the results of using alternative sources of information and methodologies. The seven member states (Germany, France, Italy, United Kingdom, Benelux) account for 88% of the GDP of the EC twelve. Extrapolation of the results in terms of the same share of GDP for the seven and twelve member states is not likely to overestimate the total for the twelve. The detailed figures in the table relate only to the seven member states because the underlying studies mainly covered those countries.

[a]This alternative estimate for the sum of steps 3 and 4 cannot be broken down between the two steps.

Source: Adapted from EC Commission, *Cecchini Report,* 1988.

Figure 10-4

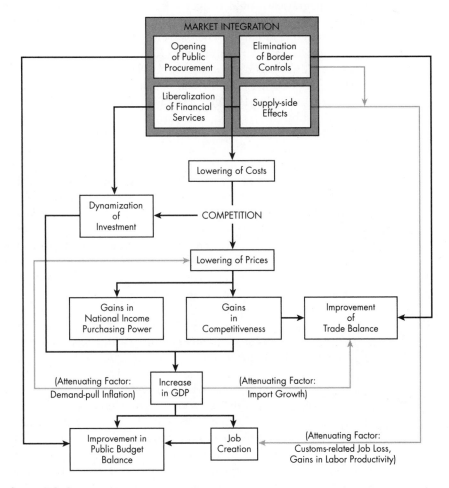

Source: EC Commission, *Cecchini Report,* 1988.

Principal Macroeconomic Mechanisms Activated in the Course of Completing the Internal Market.

transportation, energy, and communications) to suppliers throughout the Community instead of favoring local suppliers; (2) liberalizing financial services of banking, insurance, and securities firms; (3) eliminating border controls (customs) that raise costs with delays and red tape; and (4) supply-side effects that depend on business strategies in responding to the new competitive internal market.

By lowering costs and stimulating investment, market integration leads to gains in national income and competitiveness, a better trade balance, improvement in public budgets, job creation, and higher GDP. According to this analysis, market integration would trigger an increase in EC gross domestic product an average of 4.5 percent and add 1.8 million jobs. This GDP estimate is close to the microeconomic estimate of 5.3 percent. The two approaches, therefore, are in general agreement on the total gain for the Community.

Some economists believe that the Cecchini estimates are too low because they cover only static, one-time effects, ignoring dynamic effects. The *Cecchini Report* itself states that Table 10-5 does not take into full account "the overall dynamics to be unleashed by the creation of a European home market," citing business strategies and technical innovation as omissions.[12] Economists generally agree that the *dynamic* effects of EC integration are likely to exceed its static effects by a wide margin. Richard Baldwin, for instance, estimates that *medium-term* growth effects (half of which would be realized in the first ten years) would be about the same order of magnitude as the one-time static effects of the *Cecchini Report.* Moreover, dynamic effects — innovation, higher investment, economies of scale, and productivity gains — could *permanently* raise the EC growth rate over the long run by 0.3 to 0.8 percentage points, which equals a *one-time* gain of 10 to 25 percent of GDP.[13]

Both the Cecchini and Baldwin estimates assume that all 279 directives are adopted by the member countries. But the net welfare gains of Europe 1992 are dependent on a lengthy contingent process.

The first contingency is the approval of all necessary measures by the Council; the second contingency is the incorporation of those measures into the policies, laws, and regulations of all member countries; the third contingency is the effective administration of the measures by member countries; and a fourth contingency is the response of firms to market integration. This process is also subject to events outside the SEA. As we observe in the next section, the crisis over a European monetary system may well slow down completion of the internal market. Ultimately, the success of Europe 1992 depends on each member country's perceptions of the economic and noneconomic benefits and costs of a single market.

Europe 1992 has made a good start toward building a single market. Starting in 1993, for instance, trucks can move across frontiers within the Community without the need for any documentation; individuals can buy products (except for automobiles) in one EC country, pay the local tax, and then bring them home freely; a bank can open a branch in any member country under its home-country regulations; and capital can freely move throughout the Community without encountering exchange controls, with the temporary exception of some controls exercised by Greece and Portugal.

However, much remains to be done, particularly in services such as the insurance, securities, air transportation, and telephone industries. Again, the EC needs to reach agreement on the free movement of persons, which is made difficult

---

[12]Ibid.

[13]Unlike one-time gains, a permanently higher growth rate generates continuing gains year after year. The discounted value of the future stream of incremental income resulting from the single market equals its one-time value.

by illegal immigration from Eastern Europe and North Africa and by the fear of terrorism. A major challenge is the harmonization of national taxes to a degree sufficient to avoid substantial distortions of trade and investment flows among member countries. It is evident that the completion of the internal market will stretch over several years even under the most auspicious circumstances.

Creating a Monetary Union

The goal of the Community is to achieve an Economic and Monetary Union (EMU). Hence, the creation of a monetary union is linked to the creation of a single European market. A monetary union would be a formal arrangement among EC members either to fix "irrevocably" their mutual exchange rates or to use a common currency. The latter is a more ambitious union because it demands the establishment of a common central bank and the clear transfer of monetary sovereignty to that bank. It was this form of monetary union that was advanced in the Maastricht Treaty, which was approved by the leaders of all twelve member countries in December 1991. Before looking at that treaty, it is instructive to describe the present European Monetary System (EMS) on which a monetary union would be built.

The European Monetary System Following the collapse of the international monetary system in 1971, the EC countries agreed to maintain stable exchange rates among their currencies by preventing fluctuations of more than 2.25 percent. This arrangement was called the "European snake in the tunnel," because the Community currencies floated as a group against outside currencies such as the dollar. By 1978, the snake had turned into a worm, with only the West German deutsche mark, the Belgian franc, the Dutch guilder, and the Danish krone adhering to mutually stable exchange rates.[14] And so, a new effort to achieve monetary cooperation was launched in 1979 with the establishment of the European Monetary System.

The aim of the EMS is to foster "closer monetary cooperation leading to a zone of monetary stability in Europe."[15] EMS has three interrelated parts: (1) a commitment by its member countries to prevent movements greater than 2.25 percent around parity in bilateral exchange rates with other member countries;[16] (2) the European Monetary Cooperation Fund, which allocates European Currency Units (ECUs) to the members' central banks in exchange for 20 percent of the gold and dollar holdings of those central banks[17] (ECUs are used in all intrasystem

---

[14]See Chapter 19 for a description of international monetary relations during this period.

[15]International Monetary Fund, *Annual Report 1979* (Washington, D.C.: International Monetary Fund, 1979), p. 40.

[16]This is called the Exchange Rate Mechanism (ERM). A country can belong to the EMS without adhering to the ERM.

[17]The ECU is an artificial currency (with no coins or banknotes) whose value is the weighted average of the national currencies of the member countries. Hence, the U.S. dollar value of the ECU varies with changes in the exchange rates between the dollar and EC national currencies.

balance-of-payments settlements); and (3) the provision of credit facilities for compensatory financing of balance-of-payments deficits.

The Exchange Rate Mechanism works as follows. When a country's exchange rate reaches the bottom or top of its parity range, that country must keep it within the range by intervening in the foreign exchange market to buy or sell its currency for foreign currencies and/or by raising or lowering its interest rate. If such action does not work, the country needs to realign (devalue or revalue) its currency by moving to a new parity.[18]

The Maastricht Treaty The Maastricht Treaty commits the Community to establish in three stages a single currency and a single European Central Bank. In the first stage (1993), member countries would agree to coordinate their monetary policies. In the second stage (1994–1997), a European Monetary Institute would be set up as a precursor to a common central bank. The Institute would work with the member countries to bring about a convergence of their macroeconomic policies as measured by *convergence indicators* detailed in the Treaty. The third stage begins on January 1, 1997 if a majority of the member countries has attained convergence as defined by the Treaty.[19] Otherwise, a single currency will be created automatically at the start of 1999 by those countries that have met the convergence criteria. At the same time, the members will form a European Central Bank.

The Treaty is a very ambitious document. In addition to its provisions on monetary union, it has general provisions that extend the Community's responsibility to cover many fields, such as industrial, social, and environmental policies. To avert an overcentralization of power in EC institutions, the Treaty adopts the principle of *subsidiarity,* which asserts that the Community should act only where objectives cannot be sufficiently achieved by member states. The Treaty also aims to establish a common foreign and security policy on the road to political unity.

The EC in Crisis

To go into effect, the Maastricht Treaty requires ratification by all twelve member countries. The political leaders who approved the Treaty in December 1991 were confident that it would be ratified without difficulty and become operative at the start of 1993. But this was not to be. In June 1992, Denmark shocked the Community by rejecting the Treaty in a referendum, 51 percent for and 49 percent against. In September, France narrowly approved the Treaty in a referendum, 51 percent for and 49 percent against. These dispiriting events were intensified by a currency crisis in September that compelled Great Britain and Italy to leave the Exchange Rate Mechanism.

---

[18]International payments adjustment in a fixed-rate system is treated in Chapter 15.

[19]The targets of the convergence indicators are (1) an inflation rate that does not exceed by more than 1.5 percentage points the average rate of the three EC countries with the lowest rates; (2) the long-term interest rate must not exceed by more than two percentage points the average long-term rate of the three countries with the lowest inflation rates; (3) the exchange rate must stay for two years within the band of 2.25 percent above or below the parity rate; (4) the budget deficit must be under 3 percent of GDP; and (5) the public debt must be less than 60 percent of GDP.

Part I   International Trade

The disruption of ERM was caused mainly by very high interest rates in Germany designed to fight inflation stemming from the reunification. The high rates provoked a large flow of capital into Germany that pushed up the value of the deutschemark. This, in turn, weakened the value of other EC currencies, forcing the other member countries to raise their own interest rates, something they were most reluctant to do during a recession.[20] The first rupture in ERM occurred in September 1992, when Italy devalued its currency by 7 percent. This was followed a few days later by the withdrawal of Great Britain from ERM, letting the pound float freely against other currencies. A chronology of key events is offered in Table 10-6.

Table 10-6 Crisis in the European Community: A Chronology of Key Events in 1992

June 2	Denmark rejects the Maastricht Treaty in referendum by a narrow margin, putting the Treaty's ratification in jeopardy. The Treaty cannot enter into force unless all 12 members ratify it.
July 16	The German central bank (Bundesbank) raises the interest rate to 9.5 percent.
September 13	The Community authorizes Italy to devalue its currency by 7 percent.
September 14	The Bundesbank lowers the interest rate by 0.25 percent. Viewing this reduction as too little, speculators step up their attack on the pound sterling.
September 16	After raising its interest rate to 15 percent to stop speculation against the pound, Great Britain leaves the Exchange Rate Mechanism. The pound is allowed to float against other currencies.
September 17	Italy withdraws from ERM. Spain says it will devalue the peseta.
September 21	In a referendum, France approves the Maastricht Treaty by a narrow margin.
September 22	Great Britain cuts its interest rate to 9 percent to stimulate a weak economy.
September 23	France raises its interest rate from 10.5 percent to 13 percent.
September 24	France and Germany jointly act to support the franc against heavy speculation.
September 29	European currencies remain relatively stable. EC finance ministers meeting in Brussels issue a statement supporting ERM and urging all EC countries to achieve a coordinated monetary policy and a single currency by the end of the decade.

---

[20]The measures necessary to maintain stable exchange rates are discussed in Chapter 12.

The Danish veto and narrow French approval of the Maastricht Treaty, coupled with the breakdown of the Exchange Rate Mechanism have cast a pall of uncertainty over the future of the EMU. Even if the Treaty is approved by all member countries, the necessary convergence of economic conditions is only a distant possibility. The 1997 goal of a single currency has now become a dead letter. Will the Community remain a 1992-style single European market or will it become a federation of states sharing the same monetary, foreign, and defense policies and institutions? This is a question for the future.

EXTERNAL ECONOMIC RELATIONS OF THE COMMUNITY

We close our review of the European Community with some observations on its economic relations with the rest of the world.

The Community and EFTA

EFTA is an industrial *free trade area* that was fully established at the end of 1966 with the abolition of all restrictions on trade in manufactured goods among its member countries.[21] Unlike the EC, each member country retains its own tariff and quota system and follows its own trade policies with respect to third countries.

The principal motivation behind the formation of EFTA in 1960 was to set the stage for later negotiations with the EC to work toward a regional trading arrangement that would cover the whole of Western Europe. Because of the remarkable success of the EC, Great Britain opened negotiations in 1961 to enter the EC as a full member. By 1962 all EFTA members had expressed their willingness to join the EC or enter into an association with it. The United Kingdom, Denmark, and Ireland became full members of the Community at the beginning of 1973. The remaining EFTA members asked for arrangements short of full membership in the Community. In 1972, agreement was reached to establish a free trade area embracing these countries and the EC that covers industrial products but not farm products. The advent of Europe 1992 has now led to a new relationship.

After two years of negotiation, the EC and the seven EFTA countries agreed in 1991 to create the European Economic Area (EEA), encompassing 19 European countries and 380 million people.[22] The EEA allows the free movement of capital, services, workers, and industrial goods throughout the area. It covers 40 percent of world trade.[23]

---

[21]The original seven member countries of the EFTA were Austria, Denmark, Norway, Sweden, Switzerland, Portugal, and Great Britain. Finland and Iceland subsequently joined the association. The current members of EFTA are Austria, Finland, Ireland, Liechtenstein, Norway, Sweden, and Switzerland.

[22]The agreement (treaty) must be approved by nineteen national parliaments and the European Parliament before taking effect.

[23]EFTA is the EEC's main trading partner, accounting for about one-quarter of EC exports and imports. (In contrast, the United States accounts for about one-fifth of EC exports and imports.)

The EEA is basically an industrial free trade area: Both the EC and individual EFTA countries retain their own tariff schedules on imports from third countries. Also, EFTA remains outside the EC's Common Agricultural Policy. But the EEA goes beyond the scope of a pure free trade area. The EFTA countries agree to adopt many EC rules, including those on competition (antitrust), company law, consumer protection, education, the environment, and social policy. Further, there is mutual recognition of professional qualifications, allowing professional persons to live and work throughout the EEA. However, the EFTA countries will have no vote on future EC laws, and an EEA Council will decide by consensus on the application of new EC rules to EFTA countries. The EEA agreement opens the way to enlargement of the EC in the future. Already, Austria, Sweden, and Finland have applied for full membership in the Community. In sum, EEA lies somewhere between a free trade area and a common market.

Will the EEA be followed by similar arrangements with other countries? Not likely, and, in any event, not soon. The collapse of communism in Eastern Europe in 1990 has opened up the question of Community enlargement that would encompass the former communist countries. Indeed, the Community has signed "Europe Agreements" with Poland, Hungary, and Czechoslovakia that provide for transition to an industrial free trade area. But it may be twenty years or more before the EC welcomes an Eastern European country as a full member.[24] The entry of Mediterranean countries that have applied for membership (Turkey, Cyprus, and Malta) has become more distant with disruption of the Maastricht Treaty and ERM. Only EFTA countries stand a good chance of admission to the Community before the next century.

Preferential Arrangements

In addition to EEA and Association agreements with Eastern European and Mediterranean countries, the EC has entered a preferential trade arrangement with sixty-nine African, Caribbean, and Pacific (ACP) developing countries under the Lomé Convention. Renewed for a ten-year period in 1989, the Convention frees the ACP countries from all customs duties for their exports to the Community (except for temperate food products protected by CAP) while requiring no reciprocal concessions for EC exports to them.

The EC's preferential arrangements have been criticized by GATT, UNCTAD, and many third countries, notably the United States. They allege that the proliferation of these accords causes negative trade diversions (which particularly hurt tropical countries in Latin America and elsewhere that export the same products, such as coffee, cocoa, cotton, and bananas) and endangers the most-favored-nation principle (nondiscrimination). In reply, the Community points out that a preponderance of its trade is nondiscriminatory and that its preferential

---

[24]"Will More Be Merrier?" *The Economist,* October 17, 1992, p. 75.

policy is limited to agreements with European countries, countries of the Mediterranean basin, and Lomé Convention countries.

The United States and the Community

The European Community and the United States are giants of world trade. Excluding trade among its members, the enlarged Community of twelve countries accounts for about 20 percent of world exports, and the United States for about 15 percent. Furthermore, the EC's gross domestic product is comparable with that of the United States. Because of its economic size and dynamism, the external policies of the EC have a pervasive influence on the composition, direction, and volume of international trade and investment. Some comparisons between the Community and the United States are offered in Table 10-7.

The United States has consistently supported the EC in its efforts to build economic and political unity in Western Europe. At the same time, several issues have aggravated U.S.-EC trade relations, issues that first came to a head in the Kennedy Round of 1963–1967, notably the common agricultural policy and nontariff trade barriers. As we saw in Chapter 8, these same issues reappeared in the Tokyo and Uruguay Rounds.

Although the EC remains the largest U.S. export market, this country has been irritated by the trade diversion effects of the common agricultural policy and

Table 10-7 Some Comparisons Between the European Community and the United States

	European Community	United States
Population (millions)[1]	342	246
Gross domestic product (billions of dollars)[1]	7,543	6,793
Surface area (thousands of square kilometers)[1]	2,362	9,373
Inflation rate (percent)[1]	5	4.5
EC exports of goods to world (billions of dollars)[3]	529	
U.S. exports of goods to world (billions of dollars)[2]		372
EC imports of goods from U.S. (billions of dollars)[2]	107	—
EC exports of goods to U.S. (billions of dollars)[2]	96	—
U.S. direct investment in EC (billions of dollars)[2]		173
EC direct investment in U.S. (billions of dollars)[2]	230	

[1]1992

[2]1991

[3]1991; net of intra-EC trade

Source: *Facts and Figures on the European Community and the United States* (Washington, D.C.: EC Information Services, March 1992), and *OECD in Figures,* Supplement to *The OECD Observer,* June–July 1992.

EC preferential agreements in the Mediterranean. The entry of Great Britain, Ireland, and Denmark into the Community caused a sharp drop in U.S. agricultural exports to those countries, while preferential arrangements in the Mediterranean have hurt U.S. citrus exports. Conversely, the Community has frequently protested, and occasionally retaliated against, new U.S. import restrictions, and it is very sensitive to protectionism in the United States.

In the early 1990s, trade relations between the United States and the Community dramatically worsened as protectionist forces gained strength on both sides of the Atlantic, raising the spectre of a trade war between the two giants. U.S.-EC disputes on agricultural trade have been chronic since the institution of the common agricultural policy in mid-1962. As observed in Chapter 8, both the United States and the Community heavily subsidize agriculture. The U.S. proposal to eliminate *all* forms of agricultural subsidies within ten years is vigorously opposed by the EC, which favors a gradual reduction in subsidies. The two sides have failed to reach an agreement on this issue, a failure that could easily erupt into a full-scale trade war that would be fatal to the Uruguay Round.

Together the European Community and the United States account for over one-third of world trade and two-thirds of the world's gross domestic product, and they are major markets for each other. It is not too much to say that their mutual trade relations are crucial to the maintenance of an open international economy. It is imperative, therefore, that these two trading partners work out their trade differences in a spirit of understanding and cooperation, avoiding unilateral actions on issues of mutual concern.

THE NORTH AMERICAN FREE TRADE AGREEMENT

In August 1992, the United States, Canada, and Mexico concluded negotiations on the North American Free Trade Agreement (NAFTA) that will eliminate trade and investment barriers among the three countries. Formal government approval in each country is necessary before implementation of the pact.[25] NAFTA links the United States to its first-largest country trading partner (Canada) and to its third-largest (Mexico). Once operative, NAFTA will rival the European Community as the world's biggest single market, with $6 trillion in GDP and over 360 million consumers.

The precursor of NAFTA is the U.S.-Canada Free Trade Agreement, which started in 1989. This agreement is designed to (1) eliminate all tariffs by 1998 and substantially reduce other barriers to trade in goods and services between the two countries; (2) promote fair competition; (3) liberalize trade in agriculture, autos, energy, financial services, government procurement, and other areas; (4) liberalize conditions for investment; (5) establish effective administrative procedures and

---

[25]Once legislation is submitted by the president, the U.S. Congress will vote *yes* or *no* on the entire agreement with no amendments and within 90 congressional session days ("fast-track" procedure).

resolve disputes; and (6) lay the foundation for further bilateral and multilateral cooperation.[26] Each year the United States and Canada exchange more goods than any other two countries, with annual two-way trade amounting to $200 billion.

The relative size of the U.S., Canadian, and Mexican economies is shown in Table 10-8.

Table 10-8 reveals two important aspects of NAFTA. First, the U.S. economy is dominant: It accounts for nearly nine-tenths of NAFTA's gross domestic product. The U.S. economy is about ten times the size of Canada's and twenty-five times the size of Mexico's. The second aspect is the wide gap between the United States and Canada, on the one hand, and Mexico, on the other in their levels of economic development, as indicated by per capita GDP and average wage per day. In contrast, the EC has no such dominant country and its members are on about the same level of development, with the modest exceptions of Portugal and Greece. NAFTA will be the first free trade area comprising both industrial and developing countries.

Main Provisions of NAFTA

Table 10-9 summarizes the main provisions of NAFTA.

It is evident that NAFTA is more than a conventional free trade area. It moves beyond trade in goods to encompass trade in services, and it moves beyond trade to encompass direct foreign investment. Also, its provision on the environment strikes new ground.

Potential Economic Effects of NAFTA

Economists have made numerous studies of the potential impact of NAFTA on the economies of the United States, Canada, and Mexico.[27] The consensus among

Table 10-8   Relative Size of the U.S., Canadian, and Mexican Economies

	United States	Canada	Mexico
Gross domestic product (billions of dollars)	5,514	572	214
Population (millions)	250	27	86
Per capita GDP (dollars)	22,056	21,527	2,490
Average wage per day (dollars)	69.14	67.98	8.11

Source: Adapted from Nora Lustig, Barry P. Bosworth, and Robert Z. Lawrence, eds., *North American Free Trade* (Washington, D.C.: The Brookings Institution, 1992), Table 1, p. 4.

---

[26]U.S. Department of State, *U.S.-Canada Free Trade Agreement* (Washington, D.C.: June 1988).

[27]Several of these studies are detailed in Nora Lustig, Barry P. Bosworth, and Robert Z. Lawrence, eds., *North American Free Trade* (Washington, D.C.: The Brookings Institution, 1992).

Table 10-9 Main Provisions of NAFTA

General provisions on trade in goods

There will be a progressive elimination of all tariffs on goods qualifying as North American under NAFTA's rules of origin. For most goods, duties will be removed upon agreement's taking effect or phased out in five to ten years. Also, elimination of prohibitions and quantitative restrictions (such as quotas and licenses) with special rules for trade in agriculture, automotive products, energy, and textiles.

Rules of origin

Goods are deemed to originate in North America if they are wholly North American or are sufficiently transformed in the NAFTA region so as to undergo a specified change in tariff classification. In some cases, goods must include a specific percentage of North American content in addition to meeting the tariff classification requirement.

Agriculture

When the agreement goes into effect, Mexico and the United States will eliminate immediately all nontariff barriers to their agricultural trade, converting them to tariff quotas or ordinary tariffs. With a few exceptions, all tariff barriers between Mexico and the United States will be eliminated not later than ten years after the agreement takes effect. Mexico and Canada will gradually eliminate all barriers to trade in most agricultural products.

Automotive goods

Barriers to trade and investment restrictions in automotive products will be eliminated over a ten-year transition period. To qualify for preferential tariff treatment, automotive goods must contain a specified percentage of North American content ranging from 60.0 to 62.5 percent.

Textiles and apparel

Immediately or over a ten-year period, customs duties on textiles and apparel manufactured in North America that meet NAFTA's rules of origin will be eliminated.

Government procurement

A significant portion of the government procurement market in each member country will be opened gradually on a nondiscriminatory basis to suppliers in the NAFTA region.

Trade in services

A set of basic rules and obligations will be established to facilitate trade in services between the three countries, excluding government procurement and services in finance, energy, air, telecommunications, social programs, and the maritime industry.

Financial services

Financial service providers of a NAFTA country may establish banking, insurance, securities, and other types of financial operations in any other NAFTA country. Also, each country must permit its residents to buy financial services in another member country.

Table 10-9 Continued

Investment
Barriers will be removed, protection will be provided for NAFTA investors, and a mechanism will be provided to settle disputes between investors and a NAFTA country. National treatment will be accorded NAFTA investors in each member country.

Intellectual property
Each country is to provide adequate and effective protection and enforcement of intellectual property rights on the basis of national treatment.

Environment
Each country is committed to implement the agreement in a manner consistent with environmental protection and sustainable development.

Source: Claudio Loser and Eliot Kalter, *Mexico: The Strategy to Achieve Sustained Economic Growth,* Occasional Paper no. 99 (Washington, D.C.: International Monetary Fund, September 1992), pp. 34–35; and *North American Free Trade Agreement* (Washington, D.C.: Office of the U.S. Trade Representative, August 12, 1992).

analysts is that the one-time static effects of NAFTA are likely to be small for both the United States and Mexico because tariffs on their mutual trade are already low (averaging 6 percent for the United States and 13 percent for Mexico) and most NTBs are being phased out. Another reason for modest static effects is the substantial existing integration of the two economies resulting from a continuing flow of Mexican labor to the United States. In 1990, there were 4.6 million "Mexican" workers in the U.S. labor force, about 3.6 percent of the total U.S. labor force.[28] Integration has also resulted from the large number of U.S. firms manufacturing products in Mexico for subsequent export to the United States under the *maquiladora* program.[29]

Table 10-10 shows the static effects of NAFTA projected by three models using somewhat different assumptions.

Economists anticipate that NAFTA will have much larger dynamic growth effects than static resource-allocation effects. In particular, it is projected that NAFTA will induce a sustained increase in direct investment in Mexico by U.S. and other multinational firms. The resulting higher income would benefit imports of capital goods coming mainly from the United States, which account for some 70 percent of Mexican trade. This benefit would extend over several decades.

---

[28]Ibid., Table 3, p. 75. "Mexican" workers are all legal and illegal immigrants from Mexico who entered the United States between 1940 and the present and their progeny, regardless of place of birth.

[29]This program allows U.S. companies to import materials from the United States duty-free into Mexico for processing, provided that the output is exported from Mexico. The United States applies duty only on the value added in Mexico.

Part I International Trade

Table 10-10 Effect of NAFTA on Real Income: Three Static Models with Increasing Returns to Scale (Percent)

	United States	Canada	Mexico
Roland-Holst, Reinert and Shiells II[1]	2.55	6.75	3.29
Brown, Deardorff, and Stern:			
Tariffs and NTBs[2]	0.1	0.7	1.6
Tariffs, NTBs and Mexican capital inflow[3]	0.3	0.7	5.0

[1]Assumes *national* product differentiation, implying that each country has a monopoly in the market for its own national variety of a product. This constrains the possibility of intersectoral specialization as a result of liberalization.

[2]Assumes product differentiation only at the level of the firm.

[3]Assumes direct foreign investment expands Mexico's capital stock by 10 percent.

Source: Adapted from Nora Lustig and others, *North American Free Trade* (Washington, D.C.: The Brookings Institution, 1992), Table 5, p. 47.

With the poorest economy of the three member countries, Mexico is expected to gain the most from NAFTA. But to do so, it will need to make the biggest structural adjustments of the three countries. The United States is expected to gain mainly from higher growth in Mexico. Canada's gains are expected to become bigger over time as it intensifies its trade and investment ties to Mexico.

Attacks Against NAFTA in the United States

American critics of NAFTA make several charges. NAFTA will (1) cost U.S. jobs, (2) induce U.S. firms to move to Mexico, (3) increase immigration from Mexico, (4) cause Mexican exports to flood the United States, (5) let Mexico become a pollution heaven for U.S. firms, and (6) benefit only Southern border states. Some critics add that old protectionist canard: The United States cannot benefit from trade with a poor country like Mexico. Although these charges can be refuted by economic analysis, the debate over NAFTA promises to be a bitter one.

A CLOSING NOTE

The EC's drive to complete the internal market and the push to establish NAFTA are taking place at a time when the multilateral trading system—symbolized by GATT—is weakening under the blows of the new protectionism discussed in Chapters 8 and 9. The prolongation of the Uruguay Round is another sign of weakness.

Customs unions and other forms of regional integration are inherently discriminatory, favoring member countries over outside countries. To most economists, they are a "second-best" policy, the first-best policy being worldwide free trade. At the beginning of this chapter, we observed that the net effect of a customs union on world welfare depends on the balance of trade creation and trade diversion (static allocation effects) and on dynamic growth effects. From this perspective, it is critical that regional integration arrangements minimize trade diversion and, at the same time, build internal markets that generate growth beneficial to all trading countries.

But this may prove to be a counsel of perfection. Instead, will the EC and NAFTA provoke the formation of an Asian integration scheme centered on Japan? Will the multilateral trading system fragment into a tripolar system of warring trade blocs with a "fortress mentality"? Only time will tell. But there is reason to be optimistic. Led by multinational firms, global competition transcending individual countries and regions now drives international trade and investment. Only multilateral trade and investment policies can deal with this global economy in a positive way. Regional integration schemes, therefore, need to be outward-oriented, acting in support of a multilateral trading system open to all countries.

SUMMARY

1. The theory of customs unions analyzes the static, once-for-all changes in trade and welfare induced by the formation of a customs union or free trade area. The result of such changes culminates in either trade creation or trade diversion. A customs union will improve world economic efficiency and potential welfare when trade creation outweighs trade diversion. Aside from its static effects, a customs union may have many dynamic effects on economic growth and welfare: market extensions, economies of scale, competition, enterprise size, and others.

2. The European Community started its official existence at the beginning of 1958. The main feature of the EC is the creation, in planned stages, of a *customs union* for both industrial and agricultural goods. A second objective is the establishment of a *common market,* with free movement of labor, capital, and other factors of production, as well as products. A third objective is a full *economic union,* with free movement of persons, services, and capital and progressive harmonization of social, fiscal, and monetary policies. The ultimate objective is *political union* of the member countries.

3. The basic institutions of the Community are five in number: European Commission, Council of Ministers, European Parliament, Court of Justice, and European Council.

4. The EC became a full customs union in 1968, when tariffs and quantitative restrictions were completely removed on all trade among its member countries and a common tariff system was fully established vis-à-vis nonmember countries. However, nontariff barriers (such as different national technical stan-

dards, government procurement preferences, and regulations covering banking, insurance, and other services) continue to restrain trade among the member countries.

5. The EC has a common agricultural policy involving target, intervention, and threshold prices and variable import levies. Two points need stressing: There are no production controls, and the variable import levies make third countries, such as the United States, residual suppliers of farm products.

6. The EC has also built a common market with free movements of productive factors among the member countries, namely, labor, capital, and enterprise. But the common market is not complete, since several national policies and regulations continue to curtail factor movements within the Community.

7. The drive to complete the common market and move on to economic union faltered badly in the 1970s and first half of the 1980s. In 1987, the EC made a dramatic move to "relaunch" this drive by adopting the Single European Act, which commits the Community to the creation of a *single market* by the end of 1992. Such a market would resemble the U.S. market in its free movement of goods and factor services and its economic size.

8. Economists generally agree that the dynamic economic effects of Europe 1992 are likely to exceed its static effects by a wide margin. But these effects are contingent on the approval and implementation of all necessary measures by the member countries.

9. The Maastricht Treaty commits the Community to establish in three stages a single currency and a single European Central Bank by the end of the century. This Economic and Monetary Union (EMU) will supersede the present European Monetary System (EMS) that maintains exchange-rate stability among member-country currencies.

10. The Community is now in crisis. Denmark rejected the Maastricht Treaty and France narrowly approved it in national referendums held in 1992. In September of that year, a currency crisis forced Great Britain and Italy to leave the Exchange Rate Mechanism of EMS. These events have cast a pall of uncertainty over the future of EMU.

11. The EC and the European Free Trade Area (EFTA) agreed in 1991 to create the European Economic Area (EEA), a free-trade arrangement encompassing 19 European countries and 380 million people. The EC also has preferential arrangements with Mediterranean and Lomé Convention countries.

12. Trade relations between the United States and the Community have worsened in the early 1990s as protectionist forces have gained strength on both sides of the Atlantic.

13. In 1992, the United States, Canada, and Mexico concluded negotiations on the North American Free Trade Agreement (NAFTA). Once operative, NAFTA will rival the EC as the world's biggest single market.

14. It is critical to the world's welfare that regional integration schemes, such as the EC and NAFTA, minimize trade diversion and, at the same time, build internal markets that generate growth beneficial to all trading countries.

QUESTIONS AND APPLICATIONS

1. Distinguish between the following forms of economic integration: free trade area, customs union, common market, and economic union.
2. (a) Explain the meaning of *trade diversion* and *trade creation* in customs union theory.
   (b) Identify and explain the dynamic effects of a customs union.
3. Using graphical analysis, demonstrate the following proposition: When there is trade diversion in a customs union, the net welfare effect on the importing member country depends on the balance between trade creation and trade diversion.
4. Identify the institutions of the EC and describe their functions.
5. What is the structure of the common agricultural policy? How does this structure affect EC imports of farm products?
6. (a) What is the Single European Act?
   (b) What must the EC do to achieve a single market?
7. Compare the advantages and disadvantages of the concepts of *harmonization* and *mutual recognition* with reference to the completion of the single market.
8. (a) According to the *Cecchini Report,* what are the microeconomic effects of Europe 1992? The macroeconomic effects?
   (b) What are the contingencies that could limit the Cecchini estimates of Europe 1992 effects?
9. (a) Describe the main features of the Maastricht Treaty.
   (b) What are the *convergence indicators* detailed in the Maastricht Treaty?
   (c) Why is convergence of macroeconomic policies necessary to the success of EMU?
10. Using library resources, write a report titled: "The EC Currency Crisis of 1992."
11. (a) What is the EFTA?
    (b) What is the EFTA's relation to the EC?
12. Prepare an up-to-date report on trade relations between the United States and the EC.
13. (a) What is NAFTA?
    (b) Why is NAFTA more than a conventional free trade area?
    (c) How does NAFTA differ from the EC?
14. (a) Identify three charges against NAFTA by American critics.
    (b) How would you refute those three charges?

SELECTED READINGS

Abrams, Richard K., and others. *The Impact of the European Community's Internal Market on the EFTA.* Occasional Paper no. 74. Washington, D.C.: International Monetary Fund, December 1990.

Cecchini, Paolo, and others. *The European Challenge 1992: The Benefits of a Single Market*. Aldershot, England: Wildwood House, 1988.

Commission of the European Communities. *Completing the Internal Market*. White Paper from the Commission to the European Council. Luxembourg: Office of Official Publications of the European Communities, 1985.

Commission of the European Communities. *Single Market to European Union*. Luxembourg: Office of Official Publications of the European Communities, 1992.

de la Torre, Augusto, and Margaret R. Kelly. *Regional Trade Arrangements*. Occasional Paper no. 93. Washington, D.C.: International Monetary Fund, March 1992.

European Community. *Europe*. Bimonthly.

European Free Trade Association. *EFTA Bulletin*. Bimonthly.

Fratianni, Michele, and others. *The Maastricht Way to EMU*. Essays in International Finance no. 187. Princeton, N.J.: Princeton University Press, June 1992.

Giovannini, Alberto. *The Transition to European Monetary Union*. Essays in International Finance no. 178. Princeton, N.J.: Princeton University Press, November 1990.

Hufbauer, Gary Clyde, and Jeffrey J. Schott. *North American Free Trade*. Washington, D.C.: Institute for International Economics, 1992.

Hufbauer, Gary Clyde, ed. *Europe 1992: An American Perspective*. Washington, D.C.: The Brookings Institution, 1990.

Lustig, Nora, Barry B. Bosworth, and Robert Z. Lawrence, eds. *North American Free Trade*. Washington, D.C.: The Brookings Institution, 1992.

Padoa-Schioppa, Tommaso, ed. *Europe After 1992: Three Essays*. Essays in International Finance no. 182. Princeton, N.J.: Princeton University Press, May 1991.

Schott, Jeffrey J. "Trading Blocs and the World Trading System." *World Economy*, March 1991.

Swann, Dennis. *The Economics of the Common Market*. 6th ed. London: Penguin Books, 1988.

Weintraub, Sidney, ed. *U.S.-Mexican Industrial Integration: The Road to Free Trade*. Boulder, Co.: Westview Press, 1991.

INTERNATIONAL

part II

PAYMENTS

International trade and investment take place within an international monetary system composed of national monetary systems and their linkages through foreign exchange markets. Although the international monetary system is intended to facilitate flows of trade and investment, governments sometimes use (or abuse) it to restrict such flows. Part II addresses the many theoretical and policy issues that arise from the money transactions that tie together the world's countries. Our analytical focus is the adjustment processes that bring national economies into equilibrium with economic forces outside their borders. Chapters on the theory of adjustment prepare us to understand the complexities of national payments policies in the context of the contemporary international monetary system.

chapter 11

THE MECHANISM
OF INTERNATIONAL
PAYMENTS AND FOREIGN
EXCHANGE MARKETS

How are international payments made? What is the role of commercial banks in international payments? What is foreign exchange? What is the structure of the foreign exchange market in the United States? Why can we speak of a *global* foreign exchange market? What is the role of international financial centers in international payments? These are the principal questions addressed in this opening chapter on international payments. Chapter 12 continues our study by examining the determination of exchange rates in foreign exchange markets, and Chapter 13 looks at speculation and hedging in foreign exchange markets.

THE MECHANISM OF INTERNATIONAL PAYMENTS

When an American resident buys something from, say, a Japanese resident, how can the American pay the Japanese? After all, the American wants to pay in dollars while the Japanese wants to receive payment in yen. Evidently, the American needs to find someone who is willing to sell to him the required number of yen in exchange for dollars. Fortunately, it is not necessary for the American to search far and wide for that someone, because commercial banks in the United States and Japan offer facilities to transfer payments between the two countries.

Fundamentally, the mechanism of *international* payments is similar to the mechanism of *domestic* payments within the United States. Most payments in this country are made through checks drawn by persons and business firms on banks that cause shifts in the ownership of bank deposits from the payers to payees. Banknotes are used mostly for retail transactions, and even here their importance has fallen with the growth of credit cards.

Most international payments also involve shifts in the ownership of bank deposits. But these shifts are now between residents of different countries, and they are brought about by international bank transfers and bank drafts rather than by checks, because few individuals or nonbank institutions maintain deposits in *foreign*

288

banks.[1] An international *bank transfer* is an order sent (usually through an electronic network) by a bank in one country to a bank in another country instructing the latter to debit the deposit account of the former and credit the account of a designated person or institution. Banks can also make international payments through a *bank draft.* Take, for example, the American who wants to send funds to a Japanese. To do so, he can purchase a draft from a U.S. bank that orders a Japanese bank to make payment of a specified amount in yen to a designated person or institution upon presentation of the draft. Bank transfers and bank drafts are possible because banks in one country maintain deposit balances with banks in other countries. Only a small fraction of international payments (mostly tourist purchases) are made with banknotes.

International payments are more risky than domestic payments for several reasons. First, the domestic-currency value of a prospective foreign-currency payment depends on the exchange rate between the two currencies. This *foreign exchange risk* is highest when exchange rates are free to respond to market forces, as is true of the major currencies today. A second risk of international payments is the *inconvertibility risk:* the inability of the holder of a country's currency to convert it into the currency of another country because of exchange restrictions imposed by the government. A third risk is the *default risk,* the risk that the debtor will fail to pay the creditor. Although default risk is also present in domestic payments (unlike foreign exchange and inconvertibility risks), it is higher in international payments because legal action against defaulting debtors in foreign countries is more costly, more time consuming, and less successful than legal action against domestic debtors.

We shall consider how firms can hedge against foreign exchange risks in Chapter 13. International traders try to minimize inconvertibility and default risks by adapting the method of international payment to the circumstances. To understand this point, we turn to a brief description of methods of payment in international trade.

Methods of Payment in International Trade

The principal methods of payment in international trade are cash in advance, commercial letters of credit, commercial drafts drawn on the buyer, open account, and consignment. Generally, sellers (exporters) want to get paid quickly in their own currency while foreign buyers (importers) want to pay in their own currency only after delivery or resale of the goods. The method of payment agreed upon by a seller and a buyer depends, therefore, on their relative bargaining power. A strong seller can insist on cash in advance or an irrevocable letter of credit; a strong buyer can insist on open account or consignment. Payment through commercial drafts is more likely to accommodate the interests of both the exporter and the importer than other methods of payment.

---

[1]The multinational corporation is an exception to this statement, maintaining bank deposits in several countries. It is able, therefore, to make international payments by writing corporate checks.

Exporters may try to minimize buyer default risk by insisting on cash in advance or an irrevocable letter of credit or by investigating the credit standing of importers before arranging more lenient methods of payment. The risk of currency inconvertibility, however, is country-specific, not buyer-specific. A Colombian importer, for example, may be quite willing to pay an American exporter, but the importer cannot obtain a license to buy dollars from the exchange control authorities. As discussed in Chapter 17, countries may impose exchange controls in response to persistent deficits in their balance of payments. To minimize payment risks, therefore, exporters must consider not only the creditworthiness of individual importers but also the actual and prospective convertibility of the importer's currency.

Cash in Advance   This is a relatively uncommon method of international payment because of the burden that it places on the buyer. A seller may demand such terms when he judges that the credit standing of the buyer is very poor or the risk of inconvertibility is very high. However, even in those circumstances, the seller may not demand cash in advance if he would thereby lose sales to competitors.

Confirmed, Irrevocable Letter of Credit   When an exporter is not receiving cash in advance but does not want to rely on an importer's promise to pay, he may request a confirmed, irrevocable letter of credit. A letter of credit is an instrument issued by the importer's bank that obligates that bank to honor drafts drawn against it by the exporter (beneficiary) in accordance with specified terms. These terms include the amount of the credit, tenor of the draft, general description of the merchandise, documents required, and expiration date.[2] The letter of credit becomes *confirmed* when a bank in the exporter's country also promises to honor drafts drawn under it. But the bank in the exporter's country will not confirm a letter of credit unless the foreign issuing bank makes it *irrevocable* so that it cannot be cancelled or altered except with the agreement of all the parties.

Under letter-of-credit export financing, the following basic steps occur: (1) The importer's bank issues an irrevocable letter of credit covering a specific shipment of merchandise, naming the exporter as beneficiary. (2) A bank in the exporter's country confirms the letter of credit, informing the exporter about it. (3) The exporter arranges for shipment of the merchandise to the importer, receiving from the shipping company a *bill of lading*.[3] (4) The exporter draws a draft on the

---

[2]The tenor of a draft determines its time of payment. A *sight* draft is payable at the time that it is presented to the drawee (the confirming bank under a confirmed letter of credit). A *time* draft is payable a certain number of days after sight or on a certain date.

[3]The ocean (or airway) bill of lading issued by the international carrier serves three functions: (1) It is a receipt for merchandise delivered to the carrier; (2) it is a contract for services to be provided by the carrier; and (3) when made out to the order of the exporter, it is a document of title that is needed to obtain the merchandise at the point of destination. As we shall note, it is this last function that makes the bill of lading important for international payments under commercial drafts. In addition to the bill of lading, several other documents may be required by a letter of credit, notably invoices and insurance certificates.

confirming bank. (5) The exporter presents the draft (along with the bill of lading and other required documents) for payment or acceptance.[4]

In sum, payment under a confirmed commercial letter of credit is highly advantageous to the exporter, because it means payment at the time of shipment with hardly any risk of nonpayment as long as the exporter keeps to the conditions of the letter of credit. But this method is burdensome to the importer because he or she may need to make a substantial advance payment to his or her bank to arrange the letter of credit. Importers, therefore, tend to buy from exporters who offer more lenient terms. Consequently, to stay competitive, experienced exporters require letters of credit only when there are high default or inconvertibility risks.

Commercial Drafts   A commercial draft is a bill of exchange drawn by an exporter against an importer. A bill of exchange is an unconditional order in writing addressed by one party (the drawer) to a second party (the drawee), and it requires the latter to make payment of a specified sum of money at a fixed and determinable future time to a third party (the payee). A bill of exchange becomes a bill of *foreign* exchange when the drawer and drawee are residents of different countries. Bills of exchange are negotiable instruments that are transferable from one holder to another through endorsement. Such a bill is shown in Figure 11-1.

The sequence of steps in commercial draft payment is as follows: (1) The exporter draws a draft against the importer that orders payment on presentation (sight draft) or payment on a determinable date after presentation (time draft). The terms of the draft, therefore, are "documents against payment" (D/P) or "documents against acceptance" (D/A). (2) The exporter submits the draft and

Figure 11-1

A Commercial Bill of Exchange.

---

[4]A sight draft will be paid immediately by the bank; a time draft will be "accepted" by the bank, obligating it to make payment on the due date. A bank acceptance is readily sold for cash in the acceptance market.

accompanying shipping documents (including the bill of lading) to the exporter's own bank for collection. (3) The bank forwards the draft and shipping documents to its correspondent bank in the importer's country, which in turn presents it to the importer. (4) If the draft is payable on sight, then the importer must make immediate payment to the exporter in order to obtain the bill of lading, which is needed to acquire physical possession of the export shipment. (5) If the draft is payable at a certain time in the future, then the importer must "accept" the draft in order to obtain the bill of lading. This *trade acceptance* is held by the correspondent bank, and when it becomes due, it is presented to the importer for payment.

We have described what is called payment through *documentary draft*—a draft that is accompanied by documents that can be obtained by the importer only after payment or acceptance of the draft. The documentary draft is by far the most common method of financing international trade; it is also a very old method that can trace its beginnings back to the Italian city-states of the Middle Ages. The exporter's protection depends mainly on keeping title to the merchandise until the importer either pays or becomes obligated to pay.[5] But this method of payment is more risky than cash in advance or a letter of credit, for it depends on the importer (buyer) alone for payment. Even with a sight draft, the importer may refuse the shipment, leaving the exporter to incur the costs of disposing the merchandise elsewhere. With a time draft, the importer may default at maturity. Finally, documentary draft payment is subject to the risk of currency inconvertibility.

Open Account   This is a method of payment whereby the seller simply sends an invoice to the buyer, who is then expected to pay within a designated time. By far the most common method in domestic business, open account is usually restricted in international business to an exporter's own foreign sales affiliates and to intra-firm transactions of transnational corporations. It offers little protection against buyer default or currency inconvertibility. In the event of default, the exporter has no documentary evidence (draft acceptance) of the buyer's obligation to pay, and legal action to collect a debt is much more expensive and time consuming than at home. The lack of documentary evidence of the importer's obligation to pay may also make it more difficult for an importer to obtain foreign exchange when the currency is inconvertible.

Consignment   Under this method, the buyer is not obligated to pay until he has sold the merchandise. It is so disadvantageous to the seller that it is seldom used in international trade. As is true of the open account method, consignment sales are mostly limited to shipments to an exporter's own foreign affiliates. The consignment method suffers all the disabilities of the open account method and has the added disadvantage that the time of payment is uncertain.

---

[5]This protection is forgone with a *clean* draft. In that case, the documents are sent directly to the importer, and the exporter submits only his or her draft to the bank for collection. Hence the importer can obtain the merchandise without paying or accepting the draft. Clean drafts should be used only when the exporter has full confidence in the importer.

International Payments as Cross-National Transfers
in the Ownership of Bank Deposits

We can now bring together our discussion of bank transfers and methods of payment in international trade by demonstrating the mechanism of international payments with the T accounts of banks in the United States and Japan. T accounts are designed to show *changes* in assets and liabilities. To simplify our presentation, we assume that the banking system of each country is represented by a single bank.

To start, suppose an American importer wants to make a payment in yen to a Japanese exporter. The importer goes to the U.S. bank where he or she buys a draft that orders the Japanese bank to make payment of a certain sum in yen to the Japanese exporter. The American importer pays for the draft with a dollar check drawn on his or her own account with the U.S. bank, the amount being determined by the current dollar-yen rate of exchange. This transaction shows up in the T account of the U.S. bank as follows:

Assets	Liabilities
– Demand deposit in Japanese bank	– Demand deposit (American importer)

In effect, the importer purchases a yen deposit in the Japanese bank with a dollar deposit in the U.S. bank. The latter experiences a reduction in its yen-deposit assets that is offset by an equivalent reduction in its dollar-deposit liabilities as determined by the current dollar-yen exchange rate. Banks get compensated for arranging international payments by selling foreign currencies at a higher price than the price they pay for them.

The transaction appears in the T account of the Japanese bank as follows:

Assets	Liabilities
	– Demand deposit (U.S. bank) + Demand deposit (Japanese importer)

The Japanese importer gets paid with a yen deposit in the Japanese bank. This increase in the deposit liability of the Japanese bank is offset by an equal decrease in the deposit liability owing the U.S. bank.

Let us now take the example of an American exporter who receives payment in yen from a Japanese importer. The importer sends a check drawn on his or her account with the Japanese bank to the American exporter, who deposits the check with the U.S. bank. This bank then forwards it to the Japanese bank for collection. Once collection is completed, the following changes appear in the U.S. bank's T account:

Assets	Liabilities
+ Demand deposit (Japanese bank)	+ Demand deposit (American exporter)

In effect, the exporter sells a yen deposit to the American bank in exchange for a dollar deposit. The result of this transaction, therefore, is that the U.S. bank now has a yen deposit that it can sell to an American resident who needs yen.

The T account of the Japanese bank looks like this:

Assets	Liabilities
	− Demand deposit (Japanese importer + Demand deposit (U.S. bank)

The Japanese bank experiences an increase in a deposit liability owing the American bank that is offset by an equivalent decrease in the deposit liability owing the importer.

We can now see that international payments occur through shifts in the ownership of bank deposits, with banks acting as intermediaries. In our first example, a yen payment by the American importer to the Japanese exporter resulted in a shift in the ownership of a yen deposit from an American resident (the U.S. bank) to a Japanese resident (the exporter).[6] In the second example, a yen payment by a Japanese importer to an American exporter resulted in a shift in the ownership of a yen deposit from a Japanese resident (the importer) to an American resident (the U.S. bank).

THE FOREIGN EXCHANGE MARKET

The core of the foreign exchange market in the United States is a network of some 120 commercial banks, located principally in New York, that buy and sell foreign-currency bank deposits known as foreign exchange. More generally, *foreign exchange* is a financial asset that represents a money claim held by a resident of one country against a resident of another country. Foreign exchange may be banknotes (currency), bank deposits, bills of exchange, or any other highly liquid claims. Because bank deposits are the principal medium of international payment, *foreign exchange* usually refers to foreign-currency bank deposits.

---

[6]We are speaking here of a payment in *yen*. If the Japanese exporter had billed in dollars, then payment would occur through a shift in ownership of deposits in the U.S. bank: a decrease in the importer's deposit and an equivalent increase in the Japanese bank's deposit. If payment was made in a third currency, say, pounds sterling, then a deposit in a British bank would be transferred from American ownership (U.S. bank) to Japanese ownership (Japanese bank). Regardless of the currency of payment, therefore, payment occurs through transfers in the ownership of bank deposits.

Structure of the Market

Figure 11-2 depicts the foreign exchange market in the United States.

Traditionally, the foreign exchange (FX) market has comprised two sub-markets: the *FX retail market* and the *FX interbank (wholesale) market*. However, a third submarket, the *FX futures/options market,* came into existence in the 1970s with the inauguration of trading in foreign exchange futures and options by certain commodity and stock exchanges in this country. Together, these three submarkets form an integrated foreign exchange market.

Unlike the futures/options market, the FX retail and interbank markets do not have physical trading centers. They are over-the-counter markets. Customers transact business directly with local banks, and financial center banks transact business directly or through FX brokers with other financial center banks. Partici-

Figure 11-2

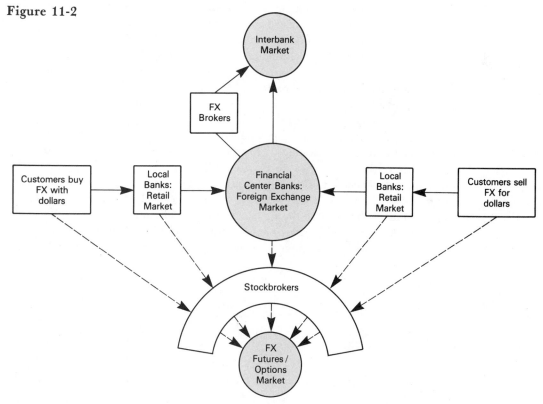

Structure of the Foreign Exchange (FX) Market in the United States. The foreign exchange market in the United States comprises three submarkets: retail, interbank (wholesale), and futures/options. In the retail market, customers (mainly individuals and international firms) deal with local banks, which, in turn, deal with financial center banks. The financial center banks deal with each other in the interbank market through FX brokers. All of these parties also participate through stockbrokers in exchanges that trade FX futures and options.

pants in the retail market are individuals, international firms, and nonbank financial institutions that buy foreign exchange from local commercial banks or sell foreign exchange to them. In turn, local banks obtain foreign exchange from and sell foreign exchange to large financial center banks mainly located in New York. Participants in the interbank market are the financial center banks. Most foreign exchange transactions are entered over the telephone between the specialist divisions of these banks, either directly or through brokers.

Foreign exchange transactions in the retail and interbank markets may be classified as spot and forward. *Spot* transactions are conducted at current exchange rates for immediate delivery of foreign exchange. Immediate delivery is over the counter in the retail market and within two business days in the interbank market. *Forward* transactions are conducted at forward exchange rates for the delivery of foreign exchange at a designated date more than two days in the future.

Nonbank customers, local banks, and financial center banks all participate through stockbrokers in exchanges that trade in FX futures and options. A FX futures contract is an agreement to purchase or sell a certain amount of designated foreign exchange at a specified price at a predetermined future time. FX contracts are of a standard size and settlement date. Before the settlement date, futures contracts may be resold at their market prices determined by trading on an organized exchange. The International Money Market (IMM) introduced trading in FX futures in 1972. IMM contracts appeal to individuals and small firms because they are convenient in size (for example, 25,000 pounds sterling, 125,000 deutsche marks, and 100,000 Canadian dollars). Delivery dates for futures contracts are the third Wednesday of March, June, September, or December.

An FX option is the *right* to buy or sell foreign exchange within a specified future time at a specified price, known as the *strike* price. A *call* option is the right to buy at the strike price; a *put* option is the right to sell at the strike price. The Philadelphia Exchange was the first to introduce FX options on spot currencies; later, the IMM offered options on FX futures contracts. We shall return to FX futures and options in Chapter 13 when we discuss hedging and speculation in foreign exchange.

Size of the Market

In 1986, for the first time, the central banks of the United States, Great Britain, and Japan—the three countries with the largest foreign exchange markets— undertook a coordinated survey of foreign exchange activities. Since then, they have made similar surveys in 1989 and 1992. The key findings are shown in Table 11-1.

The total volume of all three foreign exchange markets in New York, London, and Tokyo amounted to an astonishing average of *$623 billion each day* during April 1992. This figure does not include the activity of FX futures and options markets in those centers or the FX activity in other centers, such as Frankfurt, Zurich, Toronto, Singapore, and Hong Kong. A spokesman of the Bank of England

Table 11-1 Average Daily Trading Volume of Foreign Exchange in New York, London, and Tokyo, 1986, 1989 and 1992 (Billions of Dollars)

	March 1986	*April 1989*	*April 1992*
New York	50	129	192
London	90	187	303
Tokyo	48	115	128
Three centers combined	*188*	*431*	*623*

Source: Federal Reserve Bank of New York, Bank of England, and Bank of Japan.

estimates that the *total* daily volume of foreign exchange trading in the world averaged $1 *trillion* in April 1992![7] The foreign exchange market is now the world's biggest financial market.

The volume of foreign exchange trading has expanded at an unprecedented rate in recent years. Between 1986 and 1992, trading in New York rose from $50 billion to $192 billion a day, an increase of 284 percent. In London, the increase was 236 percent, and in Tokyo, 167 percent. For the three centers combined, the growth was 231 percent.

What explains this explosive growth? One cause is the high volatility in foreign exchange rates since the collapse of the Bretton Woods international monetary system in the early 1970s.[8] This volatility has encouraged widespread hedging and speculation by FX traders and international firms.

A second cause is the deregulation of capital markets, particularly in Western Europe and Japan. Deregulation enables holders of financial assets to move them more quickly from one country to another in search of higher yields and lower risks. In effect, a single global capital market is replacing separate national capital markets.[9]

A third cause is the technological innovation in electronic communications that has lowered the costs and increased the speed of international payments. Foreign exchange dealers are now connected worldwide by computer screens and telephone consoles. Electronic transfers have replaced checks as the principal means of payment. Each day billions of dollars of international currency transfers move in and out of New York via the Clearing House Interbank Payments System (CHIPS) operated by the New York Clearing House Association. Through CHIPS some 140 participating banks exchange irrevocable payment messages electronically throughout the day. At the end of the day, the banks settle their net positions by making or receiving a single payment to or from the CHIPS settlement account at the Federal Reserve System.

---

[7]"Currency Markets Resisting Powers of Central Banks," *The New York Times,* September 25, 1992, p. 1.
[8]See Chapter 18.
[9]Chapter 19 examines the formation of the global capital market.

Here is an example of how CHIPS works. (1) At 7 A.M. in Paris, a French vintner receives an order from a British importer for champagne to be bought with U.S. dollars. (2) At 9 A.M., the vintner orders its London warehouse to deliver the champagne to the importer. It does so. (3) At 12 noon, the importer instructs its London bank to pay the French vintner in U.S. dollars. (4) At 1 P.M., the London bank advises its New York office to pay. (5) At 3 P.M., payment is sent via CHIPS to the New York office of the vintner's French bank. (6) At 4 P.M., the French bank's New York office tells its Paris office that it has received payment. (7) At 6 P.M., the Paris bank pays the vintner.

Only a small share of the world's FX trading (10 percent or so) involves the financing of international trade in goods and services. The bulk of trading now comes from international capital flows representing currency speculation and hedging or shifts in portfolio investments responding to interest rate and risk differentials among countries. Furthermore, about 90 percent of FX turnover involves trading among the large financial center banks located mainly in New York, London, and Tokyo; only a small share of trading is generated by outside firms and individuals. The banks profit from arbitrage but mostly from "positioning"—correctly anticipating daily movements in foreign exchange rates. *Positioning* is another name for speculation.

The principal currencies traded in foreign exchange markets are the U.S. dollar, the German mark, the Japanese yen, and the British pound sterling. The U.S. dollar is the leading international currency, used in more than half of all international payments in the world. The dominant (but declining) role of the U.S. dollar is examined in Chapter 19.

A GLOBAL FOREIGN EXCHANGE MARKET: EXCHANGE ARBITRAGE

Are currency prices (foreign exchange rates) the same across the several national foreign exchange markets? For example, is the dollar price of 1 pound sterling on any given day the same in New York, London, Tokyo, and other financial centers? Surprising as it may seem, the answer is yes. The explanation of this consistency is *exchange arbitrage.*

Fundamentally, exchange arbitrage is the sale of a given currency in one foreign exchange market and the simultaneous purchase of the same currency in another foreign exchange market. Arbitrage does not involve a speculative risk, because the arbitrage trader (arbitrager) fully offsets a sale in one market with a purchase in a second market. Opportunities for arbitrage profits are transitory, for the supply-demand effects of arbitrage quickly wipe out any discrepancies in the price of a currency across foreign exchange markets.

Suppose, for example, the pound sterling is trading at $1.32 in New York and at the same time is trading at $1.30 in London. This discrepancy provides an opportunity for arbitrage profits: Traders will buy pounds with dollars in London at $1.30 and simultaneously sell pounds for dollars in New York at $1.32. An arbitrager who bought and sold one million pounds would earn profits of $20,000 ($.02 multiplied by one million). But this rate discrepancy would quickly disappear: Higher demand for sterling in London would push up its dollar price while the increased supply of sterling in New York would push down its dollar price. Arbitrage would cease when the dollar price of sterling became the same in both markets, say, $1.31. This is an example of *bilateral* arbitrage involving two currencies.

Arbitrage also maintains consistency in *cross-rates* between two currencies through a third currency. Suppose that the German mark is trading at $0.35 and the British pound sterling at $1.31 in New York. Then the mark-sterling cross-rate in New York is 3.74 marks per pound sterling. But let us further suppose that the price of sterling in Frankfurt is 3.70 marks. Because the *dollar* price of sterling at the mark-sterling cross-rate is cheaper in Frankfurt than in New York, arbitragers can profit by buying marks with dollars in New York, simultaneously selling the marks for sterling in Frankfurt, and simultaneously selling the sterling for dollars in New York. An arbitrager who undertook this set of transactions by starting with the purchase of 3.7 million marks in New York for $1.295 million would be able to sell the marks for 1 million pounds sterling in Frankfurt and then sell the sterling in New York for $1.310 million, for a profit of $.015 million (or $15,000). This is an example of *triangular* arbitrage involving three currencies.

Arbitrage creates a single integrated global market in foreign exchange. Actually, today almost all interbank transactions in foreign exchange both in the United States and abroad involve the purchase and sale of *dollars*. Thus even a British trader who wants to buy marks with sterling will first buy dollars with sterling and then sell the dollars for marks. This is done because the dollar is the principal currency for international trade and investment and the dollar market for each currency is consequently more active than the bilateral market between any pair of foreign currencies. Interbank trading directly through the dollar eliminates discrepancies between the dollar quotations of foreign currencies and their cross-rates.

Instant electronic communications have made arbitrage more effective than in the past. Arbitragers (mainly the financial center banks) rely on computer information systems and computer programs to identify and carry out arbitrage operations. Because of the time zones the major foreign exchange markets — New York, London, and Tokyo — are located in, the global foreign exchange market is open for business 24 hours each day.

INTERNATIONAL FINANCIAL CENTERS

Domestic and foreign banks are able to act as dealers in foreign exchange because they are willing to hold balances in other countries. The mechanism of international payments, therefore, is based upon a pattern of interbank debt that covers the entire world. This pattern may be decentralized, centralized, or somewhere between these two extremes.

Decentralized and Centralized Systems
of International Payment

When the banking system in one country is linked to the banking systems in all other countries by a series of bilateral debt arrangements (the number of arrangements being equal to the number of other countries) and all international payments are cleared bilaterally, the system of international payment is fully decentralized. Figure 11-3 shows a fully decentralized payments system for a world of six countries.

When, on the other hand, banks in one country are linked to banks in other countries through balances maintained at *one* financial center and all international payments are cleared through this center, then the system of international payments is fully centralized. Figure 11-4 illustrates a fully centralized system of international payments for a world of six countries.

The London Financial Center before World War I

During the half century that preceded World War I, the system of international payments was highly centralized. The focus of this system was London. Banks throughout the world maintained sterling balances in London and transferred funds from one country to another by drawing sterling bills. A Brazilian exporting

Figure 11-3

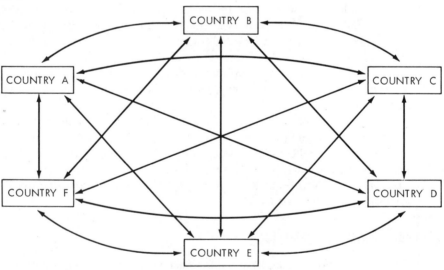

Arrows indicate reciprocal bank balances of foreign exchange dealers.

Fully Decentralized System of International Payments: Six Countries. In a fully decentralized system of international payments, banks in one country maintain balances with banks in *all* other countries. Hence, international payments are made between two countries by shifts in the ownership of balances held in each other's banks.

Figure 11-4

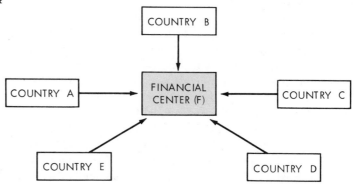

Direction of arrows indicates the location of foreign bank balances maintained by foreign exchange dealers.

Fully Centralized System of International Payments: Six Countries. In a fully centralized system of international payments, banks in different countries maintain balances with banks located in a single financial center. Hence, international payments are made via shifts in the national ownership of bank balances held in the financial center.

coffee to the United States would draw a sterling bill on the American importer, who, when the time came to buy, would remit a sterling draft. In this way international payments occurred through shifts in the ownership of sterling balances located in London. Although most countries were on the gold standard at this time, it was the pound sterling that made up most of the world's payments.

The prominence of London was due to many factors. First, Great Britain was the world's greatest importer, and its policy of free trade gave foreign suppliers easy access to its domestic market. Second, the London money market was unparalleled in its efficiency and resources — banks, acceptance houses, discount houses, dealers, and so on, made up a market in which sterling funds could be invested or borrowed on short term in any amount and at any time. Third, London was by far the paramount source of long-term investment capital; its highly evolved securities markets dealt in the securities of the entire world. First trader, first financier, and first investor of the world during a period when trade and finance were unrestricted by government policies, it was inevitable that most international payments should flow to, from, and through the London financial center.

The Rise of New York after World War I

During the 1920s New York and, to a lesser extent, Paris rose to challenge the financial supremacy of London. The blows that Great Britain had suffered during World War I and the simultaneous emergence of the United States as the leading international creditor were the main factors responsible for this development.

The resulting decentralization of the international payment system brought to the fore certain problems that had not existed in the earlier payments system centered in London. For one thing, there was less economy in the use of the world's supply of monetary gold. When there was only one dominant international financial center, there was little need for gold on the part of the peripheral countries, aside from domestic reserves, since foreign exchange could be borrowed easily from the center. When there were several financial centers, however, each center had to maintain individual gold reserves behind its international obligations, and the peripheral countries might also increase their gold holdings. In the 1920s the shortage of gold was also heightened by the large acquisitions of the United States during World War I.[10]

Another problem that arose in the 1920s was the movement of speculative capital between London and New York, stemming from the general uncertainty regarding the future course of exchange rates and from lack of faith in the ability of certain countries to maintain their newly restored gold standard. The movement of this capital was made easier by the decentralization of the international payment system; when there is only one financial center, there is less likelihood of a sudden flight of capital, since it can move only to a peripheral country. In the 1920s the volatility of short-term capital movements also heightened the gold shortage, since each financial center was compelled to maintain greater reserves behind its foreign obligations. Despite these drawbacks, the decentralized system of the 1920s, based on the London-New York axis, would probably have developed into a more workable arrangement in time. It was destroyed, however, by the onset of world depression in the early 1930s.

After World War II, the international monetary system came to rest on the dollar, and New York emerged as the dominant financial center. Foreign governments (central banks) maintained balances in New York that, together with gold, constituted their official international reserves. Private foreign banks also maintained sizable dollar balances to finance their FX transactions throughout the world.

The Emergence of Tokyo in the 1980s

In the 1980s, Japan became the world's leading exporter of capital and its greatest international creditor. At the same time, the United States became the world's leading *importer* of capital and its greatest international *debtor*. These twin developments have made Tokyo an international financial center.

Tokyo's emergence as an international financial center has been held back by regulations that prevent its markets from becoming as liquid as New York's. Investors need access to a variety of financial instruments that can be bought or sold easily at any time. Deregulation is taking place, but it has not kept pace with the growth of Japan's financial power. In sum, if the yen remains strong and the

---

[10]U.S. gold reserves rose from $1.7 billion in December 1914 to $2.7 billion in December 1918. Reserves continued to rise until December 1924, when they reached $4.1 billion. Board of Governors of the Federal Reserve System, *Banking and Monetary Statistics* (Washington, D.C.: U.S. Government Printing Office, 1943), p. 544.

dollar weak and if Tokyo's markets approach the liquidity of New York's, then Tokyo may well challenge New York (and London) in the 1990s as the premier international financial center.

SUMMARY

1. Most international payments involve shifts between domestic and foreign residents in the ownership of bank deposits. These shifts are brought about by international electronic bank transfers and bank drafts rather than by checks.
2. International payments are more risky than domestic payments because of the foreign exchange risk, the inconvertibility risk, and the default risk.
3. The principal methods of payment in international trade are cash in advance, commercial letters of credit, commercial drafts drawn on the buyer, open account, and consignment.
4. We can demonstrate the mechanism of international payments with the T accounts of U.S. and foreign banks: Payments occur through shifts in the domestic and foreign ownership of bank deposits, with banks acting as intermediaries.
5. The core of the foreign exchange market in the United States is a network of some 120 commercial banks, located principally in New York, that buy and sell foreign-currency deposits known as foreign exchange. Traditionally, the foreign exchange (FX) market has comprised two submarkets: the FX retail market and the FX interbank market. However, a third submarket, the FX futures/options market, came into existence in the 1970s.
6. Apart from the distinction between retail and interbank transactions, foreign exchange transactions may be classified as spot and forward. Only a small number of currencies — commonly referred to as international currencies — are used to effect international payments. The leading international currency is the U.S. dollar.
7. The total volume on the three principal FX markets — New York, London, and Tokyo — averaged $623 billion each day during April 1992. The explosive growth of FX markets is propelled by high volatility in exchange rates, deregulation, and electronic communication systems such as CHIPS.
8. The principal currencies traded in FX markets are the U.S. dollar, the German mark, the Japanese yen, and the British pound sterling.
9. Exchange (or currency) arbitrage is the sale of a given currency in one foreign exchange market and the simultaneous purchase of the same currency in another foreign exchange market. Bilateral arbitrage maintains the same price for a given currency across foreign exchange markets; triangular arbitrage maintains consistency in cross-rates between two currencies through a third currency. The effect of currency arbitrage is to create a single integrated global market in foreign exchange.

10. London was the dominant international financial center before World War I, and New York became the dominant center after World War II. In the 1980s, Tokyo has emerged as a new international financial center to challenge the supremacy of New York.

QUESTIONS AND APPLICATIONS

1. Why are international payments more risky than domestic payments?
2. (a) What is a confirmed, irrevocable letter of credit?
   (b) What are the advantages and disadvantages of letter-of-credit payment for the exporter? For the importer?
3. (a) What is a commercial draft?
   (b) How is the bill of lading used in documentary draft payment to protect the interests of the exporter?
4. Demonstrate with the T accounts of U.S. and foreign banks what happens when (a) a U.S. resident makes a payment to a foreign resident in the latter's currency, (b) a U.S. resident receives a dollar payment from a foreign resident, and (c) a U.S. resident makes a payment to a foreign resident in a third-country currency.
5. (a) Identify the three submarkets composing the FX market.
   (b) What are the distinctive functions of each submarket?
6. (a) What is CHIPS?
   (b) How does CHIPS work?
7. (a) How does bilateral currency arbitrage make the dollar price of a foreign currency the same in different foreign exchange markets?
   (b) How does triangular currency arbitrage keep cross-rates consistent?
   (c) Suppose the dollar price of the French franc is $0.16 in New York while at the same time it is $0.17 in Paris. What would arbitragers do?
8. Explain what a decentralized system of international payments is. Explain what a centralized system is.
9. Be prepared to debate this proposition: "Tokyo will become the dominant international financial center in the 1990s, surpassing New York."

SELECTED READINGS

See the list of readings at the end of Chapter 13.

chapter 12

FOREIGN EXCHANGE RATES
AND THEIR DETERMINATION

Foreign exchange rates are of key significance in directing the flow of merchandise, services, and capital between nations. In Chapter 11, we showed how arbitrage equates foreign exchange rates across the several national foreign exchange markets. This chapter explores the different kinds of exchange rate behavior.

THE RATE OF EXCHANGE

Foreign exchange is bought and sold in the foreign exchange market at a price that is called the *rate of exchange*. More specifically, the exchange rate is the *domestic money price of foreign money*, establishing an equivalence between dollars and British pounds sterling, dollars and French francs, dollars and Argentine pesos, and so on.[1] The daily quotations of foreign exchange are based on the price of bank (or electronic) transfers, which are the quickest means of international payment. Table 12-1 indicates the selling rates for bank transfers in New York on November 5 and November 6, 1992.

For most currencies only a "spot" rate is quoted. *Spot exchange* is foreign exchange for immediate delivery (ordinarily within one or two days). For international currencies, however, the New York market also quotes "forward" rates for foreign exchange promised for delivery at a time in the future — 30, 60, or 90 days. Unless otherwise noted, our analysis of exchange rate behavior relates to the spot rate.

---

[1]If there are *n* national currencies, then there are *n* − 1 rates of exchange relating foreign currencies to the domestic currency. Foreign exchange rates may be quoted either as the *domestic* currency price for a unit of a given foreign currency or, alternatively, as the *foreign* currency price for a unit of domestic currency. Both terms are equivalent; one is simply the reciprocal of the other. European foreign exchange markets use the second term; until recently, the U.S. foreign exchange market used only the first term, but now quotes rates in both terms, as shown in Table 12-1. To explain the determination of foreign exchange rates, we shall use the first term, specifically, the dollar price of sterling.

Table 12-1 Selling Rates of Foreign Exchange (Bank Transfers) in New York on Thursday, November 5, and Friday, November 6, 1992

11/6/92	Foreign Currency in Dollars		Dollar in Foreign Currency	
	Fri.	Thu.	Fri.	Thu.
f-Argentina	1.0100	1.0100	.9901	.9901
Australia	.6995	.6960	1.4296	1.4368
Austria	.0891	.0899	11.220	11.129
c-Belgium	.0307	.0308	32.60	32.50
Brazil	.00013	.00013	7967.00	7878.05
Britain	1.5295	1.5375	.6538	.6504
30-day forward	1.5237	1.5315	.6563	.6530
60-day forward	1.5197	1.5271	.6580	.6548
Canada	.7984	.8010	1.2525	1.2485
30-day forward	.7959	.7985	1.2564	1.2524
60-day forward	.7944	.7972	1.2588	1.2544
y-Chile	.002756	.002766	362.90	361.54
Colombia	.001648	.001652	606.90	605.20
Denmark	.1644	.1649	6.0830	6.0645
z-Ecuador	.000543	.000543	1843.01	1843.01
ECU	1.24130	1.24840	.8056	.8010
d-Egypt	.3013	.3013	3.3195	3.3195
Finland	.2000	.2013	4.9989	4.9674
France	.1853	.1869	5.3960	5.3510
Germany	.6263	.6323	1.5967	1.5815
30-day forward	.6233	.6292	1.6044	1.5892
60-day forward	.6206	.6264	1.6113	1.5964
90-day forward	.6180	.6238	1.6182	1.6031
Greece	.004846	.004874	206.35	205.15
Hong Kong	.1293	.1293	7.7330	7.7310
Hungary	.0126	.0126	79.37	79.67
y-India	.0352	.0352	28.409	28.409
Ireland	1.6610	1.6737	.6020	.5975
Israel	.3925	.3918	2.5480	2.5526
Italy	.000736	.000741	1358.25	1350.00
Japan	.008102	.008151	123.43	122.68
30-day forward	.008097	.008147	123.50	122.75
60-day forward	.008099	.008148	123.47	122.73
90-day forward	.008098	.008147	123.48	122.74
Malaysia	.3974	.3975	2.5165	2.5160
z-Mexico	.000322	.000322	3107.01	3107.01
Netherlands	.5607	.5624	1.7835	1.7780
N. Zealand	.5295	.5265	1.8886	1.8993

Table 12-1 Continued

11/6/92	Foreign Currency in Dollars		Dollar in Foreign Currency	
	Fri.	Thu.	Fri.	Thu.
Norway	.1550	.1556	6.4530	6.4285
Pakistan	.0398	.0398	25.10	25.10
y-Peru	.6623	.6623	1.510	1.510
z-Philippines	.0408	.0409	24.50	24.45
Poland	.000070	.000070	14364	14374
Portugal	.007082	.007105	141.20	140.75
a-Russia	.002506	.002506	399.00	399.00
Saudi Arab	.2667	.2667	3.7495	3.7500
Singapore	.6131	.6133	1.6310	1.6304
So. Africa	.3357	.3353	2.9790	2.9825
So. Korea	.001279	.001279	782.10	782.00
Spain	.008822	.008838	113.35	113.15
Sweden	.1678	.1683	5.9610	5.9410
Switzerland	.6960	.7060	1.4367	1.4165
30-day forward	.6943	.7042	1.4404	1.4200
60-day forward	.6926	.7027	1.4439	1.4231
90-day forward	.6910	.7013	1.4471	1.4260
Taiwan	.0394	.0394	25.40	25.39
Thailand	.03937	.03937	25.40	25.40
U.A.E.	.2723	.2723	3.6722	3.6722
f-Uruguay	.000289	.000289	3462.00	3462.00
z-Venzuela	.0130	.0130	77.1000	77.1000

ECU: European Currency Unit, a basket of European currencies.

a-auction result, Moscow Foreign Currency Exchange, c-commercial rate, d-free market rate, f-financial rate, y-official rate, z-floating rate.

Source: Adapted from *The Philadelphia Inquirer,* November 7, 1992, p. D3.

Actually, there are several spot rates of exchange for a given currency. The price of bank transfers is the *base* rate of exchange, and other means of international payment — sight and time bills — usually sell at a discounted price below this base rate. The discounts reflect varying delays or risks of payment compared to the bank transfer. Even payment by a bank draft sent airmail requires two or three days between New York and London, and during that time the foreign exchange dealer has the use of both the domestic money paid for the draft and the foreign balance against which the draft is drawn. Time drafts postpone payment for a much longer period. The discount on a given kind of foreign exchange, say a 30-day bill, will depend upon the current rate of interest since, in effect, the buyer of the bill is lending money to the seller of the bill until its maturity date. Discounts from the base rate of exchange stem also from differences in the risk of payment. For that reason trade bills are quoted below bank bills of similar maturity.

The rates of different kinds of foreign exchange are thus linked to the base rate of exchange by discounts that take into account liquidity and risk factors. Although these discounts will vary with the two aforementioned factors, the resulting pattern of exchange rates will rise and fall with the base rate. In our analysis of the determination of foreign exchange rates, therefore, we shall consider the pattern of spot rates as one rate, namely, the base rate of exchange for bank transfers.

The behavior of exchange rates will depend upon the nature of the foreign exchange market. When there are no restrictions on private trading in the market and official agencies do not stand ready to stabilize the rate of exchange, the exchange rate will fluctuate from day to day in response to changes in the supply and demand of foreign exchange. When, however, government authorities follow a policy of stabilization but do not interfere with private market transactions in foreign exchange, the exchange rate will move only within narrow limits, although these limits may be substantially altered from time to time by official action. Finally, the government may restrict private transactions by becoming the sole buyer and seller of foreign exchange; the rate of exchange is then no longer determined by supply and demand but instead is the end product of bureaucratic decisions. We now examine more closely the determination of these three types of exchange rate behavior—freely fluctuating rates, stable rates, and controlled rates.

FREELY FLUCTUATING EXCHANGE RATES

When the rate of exchange is not stabilized or controlled by government authorities, the foreign exchange market very closely approaches the theoretical model of perfect competition. Except for the liquidity and risk differentials that discounts allow for, the foreign exchange of any given country is one homogeneous product. Moreover, the number of buyers and sellers of foreign exchange is so large that a single buyer or seller cannot measurably influence the rate of exchange but must accept it as given. In a free, unstabilized market, therefore, the rate of exchange is determined by the many individual acts of buying and selling, none of which individually is able to affect it but all of which interact to set its level.

The Demand for Foreign Exchange

In a free market the rate of exchange, like any other price, is determined by the interplay of supply and demand. The foreign exchange that is demanded at any time will depend upon the volume of international transfers that require payments to foreign residents. These transfers may be purchases of goods and services (*real* transfers) or purchases of financial assets (*financial* transfers).[2]

_____

[2]The demand for foreign exchange originates in the *debit* items composing the current and capital accounts of a country's balance of payments (see Chapter 14).

The amount of foreign exchange in demand varies inversely with its price: The amount demanded at a high rate is less than the amount demanded at a low rate, provided other conditions (such as prices, interest rates, and real incomes) remain the same. A high exchange rate makes foreign goods and services and financial assets more expensive to domestic buyers, who respond by reducing the volume of their purchases from foreigners. This, in turn, lessens the amount of foreign exchange demanded by domestic residents. Conversely, a low rate of exchange increases the amount of foreign exchange demanded.

The demand relationship of foreign exchange (here represented by the British pound sterling) is indicated in Figure 12-1 by the familiar down-sloping demand schedule D–D. The schedule shows the quantity of sterling exchange demanded at each rate of exchange in the New York market; thus, it is an aggregate of all the individual demand schedules of those who wish to transfer funds abroad.

In analyzing the determination of the exchange rate, it is important to distinguish between a movement along a given demand schedule (change in the amount demanded) and a shift in the entire schedule (change in demand). We have noted that a movement along the demand schedule is downward from left to right because the exchange rate determines the domestic price of imports of goods,

Figure 12-1

Demand for Sterling Exchange in New York. The demand schedule for sterling exchange (representing foreign exchange in general) slopes downward from left to right because the *amount* of sterling demanded at a high rate is less than the *amount* demanded at a lower rate. A high rate of exchange makes foreign goods, services, and financial assets expensive to domestic buyers, and conversely. An *increase* in the demand for sterling would be indicated by a shift in the entire schedule to the right (from D–D to D'–D'); a *decrease* in demand would be indicated by a shift to the left.

services, or capital and thereby affects their volume and the amount of foreign exchange demanded to pay for them. Changes in income, costs, prices, interest rates, tastes, and other factors may, however, cause shifts in imports independent of the exchange rate. When this happens, the entire demand schedule shifts either left or right, depending on whether there has been a decrease or an increase in the volume of imports. For example, a rise in the national income of the United States will cause a rise in imports of merchandise and services, and this will shift the demand schedule for foreign exchange to the right as more foreign exchange is demanded at each rate of exchange. Such a development is shown in Figure 12-1 by $D'-D'$. Or the shift to $D'-D'$ may be caused by a rise in real interest rates abroad, which would encourage U.S. residents to buy foreign securities.

The Supply of Foreign Exchange

The supply of foreign exchange in the foreign exchange market derives from international transfers that require money receipts from foreign residents, that is, from *credit* items in the balance of payments. Unlike the amount demanded, the amount of foreign exchange supplied to the market varies directly with the rate of exchange. When the rate of exchange is high, domestic prices appear low to foreigners, since they are able to acquire a unit of domestic money with a small expenditure of their own money. This cheapness stimulates domestic exports of real and financial assets and thereby brings a larger supply of foreign exchange into the market. Conversely, a low exchange rate restricts exports and lowers the amount of foreign exchange offered to the market.

Figure 12-2 shows the supply relationship of foreign exchange by a schedule that slopes upward from left to right. A shift of the entire supply schedule either to the left or right occurs with a change in economic variables that affect receipts of foreign exchange (other than the exchange rate).

For example, a shift to the left would occur if deflation abroad caused a decrease in American exports. This would decrease the amount of foreign exchange supplied to the market at each exchange rate. A decrease in the supply of sterling exchange in the New York market is shown in Figure 12-2 by $S'-S'$.

Determination of the Rate of Exchange

The rate of exchange is determined by the intersection of the demand and the supply schedules. At this rate of exchange, and at no other rate, the market is cleared; the rate will remain stable until a shift occurs in either one or both schedules. It is unlikely that this equilibrium rate of exchange will last very long or even be attained in a free, unstabilized foreign exchange market, since continuing shifts in demand and supply will force continuing adjustments toward new equilibrium positions. Thus, the exchange rate will fluctuate continuously, just as the prices of securities traded in the security market continuously fluctuate. To simplify our analysis, however, we shall assume that there is time for the exchange rate to adjust fully to a change in demand or supply.

Figure 12-2

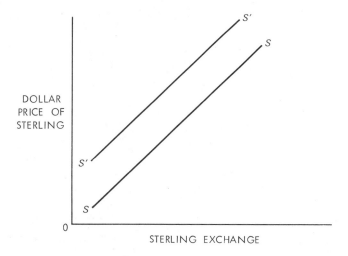

DOLLAR
PRICE OF
STERLING

0

STERLING EXCHANGE

Supply of Sterling Exchange in New York. The supply schedule for sterling exchange slopes upward from left to right: When the exchange rate moves higher, domestic prices of goods, services, and financial assets appear lower to foreign buyers. This stimulates more domestic exports and brings in a larger *amount* of foreign exchange to the market. Conversely, lower rates reduce domestic exports, bringing in a lower *amount* of foreign exchange. A *decrease* in supply would be indicated by a shift of the entire schedule to the left (from *S–S* to *S'–S'*); an *increase* in supply would be indicated by a shift to the right.

In Figure 12-3 the equilibrium rate of exchange is 0–*R*. At this rate the amount supplied is equal to the amount demanded, and both suppliers and buyers of foreign exchange are satisfied. Suppose now that the demand for sterling increases from *D–D* to *D'–D'*, as in Figure 12-4. In response to this increase, the equilibrium rate rises from 0–*R* to 0–*R'*, where once again the amounts of sterling exchange supplied and demanded are equal. This higher rate calls forth an increase in the amount supplied of *E'–E'*, since it stimulates more American exports. Similarly, a shift of the demand schedule to the left (fall in demand) will bring about a decline in the rate of exchange. On the other hand, a shift in the *supply schedule* to the left (fall in supply) will raise the exchange rate, and a shift to the right (rise in supply) will lower it.

Because foreign exchange is a store of value as well as an instrument of current payment, demand and supply schedules shift quickly in response to changes in *expectations* about the future behavior of economic variables, notably expectations about future interest and inflation rates. Suppose, for example, traders alter their expectations about future rates of inflation, and now believe that the inflation rate will become much higher in the United States than in Britain. Consequently, they regard the pound sterling as a better store of value than the dollar, moving out of dollars into sterling. This new *speculative* demand for sterling is shown as a shift in

Figure 12-3

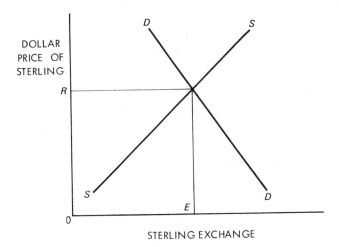

Determination of Equilibrium Sterling Exchange Rate in New York. The equilibrium rate of exchange (0–R) is determined by the intersection of the demand and supply schedules. Only at 0–R does the amount demanded equal the amount supplied. Consequently, the market clears and both buyers and suppliers of sterling exchange are satisfied.

Figure 12-4

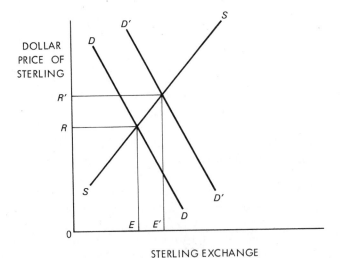

Determination of a New Equilibrium Sterling Exchange Rate in New York. When the demand for sterling exchange *increases,* as shown by the shift from D–D to D'–D', then the price of sterling rises to a new equilibrium level, 0–R'. At the new rate, the amount of sterling in demand and supply is 0–E'. The increase in the amount supplied (from 0–E to 0–E') is induced by the higher rate of exchange, which encourages domestic exports.

Part II International Payments

the demand schedule to $D'-D'$ in Figure 12-4, a rise in demand that causes a rise in the price of sterling.

In summary, the exchange rate in a free, unstabilized market is determined by the supply of and the demand for foreign exchange, which derive from exports and imports of merchandise, services, and securities (financial assets). The exchange rate itself also influences the volume of exports and imports, and this influence is shown by the shape of the demand and supply schedules of foreign exchange.[3]

STABLE EXCHANGE RATES

In this section several arguments for stable rates are presented, after which specific techniques of stabilization are discussed.

Arguments for Stable Rates

The contemporary system of fluctuating or floating exchange rates is a historical anomaly. Exchange rates have seldom been left free to vary with supply and demand. Even before World War I, when there was general agreement on the benefits of flexible market prices in merchandise, services, and securities, fluctuating exchange rates were viewed with marked distaste. At this time all of the leading trading nations were firm adherents of the gold standard, which provided fixed rates of exchange. Fluctuating exchange rates, therefore, were considered the mark of a failure to remain on the gold standard. Apart from the gold standard, however, there are strong arguments for stable exchange rates.

It is forcibly argued that the exchange rate is unlike the price of an ordinary commodity and that it is illogical to view the two in the same light. When the exchange rate varies, the prices of *all* exports are changed for foreign buyers and, simultaneously, the prices of *all* imports are changed for domestic buyers. These widespread price effects unloose a series of repercussions that extend throughout the domestic and foreign economies. This critical nature of the exchange rate, the argument runs, rules out the unlicensed freedom of the unstabilized foreign exchange market. It is also contended that fluctuating rates invite foreign exchange speculation that may intensify balance of payments difficulties. Less fundamental arguments for stable rates spring from considerations of trade and finance. Fluctuating rates provoke uncertainty in foreign payments and investments. The exporter is unable to make a sound calculation of the profit margin, since the domestic value of foreign exchange receipts depends upon an unstable rate of exchange. Lenders and borrowers are also subject to this exchange risk.[4]

Techniques of Stabilization

Unlike the controlled exchange market, the stabilized market imposes no restraints on private transactions in foreign exchange; the factors of supply and demand are

---

[3]The influence of the exchange rate on the balance of payments is an important means of adjustment to disequilibrium and is taken up in Chapter 16.

[4]The case for fluctuating rates (also referred to as flexible or floating rates) is presented in Chapter 16.

fully operative. How, then, is it possible to prevent fluctuations in the rate of exchange? The answer lies in the open-market operations of government authorities that compensate for movements in the ordinary demand and supply of foreign exchange. Successful stabilization of the rate of exchange requires that the stabilization agency be able to offset movements in market supply and demand to any desired degree. To do so, the agency must possess adequate supplies of domestic and foreign exchange.[5] Under the gold standard, stabilization is assured by the willingness of the monetary authorities to buy or sell gold without limit at a fixed price. This *passive* stabilization contrasts with *active* stabilization practices whereby government agencies buy and sell foreign exchange in the market to offset any undesired movements in exchange rates.

Passive Stabilization: The Gold Standard A country is on the *gold standard* when its basic monetary unit (dollar, pound sterling, franc, and so on) is defined in terms of a specified weight of gold and when its monetary authorities stand ready at all times to buy and sell gold in unlimited quantities at the rate fixed by the legal gold content of the monetary unit. As long as this second condition of unrestricted convertibility is observed, the gold value of the monetary unit cannot vary and the price of gold remains constant.

The minimum conditions for a true *international* gold standard are two: (1) two or more countries must adopt monetary units with a designated gold content, and (2) the monetary authorities of each country must permit the free, unlimited export and import of gold at a rate fixed by the gold content of the monetary unit. Since the gold standard creates fixed exchange rates only between countries on the gold standard, however, it makes its greatest contribution to exchange rate stability when several currencies, particularly key currencies such as the dollar and the pound sterling, are tied to gold.

Gold standard currencies hold a fixed relationship to each other because they all hold a fixed relationship to gold. Before World War I and during the last half of the 1920s, the British pound sterling was defined as 113 grains of gold and the U.S. dollar as 23.22 grains. The gold content of the pound, therefore, was 4.8665 times greater than the gold content of the dollar. This latter relationship was the *mint parity* of the pound and the dollar at the time—one pound sterling was equivalent to $4.8665. Any holder of 113 grains of gold could obtain one pound sterling from the British monetary authorities or, alternately, $4.8665 from the American authorities.

Under the gold standard, the mint parity and the exchange rate between two currencies need not be identical. Because of the costs of shipping gold from one country to another (freight, insurance, handling, and interest), the exchange rate is free to vary within narrow limits known as *gold points*. The higher the costs of

---

[5]This may be illustrated by the price stabilization of wheat. To keep the price of wheat from falling below a minimum level, the stabilization authority must have enough dollars to buy all the wheat offered at that level; to keep the price of wheat from rising above a maximum level, the authority must have enough wheat to satisfy demand at that level.

shipping gold, the greater the spread between mint parity and the gold points. The costs of shipment, when added to mint parity, establish the *gold export point;* the costs of shipment, when subtracted from mint parity, establish the *gold import point.* When the exchange rate rises to the gold export point, gold begins to flow out of the country; on the other hand, when the exchange rate falls to the gold import point, gold begins to flow into the country. These flows of gold provide the compensatory changes in the supply of and the demand for foreign exchange that are necessary to keep the foreign exchange rate from moving beyond the gold points.

This stabilizing function of gold flows under the international gold standard may be illustrated by an example. Let us assume that the mint parity of the pound sterling is $4.8665 and that shipping costs make the gold export point in New York $4.8865 and the gold import point, $4.8465. Now suppose that the rate of exchange in New York rises to the gold export point of $4.8865. The rate will not rise further because foreign exchange dealers can acquire all the pounds sterling they desire at a rate of $4.8865 by purchasing gold for dollars from the American monetary authorities, shipping the gold to London, and then selling the gold for pounds to the British monetary authorities. Thus, the supply of foreign exchange becomes perfectly elastic at the gold export point, and the rate of exchange cannot rise beyond it.[6]

Similarly, the gold import point sets a floor below which the rate of exchange cannot fall: Exchange dealers will not sell pounds at a rate below $4.8465 because they can obtain that many dollars for each pound sterling by converting pounds into gold in London, shipping the gold to New York, and then converting the gold into dollars. In other words, the demand for foreign exchange becomes perfectly elastic at the gold import point.[7]

When the rate of exchange is between the gold points, there is no longer an option on the part of dealers to acquire foreign exchange by gold exports or to dispose of foreign exchange by gold imports, since to do so would involve losses. If, in our example, the sterling exchange rate is $4.8665 (the mint parity), then to acquire or dispose of sterling by gold shipments would mean a loss of two American cents per pound sterling for each transaction (the costs of shipment). Between the gold points, therefore, the rate of exchange is determined as in a free, unstabilized market. The spread between the gold points, however, is so narrow that we may regard exchange rates under the gold standard as fixed.

It will be noted that this stabilization is achieved without any intervention in the foreign exchange market on the part of the monetary authorities, who behave simply as residual buyers and sellers of gold. Gold moves "automatically" from one country to another in response to the supply of and demand for foreign exchange.

Active Stabilization by Monetary Authorities.   A true international gold standard has not functioned since the first half of the 1930s, and since that time exchange rates, unless controlled outright or left free to float, have been stabilized by

---

[6]All the foreign exchange that is demanded at the gold export point will be supplied.
[7]All the foreign exchange that is supplied at the gold import point will be demanded.

official compensatory transactions in the foreign exchange market.[8] The policy objectives of active stabilization, however, differ considerably from the policy objectives of passive stabilization under the gold standard. Under the old gold standard, the fundamental aim of international monetary policy was to remain on the gold standard and to avoid any change in the gold content of the monetary unit. The almost incidental result of this policy was a fixed exchange rate. As a matter of fact, the exchange rates of the major trading countries were fixed at the same level for several decades preceding World War I. In contrast, active stabilization seeks to achieve stability in the exchange rate but allows for occasional adjustments in the rate to correct disequilibrium in the balance of payments. This policy of "stable, yet flexible" rates attempts to secure the advantages of stability and, at the same time, to use the exchange rate as an instrument of international adjustment.

We have already briefly described the basic mechanism of exchange rate stabilization; we now look more closely into its actual operation. To stabilize the dollar price of sterling between, say $1.73 and $1.77, the United States monetary authorities (Treasury and Federal Reserve System) would require two assets: (1) dollars and (2) sterling exchange, other foreign exchange freely convertible into sterling, or gold. The dollars would be needed so that the authorities could buy all the sterling that might be offered in New York at $1.73, that is, so that they could make the demand for sterling perfectly elastic at that rate. Foreign exchange or gold would be needed so that the authorities could satisfy any demand for sterling at $1.77 thereby providing the ability to make the supply of sterling perfectly elastic at that rate.

As part of the government, the monetary authorities would have no difficulty in obtaining sufficient dollars for their operations, but the supply of foreign exchange and gold would be limited, since the government cannot create foreign exchange and domestic gold production is small. There is another reason why American monetary authorities would not be concerned over their holdings of dollars. As we have noted, domestic currency would be necessary to put a floor under the dollar price of sterling, that is, to avert a depreciation of sterling and a simultaneous appreciation of the dollar. Ordinarily, however, domestic authorities would not support the exchange value of a foreign currency; they would be interested only in one-sided stabilization, the avoidance of depreciation of the domestic currency. In practice, therefore, the U.S. authorities would impose a ceiling over the dollar price of sterling, while at the same time the British authorities would place a floor below the dollar price of sterling.[9] This division of labor

---

[8]The first stabilization agency was the British Exchange Equalization Account, which was established in 1932 after the United Kingdom abandoned the gold standard. Upon the devaluation of the dollar in 1934, the United States also established a stabilization agency, and by the end of the 1930s, most countries had adopted a policy of exchange stabilization, whether implemented by special agencies, central banks, or treasuries.

[9]In other words, the British authorities would impose a ceiling over the pound price of dollars in London. In a stable-rate system, *depreciation* is commonly called *devaluation* (because it is a government action) and *appreciation* is called *revaluation*. We prefer to use *depreciation* and *appreciation* as the basic terms to indicate the direction of a movement in the exchange rate. Hence we shall use them for that purpose in describing both variable and stable-rate systems. With respect to the latter, we shall also use devaluation and revaluation. In the contemporary "managed-float" system, it is not always clear when a depreciation (appreciation) is a devaluation (revaluation) because of the hidden role of governments in influencing exchange rates (see Chapter 19).

Part II   International Payments

Figure 12-5

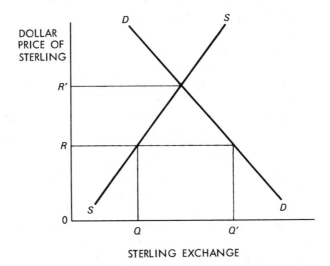

Stabilization of the Dollar-Sterling Exchange Rate. In the absence of intervention by the monetary authorities, the equilibrium rate of exchange would be 0-R'. To fix the rate at 0-R, the authorities need to supply the market with Q-Q' of sterling exchange taken from their international reserves.

would also occur under gold standard stabilization: Gold would flow out of a country to maintain an upper price limit (gold export point) on foreign exchange and would flow into a country to maintain a lower price limit (gold import point).

A diagrammatic illustration of the mechanism of exchange rate stabilization is shown in Figure 12-5. Without the intervention of monetary authorities, the exchange rate would be 0-R'. But suppose the authorities want to hold the rate to 0-R. At that rate, the amount of foreign exchange supplied the market is Q-Q' less than the amount demanded, which is the reason why 0-R is *not* the equilibrium rate. To maintain the rate at 0-R, therefore, the authorities must supply the market with Q-Q' of foreign exchange, which will close the gap between the amounts supplied and demanded.[10] In other words, they must provide *compensatory financing* of the supply deficit.

CONTROLLED EXCHANGE RATES

Neither the fluctuating rate market nor the stabilized market imposes restrictions on private transactions in foreign exchange. A wide gulf separates these two markets from the controlled foreign exchange market, which prohibits private transactions not authorized by the control authority. The controlled exchange rate

---

[10]Hence, Q-Q' is the *deficit* in the official reserves transactions balance of the country's balance of payments (see Chapter 14).

does not directly respond to shifts in supply and demand; government rationing supersedes the allocating function of the exchange rate, and the currency becomes *inconvertible*. When exchange controls are relaxed, the job of maintaining stable exchange rates is passed on to stabilization agencies or their counterparts.

We shall examine the nature and the effects of exchange control in Chapter 17. At present we are interested only in the essential mechanism of exchange control — how it works in the foreign exchange market. To simplify our analysis, we assume a completely controlled market in which the control authority is the *exclusive* buyer of foreign exchange from domestic residents and the *exclusive* seller of foreign exchange to domestic residents. All foreign exchange must be sold to the authority at its stipulated rate, and all foreign exchange must be bought from the authority at its stipulated rate. We further assume that there is only one rate of exchange, although in practice the control agency may charge a much higher rate than it pays for foreign exchange to earn a monopoly profit, or it may adopt several discriminatory rates.

The supply of foreign exchange is derived from the credit items of the balance of payments, and the control authorities have only a limited influence over it. To raise the supply of foreign exchange, steps must be taken to expand exports, encourage foreign loans, and the like. Many of these steps lie beyond the jurisdiction of the control agency. The agency, therefore, considers the supply of foreign exchange as relatively fixed with respect to its own powers, and its main task is the allocation of this fixed supply among those who demand it. This is usually done by an exchange or trade-licensing system — unless a domestic resident can obtain a license, foreign exchange cannot be secured. This rationing brings about a "suppressed disequilibrium" between supply and demand by forcibly choking off all excess demand.

The determination of the controlled rate of exchange is shown in Figure 12-6. If the market were free, the equilibrium rate of exchange would be ten pesos for one dollar where the supply and demand schedules intersect. At this equilibrium rate both the amount demanded and the amount supplied would be 0–E dollars. At the controlled rate of five pesos, however, the amount demanded (0–F) exceeds the amount supplied (0–G) by an amount of dollars (G–F); that is to say, the market is not cleared at the controlled rate. It follows that the control authority must suppress the excess demand (G–F) by issuing licenses only for the purchase of 0–G dollars; otherwise the authority will be unable to maintain the controlled rate.

We can draw the following conclusions from our analysis of the controlled rate of exchange: (1) The controlled rate is less than the equilibrium rate — the controlled rate overvalues the peso in terms of dollars; (2) the amount of dollars supplied to the market at the controlled rate is less than the amount supplied at the equilibrium rate (0–G compared with 0–E) — the controlled rate discourages exports by making them more expensive to foreign buyers; (3) the market is not truly cleared — the excess demand (G–F) is not satisfied; and (4) the purchase of dollars at the controlled rate is smaller than the purchase at the equilibrium rate (0–G compared with 0–E) — the controlled market cuts imports below the level permitted by the free market.

Figure 12-6

The Controlled Rate of Exchange: Peso Country.   If the peso were freely convertible, the exchange rate would be 10 pesos. This is the *equilibrium* rate that clears the market. To control the rate at 5 pesos, the control authority (central bank) must suppress the excess demand (*G–F*) by issuing licenses to purchase only the amount of dollars supplied at the rate of 5 pesos (0–*G*). Exchange control substitutes a bureaucratic allocation of foreign exchange to buyers for an allocation determined by the free play of market forces.

EXCHANGE SPECULATION AND CAPITAL FLIGHT

In the previous pages we have covered many of the factors that determine exchange rates: the ordinary supply of and demand for foreign exchange, gold movements, the compensatory transactions of monetary authorities, and exchange controls. We now turn to a brief description and analysis of exchange speculation and capital flight, which may provoke violent disturbances in the rate of exchange.

Speculation Proper

Speculators purposely assume an open position in the foreign exchange market with the intent of making windfall profits from fluctuations in the rate of exchange. When speculators expect the exchange rate of a specific currency to rise in the near future, they go *long* on that currency by buying it. Conversely, when they expect the exchange rate of a currency to fall in the near future, they go *short,* either by selling the currency in the *forward* market for future delivery or by borrowing the currency on short term and then exchanging it for a currency they consider stable. When the expectations of speculators are not borne out, they suffer windfall losses.

Curiously enough, however, if speculation in a currency is strong and one-sided, it may itself force the exchange rate to move in the anticipated direction.

By going long on a currency, speculators sustain its exchange rate—they increase demand and thus help ward off depreciation or even bring about appreciation. For this reason, monetary authorities, anxious to avert depreciation but not concerned about appreciation, tend to view long speculators with less distaste than short speculators.

Speculation may be *stabilizing* or *destabilizing*. Stabilizing speculation goes *against* the market. When the demand for a currency is falling (or its supply increasing), speculation helps to stabilize the exchange rate by going long and buying the currency. Conversely, when the exchange rate is rising, stabilizing speculation will retard the rise by going short and selling the currency. Stabilizing speculation was common under the gold standard before World War I, when everyone felt certain that the gold points would limit any movements in the exchange rate. Today, however, there is no such assurance, and speculation, by going *with* the market, may be destabilizing.

At times in the past, destabilizing speculation, coupled with capital flight, has swamped the ordinary transactions of the foreign exchange market and has plunged the exchange rate into a dizzy spiral of depreciation. When general confidence in the exchange rate of a currency is shaky, destabilizing speculation may become cumulative: Speculation provokes depreciation, and this in turn provokes further speculation. As was true of the German mark in the early 1920s and the Chinese yuan after World War II, this interaction may attain a truly fantastic velocity and bring about a rate of exchange that is below the true value of the currency even though domestic inflation may be running rampant.

Speculators believe that they can "outguess" the market; that is, they believe they can forecast exchange rates more accurately than market indicators such as forward exchange rates. Whether, in fact, speculators can do so is a question taken up in Chapter 13. Suffice it to say here that speculators commonly guess wrong, particularly in a floating-rate system. Since the onset of floating rates in 1973, banks in several countries have suffered massive foreign exchange losses, including the Franklin National Bank of New York (which was declared insolvent), the Herstatt Bank of West Germany (which was forced to close), the Union Bank of Switzerland, and the Lloyds Bank of London. Individual speculators have also been hurt badly by guessing wrong on the future behavior of foreign exchange rates.

Capital Flight

Unlike speculation proper, *capital flight* is initiated not by the hope of gain but by the fear of loss. When a country faces the prospect of exchange depreciation, the imposition of exchange controls, political instability, or war, domestic and foreign residents who own assets in that country seek safety by transferring funds to a country that is considered stable. The consequence may be a mass flight of capital that seriously weakens the currencies of some countries and brings unneeded foreign exchange and gold to other countries.

Speculative and flight capital movements inevitably occur when there is fear of exchange devaluation, exchange restrictions, or political instability. During the 1960s flows of speculative capital repeatedly threatened the stability of the pound sterling and the dollar. A massive flow of speculative capital out of the dollar in 1971 finally led to the abandonment of the gold convertibility of the dollar and a wholesale realignment of exchange rates, a subject which is taken up in Chapter 18.

SOME ADDITIONAL REMARKS ON THE DETERMINATION OF EXCHANGE RATES

In this chapter we have used a *balance of payments approach* to the determination of exchange rates: Exchange rates move to equilibrate the supply and demand of foreign exchange. As explained earlier, the supply of foreign exchange involves all credit transactions that appear in a country's balance of payments, and the demand for foreign exchange involves all debit transactions. But the different kinds of credit and debit transactions (current account, long-term capital account, short-term capital account, and official reserves account) do not all respond with the same speed to new economic (and political) circumstances. For that reason, we can draw a distinction between short- and long-run equilibrium in the foreign exchange market.

Flows of financial assets (including monies) that make up the short-term capital account and the official reserves account (when the monetary authorities seek to influence the exchange rate) respond quickly to international differences in interest rates and to shifting expectations of future exchange rates. Over the short run (say, up to six months), therefore, the supply and demand of foreign exchange are dominated by transfers of financial assets between the domestic and foreign countries. To explain the transfer mechanism, we must understand the forward exchange market, which is the subject of the next chapter.

In contrast to short-term financial assets, flows of goods, services, and investment capital respond more slowly to fundamental or real economic forces, such as changes in factor supply, economic growth (real income), technological innovation, productivity, and demand preferences. But these flows become the dominant influence on the long-run supply and demand of foreign exchange and, therefore, the long-run equilibrium rate of exchange.

The balance of payments approach to the determination of exchange rates is accepted by all economists. But economists may differ on the causal factors that lie behind the supply and demand of foreign exchange. Commonly, these differences relate to different emphases on short- and long-run equilibria in the foreign exchange market, but sometimes they also reflect basic theoretical disagreements. In Chapter 16 we shall take up alternative explanations of exchange rates. Our present task, however, is to complete our understanding of the balance of payments approach by looking at the flows of financial assets that determine short-run equilibrium in the foreign exchange market.

SUMMARY

1. The exchange rate is the domestic money price of foreign money. The domestic price of bank transfers is the base rate of exchange, and all other means of international payments usually sell at a discount from the base rate. Unless otherwise specified, we assume the exchange rate to be one rate, namely, the base rate. The behavior of the exchange rate will depend upon the nature of the foreign exchange market. We can distinguish three sorts of behavior: freely fluctuating rates, stable rates, and controlled rates.

2. Freely fluctuating rates result when the rate of exchange is free to respond to the movements of supply and demand. The rate of exchange is then determined by the intersection of the supply and demand schedules, which in turn are determined by the credit and debit items of the balance of payments, respectively. The rate of exchange, however, also affects the balance of payments, and there is thus a mutual interdependence between them.

3. There are several arguments in favor of stable exchange rates. Under the gold standard, international gold movements prevent any variation in the exchange rate outside the narrow limits of the gold points. Exchange rates may also be stabilized by compensatory purchases and sales of foreign exchange on the part of government agencies.

4. Controlled rates result from the monopoly purchase and sale of foreign exchange by a government agency. The available foreign exchange is distributed by a rationing system, and because the controlled rate is maintained below the equilibrium rate, there is an excess demand that is not satisfied. The exchange rate is determined by bureaucratic decision rather than supply and demand.

5. Because foreign exchange is a store of value as well as an instrument of current payment, demand and supply schedules shift quickly in response to changes in expectations about the future behavior of economic variables.

6. Exchange speculation and capital flight also influence exchange rates. Because these short-term capital movements usually undermine the exchange rate and weaken the balance of payments, monetary authorities view them with marked distaste.

QUESTIONS AND APPLICATIONS

1. What is the base rate of exchange?
2. What are the three kinds of exchange rate behavior?

3. (a) How is the exchange rate determined when it is freely fluctuating?
   (b) Why, in Figure 12-1, does the demand schedule for foreign exchange slope downward from left to right?
   (c) Why, in Figure 12-2, does the supply schedule for foreign exchange slope upward from left to right?
4. Using graphs like those in this chapter, show the effects on the exchange rate of the following:
   (a) An increase in exports of merchandise.
   (b) An increase in domestic demand for foreign securities.
   (c) An increase in sales of domestic securities to foreigners.
   (d) A decrease in imports of services.
5. (a) What are the minimum conditions of an international gold standard?
   (b) Explain how the international gold standard prevents fluctuations of the exchange rate beyond the gold points.
6. What is the function of a stabilization agency? How does it perform this function?
7. Using a graph, show how exchange control determines the rate of exchange. Why is the market not cleared under exchange control?
8. (a) Distinguish between stabilizing and destabilizing speculation.
   (b) What is capital flight?

SELECTED READINGS

See the list of readings given at the end of Chapter 13.

chapter 13

FORWARD EXCHANGE SPECULATION AND HEDGING AGAINST EXCHANGE RISKS

This chapter continues our study of the foreign exchange market by analyzing the determination of forward exchange rates and the use of the forward market to protect against exchange risks. As we shall observe, transactions in the forward market also influence spot rates of foreign exchange.

THE FORWARD RATE OF EXCHANGE

The markets that we have previously analyzed deal in foreign exchange bought and sold for immediate delivery. Closely allied to these *spot* exchange markets are the *forward* exchange markets that deal not in foreign exchange but in promises to buy or sell foreign exchange at a specified rate and at a specified time in the future, with payment to be made upon delivery. These promises are known as *forward exchange,* and the price at which they are traded is the *forward rate of exchange.*[1]

The forward exchange market resembles the futures markets found in organized commodity exchanges, such as those for wheat and coffee. The primary function of any futures or forward market is to afford protection against the risk of price fluctuations. Forward exchange markets, therefore, are most useful when the rate of exchange is freely fluctuating and when there are significant exchange risks for those who are committed to make or receive international payments. When the rate of exchange is stabilized, forward exchange is most useful when there is a strong possibility that the exchange rate will be allowed to depreciate in the near future. Since the forward exchange market must be free, it cannot function under exchange control.

Foreign exchange dealers commonly seek to balance their sales and purchases of forward exchange in a given currency to avoid the exchange risk, and they may

---

[1]The forward rates for major international currencies on November 5 and 6, 1992, are shown in Table 12-1.

refuse to enter forward contracts of long maturity because they cannot find an offsetting contract of equal maturity. At times, dealers may offset an open position in forward exchange with an opposing open position in spot exchange, a practice known as "swapping." At other times, dealers may function as professional risk bearers by deliberately assuming an open forward position in the expectation of making a speculative gain. Because of their own role as speculators, foreign exchange dealers are usually reluctant to enter forward contracts with individuals who want to speculate rather than protect themselves against an exchange risk.[2]

Two theories have been put forth to explain the determination of forward exchange rates: the traditional interest parity theory and the modern theory.

INTEREST PARITY THEORY

When short-term interest rates are higher in one national money market (say, London) than in another (say, New York), investors will be motivated to shift funds from New York to London. To do so, they must convert dollars into sterling for investment in London. But then they become exposed to an exchange risk: If the pound subsequently depreciates vis-à-vis the dollar, then when the investors convert from sterling back into dollars at the end of the investment period (maturity), they will experience an *exchange loss* that will offset, or more than offset, the gain in interest income. To avoid this possible exchange loss, therefore, dollar investors will *cover* against the exchange risk by selling sterling *forward* in an amount that fully equals their purchase of *spot* sterling plus the interest that will be earned in London. This practice is known as *interest arbitrage*. As we shall see, interest arbitrage establishes a link between the interest-rate differential of two national money markets and the forward rates of the respective currencies. This link is the basis of the interest parity theory.

Algebraic Formulation of Interest Parity Theory

The interest parity theory is most easily explained algebraically. Let us assume that a U.S. investor has A dollars to invest in 90-day Treasury bills, either in New York or in London. If A dollars are invested in New York, the return (principal plus interest) at the end of 90 days will be

$$(1) \quad A(1 + i_{US}/4),$$

where i_{US} is the annual interest rate on Treasury bills in New York. It is necessary to divide i by 4 because the maturity of the bills is 90 days, or one-fourth of a year.

---

[2]Although the traditional foreign exchange dealers (banks) continue to handle the bulk of forward exchange transactions, speculators have ample opportunities to trade in currency futures and options markets that have opened since the arrival of floating exchange rates in 1971, as described in Chapter 11. These markets appeal to the small investor who wants to speculate or to the small trader who wants to hedge against exchange risks. In contrast, the bank forward market deals primarily with the large transactions of banks, multinational companies, and big exporters and importers.

Alternatively, if our investor buys A dollars worth of bills in London and covers against the exchange risk, the return at maturity will be

$$(2)\ (A/S)(1\ +\ i_{UK}/4)F,$$

where S is the *spot* dollar-sterling rate of exchange (the dollar price of one pound sterling); i_{UK}, the interest rate in London; and F, the dollar-sterling forward rate of exchange (the dollar price of one pound sterling for delivery 90 days hence). The expression A/S is the amount of spot sterling that can be purchased with A dollars; the expression $(A/S)(1\ +\ i_{UK}/4)$ is the amount of sterling the investor will receive at the end of 90 days; and the entire expression is the amount of dollars the investor will receive when the sterling amount is converted into dollars at the 90-days forward rate of exchange.

It is evident that if $A(1\ +\ i_{US}) > (A/S)(1\ +\ i_{UK})F$, then our investor will invest funds in New York, as will short-term investors in London. Hence, funds will move from London to New York. Conversely, if $A(1\ +\ i_{US}) < (A/S)(1\ +\ i_{UK})F$, then funds will move from New York to London. To illustrate, suppose that on a given day i_{US} is 6 percent, i_{UK} is 10 percent, the dollar-sterling exchange rate is $1.70, the rate on 90-day sterling is $1.65, and A is $100,000. In which market will our investor earn the highest return on Treasury bills, assuming that our investor covers the exchange risk in the forward market? Entering the appropriate values in equation (1), we have

$$\$100,000(1\ +\ .06/4)\ =\ \$101,500.$$

Entering the appropriate values in equation (2), we have

$$(\$100,000/\$1.70)(1\ +\ .10/4)\$1.65\ =\ \$99,485.$$

Despite the higher interest rate in London, it is evident that our investor will place the funds in New York. If invested in London, the net interest gain (.04/4 or .01) would be more than offset by the loss on forward sterling. Under these conditions funds will move from London to New York.

The interest parity theory asserts that the *interest arbitrage* will cause the forward rate to adjust to the interest rate differential until it reaches an equilibrium value at which it is no longer profitable to shift funds between the two money centers. In equilibrium, therefore,

$$(3)\ A(1\ +\ i_{US}/4)\ =\ (A/S)(1\ +\ i_{UK}/4)F^*,$$

where F^* is the equilibrium ("no-profit") forward exchange rate.

Solving equation (3) for F^*, we get

$$(4) \quad F^* = \frac{S(1 + i_{US}/4)}{(1 + i_{UK}/4)}.$$

If we assume that i is adjusted for the length of the forward exchange contract, then equation (4) becomes

$$(5) \quad F^* = \frac{S(1 + i_{US})}{(1 + i_{UK})}.$$

Transposing and subtracting 1 from both sides of equation (5), we get

$$(6) \quad \frac{i_{US} - i_{UK}}{1 + i_{UK}} = \frac{F^* - S}{S}.$$

If i_{UK} is a small fraction (as it ordinarily is), then equation (6) can be approximated as

$$(7) \quad i_{US} - i_{UK} = \frac{F^* - S}{S}.$$

This equation states that at interest parity, the interest rate differential between New York and London (the New York rate *minus* the London rate) is equal to the forward-spot rate differential (the forward rate *minus* the spot rate) as a percentage of the spot rate.[3] Solving equation (7) for F^*, we have

$$(8) \quad F^* = S + S(i_{US} - i_{UK}).$$

Returning to our earlier example and assuming that the interest rates and the spot rate are autonomous (do not change) with respect to interest arbitrage, what is the equilibrium forward rate of exchange? Entering the values into equation (8), we have

$$F^* = \$1.70 + \$1.70(.06/4 - .10/4) = \$1.683.$$

At this forward rate, the investor's rate of return in New York would equal the return in London *with* forward cover. This is true because the higher net interest rate in London for 90 days (1 percent) is exactly offset by the percentage discount on 90-day forward sterling (1 percent). The discount on forward sterling ($1.683 − $1.700, or − $.017) may be expressed as an *implicit* interest rate, as shown on the right side of equation (7):

_____

[3]This equation is commonly used by arbitragers in practice.

$$\frac{F^* - S}{S} = \frac{\$1.683 - \$1.70}{\$1.70} = -.01 = 1 \text{ percent discount.}$$

This is the implicit interest rate for 90-day forward sterling; hence, the annual rate is 4 percent, which equals the annual interest rate advantage of London over New York. In other words, the forward rate is at *interest parity*. As we showed above, our investor would end up with $101,500 if the funds were invested in New York. If instead the funds were invested in London and covered against the exchange risk, the investor would receive at the end of 90 days the following *dollar* sum: ($100,000/$1.70)(1.025) × 1.6834 = $101,500 — exactly the same sum that would be received in New York.[4] Clearly, when the forward rate is at interest parity, investors in New York have no incentive to invest in London and investors in London have no incentive to invest in New York.

Graphic Demonstration of Interest Parity Theory

The interest parity theory is demonstrated graphically in Figure 13-1. The vertical axis measures the interest rate differential between New York and London. Above the origin the interest rate is higher in New York than in London; below the origin the interest rate is higher in London than in New York. The horizontal axis measures the implicit interest rate on forward sterling. To the right of the origin forward sterling sells at a premium over spot sterling; to the left of the origin it sells at a discount under spot sterling (as in our previous example). The interest parity line is drawn at a 45-degree angle to the origin (slope of 1) so that any point on it is equidistant from the two axes. According to the interest parity theory, the dollar-sterling forward rate will move to a point on the interest parity line at which the implicit interest rate equals the interest rate differential.

The forward rate F is in disequilibrium because 0–*b* (the implicit premium interest rate on forward sterling) is less than 0–*a* (the net interest advantage of New York over London). Hence, funds will move from London to New York as investors make an interest gain of 0–*a* and are able to cover the exchange risk by *buying* sterling forward (the same as *selling* dollars forward) at a premium over the spot rate that is less than their interest gain. Assuming that the interest differential is autonomous (constant), the purchase of forward sterling by interest arbitragers will raise its premium until the implicit interest reaches F^* on the interest parity line, where 0–*c* equals 0–*a*. At any forward rate lying above the interest parity line, funds will move from London to New York; at any forward rate lying below the line, funds will move from New York to London.

---

[4]To obtain full arithmetic accuracy, we have calculated the equilibrium forward rate by using the mathematically correct equation derived from equation (6):

$$F^* = S + \frac{S(i_{US} - i_{UK})}{1 + i_{UK}},$$

which gives $1.6834, as compared with $1.683, which was derived from the approximate equation (8).

Figure 13-1

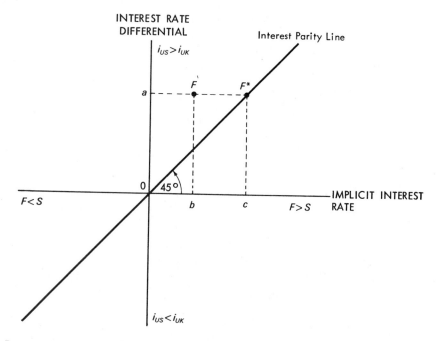

Interest Parity Theory: The Determination of the Forward Exchange Rate through Interest Arbitrage.   At every point on the interest parity line, the implicit interest rate on forward sterling ($F-S$) equals the interest rate differential ($i_{US}-i_{UK}$) between New York and London. According to the interest parity theory, the dollar-sterling forward rate will move to a point on the interest parity line. The forward rate F is in disequilibrium because the implicit premium interest rate on forward sterling ($0-b$) is less than the interest advantage of New York over London ($0-a$). Hence, funds will move from London to New York until a new equilibrium forward rate F^* makes the implicit premium interest rate on forward sterling ($0-c$) equal to New York's interest rate advantage ($0-a$).

Other Effects of Interest Arbitrage

Up to this point in our exposition of the interest parity theory, we have assumed that interest arbitrage brings about an adjustment of the forward rate to autonomous spot and interest rates. Actually, interest arbitrage will also affect those other variables. When, for example, funds move from New York to London because

$$(i_{US} - i_{UK}) < \frac{(F - S)}{S}$$

then: (1) the demand for spot sterling will push up the spot rate of exchange (S), (2) interest rates in New York (i_{US}) will rise as the supply of funds decreases, (3) interest rates in London (i_{UK}) will fall as the supply of funds increases, and (4) sales of forward sterling will lower the forward rate (F). All of these adjustments are equilibrating, helping to remove any discrepancy between the interest rate differential and the implicit interest rate.[5]

The Limitation of Interest Parity Theory

Does interest arbitrage *in practice* eliminate any discrepancy between interest rate differentials and implicit interest rates of forward exchange? The answer is no. The interest parity theory fails to explain fully the behavior of forward exchange rates because it ignores *speculation* in forward exchange. This omission is rectified by the modern theory of forward exchange that takes into account the actions of speculators and traders as well as arbitragers.

THE MODERN THEORY OF FORWARD EXCHANGE

The modern theory of forward exchange postulates that the forward exchange rate is determined by the supply and demand schedules of arbitragers, traders, and speculators. To simplify our presentation we shall assume that New York and London are the two money centers, the exchange rate is expressed as the dollar price of one pound sterling, and the interest rate differential and spot exchange rate are given (autonomous).

The Arbitragers' Schedule

Figure 13-2 depicts the arbitragers' schedule. The horizontal axis measures the quantity of forward sterling: sales to the left of the origin, purchases to the right of the origin. The vertical axis indicates the spot and forward rates of exchange.

If the forward rate is at interest parity, then arbitragers will neither buy nor sell forward sterling. This is the point (F^*) where the schedule crosses the vertical axis. The fact that F^* lies above the spot rate (S) tells us that the interest rate differential favors New York. At the forward rate F' (above F^*), arbitragers will shift funds from New York to London, selling $0–c$ forward sterling. Recall equation (7):

$$i_{US} - i_{UK} = \frac{F^* - S}{S}.$$

With a given interest differential and spot rate, if $F' > F^* > S$, then

$$\frac{F' - S}{S} > \frac{F^* - S}{S} = i_{US} - i_{UK}.$$

Thus, at F' the percentage premium on forward sterling (implicit interest rate) exceeds the interest advantage of New York over London, providing arbitragers

---

[5]In terms of Figure 13-1, $0–a$ will decrease and thus the adjustment of F to F^* will be less than $b–c$.

330   **Part II   International Payments**

Figure 13-2

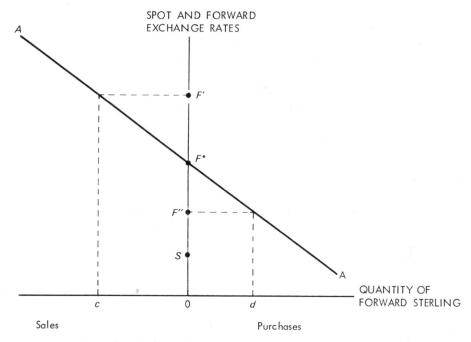

The Arbitragers' Schedule for Forward Exchange. The arbitragers' schedule indicates the sales (left of the origin) and purchases (right of the origin) of forward sterling that are undertaken by arbitragers at different spot and forward exchange rates. When the forward rate is at interest parity, then arbitragers neither buy nor sell forward sterling. This occurs at F^*, where the schedule crosses the vertical axis. Because this interest parity forward rate is above the spot rate (S), the interest rate differential favors New York. When the forward rate is at F' (above F^*), the percentage premium on forward sterling exceeds New York's interest advantage. Hence, arbitragers shift funds from New York to London, selling $0-c$ forward sterling to cover against the exchange risk. Conversely, at the forward rate of F'', arbitragers move funds from London to New York, buying $0-d$ forward sterling to cover against the exchange risk.

with an incentive to move funds from New York to London and cover with forward sales of sterling. At rate F'', arbitragers will move funds from London to New York, buying $0-d$ forward sterling to cover against the exchange risk. At that rate the premium on forward sterling is less than the interest rate advantage of New York over London. As the $A-A$ schedule shows, forward *sales* of sterling are an increasing function of the *absolute* difference $F-F^*$ when $F > F^*$. Conversely, forward *purchases* of sterling are an increasing function of the absolute difference $F-F^*$ when $F < F^*$.

The Traders' Schedule

A second actor in the forward market is the trader (exporter or importer of goods and services) who wants to hedge against an open position in foreign exchange.

For example, a U.S. importer who must pay a certain amount of sterling in 90 days for imported goods is exposed to an exchange risk: If sterling appreciates in 90 days, more dollars must be paid for the goods than otherwise. Conversely, a U.S. exporter who will receive payment for goods in sterling 90 days hence is exposed to an exchange loss if sterling depreciates in that period. In the next section we shall look at the hedging options open to the trader to eliminate the exchange risk.[6] We shall also find that the traders' schedule takes the same form as the arbitragers' schedule. Therefore, we simply add the traders' schedule (T–T) to the arbitragers' schedule (A–A) to obtain a combined schedule (AT–AT).

The Speculators' Schedule

The speculator deliberately assumes a foreign exchange risk in the expectation that future changes in the exchange rate will bring a profit. Speculation may be made in the spot or the forward market. However, deliberate speculation in the spot market requires either the purchase of a foreign currency with an immediate cash outlay (to go long) or the borrowing of a foreign currency with interest costs (to go short). In contrast, speculation in the forward market involves no cash outlay or interest cost beyond a small margin of 10 percent or less. Consequently, professional speculators choose to speculate in forward markets rather than in spot markets. Speculation in spot markets is mainly done by traders (including multinational enterprises) who fail to cover an existing foreign exchange exposure.

In our exposition of the speculators' schedule, we shall continue to use dollars and sterling. Then the speculator will *sell* sterling forward if the spot rate of sterling is expected to fall below the forward rate over the forward contract period. At the end of the contract period (say, 90 days) the speculator will buy sterling at the spot rate and sell it at the higher forward rate. Algebraically, the speculator will sell forward sterling if $E(S^t) < F$, where $E(S^t)$ is the speculator's expected spot rate at a future time t (which we take to be 90 days) and F is the price of forward sterling *now* for delivery at time t. If the speculator's expectation is realized by the market, then at time t the speculator's profit will be $A(F - S^t)$, where A is the amount of forward sterling the speculator originally sold. Assume, for example, that the current spot rate is $1.75, $E(S^t)$ is $1.65, and F for period t (= 90 days) is $1.70. The speculator expects the spot sterling rate to fall below the forward rate in 90 days. Thus, the speculator decides to sell forward $50,000 of sterling, which gives the speculator a commitment to sell £29,412 in 90 days at a rate of $1.70. Ninety days pass and the spot rate indeed falls to $1.65. Then the speculator buys £29,412 at the spot rate for $48,530 (£29,412 × $1.65) and sells those pounds for $50,000 under the terms of the forward contract, making a profit of $1,470. Of course, if the spot rate had remained above the forward rate, the speculator would have suffered a loss.

---

[6]If traders fail to hedge against the foreign exchange risk, then they become speculators in the spot market but do not influence the forward rate.

Conversely, if the speculator expects the spot rate to be above the forward rate at time t ($E(S^t) > F$), then A amount of forward sterling will be *bought*. If the expectation is realized, the profit will be $A(S^t - F)$ when the speculator buys sterling at the forward contract rate and sells it at the higher spot rate. On the other hand, if $S^t < F$, then $A(S^t - F)$ will be lost.

The speculators' schedule is depicted in Figure 13-3. If speculators expect that the spot rate of sterling at time t will equal the forward rate for period t, then they will neither sell nor buy forward sterling. This equality is at the point where the S–S

Figure 13-3

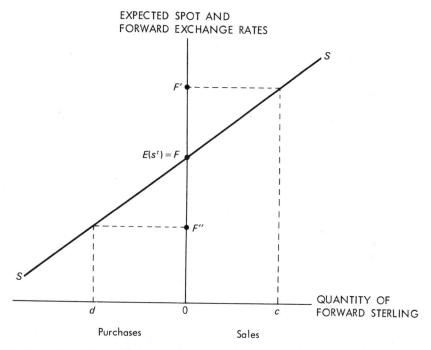

The Speculators' Schedule for Forward Exchange. The speculators' schedule shows the amounts of forward sterling purchased and sold at various differences between the expected spot and forward exchange rates. At the intersection of S–S and the vertical axis, the spot rate expected to prevail at the end of the forward contract period is equal to the forward rate [$E(s^t) = F$]. Hence, speculators neither buy nor sell forward sterling. Speculators *buy* forward sterling when the forward rate is less than the expected spot rate [$F < E(S^t)$]. The greater this difference, the greater the purchases of forward sterling, as indicated by the positive slope of the schedule to the *left* of the point of intersection. Speculators *sell* forward sterling when the forward rate is higher than the expected spot rate [$F > E(S^t)$]. The greater this difference, the greater the sale of forward sterling. Accordingly, the schedule slopes upward to the *right* of the point of intersection.

schedule crosses the vertical axis. If, however, the forward rate is $F' > E(S^t)$, then speculators will sell $0-c$ pounds forward. The greater the positive gap $F' - E(S^t)$, the greater the sales of forward sterling by speculators. Conversely, if the forward rate is F'', speculators will buy $0-d$ pounds forward. The greater the negative gap $F'' - E(S^t)$, the greater the purchases of forward sterling by speculators.[7]

The Determination of the Equilibrium Rate

The equilibrium rate of forward exchange is determined by the intersection of the $AT-AT$ and $S-S$ schedules, as shown in Figure 13-4. Since $F^* < S$, it follows that

Figure 13-4

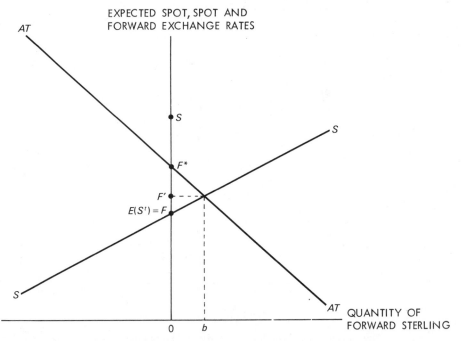

The Determination of the Equilibrium Forward Exchange Rate. The equilibrium rate of sterling forward exchange (F') is determined by the intersection of the arbitrager-trader schedule ($AT-AT$) and the speculator schedule ($S-S$). At F', arbitragers and traders want to *buy* $0-B$ of forward sterling while speculators want to *sell* $0-B$ of forward sterling. Hence, the market clears at F'. Because speculators expect a depreciation of the spot rate [from S to $F(S^t)$], the equilibrium rate F' lies below the interest parity rate F^*, at which arbitragers and traders neither sell nor buy forward sterling. A shift in either schedule causes movement to a new equilibrium rate.

---

[7]How much speculators are willing to risk depends not only on the size of the gap but also on their *confidence* in their expectations. The higher their confidence, the more speculators are willing to risk at a given gap (the more elastic is the $S-S$ schedule), and conversely.

　　　　　　　　　　　　　　　　　　　　　Part II International Payments

interest rates in London are higher than in New York. $E(S')$ lies below S, which indicates that speculators expect a sterling depreciation. The two schedules intersect to determine the equilibrium rate F'. At that rate arbitragers and traders will *buy* 0–b forward sterling while speculators will *sell* the same amount of forward sterling. Observe that the equilibrium rate (F') is below the interest parity rate (F^*) because of speculators' sales.

A shift in either schedule will bring about a new equilibrium rate. The AT–AT schedule will shift with changes in the spot rate and interest differential, because F^* would then change. The S–S schedule will shift with a change in speculators' expectations. For instance, if speculators become less bearish on the pound, then $E(S')$ will move closer to S; that is, the S–S schedule will shift upward to intersect AT–AT at a higher forward rate, since speculators will sell less forward sterling and thereby raise its price. Finally, if $E(S') = F^*$, then there is no speculation and the forward rate is at interest parity.

FORECASTING EXCHANGE RATES

Although governments continue to influence exchange rates with compensatory financing, they no longer seek to maintain them at prescribed levels (par values). Hence, exchange rates are allowed to respond to market forces much more freely than in the past. The term "dirty float" is commonly used to describe this system.

The flexibility of exchange rates today has stimulated a strong interest in forecasting exchange rates and in hedging against exchange risks. International traders, lenders, speculators, multinational companies, and governments must all make decisions that are based in some measure on their expectations of future exchange rates.

Short-Term Forecasting in a Floating-Rate System

When exchange rates are free to respond immediately to market forces, they are subject to expectations and speculation. Rates are formed in anticipation of *future* supply and demand rather than present supply and demand.

Are *forward* rates of exchange good forecasters of floating *spot* rates of exchange? The answer is no. Forward rates commonly diverge from future spot rates.

Can speculators do consistently better than the forward market in forecasting exchange rates? Most economists would say no, because they believe the foreign exchange market is an *efficient market*.

A market is strongly efficient if (1) prices immediately reflect all information, and (2) all information is public (that is, there are no traders with private "inside" information). In such a market, prices respond to the random arrival of new information, and therefore they are unpredictable. A forecaster who is trying to outsmart the market is confronted with a fatal obstacle to any systematic analysis: There is no *time lag* between the appearance of disequilibrating economic forces (such as interest rates, prices, money supply, and strikes) and adjustments in the exchange rate. A competitive, informed market immediately reflects all relevant information in the behavior of the exchange rate. Paradoxically, a forecaster who was consistently successful would be copied by others, who would then make the forecasted rate the actual market rate, thereby preventing the initial forecaster from any longer outguessing the market! In brief, the purely floating exchange rate describes a "random walk" in the same way as stock market prices. In such a market the forecaster is not likely to do any better consistently than the forward market and may do worse. Only *systematic* government intervention in the market can make short-term forecasting a successful enterprise.[8]

Although the market efficiency hypothesis has not been conclusively demonstrated, no one has found a reliable approach to forecasting exchange rates over the short run. It is for this reason that international firms are inclined to hedge against exchange risks, an activity described in the next section.

Long-Term Forecasting: The Purchasing-Power Parity Doctrine

Although forecasting exchange rates in the short term is a dubious enterprise, it is possible to forecast *long-term* changes in exchange rates with more confidence. Over a period of three to five years, the external value of a currency *tends* to reflect changes in its purchasing power relative to the purchasing power of other currencies, a relationship known as *purchasing-power parity*.

The purchasing-power parity doctrine is most easily explained with a few equations. Let us assume we are talking about the United States and Argentina. According to the doctrine, a relative change in the price levels of the two countries caused by different rates of inflation will bring about the same relative change in the external values of the U.S. dollar and Argentine peso as expressed by the exchange rate linking the two currencies:

$$(9) \quad \frac{P_{t,us}/P_{t,arg}}{P_{0,us}/P_{0,arg}} = \frac{S_t}{S_0},$$

where P is the price level in the United States (subscript *us*) and in Argentina (subscript *arg*) at time t or at a previous time 0, and S is the U.S. dollar price of the Argentine peso at time t or at time 0.

Using indexes to express price levels, suppose $P_{t,us} = 125$, $P_{t,arg} = 200$, both

---

[8]See Laurent L. Jacque, "Management of Foreign Exchange Risk: A Review Article," *Journal of International Business Studies,* Spring–Summer 1981, p. 87. When governments adhere to an agreed set of rules in managing exchange rates, such as devaluation in the face of a persistent deficit, forecasting exchange rates is comparatively straightforward and likely to be successful. Generally this was the situation with the industrial countries under the Bretton Woods international monetary system, which collapsed in 1971. Moreover, the downside risk of actions taken on the basis of forecasts was limited: Either the exchange rate decreased as expected or the government held it stable.

$P_{0,us}$ and $P_{0,arg}$ = 100, and S_0 = \$.10.[9] What, then, is S_t Using equation (9), we find that S_t = \$.0625.

The purchasing-power parity doctrine can also be formulated in terms of inflation rates. Let $r_{t,us}$ be the rate of inflation in the United States over the period t, and $r_{t,arg}$ the rate of inflation in Argentina over the same period. Then, $P_{t,us}$ = $P_{0,us}(1 + r_{t,us})$ and $P_{t,arg}$ = $P_{0,arg}(1 + r_{t,arg})$. Substituting these expressions in equation (9), we obtain

$$(10) \quad \frac{1 + r_{t,us}}{1 + r_{t,arg}} = \frac{S_t}{S_0}.$$

Suppose $r_{t,us}$ = 25 percent, $r_{t,arg}$ = 100 percent, and S_0 = U.S. \$.10. Then using equation (10), we find that S_t = \$.0625. This is the answer we got with equation (9) when using the same data expressed in terms of price levels.

Economists have raised several objections against the purchasing-power parity doctrine on both theoretical and empirical grounds. The principal theoretical objection to the doctrine lies in its inadequate coverage of the transactions that determine the rate of exchange. Only the price levels of goods are used to determine purchasing-power parities, whereas exchange rates are determined by capital transactions as well as goods transactions. On empirical grounds, the most serious objection is the question of the appropriate price indexes. To use the price indexes of export and import goods is almost a tautology: The relative price parities of homogeneous traded goods *should* be close to the actual exchange rate. Some economists also reject the use of wholesale price indexes because they may be heavily weighted with traded goods. The ideal index would be one based on the same assortment of goods in both countries, but governments do not compile such indexes. Pragmatically, the cost-of-living index would appear to be the most appropriate one to use in applying the purchasing-power parity doctrine. Other objections point to conditions that would create disparities between the purchasing-power parity exchange rate and the actual exchange rate over the short run, such as restrictions, the lagged response of officials in adjusting to payment disequilibria, the influence of exchange rate variations on the price level, and speculation.

Most critics of the purchasing-power parity doctrine do not reject it outright. It is widely accepted that in periods of rapid inflation the single most important determinant of change in exchange rates is the relative shift in the purchasing power of national currencies. Empirical studies have confirmed the usefulness of the doctrine to explain longer-term changes in exchange rates during periods of

---

[9]National price levels are a composite of many individual prices:

$$P_{US} = \sum_{i=1}^{i=n} P_i Q_i,$$

where P_i is the price of an individual good and Q_i is the quantity purchased expressed as a fraction of the total quantity purchased of all goods. This weighted price average is converted into an index number to measure changes over time.

inflation. Table 13-1 shows the application of the doctrine to the dollar-cruzeiro exchange rate during a period when Brazil experienced a high rate of inflation and made frequent devaluations of its currency.

Over the period as a whole, the U.S. price level rose 38.5 percent, while the Brazilian price level rose 160 percent. According to the purchasing-power parity doctrine, the exchange rate should fall from $.202 in 1970 to $.108 in 1975. The actual exchange rate in 1975 was $.110. This is a very close fit; the discrepancy as a percentage of the actual rate is less than 2 percent. Even on an annual basis the fit is close: The greatest discrepancy (1973) is 9.3 percent.

In sum, the purchasing-power parity doctrine is a good method to forecast exchange rates when changes in price levels are of a substantial magnitude. (Keep in mind, however, that the analyst must be able to forecast successfully the rates of inflation in the two countries.) Forecasts of long-term trends in a nation's exchange rate may be critical for international business decisions with long time horizons, such as the country location of industrial plants. But parities cannot help businessmen forecast the exchange rate of a currency three or six months from now (the time horizon of most international payments) or one year from now (the time horizon for budgetary planning in the transnational corporation). In the short run, exchange rates may diverge considerably from purchasing-power parities because they are dominated by short-term interest rates and price expectations. Also, it takes time for the demand and supply of foreign exchange to adjust to inflation. Indeed, it is this lag that makes purchasing-power parities useful for forecasting: Inflation rates become "leading indicators" of future exchange rates.

To end this discussion on a light note, we refer to the purchasing-power parity exchange rates based on Big Mac prices in different countries that have been calculated by *The Economist*, which points out that the Big Mac is one of the few products produced locally in many countries. A comparison of these prices in April 1992 reveals that the U.S. dollar is *undervalued* in Argentina, the EC countries,

Table 13-1   Comparison of the Purchasing-Power Parity Dollar-Cruzeiro Exchange Rate with the Actual Exchange Rate over the Period 1970–1975

	1970	1971	1972	1973	1974	1975
U.S. cost-of-living index	100	104.3	107.7	114.4	127.0	138.5
Brazilian cost-of-living index	100	120	140	158	210	260
Purchasing-power parity exchange rate (dollars)	.202	.176	.155	.146	.122	.108
Actual exchange rate (dollars)	.202	.177	.161	.161	.134	.110

Source: International Monetary Fund, *International Financial Statistics* (Washington, D.C.: various monthly issues).

Canada, Singapore, South Korea, Sweden, and Venezuela (where the prices of Big Macs in local currencies are higher than the U.S. dollar price when converted at the actual exchange rate) and *overvalued* in Australia, Brazil, China, Hong Kong, Hungary, and Russia (where local prices are lower than the U.S. price at the actual exchange rate). Although the Big Mac index may be hard for some economists to digest, *The Economist* believes that it offers a rough guide to how the dollar might move over the long run.[10]

HEDGING AGAINST FOREIGN EXCHANGE RISKS

Hedging is the procedure of balancing sales and purchases of an asset so there is no net open position on the market. If the hedge is perfect, the trader is protected against the risk of adverse changes in the price of the asset. In this section we examine the hedging of traders against foreign exchange risks originating in international *transactions* and the hedging of multinational companies against exchange risks originating in the *translation* of foreign currency balance sheets into dollar balance sheets. As we have demonstrated, the hedging transactions of international traders, along with the transactions of arbitragers, interact with speculators' transactions to determine the forward rate of exchange.

Hedging Against Transaction Risks

Sales contracts between international traders ordinarily call for payment at a specified future time (for example, 60 days after sight) in either the exporter's or the importer's currency. It follows that the party to whom the currency of payment is foreign is exposed to an exchange risk; that is, the amount of payment or receipt in domestic currency is subject to variations in the exchange rate between the domestic and foreign currencies. This is a *transaction* risk that arises from the international sale and purchase of goods and services.

Unless traders are willing to speculate in foreign exchange (usually they are not when, as at present, exchange rates are floating), they will eliminate the exchange risk by hedging. They may hedge in the forward exchange market or in the related foreign exchange futures and options markets. Or they may hedge through the spot exchange and money markets (borrower arbitrage). Here we examine hedging in the forward market and through borrower arbitrage.

Hedging in the Forward Market Suppose a U.S. exporter sells merchandise to a British importer for £10,000 payable in 60 days. The exporter is exposed to a transaction exchange risk: If the pound depreciates over the next 60 days, the exporter will receive fewer dollars. To hedge against this risk, the exporter proceeds as follows. Assuming the exporter wants a *dollar* payment of $17,500 for

---

[10]"Big Mac Currencies," *The Economist,* April 18, 1992, p. 81. Sophisticated estimates of purchasing-power parities also find the dollar undervalued in other industrial countries. See, for example, Kenichi Ohno, "Estimating Yen/Dollar and Mark/Dollar Purchasing Power Parities," *IMF Staff Papers,* International Monetary Fund, September 1990, Figures 1 and 2, pp. 720–21.

the merchandise, the exporter calculates the *sterling* value of that amount at the 60-day rate on forward sterling, which we take to be $1.75 ($17,500/$1.75 = £10,000). When the sales contract with the British importer is signed, the exporter *immediately sells* £10,000 forward for 60 days at $1.75. If at the end of 60 days the spot sterling rate has fallen below $1.75, the exporter is fully protected because the exporter can sell the £10,000 received from the importer for $17,500 under the forward contract, which is the dollar amount wanted by the exporter for the merchandise.

Similarly, an American importer who must pay a certain amount of sterling in 60 days to a British exporter will *immediately buy* 60-day forward sterling for that same amount. At the end of 60 days the importer will pay for the goods with sterling purchased at the forward rate under the forward contract. By using the forward market to hedge, both the exporter and the importer have transformed an *uncertain* dollar amount into a *certain* dollar amount.

Hedging through the Spot Exchange and Money Markets: Borrower Arbitrage A second hedging option for the U.S. exporter would be to borrow the present value of £10,000 in London for 60 days, immediately convert the sterling into dollars at the spot exchange rate, and then lend the funds in New York.[11] At the end of 60 days the exporter would repay the sterling loan (including interest) with the sterling received from the British importer and keep the following dollar amount:

$$\left(\frac{A}{1 + i_{UK}} \right) S(1 + i_{US}),$$

where A is the sterling amount due the exporter in 60 days (£10,000 in our example),

$$\frac{A}{1 + i_{UK}}$$

is the amount of sterling borrowed in London (the present value of A), S is the dollar-sterling spot exchange rate, and i_{UK} and i_{US} are respectively the London and New York interest rates adjusted to the 60-day period. If $S = 1.80, the annual $i_{UK} = .12$, and the annual $i_{US} = .09$, the exporter would end up with the following dollar amount at the end of 60 days:

$$\left(\frac{£10,000}{1 + .12/6} \right) $1.80(1 + .09/6) = $17,911.76.$$

---

[11]The dollar funds could be kept in the exporter's business rather than lending them. We assume that the cost of those funds kept is the interest foregone by not lending them.

In this example, the exporter would choose to hedge through the spot and money markets because only $17,500 would be received if the hedging had taken place in the forward market.

More generally, the exporter would be indifferent as to the hedging option chosen if

$$(11) \quad FA = \left(\frac{A}{1 + i_{UK}} \right) S(1 + i_{US}),$$

where the left side of the equation indicates the dollar receipts from forward hedging (the forward rate *times* the amount of sterling sold forward) and the right side represents the dollar receipts from hedging through the spot and money markets.

Solving equation (11) for F, we get

$$(12) \quad F = \frac{S(1 + i_{US})}{1 + i_{UK}}.$$

This equation is the same as equation (5), which defined the interest parity forward exchange rate. We can say, therefore, that when the exporter hedges through the spot and money markets, the exporter is behaving as an interest *arbitrager*.[12] If

$$FA < \frac{A}{1 + i_{UK}} S(1 + i_{US}),$$

then the exporter will hedge in the forward market and conversely.

Equation (11) also applies to the importer who is hedging against a sterling payment due in, say, 60 days. Instead of using the forward market, the importer can hedge as an arbitrager by borrowing in New York an amount of dollars that when converted into sterling at the spot rate and invested for 60 days in London would give the importer an amount equal to the sterling debt. But in the case of the importer we are talking of *payments* rather than *receipts*, as was true of the exporter. Thus, if

$$FA > \frac{A}{1 + i_{UK}} S(1 + i_{US}),$$

the importer will hedge as an arbitrager. Table 13-2 summarizes the hedging options of the exporter and importer.

---

[12]More precisely, the exporter is a *borrower* arbitrager (who borrows funds in one money market to transfer to another money market) rather than an *owner* arbitrager (who invests personal funds, as in our discussion of the arbitragers' schedule). Because equations (12) and (5) are the same, we added the arbitragers' and traders' schedules to get a combined schedule in our earlier presentation of the modern theory of forward exchange. The hedging actions of traders will push the forward rate toward interest parity.

Table 13-2   Hedging Options of Exporters and Importers

	$FA > \dfrac{A}{1 + i_{UK}} S(1 + i_{US})$	$FA < \dfrac{A}{1 + i_{UK}} S(1 + i_{US})$
Exporter	Sells forward	Borrows in London Lends in New York
Importer	Borrows in New York Lends in London	Buys forward

Hedging against Translation Risks

In addition to the transactions risk they encounter as international traders, multi-national enterprises with foreign subsidiaries are exposed to a foreign exchange *translation* risk because they are required to consolidate in a prescribed way the local-currency income and balance sheets of their subsidiaries with their own corporate statements.[13] Hence, they must "translate" financial statements expressed in a foreign currency into statements expressed in their home currency. Multinational corporations headquartered in different countries must conform to the accounting standards of each home country: French multinationals to French accounting rules, British multinationals to British accounting rules, and so on. In this section we shall discuss only the translation risk facing U.S. multinationals who keep their corporate accounts in dollars.

U.S. accounting rules (which became effective December 15, 1982) require U.S. companies to translate the local-currency balance sheets of their foreign subsidiaries at the exchange rate prevailing on the closing date and to translate local-currency income statements at the average rate for the period.[14] To simplify our presentation, we shall look only at the consolidation of balance sheets.

To illustrate the effects of these translation rules, Table 13-3 depicts the simplified balance sheet of the subsidiary in country X of a U.S. multinational company. To focus only on translation risk, we assume that the subsidiary has no assets or liabilities payable in foreign (nonlocal) currencies. Hence, it has no exposure to transaction risk, and the *local-currency* balance sheet will remain unaffected by variations in the exchange rate. Now suppose that the dollar price of country X's currency (francs) has depreciated 20 percent during the current quarter: On the last day of the preceding quarter, it was $.10; on the last day of the current quarter, it is $.08.

---

[13]See Chapter 22 for a description of multinational enterprises.

[14]This *current-rate* rule of the U.S. Financial Accounting Standards Board is entitled FASB 52. It replaces FASB 8, which required U.S. companies to translate the *monetary* assets and liabilities of their foreign subsidiaries at the current rates and the other items in the balance sheet (inventory and fixed assets) at historic rates in effect when the item was first added to the balance sheet.

Table 13-3 Effect of Local-Currency Depreciation on Dollar Translation of the Balance Sheet of a U.S. Company's Foreign Subsidiary in Country X

Balance Sheet Items	In Francs	In Dollars at Old Exchange Rate (1 franc = $.10)	In Dollars at New Exchange Rate (1 franc = $.08)
Assets			
Cash	100	10	8
Accounts receivable	200	20	16
Inventory	150	15	12
Fixed assets	500	50	40
Total assets	950	95	76
Liabilities and equity			
Accounts payable	50	5	4
Long-term liabilities	100	10	8
Owner's equity*	800	80	64
Total liabilities and equity	950	95	76
Translation gain or loss			− 16

*Residual item.

The first column of Table 13-3 shows the local-currency balance sheet of the subsidiary; the second column, the balance sheet translated into dollars at the *old* exchange rate according to U.S. accounting rules; and the third column, the balance sheet translated into dollars at the *new* end-of-period exchange rate, as required by the rules. Observe that the U.S. company has incurred a translation *loss* of $16 that has reduced its equity from $80 to $64. Keep in mind that it is an *accounting* loss, not a *cash* loss.

Because of the accounting rules, the net exposure of a U.S. company to translation risk is $E = A - L$, where E is net exposure, A is assets, and L is liabilities. If local-currency $A > L$, then the U.S. parent company will experience a translation *loss* when the subsidiary's currency depreciates vis-à-vis the dollar, and conversely. In Table 13-3 the net exposure is $A - L$ = F950 − F150 = F800. With this net exposure, the U.S. company incurred a translation loss when the franc depreciated − .20(F800)($.10) = $16.

Translation gains and losses can be substantial. Thus, multinational managers sometimes have a strong incentive to eliminate or limit translation risk. Multinational companies can eliminate or limit translation risk by adjusting the balance sheets of foreign subsidiaries, by hedging in the forward market, and in other ways.[15]

---

[15]Readers interested in the hedging practices of multinational companies are referred to a basic text in international finance, such as David K. Eiteman and Arthur I. Stonehill, *Multinational Business Finance,* 5th ed. (Reading, Mass.: Addison-Wesley, 1989).

Adjusting the Foreign Subsidiary's Balance Sheet A multinational enterprise can lower its *exposure* to translation risk by adjusting the asset/liability ratio of a foreign subsidiary. Under present accounting rules (FASB 52), a U.S. company can reduce its translation exposure by decreasing local-currency assets or increasing local-currency liabilities so as to reduce owner's equity. The subsidiary depicted in Table 13-3 has a net exposure of F800 (F950 − F150). By decreasing its assets to, say, F700, the U.S. parent company could reduce net translation exposure to F550. However, apart from the direct costs of adjustment (higher interest costs for local borrowing, for instance), altering the asset/liability ratio to a substantial degree may cripple the operations of the subsidiary. Balance sheet adjustment, therefore, can reduce, but not eliminate entirely, the net translation exposure.

The multinational company may try to adjust a foreign subsidiary's balance sheet not to reduce translation exposure but rather to maximize translation gains and minimize translation losses. This is speculation, not hedging. The general approach is shown in Table 13-4. The successful application of this approach depends on correct forecasts of the *direction* of movements in the foreign exchange rate.

Hedging in the Forward Exchange Market To take care of any remaining translation risk after balance sheet adjustments, the multinational company can hedge in the forward market. Suppose, for example, a U.S. company has a translation exposure of £1 million $(A - L)$ in its British subsidiary and wants to protect itself against an expected sterling depreciation over the next quarter. We assume that the current spot rate of exchange (S) is $2.00, the 90-day forward rate is $1.90, and the company expects the spot rate in 90 days $[E(S^{90})]$ to be $1.80. Then the company sells forward £1 million for $1,900,000. If at the end of the quarter the spot rate has indeed fallen to $1.80 as expected, the company will suffer a translation loss of $200,000. But it will make $100,000 in the forward market by buying £1 million in the spot market for $1,800,000 and selling it for $1,900,000 under the forward contract. Hence it has suffered a net loss of $100,000.

Table 13-4 General Approach to Increase Translation Gains and Minimize Translation Losses through Balance Sheet Adjustments of Foreign Subsidiaries

	Assets of Foreign Subsidiary	Liabilities of Foreign Subsidiary
Strong local currency*	Increase	Decrease
Weak local currency*	Decrease	Increase

*Relative to the dollar.

This example demonstrates that even when the multinational company correctly forecasts an exchange rate, it can have a net translation loss if it hedges only an amount equal to the translation exposure. In this instance the company would have to sell £2 million forward to fully offset its translation loss. A second point is that the company is behaving like a speculator: It can only make a forward profit if the spot rate at the end of the quarter is less than the forward rate ($S^{90} < F$). Otherwise it will make no profit or will even incur a loss.

More generally, a company's translation gain or loss is $E(S^0 - S^t)$, where E is the net translation exposure, S^0 is the spot exchange rate at the beginning of the quarter, and S^t is the spot exchange rate at the end of the quarter. A company's speculative gain or loss on the forward market is $A(F - S^t)$, where A is the amount hedged and F is the appropriate forward rate. Consequently, a hedge against translation risk will be perfect only when

$$(13) \ A(F - S^t) = E(S^0 - S^t).$$

To make a perfect hedge, therefore, a company must correctly forecast the end-of-period exchange rate. If its forecast is incorrect, it will make a speculative gain or loss or break even on its forward contract. In other words, to make a perfect hedge against translation risk, a company must become a speculator successful in outguessing the market.

The substantial cash losses some multinational companies have experienced in attempting perfect hedges against expected translation losses have persuaded multinational managers to use a "loss minimizing" hedge that limits translation loss but does not eliminate it. Loss minimization requires that the amount hedged in the forward market *equals* the net translation exposure. Using equation (13), we can obtain the net hedging loss (H):

$$(14) \ H = E(S^0 - S^t) - A(F - S^t).$$

By hedging on the forward market an amount equal to the translation exposure ($A = E$), equation (14) becomes

$$(15) \ H^* = E(S^0 - S^t) - E(F - S^t)$$
$$= E(S^0 - F),$$

where H^* is the loss-minimizing net hedging loss. Observe that H^* does not depend on the future exchange rate but on the difference between the current spot and forward rates, both of which are known to managers. The percentage cost of this hedge is

$$\frac{S^0 - F}{S^0},$$

which is the percentage discount on forward sterling for the period in question.

Returning to our earlier example, the company limited its translation loss to $100,000 by hedging an amount in the forward market equal to its translation exposure. The percentage cost of this protection is

$$\frac{\$2.00 \ - \ \$1.90}{\$2.00},$$

or 5 percent for 90 days. The company has replaced an uncertain translation loss with a certain loss of $100,000.

The cost of a risk-minimizing hedge has persuaded multinational managers to follow a *selective* hedging policy based on their expectations of future exchange rates. At times, therefore, they will remain deliberately exposed to a translation risk. The success of a selective policy is dependent on success in forecasting exchange rates.[16]

SUMMARY

1. Promises to buy or sell foreign exchange at a specified rate and at a specified time in the future with payment to be made upon delivery are known as forward exchange. The domestic currency price of forward exchange is the forward exchange rate.
2. Two theories have been put forth to explain the determination of forward exchange rates: the traditional interest parity theory and the modern theory. The former asserts that interest arbitrage will cause the forward rate of exchange to adjust to the interest rate differential until it reaches an equilibrium value at which it is no longer profitable to shift funds between the two money centers. In equilibrium, $F^* = S + S(i_{US} - i_{UK})$.
3. In addition to acting directly on the forward rate, interest arbitrage will also bring about adjustments in spot and interest rates that will help remove any discrepancy between the interest rate differential and the implicit interest rate.
4. The neglect by the interest parity theory of the influence of speculators on the forward rate is rectified by the modern theory of forward exchange, which takes into account the behavior of speculators (and traders) as well as arbitragers. The equilibrium rate of forward exchange is determined by the intersection of the AT-AT and S-S schedules. When there is speculative buying or selling, the equilibrium forward rate will diverge from the interest parity rate.

---

[16]We cannot take up here the question of whether translation risks *should* guide management decisions respecting foreign subsidiaries. Suffice it to say that a local-currency depreciation (or appreciation) will affect the cash flows and true economic value of a subsidiary in ways that have nothing to do with translation risk. See Chapter 16 for an analysis of the effects of exchange rate variations on a country's exports and imports.

5. Although the market efficiency hypothesis has not been conclusively demonstrated for the foreign exchange market, no one has found a reliable approach to forecasting exchange rates over the short term. However, over the long term (three to five years), the external value of a currency tends to reflect changes in its purchasing power relative to the purchasing power of other currencies, a relationship known as purchasing-power parity.

6. Hedging is the balancing of sales and purchases of an asset so there is no net open position on the market. International traders hedge against transaction foreign exchange risk. Multinational companies with foreign subsidiaries hedge against translation foreign exchange risk.

7. International traders may hedge (1) in the forward exchange market and the related futures and options markets, or (2) through borrower arbitrage. When the forward exchange rate is at interest parity, traders are indifferent between (1) and (2). Thus, the trader who hedges is behaving as an interest arbitrager.

8. Multinational companies are exposed to a translation risk because they must "translate" the financial statements of their foreign subsidiaries expressed in local currencies into corporate statements expressed in dollars. They may limit translation risk (1) by adjusting subsidiaries' balance sheet items or (2) by hedging in the forward exchange market. To avoid speculative losses in the forward market, multinational managers may use a "loss-minimizing" hedge that limits but does not try to eliminate the translation risk.

QUESTIONS AND APPLICATIONS

1. (a) How does forward exchange differ from spot exchange?
   (b) What is the primary function of the forward market?
2. (a) Define interest arbitrage.
   (b) If $A(1 + i_{US}) > A/S(1 + i_{UK})F$, will the investor place funds in New York or in London? Why?
3. (a) What is the interest parity theory?
   (b) Explain the meaning of the following equation:

$$i_{US} - i_{UK} = \frac{F^* - S}{S}.$$

   (c) Suppose $i_{US} = .10$ (annually), $i_{UK} = .14$ (annually), and $S = \$1.75$. What is the interest parity rate for 90-day forward sterling? Is it at a discount or a premium?
4. (a) Why is the forward rate at point F in Figure 13-1 in disequilibrium?
   (b) Why is a forward rate lying below the horizontal axis to the left of the interest parity line in Figure 13-1 in disequilibrium?
5. Why may interest arbitrage fail to achieve interest parity in the forward rate?

6. (a) How does the modern theory explain the determination of forward exchange rates?
   (b) In Figure 13-2, F^* lies above S. What does this tell us about the interest rate differential? Why?
7. (a) How does the speculator differ from the interest arbitrager?
   (b) If $E(S') < F$, what will the speculator do? Why?
   (c) Under which conditions will the speculator make a profit? A loss?
8. Reproduce Figure 13-4. Show what happens to the equilibrium forward exchange rate when the S–S schedule shifts downward. What would cause such a shift?
9. If the foreign exchange market is "efficient," why is successful short-run forecasting of the exchange rate impossible?
10. If 1,900 Brazilian cruzeiros exchange for one dollar today, and the U.S. annual inflation rate is 5 percent while the Brazilian annual inflation rate is 80 percent, then what will be the purchasing-power parity rate of exchange a year from now?
11. (a) What are the hedging options of the international trader against a transaction foreign exchange risk?
   (b) If

$$FA < \frac{A}{1 + i_{UK}} \, S(1 + i_{US}),$$

   which hedging option will an importer choose? Why?
12. (a) What is the net exposure of a U.S. company to translation risk?
   (b) How may a multinational company hedge its translation risk?
   (c) What is the requirement for a "loss-minimizing" hedge? Why?

SELECTED READINGS

Froot, Kenneth A., and Richard H. Thaler. "Anomalies of Foreign Exchange." *The Journal of Economic Perspectives,* Summer 1990, pp. 179–192.

Grabbe, J. Orlin. *International Financial Markets.* New York: Elsevier, 1986. Chapters 3, 7, and 8.

Hardouvelis, Gikas A. "Economic News, Exchange Rates, and Interest Rates." *Journal of International Money and Finance* (1988), pp. 23–35.

Isard, Peter. "Lessons from Empirical Models of Exchange Rates." *Staff Papers* (International Monetary Fund), March 1987, pp. 1–28.

Jacque, Laurent L. "Management of Foreign Exchange Risk." *Journal of International Business Studies,* Spring-Summer 1981, pp. 81–101.

Koedijk, Kees G., and Mack Ott. "Risk Aversion, Efficient Markets and the Forward Exchange Rate." *Review* (Federal Reserve Bank of St. Louis), December 1987, pp. 5–13.

Levich, Richard M. "Are Forward Exchange Rates Unbiased Predictors of Future Spot Rates?" *Columbia Journal of International Business,* Winter 1979, pp. 49–61.

McKinnon, Ronald I. *Money in International Exchange.* New York: Oxford University Press, 1979. Chapter 6.

Mussa, Michael L. *Exchange Rates in Theory and Reality.* Essays in International Finance. Princeton, N.J.: Princeton University Press, December 1990.

Officer, Lawrence H. "The Purchasing-Power Parity Theory of Exchange Rates: A Review Article." *International Monetary Fund Staff Papers* 23 (March 1976), pp. 1–60.

Ohno, Kenichi. "Estimating Yen/Dollar and Mark/Dollar Purchasing Power Parities." *International Monetary Fund Staff Papers,* no. 179, September 1990.

Stokes, Houston H., and Hugh Neuburger. "Interest Arbitrage, Forward Speculation, and the Determination of the Forward Exchange Rate." *Columbia Journal of International Business,* Winter 1979, pp. 86–98.

chapter 14

THE BALANCE
OF INTERNATIONAL PAYMENTS

During the course of a year the residents of one country engage in a vast number and variety of transactions with residents of other countries—exports and imports of merchandise and services, cash payments and receipts, gold flows, gifts, loans and investments, and other transactions. These transactions are interrelated in many ways, and together they comprise the international trade and payments of the national economy. Before we can analyze and evaluate a nation's international transactions, however, they must be classified and aggregated to make a balance of payments.

As a statistical classification and summary of all economic transactions between domestic and foreign residents over a stipulated period (ordinarily one year), the *balance of payments* of a nation affords an overall view of its international economic position. For this reason, the balance of payments is particularly helpful to government authorities—treasuries, central banks, and stabilization agencies—who are directly charged with the responsibility of maintaining external economic stability. Moreover, international trade is so important to many countries that the balance of payments must be carefully considered in the formulation of domestic economic policies, such as employment, wage, and investment policies.

The balance of payments of a country may also influence the decisions of business people. The experienced international trader or investor does not overlook the intimate bearing of the balance of payments upon the foreign exchange market and the course of government policy. A domestic exporter may hesitate to deal with an importer if it is suspected that the authorities of the importer's country will shortly impose or tighten exchange controls in the face of an adverse balance of payments. Dealers in foreign exchange also pay close attention to the balance of payments of countries whose currencies they handle in daily transactions. Failure to realize the close dependence of international business upon the balance of payments of the domestic and foreign countries has led to losses or even outright business failures.

350

THE COMPILATION OF THE BALANCE OF PAYMENTS

Three principles underlying the compilation of the balance of payments of a nation are worth special emphasis. First, only economic transactions between domestic and foreign *residents* are entered in the balance of payments. Second, a distinction is made between *debit* and *credit* transfers. Third, the balance of payments is a *double-entry* accounting statement.

The Concept of Residence

The balance of payments summarizes all economic transactions between domestic and foreign residents. Residence should not be confused with the legal notions of citizenship or nationality.

Individuals who represent their government in foreign countries, including members of the armed forces, are always considered residents of their own country. Thus, when a member of the American armed forces buys a glass of wine in France, an international transaction occurs that enters the balance of payments of both the United States and France.

Individuals who do not represent a government are considered to be residents of the country in which they have a permanent residence or in which they find their "center of interest." In some instances an individual's center of interest may be in doubt, but ordinarily such criteria as customary place of work, residence of employer, or principal source of income are sufficient to determine it. In the event of conflict, the permanent place of habitation takes precedence over center of interest. For example, an individual working at the United Nations in New York who does not represent a foreign government and who resides in New York permanently is treated as a resident of the United States despite the individual's foreign center of interest.

In preparing a balance of payments, the question of individual residence is much less important than the question of business residence. A corporation is a resident of the country in which it is incorporated, but its foreign branches and subsidiaries are viewed as foreign residents. Hence, shipments between an American concern and its overseas branch are international transactions and, as such, are entered in the U.S. balance of payments. At times the residence of a business may be difficult to decide. For example, a company may be incorporated in the domestic country, owned by residents of a second country, and conduct all of its business in a third country. In most instances, however, the residence of a business enterprise is readily apparent.

Government residence is the clearest of all: All government agencies are residents of their own country regardless of location.

Debit and Credit Entries in a Double-Entry System

With the exception of gifts, all international transactions represent a two-way exchange of assets between domestic and foreign residents.

Assets may be classified as *real* (goods and services) or *financial* (short- and long-term monetary claims, including money, which is the shortest-term claim). We can distinguish, therefore, three kinds of international transaction:

1. The exchange of goods or services for other goods or services. This is a *barter* transaction; both sides of the transaction are real.
2. The exchange of goods and services for money or other financial claims. These transactions are much more common than barter transactions. One side of the transaction is real and the other side is financial.
3. The exchange of financial claims, such as bonds or stock, for other financial claims, such as money. Both sides of this transaction are financial.

An international transaction, therefore, involves two opposing *transfers* of assets. Because the balance of payments is a double-entry accounting system, a transaction is entered twice: one transfer as a debit, the other transfer as a credit. *Hence, total debits and credits are always equal in a balance of payments.* This is an accounting equality that has no economic significance.

When is a transfer a debit entry? A credit entry? The accounting rules are depicted in Table 14-1.

A *debit* entry is made in a country's balance of payments for a transfer that either (1) *increases* the country's assets (something of value *owned*) or (2) *decreases* the country's liabilities (something of value *owed*). Conversely, a *credit* entry is made for a transfer that either (1) *decreases* the country's assets or (2) *increases* its liabilities.

A second way of distinguishing debit and credit transfers is as follows: A transfer that gives rise to money payments to foreign residents is a *debit* entry in the balance of payments; a transfer that gives rise to money receipts from foreign residents is a *credit* entry. This distinction, however, is less precise than the accounting distinction, and for that reason we shall use the latter in constructing the balance of payments.

Gifts are a special kind of international transaction and do not involve an exchange of assets. They are *unilateral transfers* of goods or services (gifts in kind) or of financial assets (money gifts). Despite this one-sidedness, gifts are entered twice in the balance of payments to preserve the double-entry accounting system. One entry records the actual unilateral transfer, and a second entry is made in a unilateral transfers account to record the missing side of the gift transaction.

Table 14-1 Accounting Rules for Entering Debits and Credits in the Balance of Payments

Direction of Change	International Assets	International Liabilities
Increase	Debit	Credit
Decrease	Credit	Debit

CONSTRUCTING THE BALANCE OF PAYMENTS

Table 14-2 depicts the conventional presentation of the balance of payments used by the International Monetary Fund (IMF). International transfers are grouped into three major accounts: the current account, the capital account, and the official reserves account. Entries in these accounts are recorded as *debits* or *credits*. The

Table 14-2   Conventional Presentation of a Balance of Payments (Dollars)

	Debits	Credits	Net Debit (−) or Credit (+)
A. Current account			
1. Goods	600	500	
		25	
Net balance on trade			− 75
2. Services			
(a) Transportation	100	50	
(b) Travel	75	60	
(c) Investment	50	100	
(d) Other	25	50	
Net balance on goods and services			− 65
3. Unilateral transfers	75	25	
Net balance on current account			− 115
B. Capital account			
1. Long-term capital			
(a) Direct investment	100	50	
(b) Portfolio investment	25	50	
2. Short-term capital	500	600	
	260	250	
	25	50	
	50	100	
	50	25	
		100	
Net balance on capital account			+ 215
C. Official reserves account			
1. Monetary gold (net)	5		
2. Other reserve assets (net)	100		
3. Liabilities to foreign central banks (net)		15	
Net balance on official reserves account			− 90
Net errors and omissions	10		− 10
Total debits and credits	2050	2050	

balance of payments is usually drawn up in the currency of the domestic country. Regardless of the currency in which they are made, international payments and receipts may be expressed in the domestic currency by the use of exchange rates for conversion from foreign to domestic currencies.

Current Account

All international transfers of *goods and services* are placed in the current account. Goods are physical products commonly referred to as merchandise. Services are intangible products, such as transportation, travel, capital services (as measured by interest and dividend income), construction, technical assistance, industrial property rights (as measured by income from patents, trademarks, and copyrights), and business services.

The current account also includes a *unilateral transfers* subaccount that records offsetting entries for real or financial unilateral transfers that appear elsewhere in the balance of payments. Unilateral transfers include institutional gifts for missionary and charitable purposes; personal gifts; and government transfers, such as grants to foreign countries to assist their economic development.

Table 14-2 shows three net balance entries in the current account: the net balance on trade (merchandise), the net balance on goods and services, and the net balance on current account.

Capital Account

The capital account includes all *financial* transfers between a country and the rest of the world, except for *official reserve transfers,* which are placed in a third major account.

One subaccount is *long-term capital* — financial claims and liabilities with an original maturity of more than one year. Long-term capital is further classified into direct investment and portfolio investment. *Direct investment* is defined as investment in enterprises located in one country but "effectively controlled" by residents in another country. Direct investment is a distinctive feature of international business because it usually involves the ownership of branches and subsidiaries abroad by domestic parent companies.[1]

Portfolio investment designates all long-term capital flows that do *not* give investors effective control over their investments.

Short-term capital — financial claims and liabilities, including money, with an original maturity of one year or less — includes international transfers of bank deposits and short-term securities, bank loans, and commercial claims and liabilities arising from the financing of current-account transfers.

---

[1]The U.S. Department of Commerce defines a direct investment as an investment that gives the investor at least 10 percent ownership of a foreign entity. However, this percentage is a judgmental statistical criterion, for there is no single ownership percentage that separates foreign investments that carry managerial control from those that do not (see Chapter 23).

Official Reserves Account

The official reserves account records the international financial transfers of the country's monetary authorities (the Treasury Department and the Federal Reserve System in the United States and central banks in other countries). The national monetary authorities hold the country's international reserves of gold and foreign exchange, which are used to provide residual financing of balance of payment transactions (known as "compensatory compensation") in a stable-rate system or to influence the exchange rate in a floating-rate system. These same authorities also issue currency and create the domestic reserves for commercial banks. Their responsibility for monetary policy (the cost and availability of credit) gives them a powerful role in external payment adjustment in addition to compensatory financing.

Official reserve transfers are classified as monetary gold, other reserve assets (mostly foreign exchange), and liabilities owing foreign central banks. The terminology used for monetary gold flows is identical to that used for merchandise. A monetary gold export is a credit; a monetary gold import, a debit. Since monetary gold is an international financial asset (a claim on foreigners), a gold export is equivalent to a capital inflow, while a gold import is a capital outflow. Ordinarily, however, gold movements are designated as such rather than as capital flows.

Errors and Omissions

Although the balance of payments is a double-entry account, governments do not draw up the balance of payments by recording each transaction twice. Governments simply do not have the necessary information on all of the many international transactions that take place over a year. Instead, they make single entries in the different accounts, depending on several sources of information that are not always consistent across accounts and vary in coverage and reliability. Consequently, *recorded* debits and credits are never equal in a country's balance of payments. To get that equality and thereby preserve the double-entry accounting system, an entry is made for "errors and omissions." In the balance of payments of the United States and other industrial countries, this entry is mainly attributable to inadequate coverage of service and short-term capital transfers. But in some developing countries, the major source of errors and omissions is the illegal smuggling of goods, such as the narcotics exports of Colombia.

ENTERING TRANSACTIONS IN THE BALANCE OF PAYMENTS

We can now demonstrate how transactions are entered in the balance of payments shown in Table 14-2. To facilitate our discussion, let us assume that this is the balance of payments of the United States, although the entries are illustrative only.

To make the proper entries, we need to answer five questions: (1) Is the transfer a *real* or a *financial transfer?* (2) If it is a real transfer, is it a *goods* or a *services* transfer? (3) If it is a financial transfer, is it an *official reserve* transfer or a *nonreserve* transfer? (4) If it is a nonreserve financial transfer, is it a transfer of *short-term* or *long-term* capital? (5) Is the transfer a *debit* or *credit* entry?

Entering Current-Account Transactions

We start with a U.S. merchandise export valued at $500.[2] This export is a *real* transfer that goes into the current account (item A1). It is a *credit* entry because the export of merchandise *decreases* U.S. merchandise assets. (Alternatively, it is a credit entry because it gives rise to money receipts for U.S. residents.) The payment received from the foreign resident who bought the merchandise may take the form of dollars or of another country's currency. Both forms of payment are short-term *financial* transfers that are entered under item B2 of the capital account. The payment is a *debit* entry because it either decreases U.S. dollar liabilities owing foreigners (payment in dollars) or increases U.S. foreign-currency claims owed by foreigners (payment in a foreign currency).

A U.S. merchandise import of $600 is recorded as a *debit* in the current account. Payment for this import by a U.S. resident is recorded as a *credit* in the short-term capital account. These entries are the converse of those for a merchandise export.

The purchase by U.S. residents of transportation services from foreign shipping firms ($100), travel services abroad ($75), the capital services of foreign-owned investment in the United States as measured by interest and dividends paid to foreigners ($50), and other services from foreigners ($25) are entered as *debits* in the current account. These are real transfers that increase the assets of U.S. residents. Payment for these service imports (amounting altogether to $250) is entered in Table 14-2 as a single *credit* in the short-term capital account.

Conversely, the sale of services by U.S. residents to foreign residents is entered as a *credit* in the current account. Payments received by U.S. residents for these service exports (amounting to $260) are entered in Table 14-2 as a single *debit* in the short-term capital account.

Unilateral transfers to foreigners over the past year, amounting to $75, are entered as *debits* in the unilateral transfers account (A3). Keep in mind that this account is an accounting offset to the actual unilateral transfers, which take the form of goods and services or of money. Assuming that $25 of unilateral transfers are in merchandise (for example, shipments of U.S. agricultural products under a U.S. government aid program) and $50 in money, then $25 is entered as a *credit* in the goods account and $50 as a *credit* in the short-term capital account.

In the same year, unilateral transfers received by U.S. residents ($25) are entered as a *credit* in the unilateral transfers account. Because we are assuming that the actual transfers consisted entirely of money, they are recorded in Table 14-2 as a single *debit* entry in the short-term capital account.

---

[2]A country's balance of payments is drawn up in its own currency. Hence, any transfers expressed in a foreign currency must be converted into the domestic currency at the current exchange rate.

We can now draw up the *net balances* in the current account. The net balance on trade is a *debit* of $75.[3] The net balance on goods and services is a *debit* of $65. The net balance on current account is a *debit* of $115.

Entering Capital Account Transactions

In addition to engaging in current-account transactions, U.S. residents during the year were lending to and borrowing from foreign residents. U.S. firms made *direct investments* totaling $100, as indicated by the *debit* entry in item B1(a). Direct investments abroad by U.S. firms are recorded as debits because U.S. residents *increased* their ownership claims, which constitute long-term capital assets. The firms financed their direct foreign investments in money (the most common form of payment), in goods and services, or a mix of both. We are assuming here that all payments to foreign residents for ownership claims were in money, and they are therefore recorded as *credits* in the short-term capital account.

Conversely, direct investment by foreign companies in the United States ($50) is recorded as a *credit* in item B1(a) of Table 14-2. The money received by U.S. residents from the sale of ownership rights to those foreign companies is recorded as a *debit* in the short-term capital account.

Over the year, U.S. residents also bought bonds and other long-term securities from foreign residents in the amount of $25. This *portfolio* investment is recorded as a *debit* in item B1(b) of Table 14-2 because it increases U.S. long-term claims on foreigners. Payment to foreign residents for these claims is recorded as a *credit* in the short-term capital account.

Conversely, foreign residents bought $50 of long-term securities from U.S. residents over the year. This inflow of portfolio investment is entered as a *credit* in item B1(b) because it increases U.S. long-term liabilities owing foreigners. Money receipts by U.S. residents from the sale of securities to foreigners are recorded as a $50 debit in the short-term capital account, representing an increase in U.S. short-term financial claims against foreigners.

So far all entries in the short-term capital account record payments or receipts for transfers entered in the current and long-term capital accounts. But short-term capital transfers also occur independently of those accounts. Banks, multinational enterprises, and persons located in the United States and abroad shift funds into and out of the United States to take advantage of interest-rate differentials among national money markets and to hedge against or speculate on movements in the exchange rate. Funds may also move out of countries judged to be high political risks into countries judged to be low political risks, a phenomenon called *capital flight*. Over the year, the United States received a *net inflow* of short-term capital, amounting to $100, due to these factors. This net inflow is entered as a *credit* in item B2 in Table 14-2 because it represents either a decrease in U.S. short-term claims on foreigners (as U.S. residents shift funds from abroad to the United

---

[3]A *debit* trade balance is commonly designated an *import balance* or a *trade deficit*. On the other hand, a *credit* trade balance is designated an *export balance* or a *trade surplus*.

States) or an increase in U.S. short-term liabilities owing foreigners (as foreign residents shift funds to the United States).

We can now calculate the net balance on capital account. Total debits add up to $1010; total credits, to $1225. The net balance, therefore, is a credit of $215.

Entering Official Reserves Transactions

Entries in the official reserves account are made on a net basis. Over the year, U.S. monetary authorities bought $5 of monetary gold from foreign central banks. This is regarded as a financial transfer because monetary gold is treated as a financial asset. Because an import of gold increases U.S. monetary gold assets, it is a *debit* entry. If the monetary authorities paid for this gold by crediting the accounts of the foreign central banks that sold it, then a *credit* entry is made in item C3 to record an increase in liabilities to foreign central banks.

The U.S. authorities also increased their holdings of other reserve assets (mostly foreign currencies) by a net of $100, as indicated by the *debit* entry in C2.[4] This increase in reserve assets was mostly offset by the net short-term capital inflow (credit entry) recorded in item B2. Lastly, U.S. liabilities owing foreign central banks increased by a net of $15, as shown by the *credit* entry in C3.

Entering Net Errors and Omissions

If we now add all the debit and credit entries in our balance of payments, we find that total credits exceed total debits by $10. Evidently, we have not recorded all transfers. Because the overall balance of payments *must* balance, we take care of this discrepancy by making a *debit* entry of $10 in the errors and omissions account. As noted earlier, the equality of total debits and credits has no economic significance.

Much of the errors and omissions entry derives from the comparatively poor record of private short-term capital movements. A radical shift in the size or sign of this entry from one payment period to the next is usually interpreted as a symptom of speculative or flight capital. Short-term capital may enter or leave a country outside the normal payment mechanism, especially when there is an intent to evade exchange controls and other official restrictions. In any event, short-term capital movements may either lead or lag behind the transactions they finance and thus show up in another payment period. For example, payment for a merchandise export shipped in December may not be recorded by a bank until January of the following year, or even later if the importer has received credit. Cash prepayment may cause the opposite situation.[5]

---

[4]In addition to foreign currencies (foreign exchange), other reserve assets include the U.S. reserve position with the IMF and special drawing rights (SDRs) issued by the IMF (see Chapters 18 and 19).

[5]Statistical discrepancies also appear in the balance of payments for the world as a whole. It is evident that the total of *all* countries' current-account balances should add up to zero because countries can only trade with each other. And yet there was a discrepancy of $45 billion in aggregate current-account balances in 1987. Portfolio investment income credits were $45 billion less than debits, and the gap between merchandise exports and imports was $36 billion. See "In a Maze of Numbers," *The Economist,* August 20, 1988, pp. 61–62.

BALANCE OF PAYMENTS ANALYSIS: EQUILIBRIUM AND DISEQUILIBRIUM

A balance of payments is always in accounting balance, but it is not always in *equilibrium*. The essential meaning of equilibrium is a sustainable relationship between two or more economic variables, such as the supply, demand, and price of an individual good. A balance of payments is in equilibrium when the nation's economy is in "fundamental adjustment" to the world economy. Conversely, when the balance of payments is in disequilibrium, the national economy must undergo changes in its price level, income, exchange rate, or other economic variables to restore a sustainable relationship with the rest of the world. The concept of balance of payments equilibrium is a market adjustment concept. Thus, official measures to control international transactions do not eliminate a disequilibrium but merely suppress it.

Three balances are most useful when analyzing a balance of payments: the balance on *current account,* the balance on *basic transactions,* and the balance on *official reserve transactions.* These balances are calculated by "drawing a line" at certain places in the balance of payments and then adding up all of the entries above the line. (The net balance on official reserves account equals the net balance on current and capital accounts but carries an opposite sign.) This is done in Table 14-3, which uses the same entries as appear in Table 14-2. To detect trends in

Table 14-3   Analytical Balances of the Balance of Payments (Dollars)

	Debits	Credits	Net Balance
A. Current account			
1. Goods	600	525	
2. Services	250	260	
3. Unilateral transfers	75	25	
Balance on current account			– 115
B. Capital account			
1. Long-term capital			
(a) Direct investment	100	50	
(b) Portfolio investment	25	50	
Basic balance			– 140
2. Short-term capital	910	1150	
3. Net errors and omissions	10		
Balance on current and capital accounts			+ 90
C. Official reserves account			
1. Monetary gold	5		
2. Other reserve assets	100		
3. Liabilities to foreign central banks		15	
Balance on official reserves account			– 90

these balances, it is necessary to analyze a country's balance of payments over several periods, say, each year for three to five years. However, we shall confine our analysis to a single year.

Long-Run Equilibrium

Under what conditions are a nation's external economic relations sustainable over a period of time? If we take a very long time period measured in decades, the answer is plain. In the very long run, a nation *must* pay for its imports of goods and services through its exports of goods and services. That is to say, in the very long run a nation cannot depend on international credit (whether short- or long-term) to finance a net import balance on current account. Nor can it hope to sustain a net export balance. Long-run equilibrium demands, therefore, that the net balance on goods and services become zero over the secular time period.

Long-run disequilibrium is measured by the net balance on *current account*. A net current-account *deficit* (debit balance) indicates that a country is spending more than it is earning in transactions with other countries. Conversely, a current-account *surplus* (credit balance) indicates that a country is earning more than it is spending in its international transactions. Because a current-account deficit or surplus needs to be financed, the net balance on current account also measures the *net* international lending or borrowing of a country over the year. A deficit is financed by net borrowing from foreign residents; a surplus is financed by net lending to foreign residents. In Table 14-3, the net balance on current account is a deficit of $115, indicating that the United States is spending more than it is earning internationally and, therefore, is a net borrower in the same amount from the rest of the world.

Intermediate-Run Equilibrium

Ordinarily our time frame of reference in balance of payments analysis is much shorter than decades; it seldom exceeds three to five years, or about long enough to encompass short-run cyclical variations in national income. What are the conditions of balance of payments equilibrium over this time period? It is no longer necessary for the nation to balance imports against exports: It can sustain an import balance if *long-term* credits are available to finance it. Similarly, the nation can sustain an export balance on current account if it is willing to lend (or give) an equal amount on long term to the rest of the world. In such circumstances, there are no pressures for immediate adjustment of the balance of payments. Eventually, of course, a long-term borrower must repay the lender, but this is a future contingency that can be met or prepared for over a lengthy period of time.[6]

Intermediate-term disequilibrium in the balance of payments is measured by the net *basic* balance. The basic balance is the sum of the current account balance

---

[6]A family that finances a home on a twenty-five-year mortgage offers a crude analogy. As long as the family is able to service the mortgage, it is not forced to make adjustments in income, expenditures, or savings. The situation is sustainable.

and the net movement of long-term capital. This balance is intended to measure the long-term or *structural* stability of a country's balance of payments. The transfers making up this balance are assumed to be insensitive to *short-run* changes in exchange rates and interest rates and to respond only to changes in factors of production, productivity, technology, consumer preferences, competition, and other real (nonmonetary) economic variables. A basic deficit (debit balance) or a basic surplus (credit balance) extending over several years are both indicators of an intermediate-run disequilibrium, because external payments cannot be sustained without adjustments in the economic relationship between a country and the rest of the world. Table 14-3 shows that the U.S. balance of payments is in fundamental disequilibrium with a basic deficit of $140.

Short-Run Equilibrium

In the short run (ranging from a moment to, say, a single year), equilibrium in the balance of payments exists when the monetary authorities make zero net use of international reserves: The amounts of foreign exchange in supply and demand are equal so there is no need for official intervention to sustain the exchange rate. Further, short-run equilibrium implies the absence of any government measures to adjust international payments through direct controls.

Short-run disequilibrium is measured by the net balance on *official reserves* account. As noted earlier, a country's monetary authorities use international reserves of gold and foreign exchange to maintain or influence the exchange rate. Therefore, the direction and size of the reserve transactions balance is an indicator of pressures on the exchange rate. A *credit* balance indicates that the authorities used their reserves to prevent or limit a *depreciation* of the country's currency. A *debit* balance reveals that the authorities added to reserves to prevent or limit an *appreciation* of the country's currency.

In Table 14-3, the basic deficit (a debit of $140) was more than offset by a net short-term capital inflow (including net errors and omissions) amounting to a $230 credit. The net balance on current and capital accounts, therefore, was a surplus (a credit of $90). This surplus was financed by a net *increase* of the same amount in the country's international reserves: Holdings of reserve assets (monetary gold and foreign exchange) received from foreign residents during the year rose by $105 while liabilities owing foreign central banks rose by only $15, making a *debit* net balance on official reserves account of $90.

Sources of Disequilibrium

To add further to our understanding of equilibrium and disequilibrium in the balance of payments, we offer brief descriptions of the sources of disequilibrium as classified in the following broad categories:

1. seasonal and random disequilibrium
2. cyclical disequilibrium
3. structural disequilibrium

4. destabilizing speculation and capital flight
5. other sources of disequilibrium

We shall discuss these categories as sources of *deficit* disequilibrium, but since a deficit disequilibrium in one country implies a surplus disequilibrium in one or more other countries, it should be clear that they are also sources of *surplus* disequilibrium.

Seasonal and Random Disequilibrium   A nation's exports and imports vary seasonally due to seasonal changes in production and consumption, but usually this seasonal variation is not the same for both. The result is seasonal disequilibrium in the balance of payments. Seasonal disequilibrium is ordinarily of little consequence, since it is short-lived and self-reversible: A deficit in one season offsets a surplus in another.

Irregular, nonsystematic, short-lived disturbances may also cause disequilibrium in the balance of payments. The traditional example of this kind of disequilibrium is a crop failure that curtails exports or forces a nation to import foodstuffs. Labor strikes that tie up transportation or immobilize industries can also affect exports or imports and thus the balance of payments. Other sources of random disequilibrium include natural disasters such as floods and earthquakes. The foregoing random disturbances have a once-for-all impact on the balance of payments; they cause only a short-run disequilibrium. When disturbances are of such a magnitude as to have pervasive and lasting effects on the economy and trade of a nation (war, revolution, civil strife, and so on), then they are not random in the sense that we are using the term.

Cyclical Disequilibrium   Variations in the national incomes of trading countries, whether involving changes in price levels, changes in the levels of production and employment, or both, may lead to cyclical disequilibrium in the balance of payments. In the early 1930s massive deflations in real income and production (accompanied by widespread unemployment) occurred in the industrial countries of North America and Western Europe. In the nonindustrial countries, where the agricultural sector accounted for the bulk of national income, deflation mainly took the form of a catastrophic fall in prices, wages, and terms of trade rather than in production and employment. This global deflation caused enormous payment disequilibria, wrecked the international monetary system, and forced nations into competitive depreciations and the wholesale use of trade and payment restrictions.

Since the end of World War II, the industrial countries have avoided profound deflation of the 1930s variety, but they have been far less successful in avoiding inflation generated by an effective demand running ahead of production. The situation in many developing countries has been far worse: "Runaway" inflation of 50 percent or more in a single year is not uncommon. Brazil and Argentina may be cited as examples. We can fairly say that inflation has been the single most important source of payment disequilibrium in the postwar years.

Cyclical disequilibrium may be a misnomer to denote payment disequilibrium caused by deflationary and inflationary movements in national income and price levels, because at most it is only roughly periodic. Usually, such movements are a source of intermediate-run disequilibrium lasting longer than a year.

Structural Disequilibrium Shifts in the demand for *specific* export goods, whether brought about by changing tastes, a new distribution of income in export markets, or changes in the availability or prices of competitive products offered by foreign suppliers, are common events in foreign trade. Shifts in the demand for import goods also occur for similar reasons. When a national economy is slow to adapt to these shifts, persistent structural disequilibrium appears in its balance of payments.

What is needed to remedy structural disequilibrium is a reallocation of production to conform to new patterns of demand and supply. Persistent structural disequilibrium may be viewed as a failure of the price system, which is supposed to guide and encourage reallocation in a market economy. Reallocation is sluggish when prices respond only slowly, if at all, to shifting market conditions because of monopoly, administrative pricing, price agreements, import protection, or other arrangements that limit price competition.

Adjustments in production usually demand a reallocation in the use of factors of production. In the export sector, for example, labor and other factors must move out of lines of production no longer in demand in foreign markets and into lines that enjoy a comparative advantage. When wages and the prices of other factors employed in declining export industries are hard to lower (sticky downwards), the reallocating function of factor prices is crippled and must depend on the attraction of higher factor rewards in growing industries in the export sector or elsewhere in the economy. A more serious deterrent to a prompt reallocation of factors is low factor mobility, especially labor. This creates the problem of structural unemployment.

A structural disequilibrium unprecedented in scope and severity struck the world economy when the OPEC countries quadrupled oil prices in the early months of 1974. The enormity of the payment burden suddenly imposed on the oil-importing countries was substantially responsible for the economic crisis of the mid-1970s. The further doubling of already high oil prices in 1979 undoubtedly contributed to the worldwide recession in the early 1980s. The magnitude and pervasiveness of the balance of payments adjustments to the high cost of OPEC oil places this structural disequilibrium in a class by itself.

To conclude, a wide variety of forces operating at home and abroad, such as technological and product innovations, new competition, changes in tastes, improvements in productivity, growing populations, and export cartels may cause shifts in the supply and demand of individual exports and imports that result in a structural disequilibrium in the balance of payments. Because it demands a reallocation of a country's productive capabilities, adjustment to structural disequilibrium is certain to be painful to displaced workers and industries, and therefore the restoration of international competitiveness usually takes several years. The continuing deficit disequilibrium in the U.S. balance of payments is partly structural in nature, reflecting the declining international competitiveness of the U.S. economy, as reviewed in Chapter 9.[7]

Destabilizing Speculation and Capital Flight Destabilizing speculation and capital flight (described in Chapter 12) constitute another source of payment disequilibrium. Although conceptually distinct, these short-term capital movements tend to occur together. Both intensify an existing disequilibrium, and capital flight may actually create one, since it is motivated by fears of safety that sometimes originate in conditions unrelated to the balance of payments, notably the prospect of war or revolution. In recent years the primary stimulus of destabilizing speculation and capital flight has been the expectation of depreciation in a major currency.

Other Sources of Disequilibrium The preceding four categories cover the main sources of disequilibrium, but they are not exhaustive. As we shall discover in Chapter 18, the U.S. payments deficit of the 1960s did not fit neatly into any one of these categories. And in the 1980s, an enormous current-account deficit in the U.S. balance of payments was financed by massive capital inflows induced by persistently high interest rates.

Disequilibrium may also originate in an unrealistic exchange rate, not uncommon when there is exchange control. Some economists also speak of *secular* disequilibrium, which arises from technological and other changes that occur slowly as an economy moves from one stage of growth to another over a period of decades.

Algebraic Summary of Equilibrium Conditions

In closing this section, we offer an algebraic summary of balance of payments equilibrium over the long run, the intermediate run, and the short run.

Over the long run, the equilibrium condition is $B_c = 0$, where B_c is the net balance on current account.

Over the intermediate run, the equilibrium condition is $B_c + B_{k,l} = 0$ where $B_{k,l}$ is the net balance on *long-term* capital account.

Over the short run, the equilibrium condition is $B_r = 0$, where B_r is the net balance on official reserves account.

THE NEED FOR BALANCE OF PAYMENTS ADJUSTMENT

A country's balance of payments cannot remain indefinitely in disequilibrium. But adjustment may take several forms. Over the short run, a country may adjust to an official reserves *deficit* by attracting inflows of short-term capital. But if the deficit persists, then a country must adjust in one of three ways: (1) through an internal deflation of prices and incomes relative to foreign prices and incomes, (2) through a depreciation of its rate of exchange, or (3) through an imposition of exchange

---

[7]The U.S. payments disequilibrium is also partly attributable to inappropriate macroeconomic policies. See Chapter 19.

and trade controls. Chapters 15, 16, and 17 investigate these three forms of adjustment to an international payments disequilibrium.

Market versus Nonmarket Adjustment

The first two methods of adjustment work through market processes involving changes in income, prices, exchange rates, money supplies, interest rates, and other economic phenomena. Market adjustment, however, does not imply the absence of governmental action. Indeed, successful market adjustment to an external deficit depends upon government fiscal and monetary policies directed toward reinforcing equilibrating market forces. Otherwise government monetary and fiscal policies, while not controlling or supplanting market adjustment, may counteract its equilibrating effects on the balance of payments by introducing disequilibrating changes in income, prices, and the like.

Nonmarket adjustment stands in sharp contrast to market adjustment. Government controls and regulatory devices replace the market to suppress an external deficit. Controlled adjustment is not true adjustment. Although the symptoms of disequilibrium (net official reserves balance in the balance of payments or depreciation of the exchange rate) are removed by direct controls, the causes of disequilibrium (cyclical, structural, and so on) are left untouched. The result is *suppressed disequilibrium*. Suppressed disequilibrium generally results from the widespread use of import quotas and exchange restrictions. But restrictive measures and direct controls may take any number of particular forms: tied loans and grants, ceilings on direct investment outflows, generalized tariff surcharges, domestic buying preferences, and restrictions on the purchase of foreign bonds and on bank loans to foreigners, to name only a few.

Varieties of Market Adjustment

Market adjustment to persistent disequilibrium takes two different paths depending upon whether exchange rates are stable or free to vary. When exchange rates are held stable, either through adherence to the gold standard or through official stabilization agencies, adjustment occurs in the balance of payments. When, on the other hand, the exchange rate is free to respond to fluctuations in supply and demand, disequilibrium shows up as a one-way movement of the exchange rate. Adjustment occurs within the foreign exchange market (with repercussions on domestic and foreign income and prices), and the exchange rate moves until an equality is established between the amounts of foreign exchange supplied and demanded for current-account and long-term capital transfers.

When monetary authorities try to influence exchange rates but not to peg them at a particular level (a policy known as "dirty float" in contrast to a "pure float"), then adjustment occurs in both the balance of payments and the foreign exchange market. This is the situation today for the world's major currencies.[8]

---

[8]See Chapter 19.

SUMMARY

1. The balance of payments is a statistical classification and summary of all economic transactions between residents of one country and residents of other countries over a stipulated period of time, ordinarily one year. Residence is primarily determined by permanent location and secondarily by "center of interest."

2. International transfers are grouped into three major balance of payments accounts: the current account, the capital account, and the official reserves account. Entries in these accounts are recorded as debits and credits.

3. Because the balance of payments is a double-entry accounting statement, total debits always equal total credits. This accounting equality has no economic significance.

4. An international transfer that increases a country's assets or decreases its liabilities is a debit entry in the balance of payments. Conversely, an international transfer that decreases a country's assets or increases its liabilities is a credit entry.

5. With the exception of gifts, all international transactions are two-way exchanges of assets between domestic and foreign residents. Each side of a transaction is a transfer of real or financial assets.

6. All international transfers of goods and services (real transfers) are placed in the current account. Except for official reserve transfers, all financial transfers between a country and the rest of the world are placed in the capital account. Finally, the international reserve transfers of a country's monetary authorities are placed in the official reserves account.

7. The three balances most useful in the analysis of the balance of payments are the balance on current account, the balance on basic transactions, and the balance on official reserve transactions.

8. *Long-run* equilibrium demands a zero net balance on current account ($B_c = 0$); *intermediate-term* equilibrium requires a zero net basic balance ($B_c + B_{k,l} = 0$); *short-term* equilibrium occurs when there is a zero net balance on official reserves account ($B_r = 0$). Short-term equilibrium also means equilibrium in the foreign exchange market.

9. Sources of disequilibrium in the balance of payments may be seasonal and random, cyclical, structural, speculation and capital flight, and other.

10. When a country experiences a persistent deficit in its balance of payments, it cannot rely indefinitely on net short-term capital inflows and international reserves to finance that deficit. The need for adjustment policies that will eliminate the deficit becomes critical when a country's international reserves fall to a minimal level.

11. A government may use three different modes of adjustment to remove a persistent disequilibrium in its balance of payments, either singly or in some combination: adjustment through deflation, adjustment through devaluation, and adjustment through controls.

QUESTIONS AND APPLICATIONS

1. What is the balance of international payments?
2. What determines whether a transfer is entered as a debit or a credit in the balance of payments?
3. What is the distinction between current transactions, capital transactions, and official reserve transactions?
4. Using the double-entry system, record the following international transactions in a hypothetical U.S. balance of payments: (a) an export of U.S. merchandise, valued at $500, for payment in dollars by a foreign resident; (b) the purchase of hotel services, valued at $100, by an American tourist in France; (c) the sale by the U.S. monetary authorities of gold (worth $1,000) to the Bank of England; (d) the purchase of $200 of bonds by an American resident from a foreign resident; and (e) the acquisition by a U.S. multinational corporation of a firm in a foreign country in exchange for $1,000.
5. Why is the balance of payments always in an accounting balance?
6. What is the essential meaning of balance of payments equilibrium? Of disequilibrium?
7. Describe the major sources of disequilibrium.
8. What is the economic significance of the net balance on current account? The net balance on basic transactions? The net balance on official reserve transactions?
9. (a) Why is a country compelled to take adjustment measures to eliminate a persistent deficit in its balance of payments?
   (b) Which modes of adjustment may a country use to eliminate a persistent deficit?
10. Explain the difference between market and nonmarket adjustments.

SELECTED READINGS

International Monetary Fund. *Balance of Payments Manual.* Washington, D.C.: International Monetary Fund. Latest edition.

International Monetary Fund. *Balance of Payments Yearbook.* Washington, D.C.: International Monetary Fund. Annual.

Stern, Robert M., and others. *The Presentation of the U.S. Balance of Payments: A Symposium.* Essays in International Finance no. 123. Princeton, N.J.: Princeton University Press, 1977.

United States Department of Commerce, Office of Business Economics. *Survey of Current Business.* Washington, D.C.: U.S. Government Printing Office. March, June, September, and December issues, annual.

chapter 15

INTERNATIONAL PAYMENTS ADJUSTMENT IN A FIXED-RATE SYSTEM

How do countries adjust to disequilibria in their balance of payments in an international monetary system that commits national governments to maintain fixed exchange rates? This is the question addressed in this chapter.

DETERMINANTS OF THE CURRENT AND CAPITAL ACCOUNTS

Current-account transfers and capital-account transfers in the balance of payments are influenced by different sets of economic variables.

The balance on current account depends on domestic real income, foreign real income, and the relative prices of domestically produced and foreign-produced goods and services. Expressed algebraically,

$$B_c = f(Y_d, Y_f, P/SP^*)$$

where B_c is the net balance on current account; Y_d, domestic real income; Y_f, foreign real income; P, the domestic price level; P^*, the foreign price level; and S, the spot foreign exchange rate.

The balance on capital account is dependent on the domestic interest rate relative to the foreign interest rate, the domestic profit rate relative to the foreign profit rate, and the expected exchange rate. Expressed algebraically,

$$B_k = f(i/i^*, r/r^*, E(S)),$$

where i is the domestic interest rate; i^*, the foreign interest rate; r, the domestic profit rate; r^*, the foreign profit rate; and $E(S)$, the expected exchange rate.

The combined net balance on current and capital accounts can deviate from zero only when it is financed by an opposing and equal balance on official reserves account (B_r). Compensatory financing is provided by the monetary authorities when they intervene in the foreign exchange market to maintain a fixed exchange rate. Hence, the net balance on official reserves account is *induced* by the combined net balance of the other two accounts. Expressed algebraically,

$$B_r = -(B_c + B_k).$$

To deal with the several independent variables that can play a role in the international adjustment process, we first analyze adjustment when capital is immobile among countries and then when capital is perfectly mobile among countries. In both cases, the exchange rate does not influence adjustment, because it is fixed. After this explanation of current-account and capital-account adjustment processes, we investigate the conditions of general equilibrium in an open economy.

Our first task is to examine the relationship between national income and the balance of payments.

NATIONAL INCOME, FOREIGN TRADE, AND DOMESTIC ABSORPTION

This section examines the relationships between national income and foreign trade and the conception of a balance of payments deficit (surplus) as an excess (deficiency) of domestic absorption.

The Gross National Product and Income Equations

The *gross national product* (GNP) of a nation is the market value of all final goods and services produced by the national economy over a period of time, which is usually a year. In practice, the GNP is estimated by aggregating the total expenditures on goods and services of individuals, business, government, and foreigners in the markets of the nation over the year. Since these are final expenditures, no single good or service is ever counted more than once.

In a *closed* economy with no foreign trade, all expenditures are domestic and GNP may be expressed as follows:

$$GNP = C + I + G,$$

where C represents expenditures by individuals for consumption; I, expenditures by business for gross investment (capital equipment, construction, and net additions to inventories); and G, expenditures by government for both consumption and investment.

In an *open* economy, however, GNP is affected by the exports and imports of goods and services that make up the current account of the nation's balance of payments. Exports measure the expenditures by foreigners in domestic markets and therefore are part of GNP. Imports, on the other hand, measure expenditures by domestic individuals, business, and government for goods and services produced by other nations, and they must be deducted from total expenditures to get the domestic gross national product. Hence, in an open economy GNP assumes this form:

$$(1)\ GNP = C + I + G + X - M,$$

where X represents expenditures on exports and M represents expenditures on imports. The expression $X - M$ links GNP to the balance of payments, because this expression is the net balance on goods and services, which is also the net foreign investment of the nation.[1] To show this, we can rewrite equation (1) as follows:

$$(2)\ GNP = C + I_d + G + (X - M),$$

where I_d represents *domestic* gross investment and $(X - M)$ represents net foreign investment.

The production of the goods and services making up GNP generates an equal flow of income to the factors that contribute their productive services. Some of this income is spent by individuals on consumption and some is saved by them, some is saved by business as depreciation and "retained corporate profits," and the rest is taxed away by government. Thus, we can define *gross national income* (GNI) as follows:

$$(3)\ GNI = C + S_p + S_b + T,$$

where C represents income spent on consumption; S_p and S_b, personal and business saving, respectively; and T, income taxed away by government.

Since GNP is equal to GNI, we now have this identity:

$$(4)\ C + I_d + G + (X - M) = C + S_p + S_b + T.$$

Simplifying and transposing we get

$$(5)\ I_d + G + (X - M) = S_p + S_b + T.$$
$$(6)\ S_p + S_b + (T - G) - I_d = X - M.$$

Since $(T - G)$ is the excess of tax revenue over government expenditure, or *government saving*, $S_p + S_b + (T - G) = S$, where S represents *total* domestic saving. Thus,

$$(7)\ S - I_d = X - M.$$

---

[1]To simplify our exposition, in this chapter we shall assume the absence of unilateral transfers and therefore consider the balance on current account as synonymous with the balance on goods and services.

This is a basic equation relating GNI (or GNP) to foreign trade. It states that any excess of exports over imports (current account surplus) is matched by an excess of domestic saving over domestic investment. Conversely, an excess of imports over exports (current account deficit) is matched by an excess of domestic investment over domestic saving. If domestic saving equals domestic investment, then exports also equal imports.

This discussion of GNI and GNP may take on more meaning for readers if we end it with a presentation of those two accounts for the United States in 1991.[2] This presentation is given in Table 15-1. Readers may find it instructive to insert these figures into GNP and GNI equations.

Determination of National Income

How do *changes* in GNI (GNP) affect the balance of payments? How do changes in foreign trade affect GNI? To answer these questions, we must understand how national income is determined.[3]

Although the *potential* size of the real GNP (the production possibilities fron-

Table 15-1 Gross National Product and Income of the United States in 1991 (Billions of Dollars)

Symbol	GNP	Symbol	GNI
C	3,887.7	C	3,887.7
I_d	721.1	S_p	199.6
G	1,090.5	S_b	701.9
X	741.7	T	897.2
M	− 746.0		
		Statistical discrepancy	8.6
GNP	5,695.0	GNI	5,695.0

Source: "National Income and Product Accounts," *Survey of Current Business,* August 1992, pp. 10–28.

---

[2]In 1991, the U.S. Department of Commerce replaced the gross national product with the gross *domestic* product (GDP) in its standard presentation of the national income and product accounts. The relationship between GNP and GDP is shown by the following equation: $GNP = GDP + (FR - FP)$, where FR represents international *factor receipts* (largely receipts by U.S. residents of interest and dividends and reinvested earnings of foreign affiliates of U.S. corporations) and FP represents international *factor payments* (largely payments to foreign residents of interest and dividends and reinvested earnings of U.S. affiliates of foreign corporations). In dollars for 1991: GNP ($5,695 billion) = GDP (5,677.5 billion) + [FR ($143.5 billion) − FP ($126.0 billion)] = $5,695 billion. Observe that the dollar difference between GNP and GDP is relatively small. We are using GNP in preference to GDP because we want $X - M$ to equal the net balance on current account of the balance of payments, which includes factor receipts and payments.

[3]We can offer here only a very condensed version of the theory of income determination. For a fuller treatment see any introductory text on economics.

tier) depends on the supply and productivity of the nation's factors of production, its *actual* size is determined by the level of aggregate demand—the planned expenditures of domestic consumers, investors, and government agencies *plus* the net planned expenditures of foreigners $[C + I_d + G + (X - M)]$. In Figure 15-1, GNP is determined by the intersection of the aggregate demand schedule with the aggregate (real) supply schedule at E. The equilibrium level of GNP is $0-P$, which generates an equal level of GNI; that is to say, $0-P = 0-Y$.[4] Only at E is the level of national output equal to the level of planned expenditures. At any income level below $0-Y$, aggregate demand exceeds real output. This excess demand will

Figure 15-1

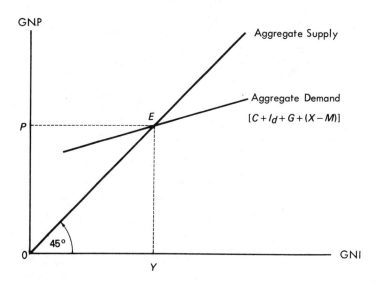

The Determination of Actual Gross National Product (Income) by Aggregate Demand. A country's GNP (national income) is determined by the intersection of the aggregate supply and demand schedules. The aggregate supply schedule shows the country's real output of goods and services. It is drawn at a 45° slope because at each point on the schedule GNP equals GNI. The aggregate demand schedule shows the *planned* expenditures of domestic consumers (C), investors (I_d), and government (G) plus the *net* planned expenditures of foreigners on domestic goods and services ($X-M$). Only at E is the level of national output (supply) equal to the level of planned expenditures, with GNP at $0-P(= 0-Y)$. At any income level below $0-Y$, aggregate demand exceeds aggregate supply. This excess demand stimulates more production of goods and services until that excess demand is eliminated at E. Conversely, at any income level above $0-Y$, aggregate demand is less than aggregate supply, forcing a contraction of national output back to $0-Y(= 0-P)$.

---

[4]Since the aggregate supply line is drawn at 45° to the origin, GNP = GNI at every point on the line. As noted above, GNP and GNI are always equal.

Part II   International Payments

stimulate producers to expand their output until the excess demand is eliminated at D. On the other hand, at any income level higher than 0–Y, aggregate demand falls short of aggregate supply. In this instance producers will respond by contracting output until the demand deficiency is eliminated at E. Hence, the only stable level of GNI is 0–Y, as determined by E.

In equilibrium, therefore,

$$(8)\ GNP = C + I_d + G + (X - M)$$
$$= GNI = C + S_p + S_b + T.$$

Although this equation appears to be the same as equation (4), it is not. The expenditures on the left side are planned or *ex ante* expenditures, whereas in equation (4) the expenditures are *ex post* expenditures that may or may not have been planned.

Any increase in planned expenditures will cause an increase in GNP and GNI, subject to the constraint of the production possibilities frontier.[5] In Figure 15-2, the initial equilibrium position is E, where aggregate demand and aggregate supply are equal. But now an increase in planned domestic investment pushes up the aggregate demand schedule, creating excess demand at the existing level of GNI. Producers respond to this excess demand by expanding output to E', where planned expenditure once again equals aggregate supply. At this new equilibrium GNP is 0–P' and GNI is 0–Y'. In similar fashion, a *decrease* in the planned expenditure causes a contraction in GNP and GNI.

Equation (8) can be rewritten as follows:

$$(9)\ \underbrace{C + I_d + G + X}_{\substack{\text{Income} \\ \text{Injections}}} = \underbrace{C + S_p + S_b + T + M}_{\substack{\text{Income} \\ \text{Leakages}}}.$$

Simply put, all increases (decreases) in expenditures on domestic goods and services will increase (decrease) national income. The different expenditures, however, do not play the same role in initiating changes in national income. Basically, changes in domestic investment and government and export expenditures are *autonomous* with respect to national income. That is to say, they are not dependent on any prior change in income but rather cause changes in income. On the other hand, changes in consumption expenditures are *induced* by prior changes in national income and do not *initiate* changes in it. In other words, consumption expenditures do not determine national income but instead are determined by it.

---

[5]In this presentation of national income determination, we are assuming a constant price level so that an increase in expenditure causes higher *real* GNP and GNI. This assumption requires that the economy be at less than full employment (below its production possibilities frontier), with the capacity to produce more goods and services. In contrast, at full employment an increase in expenditure will generate inflation with *no* increase in real output and income.

Figure 15-2

The Determination of a New Equilibrium Level of Gross National Product (Income) by an Upward Shift in Aggregate Demand. An increase in planned expenditures is shown by an *upward* shift of the entire aggregate demand schedule. The increase shown above is caused by a rise in domestic investment from I_d to I'_d that creates excess demand at $0-Y$. In response, producers increase output from E to E', where planned expenditures once again equal aggregate supply at $0-P'$ (= $0-Y'$). Conversely, a decrease in planned expenditures causes a *downward* shift in the entire aggregate demand schedule, thereby bringing about a contraction of GNP (= GNI).

Henceforth, we shall refer to autonomous expenditures (domestic investment, government expenditures, and exports) as *income injections*.

In contrast to expenditures, domestic saving, taxes, and imports act to *depress* national income. Saving is a decision not to spend, taxes lower spendable income in the hands of individuals and business, and imports divert expenditures away from domestic goods and services to foreign output. For this reason we shall call them *income leakages*.

National income is in equilibrium when the expenditures that business, government, and foreigners *intend* to make in domestic markets equal saving, taxation, and imports, that is, when

$$(10) \ \ G + I_d + X = S_p + S_b + T + M.$$

To simplify matters we can view $(T - G)$ as part of domestic saving (S), along with S_p and S_b, reducing equation (10) to

$$(11) \ \ I_d + X = S + M.$$

This equation resembles equation (7) but is not the same, because in our present discussion we are speaking of *intended* expenditures, saving, and imports. Equation (7) always holds, but equation (11) holds only when national income is in equilibrium. If, for example, businesses end up the year with unwanted or unintended additions to their inventories, then they will take steps to reduce them and thus lower income in the following year. Only when intended income injections equal income leakages is national income "determined," that is, stable. We can draw here an analogy with the balance of payments. As we have seen, the balance of payments is always in accounting balance, but it is not always in equilibrium.

Figure 15-3 indicates the determination of national income in terms of income injections and leakages [equation (11)]. The $S + M$ schedule shows how savings and imports vary with the level of national income; it is the sum of the savings

Figure 15-3

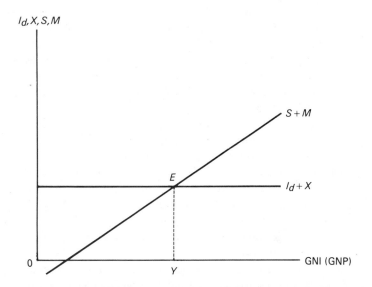

The Determination of Gross National Income: Injection-Leakage Approach. The income *injection-leakage* approach explains the determination of national income by the intersection of the combined savings and import (leakage) schedules ($S + M$) and the combined domestic investment and export (injection) schedules ($I_d + M$). Equilibrium income is 0–Y because at E the sum of leakages equals the sum of injections. The $S + M$ schedule slopes upward from left to right because leakages are a positive function of national income: The higher the income, the higher the leakages. The $I_d + X$ schedule has a zero slope because injections are autonomous (independent) with respect to national income. An upward shift in the $I_d + X$ schedule (autonomous *increase* in income injection) causes an expansion in national income to a new equilibrium level; a downward shift causes a contraction. The injection-leakage approach gives the same result as the *total expenditures* approach shown in Figure 15-1.

schedule (S) and the import schedule (M), which are not shown separately. The I_d + X schedule is the sum of the domestic investment schedule (I_d) and the export schedule (X). Since both the domestic investment schedule and the export schedule are autonomous with respect to national income, the composite I_d + X schedule is drawn parallel to the abscissa. The equilibrium level of income (0–Y) is determined by the intersection of the two composite schedules at E. An autonomous upward shift in the I_d + X schedule will bring about a higher equilibrium level of national income, whereas a downward shift will bring about a lower level. This injection-leakage approach to national income determination gives the same result as the total-expenditures approach used in Figure 15-1.

Functional Relationship of Expenditures, Saving, and Imports to Real Domestic Income

In discussing the relationships between changes in expenditures, saving, and imports, on one hand, and changes in national income, on the other, we shall be talking of *real* income changes, that is, changes that are *not* accompanied by price changes. The assumptions underlying this condition are indicated later in the chapter.

As discussed in the previous section, changes in domestic investment and exports are independent of changes in domestic national income. Investment expenditure depends on the expected return on capital (marginal efficiency of capital) interacting with the cost of capital (interest rate). Changes in exports depend upon changes in tastes and real income in foreign countries. Consumption, saving, and imports, however, are all dependent on income.

The relation between consumption and income is known as the *marginal propensity to consume* (MPC), which is expressed as dC/dY, where dY is a change in national income and dC is the change in consumption induced by the change in income. If, for example, the MPC is 0.8, then a $100 change (increase or decrease) in national income will induce an $80 change in consumption. In brief, the marginal propensity to consume is the fraction or percentage of new income that is spent on consumption.

Some of the consumption expenditure goes to buy imports. Thus, the marginal propensity to consume includes *the marginal propensity to import* (MPM), which is expressed as dM/dY. The marginal propensity to import, then, is the percentage of new income that is spent on imports. If the MPM is 0.2, then a $100 change in national income will induce a $20 change in imports.

The expression dS/dY is the *marginal propensity to save* (MPS), which relates a change in national income to the change in saving induced by the former. Since income is either spent or saved, the MPC and MPS together always add up to 1. If the MPC is 0.8, then the MPS must be 0.2.

The marginal propensities are not necessarily the same at different levels of national income. For example, as family incomes rise beyond a subsistence level, the marginal propensity to consume may decline or, to say the same thing, the marginal propensity to save may increase. For the sake of simplicity, however, we shall assume in this and later discussions that the marginal propensities are constant.

Domestic and Foreign Trade Income Multipliers

Reverting to equation (11), an autonomous shift in domestic investment or in exports will cause a change in national income in the same direction. Increases in these expenditures will raise national income; decreases will lower it. Furthermore, the resulting change in national income will be a *multiple* of the autonomous change in investment or exports. This is because the income first generated by the autonomous expenditure will be respent by its recipients, which in turn will generate another change in income, and so on. This process of income change (expansion or contraction) will come to a stop when the income leakages induced by the income change become equal to the autonomous income injection. As we have noted, this is when $I_d + X = S + M$.

This relationship between an autonomous change in domestic investment and the subsequent change in national income that it induces is called the *domestic income multiplier,* or dY/dI_d. If the domestic multiplier is 2, then a \$100 increase (decrease) in domestic investment will cause a \$200 increase (decrease) in national income. We may derive the domestic income multiplier as follows:

$$(12) \quad I_d + X = S + M.$$

Now introduce a change in domestic investment (dI) that will induce a change in domestic saving (dS) and imports (dM) via an induced change in national income. Since exports are not affected, we can rewrite equation (12):

$$(13) \quad dI_d = dS + dM.$$

Dividing both sides of equation (13) into the induced change in national income (dY), we have

$$(14) \quad dY/dI_d = \frac{dY}{dS + dM}, \text{ or}$$

$$(15) \quad dY/dI_d = \frac{1}{dS/dY + dM/dY}$$

$$= \frac{1}{MPS + MPM}.$$

This last equation tells us that the domestic income multiplier (dY/dI_d) equals the *reciprocal of the sum of the marginal propensities to save and import.* If MPS is 0.1 and MPM is 0.1, then the multiplier is 1/0.2, or 5. Thus, an autonomous change in domestic investment of, say, \$50 would cause a change of \$250 in national income. In mathematical terms,

$$(16)\ dY\ =\ (dY/dI_d)\ dI_d,$$

which says that the change in income equals the multiplier dY/dI_d times the autonomous change in domestic investment (dI_d).

The relationship between an autonomous change in exports (dX) and the induced change in national income (dY) is known as the *foreign trade multiplier*. We can derive the foreign trade multiplier in exactly the same way we derived the domestic multiplier, and it assumes the same form:

$$\frac{dY}{dX}\ =\ \frac{1}{MPS\ +\ MPM}.$$

The induced change in national income will be the autonomous change in exports *times* the multiplier $[dX(dY/dX)]$.

We may summarize this exposition by saying that changes in national income are induced by autonomous changes in domestic investment or exports. The resulting change in national income will be the product of the autonomous change in investment or exports times the income multiplier. Both the domestic and foreign trade multipliers may be expressed as the reciprocal of the sum of the marginal propensities to save and import, or the reciprocal of the sum of the *income leakages*. National income will reach a new equilibrium position (and cease to change) when intended expenditures (income injections) equal the income leakages, that is, $I_d\ +\ X\ =\ S\ +\ M$.

ADJUSTMENT WITH NO
INTERNATIONAL CAPITAL MOBILITY

In our exposition of international payments adjustment in this and the next two chapters, we shall use the net balance on official reserves account to measure disequilibrium in the balance of payments. A positive or negative balance on this account indicates that the monetary authorities are using international reserves to finance an opposing net balance on the combined current and capital accounts. When the net balance on official reserves account is zero, then the balance of payments is in *equilibrium:* $B_r\ =\ 0\ =\ B_c\ +\ B_k$.[6]

How does a country adjust to a balance of payments disequilibrium when there is no net movement of capital between it and the rest of the world? In that case, $B_k\ =\ 0$, and therefore disequilibrium appears only in the current account: $B_r\ =\ -B_c\ \neq\ 0$. The elimination of the surplus or deficit on current account to restore equilibrium occurs through changes in domestic real income (GNP) and the relative prices of domestic and foreign goods and services.

---

[6]Whether or not this equilibrium is a short-run or intermediate-run equilibrium depends on the net balance on short-term capital flows, as discussed in the previous chapter.

International Adjustment and Domestic Absorption

Let us rewrite equation (2) as follows:

$$(17) \ X - M = GNP - (C + I_d + G).$$

This tells us that when exports are greater than imports, GNP (GNI) is greater than *domestic* expenditure on goods and services $(C + I_d + G)$ by the same amount. Conversely, when imports are greater than exports, GNP is less than domestic expenditure by the same amount.

We can rewrite equation (17):

$$(18) \ B_c = Y - A,$$

where B_c is the net current-account balance $(X - M)$, Y is the gross national product, and A is the domestic *absorption* of goods and services $(C + I_d + G)$. If $X < M$, then $B_c < 0$ and $Y < A$. Hence, to correct a current-account deficit, a country must either (1) *increase* its physical output of goods and services (Y) or (2) *decrease* its real absorption of goods and services (A).

The period of time allowed for adjustment to a persistent payments deficit is limited by the availability of compensatory financing, and for most countries it is probably not more than two or three years. When an economy is fully employed, further growth in GNP must depend mainly upon an improvement in productivity, which seldom goes beyond 5 percent a year and is often less. Under full-employment conditions, therefore, it is usually not possible to raise Y to any significant degree during the period allowed for payments adjustment. Thus, adjustment under full-employment conditions calls for *a reduction in domestic absorption (expenditure) in real terms* and thus a smaller allocation of goods and services to domestic use.

When the economy is at less than full employment, it may be possible to increase output (Y). But to improve the balance of payments, output must be increased without adding equally to the level of domestic absorption (A). This requires that any new expenditure be switched from domestic absorption to expenditures by foreigners on exports and to expenditures on domestic goods that replace imports. To bring about such expenditure switching, either *prices* in the deficit country must be lowered relative to prices in the rest of the world (through internal deflation or exchange devaluation) or the reallocation must be accomplished by restrictions and controls. In the absence of switching, any increase in output will simply increase domestic absorption with no benefit to the balance of payments. If we assume that prices are fixed, then adjustment, even under less-than-full-employment conditions, must rely on *expenditure reduction* that cuts down on domestic absorption.

Equilibrating Changes in Domestic Absorption
Through Real Income Effects

We are now prepared to see how the foreign trade multiplier helps to bring about adjustment to a persistent deficit or surplus in the current account.

Operation of the Foreign Trade Multiplier   To focus our analysis in this and the next section on equilibrating changes in real expenditure, we shall assume that goods and factor prices are *fixed*. We shall further assume that the economy of the country in payments disequilibrium is at less than full employment and has excess capacity to produce real output.

How does the foreign trade multiplier function to bring about an adjustment to persistent deficit disequilibrium in the balance of payments? We can indicate income adjustment most simply with a diagram. In Figure 15-4 the initial equilibrium income level is $0-Y$, as determined by the intersection of the $X + I_d$ schedule (income injection) and the $M + S$ schedule (income leakage). The M and X schedules also intersect at $0-Y$ income: Imports equal exports, and hence the balance of payments is in equilibrium. The country is enjoying external balance

Figure 15-4

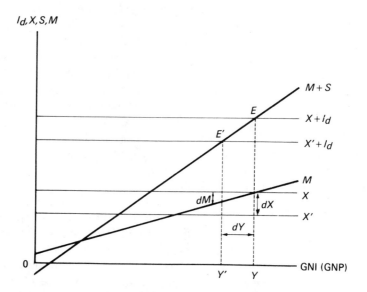

Income Adjustment to a Balance of Payments Deficit Caused by an Autonomous Decrease in Exports.   Initially, the equilibrium income level is $0-Y$, as determined by the intersection at E of the $X + I_d$ schedule (injection) and the $M + S$ schedule (leakage). It so happens that the M and X schedules intersect at income level $0-Y$. Hence, the balance of payments is also in equilibrium. Then, an autonomous decrease in the export schedule from X to X' causes a balance of payments deficit (dX) and also an equal decrease in the injection schedule from $X + I_d$ to $X' + I_d$ which forces a contraction of GNP from $0-Y$ to $0-Y'$, where income injection once again equals income leakage at point E'. The decrease in income (dY) exceeds the decrease in exports (dX) due to the foreign trade multiplier. Income adjustment to the balance of payments occurs through a decrease in imports (dM) induced by the decrease in income (dY). At the new equilibrium income $(0-Y)$, adjustment to the balance of payments deficit remains incomplete $(dM < dX)$ due to a positive savings leakage.

but not internal balance.[7] Now, however, an autonomous drop in exports from X to X' creates a balance of payments deficit (dX) and also causes an equal drop in autonomous expenditure from $X + I_d$ to $X' + I_d$. This lower injection of spending forces a contraction of output that reduces national income to a new equilibrium level of $0\text{-}Y'$. At $0\text{-}Y'$ no further changes occur in the level of income, because income injection ($X' + I_d$) once again equals income leakage ($M + S$).

Note that the decrease in income (dY) is greater than the autonomous decrease in exports (dX) as a result of the foreign trade multiplier. The multiplier is greater than one because the combined marginal propensity to import and save (the slope of the $M + S$ schedule) is less than 1. Income adjustment to the balance of payments deficit occurs through a fall in imports (dM) that is induced by the contraction in national income (dY) via the marginal propensity to import (the slope of the M schedule). In this instance, income adjustment is not sufficient to wipe out the entire deficit ($dM < dX$). As we shall observe shortly, adjustment through the foreign trade multiplier can be completed only when there is no savings leakage ($MPS = 0$). Figure 15-4 shows only the *final* effect of the foreign trade multiplier on national income and the balance of payments (imports). To gain an insight into the *process* of income adjustment, we now turn to arithmetic examples.

The Income Adjustment Process: No Savings Leakage   Let us suppose that exports of the domestic country fall \$100 because of lower foreign demand and that this fall is permanent. Assuming a prior equilibrium, the balance of payments now has a persistent deficit, and long-run adjustment is necessary. We further assume the following marginal propensities in the deficit country: MPC = 1, MPM = 0.4, and MPS = 0. Thus, all new income is spent on consumption—0.4 on imports and 0.6 on domestic output. In the same way, a drop in income induces an equal decrease in consumption spread over imports and domestic output. There is no domestic savings leakage.

We now trace the equilibrating income effects of this permanent fall in exports as they occur over income periods. An income period is the time necessary to spend the income earned in the preceding income period and to earn the income that will be spent in the next income period. (It has been estimated that an income period in the United States economy has a duration of about three months.) Turning now to Table 15-2, we observe that there is no change in the level of exports in income period 0, and consequently there are no induced changes in imports, domestic consumption, or domestic income. In income period 1, however, exports drop \$100 to a new level that is sustained throughout our example. This causes a decline of \$100 in the income received by those domestic residents who produce and sell the merchandise and services comprising the \$100 drop in exports.

---

[7]We are assuming in Figure 15-4 that full employment occurs only at a GNP higher than $0\text{-}Y$. Internal balance means that $0\text{-}Y$ is accompanied by full employment. The problem of achieving internal and external balance at the same time is explored later. Observe that at $0\text{-}Y$ there is neither internal nor external balance.

Table 15-2 Income Adjustment to a Payments Deficit with No Savings Leakage

Income Period	Period Export Income Injection	Period Import Income Leakage	Period Decrease in Domestic Consumption	Period Decrease in Consumption of Domestic Output
0	$ 0	$ 0	$ 0	$ 0
1	− 100	0	0	− 100
2	− 100	− 40	− 60	− 160
3	− 100	− 64	− 96	− 196
n	− 100	− 100	− 150	− 250

In income period 2, these residents cut their spending on imports by $40 (0.4 *times* $100) and their spending on domestic output by $60 (0.6 *times* $100). As a result, a second group of residents who produce and sell domestic goods going to the first group of residents now suffer an income loss of $60. (What is spending to the buyer is income to the seller.) The $40 drop in imports reduces foreign income but not domestic income. Thus, in income period 2 domestic income falls by $160 — an induced decline in domestic consumption ($60) plus the continuing negative export injection ($100). This process of income deflation continues into income period 3, and domestic income falls $196 below its level in period 0.

As we know, the overall contraction in domestic income is determined by the foreign trade multiplier. In this case the multiplier is the reciprocal of the marginal propensity to import, because the marginal propensity to save is zero. Thus, the multiplier is 2.5 and domestic income will fall by 2.5 *times* $100, or $250, in income period n after all the multiplier effects have taken place. This decline in domestic income induces a $100 fall in imports that exactly matches the autonomous fall in exports, thereby restoring equilibrium in the balance of payments. The process of income contraction comes to a halt in income period n because the autonomous fall in export expenditure is fully offset by an induced decline in the import leakage, that is, $dM = dX$.

The Income Adjustment Process: Savings Leakage   When spending on imports is the only income leakage, then adjustment to a balance of payments deficit (surplus) in the current account is complete: Imports fall (rise) until they exactly offset the autonomous decrease (increase) in exports. Income, however, is rarely spent entirely on consumption; part of it is generally saved, and this saving, as we have observed, constitutes a second income leakage. Because of the savings leakage, the foreign trade multiplier is too small to effect a full adjustment in the balance of payments: The induced change in imports is less than the autonomous

Table 15-3 Income Adjustment to a Payments Deficit with Savings Leakage

Income Period	Period Export Income Injection	Period Import Income Leakage	Period Savings Leakage	Period Decrease in Domestic Consumption	Period Decrease in Consumption of Domestic Output
0	$ 0	$ 0	$ 0	$ 0	$ 0
1	– 100	0	0	0	– 100
2	– 100	– 40	– 10	– 50	– 150
3	– 100	– 60	– 15	– 75	– 175
n	– 100	– 80	– 20	– 100	– 200

change in exports. Table 15-3 demonstrates this incomplete adjustment by assuming MPC = 0.9, MPM = 0.4, and MPS = 0.1.

Because the combined marginal leakage propensity (marginal import propensity plus marginal savings propensity) is 0.5, the multiplier is only 2 (1/0.5), and domestic income does not contract sufficiently to induce a fall in imports equal to the autonomous fall in exports. Actually, imports fall only $80, and thus there remains a $20 deficit (equal to the savings leakage) in the balance of payments. It is apparent, then, that the foreign trade multiplier will not effect full adjustment to disequilibrium when there is a domestic savings leakage.

The Foreign Repercussion Effect   The conclusion reached in the last paragraph is true but incomplete. To get a complete picture of income adjustment to payments disequilibrium, we must take note not only of domestic income changes induced by the balance of payments but also of income changes induced in foreign countries.

The autonomous fall in domestic exports appears to the rest of the world as a $100 fall in its imports that creates a *surplus* disequilibrium in its balance of payments. Now the foreign trade multiplier functions as soon as there is disequilibrium in the current account regardless of whether the disequilibrium results from a change in exports or a change in imports. Thus, the surplus disequilibrium in the rest of the world starts a cumulative expansive movement in foreign incomes, which in turn induces an increase in imports from the deficit country via the foreign marginal propensity to import. This complicated interaction between the foreign trade multipliers of different countries restrains the decline in income in the deficit country and the rise in income in the surplus country.

The foreign repercussion effect depends on foreign propensities to import and save. Returning to our previous example, let us now assume that the foreign propensity to import is 0.3 and the foreign propensity to save is 0.1. Then the foreign trade multiplier for the domestic country would be 1.25 rather than 2 and the domestic income would fall only $125.[8] Because in this instance we are assuming that the domestic and foreign propensities to save are both 0.1, foreign income would rise $125. Thus, the rest of the world would increase its imports from the domestic country by $37.5 (0.3 times $125) or, to say the same thing, the domestic country's exports would increase by $37.5. At the same time, the domestic country would reduce its imports by $50 (0.4 times $125). The end result of these income adjustments would be to decrease the domestic country's deficit from $100 to $12.5 because of a foreign repercussion effect of $37.5 and an induced import leakage of $50. Note that the deficit would be less than in our previous example ($12.5 compared to $20) but that adjustment would remain incomplete. This will always be the case unless the domestic savings leakage is offset by a change in domestic investment expenditure *induced* by monetary effects.

The foreign repercussion effect will be insignificant for a country whose exports and imports are only a small part of world trade. However, for major trading countries like the United States, the foreign repercussion effect must be taken into account in estimating the foreign trade multiplier.

The Domestic Income Multiplier   We have now examined adjustment via the foreign trade multiplier, noting how income changes originating in the current account work toward the establishment of a new equilibrium. But all changes in income do not proceed from disequilibrium in the balance of payments. New income may also be created (or old income extinguished) by independent shifts in domestic investment (construction, capital equipment, inventories) or domestic government expenditures. These shifts in domestic expenditure cause a multiple expansion (or contraction) of domestic income via the *domestic* income multiplier. The change in domestic income then affects the level of imports through the marginal propensity to import, and the result, assuming a prior equilibrium, is a cyclical disequilibrium in the balance of payments.

Because of the domestic income multiplier, government fiscal and monetary policies become key instruments of balance of payments adjustment. By the same token, however, these policies may delay international adjustment by bringing about changes in domestic income that counteract the equilibrating income changes of the foreign trade multiplier. This situation often occurs since nations usually place the objectives of domestic full employment and rapid economic development above that of balance of payments equilibrium.

Equilibrating Changes in Domestic Absorption Through Monetary Effects

We have seen that the foreign trade multiplier will fail to bring about full adjustment to a balance of payments disequilibrium when there is a domestic

---

[8]The foreign trade multiplier that takes account of this interaction, or foreign repercussion effect, is

$$1 \,/\, (MPS_d \,+\, MPM_d \,+\, MPM_f\,[MPS_d/\,MPS_f]) \,,$$

where MPS_d and MPM_d are the marginal propensities to save and import, respectively, of the domestic country, and MPS_f and MPM_f are the marginal propensities to save and import, respectively, of the rest of the world.

Part II   International Payments

savings leakage. Since such a leakage is almost certain to exist, how then will full adjustment be achieved when all prices are fixed and unemployment prevails in the economy? The answer to this question lies in the *monetary effects* of a balance of payments disequilibrium on real expenditure (real income).

A current account surplus or deficit is financed by an opposing and equal net balance on official reserves account when, as we are presently assuming, there is zero net international movement of capital. A current account surplus *increases* the international reserves and monetary base of the domestic country; a current account deficit *decreases* the international reserves and monetary base of the domestic country. In turn, a rise in the monetary base increases the domestic country's money supply (stock) whereas a fall in the monetary base decreases its money supply. To understand this last statement, a few words are necessary on how a country's central bank creates the money stock.

Each country's central bank (the Federal Reserve System in the United States) creates money when it buys securities (bonds) or foreign exchange from others, and it destroys money when it sells securities or foreign exchange to others.[9] When it buys securities or foreign exchange, the central bank pays for them with a check drawn against itself. The seller of bonds or foreign exchange to the central bank deposits this check with its commercial bank, which credits the seller's checking account. (The central bank then credits the account that the commercial bank maintains with it.) Hence, the *purchase* of bonds or foreign exchange by the central bank immediately creates an equal amount of money (the demand deposit of the seller). Conversely, the *sale* of bonds or foreign exchange by the central bank decreases the money stock: The buyer pays with a check drawn against its commercial bank, which debits the buyer's checking account. (The central bank then debits the commercial bank's account.)

The money creation (destruction) process does not stop with the initial creation (destruction) of the seller's (buyer's) demand deposit with its commercial bank. In the instance of a purchase of bonds or foreign exchange by the central bank, the new deposit that the commercial bank now holds in the central bank constitutes *reserves*. Because a commercial bank is required to hold reserves in the central bank that equal only a fraction of its demand deposits, an increase in reserves enables it to increase demand deposits through loans up to a multiple of the increase in reserves. If, for example, the required reserve ratio is 10 percent, then a $100 increase in the bank reserves can support a $1,000 increase in the money stock. Conversely, a decrease in bank reserves causes a multiple decrease in the money stock. In sum, the supply of money (M^s) equals the money multiplier (m) times the monetary base (B):

$$(19) \quad M^s = mB$$

---

[9]Money is a financial asset that can be used directly as a means of payment. The money stock of a country consists mostly of currency (banknotes and coins) in the hands of the public and the demand deposits of commercial banks.

The *monetary base* is composed of two elements: a *domestic* element (D) consisting of domestic credit created by the central bank (which is represented by commercial bank reserves and currency held by the nonbank public), and an *international* element (R) consisting of the domestic-currency value of the official international reserves held by the monetary authorities. In equation form,

$$(20) \quad B = D + R.$$

The monetary base is sometimes called "high-powered money" because commercial banks can create demand deposits to a multiple (m) of their reserves. This money multiplier is assumed to be independent of changes in the monetary base.

To finance a surplus in the current account, the central bank buys foreign exchange, thereby increasing R and B. Conversely, to finance a deficit in the current account, the central bank sells foreign exchange, thereby decreasing R and B. The change in R over a period equals the net balance on official reserves account which, in turn, equals the net balance on current account (ignoring sign). That is to say, $dR = B_r = -B_c$.

How can these monetary effects change real domestic absorption and thus contribute to balance of payments adjustment? Let us first take up the case of a balance of payments surplus.

A current-account surplus that raises expenditure via the foreign trade multiplier adds to the cash balances of domestic residents. At first, these higher cash balances are needed to support the higher level of real expenditure in the economy caused by the foreign trade multiplier. But after the multiplier effect on expenditure (income) has come to an end, any remaining surplus will continue to increase cash balances relative to money expenditures. Eventually the cash balances held by domestic residents will exceed their transactions demand for money, and then they will invest excess cash in securities to obtain income.[10] This purchase of securities will drive up their prices and thus lower the rate of interest. The lower interest rate, in turn, will induce businesses to increase the planned level of their investments, thus injecting new real expenditure into the economy. The resulting new income will increase imports through the marginal propensity to import (MPM). Income generated by monetary effects will continue to rise until the balance of payments surplus is completely eliminated. Only then will the supply of money stop rising and the monetary effects come to an end.

In similar fashion, the net monetary effects that continue after incomplete adjustment via the foreign trade multiplier to a current account deficit will lower cash balances below the level that domestic residents want to maintain relative to their money expenditures. To restore that level, they will sell securities, thereby lowering security prices and pushing up the interest rate. In turn, the higher interest rate will induce businesses to reduce their planned investment expenditures. The resulting drop in income will lower imports through the marginal

---

[10]Because we are assuming zero international capital mobility, excess cash is invested only in *domestic* securities. Also, we continue to assume that consumption depends only on real income.

propensity to import until the balance of payments deficit is completely eliminated. Only then will the net monetary effects become zero.

How will the burden of adjustment be shared by the foreign trade multiplier and monetary effects? To eliminate a disequilibrium caused by an autonomous change in exports, the induced change in imports must equal that autonomous change.[11] Thus, the change in real expenditure (income) required for full adjustment is the change that makes $dM = dX$. Since the change in imports is $MPM(dY)$, we have the following equation for the change in income required for full adjustment:

$$(21)\ dY\ =\ dM(1/MPM)\ =\ dX(1/MPM).$$

Now we know that the change in income (dY) that will result from the foreign trade multiplier is

$$(22)\ dY'\ =\ dX\left(\frac{1}{MPM\ +\ MPS}\right).$$

Thus, the change in income via monetary effects that is necessary to achieve full adjustment is $dY\ -\ dY'\ =\ dY''$. Algebraically,

$$(23)\ dY''\ =\ dX\left(\frac{1}{MPM}\right)\ -\ dX\left(\frac{1}{MPM\ +\ MPS}\right).$$

This reduces to

$$(24)\ dY''\ =\ dX\left(\frac{MPS/MPM}{MPM\ +\ MPS}\right).$$

Thus, the necessary change in income via monetary effects is the autonomous change in exports multiplied by the ratio of the marginal propensity to save to the marginal propensity to import divided by the sum of the two propensities.

If $MPM > MPS$, then the foreign trade multiplier will assume the larger share of the adjustment burden, and conversely.[12] If $MPM = MPS$, then the foreign trade multiplier and the monetary effects will each account for one half the adjustment. To illustrate the adjustment, let us assume that $MPM = 0.2$ and $MPS = 0.2$. Then the multiplier is 2.5. If there is an autonomous drop in exports of $100, the foreign trade multiplier will decrease income by $250. Hence, imports

---

[11]For simplicity, we are assuming the absence of any foreign repercussion effect.
[12]If $MPM > MPS$, then

$$\left(\frac{1}{MPM\ +\ MPS}\right)\ >\ \frac{MPS}{MPM}\left(\frac{1}{MPM\ +\ MPS}\right).$$

will fall by $50 [.2 ($250)], leaving a continuing deficit in the balance of payments of $50. Full adjustment will require a further decrease in income of $250 via the monetary effects that are defined by equation (24).[13]

Equilibrating Changes in Domestic Absorption Through Price Effects

Until now we have assumed fixed prices to concentrate our attention on payments adjustment through *changes in real expenditure (income)* via the foreign trade multiplier and monetary effects. We now relax this assumption to allow for some price flexibility.

In the extreme case, when prices are fully flexible (perfectly competitive markets for goods and factors), the economy is at full employment, and exchange rates are stable, a country would adjust to a balance of payments disequilibrium *solely* through price changes, with no accompanying changes in real expenditure.

It is unlikely that the fixed prices of the income theory of adjustment or the flexible prices of the classical theory of adjustment would ever exist in the actual world.[14] The relative importance of income (through both the multiplier and monetary effects) and price adjustments in a particular instance, therefore, will depend on the degree of flexibility in prices and the degree of unemployment and excess capacity in deficit and surplus countries. In periods of massive unemployment, the income-adjustment model provides a more satisfactory explanation of the actual adjustment process; in periods of full employment and inflation, the classical model gains in relevance. In both situations, however, income and price changes interact to bring about adjustment to payments disequilibrium.

Switching Real Expenditure: Tradables and Nontradables   Price effects help to eliminate a balance of payments *deficit* on current account by switching real domestic expenditure away from tradable goods and services to nontradable goods and services so as to reduce domestic absorption. Conversely, adjustment to a *surplus* involves switching real domestic expenditure away from nontradables to tradables, thereby increasing domestic absorption.

Tradable goods and services consist of exportables and importables. *Exportables* are goods and services actually exported by a country plus their close substitutes produced and consumed at home. *Importables* are goods and services actually imported by a country plus their close substitutes (import-competing goods and

---

13

$$dY'' = dX \left(\frac{MPS/MPM}{MPM + MPS} \right)$$

$$= \$100 \left(\frac{0.2/0.2}{0.2 + 0.2} \right) = \$250.$$

[14]The classical theory of adjustment is described in the following section.

services) produced and consumed at home. *Nontradables* are goods and services both produced and consumed at home. Nontradables are *not* close substitutes for tradables and, in fact, consist mostly of services.

The *domestic* supply of exportables (S_x) equals the sum of the *domestic* demand for exportables (D_x) and actual exports (X), or

$$(25)\ S_x\ =\ D_x\ +\ X.$$

Hence, exports equal the *excess domestic supply* of exportables, or

$$(26)\ X\ =\ S_x\ -\ D_x.$$

The *domestic* demand for importables (D_m) equals the sum of the domestic supply of import-competing goods and services (S_m) and actual imports (M), or

$$(27)\ D_m\ =\ S_m\ +\ M.$$

Hence actual imports equal the *excess domestic demand* for importables, or

$$(28)\ M\ =\ D_m\ -\ S_m.$$

Finally, the *domestic* demand for nontradables (D_n) equals their domestic supply (S_n), or

$$(29)\ D_n\ =\ S_n.$$

We can now derive the following equation for the net balance on current account:

$$(30)\ X\ -\ M\ =\ (S_x\ -\ D_x)\ -\ (D_m\ -\ S_m).$$

When exports equal imports, then the excess supply of exportables is equal to the excess demand for importables. When $S_x\ -\ D_x\ >\ D_m\ -\ S_m$, then the current account is in surplus, and conversely. We can restate equation (30) as follows:

$$(31)\ X\ -\ M\ =\ (S_x\ +\ S_m)\ -\ (D_x\ +\ D_m).$$

It follows that a deficit on current account can be reduced by increasing the domestic supply of tradables and, at the same time, decreasing the domestic demand for tradables. Assuming that real GNP is constant for the period in question, an increase in the supply of tradables can only occur through a transfer of resources from the production of nontradables. These supply and demand switches reduce domestic absorption, which, as we know, is necessary to reduce a deficit on current account.[15]

---

[15]The total output (Y) of the economy is the sum of the domestic production of tradables and nontradables, or $S_x\ +\ S_m\ +\ S_n$. Substituting and transposing equation (18), we get the following statement for domestic absorption: $A\ =\ S_n\ +\ D_x\ +\ D_m$. To reduce absorption, therefore, the domestic supply of nontradables and the domestic demand for tradables must decrease, as stated in the text.

Let us now trace through the price adjustments that will accompany, in small or large degree, real-income adjustment to a current-account deficit. The deficit will induce a decline in money income and spending in the deficit country, which will in turn cause a general decline in prices (although the decline may be spotty and somewhat retarded because of market imperfections). The effect of this general price deflation is to encourage exports and discourage imports: With fixed exchange rates, domestic goods and services become cheaper to foreign buyers, while foreign goods and services become more expensive to domestic buyers.

In addition to the general decline in prices, a current-account deficit will also cause the prices of tradables to rise relative to the prices of nontradables. The prices of exportables are held up by export demand; the prices of importables are determined in the world market; but the prices of nontradables are subject entirely to the deficit-induced decline in domestic spending. These relative price changes switch domestic demand away from tradables to nontradables and switch domestic supply away from nontradables to tradables.

These general and relative price changes will continue until the deficit is eliminated. At that point, there are no further effects on domestic expenditure, and the demand-supply shifts between tradables and nontradables come to an end.

Simultaneously, surplus countries will experience an expansion of money income and spending. This will cause a general rise in the price level (unless there is widespread unemployment and excess capacity) and shifts in relative prices that will encourage imports and discourage exports.

In effect, general price adjustment works through a shift in the *terms of trade* (the exchange ratio between two countries' exports and imports) of both the surplus and deficit countries. The surplus country enjoys an improvement in its terms of trade as its import prices fall and its export prices rise, while the deficit country suffers a deterioration in its terms of trade as its import prices rise and its export prices fall.

Price Elasticities   The degree to which the terms of trade must shift in favor of the surplus country to remove disequilibrium in the balance of payments will depend upon the price elasticities of supply and demand of both exports and imports.[16] When elasticities are high, a relatively small change in prices calls forth

---

[16]The price elasticity of demand is this ratio: percentage change in amount of demanded/percentage change in price. (Algebraically speaking, this ratio carries a minus sign, since the amount demanded and price are inversely related. However, following common practice, we shall ignore the sign.) When demand elasticity is one, then the percentage changes in amount demanded and price are the same, and the amount spent on the product in question stays the same after a price change. When elasticity is greater than one, total expenditure increases (decreases) with a fall (rise) in price. When elasticity lies between one and zero, then total expenditure decreases with a fall in price. When elasticity is zero, then total expenditure decreases the same percentage as the fall in price. Similarly, the quantity supplied changes the same percentage, a greater percentage, or a lesser percentage than the percentage change in price, depending on whether the elasticity of supply is one, greater than one, or less than one. It should be noted that the amount supplied and price are positively related: They change in the same direction. The use of percentages to define elasticities is a crude simplification and an approximation only. Mathematically, elasticity is $(dQ/dP)(P/Q)$, where dQ/dP is the rate of change (derivative) of Q with respect to P.

a relatively large response in the quantity of exports and imports, and the terms of trade need change little to effect adjustment. With low elasticities, however, relatively large price changes will stimulate only relatively small changes in the quantity of exports and imports, and there must be a wide swing in the terms of trade to effect adjustment.

The price elasticities of export and import supply will depend upon the mobility of productive factors within both the surplus and deficit countries. When labor and other resources are induced by only slight variations in relative wages and other factor prices to move from one industry to another, the supply of goods is *elastic:* The amount supplied can be adjusted to changing demand with relatively small changes in the supply price. When, however, productive resources are relatively immobile, supply elasticities are low and any adjustment to balance of payments disequilibrium is impeded. In a many-nation world, the price elasticity of import supply for a specific country will also depend on whether foreign suppliers have alternative markets. When the domestic demand for import goods is small compared to the world demand, it will have little or no influence over import prices, and import supply will appear highly elastic to the domestic country.

The price elasticities of export and import demand will depend on the nature of the export and import goods and the availability of domestic substitutes. Thus, the demand for luxury imports is more elastic than the demand for essential imports and, other things being equal, the demand for imports with close domestic substitutes is more elastic than the demand for imports with only distant or no domestic substitutes. In a many-nation world, substitutes for imports from a given country may also be found in imports from other countries. Hence, the demand facing the exports of a country is apt to be less elastic than otherwise when that country supplies most of the world market — that is, when foreign customers have little opportunity to obtain similar goods elsewhere. Conversely, export demand is likely to be more elastic than otherwise when the exporting country supplies only a small portion of the world market.

Obstacles to Price Adjustment   Fundamentally, international adjustment requires shifts in the level and composition of both supply and demand in the surplus and deficit countries. Equilibrating changes in prices are effective in bringing about such shifts when the price elasticities of supply and demand are high. Anything that lowers price elasticities, therefore, hinders price adjustment to balance of payments disequilibrium.

Price adjustment is undoubtedly less effective today than before World War I. As observed in Chapter 4, few contemporary markets are close to pure competition. Markets for agricultural staples, such as wheat, cotton, and coffee, are usually subject to price stabilization by government agencies, whereas the majority of markets for manufactured goods have monopolistic elements that allow the seller (or, in the case of monopsony, the buyer) some control over price. Administered pricing by large-scale oligopolistic industries and the enforcement of wage floors by powerful labor unions are common examples of price inflexibility in today's economies. Of special importance is the international cartel that outlaws price competition and fixes the pattern of foreign trade in its products. The widespread abandonment of price competition in favor of nonprice competition in quality, style, and services; government schemes to control production and marketing; and the innumerable devices used by governments to insulate the domestic economy from foreign economic influences have all diminished the importance of price adjustment.

Despite these developments, however, equilibrating changes in prices remain a significant instrument of international adjustment. The prices of many raw materials and foodstuffs in international trade remain uncontrolled and respond quickly to changes in supply and demand. Moreover, all international goods show plenty of price flexibility upward, as inflation has demonstrated time and again. We can conclude that price adjustment, when permitted, is an effective ally of income adjustment and that both are required in a fixed exchange rate system if exchange depreciation or suppressed disequilibrium is to be avoided.

The Classical Theory of Adjustment

The first coherent theory of international payments adjustment was devised by David Hume (1711–1776), British philosopher and economist extraordinary.[17] In opposition to the dominant mercantilist thought of the age, Hume asserted the impossibility of maintaining a chronic "favorable balance of trade" to acquire gold and silver (specie) from foreign countries.

The Price-Specie Flow Mechanism   Hume's theory of adjustment has come down as the *price-specie flow mechanism.* It asserts that an inflow of specie resulting from an excess of exports over imports increases the nation's money supply and that the increased money supply, in turn, increases domestic prices. These higher prices then curtail exports. At the same time there occurs a fall in the money supply and prices in the foreign countries experiencing an outflow of specie. This decline in prices stimulates the exports of those countries, including exports to the country receiving specie. In this way international specie movements eliminate any disequilibrium in the balance of payments: Higher prices in the surplus country cause its exports to fall and its imports to rise, while lower prices in the deficit country or countries cause exports to rise and imports to fall. International specie movements are, therefore, symptoms of payments disequilibrium, and they will continue until the money supplies and price levels of the trading nations achieve an equality between the exports and imports of each country.

Critique of the Price-Specie Flow Mechanism   Succeeding generations of classical and neoclassical economists (Ricardo, Mill, Marshall, Taussig, and others) added refinements to Hume's price-specie flow mechanism but made no basic changes in it. The theory was modified to take account of service or "invisible"

---

[17]This theory appeared in Hume's *Political Discourses,* published in Edinburgh in 1752.

items in the balance of payments; short-term capital movements; the fractional reserve system of banking; and the differential price behavior of export goods, import-competing goods, and nontraded goods. However, the underlying assumptions of the theory—the quantity theory of money and the effect of price changes on exports and imports—were not effectively challenged until the Keynesian revolution in economic thinking of the late 1930s.

The price-specie flow mechanism is open to all criticisms that have been leveled against the quantity theory of money. This theory assumes that a change in the quantity of money will bring about a proportionate change in the price level. A change in the quantity of money will, however, affect prices only if it affects spending, and the change in spending induced by a given change in the money supply may be relatively large or small depending on its velocity of turnover. Moreover, the influence of a given change in spending on prices will vary according to the general level of employment and output and the degree of price flexibility in the economy. Hence, there is no direct or certain price response to a change in the money supply, and under conditions of excess productive capacity and unemployment or of imperfect competition, there may be little or no response.

The main criticism of the price-specie flow mechanism, however, is its emphasis upon price adjustment to the neglect of real income adjustment. Classical and neoclassical economists understood that a deficit country underwent a decline in its purchasing power relative to a surplus country and that this decline, along with the adverse shift in its terms of trade, brought about adjustment by raising its exports and lowering its imports. But this purchasing-power or nominal income effect was viewed as the incidental accompaniment of price changes, which were the main instruments of international adjustment. There was no conception of an *autonomous* change in income unrelated to a change in prices. In the classical world of full employment and purely competitive markets, this oversight was inevitable, for under such conditions a change in spending will cause a change in prices and there are no real income effects.

Writing in 1928, Taussig, the foremost neoclassical economist in America, felt that something was missing in the price-specie flow explanation of international payments adjustment, although he was unable to lay his finger on it. In speaking of adjustment to a movement of long-term investment capital, he wrote as follows:

> What is puzzling is the rapidity, almost simultaneity, of the commodity movements. The presumable intermediate state of gold flow and price changes is hard to discern, and certainly extremely short.[18]

At another point he remarked,

> It must be confessed that here we have phenomena not fully understood. In part our information is insufficient; in part our understanding of other connected topics is also inadequate.[19]

Income and cash-balance adjustment are the keys to this puzzle.

---

[18]Frank W. Taussig, *International Trade* (New York: Macmillan, 1928), p. 260.
[19]Ibid., p. 239.

ADJUSTMENT
WITH INTERNATIONAL
CAPITAL MOBILITY

In our treatment of current-account adjustment through changes in income and the price level, we have assumed until now that capital does not move between the domestic country and the rest of the world. But if in fact capital does so move, then a net balance on current account may be financed by an opposing net balance on capital account. When $B_c = -B_k$, then $B_c + B_k = 0$ and $B_r = 0$. Capital flows, therefore, can restore *temporary* equilibrium in the balance of payments.

International Differentials in Short-term Interest Rates

How is the adjustment process affected by international capital mobility? Let us trace adjustment to a current-account deficit. We continue to assume fixed exchange rates and, to simplify the presentation, we also assume fixed price levels. Under these assumptions, a decrease in the money stock induced by the current-account deficit is also a decrease in the *real* money stock of the deficit country.[20] This decrease will cause a *rise* in the short-term interest rate as residents of the deficit country try to restore their cash balances by selling financial assets (securities), thereby lowering the price of those assets. The higher interest rate in the deficit country creates a real interest-rate differential between it and the rest of the world that attracts an inflow of capital, thereby creating a surplus on capital account in the balance of payments. (Earlier, when we assumed *no* international capital mobility, a change in the interest rate in the deficit country could only induce a change in domestic investment.)

Not all forms of international capital transfer are sensitive to interest-rate differentials. Short-term capital (securities with a maturity of one year or less) moves quickly in response to differentials, as indicated in our presentation of interest arbitrage in Chapter 13. At the extreme of *perfect* international capital mobility, even a very small change in the rate of interest would cause massive short-term capital flows. In contrast, flows of direct foreign investment capital are *insensitive* to interest-rate differentials, responding instead to profit-rate differentials and other factors.[21] Flows of other long-term investment capital (evidenced by debt securities with distant maturities) respond to long-term interest rates that reflect the marginal productivity of real capital used to create wealth. Hence, under conditions of fixed exchange rates and price levels, international flows of direct foreign investment and other long-term capital are *autonomous,* remaining unaffected by changes in short-term interest rates.

Because only short-term capital flows are sensitive to the *liquidity effect* of changes in the money stock, the adjustment process in the capital account achieves

---

[20]The real money stock is the *nominal* money stock adjusted for the rate of inflation. In our example, the rate of inflation is zero because the price level is fixed. Hence, the real money stock equals the nominal money stock.

[21]For a review of the theory of foreign direct investment, see Chapter 23.

only *temporary* equilibrium, which eliminates the need for net official reserve transfers but does not eliminate the source of *persistent* disequilibrium in the current account. The inflow of short-term capital comes to a halt when a rising interest rate equilibrates the demand and supply of money. This money market equilibrium will be coupled with equilibrium in the short-term capital market that (assuming perfect international mobility) occurs when there is no longer a differential in real interest rates between the deficit country and the rest of the world. Expressed algebraically,

$$(32)\ i - i^* = 0,$$

where i is the domestic interest rate and i^* is the foreign interest rate. (Keep in mind we are still assuming fixed exchange rates and price levels.)

If the current account deficit continues after equilibrium is established in the money and short-term capital markets, then the money stock will decrease further, causing a new round of adjustment in the capital account. Only when the combined net balance on the current account and the *autonomous* capital account (direct foreign investment and other long-term capital) equals zero will the balance of payments reach stable, intermediate-run equilibrium.

The International Portfolio Effect

The riskiness of a combination or portfolio of securities (as measured by the variability of returns) is less than the riskiness of the individual securities making up the portfolio when the riskiness of each security is in some degree independent of the riskiness of the others. Through diversification of their security holdings, therefore, investors can achieve lower risk at any given rate of return. The theory of *international* diversification predicts that capital will flow among countries even when interest rates are identical if the riskiness of financial assets is *not* perfectly correlated across countries. By diversifying internationally, investors seek to maximize their risk-adjusted returns. It follows that a higher interest rate in a deficit country will immediately cause an inflow of short-term capital as investors throughout the world rearrange their holdings of securities so as to achieve new optimal portfolios. Once these optimal portfolios are established, capital movements will cease.

If financial assets denominated in different currencies also differ in riskiness, then investors will demand a *risk premium* for a higher risk. Hence, the equilibrium condition of equation (32) becomes

$$(33)\ i - i^* = v,$$

where v represents a risk premium expressed at an annual rate.

The short-term capital market is in equilibrium only when any remaining interest-rate differential is fully matched by a risk premium. When investors judge short-term financial assets in the deficit country to have the *same* degree of riskiness as in the rest of the world, then $v = 0$ and equation (33) reduces to equation (32). The international portfolio effect remains positive, however, even when the riskiness (variability of returns over time) of financial assets denominated in different currencies is the same—as long as that riskiness is not perfectly correlated over time.

The International Expectations Effect

As discussed earlier, an increase (decrease) in a country's money stock causes a decrease (increase) in real short-term interest rates through the *liquidity effect*. But if we drop our assumption of fixed price levels, then a change in the money stock can alter expectations about future price levels. This *expectations effect* opposes the liquidity effect. When investors expect inflation, they demand an *inflation premium* in the form of a higher interest rate, and conversely. Suppose that an increase in the money stock of a *surplus* country triggers expectations of a higher price level over the next year. Then, the liquidity effect, which acts to *lower* the interest rate, would be offset in some degree by the expectations effect, which acts to *raise* the interest rate. The latter might overwhelm the former so that the interest rate would rise in the surplus country rather than fall! The expectations effect, therefore, weakens the adjustment process: Movement toward equilibrium in the short-term capital market will require larger changes in the money stock and interest rate than would otherwise be the case.

When the price level is free to move, the equilibrium condition expressed by equation (33) becomes

$$(34) \quad i - i^* = v + \frac{E(P/P^*) - P/P^*}{P/P^*},$$

where $E(P/P^*)$ is the expected ratio between the domestic price level (P) and the foreign price level (P^*) over next year. Any remaining interest-rate differential equals the sum of the risk premium and the inflation premium (which is the expected annual change in the domestic price level relative to the foreign price level). The inflation premium is positive when the domestic country is expected to experience more inflation than the rest of the world. As we know from the purchasing-power parity doctrine, an international inflation differential eventually leads to an equal adjustment in the exchange rate. Hence,

$$\frac{E(P/P^*) - P/P^*}{P/P^*}$$

is equivalent to $[E(S) - S]/S$, which in turn is equivalent to $(F^* - S)/S$. Hence, equation (34) is equivalent over the longer run to the interest-parity equation (7) in Chapter 13, except for the risk premium, which is ignored in that equation.[22]

---

[22]Equation (7): $i_{US} - i_{UK} = (F^* - S)/S$.

Part II   International Payments

BALANCE OF PAYMENTS POLICY:
INTERNAL AND EXTERNAL BALANCE

In Chapter 1 we spoke about the diversity and conflict of goals in foreign economic policy. Both internal and external goal conflicts make it impossible for a nation to fully achieve a particular goal without sacrificing in some degree the achievement of other goals. In no area of foreign economic policy is goal conflict more apparent than in balance of payments policy in a fixed system. It comes about when the goal of *internal balance* (full employment with price stability) is perceived by policymakers as incompatible with the goal of *external balance* (balance of payments equilibrium), or conversely. Here we call attention to this potential conflict, whose impact on the international monetary system is described in Chapters 18 and 19.

Inflation and recession are the two internal imbalances and deficits and surpluses are the two external imbalances. Conflict arises when the two goals become inconsistent so that an effort to achieve one goal renders more difficult or impossible the achievement of the other. Figure 15-5 depicts in summary fashion the incidence of conflict.

The three conditions relating to internal balance (inflation, recession, and balance) combine with the three conditions relating to external balance (deficit, surplus, and balance) to make a nine-cell matrix whose entries indicate when the policy requirements for internal and external balance (contraction, expansion, or none) are consistent or in conflict. With generally inflationary situations in many countries, a common policy conflict is located in cell 1.2 — inflation at home

Figure 15-5

DOMESTIC ECONOMY ↓	BALANCE OF PAYMENTS → POLICY REQUIREMENT →	Deficit / Contraction	Surplus / Expansion	Balance / None
Inflation	Contraction	No conflict 1.1	Conflict 1.2	Conflict 1.3
Recession	Expansion	Conflict 2.1	No conflict 2.2	Conflict 2.3
Balance	None	Conflict 3.1	Conflict 3.2	No conflict 3.3

The Internal Conflict of Goals: Internal and External Balance.   Goal conflict in balance of payments policy occurs when the goals of *internal balance* (high employment with price stability) and *external balance* (balance of payments equilibrium) become incompatible. Failure to resolve goal conflict with monetary and fiscal policies leads to an alteration in the exchange rate or to exchange control.

combined with a persistent balance of payments surplus. In the late 1950s, the early 1960s, the 1970s, and again in the early 1990s, the United States faced the policy conflict located in cell 2.1—unemployment at home with a persistent balance of payments deficit. This second policy dilemma is felt more keenly by governments than the first one, because both unemployment and a balance of payments deficit are widely viewed as more serious than inflation or a balance of payments surplus (which is often viewed as highly desirable).

When governments fail to resolve the conflict between internal and external balance in a fixed-rate system with monetary and fiscal policies, they resort to other policy instruments, most notably an alteration in the exchange rate or the suppression of balance of payments disequilibrium with exchange controls. Flexible exchange rates and exchange control are the subjects of the next two chapters.

THE MONETARY APPROACH
TO THE BALANCE OF PAYMENTS

In the 1970s, a period marked by high rates of inflation in the world economy, some economists advanced a new approach to the balance of payments. Although new, the monetary approach can trace its lineage back to Hume's price-specie flow mechanism, which explained payments adjustment in terms of changes in the money supply. But unlike Hume, today's monetarists do not rely on price effects to achieve equilibrium.

According to the monetary approach, the balance of payments is a monetary phenomenon determined by the demand and supply of money stocks. Whereas the conventional approach explains current-account adjustment by changes and switches in real expenditure, the monetary approach explains adjustment of the entire balance of payments by changes in the demand and supply of money.

In conventional balance of payments analysis, transfers in the current and long-term capital accounts are regarded as *autonomous* and transfers in the short-term capital and official reserves accounts are regarded as *compensatory,* passively financing the net balance on autonomous transactions. The monetary approach takes the opposite view: The official reserve transfers are *active* (or autonomous), responding to changes in the demand and supply of money, whereas all other transfers in the balance of payments are *passive,* adjusting to the official reserves balance. In sum, the conventional approach looks at the balance of payments from the "top down" and the monetary approach looks at the balance of payments from the "bottom up."

Money Demand and Supply

The monetary approach postulates that the cause of an international payments imbalance (defined as a nonzero balance on the official reserves account) is an excess demand or excess supply of money. An excess demand causes a payments surplus; an excess supply, a payments deficit. Balance of payments equilibrium is achieved only when the demand and supply of money are equal.

For monetarists, the demand for money (currency and demand deposits held by the public) is a stable function of a few macroeconomic variables:

$$(35)\ M^d\ =\ L(P, Y, i),$$

which states that the demand for nominal money balances (M^d) is a function (L) of the price level (P), real income (Y), and the interest rate (i).[23] An increase in P or Y causes an increase in M^d, because individuals and business firms need to finance a larger value of transactions—the so-called *transactions* demand for money. However, an increase in i causes a decrease in the demand for money, because it raises the opportunity cost of holding money—the so-called *hoarding* (or precautionary/speculative) demand for money.

The supply of money (M^s) equals the money multiplier (m) times the monetary base (B):

$$(36)\ M^s\ =\ mB\ =\ m(D\ +\ R).^{24}$$

Adjustment to Balance of Payments Disequilibrium

Equilibrium in the money market is an equality between the stock demand and stock supply of money:

$$(37)\ M^d\ =\ m(D\ +\ R).$$

Assuming a constant money multiplier, monetarists consider changes in the demand for money (ΔM^d) and in the domestic element of the monetary base (ΔD) as the initiating forces causing disequilibrium in the money market. Under fixed exchange rates, equilibrium is restored by changes in the international element of the reserve base (ΔR) that are expressed in the balance of payments as a net balance on official reserves account. We have, therefore,

$$(38)\ m\Delta R\ =\ \Delta M^d\ -\ m\Delta D,$$

which, in turn, equals the net balance on official reserves account.

The monetary approach explains payments adjustment in a fixed-rate system in the following way. Changes in the demand for money can occur quickly with changes in the price level, real income, or the interest rate. Also, changes in the domestic supply of money ($m\Delta D$) can occur quickly through the open-market operations of the central bank. Such changes create either an excess stock demand for money ($\Delta M^d > m\Delta D$) or an excess stock supply of money ($\Delta M^d < m\Delta D$). (Keep

---

[23]This and the following equations are taken from Mordechai E. Kreinin and Lawrence H. Officer, *The Monetary Approach to the Balance of Payments,* Princeton Studies in International Finance, no. 43 (Princeton, N.J.: Princeton University Press, 1978), pp. 5 ff.

[24]See equations (19) and (20).

in mind that ΔM^d and ΔD are *not* flows over time but rather one-time changes in stocks.)

Any divergence between the demand and supply of money (disequilibrium in the money market) is eliminated by a one-time change in the international element of the monetary base (ΔR). Suppose $\Delta M^d > m\Delta D$, then the excess demand for money by individuals and business firms will cause them to build up their money stocks by cutting their purchases of foreign goods and services, by liquidating their foreign investments, or by borrowing from foreigners. These actions will draw foreign funds into the country and thereby create a balance of payments surplus. Monetarists are not concerned with where the official reserves account is offset in the remainder of the balance of payments. The important point is that the surplus will disappear as soon as the stock supply of money satisfies the stock demand for money balances.

Conversely, when $\Delta M^d < m\Delta D$, then individuals and firms act to reduce their money stocks by increasing their purchases of foreign goods and services, investing abroad, or lending to foreigners, thereby creating a balance of payments deficit. The deficit, therefore, is regarded as a spillover of the excess supply of money, and it will cease to exist when stock equilibrium is restored in the money market.

To monetarists, a *continuing* disequilibrium in the balance of payments is possible only when the monetary authorities offset ("sterilize") a change in international reserves with an opposing change in domestic credit created (or destroyed) by the central bank. The self-correcting mechanism takes time to work, but the monetarists have said little about the dynamic adjustment process of the economy necessary to reestablish equilibrium (or the time required). The monetary approach, therefore, deals only with the final, equilibrium position of the balance of payments and money market.

Some Closing Remarks About the Monetary Approach

The monetary approach to the balance of payments is posed as a direct challenge to the conventional approach. In sum, the monetarists argue that the demand for money balances relative to supply determines the level of real expenditure on goods and services, rejecting the conventional view that real expenditure decisions are the initiating forces and money is only a passive agent to finance expenditures.

The monetary approach has made an undeniable contribution to the theory of balance of payments adjustment by emphasizing the role of money, which has often been ignored in the real-expenditure approach. In so doing, it has made the theory more relevant to the inflationary conditions of recent years. For example, the monetary approach demonstrates a direct connection between excessive domestic credit creation and a balance of payments deficit.

But the monetarists would appear to have gone too far in singling out monetary variables as the *only* explanation of balance of payments disequilibria and in claiming that their approach is a *complete* substitute for the conventional approach. After all, *real* factors, such as economic growth, technological innovation, and shifts in international competitiveness (comparative advantage) can generate structural payments imbalances, and these real factors are not related to money variables in any systematic way.

By ignoring the *composition* of the balance of payments, the monetarists have also gone too far. For example, a current-account deficit has very different implications for the domestic economy (and calls for different policy responses) than a deficit on long- or short-term capital accounts. Also, the monetarists fail to distinguish between financing a current-account deficit through inflows of long-term capital and through inflows of short-term capital. As discussed in Chapter 14, short-term capital flows can provide only short-run adjustment.

Are the two approaches irreconcilable? Almost certainly, no. Economists have always recognized that there are two sides to transactions in goods, services, and securities, and in a monetary system (in contrast to a barter system), one of those sides is money. Hence, when the conventional approach looks at the real side of transactions and the monetary approach looks at the money side of transactions, they are looking at the same phenomenon. It remains true, therefore, that an imbalance on current account can be eliminated only by changing domestic absorption or (less likely) by changing physical output. We can justifiably view the monetary approach, therefore, as an additional explanation of the absorption process of adjustment.

GENERAL EQUILIBRIUM IN AN OPEN ECONOMY

Equilibrium in the balance of payments requires simultaneous equilibrium in a country's goods and money markets. We offer here in summary form a graphical depiction of general equilibrium in these three markets.

The IS Schedule

The IS schedule shown in Figure 15-6 indicates equilibrium in the goods market: It contains all combinations of interest rates and levels of national income that equate aggregate demand and supply. Alternatively, it contains all combinations of interest rates and national income that equate income injections and leakages: $I + X = S + M$. This equilibrium condition may be rewritten as follows: $I + (X - M) = S$.

The IS curve slopes downward from left to right because equilibrium at higher levels of national income requires lower interest rates to induce higher domestic investment. At any point below and to the left of the IS schedule, $I + (X - M) > S$; at any point above and to the right of the IS schedule, $I + (X - M) < S$.

The IS schedule assumes that government spending (G) and X and M are fixed. Autonomous changes in any of these variables will cause a shift to the left or right of the entire IS schedule.

The LM Schedule

The LM schedule shown in Figure 15-7 depicts equilibrium in the money market. At each point on the schedule, the quantity of money demanded (L) equals the

Figure 15-6

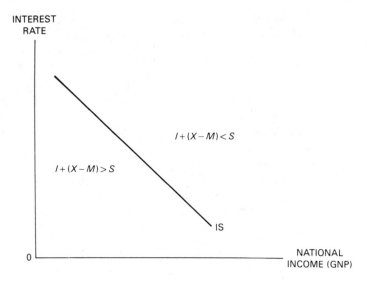

The IS Schedule. The IS schedule shows all the combinations of interest rates and levels of national income that equate aggregate demand and supply. The schedule slopes downward from left to right because equilibrium at higher levels of national income requires lower interest rates to induce higher domestic investment.

money stock (M). The LM schedule slopes upward from left to right because as national income rises more money is demanded to support the greater volume of transactions in goods and services. With the money stock fixed, individuals try to obtain additional cash balances by selling securities, which lowers their price and thus pushes up the interest rate. Higher interest rates reduce the amount of money demanded by raising the opportunity cost of holding money, namely, the interest that could otherwise be earned from securities. Interest rates will raise until the money demanded once again equals the money stock. Hence, national income and interest rates must move in the same direction to maintain equilibrium in the money market.

Above and to the left of the LM schedule, the amount of money demanded is less than the money stock ($L < M$); below and to the right of the schedule, the amount of money demanded is greater than the money stock ($L > M$). Because the LM schedule assumes a fixed money stock, any increase in the money stock shifts the entire schedule to the right, and conversely.

The BOP Schedule

The BOP schedule presented in Figure 15-8 is the locus of all combinations of interest rates and national income levels at which the balance of payments is in equilibrium: $B_c + B_k = 0$. The foreign exchange market is also in equilibrium

Figure 15-7

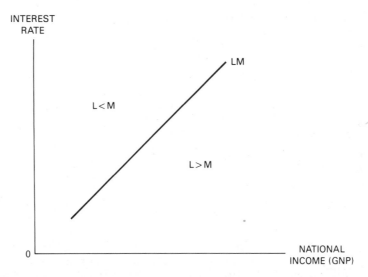

The LM Schedule. The LM schedule depicts equilibrium in the money market: At each point on the schedule, the quantity of money demanded (L) equals the money stock (M). The schedule slopes upward from left to right because the quantity of ymoney demanded rises with a rise in national income and a new equilibrium can be achieved with a fixed stock of money only through a rise in the interest rate, which increases the opportunity cost of holding money.

(with a zero net flow of foreign exchange into or out of the domestic country), because $B_r = 0$. The BOP curve slopes upward from left to right because at a fixed exchange rate higher levels of national income induce more imports (via the marginal propensity to import), which worsens the current account balance, and higher interest rates induce inflows of short-term capital, which improves the capital account balance.

At the lower end of the BOP schedule, low income levels create a surplus in the current account that is fully offset by a deficit on capital account induced by low interest rates: $B_c = -B_k$. At the higher end of the schedule, high income levels cause a deficit in the current account that is fully offset by a surplus on capital account resulting from capital inflows induced by high interest rates: $-B_c = B_k$. It follows that above and to the left of the BOP schedule the balance of payments is in *surplus disequilibrium* (BOP > 0), whereas below and to the right of the schedule the balance of payments is in *deficit disequilibrium* (BOP < 0).

The BOP schedule assumes fixed values for foreign income (Y_f), the relation between foreign and domestic prices as determined by both local-currency price levels and the foreign exchange rate (P/SP^*), the relation between domestic foreign profit rates (r/r^*), and the expected exchange rate [$E(S)$]. Changes in any of these variables will cause the entire schedule to shift to the left or right.

Figure 15-8

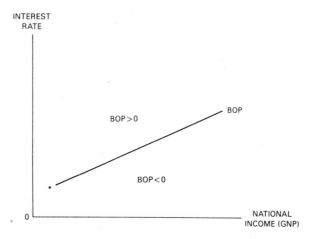

The BOP Schedule.   The BOP schedule shows all combinations of interest rates and national income levels at which the balance of payments is in equilibrium, with a zero net balance on official reserves account. (At the same time, the foreign exchange market is in equilibrium.) The schedule slopes upward from left to right because at a fixed exchange rate a rise in national income worsens the *current-account* balance, putting the balance of payments in deficit disequilibrium. A new equilibrium can be achieved only through a rise in the interest rate, which improves the *capital-account* balance.

Figure 15-9

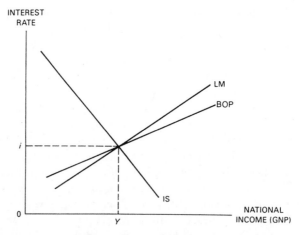

General Equilibrium in an Open Economy: The Intersection of the IS, LM, and BOP Schedules.   General equilibrium in an open economy is determined at the point of intersection of the IS, LM, and BOP schedules. Simultaneous equilibrium in the goods, money, and balance of payments (foreign exchange) markets occurs only at that point. General equilibrium occurs at an interest rate *i* and a national income level *Y*.

Determination of General Equilibrium

General equilibrium in an open economy is determined graphically at the point of intersection of the IS, LM, and BOP schedules, indicating simultaneous equilibrium in the goods market, the money market, and the balance of payments (foreign exchange) market. In Figure 15-9, general equilibrium is determined at the rate of interest i and the national income level Y.

To conclude, the general equilibrium model demonstrates that balance of payments equilibrium requires simultaneous equilibrium in the goods and money markets. If one or both of these markets is in disequilibrium, then continuing changes in the interest rate and the level of national income will prevent the balance of payments from reaching equilibrium. But it is important to keep in mind that this model concerns only general equilibrium over the short run. As pointed out earlier, *intermediate* and *long-run* equilibrium in the balance of payments cannot be sustained with net flows of short-term capital.

SUMMARY

1. The balance on current account depends on domestic real income, foreign real income, and the relative prices of domestic and foreign goods and services as determined by local-currency price levels and the rate of foreign exchange. The balance on capital account is dependent on the domestic interest rate relative to the foreign interest rate, the domestic profit rate relative to the foreign profit rate, and the expected exchange rate.

2. The gross national product (GNP) is the market value of all final goods and services produced by the national economy over the year; it is equal to the gross national income (GNI). $S - I_d = X - M$ is a basic equation relating GNI (or GNP) to foreign trade.

3. National income is in equilibrium when intended expenditures equal income leakages, that is, $I_d + X = S + M$. The foreign trade multiplier equals the reciprocal of the marginal propensities to save and import, or

$$\frac{dY}{dX} = \frac{1}{MPS + MPM}.$$

4. For our exposition of international payments adjustment in this and the next two chapters, we define balance of payments equilibrium as a zero net balance on official reserves account.

5. When the exchange rate is fixed and there is zero international mobility of capital, disequilibrium in the balance of payments appears as a surplus or deficit in the current account. Algebraically, $B_c = Y - A$. Adjustment to a *persistent deficit* in the current account requires the elimination of excess domestic absorption (reduction in real expenditure).

6. When prices are fixed, equilibrating changes in domestic absorption occur through changes in real income via the foreign trade multiplier and monetary effects.
7. When there is a savings leakage, adjustment to a payments disequilibrium via the foreign trade multiplier is incomplete, even after allowance is made for the foreign repercussion effect.
8. When prices are fixed and there is a savings leakage that causes incomplete adjustment via the foreign trade multiplier, the remaining adjustment depends on the monetary effects on real income.
9. When prices are flexible, adjustment to a balance of payments disequilibrium also occurs through changes in prices that *switch* expenditures among exportables, importables, and nontradables. Price elasticities determine the effectiveness of price adjustment.
10. The classical theory of adjustment in a fixed exchange rate system (the gold standard) is the price-specie flow mechanism, which stresses the equilibrating role of price changes but ignores changes in real income and cash balances.
11. When capital is internationally mobile, then adjustment can occur in the capital account, because interest-rate differentials stimulate short-term capital flows between deficit and surplus countries. In addition to current interest-rate differentials, portfolio and expectations effects influence the international movement of capital.
12. Balance of payments policy in a fixed-rate system is often constrained by a conflict between internal and external balance.
13. The monetary approach explains a balance of payments deficit as an excess supply of money stocks and a surplus as an excess demand for money stocks.
14. Equilibrium in the balance of payments requires simultaneous equilibrium in a country's goods and money markets.

QUESTIONS AND APPLICATIONS

1. Explain the following equation: $B_r = -(B_c + B_k)$.
2. (a) What are the components of gross national product and gross national income?
   (b) Why is GNP equal to GNI?
   (c) Derive the equation $I_d + X = S + M$ from the GNP and GNI equations.
3. (a) What are the equilibrium conditions of national income?
   (b) Derive both the domestic and foreign trade multipliers from the equation $I_d + X = S + M$.
4. Explain the following equation: $B_c = Y - A$.
5. (a) How does the foreign trade multiplier explain income adjustment to a current-account disequilibrium in the balance of payments?
   (b) When is income adjustment complete? Incomplete?

6. Explain the following equations: (1) $M = mB$ and (2) $B = D + R$.
7. (a) How do the monetary effects of a current-account deficit bring about equilibrating changes in domestic absorption?
   (b) Assuming fixed prices, what change in income via monetary effects is *necessary* to restore equilibrium after an autonomous change in exports?
8. (a) What determines the effectiveness of a shift in the terms of trade in bringing about adjustment in the balance of payments?
   (b) What are the obstacles to price adjustment?
9. Under what conditions is income adjustment likely to dominate adjustment to a net balance on current account when exchange rates are fixed? Under what conditions is price adjustment likely to dominate?
10. (a) Describe the classical theory of adjustment.
    (b) What is the main criticism of this theory?
11. (a) How does adjustment to a current-account surplus occur when there is international capital mobility?
    (b) Why does the adjustment process in the capital account restore only *temporary* equilibrium in the balance of payments?
12. Explain the following equation:

$$i - i^* = v + \frac{E(P/P^*) - P/P^*}{P/P^*} .$$

13. Explain why there is a policy conflict in cell 3.1 of Figure 15-5. Why is there no conflict in cell 2.2 of Figure 15-5?
14. (a) According to the monetary approach, what is the process of adjustment to a balance of payments *deficit?*
    (b) How does this explanation differ from the conventional explanation?
15. Using the monetary approach, trace the effect on the balance of payments of an increase in the interest rate.
16. (a) Define the IS, LM, and BOP schedules.
    (b) Why is equilibrium in an open economy determined by the intersection of these three schedules?

SELECTED READINGS

See the list of readings at the end of Chapter 16.

chapter 16

INTERNATIONAL PAYMENTS ADJUSTMENT IN A VARIABLE-RATE SYSTEM

In a variable-rate system, adjustment to a payments disequilibrium occurs through an alteration in the rate of exchange. There are many possible kinds of variable-rate systems. At one extreme is the system of *flexible rates* (or purely floating), in which the rate of exchange is determined solely by supply and demand in the foreign exchange market with no attempt by government authorities to limit or moderate fluctuations.[1] At the other extreme is the *adjustable-peg* system, in which rates are fixed by government authorities in the short run and then adjusted once-and-for-all to a new stabilized level.[2] In between these two extremes there are any number of variant systems that have more rate variability than the adjustable-peg system but less variability than the flexible-rate system. We shall call these middle variants *managed floating-rate systems,* because the rate of exchange may vary beyond the limits imposed on fixed rates but is constrained within wider limits decided by monetary authorities. These limits may or may not change in line with market trends. In all of these systems, however, the rate of exchange continuously or occasionally varies and, in so doing, influences the balance of payments. This variability distinguishes them from a fixed-rate system.

After some introductory remarks, we shall take up, in turn, three different explanations of how exchange rates effect adjustment in the balance of payments: the elasticities approach, the absorption approach, and the monetary approach. In the final section, we shall look at general equilibrium in an open economy with flexible exchange rates.

---

[1]The determination of flexible (freely fluctuating) rates was examined in Chapter 12.

[2]Since the adjustable-peg system involves both fixed and variable exchange rates, it may be considered a variant of either the fixed-rate or variable-rate system. In Chapter 12, we described briefly the adjustable-peg system in our treatment of active stabilization. In this chapter our interest lies in the variable-rate element of the adjustable-peg system.

VARIABLE RATES: INTRODUCTION

It is important to distinguish between the continuous exchange rate adjustments in a flexible-rate system and occasional exchange rate adjustments in an adjustable-peg system. In both instances, exchange rates are used as an instrument for international payments adjustment, but the circumstances and theoretical arguments are different.

Adjustment Through Flexible Rates

Flexible (purely floating) exchange rates bring about an instantaneous adjustment of the amounts of foreign exchange demanded and supplied in the market. Over time, movements in the exchange rate achieve a succession of short-run equilibria that clear the market. Short-run disequilibrium does not appear in the balance of payments because there are no official reserve transfers to finance a deficit or surplus on the combined current and capital accounts. Algebraically, $B_r = 0$, and consequently $B_c + B_k = 0$.

Adjustment Through Occasional Devaluation or Revaluation

What we have just said applies to a system in which exchange rates are *always* free to respond to changes in supply and demand. It does not apply to a payments system in which exchange rates are *occasionally* varied from one stable level to another stable level. In this system, short-run adjustment occurs as under a fixed-rate system, while a planned and limited variation in the exchange rate effects a longer-run adjustment. Under these conditions a variation in the exchange rate will have income and price effects, since it is closing a gap in the balance of payments—a gap that could not exist in a flexible-rate system due to the lack of any compensatory financing. In this adjustable-peg system, adjustment to persistent disequilibrium takes the form of *exchange devaluation* or *exchange revaluation*—a limited decrease or limited increase in the domestic price of foreign money.

Deciding on the Equilibrium Rate With purely floating rates, the equilibrium rate is determined by the impersonal tug and pull of supply and demand. When, however, a nation that normally stabilizes its exchange rate decides to devalue to correct a deficit disequilibrium, the equilibrium rate of exchange is not known in advance, even though successful devaluation requires depreciation to the equilibrium rate. The exchange rate will otherwise continue to be too low, with domestic currency overvalued, or too high, with domestic currency undervalued.

One solution to this difficulty is to free the exchange rate to find its equilibrium rate in the market and then, when equilibrium is restored, to stabilize the rate at the new level. When exchange controls are in existence, either the illegal black market rate or the official "free" rate is sometimes taken to be the equilibrium rate of exchange.[3] Although these rates will usually reveal whether the domestic currency is overvalued or not, they are apt to be unreliable indicators of the equilibrium rate, since the forces of supply and demand acting to determine them often diverge widely from the forces that would exist in a purely floating-rate market.

To estimate the equilibrium rate of exchange, the monetary authorities may apply the *purchasing-power parity doctrine,* a subject treated in Chapter 13. Or they can evaluate the many factors that determine the rate of exchange, including the likely responses of those same factors to a variation in the exchange rate itself.

We learned in Chapter 12 that there is a mutual interdependence between the exchange rate and the balance of payments. When changes in the balance of payments place it in deficit disequilibrium, exchange devaluation is successful only if it reverses those changes or induces new compensating changes. An intelligent policy of devaluation, therefore, depends upon a careful appraisal of the sources of disequilibrium in the balance of payments and of the conditions (supply and demand elasticities, income, price, and monetary effects, and so on) that will determine the efficacy of a given devaluation in overcoming a specific disequilibrium. Even then, the dynamic nature of economic phenomena makes impossible any certain discovery of the equilibrium rate of exchange and any firm guarantee of successful devaluation. Deciding upon the equilibrium rate of exchange, then, is partly economic analysis and partly hunch.

Competitive Depreciation and Overvaluation   Depreciation stimulates exports and simultaneously deters imports. During the 1930s many countries took advantage of this fact by depreciating their currencies beyond the equilibrium rate of exchange. Their purpose was to create a surplus in the balance of payments and thereby foster greater income and employment in the domestic economy. Since this policy required a deficit disequilibrium in the balance of payments of other countries that also faced depression, it amounted to exporting unemployment. For this reason, the attempt to depreciate more than other countries — *competitive depreciation* — has received the uncomplimentary designation of "beggar-my-neighbor policy." Competitive depreciation is not likely to be effective in the long run, since other countries will also depreciate in retaliation. The result for a country is usually a disruption of its foreign trade rather than any improvement in the domestic economy.

Competitive depreciation developed out of the rigors of international depression. In our own day, widespread inflation has led to *overvaluation* of the exchange rate through exchange control, especially in developing countries. Depreciation is feared for its inflationary impact on the domestic economy, and it is avoided even when overvaluation of the currency perpetuates a deficit in the balance of payments.

---

[3]See Chapter 17 for a description of the official "free" market with fluctuating exchange rates in multiple-rate systems of exchange control.

Arguments for Variable Exchange Rates

In Chapter 12 we noted some of the arguments for fixed exchange rates. We now turn the tables and present the argument for flexible exchange rates.

There is a strong theoretical case for flexible exchange rates. In highly simplified terms, it assumes this form. In a fixed-rate system, adjustment to a deficit is carried out by deflationary movements in domestic income and prices that contract real expenditure. All goes well if wages and prices are flexible downward, for then employment and output are sustained at their previous levels. But if wages and prices are *inflexible* downward, then a contraction in real expenditure involves a fall in employment and output. There is abundant evidence indicating that the second course of events is the more likely to happen in contemporary national economies. Unions set floors under wages that are supplemented by official minimum wage policies. Oligopolistic industries set administered prices that do not respond to a decline in effective demand. The decline is met instead by a cutback in production. Under these conditions, current-account adjustment in a fixed-rate system will cause a downward spiral in employment and output. On the other hand, governments are pledged to the maintenance of a high-employment economy. Hence, they will act to frustrate any deflation induced by a deficit in the balance of payments by making use of expansionary fiscal and monetary policies that sustain the level of real expenditure necessary for high employment.

Given contemporary government policies with respect to employment and economic stability, then, current-account adjustment in a fixed-rate system is not likely to be effective. There are two ways out of this impasse: (1) impose controls on trade and payments, or (2) devalue the rate of exchange. Controls, however, are incompatible with a market economy, and they provoke hostility and retaliation in foreign countries. We are left, then, with depreciation or, more comprehensively, variable exchange rates as the only mode of payments adjustment that is compatible both with domestic high-employment policies and the principle of free competition in world markets. Free exchange rates respond to disequilibrating forces and achieve a continuous adjustment in the balance of payments. This gives governments the freedom to follow domestic policies of high employment and growth without worrying about payments deficits.

The theoretical argument for an adjustable-peg system is less strong, because adjustment in the exchange rate is apt to be delayed and the degree of rate variation is determined by a government under circumstances that make the choice of the correct equilibrium rate a very difficult one. Delay in devaluing the exchange rate to correct a deficit is likely to occur in an adjustable-peg system for several reasons. The government often demonstrates a "fixed-rate complex" and makes the mistake of identifying its prestige with the maintenance of the existing rate. Or the government may repeatedly postpone rate adjustment in the renewed expectation that the disequilibrium will prove to be "temporary" after all. Or, having decided in principle on devaluation, the government may take a long time to reach a political consensus on the appropriate amount of devaluation. All this adds up to the fact that there is a strong probability that a government will put off devaluation until it is forced to act because its official reserves are running out and its international credit is exhausted. By that time it is clear to everyone that devaluation (or controls) is imminent, and this will stimulate massive capital flight and destabilizing speculation that will intensify the drain on reserves. In these circumstances a government may feel compelled to undertake a very large devaluation to put a stop to speculative activity. In the end the government devalues the exchange rate and blames the speculators for its troubles.[4]

To sum up, in an adjustable-peg system, devaluation to eliminate a deficit is likely to come too late and be too big. Moreover, the deficit country must do most of the adjusting because there is little or no incentive for surplus countries to revalue their exchange rates. These drawbacks do not appear in a flexible-rate system shared by several countries: The exchange rates of all countries respond quickly to disturbances, and these prompt adjustments sustain a continuing equilibrium in international payments.

Despite the strong theoretical case for flexible exchange rates, governments and central bankers traditionally have been hostile to a flexible-rate system. Unfortunately the reputation of flexible rates has suffered from bad company in the past. Until the 1970s, flexible rates involving several major currencies had appeared two times during this century, but only by default: in the period following World War I, before European countries returned to the gold standard in the middle 1920s, and in the 1930s, when global depression forced the wholesale abandonment of the international gold standard. Grave instability in international trade and payments characterized both periods. Not surprisingly, speculation and capital flight were rife; exchange rates behaved erratically, making sharp and sudden movements. Thus, flexible exchange rates came to be associated with instability, speculation, and generally bad times.

This presumed association rests on a confusion of symptom and cause. When underlying conditions are very unstable, then exchange rates will mirror this instability. The same conditions will provoke capital flight and unwanted shifts in domestic income and prices in a fixed-rate system. When underlying conditions are only moderately unstable, then fluctuations in exchange rates will also be moderate.

There is also a widespread belief that fluctuating rates introduce exchange risks that hinder international trade and investment. The rebuttal is that forward exchange markets quickly develop in a flexible-rate system, making possible the hedging of foreign exchange risks. Moreover, there are trading risks of another kind in a fixed-rate system caused by income and price adjustments, to say nothing of trade restrictions stemming from a failure, or rather frustration, of the market adjustment process.

Despite the traditional hostility to flexible rates, the collapse of the Bretton Woods (adjustable-peg) international monetary system at the end of 1971 was followed by the contemporary *managed* floating-rate system, which is characterized

---

[4]The disruption of the Exchange Rate Mechanism of the European Monetary System in September 1992 (described in Chapter 10) offers a recent example of delayed adjustment in an adjustable-peg system.

by a far higher degree of exchange rate flexibility. When we examine the operation of the contemporary system in Chapter 19, we shall encounter once again the debate on fixed versus flexible exchange rates.

ELASTICITIES APPROACH
TO EXCHANGE RATE ADJUSTMENT

The primary effect of an alteration in the exchange rate on the balance of payments depends on the sensitivity of the demand and supply of foreign exchange to the new price of foreign exchange. When demand and supply are very sensitive, or highly elastic, then a small movement in the exchange rate can be very effective in removing a disequilibrium. But when elasticities are low, a large movement in the exchange rate is necessary to restore or maintain equilibrium. Let us examine the role of elasticities for a depreciation (devaluation) of the exchange rate.

This effect of exchange depreciation is shown in Figures 16-1 and 16-2. We take as our example a depreciation of the French franc as viewed in the French foreign exchange market, where the foreign exchange rate is the franc price of dollars. Suppose the French government decides to devalue the franc to remove a deficit in the balance of payments. If, as in Figure 16-1, the elasticities of the demand and supply of foreign exchange (dollars) are high, then the devaluation

Figure 16-1

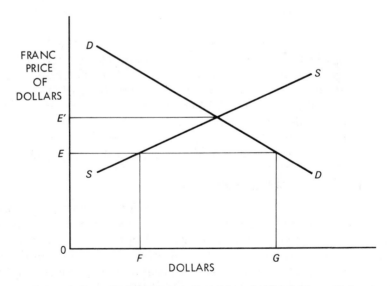

Exchange Depreciation with High Demand and Supply Elasticities.   Before devaluation, the exchange rate is 0–E and the deficit is F–G. Because the elasticities of demand and supply are high, only a small devaluation from 0–E to 0–E' is needed to eliminate the deficit.

Figure 16-2

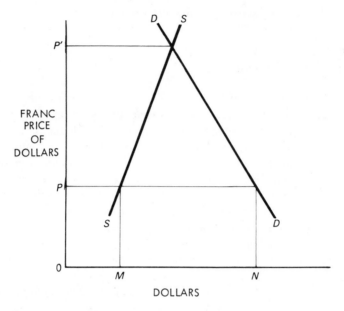

Exchange Depreciation with Low Demand and Supply Elasticities. Before devaluation, the exchange rate is 0-P and the deficit is M-N (equal to F-G in Figure 16-1). Because the elasticities of demand and supply are low, a much larger devaluation from 0-P to 0-P' is needed to wipe out the deficit than was needed in Figure 16-1.

will be very effective and will not need to be great. In Figure 16-1, the exchange rate before depreciation is 0-E and the deficit is F-G. This deficit is closed by a relatively slight devaluation from 0-E to 0-E'. On the other hand, when elasticities are low, a considerable devaluation is needed to bring about adjustment. In Figure 16-2, the exchange rate before devaluation is 0-P and the deficit is M-N. To wipe out this deficit, the franc must be devalued from 0-P to 0-P'. Note that despite the fact that the deficit in Figure 16-2 is equal to the deficit in Figure 16-1, the exchange depreciation is much larger in the former case.

The Elasticity of Foreign Exchange Supply

The elasticity of the supply of foreign exchange is mainly dependent on the elasticity of foreign demand for domestic exports. Upon devaluation, the foreign exchange price of exports falls. When foreign demand is elastic, this decline in export prices will stimulate an expansion in the quantity exported that will be sufficient to enlarge total receipts of foreign exchange despite the lower prices in terms of foreign exchange. On the other hand, when the elasticity of foreign demand is low, total receipts of foreign exchange may even be smaller after devaluation. In this unlikely event, devaluation will widen the deficit insofar as the supply of foreign exchange is concerned.

We can distinguish three cases that demonstrate the influence of the elasticity of export demand on the elasticity of foreign exchange supply. (When *domestic* export prices do not change after devaluation because export *supply* is perfectly elastic, then the export demand elasticity *fully* determines the supply elasticity of foreign exchange.)

1. When the elasticity of export demand has a value of *one* (unit elastic), then a 10 percent devaluation causes a 10 percent increase in the quantity of exports.[5] Hence, the receipts of foreign exchange are the same before and after devaluation. The elasticity of *foreign exchange supply,* therefore, is zero—foreign exchange receipts do not respond to a variation in the exchange rate—and the effect of devaluation on the supply of foreign exchange is neutral.

2. When the elasticity of export demand is greater than one, then a 10 percent devaluation causes an increase of more than 10 percent in the quantity of exports. Receipts of foreign exchange, therefore, increase and help close the deficit in the balance of payments. In this case the elasticity of foreign exchange supply is greater than zero—foreign exchange receipts respond positively to a higher domestic price of foreign money.

3. When the elasticity of export demand is zero, then a 10 percent devaluation causes no increase in the quantity of exports and foreign exchange receipts fall by 10 percent. When the elasticity lies between zero and one, then the percentage increase in the quantity of exports is less than the percentage devaluation. In both instances devaluation causes a fall in the receipts of foreign exchange that worsens the deficit. Thus, the elasticity of foreign exchange supply is less than zero, or negative—on a graph the supply schedule slopes *downward* from left to right, unlike the normal supply schedule.

In summary, when the elasticity of export demand is greater than one (elastic), then devaluation causes an increase in the receipts of foreign exchange and helps close the deficit. When, on the other hand, the elasticity of export demand is less than one, or zero (inelastic), then devaluation lowers foreign exchange receipts and, insofar as the supply of foreign exchange is concerned, worsens the deficit. The elasticities of foreign exchange supply that we have discussed are shown in Figure 16-3, where e_s is the appropriate elasticity.

Under what conditions is export demand likely to be elastic? We can make only a few pertinent comments relating to the composition of exports, the relative importance of a nation's exports in world trade, and the presence of trade restrictions.[6] Generally speaking, the demand for manufactured products (especially "luxury-type" products) is more elastic than the demand for agricultural and other primary products, which is often inelastic. Many primary products satisfy basic needs and their consumption is relatively insensitive to price changes. The same is

---

[5] For a definition of price elasticities, see footnote 17 in Chapter 15.
[6] See also Chapter 15.

Figure 16-3

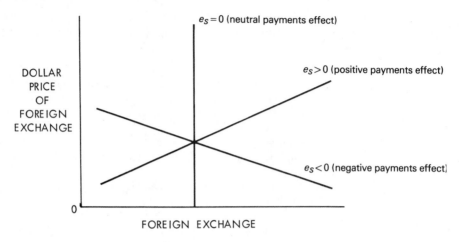

Elasticities of Foreign Exchange Supply. When the elasticity of *export demand* has a value of *one,* then the elasticity of *foreign exchange supply* is *zero,* as shown by the vertical supply schedule. When the elasticity of *export demand* is *more than one,* the elasticity of *foreign exchange supply* is *greater than zero,* as shown by the schedule sloping upward from left to right. When the elasticity of *export demand* lies *between zero and one,* then the elasticity of *foreign exchange supply* is *less than zero* (negative), as shown by the schedule sloping downward from left to right.

true of intermediate goods that are purchased as raw materials, semimanufactures, and the like, when these goods contribute only a small share to total costs of production. Such products face a derived demand that tends to be inelastic.

The demand facing a product with many substitutes is likely to be more elastic than a product with few or no substitutes. That is why a country whose exports are only a small fraction of world exports experiences a more elastic demand (other things equal) than a country like the United States, whose exports bulk large in world trade. There is a greater opportunity for substitution between a country's exports and the competitive exports of other countries when the country holds only a modest share of foreign markets.

One final point: Tariffs, quotas, cartels, and other restrictions that inhibit the free play of competition in world markets act to lower effective demand elasticities by limiting the role of price in buying decisions.

The Elasticity of Foreign Exchange Demand

The elasticity of the demand for foreign exchange depends mainly on the elasticity of the domestic demand for imports. When higher import prices in domestic currency cause a fall in the quantity of imports, then devaluation improves the balance of payments on the demand side. At the very worst, when the quantity of imports stays the same, devaluation has no effect on the balance of payments as far as foreign exchange demand is concerned.

When the *foreign exchange* price of imports does not change after devaluation (import *supply* is perfectly elastic), then the elasticity of import demand *fully* determines the demand elasticity of foreign exchange. We can distinguish two important cases:

1. When the import demand elasticity is *greater than zero,* then the quantity of imports decreases after devaluation and (given an unchanged foreign exchange price of imports) the quantity of foreign exchange demanded therefore also decreases. The higher the import elasticity, the greater the decline in the amount of foreign exchange in demand. In this case devaluation improves the balance of payments on the demand side.
2. When the elasticity of import demand is *zero,* then the quantity of imports does not change after devaluation and the *foreign exchange* value of imports is constant. In this case the demand for foreign exchange is perfectly inelastic (zero), and devaluation neither helps nor worsens the balance of payments on the demand side.

Figure 16-4 illustrates these two cases.

Figure 16-4

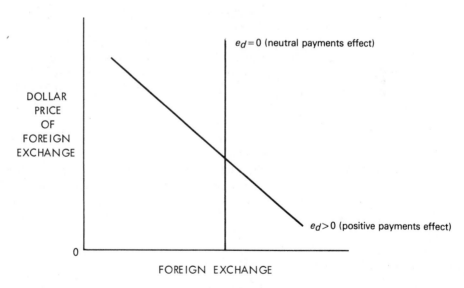

Elasticities of Foreign Exchange Demand. When the elasticity of *import demand* is *greater than zero* (disregarding sign), then the elasticity of *foreign exchange demand* is also *greater than zero,* as shown by the demand schedule sloping downward from left to right. When the elasticity of *import demand* is *zero,* then the elasticity of *foreign exchange demand* is also *zero,* as shown by the vertical demand schedule.

The elasticity of import demand will tend to be high when the composition of imports is heavily weighted with luxury-type consumer goods (such as automobiles and household equipment) and expensive capital goods (such as heavy machinery and transport equipment). Conversely, elasticity will tend to be low when most imports are raw materials, foodstuffs, and semimanufactures. Another factor is the degree of substitutability between import goods and domestic goods. When domestic substitutes are widely available at reasonable prices, then higher domestic prices for imports after depreciation will cause a switch to domestic sources of supply, thereby increasing the elasticity of import demand.

Elasticities of Export and Import Supply

In our analysis of the demand elasticities of export and imports, we assumed that export and import *supply* elasticities were infinite or perfectly elastic. Thus, the domestic price of exports and the foreign exchange price of imports did not respond to depreciation. This is an unrealistic assumption, and we must now take into account less-than-perfect elasticities of export and import supply.

The significance of supply elasticities may be understood if we make another unrealistic assumption, namely, perfectly inelastic (zero) export and import supplies. In that event devaluation has *no effect* on the balance of payments *regardless* of the demand elasticities. An export supply of zero elasticity means that the quantity of exports cannot be increased. Hence, a devaluation of 10 percent is promptly offset by a 10 percent *increase* in the domestic export price as foreign buyers bid for the same quantity of export goods. Thus, the *foreign exchange* price of exports remains the same, and there is no change in foreign exchange receipts. Similarly, an import supply of zero elasticity means that a 10 percent devaluation is promptly matched by a 10 percent cut in the foreign exchange price of imports as foreign suppliers strive to maintain sales in the devaluing country. Thus, the domestic price of imports stays the same after devaluation, and there is no effect on foreign exchange expenditures.

It would be tedious to recount the many combinations of demand and supply elasticities and their effects on the balance of payments. Suffice it to say that when demand elasticities are high, the effects of devaluation are most beneficial if supply elasticities are also high. Then lower foreign exchange prices can expand exports and higher domestic import prices can contract imports. On the other hand, when demand elasticities are low, devaluation is most beneficial (or least harmful) if supply elasticities are low, for then foreign exchange export prices fall less and domestic import prices rise less than otherwise.

When Is Exchange Depreciation Successful?

If the foreign exchange market is in stable equilibrium, then devaluation lessens or eliminates a deficit in the balance of payments, as shown in Figures 16-1 and 16-2. But if the foreign exchange market is in *unstable* equilibrium, then devaluation hurts rather than helps the balance of payments in deficit. Figure 16-5 shows that

Figure 16-5

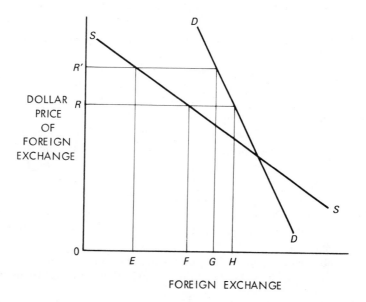

Unstable Equilibrium in the Foreign Exchange Market. The schedule of foreign exchange supply (*S–S*) has a negative slope and cuts the schedule of foreign exchange demand (*D–D*) from below. Hence, the sum of the supply and demand elasticities is negative, putting the market in *unstable* disequilibrium. A devaluation from 0–*R* to 0–*R′* *widens* the balance of payments deficit from *F–H* to *E–G* instead of helping to close it. *Stable* disequilibrium requires that the sum of the *export* and *import* demand elasticities be greater than one (Marshall-Lerner condition). In that event, devaluation reduces a payments deficit and revaluation reduces a payments surplus.

unstable equilibrium occurs when the supply curve has a negative slope and cuts the demand schedule from *below*.[7]

At the exchange rate 0–*R*, foreign exchange demanded exceeds foreign exchange supplied by *F–H*. In the attempt to wipe out this deficit, the exchange rate is devalued to 0–*R′*. But this only makes matters worse as the deficit increases in size to *E–G*.

What, then, is the requirement for stable equilibrium in terms of export and import elasticities? Devaluation *always* helps to lessen a deficit in the balance of payments if the sum of the *absolute* values of export and import demand elasticities is greater than one, that is, $e_x + e_m > 1$. This is known as the Marshall-Lerner condition, and we may demonstrate its validity by citing two extreme examples. (The Marshall-Lerner condition assumes perfect elasticities of export and import

---

[7]In that event the sum of the supply and demand elasticities is negative. See Figures 16-3 and 16-4.

supply.) Suppose the elasticity of export demand is zero and there is a 10 percent devaluation. Then foreign exchange receipts drop 10 percent; but if import demand elasticity is greater than one, foreign exchange expenditures decrease by more than 10 percent. Thus, the deficit becomes less. Again, suppose the elasticity of import demand is zero. Then foreign exchange expenditures do not change after depreciation; but if export demand elasticity is greater than one, a 10 percent devaluation leads to a greater than 10 percent increase in the quantity of exports and consequently an increase in foreign exchange receipts. Once again, the balance of payments improves.

When we introduce supply elasticities, we discover that the Marshall-Lerner condition is sufficient but not necessary. Even if the sum of demand elasticities is somewhat below one, the balance of payments can improve, provided that the supply elasticities are small enough.

What is the probability that the demand elasticities of exports and imports of a country will add to a sum greater than one? Today most economists believe the probability is high.[8] As far as elasticities are concerned, therefore, a country can be reasonably confident that devaluation will improve its balance of payments. But elasticities are not the whole story. Devaluation also induces income and general price effects in the devaluing country that may nullify or compromise its effectiveness in remedying a payments deficit.

The Effect of Devaluation on the Terms of Trade

The effect of devaluation on the commodity terms of trade (the exchange ratio between two countries' exports and imports) is uncertain. It may seem obvious that devaluation *worsens* the terms of trade of the devaluing country: The foreign exchange price of its exports drops while the foreign exchange price of its imports usually stays the same. But this price behavior is by no means certain. We can see why if we understand that an exchange devaluation of, say, 10 percent is equivalent to a *duty* of 10 percent on all imports and a *subsidy* of 10 percent on all exports. An import tariff tends to *improve* the terms of trade by lowering the foreign exchange price of imports, but an export subsidy tends to *worsen* the terms of trade by lowering the foreign exchange price of exports. The net effect of *both* duty and subsidy on the terms of trade depends on the interaction of the supply and demand elasticities of both imports and exports.

---

[8]The IMF World Trade Model, covering a period through 1977, indicates a range of -0.5 to -1.0 for total imports and 0.5 to 1.5 for total exports. See Michael C. Deppler and Duncan Ripley, "The World Trade Model: Merchandise Trade Flows," *IMF Staff Papers,* March 1978, pp. 147–206. The IMF also estimates that the sum of long-run export and import elasticities for trade in manufactured goods is greater than one for all industrial countries except Switzerland, where it is 0.98. See Jacques R. Artus and Malcolm D. Knight, *Issues in the Assessment of the Exchange Rates of Industrial Countries,* Occasional Paper no. 29 (Washington, D.C.: International Monetary Fund, July 1984), Table 4. The median estimates of six independent econometric models of the long-run price elasticity for U.S. imports is 1.1 and for U.S. exports, 0.8. See Paul R. Krugman, "Has the Adjustment Process Worked?" in C. Fred Bergsten, ed., *International Adjustment Financing* (Washington, D.C.: Institute for International Economics, 1991), Table 2, p. 283.

The general rule states that a devaluation worsens the terms of trade if the product of the two supply elasticities is *greater* than the product of the two demand elasticities, or $(e_{sx})(e_{sm}) > (e_{dx})(e_{dm})$. Otherwise the terms of trade remain unchanged (the two products are equal) or improve (the product of the two supply elasticities is *less* than the product of the two demand elasticities).

ABSORPTION APPROACH
TO EXCHANGE RATE ADJUSTMENT

In Chapter 15 we stated that adjustment to a current-account deficit under full-employment conditions calls for a reduction in real domestic expenditure regardless of whether adjustment occurs in a fixed-rate or a variable-rate system. Recall equation (18) in Chapter 15:

$$(1)\ B_c\ =\ Y\ -\ A.$$

When B_c is in deficit (negative), then A exceeds Y. Adjustment to a deficit demands, therefore, either (1) an increase in real Y, or (2) a decrease in real A. Since physical output cannot be expanded in the short run with full employment, adjustment to a deficit in such a situation requires a reduction in the real absorption of goods and services (an *increase* in real saving) to allow for higher exports and lower imports.

As we have seen in Chapter 15, income adjustment to a deficit on current account involves a decline in the level of aggregate demand. Thus, income adjustment via the foreign trade multiplier and monetary effects or via restrictive monetary and fiscal policies (the domestic multiplier) is *expenditure reducing*. In contrast, exchange depreciation is *expenditure switching:* It shifts domestic expenditures away from tradables by raising their prices in domestic currency relative to the price of nontradables.[9]

Expenditure Switching and Real Output

Where does the real output come from to support this expenditure switch? With full employment it can come only from a reduction in domestic absorption (A) that releases resources for the production of exportables and importables. Recall the statement for domestic absorption in terms of tradables and nontradables:

$$(2)\ A\ =\ S_n\ +\ D_x\ +\ D_m.\text{[10]}$$

Hence, lower absorption requires a decrease in the domestic *supply* of nontradables accompanied by a decrease in the domestic *demand* for tradables. Putting the

---

[9]The role of relative price changes in effecting switches in real expenditure was explored in Chapter 15.
[10]See footnote 15 in Chapter 15.

matter somewhat differently, devaluation with full employment can be successful only if it is accompanied by an increase in domestic saving that matches the improvement in the balance of payments.[11] Can devaluation be expected to bring about the requisite increase in saving? The general answer is negative, because depreciation exerts no direct influence on saving.

In failing to increase saving and thereby decrease domestic absorption, devaluation with full employment will cause an inflationary rise in the price level that will partly or fully offset its initial effects on exports and imports. When devaluation raises exports and lowers imports, it injects income into the domestic economy and starts a cumulative expansion of money income. This higher money income stimulates higher expenditures on domestic goods whose supply cannot be expanded under full employment. The consequence, therefore, is inflation. If this general price rise is of the same order as the devaluation (say 10 percent), then the initial effects of devaluation are completely vitiated and the payments deficit remains the same. Devaluation may also stimulate a general price rise on the cost side. Higher domestic prices paid for imports of raw materials, capital equipment, and the like, may impose an upward pressure on domestic costs of production and the price level. The higher prices of imported consumer goods may encourage labor unions to ask for higher wages—and in countries where the wages of most workers are linked to a consumer price index, higher wages inevitably result when there is a substantial dependence upon such imports. It should be noted, however, that cost-push inflation would not occur in the absence of new money created by the government to finance it.

Under full-employment conditions, therefore, the income and price effects of devaluation limit its effectiveness, and in some instances they may nullify it entirely. Exchange rate adjustment provides an initial impulse for a switch in a country's resources from domestic to external use, but it does not guarantee that such a switch will actually take place. Hence, expenditure-switching policies must be supported by expenditure-reducing policies. Unless the domestic government contracts real absorption through monetary, fiscal, and (possibly) wage-price policies, depreciation can only lead to inflation and a perpetuation of the balance of payments deficit.

Because of its price and income effects, devaluation is likely to be more effective in removing a payments deficit when the domestic economy has substantial unemployment and excess capacity. Then the rise in money income and expenditure provoked by the depreciation will cause an expansion of real gross national product (Y). As noted earlier, governments tried to utilize the "employment effect" of depreciation by overdepreciating their currencies in the 1930s. In this situation it may be possible to have one's cake and eat it too, that is, to achieve an improvement in the balance of payments and an increase in real domestic expenditure at the same time. But this does not necessarily happen, because some of the increase in real expenditure induces higher imports via the marginal

---

[11]Recall that $X - M = S - I_d$. Assuming that I_d is autonomous, then a change in $X - M$ requires an equal change in S in the same direction, or $d(X - M) = dS$.

propensity to import. Even under conditions of widespread unemployment and excess capacity, therefore, the effectiveness of devaluation may be constrained by its income effects, although these are unlikely to fully offset its elasticity effects.

In sum, devaluation under full-employment conditions can effect adjustment in the balance of payments only when it is accompanied by expenditure-reducing policies that contract real domestic absorption. In the absence of such policies, devaluation will simply cause inflation that will nullify its initial balance of payments effects. Successful devaluation demands, therefore, more than a manipulation of the exchange rate; it must be part of a broader policy of international adjustment.[12]

The Dynamic Path of Exchange Rate Adjustments: J-Curve, Pass-Through Effect, and Hysteresis

So far, in discussing the elasticity and absorption approaches to exchange rate adjustment, we have ignored the *time* it takes for full adjustment to occur. Changes in exchange rates do not effect an instantaneous adjustment of a current account deficit or surplus. The required change in domestic absorption may take more than two years, even when expenditure switching is supported by expenditure-reducing policies. Consequently, the initial impact of a *depreciation* (appreciation) is to *worsen* (improve) the current account. For some time after depreciation (devaluation), foreign exchange expenditures on imports fall only a little, while foreign exchange receipts may actually decline as the same export volume is sold at lower foreign currency prices. Eventually import and export volumes adjust to the new exchange rate, with a corresponding improvement in the current account. The time path of adjustment, therefore, is described by a *J-curve,* as depicted in Figure 16-6.

The delayed effects of a change in the exchange rate are traceable to two sources. First, a change in the exchange rate is transformed into changes in the *domestic currency* prices of imports (known as the "pass-through effect") only after some time. Full pass-through may be delayed indefinitely when *hysteresis* is present. Second, even when a change in the exchange rate is passed through to importables and exportables, domestic and foreign buyers may be slow to respond to the new prices. That is to say, short-run price elasticities can be much smaller than long-run elasticities. We offer here a brief explanation of pass-through effects and hysteresis to further our understanding of the J-curve phenomenon.

Pass-Through Effect   Pass-through is the degree to which import prices (expressed in the domestic currency) reflect movements in the exchange rate. The pass-through ratio, therefore, is the percentage change in domestic-currency im-

---

[12]We are speaking here of devaluation to overcome an actual deficit in the balance of payments, which implies an adjustable-peg or managed-float system. In a flexible-rate (purely floating) system such a deficit would not appear because of continuous equilibrating adjustments in the exchange rate. Hence, there would be no income and price-level effects. The latter result from the elimination of a deficit caused by compensatory financing and a prior stabilization of the exchange rate.

Figure 16-6

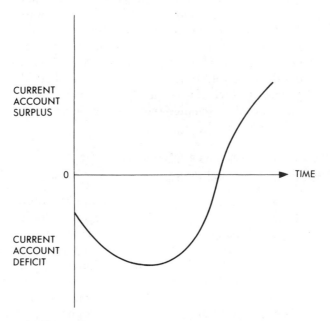

CURRENT ACCOUNT SURPLUS

0

TIME

CURRENT ACCOUNT DEFICIT

J-Curve: Delayed Effects of a Devaluation on Current Account. Because of the J-curve effect, a devaluation initially increases a deficit on current account rather than decreasing it. This happens because the *quantities* of exports and imports take time to respond to the new exchange rate. Hence, foreign exchange receipts decline and foreign exchange expenditures decline only a little. Eventually, when export and import volumes adjust progressively to the new exchange rate, the J-curve rises and devaluation improves the balance on current account.

port prices divided by the percentage change in the exchange rate. If, for example, a country's exchange rate depreciates 20 percent but domestic-currency import prices rise by only 10 percent, then the pass-through ratio is 0.5.

Low pass-through ratios are caused by the existence of imperfect competition in international trade: product differentiation, economies of scale, and oligopoly. Firms in oligopolistic markets may use price to keep or expand market share, rather than maximize short-run profits, in the belief that market share brings economies of scale that benefit the firm in the long run. Hence, faced with a dollar depreciation, foreign firms exporting to the United States may lower their own domestic-currency prices to keep the dollar prices of their products constant and thereby maintain market share. To do so, they must accept lower profit margins.[13]

---

[13]At the same time, U.S. exporting firms may *raise* their dollar prices to keep the foreign currency price constant in importing countries, because they are reluctant or slow to invest in new production or incur higher distribution and other export marketing costs. Instead, they prefer to enjoy the windfall gains from higher profit margins. This pass-through effect means that a dollar depreciation would not show up in the domestic currency prices of imports from the United States.

This behavior, known as "pricing to market," holds foreign currency prices constant despite volatile exchange rates. Japanese exporting firms in the general machinery industry during the 1980s exhibited this pricing strategy, as shown in Figure 16-7.

Figure 16-7 tracks the annual percentage changes in the domestic and export prices of Japanese firms. "Foreign currencies" denotes a currency basket weighted by the country destinations of Japanese manufactured exports. The stable *domestic* yen price contrasts sharply with variable export prices in yen and foreign currencies.[14] Observe that the movements in the yen export price and the foreign-

Figure 16-7

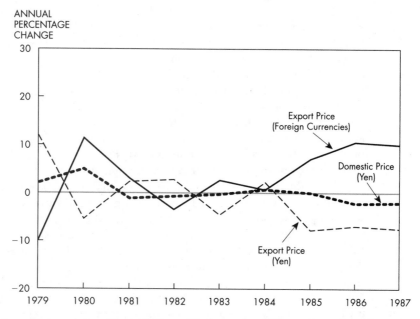

Source: Adapted from Kenichi Ohno, "Exchange Rate Fluctuations, Pass-Through, and Market Share," *IMF Staff Papers* (International Monetary Fund, June 1990), Figure 1, p. 296.

Pricing to Market: Changes in Domestic and Export Prices in the Japanese General Machinery Industry, 1979–1987. The generally stable domestic yen price contrasts with the variability of both the yen export price and the foreign currency export price. But the opposing patterns of the yen and foreign currency export prices indicate that the Japanese firms were pricing to market by adjusting the yen export price so as to moderate changes in the foreign currency export price resulting from volatile exchange rates. This adjustment limited the pass-through ratio to about 0.5 over the period.

---

[14]In other words, Japanese manufacturers practice price discrimination between domestic and foreign markets. When the yen appreciates, this results in dumping in foreign markets.

currency price are offsetting. For instance, in 1980, when the yen was strong, Japanese exporters lowered the yen export price to moderate the rise in the foreign currency export price, and in 1981, when the yen depreciated, exporters raised the yen export price to moderate the decline in the foreign currency price. In sum, the Japanese exporters adjusted their yen export prices so as to limit the pass-through ratio to about 0.5 over the period.

Hysteresis *Hysteresis,* a word used by physicists, is defined by *The American Heritage Dictionary* as the "lagging of an effect behind its cause."[15] Applied to international economics, hysteresis means that the effects of a prolonged real change in the exchange rate are *not* fully reversed when the exchange rate later returns to its original level.

Hysteresis is offered as an explanation for the pattern of exchange rate adjustment for the United States during the 1980s.[16] In the first half of that decade, the real value of the U.S. dollar rose sharply against the Japanese yen and other major currencies. This appreciation gave Japanese and other foreign exporters an extraordinary opportunity to expand sales to the United States: Simply by holding their domestic currency export prices constant, they were able to offer lower dollar prices to American customers. Because the dollar appreciation lasted several years, foreign firms invested in new products adapted to American tastes and strengthened their marketing efforts in the United States, as with new distribution facilities and heavy promotion. At the same time, U.S. firms lost market share in face of the cost advantage of foreign firms.

When the dollar lost value in the second half of the 1980s, foreign firms were unwilling to give up the increasing returns generated by their larger U.S. market shares and stronger marketing systems. After all, the marketing investments they made in the first part of the decade were now sunk costs that did not affect the current costs of maintaining market shares. Accordingly, these firms kept their dollar prices constant by cutting back on profit margins. Hence, the U.S. market shares of foreign exporters, particularly the Japanese, remained higher despite the fact that the real value of the dollar was about the same at the end of the decade as it was at its beginning. At the same time, many domestic firms were unwilling to invest in the new products and marketing effort necessary to recapture lost market share.

We can now understand why hysteresis is also called the "beachhead effect": The prolonged dollar appreciation allowed foreign exporters to establish beachheads in the U.S. market that they were able to sustain even when the dollar returned to its old level. To conclude, hysteresis (or beachhead effect) not only lowers the pass-through ratio but also brings about lasting *structural* changes in trade patterns resulting from prolonged variations in the exchange rate.

---

[15] *The American Heritage Dictionary.* 3d ed. (New York: Houghton Mifflin Company, 1992), p. 891.
[16] This behavior is discussed in Chapter 19.

MONETARY APPROACH
TO EXCHANGE RATE ADJUSTMENT

The elasticities approach to exchange rate adjustments is a *partial-equilibrium* analysis that deals only with the export and import sectors while ignoring the macroeconomic effects of a change in the exchange rate on the general price level and on real income. As pointed out earlier, the elasticities approach needs to be supplemented (or validated) by the absorption approach, which offers a *general-equilibrium* analysis that covers macroeconomic effects. Both of these approaches focus on current-account or "real" adjustment, with little attention to the remainder of the balance of payments, which is thought to passively accommodate the current account. In contrast, the monetary approach is a general-equilibrium analysis that explains exchange rate adjustment in terms of its effect on the money market, which in turn brings about equilibrating changes in both the current and capital accounts of the balance of payments.

In the following sections we look first at the monetary explanation of adjustment through an occasional devaluation or revaluation in an adjustable-peg or managed-float system. Then, as promised in Chapter 12, we take up the monetary explanation of exchange rate determination, particularly in a flexible-rate system.

Adjustment Through Devaluation[17]

Let us assume that at a given exchange rate a country is running a deficit in its balance of payments as measured by a net balance on official reserves account. As we know, to monetarists this means that there is an excess supply of money ($M^s > M^d$) and the money market is in disequilibrium. Now suppose the government devalues its currency. Clearly, devaluation can eliminate the balance of payments deficit only if it can eliminate the excess supply of money. How is this possible?

We can explain the monetary version of the effects of devaluation in two steps. First, devaluation *raises* the domestic currency prices of tradables and also of nontradables, although to a lesser extent. This price inflation increases the demand for nominal money balances.[18] Second, the resulting higher demand for money causes an inflow of money from abroad as individuals and firms seek to restore their *real* money balances by cutting expenditures on imports of goods and services, by liquidating foreign financial assets (securities), or by borrowing from foreign lenders. These actions eliminate the balance of payments deficit or, if the devaluation is large enough, create a surplus.

The improvement in the balance of payments resulting from a devaluation continues only until *stock* equilibrium is restored in the money market, that is, until $M^d = M^s$. To monetarists, therefore, the effect of devaluation is *temporary;* over the

---

[17]This and the following subsections draw on the presentation in Mordechai E. Kreinin and Lawrence H. Officer, *The Monetary Approach to the Balance of Payments: A Survey,* Princeton Studies in International Finance, no. 43 (Princeton, N.J.: Princeton University Press, 1978), Chapters 4 and 5.

[18]See equation (35) in Chapter 15.

long run it only raises the price level without affecting real economic variables. For that reason, monetarists argue that devaluation (or revaluation) is unnecessary in an adjustable-peg system; instead, authorities should reduce the domestic-credit element of the monetary base (D) or, in dynamic terms, restrain its growth rate below that of its trading partners.

To monetarists, the temporary effect of devaluation does not depend on changes in the country's terms of trade or on the demand and supply elasticities of tradables. The only requirement for adjustment is that the decrease in real money stocks causes a decrease in real absorption out of a given real income.

The monetarists use the same mechanism to explain adjustment to a balance of payments surplus through revaluation. A payments surplus means an excess demand for money ($M^d > M^s$) in the surplus country. By *lowering* the general price level, revaluation decreases the demand for money. Individuals and firms cut their money balances by buying more from abroad or investing and lending abroad. Once again, the effect is temporary, ceasing when equilibrium is restored in the money market.

The monetary approach to devaluation and revaluation can be reconciled with the absorption approach by recognizing that when absorption exceeds income (a deficit on current account), then the supply of domestic money stock exceeds its desired level, and conversely. Both the absorption and monetary approaches agree that exchange rate adjustment depends critically on the absence of new domestic money creation that would offset its effect on real money balances.

The assertion by monetarists that a change in the exchange rate will have *no* effect on real variables over the long run follows from their assumption of the *law of one price* in global markets for goods and services and for money and other financial assets. If, indeed, national markets were fully integrated with global markets through perfect international arbitrage, then the prices of importables and exportables would always remain in line with world prices. For instance, after a 10 percent devaluation, the domestic currency prices of exports and import-competing goods would also rise 10 percent, thereby foreclosing any switching through price effects. Insofar as the law of one price does not hold (and the empirical evidence says it does not, particularly in markets for differentiated goods and services), then a change in the exchange rate can have long-run switching effects on trade flows and other real economic variables.[19] And in that case, the elasticities approach can be useful in tracing and forecasting the magnitude of the switching effects. We shall have more to say about the law of one price in the next section.

---

[19]Himarios examined the relationship between nominal and real devaluation for fifteen countries covering a variety of exchange rate systems over the period 1953–1973 and the same relationship for a second sample of fifteen countries over the period 1975–1984. He concluded that over a relevant policy horizon (three years) a *nominal* devaluation changes relative prices (becoming thereby a *real* devaluation) and affects the trade balance "positively and significantly." In over 80 percent of the cases, devaluation caused a long-run net improvement in the trade balance. See Daniel Himarios, "Do Devaluations Improve the Trade Balance? The Evidence Revisited," *Economic Inquiry*, January 1989, pp. 143–68.

Determination of Exchange Rates
in a Freely Fluctuating Rate System

Monetarist and nonmonetarist economists agree that fully flexible exchange rates keep the balance of payments in continuing equilibrium. However, the monetarists do not believe that fluctuating rates are necessary to maintain long-run payments equilibrium, because they regard payments imbalances as self-correcting in a fixed-rate system. As we learned in Chapter 15, the money supply in a fixed-rate system adjusts gradually through changes in international reserves until equilibrium is restored in the money market. In a freely fluctuating rate system, however, equilibrium is continuously maintained in the money market through domestic price changes that affect the real value of money stocks. But how are exchange rates determined in such a system?

Monetarists answer that question in the first instance by saying that exchange rates, as the relative prices of national monies, are determined by the demand and supply of stocks of the several national monies.[20] Real factors, such as relative changes in national productivity, influence the exchange rate, but they work through monetary channels. A simple model can depict the fundamental reasoning of the monetary approach to exchange rate determination.

Monetarists begin with the proposition that the exchange rate, defined as the domestic currency price of a unit of foreign currency, is the ratio between domestic and foreign price levels:

$$(3) \ r \ = \ P/P^*,$$

where r is the exchange rate, P is the domestic price level, and P^* is the foreign price level. This equation is a statement of the purchasing-power parity doctrine that was described in Chapter 13. But monetarists do not assert, as does the doctrine, that relative price levels determine the exchange rate. Instead, equation (3) is simply a statement of the *law of one price* in a global market: Perfect commodity arbitrage makes the price levels of all countries equal when the levels are expressed in a common currency.

The domestic price level must also satisfy the conditions of equilibrium in the money market:

$$(4) \ M^{dr} \ = \ M^s/P,$$

where M^{dr} is the demand for *real* money stocks and M^s is the nominal money stock. Solving equation (4) for P, we get

$$(5) \ P \ = \ M^s/M^{dr}.$$

---

[20]The balance of payments approach to exchange rate determination, which was presented in Chapter 12, views exchange rates as the relative prices of *national outputs*. The equilibrium rate is determined by *flows* of funds, not stock adjustments.

Substituting this expression for P and a similar one for the foreign price level in equation (3), we obtain

$$(6) \; r \; = \; \frac{M^s/M^{dr}}{M^{s*}/M^{dr*}} \, ,$$

where M^{s*} is the foreign money stock and M^{dr*} is the foreign demand for real money balances. This equation states that the exchange rate equals the money supply/real money demand ratio in the domestic country divided by the foreign money supply/real money demand ratio.

The demand for real money balances is dependent on real income and the nominal interest rate, or

$$(7) \; M^{dr} \; = \; f(y,i).$$

Substituting this expression for real money demand in equation (6) we get

$$(8) \; r \; = \; [M^s/M^{s*}]^s \; [f(y^*)/f(y)][f(i^*)/f(i)],$$

where the asterisks indicate the foreign real income and nominal interest rate. Hence, the exchange rate equals the ratio of the foreign and domestic money stocks *times* the ratio of the foreign and domestic real income functions *times* the ratio of the foreign and domestic nominal interest rate functions.

The nominal rate of interest is composed of a *real* rate, which monetarists assume is the same in all countries (perfect international mobility of funds), and an *inflation* premium, which is the expected rate of increase in the domestic price level.

$$(9) \; i \; = \; i^r \; + \; E(p),$$

where i^r is the real rate of interest and $E(p)$ is the expected rate of inflation. And

$$(10) \; i^r \; = \; i^{r*},$$

where i^{r*} is the foreign real rate of interest.

Substituting the expression of i in equation (9) and a similar expression for the foreign interest rate (i^*) in equation (8), we arrive at:

$$(11) \; r \; = \; [M^s/M^{s*}][f(y^*)/f(y)][[f[i^r \; + \; E(p)^*]/f[i^r \; + \; E(p)]]$$

This equation shows the basic relationships of the monetary approach to the determination of exchange rates. Exogenous shifts in the domestic money stock or real income *relative* to the foreign money stock or real income and shifts in expected rate of domestic inflation *relative* to the expected rate of foreign inflation cause changes in the exchange rate.

In the short run, price expectations are the dominant influence on exchange rates because expectations are much more volatile than money stocks and real income. But fueling these expectations are divergent money/real income ratios among countries caused by divergent national monetary policies. Hence, a necessary condition for exchange rate stability is consistency among national monetary policies. Equation (11) also indicates that the most effective way to stop a depreciation in the exchange rate is a *permanent* reduction in the rate of growth of M^s announced by the monetary authorities in advance. Such an announcement (when it is believed by participants in the money market) will immediately lower the inflation premium on the interest rate and thereby cause an appreciation in the exchange rate.

Overshooting Exchange Rates

The monetary approach assumes *instantaneous* adjustment in international payments through movements in the exchange rate. As we observed in Chapter 15, adjustment can indeed occur rapidly through short-term capital flows as holders of financial assets (securities) respond to international shifts in interest rates, risks, and expectations. But adjustment in the goods market is another matter: Equilibrating changes in the volume and composition of expenditures on tradables and nontradables occur comparatively slowly. It is this lagged response that gives rise to the J-curve effect.

The lagged equilibrating response of the goods market (current account) in a flexible-rate system places the burden of *initial* adjustment entirely on the capital account. Hence, the initial change in the exchange rate (whether depreciation or appreciation) is greater than will be necessary to restore equilibrium when eventually the current account takes up some or all of the adjustment burden. This phenomenon is called "overshooting."

Let us trace the adjustment path in a flexible-rate system according to the monetary approach. We start with an increase in the domestic money stock that causes lower domestic interest rates and raises expectations of an eventual depreciation of the domestic currency. The resulting outflow of short-term capital from the domestic country due to interest-rate differentials, the portfolio effect, and the expectations effect (as described in Chapter 15) causes an *immediate* depreciation of the domestic currency. Subsequently, however, the domestic currency will *appreciate* throughout the rest of the adjustment that progressively occurs in the current account. This appreciation, however, will be less than the initial depreciation. In sum, the depreciation needed to clear the financial-asset market in the short run is greater than the depreciation needed to clear *both* the financial-asset and the goods markets in the longer run. Overshooting intensifies the volatility of exchange rates in a floating-rate system.

GENERAL EQUILIBRIUM IN AN OPEN ECONOMY
WITH FLEXIBLE EXCHANGE RATES

As was true of a fixed-rate regime, equilibrium in the balance of payments (foreign exchange market) requires simultaneous equilibrium in a country's goods and money markets. General equilibrium is depicted graphically in Figure 15-9 in Chapter 15. It occurs at the point of intersection of the IS, LM, and BOP schedules.

In a flexible-rate system, the exchange rate varies continually to keep the balance of payments in equilibrium. General equilibrium is achieved by shifts in the IS and BOP schedules induced by exchange rate movements until the two schedules intersect on the LM schedule, which remains unaffected by such movements.

Figure 16-8 shows the markets for goods and money in equilibrium at point E, with an interest rate i and national income Y. However, the balance of payments is in *deficit* disequilibrium at E, given the initial exchange rate S. (Remember: All points *below* the BOP schedule indicate a deficit [BOP $<$ 0].) This disequilibrium cannot endure. Because the amount of foreign exchange demanded exceeds the amount supplied at E, the domestic currency depreciates from S to S'. This depreciation causes a decline in imports and a rise in exports (an increase in $X–M$),

Figure 16-8

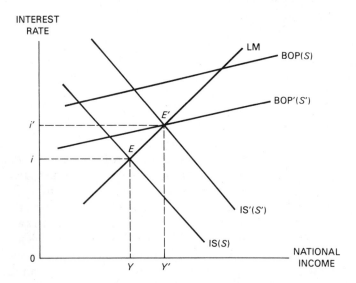

Adjustment to General Equilibrium Starting from a Balance of Payments Deficit in a Flexible-Rate System. The goods and money markets are in equilibrium at $E(IS = LM)$, but the balance of payments is in deficit at $E(BOP < 0)$, given the original exchange rate S. General equilibrium is restored at E' after a depreciation from S to S' causes the IS schedule to shift to IS' and the BOP schedule to shift to BOP'. At E', $BOP = 0$.

which raises national income via the foreign trade multiplier. Consequently, the IS schedule shifts to the right from *IS* to *IS'*. Aggregate demand and supply are now equated at a higher income level for any given interest rate. At the same time, the BOP schedule shifts downward: Equilibrium now occurs at a combination of lower interest rates and higher income levels than it did at the initial exchange rate *S*. General equilibrium is established at *E'*, with national income at *Y'*, the interest rate at *i'*, and the exchange rate at *S'*.

SUMMARY

1. There are many possible kinds of variable-rate systems, ranging from a flexible-rate (purely floating) system to an adjustable-peg system. In a flexible-rate system, movements in the exchange rate achieve a continuing short-run equilibrium in the balance of payments. In the adjustable-peg system exchange rates are occasionally varied by government action from one fixed level to another, and the choice of a new equilibrium rate is difficult.

2. The basic argument for flexible exchange rates is that they are the most effective means of market adjustment to balance of payments disequilibrium in the kind of world in which we live. It is alleged by proponents of flexible rates that long-run adjustment in a fixed-rate system is likely to be vitiated by domestic government policies of high employment and stability. The theoretical argument for an adjustable-peg system is less strong, because exchange rate adjustment is apt to come too late and be too big.

3. Economists have developed three different approaches to exchange rate adjustment: the elasticities, absorption, and monetary approaches.

4. According to the elasticities approach, the effects of depreciation on the balance of payments depend on the elasticities of demand and supply of both exports and imports. Depreciation *always* improves the balance of payments when the sum of export and import demand elasticities is greater than one (Marshall-Lerner condition). Even if this sum is below one, depreciation improves the balance of payments, provided supply elasticities are small enough.

5. The effect of depreciation on the commodity terms of trade is uncertain. It depends on the size of the product of the two supply elasticities of exports and imports as compared with the product of their demand elasticities.

6. The absorption approach demonstrates that regardless of elasticities, depreciation with full employment can be successful only when it is accompanied by expenditure-reducing policies that contract real domestic absorption.

7. The J-curve illustrates that the initial short-run impact of depreciation is to worsen — not improve — the current account of the balance of payments. The delayed effects of a depreciation are traceable to the pass-through effect (intensified by hysteresis) and to low *short-run* price elasticities.

8. The monetary approach explains the effects of depreciation on the balance of payments through its alteration of real money balances.

9. According to the monetary approach, exchange rates are determined by shifts in the domestic money stock or real income relative to the foreign money stock or real income and by shifts in the expected rate of domestic inflation relative to the expected rate of foreign inflation.

10. The lagged equilibrating response of the current account in a flexible-rate system places the burden of *initial* adjustment entirely on the capital account. Hence, the initial change in the exchange rate is greater than is needed for long-run equilibrium. This phenomenon is called "overshooting."

11. As was true of a fixed-rate regime, equilibrium in the balance of payments (foreign exchange market) requires simultaneous equilibrium in a country's goods and money markets.

QUESTIONS AND APPLICATIONS

1. (a) How does adjustment occur in a flexible-rate system?
   (b) How does it occur in an adjustable-peg system?

2. What is the basic argument for flexible exchange rates? Why have governments traditionally opposed flexible exchange rates?

3. (a) Assuming infinite supply elasticities, construct a graph to show the effects of depreciation when the elasticity of export demand is zero and the elasticity of import demand is zero. Does depreciation improve the balance of payments?
   (b) Using graphs, show how the effectiveness of exchange depreciation is determined by the elasticities of the supply and demand of foreign exchange.
   (c) What is the Marshall-Lerner condition?

4. "The effect of depreciation on the commodity terms of trade is uncertain." Explain.

5. (a) Using the absorption approach, explain why devaluation to eliminate a current-account deficit will be unsuccessful unless it is accompanied by higher domestic saving that matches any improvement in the balance of payments.
   (b) What steps can a government take to increase saving and thereby make devaluation effective?

6. (a) What is the "J-curve"?
   (b) What are the two general sources of the delayed effects of a change in the exchange rate?
   (c) What is "pricing to market"? How does it lower the pass-through ratio?

7. What is *hystersis* or the "beachhead effect"?

8. What is the monetary explanation of an exchange devaluation? An exchange revaluation?

9. (a) What is the law of one price?
   (b) Explain how the law of one price underlies the monetarist assertion that a change in the exchange rate will have no long-term effects on the international trade balance.
10. Using equation (11), show the effect on the exchange rate of (a) an increase in the domestic money stock, (b) an increase in foreign real income, and (c) a fall in the expected domestic rate of inflation.
11. Explain the phenomenon of "overshooting."
12. (a) Using IS, LM, and BOP schedules, indicate a situation in which the goods and money markets of a country are in equilibrium but its balance of payments is in *surplus*.
   (b) Illustrate graphically how general equilibrium is restored after an *appreciation* of the country's exchange rate.

SELECTED READINGS

Allsop, Christopher, Tim Jenkinson, and Terry O'Shaugnessy. "The Assessment: The Balance of Payments and International Economic Integration." *Oxford Review of Economic Policy,* no. 3, 1990, pp. 1–17.

Baldwin, Richard, and Paul Krugman. "Persistent Trade Effects of Large Exchange Rate Shocks." *The Quarterly Journal of Economics* (November 1989), pp. 635–654.

Begg, David. "Floating Exchange Rates in Theory and Practice." *Oxford Review of Economic Policy,* no. 3, 1989, pp. 24–39.

Bergsten, C. Fred, ed. *International Adjustment Financing.* Washington, D.C.: Institute for International Economics, 1991, Chapters 6 and 8.

Broughton, James M. *The Monetary Approach to Exchange Rates: What Now Remains?* Essays in International Finance, no. 171. Princeton, N.J.: Princeton University Press, October 1988.

Corden, W. M. *Inflation, Exchange Rates and the World Economy.* 3d ed. Chicago: The University of Chicago Press, 1986. Chapters 1, 2, and 3.

Deyak, Timothy A., and W. Charles Sawyer. "The Effects of Exchange Rate Changes on Prices and Quantities in U.S. Foreign Trade." *The International Trade Journal,* Fall 1990, pp. 77–92.

Friedman, Milton. "The Case for Flexible Exchange Rates." In *Essays in Positive Economics.* Chicago: University of Chicago Press, 1953, pp. 157–87.

Genberg, Hans, and Alexander K. Swoboda. "Policy and Current Account Determination under Floating Exchange Rates." *International Monetary Fund Staff Papers* 36 (March 1989), pp. 1–30.

Isard, Peter. "Lessons from Empirical Models of Exchange Rates." *International Monetary Fund Staff Papers* 34 (March 1987), pp. 1–28.

Johnson, Harry G. *Money, Balance of Payments Theory, and the International Monetary Problem.* Essays in International Finance, no. 124. Princeton, N.J.: Princeton University Press, 1977.

Kamin, Steven B. *Devaluation, External Balance and Macroeconomic Performance: A Look at the Numbers.* Princeton Studies in International Finance, no. 62. Princeton, N.J.: Princeton University Press, August 1988.

Kreinen, Mordechai, and Lawrence H. Officer. *The Monetary Approach to the Balance of Payments: A Survey.* Princeton Studies in International Finance, no. 43. Princeton, N.J.: Princeton University Press, 1978.

Krueger, Anne O. *Exchange-Rate Determination.* Cambridge: Cambridge University Press, 1983.

Mussa, Michael L. *Exchange Rates in Theory and Reality.* Essays in International Finance, no. 179. Princeton, N.J.: Princeton University Press, December 1990.

chapter 17

NONMARKET SUPPRESSION OF EXTERNAL PAYMENTS DISEQUILIBRIUM: EXCHANGE CONTROL

In Chapter 6 we examined tariff and nontariff restrictions on trade. A government may employ any of these restrictions to suppress a deficit in the balance of payments and foreign exchange market by lowering imports and thus the demand for foreign exchange. A government may also use export subsidies to stimulate export sales and thereby increase the supply of foreign exchange.[1] However, the most direct and comprehensive policy instrument to suppress a payments deficit is *exchange control.* In effect, exchange control replaces the free operation of the market with official decisions that determine the uses and availabilities of foreign exchange for all or specific transactions. When exchange control covers all transactions, then the government becomes a pure monopsonist and monopolist of foreign exchange.

THE ORIGINS OF EXCHANGE CONTROL

Exchange control was initially adopted by many governments during World War I, when it became necessary to conserve scarce supplies of gold and foreign exchange for the financing of imports vital to the national economy. Following the war, however, exchange control was abandoned everywhere, and by the second half of the 1920s most nations had returned to the gold standard and the full convertibility that characterized the prewar system of international payments. At that time it was widely believed that only the exigencies of war justified the use of exchange control, and few observers expected to witness its revival in a period of peace. Yet, within a few years several governments had resurrected exchange control in the face of an event that was almost as convulsive as war in the suddenness of its impact on the international payments system—the international financial crisis of 1931.

---

[1]The variety of measures taken by the U.S. government in the 1960s to suppress a balance of payments deficit are described in Chapter 18.

437

The first peacetime use of exchange control by industrial countries arose as a response to the crisis of 1931, which unloosed a panicky run on the gold and foreign exchange reserves of one country after another.[2] The crisis began inconspicuously when the Credit-Anstalt bank in Vienna was declared insolvent in the summer of 1931. This caused a loss of confidence in the ability of Austria to honor its international short-term obligations, and there was an immediate large-scale withdrawal of funds from that country. Upon the failure of a large German bank in early July, the run by foreign creditors spread to Germany and to many Eastern European countries that had borrowed heavily on short term during the 1920s. Fearful of an exhaustion of its reserves, the German government stopped the flight of capital funds by introducing exchange control in August. By the end of the year, most countries in Eastern Europe, as well as Denmark and Iceland, had also applied exchange control to halt an outflow of capital. Foreign-owned balances in the exchange control countries were now "frozen" and could no longer be freely transferred into gold or convertible foreign exchange. Similarly, residents of the exchange control countries were no longer able to send capital abroad.

The institution of exchange control in Germany next started a run on the British pound sterling. The large short-term loans that the United Kingdom had made to Germany were now immobilized by exchange control, and this created a doubt as to the capacity of the United Kingdom to liquidate its own heavy short-term international indebtedness. The panic rapidly depleted British reserves, but instead of following the example of Germany, the United Kingdom went off the gold standard in September 1931 and allowed the pound sterling to depreciate. In June of the following year, the British government established the Exchange Equalization Fund to stabilize the pound at a level below its former gold parity. A number of other countries allowed their currencies to depreciate along with the pound sterling and in this way gave birth to the Sterling Area.

By 1935 the international financial crisis and the global depression had split the international payments system into five groups:[3]

1. The *Sterling Area,* comprising principally the British Commonwealth and Scandinavian countries.
2. The *Dollar Area,* comprising the United States and most of the countries of Central America and northern South America.
3. The *Gold Bloc* countries of Western Europe.
4. The *Yen Area,* comprising Japan and Japan's possessions.
5. The *Exchange Control Area* of central and southeastern Europe, dominated by Germany.

Some countries, such as Canada, Argentina, Brazil, and Chile, did not fall completely into any one currency area. The Canadian dollar was depreciated about 10 percent against the dollar but remained convertible. The other three

---

[2]In 1929 and 1930 a number of raw material exporting nations imposed exchange control to meet current account deficits brought on by the onset of depression in the industrial countries.

[3]League of Nations, *International Currency Experience* (Geneva: League of Nations, 1944), p. 198.

countries also depreciated but adopted exchange control that rendered their currencies inconvertible.

Exchange control was practiced by Germany, the Eastern European countries, and many countries in Latin America throughout the 1930s, long after the international financial crisis of 1931 had become history. Many new uses were found for exchange control, and this served to perpetuate its existence. The currencies of the Dollar Area, the Sterling Area, the Yen Area, and the principal countries of Western Europe (excluding Germany and Italy) remained fully convertible, however, up to the outbreak of World War II. During the war, all countries exercised tight control over their economies, and exchange control was only one of several instruments employed for that purpose.

After World War II most countries of the noncommunist world continued to restrict both current and capital transactions by means of exchange control.[4] In 1958 only eleven countries — all located in the Western Hemisphere — had *fully* convertible currencies that any holder could transfer freely into other currencies. All other currencies were inconvertible to one degree or another. This widespread use of exchange control had profound effects upon international trade and payments. It sharply limited the scope of multilateral trade and divided the free world into distinct currency areas. To the individual trader, exchange control meant that it was no longer possible to buy in the low-price market and sell in the high-price market without permission of the authorities. At times this permission was denied outright, and it was almost always limited in some way.

A massive liberalization of exchange restrictions started at the close of 1958, when ten countries in Western Europe established nonresident convertibility of their currencies on current account. In the early 1960s other industrial countries (including Japan) eliminated exchange restrictions on merchandise trade and, in most instances, on other current transactions as well. The industrial countries also greatly moderated their restrictions on capital transactions, and some removed them entirely. Exchange control, therefore, is no longer a significant policy instrument for the countries of the industrial West.

The less-developed countries have not matched the liberalization of the developed countries. The majority still retain exchange restrictions on trade and other transactions. For the developing countries, then, exchange control continues to be a major tool of foreign economic policy.

THE OBJECTIVES OF EXCHANGE CONTROL

Although the suppression of balance of payments disequilibrium has been the dominant objective of exchange control, it may also serve other important national objectives, such as the facilitation of national planning, the protection of domestic industries, and the creation of government revenue.

---

[4]Since all international transactions of communist countries were channeled through state agencies, exchange control was an integral element of communist trading systems.

The Suppression of Balance of Payments Disequilibrium

When a nation is unwilling or unable to adjust to a persistent deficit in its balance of payments by deflating the domestic economy, by depreciating its rate of exchange, or by any other domestic measure of a fiscal or monetary nature, it must suppress the deficit by imposing direct controls over its international transactions. As noted earlier, the most important direct control utilized by contemporary governments is exchange control, which regulates the acquisition and disposition of foreign exchange. Other forms of direct control—import quotas and import licenses—usually supplement exchange control, although at times they may be used as substitutes.

Exchange control was first used in peacetime mainly for suppression of the unique sort of disequilibrium that is provoked by a flight of capital. When exchange control is used solely for this purpose, there is no reason to restrict imports of merchandise and services, because the trouble is not in the current account. Moreover, exchange control need only be temporary, for once the panic has subsided it may be lifted, and most of the capital will return of its own accord. This last statement presupposes, however, a widespread belief that exchange control will not be reimposed. If there is doubt on this score, the cessation of exchange control will itself renew the capital flight. In this way, exchange control may perpetuate the loss of confidence and the speculative attitudes that engendered the original flight of capital. Fearing this consequence, governments tend to maintain exchange control long after the danger of capital flight is past.

There is another reason why exchange control that is imposed to restrain a capital flight may continue as a permanent feature of a nation's foreign economic policy. By maintaining an overvalued exchange rate, exchange control may itself create a current-account deficit in the balance of payments and induce further disequilibrium in the balance of payments. This is why many nations, once they have adopted exchange control, dare not abandon it.

The Facilitation of National Planning

Governments may use exchange control as a policy instrument (along with others) to attain certain national economic goals, such as full employment and economic development.

Until recently, China and countries in Eastern Europe had centrally planned economies directed toward specific goals by communist regimes. This was accomplished through a comprehensive set of controls that determined the allocation of productive factors and the national product.[5] Because private enterprise was

---

[5]The once-communist countries of Eastern Europe are now in transition to market economies, as is still-communist China. We explore this transition (which will have profound effects on the world economy) in Chapter 21.

forbidden, state enterprises executed national plans, including those for international trade, which was conducted exclusively by state trading agencies.

National planning in market economies differs significantly from central planning in nonmarket economies. In market economies, production rests largely in the hands of private entrepreneurs, and the price system is the main instrument in deciding the allocation of production and consumption. Consequently, governments depend principally (although not exclusively) on fiscal and monetary policies instead of direct controls to implement their national economic programs. But since these programs are conceived in national terms, they sometimes demand an insulation of the national economy from the world economy. To achieve this insulation, governments may impose exchange and trade controls that are supplemented, at times, by state trading in specific commodities.

Since World War II the governments of less-developed countries in Latin America, Asia, and Africa have made economic development their preeminent policy goal. The policies associated with that goal have tended to create inflationary pressures that have, in turn, induced deficits in the balance of payments. Lacking adequate reserves, many countries have been forced to make immediate adjustments to these external deficits. Because of the objectives of national planning, however, the choice of methods of adjustment has been narrowly circumscribed. Deflation has been avoided because it would slow down the rate of economic growth. Similarly, exchange depreciation has promised little help because any subsequent domestic inflation would offset its effects on international payments. Rather than moderate the goals of national planning, governments have used exchange control and other direct measures to insulate the domestic economy from international repercussions. Apart from its insulation effect, the governments of less-developed countries have utilized exchange control to penalize imports of "nonessential goods" and favor imports of "essential goods" in accordance with criteria laid down by national development plans.

The Protection of Domestic Industries

By restricting imports, exchange control inevitably protects domestic producers against foreign competition. Therefore, exchange control will be supported by protectionist groups, which will seek to enhance its protective features. When exchange control is not consciously oriented toward protection but is set up simply to suppress an external deficit, it will not discriminate against those imports that have close domestic substitutes. All imports will be viewed indiscriminately as a drain on foreign exchange, and they will be restricted only to stop that drain. When, however, exchange control also has a protectionist purpose, it will curtail imports of competitive products more stringently than imports of products not produced at home or in sufficient quantities. Once exchange control is established, it usually evolves in the direction of greater protection as a result of the lobbying activities of vested interests. This is also true of the import quotas and licenses that ordinarily accompany exchange control.

The Creation of Government Revenue

Exchange control is used in some countries to collect revenue for the government. In most instances this occurs where the exchange control authority sets the price at which it will buy foreign exchange below the price at which it will sell foreign exchange. For example, if the authority forces exporters to surrender dollar exchange at a rate of 10 pesos to the dollar and then sells dollar exchange to importers at a rate of 15 pesos to the dollar, it pockets 5 pesos for each dollar that it buys and sells.

Exchange control is used as a source of revenue mainly by developing countries. The reliance of nonindustrial countries on exchange control to provide government revenue is largely due to the difficulty of collecting income and other direct taxes. Many of these countries do not have the personnel and skills required to administer direct taxes, and often it is politically impossible to impose such taxes on wealthy individuals. By way of contrast, an exchange control system offers a ready-made apparatus for the collection of revenue with only slight additional administrative expense. Moreover, the tight regulations of exchange control make it more difficult to avoid the tax, whether in the form of a penalty exchange rate or an exchange tax.[6]

SINGLE-RATE SYSTEMS OF EXCHANGE CONTROL

No two nations have identical systems of exchange control. Some systems are lenient and have almost fully convertible currencies, whereas others carefully police all uses of foreign exchange and may strongly discriminate against certain currencies. Many other variations in systems of exchange control are attributable to differences in objectives, differences in administrative competence, and differences in economic conditions. It is possible, however, to classify exchange control systems into two broad categories depending upon whether they employ one or several exchange rates.

Single-rate systems are administered by an exchange control authority that is the sole buyer and seller of foreign exchange. All foreign exchange transactions are carried on at one official rate of exchange. Exporters and others who receive foreign exchange from foreign residents are compelled to surrender it to the control authority at the official rate. Importers and others who must make payments to foreign residents must obtain permission to buy foreign exchange from the control authority at the official rate. The control authority also regulates the use of domestic currency (bank accounts) owned by foreign residents. Commercial banks are usually authorized to act as buying and selling agents of the exchange control authority. The key to the system of control is the requirement that all foreign exchange transactions involving domestic or foreign residents must pass through authorized banking channels.

---

[6]An exchange tax is a charge levied on transactions in foreign exchange.

The Surrender of Foreign Exchange Receipts

To regulate the expenditure of foreign exchange, the exchange control authority must make certain that all foreign exchange received by the nation's residents is actually surrendered to it. Otherwise foreign exchange that is not captured by the authorities may be used for illegal purposes, such as exporting capital, and thus it is not available to finance imports that the authorities consider desirable. Hence, surrender requirements must apply to all credit transactions in the balance of payments.

The surrender of foreign exchange to the control authority is usually accomplished in one of two ways. Under one method, all exports may be licensed by a trade control authority, and before the merchandise is allowed to pass through customs, the export license must be validated by an authorized bank. To obtain license validation, the exporter is required to inform the bank of the destination of the export shipment as well as the amount of the payment and the currency in which it is to be made. The exporter also agrees to surrender to the bank all receipts of foreign exchange. When the exporter arranges for payment by drawing a bill of exchange against the foreign importer or against a bank, the bill must be either discounted with the authorized bank or sent through that bank for collection. Thus, the authorized bank is certain to acquire the foreign exchange when payment is made on the bill.

In the second method, the surrender of foreign exchange receipts is insured by requiring the exporter to secure a sworn declaration from an authorized bank before the exports are allowed to pass customs. In obtaining the declaration, the exporter must inform the bank of the destination of the exports and the amount and kind of payment to be received for them. The exporter also agrees to surrender to the bank all receipts of foreign exchange within a stipulated period.

These two methods of effecting the surrender of foreign exchange receipts apply to merchandise exports only. It is more difficult for the control authority to capture foreign exchange receipts arising out of exports of services, gifts, and capital movements. Close watch must be kept over all foreign-owned bank balances in the exchange control country, foreign securities owned by domestic residents must be registered with the control authority and sometimes held by an authorized bank, and the international mails must be screened for domestic and foreign bank notes.

Failure to surrender foreign exchange in accordance with the regulations of the control authority is a criminal act. The guilty party may be punished by the imposition of a fine or, in the case of an exporter, denied permission to export in the future. Violations of the exchange control laws of Nazi Germany carried the death penalty. Nevertheless, evasions of exchange control are widespread, and the surrender procedures are never 100 percent effective.

The Allocation of Foreign Exchange Receipts

The exchange control authority is faced with several problems in the allocation of foreign exchange. First, it must decide how much foreign exchange to allot to the main categories of debit transactions of the balance of payments: merchandise imports, transportation services provided by foreigners, the servicing of foreign debts, travel expenditures of domestic residents, capital investment, and so on.

After reaching a decision on the overall amount of foreign exchange to be distributed to each of these categories, the control authority must next decide on the allocation of foreign exchange to the individual items within each category. It must also determine the applicants who will receive foreign exchange and the amounts they will be granted.

Finally, the exchange control authority must often decide upon the allocation of foreign exchange by countries or by currency areas, since it may have abundant supplies of some currencies and only scarce supplies of others. If all foreign currencies were convertible, this would not matter, but when several other countries also employ exchange control, it is no longer possible to settle a deficit through multilateral transfers.

Ordinarily the official rate of exchange *overvalues* the domestic currency. Regardless of the criteria used to allocate foreign exchange, therefore, it is not possible to satisfy the entire demand. The criteria of allocation will reflect the objectives of exchange control and current economic conditions. Imports that are considered vital to the nation's well-being will be afforded generous allotments of foreign exchange, while imports of "nonessential" items will receive only scanty allotments. Convertible currencies will be hoarded by the exchange control authority and released only for high-priority imports. On the other hand, inconvertible currencies may be sufficiently abundant to permit their use for low-priority imports.

The individual importer is particularly concerned with the method used to allocate foreign exchange to the applicants within each category. Among the several methods employed are the following:

1. individual allocation
2. exchange quotas
3. waiting list
4. prohibitions
5. tie-in import arrangement

The method of *individual allocation* involves the examination of each individual request for foreign exchange and, upon approval, the issuance of a license that permits the holder to buy a stipulated amount of foreign exchange from an authorized bank. The virtue of this technique is its flexibility. However, it encourages the bribery and corruption of officials, and it places in their hands the powers of life and death over the business enterprises engaged in importing. Efforts are often made to limit the arbitrary nature of individual allocation by requiring the authorities to use the past imports, capital, taxes paid, and so on, of the importing firm in deciding its exchange allotment. This procedure has the disadvantage of establishing fixed quotas for individual firms, and unless safeguards are established, it may create a special hardship for new or growing concerns.

Another method of allocation among applicants is the establishment for each category of imports of *exchange quotas* derived from estimates of the amount of foreign exchange that will be forthcoming over a specified period. Foreign exchange is then sold freely to all applicants on a first-come, first-served basis until the respective quotas are exhausted. Although this technique limits the exercise of discretion on the part of officials, it suffers from inflexibility.

The *waiting-list* method resembles the quota method. The exchange control authority places each application on a waiting list and takes care of it when the foreign exchange becomes available. Hence, no application is rejected, but the importer may have only a vague idea as to when foreign exchange will be obtained. Unless the priority of exchange allocation is strictly decided by the date of application, the waiting-list technique becomes as arbitrary as the individual allocation of exchange.

Prohibitions are often used to rule out any foreign exchange for certain import items from specific countries or from all countries. Prohibitions are actually zero exchange quotas, and the same effect may be obtained by not issuing licenses when the method of individual allocation is used by the control authority.

Finally, mention should be made of the *tie-in import arrangement,* whereby foreign exchange is allocated for specified imports on the condition that the importer buy complementary or similar domestic products in a certain proportion. The object here is to stimulate particular kinds of domestic production rather than to protect the balance of payments. This method of exchange allocation is very similar to the mixing quotas discussed in Chapter 6.[7]

Import Quotas and Licenses

Single exchange-rate systems are usually strengthened by a system of *import quotas* or *import licenses.*[8] The most common procedure is to require that the importer first obtain an import license from the trade control authority. Import licenses will be issued in accordance with import quotas for specified imports or on an individual ad hoc basis in the absence of import quotas. Ordinarily the import license also serves as an exchange license, permitting the importer to buy the foreign exchange necessary to finance the import shipment. In some countries, however, an exchange license may be needed in addition to an import license; that is, the import license does not provide the importer with an automatic right to buy foreign exchange. The methods used to distribute import licenses among importers are similar to those used to allocate foreign exchange licenses.

As far as merchandise imports are concerned, import quotas or import licenses can do the same job as exchange control. In fact, they may do a better job. Import quotas and licenses allow only fixed quantities of merchandise to enter the country over a certain period, whereas exchange control simply limits the amounts of foreign exchange available for specified merchandise imports over a certain pe-

---

[7]The tie-in import arrangement is also related to *countertrade arrangements* that allow imports into a country only if foreign suppliers also buy products from the importing country.

[8]The use of *export licenses* to compel surrender of foreign exchange receipts has already been mentioned. Export licenses may be used for several other purposes unrelated to exchange control, such as limiting exports of strategic military significance or conserving scarce commodities for use at home.

riod. Under exchange control, therefore, variations in import prices or in the credit extended by foreign suppliers can lead to variations in the quantities of imports even though there is a fixed allotment of foreign exchange. This difficulty is avoided when exchange control is supplemented by import quotas and licenses. Of course, exchange control is more comprehensive than direct trade control, since it covers service and capital transactions in addition to merchandise transactions. The importance of merchandise, however, as compared to other items in the balance of payments, makes a widespread application of import quotas and licenses a very close substitute for exchange control, with similar effects on international trade.

As has been noted, exchange control and quantitative import restrictions ordinarily are parts of the same overall system of direct control that is established by governments to suppress an external deficit. It follows, then, that international measures to remove or to reduce exchange control are likely to be ineffective unless steps are also taken to limit the use of import quotas and licenses.[9]

The Control of Nonresident Accounts

When a country employs exchange control to suppress a deficit in its balance of payments, it must regulate not only the foreign exchange transactions of its residents but also the use of domestic bank accounts owned by foreign residents. This is especially the case when the exchange control country is an international financial center such as the United Kingdom, for then a large proportion of its international receipts and expenditures are made by debiting and crediting accounts maintained in its banking system by foreign residents.

At the end of 1958 the United Kingdom and several other European countries took a long step toward full convertibility by making freely transferable all nonresident accounts arising out of current transactions. Previously, the British government did not allow foreign residents of nondollar countries to transfer their sterling balances to residents of dollar countries, although they were free to transfer such balances to residents of a nondollar country other than their own to finance transactions on current account. This procedure was necessary to ensure that all British exports to dollar countries were paid for in dollars. Otherwise, say, a French resident might have used a sterling account to finance imports from the United States, and this sterling could then have been used by an American resident to finance imports from the United Kingdom. Thus, the United Kingdom would have lost the opportunity to earn the dollars the American importer would have had to pay if sterling had not been acquired from the French resident.

MULTIPLE-RATE SYSTEMS OF EXCHANGE CONTROL

In a single-rate system of exchange control, the exchange rate itself plays no role in the allocation of foreign exchange among transactions, applicants, currencies, and countries. Indeed, the overvaluation of the exchange rate intensifies the task of

---

[9]The tariff is also an import restriction, but the uncertainty of its effects and the difficulties involved in changing it to meet new conditions make it a poor instrument of balance of payments adjustment.

allocation by diminishing the amount of foreign exchange in supply and, at the same time, increasing the amount of foreign exchange in demand.

In multiple-rate systems of exchange control, however, two or more exchange rates are used to effect the allocation of foreign exchange, although they are usually used in conjunction with exchange licenses and direct trade controls. Because the task of allocation is at least partially carried out by differential exchange rates, multiple-rate systems rely far less upon administrative action than do single-rate systems. It is not surprising, therefore, that multiple-rate systems are associated with less-developed countries, which may also find them attractive as devices to raise revenue.

Multiple-rate systems exhibit a bewildering variety. At one extreme are the systems that depend upon two or more "free" markets to allocate foreign exchange, with few direct controls of any kind. At the other extreme are the systems that use two or more fixed official rates that are supplemented by exchange licenses, import quotas, and other quantitative controls characteristic of single-rate systems. Our description is confined to remarks about those features peculiar to multiple-rate systems: penalty and preferential rates, fluctuating "free" market rates, mixing rates, and exchange taxes and subsidies.

When multiple-rate systems use fixed official rates of exchange, the simplest form occurs when the exchange authority sells foreign exchange at a single rate that differs from the single rate at which it buys foreign exchange. When the selling rate is higher than the buying rate in domestic currency (the usual case), the difference accrues to the government as revenue.[10] More than two rates result when the exchange authorities buy exchange received for specific export goods at low *penalty* rates or at high *preferential* rates or sell exchange for "nonessential" imports at high penalty rates and for "essential" imports at low preferential rates. Ordinarily, penalty buying rates are applied only to exports that face an inelastic foreign demand that enables exporters to escape the incidence of the penalty rate by passing it on to foreign buyers. Sometimes mistakes are made, however, and then penalty rates depress the affected exports.

Many multiple-rate countries allow designated transactions in foreign exchange to be effected in a *free* market. In such a market, a floating rate of exchange adjusts the amount of foreign exchange in demand to the amount in supply. Since floating rates are ordinarily considerably higher than the official rate, they favor sellers of foreign exchange and hence encourage those transactions whose exchange receipts may be sold at floating rates. By the same token, buyers of foreign exchange at floating rates are penalized, and this tends to restrict transactions that must be financed in a floating-rate market. Floating-rate markets are used most frequently for invisible (service) and capital transactions and for high-priority exports and low-priority imports. At times, however, a country may use two or more floating-rate markets for most, if not all, foreign exchange transactions.

---

[10]The foreign exchange rate is defined here as the price in domestic currency of a single unit of a foreign currency. If the exchange authorities sell at an official rate of, say, 5 pesos per U.S. dollar and buy at an official rate of, say, 4 pesos per U.S. dollar, then they reap a gain of 1 peso for every U.S. dollar they sell.

When a multiple-rate country wants to discriminate finely among different transactions by applying a large number of exchange rates, it may do so by *mixing* official rates with floating rates in varying proportions. Exporters are allowed to sell different percentages of their foreign exchange receipts on the "free" market, depending on their products. The higher the percentage, the greater the preferential treatment accorded to an exporter, because the free rate of exchange is ordinarily much higher (when expressed in domestic currency) than the official rate. Conversely, importers are penalized by making them buy a high percentage of their foreign exchange in the free market. The device of mixing rates enormously heightens the power of the control authority to discriminate between narrow classes of exports or imports: Minute variations in effective exchange rates become possible. It should be noted, however, that mixing rates also demand closer administrative supervision of specific export or import items than do rates that apply to a broad class of items.

Countries may *tax* or *subsidize* certain transactions in foreign exchange for revenue or control purposes. The effect is to alter the buying rates of exchange for the transactions in question, thereby creating multiple rates. In 1990, for instance, Colombia imposed a 6.5 percent tax on exchange receipts from coffee exports while, at the same time, it gave tax credits on exchange receipts from several other export products.[11]

THE EFFECTS OF EXCHANGE CONTROL

We have investigated the origins, objectives, and nature of exchange control. What of its effects? The answer to this question is not simple. For one thing, the effects are manifold; for another, the effects vary greatly in intensity depending on the severity and comprehensiveness of exchange control. Here we can only briefly evaluate the principal effects of exchange control on international payments.

Inconvertibility and Bilateralism

By making a currency inconvertible, exchange control strikes at the heart of multilateral settlement, which permits a country to offset a deficit in one direction with a surplus in another direction. To illustrate, suppose that country A has traditionally run a deficit with country B that has been financed by a surplus with country C. But now country C imposes exchange control and no longer allows residents of country A to use its currency to buy the currency of country B. The effect is to force country A to balance its trade *bilaterally* with country B, either by cutting its imports from or raising its exports to country B. Usually the first alternative is adopted, and, as a result, country B suffers a loss of exports to country A that may force it to restrict imports from a third country. Thus,

---

[11]The *ad valorem* tax on coffee exports was eliminated in January 1991 and replaced by a "coffee contribution" determined by the difference between the export value of coffee surrendered and its estimated cost. See *Exchange Arrangements and Exchange Restrictions,* Annual Report 1991 (Washington, D.C.: International Monetary Fund, 1991), p. 113.

exchange control, by disrupting the pattern of multilateral settlement, may compel other countries, one after another, to restrict imports and even to adopt exchange control in turn. A lower volume of trade is not the only consequence of this train of events. The *quality* of trade is also worsened, because it is no longer possible for the exporter to sell in the most profitable market or for the importer to buy in the least expensive market. The truth of this remark becomes clearer when we consider bilateral payments agreements.

Bilateral Payments Agreements

When several countries employ exchange control, there is usually an accumulation of bank balances owned by nonresidents that cannot be freely converted into other currencies. To liquidate these "blocked" balances and to avoid as much as possible the use of convertible currencies in the financing of trade, countries enter into bilateral payments agreements. In the 1950s the majority of trade between nondollar countries was financed in accordance with such agreements, which were often accompanied by trade agreements that specified the goods to be exchanged by the participating countries.

In the words of one authority, a bilateral payments agreement "provides a general method of financing current trade between two countries, giving rise to credits which are freely available for use by one country in making payments for goods and services imported from the other.[12] Bilateral payments agreements contain provisions relating to the unit or units of account that are to be used to finance the net balances of either country, the settlement of balances not covered by credits, the settlement of final balances at the conclusion of the agreement, the tenure of the agreement, and the transferability of balances. The credit and transferability provisions are of particular importance.

Most bilateral payments agreements establish reciprocal credits known as *swing credits*. These credits permit each country to have a deficit in its trade with the partner country up to a specified limit before settlement must be made in gold or dollars or in another agreed manner. At the conclusion of the agreement (which may run for several years), any outstanding balances must be settled in similar fashion. The presence of swing credits lessens the need of the partner countries to achieve an exact balance in their mutual trade, but it may expose the deficit country to a loss of gold or convertible currencies.

All bilateral payments agreements restrict in one way or another the transferability of domestic currency held by residents of the other partner country. This must be done if the agreement is to achieve its main function: the financing of trade with inconvertible currencies. The degree of transferability, however, may vary significantly in different agreements.

At one extreme are the restrictive *bilateral offset agreements* that allow no transferability to third currencies. Under this sort of agreement, usually found only

---

[12]Raymond F. Mikesell, *Foreign Exchange in the Postwar World* (New York: Twentieth Century Fund, 1954), p. 86.

between communist countries, any net balances are settled by an export of goods from the debtor country. Bilateral offset agreements, like barter, effectively prevent any multilateral settlement by destroying its very basis.

Exchange settlement agreements, as their name implies, allow for the settlement of final balances, and of balances beyond the swing credit, in gold, convertible currencies, or other agreed currencies. Although these agreements do not rigidly bilateralize trade, they do encourage bilateral settlement, since each partner country seeks to avoid having to pay gold or third currencies to the other.

The restoration of current-account convertibility by the important trading nations of Europe at the close of 1958 led to the dissolution of many payments agreements. Although forty-five agreements were in force at the end of 1990 between member countries of the International Monetary Fund, none involved a major trading country. Of some thirty-one agreements between member and nonmember countries, nearly all involved communist or former-communist countries. As these countries become market economies in the 1990s, we can reasonably anticipate the near disappearance of bilateral payments agreements.

The Redistribution of Money Incomes

The redistribution of money incomes that results from exchange control will vary depending upon the circumstances. Money income is diverted to the government by penalty selling rates of exchange, exchange taxes, exchange auctions, and the like. On the other hand, exporters and other sellers of foreign exchange may reap windfall profits when they are allowed to sell their exchange in floating-rate markets. In contrast, importers are apt to enjoy windfall profits in a single-rate system because the restriction of imports will push up their domestic prices. When exchange control protects domestic industry, its redistribution effects are similar to those of protective tariffs and quotas (see Chapter 6). In the last analysis, the consumer is likely to bear the incidence of exchange control in the form of higher prices for imports and their domestic substitutes.

The Evasion of Exchange Control

Exchange control encourages widespread evasion on the part of residents and nonresidents alike. Evasion of exchange regulations by residents is criminal, since it flouts domestic law. The exchange control country, however, has no jurisdiction over nonresidents who are located outside its boundaries and who may also evade its exchange regulations.

Bilateral payments agreements are often designed to lessen evasion of the exchange control of one partner country by residents of the other partner country, but the success of payments agreements in this respect depends upon the willingness and the ability of the government of the partner country to fulfill its obligations. The residents of free exchange countries, such as the United States, are able to evade the exchange regulations of other countries without violating domestic laws, since their governments are usually unwilling to enter into bilateral payments agreements with an evasion clause. Even if exchange control were fully effective in regulating all foreign exchange transactions within the exchange control country, it would not restrain much of the evasion practiced by nonresidents located abroad.

The number of evasion techniques is legion, including bribery and corruption of officials, false invoicing of exports and imports, and black market operations. False invoicing may involve the *underinvoicing* of exports so that part of the actual foreign exchange receipts is withheld from the control authority and placed by the importer or other agent in a foreign bank to the account of the exporter. The same thing may be accomplished through the *overinvoicing* of imports so that the importer obtains more foreign exchange than is needed to pay for the imports, the excess ending up in the importer's private bank account in a foreign country. Black market operations cover any illegal transactions in foreign exchange.

A SYNOPTIC VIEW
OF CONTEMPORARY EXCHANGE
CONTROL PRACTICES

Table 17-1 offers a synoptic view of the exchange control systems employed by members of the International Monetary Fund (IMF), which embraces 166 countries. All the *highly industrialized developed* countries have now accepted Article VIII of the IMF agreement, which obligates them to refrain from restrictions on current payments.[13] However, one less-advanced developed country (Greece), along with 62 percent of the developing countries, remains under Article XIV, which allows them to retain current account restrictions. At the end of 1990, three developed countries and eighty developing countries had such restrictions. However, no developed country had more than one rate of exchange for current transactions, while twenty-six developing countries had multiple-rate systems. Restrictions on capital transactions are prevalent throughout the world: Only ten developed countries and twenty-nine developing countries (mostly oil-exporting and newly industrializing countries) did *not* have them. Also, only about one-quarter of IMF countries do *not* require their exporters to surrender or repatriate foreign exchange receipts. Although there was some liberalization of exchange restrictions during the 1980s, it is evident that exchange controls of one sort or another remain very common in the world economy. Apart from their broad economic effects, such controls generate constraints and risks for international business enterprise, which must somehow learn to cope with them.

Is exchange control economically justified? The argument against exchange control is that its use raises obstacles to gainful international trade by restricting the convertibility of currencies, distorting price and cost relationships, discriminating among countries and currency areas, perpetuating balance of payments disequilibrium, and creating uncertainty and confusion. Hence, exchange control

---

[13]Article VIII and other features of the IMF Agreement are treated in Chapter 18.

Table 17-1   Summary Features of Exchange Control Systems of IMF Countries at the End of 1990

	Developed Countries[1]	Developing Countries[2]	Communist and Former-Communist Countries[3]
Article VIII status	22	51	0
Article XIV status	1[a]	83	9
Restrictions on current transactions[4]	3[b]	80	9
Restrictions on capital transactions[5]	12	105	9
Import rate(s) different from export rate(s)	0	26	8
Surrender or repatriation of export proceeds	9	106	9
Bilateral payments arrangements with IMF countries	1[c]	36	8
Bilateral payments arrangements with non-IMF countries	1[c]	21	9

[1]Twenty-three countries: United States, Canada, sixteen Western European countries, Japan, Australia, New Zealand, South Africa, and Finland.

[2]One hundred and thirty-four countries in Asia, Africa, and Latin America.

[3]Bulgaria, China, Czechoslovakia, Hungary, Laos, Poland, Romania, Viet Nam, and Yugoslavia.

[4]Other than restrictions for security reasons.

[5]Other than restrictions for security reasons. Resident-owned funds.

[a]Greece.

[b]Greece, Iceland, and South Africa.

[c]Finland.

Source: Derived from *Exchange Arrangements and Exchange Restrictions,* Annual Report 1991 (Washington, D.C.: International Monetary Fund, 1991), pp. 580–85.

interferes with international specialization and trade in accordance with comparative advantage.[14]

Despite this serious indictment, we have seen that exchange restrictions on current transactions have become a way of life for over half of the developing countries. The main explanation for the persistence of exchange control is that, although most nations pay lip service to the objective of free multilateral trade, they are unwilling to accept the monetary and fiscal disciplines necessary to sustain the convertibility of their currencies. Other objectives—full employment, eco-

---

[14]Peter J. Quirk, "The Case for Open Exchange Systems," *Finance & Development,* June 1989, p. 30.

nomic development, national planning, and so on—are placed ahead of the attainment of international equilibrium. Exchange control then becomes a mechanism used to defend national policies against international repercussions, and under some circumstances exchange restrictions on current account may be justified as a second-best policy.

The achievement of a multilateral trading system does not require the abandonment of all forms of exchange control. Currencies used to finance current transactions in merchandise and services as well as in investment capital must be fully convertible. Exchange control, however, may be used to restrain an occasional capital flight without endangering multilateral trade. Another legitimate use of exchange control is its *temporary* employment to allow a nation enough time to make a fundamental adjustment to a persistent deficit in its balance of payments, assuming that its reserves are inadequate to perform the same task. Since the longer-term elasticities of the supply and demand of foreign exchange are ordinarily greater than their short-term elasticities, the temporary use of exchange control may also be justified as a policy instrument to ease adjustment after a devaluation. As we have observed, however, the *temporary* exchange control system commonly becomes a permanent system because of the vested interests that benefit from it.

SUMMARY

1. The direct interference of governments in the foreign exchange market is known as exchange control. Exchange control restricts the right of holders of a currency to exchange it for other currencies. It thereby renders a currency inconvertible.

2. Aside from its use during World War I, the first peacetime application of exchange control by industrial countries occurred in response to the capital flight unloosed by the international financial crisis of 1931. During the 1930s the exchange control area was centered in Germany and Eastern Europe, although several countries in Latin America also adopted exchange restrictions in the face of balance of payments difficulties.

3. After World War II most countries continued to restrict both current and capital transactions by means of exchange control. However, a massive liberalization by the industrial countries began at the close of 1958, when ten European countries established nonresident convertibility of their currencies on current account. The majority of developing countries still retain exchange control as a major tool of foreign economic policy.

4. There are many objectives of exchange control. Foremost among them are the suppression of balance of payments disequilibrium, the facilitation of national planning, the protection of domestic industries, and the creation of government revenue. The versatility of ends that may be served by exchange control

is an important factor behind its continued use in contemporary international trade.

5. A useful distinction may be made between single-rate systems of exchange control and multiple-rate systems. In single-rate systems, all foreign exchange transactions are carried on at one official rate of exchange. All foreign exchange receipts are surrendered to an exchange control authority that allocates foreign exchange expenditures by types of important transactions, by countries and currency areas, and by applicants. Single-rate systems make use of import licenses and quotas in allocating foreign exchange.

6. In a multiple-rate system of exchange control, two or more legal exchange rates apply to different foreign exchange transactions. Because at least part of the task of allocating foreign exchange to different uses is carried out by differential exchange rates, multiple-rate systems rely on administrative action far less than do single-rate systems. There is a bewildering variety of multiple-rate systems.

7. The most important effect of exchange control is its disruption of multilateral settlement and the forcing of international trade into bilateral channels. Exchange control thus limits the advantages to be gained from international specialization in a competitive world market. When several countries practice exchange control, blocked balances and the scarcity of convertible currencies raise formidable obstacles to trade. To liquidate blocked balances and to avoid the use of convertible currencies in the financing of mutual trade, exchange control countries negotiate bilateral payments agreements.

8. Exchange control also redistributes money incomes, since exporters, importers, or the government are able to enjoy monopoly profits depending upon the nature of the system.

9. Exchange control is evaded by both residents and nonresidents in many ways, including bribery and corruption of officials, false invoicing of exports and imports, and black market operations.

10. The main indictment of exchange control is its interference with international trade based on comparative advantage. The achievement of a multilateral trading system, however, is compatible with the use of exchange control to stop a capital flight and with its temporary use to provide time for fundamental adjustment to an external payments deficit.

QUESTIONS AND APPLICATIONS

1. What is exchange control?
2. (a) Trace the origins of exchange control in the 1930s.
   (b) What is the present situation in the world economy with regard to exchange control?

3. (a) What are the principal objectives of contemporary exchange control systems?
   (b) How does exchange control serve these objectives?
4. (a) Describe the single-rate system of exchange control.
   (b) What is the key to this system of control?
   (c) How may the control authority ensure the surrender of foreign exchange?
   (d) What allocation problems does the control authority face?
   (e) What methods may be used to allocate foreign exchange to applicants?
5. What is the role of import quotas and licenses in single-rate systems of exchange control?
6. Why does exchange control involve the control of nonresident accounts?
7. (a) How does the multiple-rate system of exchange control differ from the single-rate system?
   (b) What features are peculiar to multiple-rate systems?
8. Distinguish between preferential and penalty buying and selling rates of exchange.
9. In the multiple-rate system, what is the function of floating market rates? Of mixing rates? Of exchange taxes?
10. Enumerate the principal effects of exchange control.
11. Describe the purpose and nature of bilateral payments agreements. Comment specifically on their credit and transferability provisions.
12. What is the "proper" use of exchange control?

SELECTED READINGS

Annual Report on Exchange Arrangements and Exchange Restrictions. Washington, D.C.: International Monetary Fund.

Bhagwati, Jagdish. *Anatomy and Consequences of Exchange Control Regimes.* Cambridge, Mass.: Ballinger, 1978.

League of Nations. *International Currency Experience.* New York: Columbia University Press, 1944.

Lizondo, Jose S. "Unifying Multiple Exchange Rates." *Finance & Development,* December 1985, pp. 23–24.

Nowak, Michael. "Black Markets in Foreign Exchange." *Finance & Development,* March 1985, pp. 20–23.

Quirk, Peter J. "The Case for Open Foreign Exchange Systems." *Finance & Development,* June 1989, pp. 30–33.

Trued, M. N., and R. F. Mikesell. *Postwar Bilateral Payments Agreements.* Princeton Studies in International Finance, no. 4. Princeton, N.J.: Princeton University Press, 1955.

THE BRETTON WOODS INTERNATIONAL MONETARY SYSTEM AND ITS COLLAPSE (1945–1971)

For 25 years after World War II, the international monetary system, known as the Bretton Woods system, was based on stable and convertible exchange rates, with occasional devaluations of individual currencies to correct "fundamental" disequilibria in the balance of payments. This system had several strengths, but it also had flaws that were to prove fatal. Mounting pressures in the 1960s culminated in the collapse of the Bretton Woods system in 1971 and its unintended replacement with a regime of floating exchange rates. In this and the following chapter we examine the leading features of the Bretton Woods system, the reasons for its collapse, the nature and performance of the contemporary floating-rate system.

The Bretton Woods international monetary system was sustained by two institutions: the International Monetary Fund and the central reserve role of the U.S. dollar.

THE INTERNATIONAL MONETARY FUND (IMF)

While war still raged in Europe and Asia, representatives of the United States, Great Britain, and other Allied countries met at Bretton Woods, New Hampshire, in 1944 to reach final agreement on the postwar international monetary system. The delegates to the conference, who included the eminent British economist John Maynard Keynes, were mindful of the rise and fall of international monetary systems in the past and particularly of the monetary chaos that preceded the war. From 1870 to 1914, the international gold standard (centered in London) had reigned supreme, only to be abandoned at the outbreak of World War I.[1] Among the major countries, only the United States maintained the gold convertibility of its currency during that conflict. After a period of freely fluctuating exchange

---

[1]The mechanics of the international gold standard are discussed in Chapter 12.

rates, the gold standard was painfully restored in the 1920s, but only in the modified form of a gold exchange standard whereby central banks held some or all of their reserves in sterling, dollars, or francs rather than in gold. Global depression, heightened by massive flows of speculative capital, forced the collapse of this system in the early 1930s; Great Britain halted the gold convertibility of the pound in September 1931, and the United States devalued the dollar by raising the price of gold from $20.67 to $35.00 an ounce in 1933. There followed a scramble by each country to protect its currency and trade vis-à-vis other countries. Competitive depreciations to promote exports and curb imports, inconvertible currencies, exchange control, currency blocs, and bilateral trade agreements became the order of the day.[2] Then came World War II.

The delegates at Bretton Woods were convinced that only an unprecedented degree of international monetary cooperation could hope to forestall a repetition of the 1930s. The outcome of their deliberations was the establishment of the International Monetary Fund, an international agency to administer a code of fair exchange practices and provide compensatory financial assistance to member countries in balance of payments trouble.[3]

The purposes of the IMF were clearly set forth in Article I of its Articles of Agreement:

1. To promote international monetary cooperation through a permanent institution which provides the machinery for consultation and collaboration on international monetary problems.
2. To facilitate the expansion and balanced growth of international trade, and to contribute thereby to the promotion and maintenance of high levels of employment and real income and to the development of the productive resources of all members as primary objectives of economic policy.
3. To promote exchange stability, to maintain orderly exchange arrangements among members, and to avoid competitive exchange depreciation.
4. To assist in the establishment of a multilateral system of payments in respect of current transactions between members and in the elimination of foreign exchange restrictions which hamper the growth of world trade.
5. To give confidence to members by making the Fund's resources available to them under adequate safeguards, thus providing them with the opportunity to correct maladjustments in the balances of payments without resorting to measures destructive of national or international balances of payments of members.

Code of Fair Exchange Practices

Upon entering the Fund, a country submitted a *par value* of its currency expressed in terms of gold or in terms of the U.S. dollar value of the weight and fineness of gold in effect on July 1, 1944. All exchange transactions between member coun-

---

[2]The collapse of the gold exchange standard in the 1930s is briefly treated at the beginning of Chapter 17.
[3]The Articles of Agreement of the Fund entered into force in December 1945. A second Bretton Woods agreement established the International Bank for Reconstruction and Development.

tries were to be effected at a rate that diverged not more than 1 percent from the par values of the respective currencies.

A member could change the par value of its currency only to correct a *fundamental* disequilibrium in its balance of payments and only after consultation with the Fund. If the Fund objected to the change but the member nevertheless went ahead with it, the Fund could declare that member ineligible to use its resources.[4] Although the Fund could object to a proposed change in the par value of a currency, it could not formally propose a change of its own accord. These provisions envisaged, therefore, a system of fixed exchange rates with an occasional devaluation (depreciation) or revaluation (appreciation) to remove a persistent disequilibrium in the balance of payments.[5]

Article VIII of the agreement forbade members to restrict current (account) payments or to discriminate in their currency practices without the approval of the Fund. Members were also obligated to maintain the convertibility of foreign-held balances acquired or used in connection with current transactions. Thus, Article VIII clearly outlawed exchange control over international payments for merchandise and services. On the other hand, Article VI allowed members to control capital movements as long as current transactions remained unaffected.

There were two exceptions to the provisions of Article VIII. One exception occurred when the Fund declared a currency to be scarce because the demand for the currency threatened the Fund's ability to supply it. A scarce currency declaration authorized member countries to impose exchange control over all transactions in the scarce currency. The scarce currency provision explicitly recognized that free convertibility could not be sustained if most countries had persistent deficits with the same surplus country, for in that event multilateral settlement of the deficits was out of the question. This provision also applied pressure on the surplus country to take remedial measures to avoid discrimination against its trade.

The most important exception to the provisions of Article VIII, however, was found in the provisions of Article XIV. This article allowed a member country to retain exchange restrictions on current international transactions in effect when that country entered the Fund. Moreover, these restrictions could be adapted to changing circumstances to deal with balance of payments difficulties. The decision to abandon exchange restrictions permitted under Article XIV was left to the member country, but it was supposed to occur when such restrictions were no longer necessary to settle the balance of payments without undue dependence on the Fund's resources. Once a member abolished its exchange control over current payments and accepted the obligations of Article VIII, it could not reimpose similar exchange restrictions without the approval of the Fund.

Article XIV was conceived as a "transitional arrangement" that would not be necessary once the member countries had overcome the problems of readjustment that immediately followed World War II. Events proved otherwise, however, and

---

[4]If the proposed change, together with all previous changes, whether increases or decreases, did not exceed 10 percent of the initial par value of the member's currency, the Fund would raise no objection.

[5]This is the adjustable-peg system described in the section "Variable Rates: Introduction" in Chapter 16.

it was not until 1961 that the major countries in Western Europe were able to accept the obligations of Article VIII. The last big trading country, Japan, came under Article VIII in 1964.[6] The remaining Article XIV countries were obliged to consult annually with the Fund on the continuance of exchange restrictions, but, as we noted earlier, the Fund had no power to decree their abolition. Nor did the Articles of Agreement specify the duration of the transition period.

Compensatory Financing by the Fund

In addition to administering a code of fair exchange practices, the Fund was also a source of compensatory financing for a member country experiencing a *temporary* disequilibrium in its balance of payments. The resources of the Fund came from the gold and currency subscriptions of its member countries.[7] Upon entering the Fund, each country was allotted a quota in accordance with its relative economic size. Twenty-five percent of a country's quota was paid to the Fund in gold and the remainder in the country's own currency.[8] Since quotas were calculated in the 1944 U.S. dollar, the dollar equivalents of nondollar currencies were determined by their respective par values. The Fund started operations in 1947 with aggregate quotas of $8 billion, but successive quota increases had raised the total to $28.5 billion by 1971. The largest quota was subscribed by the United States ($6.7 billion); the next largest by Great Britain ($2.8 billion).

The size of a country's quota was significant in two respects. First, it determined, approximately, the voting power of a member's executive director. Thus, the executive director of the United States had 21.9 percent of the voting power of the executive directors; the executive director of the United Kingdom had 9.2 percent. This gave these two countries a dominant voice in the operation of the Fund. Second, the size of a country's quota determined the overall amount that it could draw from the resources of the Fund.

A member country was entitled to buy from the Fund, with its own currency, the currency of another member subject to the following conditions:

1. The member desired to buy a currency to make currency payments consistent with the provisions of the Articles of Agreement.
2. The Fund had not given notice that its holdings of the desired currency were scarce.
3. The proposed purchase did not cause the Fund's holdings of the purchasing member's currency to increase by over 25 percent of its quota during the twelve-month period ending on the date of such purchase nor to exceed 200 percent of its basic quota.

---

[6]By April 1971, thirty-five countries had accepted Article VIII. The Fund never invoked the scarce currency provision.

[7]In 1971, 117 countries of the noncommunist world were members of the Fund.

[8]When a country's gold reserves were low, it was permitted to join the Fund without full payment of its gold subscription, using its own currency as a substitute. Full payment was expected, however, when the country's gold reserves became adequate.

4. The Fund had not previously declared that the member desiring to purchase was ineligible to use the resources of the Fund.

In practice, the Fund freely allowed member countries to purchase other currencies up to the first 25 percent of their quotas (often called the *gold tranche*).[9] It also waived the twelve-month requirement in many instances. The Fund would not permit a country to draw beyond 25 percent of its quota, however, unless convinced that the country in question was following policies directed toward the eventual achievement of convertibility or the avoidance of exchange restrictions. Convertibility was a principal objective of the Fund, and it employed its resources accordingly.

The Fund also encouraged liberal exchange policies by negotiating *standby agreements* with interested member countries. Through these agreements, member countries received the Fund's guarantee that they would be allowed to draw on the Fund for the currency or currencies covered by the agreement within a specified period of time.

In addition to drawings under these general arrangements, a country could apply for a special drawing to obtain compensatory financing for a temporary decline in its export earnings. Intended to assist developing countries, such special drawings did not normally exceed 25 percent of a country's quota, but they could bring the Fund's holdings of a country's currency over the limit of twice its quota.

The resources of the Fund were intended to supplement the reserves of a country when it was faced with a temporary deficit in the balance of payments. Hence, the Fund provided only *short-term* financial assistance that was to be repaid by the borrowing country within the near future (three to five years). The Fund was not a source of capital like the World Bank, and no member country could look to it for more than stopgap compensatory financing of an external deficit.

In 1962 the Fund's resources were supplemented by the *General Arrangements to Borrow,* which were negotiated by ten industrial countries. Under this agreement the Fund could borrow up to $5.9 billion from the "Group of Ten" to provide compensatory financial assistance to one or more of the participating countries.[10] In 1970, the Fund activated an entirely new facility to supply reserve assets to its members, known as *Special Drawing Rights (SDRs).* SDRs are treated later in the chapter.

Evaluation of the Fund

The IMF was originally intended to carry out its functions in a world economy enjoying a substantial degree of overall equilibrium and free of any persistent

---

[9]A country's *reserve position in the Fund* equaled its gold tranche *minus* any current utilization of its drawing rights *plus* the Fund's use of its currency to finance the drawings of other countries or to purchase gold. This reserve position was considered an unconditional asset that was part of a country's international reserves.

[10]Participants in the General Arrangements to Borrow, known as the "Group of Ten," were Belgium, Canada, France, West Germany, Italy, Japan, the Netherlands, Sweden, the United Kingdom, and the United States. In 1964 Switzerland became an associate member.

maladjustments, such as the dollar shortage or subsequent dollar glut. In such an economy, countries would adjust to temporary deficits in their balance of payments by resorting to their own reserves and, if necessary, to the resources of the Fund. Free convertibility would be maintained by all countries and exchange rates would be altered, after consultation with the Fund, only to correct a fundamental disequilibrium. In this way, the advantages of the gold standard — convertibility and fixed exchange rates — would be gained, while an occasional exchange devaluation would maintain equilibrium without the disadvantage of internal deflation. More specifically, the Fund was conceived as an antidote to the conditions of the 1930s. In those years convertibility was maintained between the dollar and the pound sterling (the key trading currencies), but its effects were compromised by disorderly exchange practices, including competitive depreciation and the spread of exchange control to Central and Eastern Europe and to Latin America.

In light of these observations, it is not surprising that the Fund could not fulfill its intended functions in the first decade of its existence. During those years nondollar countries showed persistent payments deficits and continued to restrict dollar payments. Moreover, unlike in the 1930s, inflation rather than depression was the principal obstacle to external stability after World War II, and with few exceptions exchange rates were controlled to avert depreciation. During this period of restrictions and inconvertibility, the Fund was mostly a bystander, and little use was made of its resources. This passive role ended abruptly with the Suez crisis in 1956–1957.

We can now see in retrospect that the Suez crisis coincided with the end of the dollar shortage: In 1958 the U.S. balance of payments suffered the first of a continuing series of big deficits that replaced the dollar shortage with a dollar glut. When called upon at the end of 1956, the Fund quickly responded with compensatory financial assistance that was needed to overcome the trade disruptions and fears of the time. The resumption of convertibility by Western European countries at the end of 1958 carried with it the widespread abandonment of exchange controls on current transactions and later on capital transactions. With the accession of Japan to Article VIII in 1964, the Fund nearly achieved one of its basic purposes — the elimination of exchange controls for the bulk of world trade.

The return of convertibility, however, brought another problem in its wake: sudden, massive movements of speculative and flight capital among the financial centers of North America and Western Europe. As we shall see, this new source of instability, together with a progressive weakening of the dollar during the 1960s, ultimately forced a profound disruption of the Fund's par value system in 1971. We now turn to another aspect of the Bretton Woods monetary system as it evolved after World War II: the central reserve role of the U.S. dollar.

THE CENTRAL RESERVE ROLE OF THE U.S. DOLLAR

The Fund agreement laid the basis for the international monetary system after World War II. But the system evolved in a way that was not envisaged in that agreement. During the 1950s the United States emerged as the prime reserve country, with the dollar increasingly taking over the function of gold as an international reserve asset. No one planned this development; it arose as a response to the dominant postwar position of the United States in international trade and finance.[11] With well over half of all international money transactions being financed in terms of dollars, it became necessary for banks and business enterprises throughout the world to maintain dollar working balances.

In the early 1950s, as the European countries began to enjoy reserve surpluses, the most natural course of action for central banks was to convert those surpluses into dollar reserves rather than into gold. After all, interest could be earned on dollar assets and they could always be converted into gold at $35 per ounce if that ever became necessary.

The gold-exchange system that emerged in the 1950s is depicted in Figure 18-1. All of the noncommunist countries maintained a stable relationship between their currencies and the dollar either directly or through the British pound. For members of the Fund this relationship was expressed in the par values of their currencies; for nonmembers (the most important being Switzerland) it was a result of an autonomous stabilization policy. The U.S. dollar stood at the center of this system, and it was the only currency directly convertible into gold for official monetary purposes. Before World War I the pound sterling performed a similar function, but the sterling area had shrunk to a small number of countries with mostly minor currencies. In this limited fashion, the United Kingdom also operated as a central reserve country. As the Bretton Woods system evolved, however, the reserves of most countries became a mixture of gold and dollars, with a growing dominance of the latter.[12]

The extraordinary role of the dollar in the international monetary system gave the U.S. balance of payments a significance far transcending that of other countries' balances of payments. And it was the inability of the United States to restore equilibrium after more than a decade of deficits that proved the undoing of the Bretton Woods system.

THE U.S. BALANCE OF PAYMENTS DEFICIT

In the 1960s the international monetary system was shaken by a series of crises in foreign exchange and gold markets. Although speculation against the dollar started as early as 1960, these crises became more frequent and more intense in the second half of the decade. Some of these crises were provoked by balance of payments disequilibria in nondollar currencies accompanied by massive shifts of speculative funds among the major financial centers. But the most pervasive source of instability was the weakness of the dollar, which, given its role as the central reserve currency, raised doubts about the viability of the entire system.

---

[11]As one writer put it, the dollar and the pound sterling "became international currencies neither by Act of Congress (Parliament) nor by Act of God, but rather because they met various needs of foreign official institutions and foreign private parties more effectively than other financial assets could." See Robert Z. Aliber, *The Future of the Dollar as an International Currency* (New York: Frederick A. Praeger, 1966), p. 8.

[12]See Table 18-6.

Figure 18-1

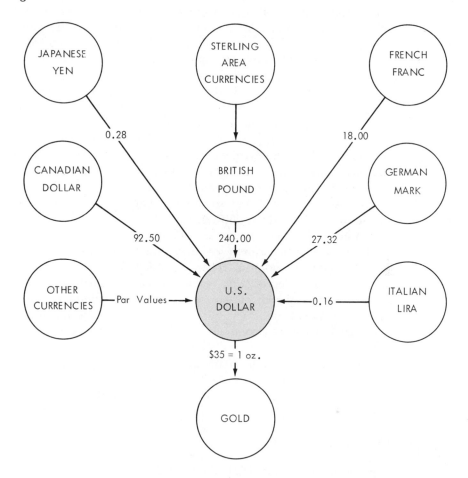

Note: Par values as of August 15, 1971, expressed as U.S. cents per currency unit.

The Central Reserve Role of the U.S. Dollar in the Bretton Woods International Monetary System. In the Bretton Woods international monetary system, all IMF countries were obligated to maintain stable par values of their currencies expressed in terms of gold or in terms of the 1944 U.S. dollar. The U.S. dollar was the only currency convertible into gold (at a fixed price of $35 per ounce) for official monetary purposes. In practice, nondollar currencies were pegged to the dollar at rates of exchange that were altered only to adjust to a "fundamental disequilibrium" in a country's balance of payments. Hence, the designation of the Bretton Woods system as an "adjustable-peg" system.

During the period 1958–1971, the United States experienced a persistent deficit in its balance of payments. At first, the tendency was to regard these annual deficits as temporary in nature and not calling for any extraordinary measures by U.S. authorities. But by the fall of 1960 it had become obvious that the United States was facing a payments situation that was not self-corrective and showed signs of disconcerting permanency.

The complexity of the U.S. balance of payments, the mutual interdependence of its individual items, the many factors— economic and political—that have a causal bearing on international transactions, and, in some instances, the lack of sound quantitative data rendered impossible a precise determination of the cause or causes of the successive deficits. This is hardly surprising when we realize that a balance of payments is a summary of *all* the economic transactions between one country and the rest of the world over the year. It is also not surprising that economists disagreed—and sometimes sharply—as to the underlying cause or causes of the U.S. disequilibrium.

Analytical disagreements inevitably engendered policy disagreements. All sorts of remedial measures were urged upon the U.S. government by American and European economists. These included the "classical medicine" of internal deflation, dollar depreciation, gold appreciation, floating exchange rates, capital issues control, orthodox measures to increase world liquidity, and a basic reform of the international monetary system. These policy recommendations were often supported by cogent reasoning, but all of them were controversial in one way or another.

Table 18-1 shows the basic, net liquidity, and official reserves deficits of the U.S. balance of payments in 1970.[13] Table 18-2 indicates the net liquidity, official reserves, and basic deficits of the U.S. balance of payments during the period 1960–1971.

Financing the U.S. Deficits

During the years 1958–1971, the United States experienced a cumulative reserve deficit of $56 billion. The United States financed this deficit by drawing on its gold reserves and by incurring liquid liabilities to foreign central banks. Table 18-3 records the changes in U.S. reserve assets during those years.

As a central reserve country, the international reserves of the United States consisted mainly of gold. Gold reserves fell from $22.9 billion in 1957 to $10.2 billion at the end of 1971, or a total reduction of $12.7 billion. Exports of monetary gold, therefore, financed some 23 percent of the cumulative deficit. The other reserve assets provided only minimal compensatory financing for the period as a whole. The United States started using the currencies of other countries (mainly

---

[13]The basic and official reserves transactions balances are described in Chapter 14. The *net liquidity balance* was intended to measure changes in the liquidity position of the United States by distinguishing *nonliquid* private short-term capital from *liquid* private short-term capital.

Table 18-1   U.S. Balance of Payments in 1970 Showing the Basic, Net Liquidity, and Official Reserve Deficits (Billions of Dollars)

1.	Net balance on goods and services[1]	3.6
2.	Remittances, pensions, and other transfers	− 1.4
3.	U.S. government grants[2]	− 1.7
4.	Long-term U.S. government capital flows, net	− 1.8
5.	Long-term private capital flows, net	− 1.5
6.	*Basic balance* (1 + 2 + 3 + 4 + 5)	− 3.0
7.	Nonliquid short-term private capital flows, net[3]	− 0.5
8.	Allocations of Special Drawing Rights (SDRs)	0.9
9.	Errors and omissions, net	− 1.1
10.	*Net liquidity balance* (Basic balance + 7 + 8 + 9)	− 3.8
11.	Liquid private capital flows: claims[4]	0.2
12.	Liquid private capital flows: liabilities[5]	− 6.2
13.	*Official reserves transactions balance* (net liquidity balance + 11 + 12)	− 9.8
14.	Nonliquid liabilities to foreign official agencies	− 0.3
15.	Liquid liabilities to foreign official agencies	7.6
16.	U.S. official reserve assets	2.5

(a)	Gold	0.8
(b)	SDRs	− 0.9
(c)	Convertible currencies	2.2
(d)	Gold tranche position in IMF	0.4

Note: Figures may not add because of rounding.

[1]Excludes military transfers under grants.

[2]Excludes military grants.

[3]Nonliquid short-term capital flows include changes in loans, collections, acceptance credits, and other credits to finance international trade.

[4]Changes in time and demand deposits and other negotiable instruments held abroad by U.S. residents.

[5]Changes in time and demand deposits and other negotiable instruments held in the United States by foreigners.

Source: Federal Reserve Bulletin (Washington D.C.: U.S. Government Printing Office, December 1971), Table 1, p. A74.

through bilateral swap agreements with foreign central banks) only in 1961, and SDRs were not activated until 1970.

The remaining cumulative deficit was financed primarily by an increase in liquid liabilities to official monetary institutions, as shown in Table 18-4. These liabilities rose from $7.9 billion in 1957 to $47.1 billion at the end of 1971, an

Table 18-2 Basic, Net Liquidity, and Official Reserve Deficits in the U.S. Balance of Payments, 1960–1971 (Billions of Dollars)

Year	Net Liquidity Deficit	Official Reserves Deficit	Basic Deficit
1960	– 3.7	– 3.4	– 1.2
1961	– 2.3	– 1.3	0.0
1962	– 2.9	– 2.7	– 1.0
1963	– 2.7	– 1.9	– 1.3
1964	– 2.7	– 1.5	0.0
1965	– 2.5	– 1.3	– 1.8
1966	– 2.2	+ 0.2	– 1.7
1967	– 4.7	– 3.4	– 3.3
1968	– 1.6	+ 1.6	– 1.4
1969	– 6.1	+ 2.7	– 3.0
1970	– 3.9	– 9.8	– 3.1
1971	– 22.0	– 29.8	– 9.4

Source: *U.S. Balance of Payments Trends* (St. Louis: Federal Reserve Bank of St. Louis, April 1973), p. 3.

increase of $39.2 billion.[14] This extraordinary rise in official liquid liabilities was possible only because of the central reserve role of the dollar. Dollars accumulated by foreign central banks were regarded as international reserve assets. A non-reserve country did not have this source of compensatory financing; it was compelled to rely on its own reserve assets and limited external assistance from the Fund and other agencies. Although foreign central banks became increasingly reluctant to add to their dollar reserves in the 1960s, as a group they had no alternative. By 1963 U.S. gold reserves barely covered liabilities to foreign central banks, and by the end of 1970 coverage had fallen to 55 percent. Any concerted attempt by central banks to convert their dollar holdings into gold, therefore, would have forced the United States to abandon gold convertibility, which was the foundation of the Bretton Woods system. As it turned out, a massive flight from the dollar in 1971 (financed by a truly fantastic increase in official liabilities, from $20.1 billion at the end of 1970 to $40.7 billion at the end of August 1971) persuaded the United States to halt gold convertibility on its own initiative on August 15, 1971.

---

[14]Additional compensatory financing was supplied by an increase in nonliquid liabilities to foreign official agencies (item 14 in Table 18-1) and by liabilities to the IMF arising out of gold transactions.

Table 18-3 Reserve Assets of the United States, 1957–1971

End of Period	Total Reserve Assets	Convertible Currencies	Reserve Position in IMF	SDRs	Gold Stock	Gold Stock as Fraction of Official Liquid Liabilities
1957	24.8		2.0		22.9	2.90
1960	19.4		1.6		17.8	1.75
1963	16.8	0.2	1.0		15.6	1.08
1966	14.9	1.3	0.3		13.2	0.96
1967	14.8	2.3	0.4		12.1	0.78
1968	15.7	3.5	1.3		10.9	0.88
1969	17.0	2.8	2.3		11.9	0.99
1970	14.5	0.6	1.9	0.9	11.1	0.55
1971	12.2	0.2	0.6	1.1	10.2	0.22

Source: Federal Reserve Bulletin (Washington, D.C.: U.S. Government Printing Office, September 1969), Table 4, p. A75, and (January 1974), Table 4, p. A75. Liquid liabilities to official institutions are shown in Table 18-4.

Table 18-4   U.S. Liquid Liabilities to Foreign Countries, 1957–1971 (Billions of Dollars)

End of Period	Official Institutions	Banks and Other Private Foreigners	Total Liabilities
1957	7.9	5.7	13.6
1960	10.2	7.6	17.8
1963	14.4	9.2	23.6
1966	13.7	14.2	27.9
1967	15.6	15.8	31.4
1968	12.4	19.4	31.8
1969	12.0	28.2	40.2
1970	20.1	21.8	41.9
1971	47.1	15.1	62.2

Source: Federal Reserve Bulletin (Washington, D.C.: U.S. Government Printing Office, December 1971), Table 6, p. A78, and (January 1974), Table 6, p. A75.

Remedial Measures Taken by the U.S. Government
Before August 15, 1971

As we learned in earlier chapters, a country may adjust to a persistent deficit in its balance of payments in three broad ways: (1) through an internal deflation of prices and incomes relative to foreign prices and incomes; (2) through a devaluation of its exchange rate; or (3) through direct, nonmarket measures such as export promotion, exchange controls, and restrictions on trade and investment. In the 1960s the U.S. government chose the third way by adopting an extraordinary variety of measures to directly influence all of the major classes of transactions making up the balance of payments. They included measures to increase exports through promotional activities, measures to reduce U.S. government outlays abroad, measures to restrain private capital exports, and measures taken by the U.S. monetary authorities. Here we describe only capital restrictions and compensatory financing arrangements.

The first direct action to lessen the outflow of private capital was the imposition in mid-1963 of an *interest equalization tax* on the value of foreign securities bought by U.S. residents. This tax was effective in curbing the outflow of portfolio investment even though Canada, developing countries, and international financial agencies were granted exemptions. The tax forced foreign borrowers to raise funds locally or in European capital markets.

The curtailment of U.S. portfolio investment after mid-1963 was more than offset in 1964 by a big jump in U.S. bank loans to foreign borrowers and a further growth in U.S. direct investments. This precipitated a series of measures called the *voluntary restraint program.*

In a special balance of payments message to Congress in February 1965, President Johnson proposed a series of new steps to eliminate the payments deficit, including the application of the interest equalization tax to bank loans to foreigners of one year or more (except export credit), the voluntary cooperation of U.S. banks to limit their lending abroad, and the enlistment of U.S. business in a national campaign to limit direct investments abroad. Shortly thereafter, the Federal Reserve System and the Department of Commerce issued guidelines to commercial banks and business corporations, respectively, requesting them to achieve specified goals in restraining loans and investments abroad. Although the voluntary program was successful in limiting the outflow of direct investment capital, it was replaced in 1968 by *mandatory investment controls.*[15]

Although compensatory financing is not an adjustment to a persistent deficit, the U.S. monetary authorities sought to lessen the gold drain and forestall speculation by initiating measures that were described as the "first line of defense" for the dollar. Traditionally the United States had supported the dollar through a policy of passive stabilization. This policy shifted in May 1961, when the U.S. Treasury actively intervened in the foreign exchange market for the first time since the early 1930s. Using its Exchange Stabilization Fund, the Treasury's first intervention

---

[15]Restrictions on capital outflows were not lifted until 1974.

was limited to sales of forward West German deutsche marks to prevent excessive speculation in that currency, which could lead to a flight from the dollar. Later it extended its operations to other currencies in both spot and forward markets. Active stabilization of the dollar was massively reinforced in March 1962, when the Federal Reserve System entered the foreign exchange market on its own account (for the first time since the late 1920s) rather than simply acting as an agent of the Treasury. In the ensuing years the U.S. monetary authorities engaged in numerous transactions in all the leading currencies, mainly to prevent or moderate speculative capital movements in both the dollar and foreign currencies, especially the pound sterling.

As part of its new intervention activity, the Federal Reserve System entered into a series of reciprocal currency arrangements (commonly called *swap agreements*) with the central banks of Western Europe, Canada, and Japan. Under these bilateral arrangements a foreign central bank provided standby credits to the Federal Reserve System in return for an equal amount of standby credits. At the end of 1964 the total amount of swap standby credits was over $2.3 billion; by 1971 it had climbed to $11.7 billion. The swap network benefited foreign countries, such as Italy and Great Britain, by supplementing their reserves with an assured access to dollars and, at the same time, afforded the United States a buffer to absorb sudden speculative drives on the dollar and thereby protected its gold reserves.

To reduce the "overhang" of U.S. liquid liabilities owing to foreign central banks, the U.S. Treasury issued a series of medium-term bonds payable in dollars or in specified foreign currencies for sale to foreign governments and central banks. In effect, these sales of medium-term bonds relieved pressure on U.S. gold reserves by giving foreign central banks an opportunity to acquire an earning asset payable in their own currencies.

None of the foregoing measures introduced by the U.S. monetary authorities reduced the U.S. basic deficit. But they lessened the gold drain and dampened speculative capital outflows by influencing spot and forward rates of exchange (especially forward rates), by interposing a buffer of foreign central bank credits, and by converting a part of U.S. liquid liabilities to a less liquid, more stable form.

Constraints Imposed on U.S. Payments Policy

In the 1960s, U.S. policymakers perceived many constraints that prevented them from making a fundamental adjustment to the balance of payments deficit. Conscious of U.S. leadership of the noncommunist world, they refused to cut back on military forces abroad or abandon foreign assistance to developing countries. Quite understandably, they also refused to deflate the economy to improve the balance of payments. In the first half of the 1960s, U.S. domestic policy was geared to expansion rather than contraction. Only in the late 1960s, when inflation got out of hand, did U.S. policymakers adopt anti-inflationary policies.

Why, then, did the United States not devalue the dollar in the 1960s? The answer to this question lies in the unique role of the dollar as a central reserve currency. This role conferred both benefits and costs on the United States. The clearest benefit was the willingness of foreign central banks to add dollars to their reserves, thus giving the United States a virtually unlimited and automatic access to compensatory finance and allowing it to postpone fundamental adjustment. The cost of this benefit was the commitment (as perceived by U.S. policymakers) to maintain a fixed link between the dollar and gold. Hence, the United States was not able to *initiate* a change in the external value of the dollar, which instead was dependent on the devaluations and revaluations of other currencies. It was also widely held that even if the United States did devalue the dollar by raising the price of gold, other countries would respond by devaluing their own currencies to the same extent and would thereby neutralize the effects of dollar devaluation on the balance of payments. There was also fear that a dollar devaluation would set off immense speculative activity endangering all countries. Only the monetary crisis of 1971 forced an abandonment of these perceptions and the undertaking of drastically new policies in August of that year.

MONETARY CRISES IN THE LATE 1960s

In the middle 1960s, the continuing weakness of sterling (the second central reserve currency) was a major cause of disturbances in foreign exchange markets. Starting in June 1967, tremendous speculative pressures built up against sterling, and in November it was officially devalued from $2.80 to $2.40. This action did not, however, restore stability in foreign exchange markets. Early in 1968, speculators turned to the London gold market in the expectation of a rise in the official price of gold. To maintain the London price at the official price of $35 an ounce, the United States and other members of the "gold pool" sold gold to the private market out of their own reserves.[16] During the first quarter of 1968, the United States lost $1.3 billion in gold, three-fourths of which went to support the London market.

This drain of official gold reserves to private speculators was stopped in March 1968, when the gold pool members agreed to abstain from any further sales to the London market and also not to buy private gold in the future. In this way there emerged the "two-tier" gold arrangement: an official price of $35 an ounce and a private price determined by private supply and demand. The decision to abandon all intervention in the London gold market served to freeze the amount of gold in official reserves — another step away from a gold-exchange standard and toward a dollar standard. Henceforth, central banks would engage in gold transactions only with other central banks.

Scarcely had the gold crisis abated when France was wracked by widespread student and worker protests in May and June 1968. This political instability sparked a capital flight from the franc, especially into the West German deutsche

---

[16]The gold pool was devised in 1961 by the United States, the United Kingdom, Belgium, West Germany, Italy, the Netherlands, and Switzerland. The members of the pool agreed to share in the support of the London gold market.

mark. Although the French reserves fell drastically (France lost $2.8 billion in gold in 1968), the French government opted for exchange restrictions instead of devaluation. In 1969 there was a mounting expectation that the French deficit would force a devaluation of the franc while the West German trade surplus would force a revaluation of the deutsche mark. Stability was eventually restored by a franc devaluation of 11.1 percent in August and the declaration of a higher par value for the deutsche mark in October.

THE INTERNATIONAL MONETARY CRISIS OF 1971

Unlike the crises of the late 1960s, the crisis of 1971 was directly inspired by a loss of confidence in the dollar. In the third quarter of 1970, funds began to move at an enormous rate from the United States to financial centers in Europe and Japan. At first, these short-term capital flows were largely a response to interest-rate differentials, but in March 1971 (when interest-rate differentials had narrowed), expectations of changes in exchange rates began to feed a growing speculation against the dollar. The ensuing sequence of events is presented in Table 18-5.

The actions taken by the United States on August 15 marked the end of the Bretton Woods system. On that day (a Sunday), President Nixon suspended "temporarily" the gold convertibility of the dollar and imposed a "temporary" surcharge on dutiable imports into the United States. He justified the suspension of convertibility as necessary to "defend the dollar against speculators" who "have been waging all-out war on the American dollar." But the more important purpose was to compel foreign governments to raise the value of their currencies against the dollar. In effect, foreign governments were offered a simple choice: Continue to maintain existing exchange rates by accumulating more dollars without gold convertibility *or* revalue exchange rates. The import surcharge was intended to place further pressure on them; it would not be taken off until foreign governments altered their "unfair" exchange rates.

The immediate response to the U.S. actions was a closing of foreign exchange markets in Europe and Japan. When they reopened, all of the major foreign currencies were left to float vis-à-vis the dollar, with the exception of the French franc. Hence, the system depicted in Figure 18-1 no longer existed; the Bretton Woods system had died, and a new system was waiting to be born.

THE SMITHSONIAN AGREEMENT

The weeks following August 15 were rife with uncertainty, rumor, and tension. Taking a hard line, the U.S. government pressed the view that the dollar's troubles arose from the undervalued exchange rates, protectionist trade policies, and the inadequate defense-sharing expenditures of foreign governments. It demanded unilateral concessions in all three areas. Put on the defensive, the European and Japanese governments firmly resisted any change in the par values of their currencies, fearing the harmful consequences of revaluation on their exports and domestic economic situations. If the dollar is overvalued, they argued, then the United States should find a way to carry out a unilateral devaluation.

Chapter 18   The Bretton Woods International Monetary System and Its Collapse   471

**Table 18-5 Collapse of the Bretton Woods System:
A Chronology of Events in 1971**

January February	Large movement of interest-sensitive funds from the United States to Europe, pushing European currencies against dollar ceilings.
March April	Overt speculation appears in foreign exchange markets. A strong trade surplus and restrictive credit policy intensify buying pressure on the deutsche mark. U.S. official reserve deficit for first quarter reaches $5.5 billion.
May 3–4 May 5	Bundesbank forced to absorb a capital inflow of $1 billion. Bundesbank suspends support of the dollar after absorbing $1 billion in the first forty minutes of trading. Central banks of the Netherlands, Switzerland, Belgium, and Austria also terminate support of the dollar.
May 10	When foreign exchange markets reopen, the Swiss franc and Austrian schilling are revalued 7.07 percent and 5.05 percent, respectively, while the West German deutsche mark and Dutch guilder are allowed to float. Belgian market is split between official and financial markets.
June July	U.S. official reserves deficit soars to $11.3 billion for first half of year. U.S. trade deficit for second quarter is $1.0 billion. Outflow of speculative capital from United States continues. U.S. gold stock falls close to $10 billion.
August 1–14	U.S. Congressional subcommittee asserts the dollar is overvalued; calls for general realignment of exchange rates. Abrupt acceleration of capital flight from the dollar, which sells at its lowest level against the deutsche mark in twenty-two years.
August 15	President Nixon announces major new program: ninety-day freeze on wages and prices, new tax measures, 10 percent temporary surcharge on dutiable imports, and "temporary" suspension of the dollar's convertibility into gold.
August 16–20	West European governments keep their exchange markets closed. Fail to develop a coordinated response to U.S. measures.
August 23	European governments open foreign exchange markets on uncoordinated basis; each continues to adhere to pre-August 15 parity, but all except the French government cease to support the dollar. The French support commercial transactions market but not financial transactions market.
August 28	Japanese government suspends official intervention in the foreign exchange market. Yen immediately rises 4.7 percent.

Table 18-5 Continued

September	Exchange rates of major trading currencies rise against the dollar, except commercial rate for French franc. But it is not a "pure" float: Many central banks continue to intervene on an ad hoc basis and some apply exchange restrictions.
September 15	Meeting of Finance Ministers of Group of Ten countries ends in total disagreement; U.S. demands — revaluation of other currencies, reduction in trade barriers, and more sharing of international defense burdens — shock foreign officials.
September 16	GATT urges the United States to end import surcharge.
October November	Pressure builds on the United States to end crisis; there is talk of retaliation in foreign countries. U.S. official reserves deficit reaches $12.1 billion for the first three quarters of year. Speculation intensifies.
December 1	U.S. Secretary of the Treasury surprises Group of Ten Finance Ministers at a meeting in Rome by suggesting a 10 percent dollar devaluation (rise in price of gold) as basis for negotiation.
December 14	At a meeting in the Azores, President Nixon and President Pompidou of France agree to work toward "prompt realignment of currencies through devaluation of the dollar and revaluation of some other currencies."
December 17–18	Group of Ten Finance Ministers meet at Smithsonian Institution in Washington, D.C. United States agrees to 8.57 percent devaluation of the dollar (rise in price of gold per ounce from $35 to $38) and end of surcharge in return for revaluation of other currencies. President Nixon hails outcome as "the most significant monetary agreement in the history of the world."

Meanwhile most of the leading currencies were floating at higher dollar values, but it was not a "clean" float, as central banks intervened in the market to prevent a full appreciation. France refused to float its currency for commercial transactions, although it permitted a floating rate for financial transactions. Foreign governments were reluctant to let their currencies float freely because they hoped to persuade the United States to devalue the dollar by raising the price of gold.

International monetary negotiations were undertaken within the framework of the Group of Ten. After several meetings, the United States agreed in mid-December to include a dollar devaluation in a general realignment of currencies. The details of this realignment were worked out by the Group of Ten on December 17 and 18 in a meeting at the Smithsonian Institution in Washington, D.C. The

Smithsonian Agreement was then formalized by the IMF, which established a "temporary regime" allowing member countries to vary their exchange rates within margins of 2.25 percent on either side of the new "central rates" resulting from the currency realignment. In return for the revaluation of other currencies, the United States agreed to raise the price of gold from $35 an ounce to $38 an ounce (a dollar devaluation of 8.57 percent) and to immediately "suppress" its 10 percent import surcharge.

The Smithsonian Agreement gave the United States the currency realignment it had requested in return for a modest rise in the price of gold, a concession having no economic significance while the dollar remained inconvertible to gold. More important, it was an achievement of international monetary cooperation, a triumph of enlightened self-interest over economic nationalism. It reflected the universal acceptance of the need for agreed rules to govern exchange rates and exchange practices. Hence, the collapse of the Bretton Woods system on August 15 did not degenerate into chaos, as did the collapse of the international gold standard in the early 1930s. For all of its weaknesses, the Bretton Woods system had fostered intimate monetary cooperation on an unprecedented scale through the institutional machinery of the IMF and the Group of Ten. When the crunch came, this machinery proved equal to the challenge.

Although the Smithsonian Agreement prevented competitive exchange-rate behavior, it did not tackle the problems of durable international monetary reform. In retrospect, it was a futile attempt to perpetuate the adjustable-peg system, albeit with new currency alignments. With the second devaluation of the dollar in February 1973, the Smithsonian Agreement fell apart as other currencies were left to float against the dollar, thus marking the beginning of the contemporary international monetary system.

WEAKNESSES OF THE BRETTON WOODS SYSTEM

The poor performance of the Bretton Woods system in the 1960s is attributable mainly to three interrelated causes: (1) the problem of international liquidity formation centered on the dollar, (2) delays in balance of payments adjustment, and (3) disequilibrating short-term capital movements.

The Problem of International Liquidity Formation

International liquidity consists of (1) the world's supply of gold, foreign exchange, and other assets ("owned" reserves) that are freely usable to finance payments deficits and (2) available facilities for borrowing them ("borrowed" reserves). Over the longer run, the growth of international liquidity is dependent on the growth of international reserve assets or owned reserves. Table 18-6 depicts the growth and composition of reserve assets between the end of 1959 and the end of September 1971.

The most striking feature of Table 18-6 is the prominence of the U.S. dollar. During this period, nearly all the growth in total reserves ($59.9 billion) came from

Table 18-6 Growth and Composition of International Reserves of IMF Countries, 1959–1971 (End of Period—Billions of Dollars)

Reserve Asset	1959	1965	1968	1969	1970	1971*	Increase (+) or Decrease (–) 1959–1971
Gold	37.9	41.9	38.9	39.1	37.2	36.2	– 1.7
Foreign exchange	16.2	23.8	31.9	32.3	44.5	68.9	+ 52.7
U.S. dollar	10.1	15.8	17.5	10.0	23.9	45.7	+ 35.6
U.K. pound	7.0	7.1	9.7	8.9	6.6	7.1	+ 0.1
Difference	– 0.9	0.9	4.7	7.4	14.0	16.2	+ 17.1
Reserve positions in Fund	3.2	5.4	6.5	6.7	7.7	6.3	+ 3.1
Special Drawing Rights (SDRs)	–	–	–	–	3.1	5.9	+ 5.9
Total reserves	57.4	71.0	77.3	78.2	92.5	117.3	+ 59.9

*End of September 1971.

Source: International Financial Statistics (Washington, D.C.: International Monetary Fund, February 1970), pp. 13, 15, and (February 1972), pp. 18, 23.

General Note: Total may not add because of rounding. *Foreign exchange* mostly consists of U.S. liabilities to foreign official holders and, to a much lesser extent, U.K. liabilities to foreign official holders. From 1968, most of the *difference* is attributable to official holdings of Eurodollars, which do not appear as U.S. liabilities to official holders. *Reserve positions in the Fund* equal member countries' gold tranches plus the Fund's use of their currencies for drawings or gold purchases. *SDRs* are unconditional reserve assets created by the Fund.

an increase in the dollar holdings of foreign central banks—an increase of $35.6 billion in recorded U.S. liabilities and an increase of $17.1 billion in the "difference," which consists mostly of Eurodollar holdings.[17] The remaining growth ($7.2 billion) came from increases in reserve positions in the IMF and the creation of SDRs after 1969. Sterling reserves were stable over the period, while gold reserves actually decreased by $1.7 billion. As noted earlier, no gold was purchased by the major central banks from private sources after the agreement of March 1968.

As the Bretton Woods system actually functioned, therefore, most of the growth in international reserves came from an increase in U.S. liabilities to foreign central banks. This growth was not planned; it was the result of U.S. balance of payments deficits. In particular, the growth had nothing in common with the required level of international liquidity. If the U.S. deficit were to turn into a surplus, then dollar reserves would fall regardless of the need for international liquidity. More fundamentally, the dollar could not supply new reserves on a sustainable basis over the long run because of an inherent *contradiction* of the gold-

---

[17]The Eurodollar market is discussed in "The Eurocurrency Market" in Chapter 19.

exchange standard. A sustained increase in the official liabilities of the central reserve country would eventually reduce the gold cover below 100 percent (as happened to the dollar in the mid-1960s), and a continuing increase would cause a progressive loss of confidence in the gold convertibility of the reserve currency. At some point, foreign central banks would force a breakdown of the system by demanding gold from the central reserve country, or the central reserve country itself would declare its currency no longer convertible into gold. As we have seen, the latter happened on August 15, 1971, and its effect was to transform the international monetary system from a gold-dollar standard into a pure dollar standard, a most fragile arrangement because of the reluctance of foreign central banks to add more dollars to their reserves.

The liquidity problem of the Bretton Woods system, therefore, was twofold. In the short run, the amount of liquidity was dependent on erratic swings in the U.S. balance of payments, and in the long run, the dollar could not be counted on to supply new liquidity.

How much international liquidity is needed in a fixed-rate system? There is no simple answer to this question because it depends on the level of reserves each country *thinks* it should hold and the level it *actually* holds as a consequence of its policies. More generally, too much international liquidity is inflationary because countries are under little compulsion to make fundamental adjustments to deficits. Too little liquidity, on the other hand, forces countries to respond quickly to deficits by imposing restrictions, deflating their economies, or devaluing their exchange rates. If the supply of international liquidity does not keep pace with demand, then countries will seek to obtain reserves from each other, with the danger that they will slow down real economic growth to generate export surpluses or use restrictions to protect existing reserves.

In the 1960s there was widespread concern over the adequacy of international liquidity because of the expectation that the dollar would not continue to supply new reserves. Facilities for borrowed reserves were improved, notably by increasing the IMF quotas and strengthening the swap network among central banks. But borrowed reserves make no permanent contribution to the world's liquidity. Hence, attention was devoted to a scheme for the deliberate creation of a new reserve asset that came to be known as Special Drawing Rights (SDRs).

SDRs constitute international reserve assets that may be used in the settlement of balance of payments deficits by countries participating in the Special Drawing Account administered by the IMF. A decision to create SDRs requires the approval of a majority of the member countries holding 85 percent of the weighted voting power of the Fund. Once created, SDRs are distributed to participants in proportion to their Fund quotas. In 1969 it was agreed to allocate SDRs to the 104 participants in three annual stages: January 1, 1970 (SDR 3.4 billion); January 1, 1971 (SDR 2.95 billion); and January 1, 1972 (SDR 2.95 billion).[18]

---

[18]At the time one SDR unit was equal to one U.S. dollar. The SDR, now defined in terms of a bundle of currencies, was worth $1.40 in April 1993. As of April 1992, total SDR allocations were SDR 21.4 billion. The SDR has now become the official unit of account for the International Monetary Fund.

Actually SDRs are merely computerized bookkeeping entries. What makes them a reserve asset is the commitment of the participating countries to accept SDRs in exchange for a convertible currency up to an amount equal to three times their own SDR allocations. Only one constraint is placed on a country's use of its SDRs for balance of payments settlements. It is expected to maintain over a five-year period average holdings of SDRs equal to 30 percent of its cumulative allocations. A country does not buy its SDRs, but all allocations of SDRs are subject to a market rate of interest, while member holdings of SDRs earn the same rate of interest.[19] Once placed on the books of the IMF, SDRs remain in existence as a permanent addition to the world's reserve assets.

Ironically, the first activation of SDRs coincided with a massive buildup of dollar reserves as short-term capital moved out of the United States in 1970 and 1971. As Table 18-6 indicates, total reserves rose from $78.2 billion to $117.3 billion between the end of 1969 and September 1971. Instead of a liquidity shortage, there was a liquidity surplus. Although the SDR facility did not solve the liquidity problem, it opened up the possibility of a gradual replacement of dollars with SDRs in international reserves. In that event, the dollar would eventually lose its role as a reserve currency, and reserve creation would no longer be dependent on U.S. deficits but rather on the collective judgment of the IMF member countries.[20]

Inadequate Adjustment Mechanism

In accordance with the Bretton Woods Agreement, countries were expected to maintain fixed exchange rates (within a band of 1 percent on either side of par values) and alter the par values of their currencies only to adjust to a fundamental disequilibrium in the balance of payments. In practice, the U.S. dollar emerged as the central reserve currency with a fixed parity, while the other major currencies tended to maintain their parities even in the face of prolonged disequilibria. This almost rigid adherence to exchange parities encouraged speculation, provoked crises, and delayed adjustment.

Movements in the parities of the major currencies are depicted in Figure 18-2 for January 1947 to June 1970. Note the small number of parity adjustments. Furthermore, when parity changes were made, they were usually in a downward direction that devalued the currencies vis-à-vis the dollar. For the period as a whole, all currencies lost value vis-à-vis the dollar except the Swiss franc and Japanese yen, which maintained the same parity. As a consequence, the dollar became substantially revalued in terms of other major currencies, and even when it became apparent in the 1960s that the dollar had become overvalued, upward adjustments in parities occurred only rarely in crisis situations. Ultimately, the

---

[19]Thus, a country that does not use its SDRs comes out even.

[20]The dollar would still remain the major *intervention* currency (the currency used by central banks to influence exchange rates) and the major *vehicle* currency (the currency used in the settlement of private international commercial and financial transactions).

Figure 18-2

[1]The rates indicated are the par values agreed with the Fund except in the following cases: Swiss franc (nonmember currency); Japanese yen, to May 1953; Italian lira, to March 1960; French franc, January 1948 to December 1960; Canadian dollar, see footnote 2.
[2]Fluctuating rate, September 30, 1950 to May 1, 1962; and June 1, 1970–.
[3]Fluctuating rate, September 20 to October 24, 1969.
Source: The Role of Exchange Rates in the Adjustment of International Payments, A Report of the Executive Directors (Washington, D.C.: International Monetary Fund, 1970), p. 9.

Movements in Parities of Currencies of Selected Industrial Countries, January 1947 to June 1970 (January 1947 = 100). Over nearly a quarter century, most currencies *devalued* with respect to the dollar. Only the Japanese yen and the Swiss franc maintained a constant parity with the dollar. Upward movements of nondollar currency parities occurred only in crisis situations and then only in modest amounts for a few currencies. Because of this devaluation bias, the U.S. dollar had become overvalued by the 1960s—a failure of the international adjustment mechanism.

United States was compelled to take unilateral action to achieve a currency realignment.

Disequilibrating Short-Term Capital Movements

A third source of weakness in the Bretton Woods system as it functioned in the 1960s was the enormous flow of disequilibrating short-term capital between the major financial centers. The emergence of a truly integrated international capital market based on Eurodollars created a growing pool of liquid funds that could be rapidly switched from one center to another in response to interest rate differentials (interest arbitrage) or to expected adjustments in exchange rates.

The quick transfer of billions of dollars from one center to another had two broad consequences. First, it limited the freedom of national authorities to use monetary policy for domestic stabilization by intensifying the conflict between external and internal balance as depicted in Figure 15-5. When interest rates in one center rose above those in other centers, funds immediately left the country with the lower rates, and vice versa. More often than not, these shifts of funds were disequilibrating for the domestic economy or the balance of payments. In 1969 high interest rates in the United States attracted billions of dollars from European centers. Although this inflow improved the official reserves balance, it also partly nullified anti-inflationary policies of the U.S. government by swelling the money supply. In 1971 high interest rates in West Germany (induced by a restrictive monetary policy to impede inflation) drew in billions of dollars from abroad, thereby inducing further inflation and adding to a huge balance of payments surplus. Indeed, liquid funds became so sensitive to money market conditions in major-currency countries that some economists advocated using monetary policy primarily for balance of payments purposes and leaving domestic stabilization to fiscal policy.

A second consequence of the high international mobility of liquid capital was its disequilibrating impact on foreign exchange markets. In the 1960s speculation *against* currencies was demonstrably generated by delays in exchange rate adjustments. Deficit countries refused to devalue until it became obvious that they had to do so. Thus, speculators enjoyed a "no-lose" situation, since the *direction* of any adjustment was certain (if not the precise timing) and the adjustment most probably would be substantial.

Many industrial countries (including the United States) tried to influence or restrict short-term capital flows through a variety of special techniques: imposing selective taxation, limiting the foreign lending or borrowing of domestic commercial banks, prohibiting the payment of interest on foreign-held demand and time deposits, imposing reserve requirements on the foreign borrowings of domestic banks, intervening in forward markets, imposing selective exchange controls, and others. These techniques often proved effective in influencing changes in the foreign assets and liabilities of domestic commercial banks, but they had little or no effect on the short-term borrowing and lending by domestic nonbank business firms, to say nothing of leads and lags in international payments.

By and large, the industrial countries avoided comprehensive exchange controls over short-term capital movements even though they were permissible under the IMF Articles of Agreement. This reluctance stemmed from serious doubts about their feasibility and desirability. Short-term capital can move into and out of a country in so many ways that any attempt at full control requires a close regulation of all international transactions, current as well as capital. Hence, comprehensive exchange controls run the grave risk of "throwing the baby out with the bath water" by restricting legitimate international trade and investments and by curbing all short-term capital flows, not just speculative flows. The feasibility of unilateral controls is also limited; no single country can hope to control or even greatly influence the international capital market because of its size. Most fundamentally, controls attack only the symptoms of disequilibrium rather than the causes.

SUMMARY

1. Agreement on the postwar international monetary system was reached at Bretton Woods, New Hampshire, in 1944. An international agency, the International Monetary Fund, was established to administer a code of fair exchange practices and provide compensatory financial assistance to member countries in balance of payments trouble.

2. In 1962, the Fund's resources were supplemented by the *General Arrangements to Borrow,* which enabled the Fund to borrow up to $5.9 billion from ten industrial countries (known as the "Group of Ten") to provide compensatory financial assistance to one or more of them. In 1970, the Fund activated an entirely new facility to supply to its members reserve assets, known as Special Drawing Rights (SDRs).

3. After World War II, the international monetary system evolved in a way that was not envisaged by the Bretton Woods agreement. In the 1950s, the United States emerged as the prime reserve country, with the dollar increasingly taking over the function of gold as an international reserve asset.

4. After 1958, the United States experienced a persistent deficit in its balance of payments. Three concepts of surplus and deficit were used by U.S. authorities in measuring disequilibrium in the balance of payments: the basic balance, the net liquidity balance, and the official reserves transactions balance.

5. During the years 1958–1971, the United States experienced a cumulative reserve deficit of $56 billion, which was financed by drawing down its gold reserves and by incurring liquid liabilities to foreign central banks.

6. In the 1960s, the United States undertook a variety of measures to remedy its balance of payments deficit. These included efforts to expand exports, to reduce U.S. government outlays abroad, to restrain U.S. private capital exports, to lessen the gold drain, and to discourage speculation. None of these measures involved a fundamental adjustment in the balance of payments. U.S. policymakers refused to cut back on military forces abroad, abandon foreign assistance to developing countries, deflate the economy, impose import restrictions, or devalue the dollar.

7. In the 1960s, the international monetary system was shaken by a series of crises in foreign exchange and gold markets. Although other currencies were involved in these crises (notably the British pound and French franc), the pervasive source of instability was the weakness of the dollar.

8. The international monetary crisis of 1971 was directly inspired by a loss of confidence in the dollar. Confronted with an enormous speculative run on the dollar, the United States suspended the gold convertibility of the dollar on August 15 and thereby forced the collapse of the Bretton Woods system. The United States also imposed domestic wage and price controls, as well as a 10 percent surcharge on all dutiable imports.

9. The immediate response to the U.S. actions was a closing of foreign exchange markets in Europe and Japan. When they reopened, all of the major foreign currencies (with the exception of the French franc) were left to float vis-à-vis the dollar. However, foreign governments were reluctant to let their currencies float freely to higher dollar values because they hoped to persuade the United States to devalue the dollar by raising the price of gold. Hence, central banks continued to intervene in foreign exchange markets and, in some instances, further appreciation vis-à-vis the dollar was prevented by exchange restrictions.

10. After weeks of uncertainty, the Group of Ten countries negotiated the Smithsonian Agreement on December 18, 1971. In return for the revaluation of the other currencies, the United States agreed to raise the price of gold from $35 an ounce to $38 an ounce. However, this agreement did not tackle the problems of fundamental international monetary reform.

11. The poor performance and eventual collapse of the Bretton Woods system is attributable to three interrelated causes: (1) the problem of international liquidity formation centered on the dollar, (2) delays in balance of payments adjustment, and (3) disequilibrating short-term capital movements.

12. In response to widespread concern over the adequacy of international liquidity, agreement was reached in the late 1960s on facilities to create a new international reserve asset (SDRs). SDRs were first activated at the beginning of 1970.

QUESTIONS AND APPLICATIONS

1. (a) What were the purposes of the International Monetary Fund?
   (b) What was the par value system of exchange rates?
   (c) What were the implications of the IMF rules on exchange rates?
2. Explain the compensatory financing system of the IMF.
3. "As the Bretton Woods system evolved, however, the reserves of most countries became a mixture of gold and dollars, with a growing dominance of the latter." Why did this development occur?
4. (a) Describe the remedial measures undertaken by the U.S. government before August 15, 1971, to overcome the deficit in the U.S. balance of payments.

(b) Why did the United States not make a fundamental adjustment to its payments deficit in the 1960s by (1) deflating the domestic economy or (2) devaluing the dollar?

5. (a) Describe the actions of the United States on August 15, 1971.
   (b) Why did these actions bring about a collapse of the Bretton Woods system?

6. Be prepared to defend or criticize the U.S. decision to abandon the gold convertibility of the dollar on August 15, 1971.

7. (a) What was the Smithsonian Agreement?
   (b) Why was it only an "interim" agreement?

8. What was the problem of international liquidity formation? How was it related to the dollar? What is meant by the "inherent contradiction of the gold-exchange standard"?

9. What are SDRs? How are they created?

10. When are short-term capital movements "disequilibrating"?

SELECTED READINGS

See the list of readings given at the end of Chapter 19.

THE CONTEMPORARY INTERNATIONAL MONETARY SYSTEM, THE U.S. BALANCE OF PAYMENTS, AND GLOBAL CAPITAL MARKETS

The second devaluation of the dollar in February 1973 brought in its wake floating exchange rates and a new international monetary system. Against the background of the Bretton Woods collapse, we describe in this chapter the principal features of the contemporary system and its performance, the persistent deficit in the U.S. balance of payments, and the emergence of global capital markets.

FOREIGN EXCHANGE ARRANGEMENTS

Figure 19-1 depicts the foreign exchange arrangements of countries in the contemporary international monetary system. The reader should compare Figure 19-1 with Figure 18-1, which depicts exchange practices under the Bretton Woods system. Under the Bretton Woods system, all foreign currencies were pegged to the dollar or to gold through the dollar. In sharp contrast, today the currencies of other industrial countries are floating with respect to the dollar, as shown by the dashed lines in Figure 19-1. Beyond that dominant feature, the contemporary international monetary system is a mixture of exchange rate arrangements. The Swiss franc, the Canadian dollar, the Japanese yen, and the U.S. dollar are floating against all other currencies. Eleven European currencies are aligned within margins of 2.25 percent, but they jointly float against the dollar and other currencies.[1] Sixty-nine other currencies (sixty-six developing and three industrial countries) are either floating independently or adjusted according to a set of indicators. The remaining currencies of developing countries (LDCs), however, are pegged either on a major currency or on a "basket" of currencies: twenty-four are pegged on the U.S. dollar, fourteen are pegged on the French franc, five are

---

[1]This is the Exchange Rate Mechanism of the European Monetary System described in Chapter 10. As related in that chapter, Great Britain and Italy withdrew from ERM in September 1992, allowing their currencies to float freely.

Figure 19-1

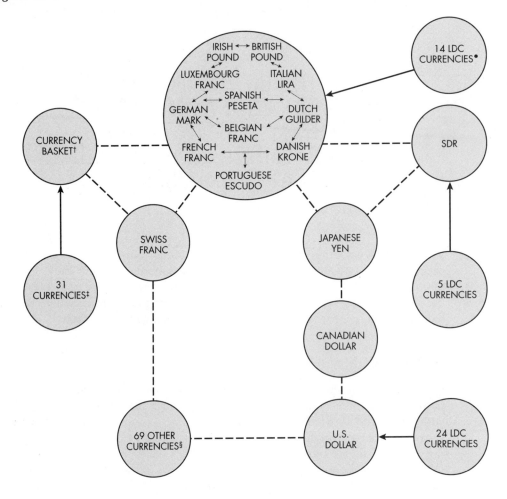

Legend: Floating rate---; Pegged rate →.
* Pegged on the French franc.
† Other than SDR.
‡ Twenty-five LDCs; four industrial countries, and two East European countries.
§ Sixty-six LDCs and three industrial countries. Exchange rates are floating independently or adjusted according to a set of indicators.
Source: International Monetary Fund, *IMF Survey,* October 26, 1992, p. 328.

Exchange Rate Arrangements, June 30, 1992. The contemporary international monetary system may be described as a system of currency areas, primarily centered on the U.S. dollar, the European Monetary System, and the French franc. Its basic difference from the Bretton Woods system is the floating dollar.

pegged on the SDR basket, and thirty-one on non-SDR baskets.[2] In this respect, therefore, the contemporary system is a system of *currency areas:* the U.S. dollar area, the European Monetary System, and the French franc area. Exchange rates are stabilized within each area through occasional devaluations and revaluations but are allowed to float freely among the areas. The signal departure from the Bretton Woods system is the flotation of the U.S. dollar against other key currencies.

EXCHANGE RATE BEHAVIOR

As we know from our analysis of the determination of exchange rates in Chapters 12 and 13, exchange rates respond immediately to market forces in a floating-rate (or flexible-rate) system. In the short run, capital flows dominate current account payments in foreign exchange markets, making floating exchange rates highly volatile. Figure 19-2 shows the monthly swings in nominal exchange rates among the U.S. dollar, West German mark, and Japanese yen. Observe the contrast in exchange rate behavior during the period 1962–1971, when the Bretton Woods system was fully operating, with the years after its collapse. It is evident that a distinctive feature of the contemporary system is the extraordinary short-term volatility in exchange rates. Is this short-term volatility matched by longer-term variability? And are *real* exchange rates also variable?

Figure 19-3 traces the time paths of the three leading currencies on a quarterly basis over the years 1975–1990 for both nominal and real effective exchange rates.[3] Our first observation is that the longer-term variability of *nominal* exchange rates is high for the three currencies. The dollar took a roller coaster ride in the 1980s, rising sharply in the first half of the decade, and then falling back to its 1980 level by 1987 and even further by 1990. The yen's behavior was almost a mirror image of the dollar's, while the mark was less variable than the other two currencies.

Our second observation is that *real* exchange rates were also highly variable during the 1980s, reflecting the variability of nominal exchange rates.

What caused the longer-term variability of *nominal* exchange rates in the 1980s? In the 1970s, the major influence on nominal rates was divergent rates of inflation. Because Japan and Germany experienced lower rates of inflation than the United States, the yen and mark appreciated while the dollar depreciated over that decade. This behavior validated the purchasing-power parity doctrine, which states that changes in nominal exchange rates keep *real* exchange rates constant over the longer run.[4] But divergent rates of inflation cannot explain the behavior

---

[2]The SDR basket contains different percentages of five currencies: the U.S. dollar, British pound, West German mark, Japanese yen, and French franc. The currency mix of non-SDR baskets is particular to each country.

[3]*Nominal* exchange rates are actual rates of exchange; *real* exchange rates are nominal rates adjusted for relative changes in the purchasing power of the respective currencies. In this instance, the adjustment uses relative changes in unit labor costs. *Effective* rates are weighted rates that take into account the relative importance of a country's trading partners in direct bilateral relations with them. In this instance, the indices measure changes in the value of each of the three currencies against the currencies of seventeen other industrial countries.

[4]See Chapter 13 for an explanation of the purchasing-power parity doctrine.

Figure 19-2

PERCENTAGE CHANGE FROM PREVIOUS MONTH

Source: Adapted from Morris Goldstein and others, *Policy Issues in the Evolving International Monetary System,* Occasional Paper 96 (Washington, D.C.: International Monetary Fund, June 1992) Chart I, p. 17.

Monthly Swings in Nominal Bilateral Exchange Rates for the United States, West Germany, and Japan, 1962–1990. In contrast to their stability during the years 1962–1971, when the Bretton Woods system was in effect, exchange rates of the three dominant currencies have been highly volatile, with large monthly swings in the contemporary international monetary system.

Figure 19-3

INDEX NUMBER

Source: Adapted from Morris Goldstein and others, *Policy Issues in the Evolving International Monetary System,* Occasional Paper 96 (Washington, D.C.: International Monetary Fund, June 1992) Chart 3, p. 19.

Nominal and Real Effective Exchange Rate Indices for the United States, Japan and Germany, 1975–1990 (1975 = 100). The high variability of the *nominal* exchange rates of the three countries over the period is mainly owing to divergent macroeconomic monetary and fiscal policies expressed in *real* interest-rate differentials. The high variability of *real* exchange rates is owing to the slow responses in national prices and costs to variations in nominal exchange rates.

of nominal exchange rates in the 1980s. Indeed, that behavior appears to contradict the purchasing-power parity doctrine. When the U.S. inflation rate was relatively high in the early years of the decade, the dollar appreciated rather than depreciated, and when the U.S. inflation rate was relatively low in the late years of the decade, the dollar depreciated rather than appreciated.

What then is the explanation of the variability in nominal rates? The basic answer to this question is the markedly divergent macroeconomic policies of the United States and the other industrial countries in the 1980s. These divergent policies brought about large international differentials in *real* interest rates, as indicated in Figure 19-4.

Figure 19-4

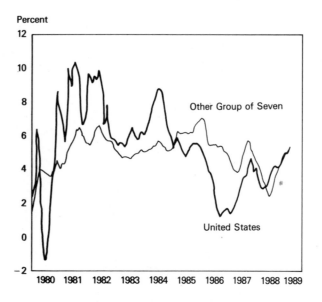

Note: The Group of Seven includes Canada, France, Italy, Japan, the United Kingdom, and West Germany. The seventh country is the United States. The interest rates are monthly rates on money market instruments of about ninety days maturity deflated by the private domestic demand deflator. The interest rate for the other countries in the Group of Seven is the weighted average of individual rates.

Source: World Economic Outlook (Washington, D.C.: International Monetary Fund, April 1989), Chart 32, p. 98.

Real Short-Term Interest Rates of the United States and Other Countries in the Group of Seven, 1980–1989. Because of divergent macroeconomic policies between the United States and the other industrial countries in the 1980s, *real* interest-rate differentials opened up between them. In the first half of the 1980s, high real rates in the United States induced a massive net inflow of short-term capital that caused a dollar appreciation. The converse occurred in the second half of the 1980s.

The relationships between interest rates and exchange rates is not a simple one. Both are influenced by changes in the supply and demand of money and other financial assets and by price expectations. Both, therefore, depend on national monetary and fiscal policies. Can interest-rate differentials, then, *cause* changes in exchange rates? The answer is *yes* when the differentials are real, but *no* when differentials are merely nominal. In the first instance, real differentials and exchange rates move in the same direction: A more positive (less negative) differential is accompanied by an appreciation in the currency, and conversely. In the second instance, nominal differentials and exchange rates move in opposite directions: A more positive (less negative) differential is accompanied by a depreciation in the currency, and conversely.

When interest-rate differentials among countries express *only* expected rates of inflation, they offer no inducement for persons and institutions to switch money and other financial assets from one currency to another, that is, they do not induce an inflow of short-term capital into the high-interest-rate country. Nominal differentials, therefore, do not influence the exchange rate. However, when differentials arise from factors other than price expectations, they do offer an inducement to switch money and other financial assets to the high-interest-rate country, thereby causing an appreciation of that country's currency.

This happened to the dollar in the 1981–1985 period, when real short-term interest rates in the United States were significantly higher than real rates in other leading industrial countries. This provoked a massive net inflow of short-term capital that pushed up the external value of the dollar. In the second half of the decade, the net inflow became a net outflow as U.S. real interest rates fell below those of other industrial countries, causing a dollar depreciation. Because these capital flows were so much larger than trade flows, they exerted the dominant influence on the dollar's exchange value.

What explains the variability of the *real* exchange rates depicted in Figure 19-3? The answer is the variability of the nominal rates together with sluggish ("sticky") responses of national prices and costs to that variability. Prices and costs adapted too slowly to prevent the variability in nominal rates from translating into real rates. (Sticky responses to changes in exchange rates were discussed in Chapter 16 as J-curve effects, delayed pass-through effects ["pricing to market"], and hysteresis.) If national prices and costs had reacted quickly to variations in nominal exchange rates, then the real exchange rate would have remained close to 100 over the period in Figure 19-3. Another way of making this point is to say that the restoration of purchasing-power parity was prevented by sluggish responses in national prices and costs to continuing changes in nominal exchange rates. Purchasing-power parity was never able to catch up to the dynamic path of nominal rates.

The prolonged variations in the real values of the dollar, yen, and mark have created huge imbalances in the current accounts of the respective countries by directly affecting international competitiveness. As indicated in Figure 19-5, the United States has run a deficit on current account (expressed as a percentage of GDP) for the entire period 1981–1993, except for 1991 when it received extraordi-

Figure 19-5

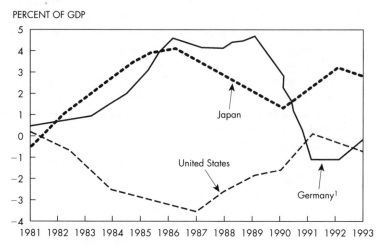

PERCENT OF GDP

Note: Data for 1992 and 1993 are IMF staff projections.

[1]Prior to July 1990, the current account balance of West Germany, excluding the bilateral balance with East Germany; from July 1990, the current balance of Unified Germany. Data are in terms of GNP.

Source: Adapted from *IMF Survey,* September 1992, p. 276.

Current Account Imbalances of the United States, Japan, and Germany, 1981– 1993. The current account imbalances of the United States, Japan, and Germany are a consequence of divergent macroeconomic policies. The convergence of the imbalances toward the end of the period offers evidence of an adjustment process under way.

nary payments from its allies in the Gulf War. This deficit widened in the mid-1980s, but then returned to about the same level as in the early 1980s. Except for 1981, Japan ran a surplus over the period that was much larger in the early 1990s than a decade earlier. Germany's large surplus of the middle 1980s changed to a deficit in the early 1990s. This turnaround was caused by the heavy costs of absorbing the former East Germany. The convergence of the imbalances in the 1990s offers some evidence of an adjustment process under way.

THE PERSISTENT DEFICIT
IN THE U.S. CURRENT ACCOUNT

We have observed that the longer-term variability of nominal exchange rates in the 1980s translated into prolonged changes in their real values, owing to a divergence between U.S. fiscal and monetary policies and those of other industrial countries (notably Japan and Germany), together with sluggish responses of national prices and costs to exchange rate movements.

This macroeconomic divergence was initiated in late 1979 when the Federal Reserve tightened monetary policy in an effort to lower a double-digit rate of inflation. But it was magnified in 1981 when the new U.S. administration simultaneously started a long-term program of higher military expenditures, gave business firms more incentive to invest (through more generous depreciation allowances and investment tax credits), and gave consumers more disposable income to spend through cuts in personal taxes. Consequently, total domestic absorption rose at an average annual rate of 8.5 percent from 1981 through 1985 while gross national product rose at a lower annual rate of 7.9 percent. Total domestic absorption (national expenditure) rose from less than 99 percent of GNP in 1980 to 102 percent in 1985. This excess expenditure was possible only through a deficit on current account of the same amount. Recall equation (18) in Chapter 15: $B_c = Y - A$, where B_c is the net balance on current account, Y is the gross national product, and A is the domestic absorption of goods and services (consumption, domestic investment, and government expenditures). In short, the mix of new U.S. fiscal and monetary policies at the start of the 1980s caused excess domestic absorption and a corresponding current-account deficit.

But why did not the expansion of national spending induce a higher domestic output (Y) and thereby avoid a current-account deficit? The reason is the high real interest rates induced by both fiscal and monetary policies. The change in fiscal policy increased the demand for credit, leading to higher interest rates. (This effect was exacerbated by a decline in the already low personal savings rate.) At the same time, tight monetary policy sharply lowered inflation expectations, making *real* interest rates even higher. These rates made U.S. financial assets more attractive to foreign investors, who then shifted funds to the United States from other countries (portfolio effect). But to do so, they needed to buy dollars, which pushed up their external value. In turn, the dollar appreciation discouraged U.S. exports and encouraged U.S. imports. In sum, the dollar's appreciation *switched* U.S. national spending toward foreign goods and services (increasing U.S. imports) and, at the same time, *switched* foreign national spending away from U.S. goods and services, thereby decreasing U.S. exports.

Figure 19-6 depicts the relationship between the U.S. real exchange rate and its current-account deficit. The rapid ascent of the real exchange rate starting in 1980 brought about a comparable increase in the current-account deficit after a lag of about two years. The real exchange rate reached a peak at the start of 1985 and then began a steep decline lasting until 1988. The deficit continued to climb until 1987, demonstrating again a two-year response lag. The deficit shrank for the rest of the decade, but the dollar's value increased in 1989 and then fell back in 1990 to its 1988 level. This experience shows that dollar depreciation has brought about payments adjustment, but only after a two-year lag and only to a degree that falls short of full elimination of the deficit.

The macroeconomic policies followed by the United States in the 1980s had several unfortunate consequences. The 50 percent appreciation of the dollar between 1980 and 1985 (1) badly hurt U.S. export- and import-competing indus-

Figure 19-6

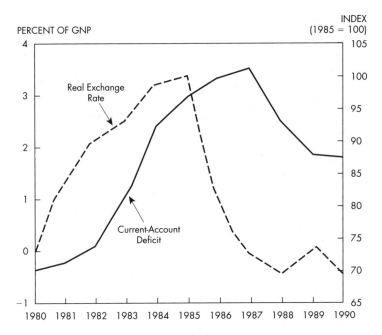

Note: The left scale indicates the current-account deficit as a percentage of U.S. GNP; the right scale indicates the U.S. real exchange rate expressed as an index number with a 1985 base.

Source: International Monetary Fund, *International Statistics,* various issues; and OECD, *Main Economic Indicators,* various issues.

U.S. Current-Account Deficit and Real Exchange Rate, 1980–1990. The U.S. current-account deficit responded to movement in the real exchange rate, but only after a two-year lag. Also, depreciation in the second half of the decade was not able to eliminate the deficit.

tries, notably steel, automobiles, and nonelectrical machinery, and (2) magnified demands for U.S. import protection and generated trade disputes with Japan, the European Community, and other countries. High U.S. real interest rates (1) induced an enormous inflow of capital, making the United States the world's biggest debtor;[5] (2) slowed U.S. *domestic* investment; and (3) made it more difficult for Third World countries to manage their external dollar debts.[6]

---

[5]Some of this capital inflow took the form of direct investment, including the acquisition of U.S. firms, office buildings, land and other real assets. See Chapter 23 for a discussion of foreign direct investment in the United States.

[6]See Chapter 20.

It cannot be safely assumed that the rest of the world will continue to finance the U.S. current-account deficit indefinitely.[7] At some point, foreign investors and central banks may refuse to transfer more capital to the United States. The nightmare scenario is an incident that provokes a massive capital flight from the dollar, pushing the dollar into a free fall and plunging the world into a financial crisis. To avert the possibility of this catastrophe, the United States needs to cut its domestic absorption by reversing its fiscal policy through some mix of lower government spending, higher taxes, and personal savings incentives. This contractionary fiscal policy would allow an easier monetary policy, reducing real interest rates. Unfortunately, this policy demands austerity and does not appeal to U.S. policymakers. Adjustment would be considerably eased by opposing changes in the macroeconomic policies of Japan and West Germany: tax cuts and higher real interest rates.

CENTRAL BANK INTERVENTION IN FOREIGN EXCHANGE MARKETS

Any inference from Figures 19-1 and 19-2 that the key currencies have been left to float freely against each other in response *only* to market forces would be erroneous. As a matter of fact, central banks have actively intervened in foreign exchange markets with compensatory financing intended to influence foreign exchange rates. Indeed, the amount of compensatory financing by central banks in the new system may well exceed the amount in the Bretton Woods system over a similar period of time. Intervention has been financed by central banks out of their international reserves, short-term borrowings from other central banks ("swap credits"), IMF credits, and borrowings from private banks. In light of this central bank activity, the contemporary system is correctly designated as a "managed float" rather than a "pure float."[8]

Arguments for Intervention

Why have national monetary authorities refused to allow exchange rates to respond freely to market forces? In theory, there would be no need for central bank intervention in a floating-rate market. Under conditions of perfect competition, exports and imports would respond immediately to changes in exchange rates so as to maintain current-account equilibrium in the balance of payments. As we have seen, however, the response of exports and imports is not spontaneous; it occurs only after a lag, which can take two years. Also, when macroeconomic policies diverge radically among the leading industrial countries, current account imbalances may persist for several years.

---

[7]It may be argued that it is *unethical* for a rich country like the United States to borrow from the rest of the world; rather, it should be lending to the rest of the world.

[8]The terms "dirty float" and "clean float" are also used, respectively.

During the period of adjustment, therefore, surpluses and deficits appear in the balance of payments (as they do in a fixed-rate system) that are financed by the central monetary authorities. In the absence of such compensatory financing, it is argued, exchange rates during the adjustment period would fluctuate in response to speculation and other temporary factors in ways that could inhibit adjustment in exports and imports. Thus, there is justification for official compensatory action to "smooth" the short-run behavior of exchange rates as long as such action does not counteract fundamental economic forces and thereby delay real adjustment.

Another explanation for managed floating is the unwillingness of governments to let exchange rates float freely without limit when they perceive undesirable effects on employment, inflation, international competitiveness, and other matters of official policy concern. Hence, central banks may go beyond smoothing daily and weekly fluctuations in exchange rates to maintain them at levels that conform to their policy targets. In that event, a managed float takes on some of the characteristics of an adjustable-peg system by delaying fundamental adjustment and inviting speculation.

Economists generally advocate a standard of intervention that is called "leaning against the wind." Using this standard, a central bank opposes exchange rate movements but does not reinforce them: The bank sells foreign exchange when its currency is depreciating and buys foreign exchange when its currency is appreciating. Furthermore, a central bank does not try to maintain a target rate of exchange; it seeks to moderate the strength of the wind, not neutralize it. Again, a central bank intervenes "symmetrically" by leaning against both upward and downward movements of the exchange rate. In sum, intervention in accordance with this standard acts to smooth short-run fluctuations but does not attempt to influence the long-term trend of exchange rates that responds to changes in purchasing-power parities and real factors that affect international competitiveness.

Intervention in the 1980s

During the first half of the 1980s, U.S. officials saw no need to influence the dollar's value. Indeed, they treated the dollar's appreciation as a welcome vote of confidence in the U.S. economy. But this laissez-faire policy was abandoned in September 1985, when the U.S. Treasury Secretary invited the finance ministers of Japan, West Germany, France, and the United Kingdom (these, plus the United States, are the G-5 countries) to a weekend meeting at the Plaza Hotel in New York. In the resulting *Plaza Agreement,* the ministers announced that the dollar was overvalued and that coordinated action was necessary to push down its value. However, no commitments were made to alter macroeconomic policies.

Table 19-1 describes four phases of the dollar's depreciation. In phase 1, the dollar's value reached a peak (in February 1985) and then started to fall. By the time of the Plaza Agreement, it had fallen by 9 percent. After U.S. central bank sales of dollars (through purchases of foreign currency) in February and March, intervention played little role in the subsequent decline. In phase 2, the dollar's

Table 19-1 Four Phases in Depreciation of U.S. Dollar, February 1985 to February 1988

Phase		Average Monthly Nominal Depreciation* (Percent)	Cumulative Real Depreciation to Last Month of Period† (Percent)	Average Monthly Increase in Reserves of Group of Seven, excluding U.S.‡ (Billions of U.S. Dollars)	Intervention by U.S. Authorities
1. Pre-Plaza Agreement	February to September 1985	1.3	9	1.3	$565 million purchases of foreign currency, February–March.
2. Post-Plaza Agreement	September 1985 to May 1986	2.3	25	2.0	$3,301 million purchases of foreign currency, September–November.
3. Pre-Louvre Accord	May 1986 to February 1987	1.1	34	5.4	$50 million sales of foreign currency, January 1987.
4. Post-Louvre Accord	February 1987 to February 1988	0.8	40	7.1§	Purchases of foreign currency: $30 million in March, $631 million in August. Sales of foreign currency: $4,870 million, April–June; $5,040 million, August–January.

*In term of nominal effective exchange rate of U.S. dollar (weights from the Fund's Multilateral Exchange Rate Model), monthly averages.
†Real effective exchange rate for U.S. dollar defined in terms of normalized unit labor costs.
‡Foreign exchange reserves, aggregated over the six countries, end-monthly data.
§Average for February 1987 to January 1988.

Source: World Economic Outlook (Washington, D.C.: International Monetary Fund, April 1988), Table 21, p. 55.

decline picked up speed; by May 1986, its cumulative real depreciation reached 25 percent. To help push the dollar down, the U.S. monetary authorities bought $3.3 billion in foreign currencies. Initially, foreign central banks sold dollars, but by the end of this phase they had added $2 billion a month on the average to their international reserves. In phase 3, the earlier consensus that the dollar was overvalued dissipated. There was little U.S. intervention, but foreign central banks at times intervened heavily to support the dollar, increasing their reserves by $5.4 billion a month on the average. In this phase, the rate of depreciation slowed down; by February 1987, the cumulative real depreciation reached 34 percent.

In February 1987, the G-5 countries and Canada met in Paris and adopted the *Louvre Accord*. The central objective of the accord was to stabilize the dollar's value through equilibrating changes in macroeconomic policies and to prevent undue volatility in exchange rates through market intervention. In phase 4, the rate of dollar depreciation slowed considerably; the cumulative real depreciation reached 40 percent by February 1988. Large interventions were undertaken by the central banks in support of the dollar: Foreign central banks bought $7.1 billion on the average each month, and the U.S. monetary authorities sold $4.9 billion of foreign currencies in the April–June period and $5.0 billion in the August–January period.

How much central bank intervention influenced the behavior of the dollar over the 1985–1988 period is debatable. The purchase and sale of foreign exchange by central banks can add to or subtract from commercial bank reserves and, therefore, the money supply. But this monetary effect is nullified when changes in bank reserves resulting from intervention are "sterilized" by offsetting open market operations (the sale or purchase of securities by the central bank), a practice generally followed by the U.S. monetary authorities. Most economists agree that intervention can smooth short-run fluctuations in exchange rates but cannot stop a shift in rates to a new market equilibrium. Central bank reserves are simply too small compared with the funds available to private international investors. Intervention, therefore, is *not* a substitute for macroeconomic policy.

The depreciation of the dollar after February 1985 was market-driven. Although intervention affected the dollar's short-run behavior, it is almost certain that the 40 percent depreciation reached in February 1988 would have occurred without central bank intervention.

The Need for Policy Coordination

To repeat an earlier statement, the fundamental cause of the current-account imbalances and associated swings in the real values of the dollar, yen, and mark is the continuing divergence of the macroeconomic policies followed by the United States, Japan, and West Germany. So far, these three countries have failed to live up to their commitments in the Louvre Accord to achieve policy coordination. The chief culprit is the United States: Its seeming inability to eradicate the budget deficit (coupled with low private savings) ensures a continuation of the international payments disequilibrium.

International policy coordination is based on formal agreements among countries to carry out specific policies in concert. Such coordination among the major industrial countries can greatly lower the adjustment costs of eliminating imbalances as compared with unilateral policy actions. With coordination, both deficit and surplus countries share the adjustment burden. This is not to gainsay the many pitfalls that can limit the effectiveness of policy coordination, including disagreements on how the world economy operates and should operate, imperfect information and forecasts, and the inability of governments to keep their promises because of national politics. Nor is international policy coordination a substitute for intelligent national policies.[9]

It is evident that further depreciation of the dollar alone cannot eliminate current-account imbalances. What is needed is international policy coordination that achieves a *decrease* in domestic absorption by the United States and, simultaneously, an *increase* in domestic absorption by Japan and West Germany.

THE CONTINUING ROLE
OF THE INTERNATIONAL MONETARY FUND

The International Monetary Fund did not disappear with the demise of the Bretton Woods system. Indeed, it can be argued that the Fund's role in the contemporary international monetary system has become more important, not less so. The Fund has replaced its code of fair exchange practices with a program of surveillance over exchange rate policies and has greatly stepped up its financial assistance to member countries in balance of payments difficulties. We offer here a brief review of the Fund's activities to bring up to date our earlier discussion of the Fund in Chapter 18.

Surveillance of Exchange
Rate Policies

In 1978, the IMF adopted a new Article IV to replace the old article, which obligated member countries to maintain par values for their currencies. Under the new article, each member country is free to choose its own exchange arrangement, including the freedom to float. Member countries, however, undertake a general obligation to collaborate with the Fund and with other members to ensure "orderly" exchange arrangements and to promote a *stable system* of exchange rates (but not a system of *stable exchange rates*). More specifically, members are "to avoid manipulating exchange rates or the international monetary system in order to prevent effective balance of payments adjustment or to gain an unfair competitive advantage over other members." The Fund is to exercise "firm surveillance" of the

---

[9]Martin Feldstein, *Rethinking International Economic Coordination,* Oxford Economic Papers, 40, 1988, pp. 205–19.

exchange rate policies of its members and is to adopt principles for their guidance.[10]

To undertake surveillance of exchange rate policies, the Fund has devised three principles for the guidance of member countries in their exchange rate policies:

(1) A member shall avoid manipulating exchange rates or the international monetary system in order to prevent effective balance of payments adjustment or to gain an unfair competitive advantage over other members.

(2) A member should intervene in the exchange market if necessary to counter disorderly conditions which may be characterized inter alia by disruptive short-term movements in the exchange value of its currency.

(3) Members should take into account in their intervention policies the interests of other members, including those of the countries in whose currencies they intervene.[11]

The Fund has also adopted principles and procedures for surveillance itself. The principles list "developments" that could trigger discussions between the Fund and a member country, including (1) protracted, large-scale intervention in one direction in the exchange market, (2) an unsustainable level of borrowing or lending for balance of payments purposes, (3) restrictions on current- and capital-account transactions, and (4) exchange rate behavior unrelated to underlying economic and financial conditions.

In practice, surveillance occurs on both global and country levels. Global surveillance is intended to ascertain whether or not the balance of payments and exchange rate policies of member countries are mutually consistent. Country surveillance calls for identifying and encouraging the correction of inappropriate exchange rates and exchange rate policies of individual countries. Under Article IV, each country is required to notify the Fund promptly of any changes in its exchange arrangements and to hold annual consultations with the Fund.

In the 1980s, the behavior of exchange rates highlighted the relationship between exchange rates and demand management (monetary and fiscal policies) as well as the role of exchange rates in the adjustment process. A fundamental precept motivating the Fund's surveillance, therefore, is that stability in the exchange market should be accomplished through achievement of *domestic* economic stability. The Fund strives for greater coordination of domestic economic policies among its members, and to that end it applies surveillance to countries in payments surplus as well as those in payments deficit. But the Fund has no powers to *make* a member country adopt domestic policies that will support stability in the exchange market and international adjustment. As we know, widely divergent

---

[10]Amendments to other articles in 1978 (1) reduce the role of gold by abolishing its official price and eliminating it as a unit of account in any par value system, and (2) obligate members to follow policies that will make the Special Drawing Right the "principal reserve asset" in the international monetary system. Collectively, the changes made in the Fund's Articles of Agreement in 1978 are known as the Second Amendment. The First Amendment in 1969 instituted the SDR.

[11]Executive Board Decision no. 5392-(77/63), adopted April 29, 1977.

monetary and fiscal policies have induced highly variable exchange rates in the contemporary system. The Fund sometimes can exert a strong influence on member countries that come to it for assistance, but its influence rests generally on the willingness of countries to live up to their responsibilities as members.

In recent years, the Fund has vigorously pushed for the use of indicators to promote policy coordination compatible with floating exchange rates. These indicators include GNP growth rates, inflation rates, interest rates, unemployment rates, fiscal deficit ratios, current-account and trade balances, monetary growth rates, reserves, and exchange rates. The Fund now uses these indicators in its surveillance activities, with the addition of a commodity price indicator.[12]

Payments Adjustment Assistance

In the 1980s, the need of developing countries for assistance in financing balance of payments deficits grew enormously under the impact of high oil prices, inflation, a general slowdown in the world economy, and the extraordinary growth of international debt in the Third World. The Fund responded to this need by adding to its resources with quota increases supplemented by borrowed funds and by enlarging the access of member countries to those resources. Table 19-2 shows the outstanding Fund credit by facility and policy for the period 1986–1992.

Table 19-2 Outstanding Fund Credit by Facility and Policy for the Financial Years 1986, 1988, 1990, 1992 (Billions of SDRs)[1]

	1986	1988	1990	1992
Standby arrangements	15.4	13.3	10.0	9.5
Extended Fund facility arrangements	12.8	10.2	8.3	8.6
Compensatory and contingency financing	6.4	4.3	3.8	5.3
Subtotal (General Resources Account)	*34.6[a]*	*27.8[b]*	*22.1*	*23.4*
Structural Adjustment Facility (SAF) arrangements	—	0.6	1.3	1.5
Enhanced Structural Adjustment (ESAF) arrangements	—	—	0.7	1.6
Trust Fund	2.2	1.1	0.3	0.2
Total	*36.9*	*29.5*	*24.4*	*26.7*

[1]Financial year ends April 30.
[a]Includes SDR 73 million in buffer stock financing.
[b]Includes SDR 3 million in buffer stock financing.
Note: Totals may not add because of rounding.
Source: Derived from *Annual Report 1992* (Washington, D.C.: International Monetary Fund), Table II.9, p. 102.

---

[12]For a review of recent surveillance activity, see the Fund's latest *Annual Report.*

Until 1962, member countries obtained Fund credit only through the "purchase" of foreign currencies under quota arrangements, as described in the previous chapter. But subsequently, the Fund established facilities to finance specific needs of members, such as the oil facility set up in 1974 with borrowed funds to help oil-importing developing countries. Most recently, the Fund established a Structural Adjustment Facility and an Enhanced Structural Adjustment Facility. Table 19-3 explains the types of Fund assistance. The traditional source of Fund credit through tranches (ordinary resources) accounted for only about one-fifth of total outstanding credit in 1992. A second departure from past practice is longer credit terms, ranging from five and a half to ten years in the case of the Enhanced Structural Adjustment Facility. Longer credit terms have moved the Fund toward the kind of development assistance provided by the World Bank, which is discussed in Chapter 20.

Periodic increases brought total quotas in the Fund to SDR 97 billion at the end of 1992. Quotas are scheduled to rise to SDR 145 billion (about $210 billion) in 1993. The first 25 percent of a member's quota (formerly subscribed in gold but now subscribed in SDRs or convertible currencies acceptable to the Fund) is known as the *reserve tranche*. [13] A member can obtain unconditionally from the Fund an amount of currency equal to its *reserve position,* which in turn equals its reserve tranche *plus* the Fund's use of its currency to finance the drawings of other countries *minus* any current utilization of its drawing rights. Because reserve tranches are considered the owned reserves of member countries rather than Fund credit, their use does not appear in Figure 19-2.

Table 19-3   Types of Financial Assistance Provided by the International Monetary Fund

---

The facilities and policies through which the Fund provides financial support to its members differ, depending on the nature of the macroeconomic and structural problems they seek to address and the degree of conditionality atttached to them.

Regular Facilities

- *Tranche policies.* The Fund's credit under its regular facilities is made available to members in four tranches or segments of 25 percent of quota each. For *first credit tranche purchases,* members are required to demonstrate reasonable efforts to overcome their balance of payments difficulties. Performance criteria are not applied and repurchases (or repayments) are made in $3\frac{1}{4}$ to 5 years. *Upper credit tranche purchases* are normally associated with *stand-by arrangements*. These typically cover periods of one to two years and focus on macroeconomic policies — such as fiscal, monetary, and exchange rate policies — aimed at overcoming balance of payments difficulties. Performance criteria to assess policy implementation — such as budgetary and credit ceilings, reserve and external debt targets, and avoidance of restrictions on current payments and trans-

---

[13]The reserve tranche was formerly called the gold tranche. See Chapter 18.

Table 19-3   Continued

---

fers — are applied during the period of the arrangement, and purchases (or drawings) are made in installments. Repurchases are made in $3\frac{1}{4}$ to 5 years, except in the case of purchases made with resources borrowed by the Fund under the enlarged access policy.

• *Extended arrangements.* Under extended arrangements, the Fund supports medium-term programs that generally run for 3 years (up to 4 years in exceptional circumstances) and are aimed at overcoming balance of payments difficulties stemming from macroeconomic and structural problems.

• *Enlarged access policy.* Introduced as a temporary policy, the enlarged access policy is used to increase the resources available under stand-by or extended arrangements for programs that need substantial Fund support.

Special Facilities

• *Compensatory and contingency financing facility (CCFF).* The purpose of this facility is twofold. The compensatory element provides resources to members to cover shortfalls in export earnings and services receipts and excesses in cereal import costs that are temporary and arise from events beyond their control. The contingency element helps members with Fund arrangements to maintain the momentum of reforms when faced with a broad range of unforeseen adverse external shocks, such as declines in export prices, increases in import prices, and fluctuations in interest rates.

• *Buffer stock financing facility.* Under this facility the Fund provides resources to help finance members' contributions to approved buffer stocks. Repayments are made within $3\frac{1}{4}$ to 5 years, or earlier.

Emergency Assistance

In addition to balance of payments assistance under its tranche policies and special facilities, the Fund provides emergency assistance in the form of purchases of help members meet payments problems arising from sudden and unforeseeable natural disasters. Such purchases do not involve performance criteria or the phasing of disbursements, and must be repurchased in $3\frac{1}{4}$ to 5 years.

Facilities for Low-Income Countries

• *Structural adjustment facility* (SAF) arrangements. These enable the Fund to provide resources on concessional terms to support medium-term macroeconomic adjustment and structural reforms in low-income countries facing protracted balance of payments problems.

• *Enhanced structural adjustment facility* (ESAF) arrangements. The objectives, conditions for eligibility, and program features under these arrangements are similar to those under SAF arrangements. However, ESAF arrangements differ in the scope and strength of structural policies, and in terms of access levels, monitoring procedures, and sources of funding.

Source: Derived from *Annual Report 1992* (Washington, D.C.: International Monetary Fund, 1992), pp. 50–51.

When a country obtains currencies in an amount beyond its reserve tranche, it uses its *credit tranche*. But this credit is conditional. To get it, a member must conclude an agreement with the Fund that commits that member to follow certain adjustment policies, including monetary and fiscal policies. The broad objective of Fund *conditionality* is the restoration and maintenance of equilibrium in the balance of payments in an environment of stable prices and sustainable rates of economic growth without resort to controls on trade or capital flows. In applying conditionality, the Fund sets quantifiable targets in its credit agreements for major adjustment variables, such as domestic credit growth and foreign borrowing. Conditional assistance is disbursed in installments and may be halted if the member fails to meet the agreed targets. Conditionality can give the Fund a strong leverage on member-country policies, but it is limited to countries that need to borrow from the Fund.

EMERGENCE OF A GLOBAL CAPITAL MARKET

A global capital market first emerged in the 1950s in the form of the *Eurocurrency* market. The movement to liberalize the *national* capital markets of the industrial countries started in the 1970s and gathered force in the 1980s. These developments stimulated a rapid growth of international capital movements, which have progressively integrated national capital markets and the Eurocurrency market to create a single global capital market with enormous financial resources. We offer here a brief description of the Eurocurrency market and then go on to identify the consequences of a global capital market for the operation of the international monetary system and national macroeconomic policies.

The Eurocurrency Market

The largest Eurocurrency market by far is in Eurodollars.[14] What are Eurodollars? Quite simply, *Eurodollars* are dollars that are deposited in foreign commercial banks, including the foreign branches of U.S. banks mainly located in Europe. It is the foreign location of the banks that distinguishes Eurodollars from ordinary dollar deposits in U.S. banks.[15]

Eurodollars come into existence when someone transfers dollars from a U.S. bank to a foreign bank or when someone converts a foreign currency into dollars that are then deposited in a foreign bank. Actually the dollars underlying the Eurodollars resulting from such transfers never leave the U.S. banking system. A

---

[14]Any currency can assume "Euro" form when it is held as commercial bank deposits outside the home country. Deutsche marks, yen, pounds sterling, and Swiss francs are the most common nondollar currencies used in this way. Hence, the Eurodollar market is correctly described as a "Eurocurrency" market. But even this designation is somewhat misleading, because some Eurocurrency deposits are held by banks located outside Europe, such as in Singapore. In brief, the Eurocurrency market has become a market for borrowing and lending the world's major convertible currencies.

[15]Hence, the Eurodollar market is referred to as an "offshore" market, in contrast to domestic "onshore" markets.

foreign bank accepting dollar deposits acquires a dollar balance in a U.S. bank, and when it lends Eurodollars, it draws down its U.S. dollar balance. Hence, transactions in the Eurodollar market involve shifts in the ownership of bank balances in the United States. We can demonstrate this fundamental fact with T accounts of participating banks.

Suppose a deposit holder (H) in a U.S. bank transfers $1 million to a Eurobank, for example, one located in London. Initially, let us assume also that the Eurobank maintains a demand account in the same U.S. bank. This transaction appears as follows in the U.S. bank's T account:

Assets		Liabilities	
		Demand deposit (H)	– $1 million
		Demand deposit	
		(Eurobank)	+ $1 million
Net change	$0	Net change	$0

Observe that the levels of the U.S. bank's assets and liabilities do not change: The ownership of a demand deposit simply shifted from H to the Eurobank. The same transaction appears as follows in the Eurobank's T account:

Assets		Liabilities	
Dollar deposit		Time deposit (H)	+ $1 million
(with U.S. bank)	+ $1 million		
Net change	+ $1 million	Net change	+ $1 million

But now suppose that the Eurobank does *not* maintain a demand account with the U.S. bank (Bank I) but with another U.S. bank (Bank II). Then Bank I loses reserves to Bank II, as shown in its T account:

Assets		Liabilities	
Reserves	– $1 million	Demand deposit (H)	– $1 million
Net change	– $1 million	Net change	– $1 million

The T account of Bank II shows the following changes:

Assets		Liabilities	
Reserves	+ $1 million	Demand deposit	
		(Eurobank)	+ $1 million
Net change	+ $1 million	Net change	+ $1 million

Note that the level of assets and liabilities for the U.S. banking system as a whole remains the same: A deposit has merely moved from one U.S. bank to another.

(Bank I, of course, is unhappy with the arrangement; it will seek to attract new deposits and hold on to existing deposits.)

The Eurobank may use the $1 million to convert into another currency for any purpose, lend dollars to nonbank borrowers, or, most likely, lend dollars to another Eurobank. Suppose the Eurobank (Eurobank I) decides to lend to a second Eurobank (Eurobank II) in the interbank market. The T account of Eurobank I shows the following changes:

Assets		Liabilities	
Demand deposit		Time deposit (H)	+ $1 million
(with U.S. bank)	+ $1 million		
	– $1 million		
Interbank loan			
(to Eurobank II)	+ $1 million		
Net change	+ $1 million	Net change	+ $1 million

Eurobank's II's T account looks like this:

Assets		Liabilities	
Demand deposit		Interbank loan	
(with U.S. bank)	+ $1 million	(from Eurobank I)	+ $1 million
Net change	+ $1 million	Net change	+ $1 million

When one Eurobank lends dollars to another Eurobank, therefore, there is no effect on the level of assets and liabilities for the entire U.S. banking system: Ownership of a demand deposit simply shifts between the Eurobanks. As we have seen, one U.S. bank loses reserves to another when this deposit shift moves funds from the first U.S. bank to the second. In practice, Eurobank I will lend out somewhat less than $1 million, keeping the remainder as a transactions/precautionary reserve. But the reserve will be less than would be required by national monetary authorities for a deposit in domestic currency.

Although centered in London, the Eurocurrency market is dominated by the European branches of the leading American banks. Banks seek out Eurocurrency deposits from individuals, banks, international traders, multinational corporations, and government agencies throughout the world by offering higher rates of interest than domestic banks. In turn, banks lend Eurocurrencies to the same groups at rates that are frequently lower than domestic rates. This is possible because the spread between borrowing and lending rates is smaller than in domestic markets as a consequence of the large size of most Eurocurrency transactions, intense competition, and the lower costs of smaller reserves against Eurocurrency deposits.

Apart from the rapid growth of the Eurocurrency market, the globalization of *national* ("onshore") capital markets has proceeded smartly as governments have deregulated securities markets and liberalized controls constraining international capital flows.[16] The linking of onshore and offshore markets has created a vast global capital market. For instance, between 1974 and 1988, the annual gross flows of international bank lending rose 7.5 times, from $57 billion to $425 billion, and the annual flows of international bonds (net of redemptions) rose 2.5 times between 1980 and 1988 from $58 billion to $144 billion.[17]

Implications of a Global Capital Market

The progressive formation of a global capital market now and in the future holds several consequences for the behavior of the international monetary system and the autonomy of national macroeconomic policies.

The most evident consequence of international financial integration is the enormity of short-term capital flows among the principal industrial countries. In the 1980s international flows of money overwhelmed international flows of goods and services in determining exchange rates. Because funds move quickly in response to actual and anticipated changes in interest and foreign exchange rates, international capital mobility has intensified the volatility of exchange rates.

Has the globalization of capital markets weakened the linkage between the instruments of U.S. monetary policy (discount rate and open market operations) and U.S. short-term interest rates? Economic theory supports the proposition that the integration of capital markets makes both the demand and supply of dollars more *interest-elastic*. Short-term securities issued by foreigners become closer substitutes for short-term dollar securities. Hence, on the demand side, both U.S. and foreign investors become more sensitive to interest-rate differentials in arranging their portfolios. On the supply side, borrowers have the option of issuing short-term securities either in the U.S. or foreign capital markets.

Higher interest elasticity in the demand and supply of dollars implies that changes in U.S. bank reserves induced by actions of the Federal Reserve will have a smaller impact on U.S. short-term interest rates (and therefore less policy effectiveness) than formerly, when capital markets were more independent. Has this actually occurred? One study concludes that there is some evidence that the emergence of a global capital market has loosened the linkage between changes in bank reserves and short-term interest rates in the United States and has therefore "complicated" the use of monetary policy. Also, the greater influence of foreign economic factors in determining U.S. short-term rates has created more uncertainty about the impact of a change in U.S. monetary policy.[18] A widely accepted

---

[16]For a recent review that discusses the sharp expansion in the scale of net and gross capital flows and the globalization and integration of offshore and major financial markets, see *Determinants and Systematic Consequences of International Capital Flows*, Occasional Paper 77 (Washington, D.C.: International Monetary Fund, March 1991).

[17]Ibid., Table 3, p. 6.

[18]Lawrence J. Radecki and Vincent Reinhart, "The Globalization of Financial Markets and the Effectiveness of Monetary Policy Instruments," *Quarterly Review* (Federal Reserve Bank of New York), Autumn 1988, pp. 18–27.

proposition is that international financial integration reduces interest-rate disparities among similar securities traded in different national capital markets. But we have seen that interest-rate differentials among industrial countries persisted throughout the 1980s. Is this proposition, then, false?

International financial integration means lower institutional barriers to the movement of funds in and out of national capital markets. Since the 1970s, such barriers have been dismantled in the industrial countries by deregulating national capital markets to make them more competitive and open to foreigners and by eliminating foreign exchange restrictions on the international flow of funds.[19] But this liberalization has not wiped out interest-rate differentials among those countries, because financial integration remains incomplete as long as each country has an independent monetary system with its own currency.

Because the global capital market remains *segmented* by different national currencies, shifts of funds from one national capital market to another assume an *exchange* risk. This risk prevents the equalization of interest rates. Interest parity theory states that equilibrium is achieved when an interest-rate differential is exactly offset by the cost of hedging.[20] And, as demonstrated in Chapter 13, speculation may prevent interest parity equilibrium. Even if institutional barriers become zero, therefore, interest rates will fail to equalize across countries because of the foreign exchange risk.

The significance of exchange risk is shown by the fact that short-term interest rates in the U.S. capital market track very closely with *Eurodollar* rates, as do the short-term rates in other major capital markets with their counterparts in the Eurocurrency market (yen rates with Euroyen rates, pound sterling rates with Eurosterling, and so on). In these cases, the near absence of institutional barriers between national markets and the Eurocurrency market and the absence of any exchange risk come close to complete financial integration. The answer to our question, therefore, is that the elimination of institutional barriers reduces the divergence of interest rates among national capital markets for the same class of security. But as long as the global capital market falls short of complete integration with a single currency, it will fail to eliminate interest-rate differences across countries. Summing up, the emergence of a global capital market has made exchange rates more volatile and more sensitive to national macroeconomic policies. High capital mobility has made national economies more interdependent and, for that reason, has weakened the autonomy of national policymakers in spite of the existence of floating exchange rates.

PERFORMANCE OF THE CONTEMPORARY SYSTEM

How has the contemporary system performed since it began in 1973? The answer to this question cannot be a simple "poorly" or "well," because it depends on assumptions about how an ideal floating-rate system *should* perform or how an

---

[19]Institutional barriers remain high in the developing countries.
[20]Recall equation (7) in Chapter 13: $i_{US} - i_{UK} = (F^* - S)/S$.

alternative system *would* have performed, as well as the *actual* performance of the contemporary system. In short, the answer to this question is a value judgment. Our response to this question, therefore, is the modest one of making some relevant observations.

The actual performance of the contemporary system has fulfilled neither the dire prophecies of fixed-rate advocates nor the fond expectations of floating-rate advocates. On the one hand, floating rates have *not* inhibited international trade and investment or caused a disintegration of international capital markets. Traders, bankers, multinational enterprises, and others have learned to manage their affairs in a floating-rate environment. On the other hand, floating rates have *not* brought about quick adjustments in trade flows through smooth changes in exchange rates. Instead, rates have been extremely volatile, while current-account adjustments in response to changes in relative prices and costs have occurred only slowly. Nor have floating rates enabled governments to pursue national policies without regard to their international consequences. Instead, governments have encountered difficulties with national policy autonomy because of the international integration of money and capital markets.

The high short-run volatility of exchange rates has intensified the debate on stable versus variable rates. Fixed-rate advocates argue that exchange rates in the contemporary system "overshoot" their proper equilibrium levels, causing excessive adjustments in national economies. But there is now substantial agreement among economists that short-run volatility in exchange rates is caused by volatile expectations about future rates and government policies that influence them. As "efficient" markets, foreign exchange markets respond to all available information, and they continuously receive new information that alters existing exchange rates. Moreover, although exchange rates have been more volatile than national price levels, they have been *less* volatile than the prices of other financial assets (stocks and bonds) and gold, which are also traded in organized markets.

The contemporary system has now operated through a turbulent quarter-century — about the same amount of time as the Bretton Woods system — marked by high but uneven rates of inflation, divergent national monetary and fiscal policies, two oil-pricing shocks, a slowdown in economic activity with rising unemployment, an international stock market crash, and several political crises, most recently the collapse of the Soviet Union and other communist regimes in Europe, the Gulf War, and civil war in Yugoslavia. It is doubtful that any fixed-rate system could have survived such turbulence without the imposition of stringent controls over international trade and capital movements by at least some of the major industrial countries.[21] Highly variable exchange rates have been a response to turbulence, not its cause.

The exchange rate is only one of several macroeconomic variables. In particular, exchange rates are strongly influenced by national monetary policies. Divergent monetary policies among countries, as we have seen, can create *real* interest-

---

[21]The alleged drawbacks of the contemporary system remind one of a saying attributed to Winston Churchill: "Democracy is a terrible form of government — except when compared to all the others!"

rate differentials (as well as nominal differentials) that instigate international flows of money and other financial assets. More profoundly, divergent monetary policies create different rates of inflation among countries and, therefore, shifting purchasing-power parities. Hence, exchange rate behavior should not be evaluated in isolation from other macroeconomic variables.

The experience of the 1980s demonstrates that countries need to coordinate their macroeconomic policies in the contemporary system (even though they have somewhat more flexibility than in a fixed-rate system) if they want less variable exchange rates over the longer term. But coordinated policies will not ensure stable foreign exchange markets: They are a necessary but not sufficient condition for stability. As long as the international environment remains turbulent, exchange rates will remain highly variable. This is as it should be in a system in which exchange rates are the principal instrument of international adjustment. But coordinated national policies would certainly lessen exchange rate variability.

The world economy in the 1980s experienced large swings in current-account balances and accompanying capital movements in an environment of uneven rates of inflation, general economic slowdown, and unemployment. With these conditions, a return to a fixed-rate system is most improbable. But if the leading industrial countries succeed in establishing low-inflation, high-employment economies and are willing to coordinate their domestic economic policies, then we can expect growing support for a fixed-rate system. The main threat today, however, is not a collapse of the international monetary system but rather protectionism. This new protectionism, which is spawned by divergent macroeconomic policies and structural maladjustments, will stifle international trade and investment in the 1990s if it is not successfully combatted.

SUMMARY

1. In sharp contrast to the Bretton Woods system, the currencies of other industrial countries are now floating with respect to the U.S. dollar.
2. Exchange rates were highly variable in the 1980s. Changes in *nominal* exchange rates among the dollar, yen, and mark cannot be explained by divergent rates of inflation. Rather, they were due to divergent macroeconomic policies that brought about large international differentials in real interest rates.
3. The high variability of *real* exchange rates in the 1980s was owing to the high variability of nominal exchange rates and the sluggish responses of national prices and costs to changes in nominal rates.
4. The macroeconomic policies followed by the United States in the 1980s had several unfortunate consequences. The 50 percent appreciation of the dollar between 1980 and 1985 hurt U.S. export- and import-competing industries and magnified demands for import protection. High U.S. real interest rates induced an enormous inflow of capital (making the United States the world's biggest debtor), slowed U.S. domestic investment, and increased the burden of servicing the external debts of the Third World.

5. Central banks have continued to intervene in foreign exchange markets, and thus the contemporary system is best described as a *managed-float* system. In general, intervention has followed the standard of "leaning against the wind."

6. Abandoning its laissez-faire attitude, the United States, together with other major industrial countries, announced the Plaza Agreement in September 1985. This agreement was intended to push down the value of the dollar. Actually, the dollar had started to fall in February of that year. The Louvre Accord of February 1987, agreed to by the G-5 countries and Canada, sought to stabilize the dollar's value through equilibrating changes in macroeconomic policies. But the Louvre Accord has so far failed to reduce significantly the divergence of macroeconomic policies, which is the fundamental cause of the huge current-account deficits of the United States.

7. Further depreciation of the dollar alone cannot eliminate current-account imbalances. What is needed is international policy coordination that achieves a decrease in U.S. domestic absorption and an increase in the domestic absorption of Japan and West Germany.

8. The International Monetary Fund continues to play a role in the contemporary international monetary system. It undertakes surveillance of the exchange rate policies of member countries and extends far more adjustment assistance to developing countries than in the past. Conditionality gives the Fund strong leverage over the policies of the countries that use its credit.

9. A global capital market first emerged in the 1950s in the form of the Eurocurrency market. The liberalization of national capital markets started in the 1970s and gathered force in the 1980s. This movement has progressively integrated national capital markets and the Eurocurrency market to create a single global capital market. The resulting high international mobility of capital has made national economies more interdependent and, for that reason, has weakened the autonomy of national policymakers.

10. The contemporary international monetary system has functioned through two decades of economic and political turbulence. It is doubtful that a fixed-rate system could have survived such turbulence. As long as the major industrial countries remain unwilling or unable to coordinate macroeconomic policies, a return to a fixed-rate system is unlikely.

QUESTIONS AND APPLICATIONS

1. (a) Describe the structure of the contemporary international monetary system.
   (b) How does this system differ from the Bretton Woods system?
   (c) Some observers have described the contemporary system as a "non-system." Do you agree or disagree? Why?

2. Define *nominal effective exchange rate* and *real effective exchange rate*.

3. Why did the dollar, yen, and mark exhibit prolonged changes in *real* exchange rates in the 1980s?

4. What is the relationship between interest rates and exchange rates?
5. (a) Why did U.S. domestic absorption rise so strongly after 1980?
   (b) Explain how this rise in absorption was possible only through a deficit of the same amount in the U.S. current account.
   (c) Why did not the increase in U.S. absorption after 1980 induce higher output and thereby avoid a current-account deficit?
6. (a) Why have central banks intervened in foreign exchange markets in the contemporary system?
   (b) Distinguish a "managed float" from a "pure float."
   (c) Explain the intervention standard known as "leaning against the wind."
7. (a) What is the Plaza Agreement? The Louvre Accord?
   (b) What was the effect of central bank intervention during the period February 1985 to February 1988?
8. (a) What is international policy coordination?
   (b) Explain the reasoning behind this statement: "Further depreciation of the dollar alone cannot eliminate current-account imbalances. What is needed is international policy coordination."
9. Which principles guide the International Monetary Fund's surveillance of exchange rate policies?
10. What is IMF "conditionality"? Can it be applied equally to deficit and surplus countries? Why or why not?
11. (a) What are Eurocurrencies?
    (b) How does the Eurocurrency market differ from national capital markets?
    (c) How does the Eurocurrency market facilitate the international transfer of funds?
12. Using T accounts, show what happens to bank assets and liabilities when (a) a deposit holder switches a dollar deposit from a Eurobank to a U.S. bank; (b) a multinational enterprise borrows from a U.S. bank and then deposits the dollars in a Eurobank.
13. (a) Why should a global capital market make the demand and supply of dollars more interest-elastic?
    (b) What are the implications for U.S. monetary policy of higher interest elasticity?
14. Why has not the emergence of a global capital market eliminated interest-rate disparities among the industrial countries?
15. Evaluate the prospects for a return to a fixed-rate international monetary system.

SELECTED READINGS

Cooper, Richard N. *Economic Policy in an Interdependent World.* Cambridge: MIT Press, 1986.

De Vries, Margaret G. *The IMF in a Changing World, 1945–85.* Washington, D.C.: International Monetary Fund, 1986.

DeVries, Margaret G. *Balance of Payments Adjustment, 1945 to 1986: The IMF Experience.* Washington, D.C.: International Monetary Fund, 1987.

Eichengreen, Barry, ed. *The Gold Standard in Theory and History.* New York: Methuen, 1985.

Federal Reserve Bank of New York. "Treasury and Federal Reserve Foreign Exchange Operations." *Quarterly Review.* Each issue.

Federal Reserve Bank of New York. "Studies in U.S. External Imbalances." *Quarterly Review,* Winter–Spring, 1989, pp. 1–82.

Frankel, Jeffrey A. *Obstacles to International Macroeconomic Policy Coordination.* Princeton Studies in International Finance, no. 64. Princeton, N.J.: Princeton University Press, December 1988.

International Monetary Fund. *Annual Report.* Washington, D.C.

International Monetary Fund. *Articles of Agreement.* Washington, D.C.: International Monetary Fund. Latest edition.

International Monetary Fund. *IMF Survey.* Biweekly.

International Monetary Fund. *International Capital Markets.* Washington, D.C.: International Monetary Fund. No fixed issue date.

International Monetary Fund. *International Financial Statistics.* Washington, D.C.: International Monetary Fund. Monthly.

International Monetary Fund. *Strengthening the International Monetary System: Exchange Rates, Surveillance, and Objective Indicators.* Occasional Paper 50. Washington, D.C.: International Monetary Fund, February 1987.

International Monetary Fund. *World Economic Outlook.* Washington, D.C.: International Monetary Fund. No fixed issue date.

Meese, Richard. "Currency Fluctuations in the Post-Bretton Woods Era." *Journal of Economic Perspectives,* Winter 1990, pp. 117–134.

Solomon, Robert. *The International Monetary System, 1945–1976.* New York: Harper & Row, 1977.

Von Furstenberg, George M., and Joseph P. Daniels. *Economic Summit Declarations 1975–89: Examining the Written Record of International Cooperations.* Princeton Studies in International Finance, no. 72. Princeton, NJ: Princeton University Press: February 1992.

INTERNATIONAL

part III

DEVELOPMENT

Over half of the world's peoples live in the developing countries of Asia, Africa, and Latin America at levels of income that remain far below those enjoyed by peoples in the industrial countries of North America, Western Europe, and Japan. Another third of the world's peoples live poorly in the communist and once-communist countries of Eastern Europe and Asia, notably the former Soviet Union and China. These countries have entered a historic transformation of their centrally planned economies into market economies, which will have profound consequences for the world economy. In Chapter 20, we look at the role of the developing countries in the world economy. In Chapter 21, we address the policy issues facing centrally planned economies in their efforts to build market economies.

chapter 20

THE DEVELOPING COUNTRIES
IN THE WORLD ECONOMY

One-fifth of the world's people live a daily round of grinding poverty.[1] Occupying the vast stretches of Asia, Africa, and Latin America, these people inhabit more than one hundred countries that are committed to programs of economic development intended to break the vicious circle of poverty. Industrialization has become the supreme national goal of these developing countries; it dominates their economic policies and will probably continue to do so for generations to come. In particular, the drive for economic development shapes the attitudes, policies, and expectations of the developing countries in the areas of international trade, external assistance, and international investment.

In this chapter, we examine the role of international trade in economic development and the trade policies of the developing countries. We also look at the response that industrial countries are making to the needs and demands of the developing countries. But first we must comprehend the economic situation of the poor countries and the major obstacles to a betterment of their low standards of living, for it is this situation that generates the drive for development and the policies directed toward international trade and investment.

THE ECONOMIC SITUATION
OF THE DEVELOPING COUNTRIES

Which are the developing countries? What are their major obstacles to further development? What is the record of three decades of development?

---

[1]In 1990, 1.1 billion people in the developing countries (three-tenths of their population) had incomes below a poverty line of $370 annual income in 1985 purchasing-power parity dollars. (In 1990 prices, the poverty line would be $420 annual income per capita.) See The World Bank, *World Development Report 1992* (New York: Oxford University Press, 1992), Table 1.1, p. 30.

Which Are the Developing Countries?

The most commonly used indicator to distinguish the developing from the industrial countries is gross national product (income) per capita.[2] Table 20-1 classifies countries according to this indicator.[3]

Economic development and underdevelopment are complex phenomena with social, cultural, and political dimensions as well as an economic dimension. Hence, they cannot be fully measured by any single indicator. Nonetheless, most observers would agree that countries with per capita GNPs below $1,500 in 1990 are unquestionably nonindustrial countries. These poor countries, classified as low-income and lower-middle-income developing countries, account for 84 of the 125 countries listed in Table 20-1. At the same time, several countries in the upper-middle-income group, such as Brazil, Mexico, and Korea, can hardly be described as modern industrial economies. This is also true of *high-income oil exporters*, whose per capita incomes have shot up since the quadrupling of oil prices at the beginning of 1974 but whose economies continue to bear the hallmarks of developing countries, which are discussed later in this chapter. Although the United Arab Emirates and Kuwait are in the highest per capita income category,

Table 20-1 Population, Per Capita GNP, and Energy Consumption by Country Groups in 1990

Country Group[1]	Population (Millions)	Per Capita GNP (Dollars)	Per Capita Energy Consumption (Kilograms of Oil Equivalent)
Low-income	3,058	350	339
China and India	1,983	360	440
Other low-income	1,075	320	153
Lower-middle-income	629	1,530	1,025
Upper-middle-income	458	3,410	1,818
High-income countries	816	19,590	5,158

[1]In terms of 1990 GNP per capita, the country groups are defined as follows: low-income—$610 or less; lower-middle-income—$611–$2,465; upper-middle-income—$2,466–$7,619; and high-income—$7,620 or more.

Note: Only countries with a population of one million or more are included in this table.

Source: Based on data in The World Bank, *World Development Report 1992* (New York: Oxford University Press, 1992), Table 1, pp. 218–19, and Table 5, p. 226.

---

[2]Several terms are used to denote the developing countries: *poor, nonindustrial, underdeveloped, less-developed (LDC), South* and *Third World*. These terms are used interchangeably in this and other chapters.

[3]Note that Table 20-1 includes the communist or once-communist countries, all of whose per capita GNPs lie below the high-income group.

they remain largely preindustrial societies badly in need of social and economic development.

It is impossible, therefore, to draw a line in Table 20-1 separating developing from developed countries. Per capita GNP is only a partial indicator of economic development. More fundamentally, the *developed* countries have not only surpassed the "threshold" level of annual per capita GNP (say $7,500) but have also demonstrated a capacity for sustained economic growth over a long period without concessional assistance (grants or low-interest, easy-payment loans) from external sources. However, the per capita GNP indicator offers certain advantages as a criterion of economic development: It distinguishes the least-developed from the most highly developed countries, it is quantitative, and it rests upon the empirical truth that a threshold level of per capita income is necessary, if not sufficient, for economic development. Furthermore, per capita GNP correlates highly with other indicators of development, such as per capita energy consumption which is also shown in Table 20-1.

The developing countries make up a highly heterogeneous group. In size of population they range from China, with over one billion inhabitants, to the many developing countries, such as Barbados, with less than one million inhabitants. Some are highly endowed with minerals or fertile agricultural lands; others consist mainly of arid desert or tropical rain forest. Some are much further advanced than others: Brazil possesses a major industrial center in its Sao Paulo region, Argentina has ten times the per capita GNP of the least-developed countries, and the oil-exporting countries constitute a distinctive subset.

The developing countries also exhibit broad cultural, social, and political differences. Despite this diversity, they generally (but not always) share common features: low levels of industrialization, low per capita incomes (except the oil-exporting countries), high illiteracy rates, a predominance of agriculture and other primary production, and a dependence on commodity exports. These common features set them off from the economically advanced countries located mainly in Western Europe and North America. Nonetheless, the developing countries can be adequately described today only in terms of three subgroups: (1) high-income oil exporters, (2) upper-middle-income economies, and (3) lower-middle-income and low-income economies. The upper-middle-income economies include the "newly industrializing economies" or NICs (notably, Brazil, Hong Kong, Mexico, Singapore, South Korea, and Taiwan), which have switched from commodity to manufactured exports and which possess high rates of industrial growth that are making their economies resemble more closely those of the industrial economies than those of other developing countries.

The *regional* economic performance of the developing countries is also highly diverse. As shown in Table 20-2, the per capita GNP of East Asia and the Pacific (which embraces the four NICs: Korea, Taiwan, Hong Kong, and Singapore) grew at an annual rate of 6.3 percent during the 1980s. At the other extreme, the Middle East and North Africa *declined* at an annual rate of 1.5 percent during the same decade.

Table 20-2 Average Annual Growth of the Developing Countries' GNP Per Capita by Region, 1980–1990 (Percent)

Region	Percent
East Asia and the Pacific	6.3
South Asia	2.9
Europe	1.0
Latin America and the Caribbean	0.5
Sub-Saharan Africa	– 1.1
Middle East and North Africa	– 1.5

Source: The World Bank, *World Development Report 1992* (New York: Oxford University Press, 1992), Table A.2, p. 196.

The inequality of per capita income among the world's nations is enormous. Figure 20-1 depicts this inequality with a Lorenz curve. If national per capita incomes were absolutely *equal,* the income distribution curve would be the diagonal line 0–*P.* For then 20 percent of the world population would earn 20 percent of the world income; 40 percent, 40 percent; and so on. (The curve of absolute *inequality* is the bottom and right sides of the figure.) The curve of *actual* income distribution determines the zone of income inequality, as shown in Figure 20-1. This zone is a large fraction of the entire space lying below the diagonal, indicating a high degree of income inequality. To demonstrate this inequality specifically, we have partitioned the income distribution curve into three income groups.

0–*L* represents the 43 low-income countries that have 57.9 percent of the world's population but only 4.8 percent of its income (GNP). *L–N* denotes the 61 lower- and upper-middle-income countries that have 26.7 percent of the world's population and 23.0 percent of its income. *N–P* represents the 24 high-income countries that have 15.4 percent of the world's population but enjoy 72.2 percent of the world's income.[4]

The poverty of the developing nations is not new; it has been a way of life for untold generations. What is new is the bitter awareness of poverty, the knowledge that it is not inevitable, and the determination to raise living standards one way or another. Many of the countries of Asia and Africa emerged from a colonial status to full political independence only after World War II. Independence has been

---

[4]Nineteen of these high-income countries are *industrial* countries which together with Greece, Iceland, Portugal, Luxembourg, and Turkey, are the OECD countries. The OECD is the Organization for Economic Cooperation and Development. It has the following member countries: Australia, Austria, Belgium, Canada, Denmark, Finland, France, Germany, Greece, Iceland, Ireland, Italy, Japan, Luxembourg, the Netherlands, New Zealand, Norway, Portugal, Spain, Sweden, Switzerland, Turkey, the United Kingdom, and the United States. *OECD* is another designation for the developed or industrial countries. This group is also called the *West* or *North.* These terms are used interchangeably in this and other chapters.

Figure 20-1

Source: Based on data in The World Bank, *World Development Report 1992* (New York: Oxford University Press, 1992), Table A.2, p. 196.

International Inequality of Income in 1990. The international distribution of income is depicted by the $0-L-N-P$ curve. If per capital incomes among countries were absolutely equal, then income distribution would fall on the $0-P$ line: 20 percent of the world's population would earn 20 percent of the world's income, and so on. Hence, the gap between the $0-P$ line and the $0-L-N-P$ curve indicates income inequality.

accompanied by a virulent nationalism, high expectations, and, in some cases, antagonism toward the West.

What has been called "the revolution of rising expectations" is cause for both hope and fear. Of hope, for after centuries of stagnation the developing countries are now striving to create the conditions essential to economic and social progress. Of fear, for the frustration of their high expectations may turn these peoples toward violent revolution (as it has already done in some instances) and against the West.

Obstacles to Economic Development

The developing countries need to overcome many obstacles to match the sustained economic growth and rising living standards of the industrial countries. These obstacles are a complex set of internal and external factors. Although it is widely agreed that the basic restraints on growth derive from the structure of the poor societies, external conditions that hinder the exports of developing nations or limit the availability of financial assistance from abroad also can restrain growth.

To become mature economies, the developing nations must undertake a massive transformation of their societies, and this can be accomplished only by their own peoples and national leaders. To succeed, however, they need the capital goods and technology of the developed, industrial countries. This section looks at major obstacles to growth *within* the developing countries themselves; international trade and financial conditions that limit growth are taken up later.

The situation of developing countries has been aptly described as interlocking sets of vicious circles that perpetuate economic stagnation and poverty. One of these vicious circles involves the savings-investment gap:

1. Productivity is low because investment is low.
2. Investment is low because saving is low.
3. Saving is low because income is low.
4. Income is low because productivity is low.

Thus, in a very real sense the poor nations are poor because they are poor.

Lack of Social Overhead Capital Social overhead capital supplies the services — power, transportation, storage, communications, education, and so on — that are indispensable to modern industry and agriculture. The lack of this capital in the poor nations is a bottleneck to economic development. Inadequate transportation and communication facilities block the exploitation of attractive resources located in the interior regions of many countries in Latin America, Asia, and Africa. A country like India may lose up to one-third of its agricultural output because it lacks storage facilities to protect against spoilage, rodents, and other wastage. The absence of electrical power thwarts the establishment of the many industries dependent on it, as well as impeding community and urban development.

Educational facilities are a vital element of social overhead capital. The majority of the people in the low-income nations are illiterate. Lacking the basic skills and training necessary for industrial production or modern agriculture, these people can make little contribution to economic development. The developing countries must stamp out illiteracy mainly by educating the new generation; unless this is done, there is little hope for the future.

Lack of Entrepreneurs and Managers The efforts of countless, mostly private, entrepreneurs gave Western Europe and North America the momentum to move into and beyond the takeoff stage of economic growth. Eagerly searching for new profit opportunities, these entrepreneurs combined factors of production in new ways and on a broader scale than ever before in history to produce new products for emerging markets. Later, a large class of business managers arose to promote and administer the expanding private enterprise sectors of these economies. Today, professional preparation for careers in business is commonplace in the United States, Western Europe, and Japan.

In contrast, the developing nations generally lack a business class that is willing to invest in new industrial enterprises and has the know-how to manage them. Their business people are likely to be traders and merchants engaging in foreign trade, wholesaling, and retailing rather than in manufacturing. They tend to be speculative, looking for quick profits in real estate or monopoly market situations. Frequently the upper class in the poor societies disapproves of business, preferring to invest in land and rearing its children to be land-owning aristocrats, soldiers, lawyers, and diplomats instead of business executives.

Cultural Blocks to Economic Growth   Old ways and new ways live side by side in the developing societies, and in many, the old ways remain dominant. Preindustrial attitudes toward work and belief in traditional ways are very hard to change. And yet they must be changed if the economy is ever to achieve takeoff: Workers must develop the motivation and discipline essential to industrial production, and peasants must become commercial farmers, open to technological innovations in agriculture.

Poor motivation, high turnover, absenteeism, and generally sloppy performance characterize the industrial workers of many developing nations. In the early stage of industrialization, an increase in wages may actually cause absenteeism because people work only to maintain a traditional standard of living, having no conception of a rising standard.[5] Peasants can offer stubborn resistance to changing their ways. Getting them to use commercial fertilizers, improved seed strains, crop rotation schemes, and so on, requires a time-consuming educational process that is likely to be only partially successful, as witnessed by the community development programs in India and Latin America.

Cultural blocks are often elusive and hard to identify. Once identified, they are hard to overcome. Nevertheless, they must be overcome, because prescientific, traditional attitudes and beliefs act to reinforce the vicious circles of poverty that plague the developing nations.

The Population Explosion   It was not until 1800 that the world's population reached one billion. But then it took only 120 years to add a second billion; 35 years to add a third; and 15 years to add a fourth. Today, the world's population exceeds five billion, and it grew in the 1980s at an average annual rate of 1.7 percent. Most of that growth occurred in the developing countries whose population grew at an annual average rate of 2.0 percent. At that rate, population

---

[5]This causes a "backward sloping supply schedule" for labor. This situation is not likely to last very long, particularly in urban areas where newly arrived workers are exposed to examples of higher standards of living.

doubles every 35 years. Demographers anticipate a leveling off of population at somewhat over ten billion at the end of the next century.[6]

The issue here is not whether this vast number of people in the developing countries will be able to survive but rather how fast economic development would be able to proceed at a lower rate of population growth. The evidence is now conclusive that population growth at the rapid pace of most of the developing world slows development.[7] When population grows rapidly, the bulk of domestic investment is devoted to simply maintaining the current level of per capita income rather than increasing it. In other words, much of the increase in production of the poor countries is being consumed by the newly born.

Fundamentally, the population explosion is a consequence of the "public health" revolution in the poor countries. The introduction of modern medicine has cut death rates drastically (mainly in the early years of life) but has had little influence on birth rates, which often remain at the traditional high levels. Paradoxically, modern medicine, by saving lives, is making it more difficult to lift those lives out of poverty. Only recently have some governments of developing countries responded to this critical situation.

Three Decades of Development

Table 20-3 shows the rates of growth in population, GNP, and per capita GNP for the developing countries of the South and the industrial countries of the North over the period 1965 to 1990.

The GNP growth rates of the low-income countries matched or exceeded world GNP rates in all three decades. Despite high growth rates in population, percentage growth of the per capita GNP in these countries exceeded the world's in the 1970s and 1980s. The GNP and per capita GNP growth rates of the middle-income countries were far higher than world rates in the 1960s and 1970s. But this progress was abruptly halted in the 1980s under the impact of the international debt crisis. In that decade, the GNP growth rate of the middle-income countries barely exceeded their population growth rate. All in all, however, the performance of the developing countries over three decades compares very favorably with the average annual historical growth rate of 2 percent experienced by the industrial countries over the last century.

It is evident that three decades of development have brought substantial economic progress to the developing countries. This progress does not support those who believe that the LDCs are permanently sunk in hopeless poverty, and it offers encouragement to those who are committed to development. But the *absolute* levels of per capita income remain depressingly low for the least-developed countries. Even if the very high per capita growth rate achieved by the low-income

---

[6]Allen C. Kelley, "Economic Consequences of Population Change in the Third World," *Journal of Economic Literature,* December 1988, p. 1685.

[7]The World Bank, *World Development Report 1984* (New York: Oxford University Press, 1984), p. 105.

Table 20-3 Growth of Population, GNP, and Per Capita GNP of the Developing and Industrial Countries, 1965–1990 (Average Annual Percentage Changes)

	1965–1973			1973–1980			1980–1990		
	Population	GNP	Per Capita GNP	Population	GNP	Per Capita GNP	Population	GNP	Per Capita GNP
Low-income developing countries	2.5	4.9	2.4	2.0	4.7	2.7	2.0	6.0	4.0
Middle-income developing countries	2.3	7.6	5.3	2.3	4.7	2.4	2.0	2.4	0.4
High-income OECD countries	0.9	4.6	3.7	0.7	2.8	2.1	0.6	3.1	2.5
World	2.1	4.9	2.8	1.8	3.1	1.3	1.7	3.1	1.4

Note: The GNP growth rate was derived from the summation of the population and per capita GNP growth rates.
Source: Based on data in The World Bank, *World Development Report 1992* (New York: Oxford University Press, 1992), Tables A.1 and A.2, p. 196.

countries in the 1980s were to continue, it would take some 18 years to double their average per capita income of $350.

CAPITAL FORMATION, ECONOMIC GROWTH, AND CONSTRAINTS ON DOMESTIC INVESTMENT

Capital formation—the creation of transportation, communications, and power facilities; the construction of factories; the acquisition of machines, tools, and other instruments of production—is an essential condition of economic growth. The harnessing of mechanical energies, the organization of mass production, the utilization of modern technology, the education and training of workers—all of these are dependent on the formation of capital. In the developed countries, capital resources per capita are high; in the developing countries, they are low.

Investment and National Output

To increase its stock of capital, a country must invest a part of its national product.[8] Investment reduces the resources available to satisfy immediate consumption, but it raises the level of consumption in the future by enhancing economic productivity. The relationship between new investment and a subsequent increase in real output depends on the marginal productivity of capital, which may be expressed as the *incremental capital-output ratio, or k.*

$$(1) \quad k = I_t / \Delta V_{t+1}.$$

I_t is the investment in period t and ΔV_{t+1} is the resulting increment in real national output (gross domestic product) in the next period, which we shall take to be the following year. If, for example, $6 million of investment causes a $2 million increase in national output, then the capital-output ratio is 3.[9]

Given k, we can calculate the growth rate of a country's output once we know the annual rate of investment (r) expressed as a fraction (or percentage) of current national output.

$$(2) \quad r = I_t / V_t.$$

Hence, the growth rate (g) of gross domestic product is r/k:

$$(3) \quad g = r/k = (I_t / V_t)(\Delta V_{t+1} / I_t) = \Delta V_{t+1} / V_t.$$

To illustrate, if a country is investing 15 percent of its gross domestic product on an annual basis and its incremental capital-output ratio is 3, then its rate of growth is 15 percent/3, or 5 percent.

---

[8]More precisely, a country must invest an amount beyond that needed to maintain its existing capital stock (capital consumption is measured by depreciation) if it is to add to its capital stock. In the subsequent discussion we shall ignore the distinction between gross and net investment.

[9]In both developed and developing countries, the incremental capital-output ratio generally falls between 2 and 5.

In measuring the progress of the developing countries, we are particularly interested in the *per capita* growth rate (w). If p is the annual rate of growth in population, then

$$(4) \; w = g - p = (r/k) - p.$$

(Strictly speaking, we should calculate w by dividing the index of gross domestic product by the population index, but when the population growth rate is less than 5 percent, which is empirically true, equation (4) will render a close approximation of the true value and is much simpler to compute.)

Returning to our previous example, if the annual rate of population growth is 2 percent, then the per capita growth rate in terms of equation (4) is

$$w = (15\%/3) - 2\% = 3\%.$$

Equation (4) tells us that a country can increase its rate of per capita growth by lowering its incremental capital-output ratio (k), by lowering its rate of population growth (p), or by raising its rate of investment (r). The incremental capital-output ratio is determined by many dynamic factors: As a country's capital stock increases relative to other productive agents, diminishing returns act to raise k, while a better allocation of investment, new technology, and improvements in human skills act to lower k by increasing the productivity of capital. Studies of long-term economic growth in the developed countries indicate that increases in productivity (decreases in k) account for a greater share of per capita income growth than the mere increase in capital utilized per worker at a constant level of technology.[10] It follows that the developing countries must continually work to lower k if they are to match the development experience of the advanced countries. As for population, we have already spoken about this growth constraint in the preceding section.

Given k and p, a country can increase its rate of growth by raising its rate of domestic investment (r). Negatively expressed, a country may fail to achieve a target rate of growth (say, 2 percent per capita per year) because r is too low. Suppose, for example, a country has an incremental capital-output ratio of 3, a rate of investment of 9 percent (rather than 15 percent as in our previous example), and an annual rate of population growth of 2 percent. Then

$$w = (9\%/3) - 2\% = 1\%.$$

The relationship between domestic investment and economic growth has been emphasized by economists in growth models because it can be quantitatively

---

[10]For the 1929–1957 period in the United States, Denison attributes only 42 percent of the increase in output per worker to an increase in inputs (quality improvements in labor, more land, and more capital) and 58 percent to an increase in output per unit of input that mainly resulted from technological innovation and economies of scale. The increase in capital per worker (technology constant) explains only 9 percent of the growth rate. See Edward F. Denison, *The Sources of Economic Growth in the United States and the Alternatives before Us* (New York: Committee for Economic Development, 1962), Table 33, p. 270.

defined, whereas the relationships between social and political factors and economic growth are hard to quantify and fall outside the disciplinary boundaries of economics. Economists recognize, however, that investment is a *necessary* condition but not a *sufficient* condition for economic development. Investment must be accompanied by appropriate changes in attitudes, values, and institutions if an economy is to achieve a self-sustaining growth. Economic growth is only one element in the modernization of a traditional society. The foregoing remarks are not intended to dispute the importance of capital formation in the developing countries. Capital formation is the major instrument for the transformation of technical knowledge into technological innovation: Infrastructure investment in transportation and communication makes possible economies of scale, and social investment in education is necessary to improve human skills. It is correct, therefore, to view the rate of investment as a critical factor in economic development, although it is by no means the only critical factor. From this perspective, we now turn to a consideration of the constraints that may limit the growth of investment in the developing countries.

Constraints on Domestic Investment Faced by Developing Countries

The rate of domestic investment in a developing country may be constrained in three principal ways: (1) by the capacity of the country to absorb additional capital, (2) by the level of its domestic savings, or (3) by the availability of foreign exchange. With a given k, any one of these three constraints may impose a ceiling on the level of investment and, therefore, on the rate of growth in gross domestic product.

The *capital-absorption capacity* of a country depends on the availability of human factors (labor, managerial, and administrative) embodying skills that are necessary to transform investment funds (savings) into real investment. It also depends on the presence of an effective demand for the output resulting from investment. Suppose the target rate of growth is $\bar{g}$ and the rate of investment required to achieve this target rate is $\bar{r}$. Now let a be the country's current rate of capital-absorption capacity (expressed as a percentage of gross domestic product). Then if $\bar{r} > a$, absorptive capacity places a limitation on the rate of growth. Absorptive capacity is likely to be a critical constraint for an economy as a whole only when a country is in the early stages of growth.

In an open economy, gross *domestic* product assumes this form:

$$(5)\ GDP\ =\ C\ +\ I\ +\ G\ +\ (X\ -\ M).$$

This identity equation may be compared to that for gross *national* product, which is stated as equation (1) in Chapter 15. The only difference between the two is that exports (X) and imports (M) in the GDP identity are defined so as to exclude factor payments received from or paid to the rest of the world. Thus, GNP measures total output resulting from factors of production owned anywhere by the country's residents, whereas GDP measures all output resulting from factors of production located on the country's territory regardless of their ownership.

Since gross domestic product equals gross domestic income (the sum of domestic consumption and domestic saving), it follows that domestic investment equals the sum of domestic saving and the import balance on current account (excluding factor payments and receipts) that is financed by net borrowing from abroad:

$$(6)\ I\ =\ S\ +\ (M\ -\ X).[11]$$

In the absence of any net foreign borrowing ($M = X$), then $I = S$, the rate of investment (r) equals the rate of domestic saving (s), and $r/k = s/k$. Now assume that a country's target rate of growth is $\bar{g}$ and the required rate of investment is $\bar{r}$ while the rate of domestic savings is s. Then if $s < \bar{r}$, there is a *domestic savings gap* that will prevent the attainment of the target rate of growth: $g = s/k = r/k < \bar{r}/k = \bar{g}$.

When its savings gap is financed by net borrowing from abroad that permits an excess of imports over exports, then a country is able to achieve its target rate of growth: $\bar{I} = S + (M - X)$, where $\bar{I}$ is the required level of investment. If b is ($M - X$) expressed as a percentage of gross domestic product (the rate of foreign borrowing), then $\bar{g} = s/k + b/k = \bar{r}/k$.

In the absence of capital-absorption and savings gaps, the growth rate of a developing country may still be constrained by a *foreign exchange (trade) gap*. That is to say, domestic savings are a necessary condition but may not be a sufficient condition for raising investment in a developing country to a desired level. The explanation of this situation rests on the import requirements of real capital formation coupled with the structural inability of a developing economy to transform savings into foreign exchange through an increase in exports or a decrease in imports. In order to invest, a developing country must acquire from abroad the capital equipment and other investment goods (such as structural steel) that it is unable to produce at home. If the output released by domestic savings can be allocated to exports or import substitution, then the foreign exchange necessary to purchase investment goods from abroad is forthcoming. In that event, there is no foreign exchange gap distinct from a savings gap, a situation that is true of the advanced, developed economies. But in developing countries, the capacity to reallocate resources is commonly limited by internal structural obstacles as well as external obstacles that curb export growth.

Because of the foreign content of capital formation, a developing country will require a certain level of imports ($\bar{M}$) to sustain a desired level of investment ($\bar{I}$). In the absence of external borrowing, a country can only obtain $\bar{M}$ through exports (X). If, therefore, $\bar{M} > X$, there is a trade or foreign exchange gap that blocks the attainment of $\bar{I}$. The foreign exchange gap ($\bar{M} - X$) will place a ceiling on actual

---

[11]The derivation of this identity is the same as the derivation of equation (7) in Chapter 15. For the distinction between GDP and GNP, see footnote 2 in Chapter 15.

investment. As was true of the savings gap, the foreign exchange gap may be closed by external assistance (b). When it is fully closed ($b = \overline{M} - X$), then the foreign exchange gap no longer constrains the desired level of investment and growth.

Figure 20-2 offers a schematic representation of the three investment constraints. It is reasonable to hypothesize that in the early stages of economic development the critical constraint is absorptive capacity. At E, however, the critical constraint becomes the availability of foreign exchange. In late stages of development, an economy exhibits diversified production and has the capacity to adjust its exports and imports to the desired gap between investment and domestic saving. In Figure 20-2, this capacity is realized at L; after L, domestic saving becomes (and remains) the critical constraint on the rate of investment.

Broadly speaking, two courses of action are open to the developing countries in the face of exchange gaps that will prevent the achievement of a target growth rate. The first course of action involves the use of policy instruments intended to reduce or eliminate the foreign exchange gap by expanding exports or contracting the level of required imports through import substitution. The second course of action is to obtain external financing of the foreign exchange gap from private and official sources.

Figure 20-2

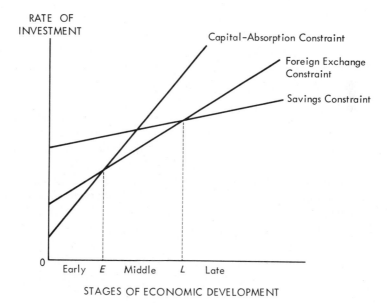

Capital-Absorption, Foreign Exchange, and Savings Constraints on the Rate of Investment.   In the early stages of development, the critical constraint on investment is capital absorption. At E, however, foreign exchange becomes the critical constraint. In the late stage of development at L, savings become the critical constraint.

We shall argue later that the most effective way of overcoming constraints on investment in the developing countries is through the operation of competitive markets in an open economy that encourages exports and creates an attractive investment climate for domestic and foreign firms.

TRADE POLICIES OF THE DEVELOPING COUNTRIES

After World War II, the developing countries generally relied on a mix of import-substitution trade policies and external financing. But in the 1980s, they shifted toward export-oriented policies as the availability of external financing diminished and import-substitution policies offered few, if any, opportunities to save foreign exchange.

This new direction of trade policies in the developing countries is the principal theme of this section.

International Trade and Economic Development

A foreign exchange or trade gap can constrain growth in a developing country, but can foreign trade also be an *autonomous* source of economic growth? The answer to this question is not a simple yes or no. Since international trade and economic growth are interdependent, trade may lead growth or growth may lead trade, depending on the circumstances.

In Chapter 3 we examined the effects of changes in factor endowments (which are associated mainly with economic growth) on international trade and showed that growth may be neutral, antitrade, or protrade.[12] We concluded that factor changes are a continuing phenomenon within countries, causing shifts in factor proportions and in comparative cost structures. We now reverse our analytical direction to look at the effects of changes in trade on economic growth and development.[13]

Conventional international trade theory (the Heckscher-Ohlin model) has ignored the growth effects of trade by assuming fixed supplies of homogeneous factors of production, the absence of technological innovation, and the sameness of production functions in different countries. By focusing on allocation effects, this theory demonstrates how international trade leads to a more efficient use of *existing* factor of production, thereby enabling countries to consume at a level beyond their production possibilities (transformation) curves. But it does not demonstrate whether or not international trade can shift the production possibilities curve outward as an independent agent of economic growth.

Although the H-O model is silent on the growth effects of trade, the classical and neoclassical stream of comparative advantage theory (to which the H-O model

---

[12]See Chapter 3.
[13]The effects of factor transfers (foreign investment and technology) on growth and development are treated in Chapter 24.

belongs) has argued that economic growth is stimulated by international specialization resulting from the free play of market forces. That is to say, free trade not only utilizes existing factors of production more efficiently but also contributes to the quantity and quality of those factors. Rising exports lead to higher production in export industries, which in turn encourages higher investment to expand productive facilities and achieve economies of scale. Growing export industries open up new opportunities for employment and create new labor skills. This growth impulse spreads to the rest of the economy in a variety of ways: Other sectors are stimulated to provide inputs (raw materials, supplies, and capital equipment) to the export sector; the general economy is stimulated as the income effects of the dynamic export sector raise effective demand; and externalities (transportation, power, communication, and financial facilities created to support export industries), as well as labor and management skills, benefit the rest of the economy. Growing exports also finance growing imports, which stimulate growth by bringing in new products and technology and by compelling local import-competing industries to become more productive.

The majority of economists believe that international trade can be an "engine of growth" in the classical and neoclassical sense. To support this position, they can appeal to history, for the evidence is strong that in the nineteenth century exports led growth in Great Britain and several other now-advanced countries and have also done so since World War II in Western Europe and Japan.

Export Performance of the Developing Countries

Figure 20-3 depicts the annual export growth of the developing countries by region in the 1980s. What is striking is the wide disparities in export growth across the regions. At one extreme, East Asia and the Pacific grew at an average annual rate of almost 10 percent while exports of the Middle East and North Africa *declined* at a rate of more than 1 percent. Also, exports of Sub-Saharan Africa hardly grew, and exports of Latin America grew at a rate well below the world rate.

Over the past quarter century, developing-country exports have shifted toward manufactures for all income groups, as shown in Table 20-4. In the low-income countries (excluding China and India), manufactures rose from 11 percent in 1965 to 29 percent in 1990. The big populations of China and India are still mainly in low-income agricultural pursuits, but these countries also have manufacturing sectors of a large *absolute* size. In 1990, their exports of manufactures were 73 percent of total exports. Except for their relatively high dependence on fuels, minerals, and metals, the export structure of the upper-middle-income group in 1990 was quite similar to that of the OECD countries. Several middle-income countries have become major exporters of machinery and transport equipment — not only manufactures of consumer goods, such as textiles. These structural changes in LDC exports reflect significant economic development since 1965. Developing countries can no longer be described as exporters of commodities and importers of manufactures.

Figure 20-3

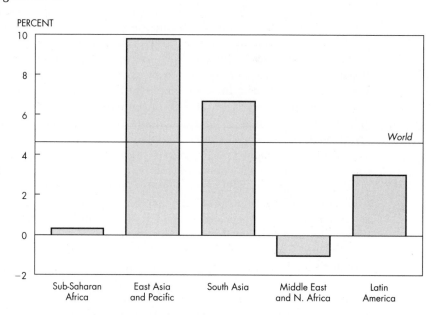

Source: The World Bank, *Global Economic Prospects and the Developing Countries* (Washington, D.C.: World Bank, 1992), p. 57.
Annual Growth of Developing Countries' Exports by Region, 1980–1990. The annual growth rates of developing-country regions were highly divergent in the 1980s.

Table 20-4   Structure of Merchandise Exports by Country Group, 1965 and 1990 (Percent)

Country Group	Fuels, Minerals, and Metals		Other Primary Products		Machinery and Transport Equipment		Other Manufactures	
	1965	1990	1965	1990	1965	1990	1965	1990
Low-income	17	27	52	20	3	9	28	45
China and India	13	10	29	17	6	15	52	58
Other low-income	21	48	69	24	1	1	10	28
Lower-middle income	30	32	52	30	7	11	9	27
Upper-middle income	44	32	26	13	14	20	18	37
High-income OECD	9	7	21	12	31	42	38	39

Source: The World Bank, *World Development Report 1992* (New York: Oxford University Press, 1992), Table 16, pp. 248–49.

The export performance of the developing countries would be better if the European Community, Japan, and the United States lowered their trade barriers. As shown in Table 20-5, a 50 percent reduction in those barriers would raise LDC exports to those countries by $50 billion. But over half of this export gain would be enjoyed by East Asia, which is the region of fastest export growth. In contrast, Sub-Saharan Africa would get only 4.4 percent of the export gain, and the Middle East and North Africa, 5.2 percent. This disparate response of the LDC regions indicates that export performance depends critically on *internal* market conditions that are greatly influenced by LCD policies, to which we now turn.

Comparative Analysis
of Outward- and Inward-Oriented Trade Strategies

Until recently, we have lacked empirical data on the relationship between trade strategies and economic performance. But now this deficiency has been corrected by economists at the World Bank.[14] The World Bank study classifies forty-one developing countries according to the orientation of their trade strategies in two periods, 1963–1973 and 1973–1985. (These countries accounted for two-thirds of

Table 20-5   Estimated Increase in Developing Countries' Exports Under a 50 Percent Reduction in Trade Barriers by the European Community, Japan, and the United States

Region	Amount (Billions of Dollars)	Share (Percent)
East Asia	27.1	54.2
Eastern Europe	3.8	7.6
Latin America and Caribbean	9.6	19.2
Middle East and North Africa	2.6	5.2
Other Europe	0.2	0.4
South Asia	4.5	9.0
Sub-Saharan Africa	2.2	4.4
All developing countries	*50.0*	*100.0*

Note: These projections are based on 50 percent cuts in applied tariffs and available estimates of NTB ad valorem equivalents.

Source: The World Bank, *Global Economic Prospects and the Developing Countries 1992* (Washington, D.C.: World Bank, 1992), Table 2-10, p. 23.

---

[14]See The World Bank, *World Development Report 1987* (New York: Oxford University Press, 1987), pp. 78–112.

the total output of all developing countries in 1985.) Trade strategies are classified into four categories:

1. A *strongly outward-oriented strategy* does not use trade controls or uses only low-level ones. Also, the exchange rate does not discriminate between importables and exportables. Hence, production for the domestic market is not favored over production for export, and conversely.

2. A *moderately outward-oriented strategy* is biased toward production for domestic rather than export markets. But the average rate of effective protection is low, and the effective exchange rate is only slightly higher (the domestic price of a unit of foreign currency is lower) for imports than for exports.

3. A *moderately inward-oriented strategy* has an overall incentive structure that distinctly favors production for the domestic market. Effective protection is relatively high, the use of import controls and licensing is extensive, and the exchange rate is clearly overvalued.

4. A *strongly inward-oriented strategy* greatly favors production for the domestic market. The rate of effective protection is high, direct control and licensing disincentives to the traditional export sector are pervasive, positive incentives to nontraditional exportables are few or nonexistent, and the exchange rate is significantly overvalued.

The World Bank study demonstrates that trade strategies have a marked influence on industrial performance, manufactured exports, capital-output ratios, and gross domestic product.

Table 20-6 shows the average annual percentage growth of real manufacturing value added for the forty-one developing countries grouped by trade orientation (strategy). The table also lists the countries belonging to each group in the two periods. In the first period (1963–1973), the average growth rate of the strongly outward-oriented countries was 15.6 percent compared with only 5.3 percent average growth rate for the strongly inward-oriented countries. In the second period (1973–1985), growth rates were 10.0 and 3.1 percent, respectively.

Figure 20-4 is hardly surprising. Between 1965 and 1973, manufactured exports of the strongly and moderately outward-oriented countries grew by 14.8 and 16.1 percent, respectively. This compares with 10.3 and 5.7 percent for the moderately and strongly inward-oriented countries, respectively. In the later period (1973–1985), growth rates were 14.2 and 14.5 percent compared with 8.5 and 3.7 percent.

Figure 20-5 indicates that the outward-oriented countries made more efficient use of their incremental capital resources than the inward-oriented countries. In both periods, the incremental capital-output ratio (the ratio of gross investment to the increase in GDP) was lower for the two outward-oriented groups than for the inward-oriented groups. In the first period, the ratio for the outward-oriented countries was 3.3 and for the inward-oriented countries, 5.2. Although the capital-

Table 20-6 Average Annual Percentage Growth of Real Manufacturing Value Added for Forty-One Developing Countries by Trade Orientation, 1963–1973 and 1973–1985

	1963–1973	1973–1985
Outward-oriented	10.3	5.2
Strongly outward-oriented[1]	15.6	10.0
Moderately outward-oriented[2]	9.4	4.0
Inward-oriented	6.8	4.3
Moderately inward-oriented[3]	9.6	5.1
Strongly inward-oriented[4]	5.3	3.1

Note: Although Yugoslavia is listed as a moderately inward-oriented country for both periods, the percentages in this table exclude it for lack of data.

[1]For 1963–1973 and 1973–1985: Hong Kong, South Korea, and Singapore.

[2]For 1963–1973: Brazil, Cameroon, Colombia, Costa Rica, Ivory Coast, Guatemala, Indonesia, Israel, Malaysia, and Thailand. For 1973–1985: Brazil, Chile, Israel, Malaysia, Thailand, Tunisia, Turkey, and Uruguay.

[3]For 1963–1973: Bolivia, El Salvador, Honduras, Kenya, Madagascar, Mexico, Nicaragua, Nigeria, Philippines, Senegal, Tunisia, and Yugoslavia. For 1973–1985: Cameroon, Colombia, Costa Rica, Ivory Coast, El Salvador, Guatemala, Honduras, Indonesia, Kenya, Mexico, Nicaragua, Pakistan, Philippines, Senegal, Sri Lanka, and Yugoslavia.

[4]For 1963–1973: Argentina, Bangladesh, Burundi, Chile, Dominican Republic, Ethiopia, Ghana, India, Pakistan, Peru, Sri Lanka, Sudan, Tanzania, Turkey, Uruguay, and Zambia. For 1973–1985: Argentina, Bangladesh, Bolivia, Burundi, Dominican Republic, Ethiopia, Ghana, India, Madagascar, Nigeria, Peru, Sudan, Tanzania, and Zambia.

Source: Based on The World Bank, *World Development Report 1987,* Table 5.1, p. 87.

Figure 20-4

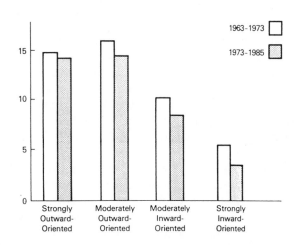

Source: Derived from the World Bank, *World Development Report 1987,* Figure 5.2, p. 84. **Average Annual Percentage Growth of Manufactured Exports of Forty-One Countries Grouped by Trade Orientation.** Manufactured exports of outward-oriented developing countries grew much more rapidly than those of inward-oriented developing countries in both the 1963–1973 and 1973–1985 periods.

Figure 20-5

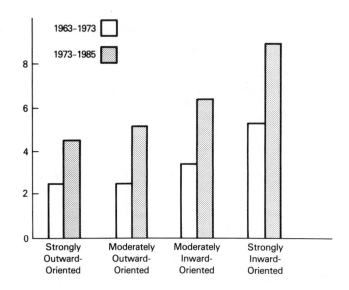

Source: Derived from The World Bank, *World Development Report 1987,* (New York: Oxford University Press, 1987), Figure 5.2, p. 84.

Average Annual Incremental Capital-Output Ratio of Forty-One Developing Countries Grouped by Trade Orientation. The outward-oriented countries made more efficient use of their incremental capital investment than the inward-oriented countries.

output ratio deteriorated for all groups in the 1973–1985 period, it remained significantly lower for the inward-oriented groups.

Figure 20-6 shows a decline in the growth of real gross domestic product for both outward-oriented and inward-oriented countries. In the 1963–1973 period, the annual average growth for the strongly outward-oriented group was 9.5 percent, more than twice the 4.1 percent achieved by the strongly inward-oriented group. This gap widened in the 1973–1985 period (7.7 percent and 2.5, respectively).

It is evident that over the past quarter century the economic performance of developing countries following outward-oriented trade strategies has been superior to that of developing countries following inward-oriented strategies. This advantage of outward-oriented strategies is owing to the greater effectiveness of open markets than of controlled markets in stimulating economic growth. The World Bank study demonstrates that open markets avoid the costs of protection, introduce international competition to domestic markets, and improve the efficiency of capital allocation.

Figure 20-6

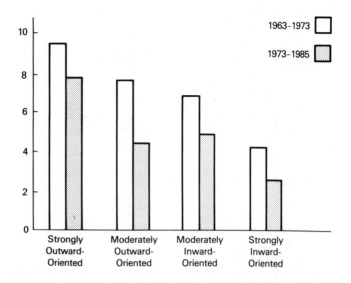

Source: Derived from the World Bank, *World Development Report 1987* (New York: Oxford University Press, 1987), Figure 5.2, p. 84.

Average Annual Percentage Growth of Real Gross Domestic Product of Forty-One Countries Grouped by Trade Orientation. Although the growth rate of real GDP declined from the 1963–1973 period to the 1973–1985 period, it was far higher for the strongly outward-oriented countries than for the strongly inward-oriented countries.

Regional Economic Integration

The great majority of the developing countries in Africa, Asia, and Latin America have small populations and national incomes. Consequently, their domestic markets are also small. Furthermore, autarkic economic development relying on import substitution is not possible: Small markets quickly limit growth, diversification, and economics of scale. In order to industrialize, therefore, small countries must find export outlets for their manufactures. It is not surprising, therefore, that developing countries seek to create institutional arrangements that will encourage mutual trade in manufactured goods. The most notable efforts in this regard are the regional schemes for economic integration that have been inspired by the outstanding success of the European Community. Table 20-7 identifies the principal integration efforts.

Figure 20-7 depicts the intraregional exports of selected regional trade arrangements of both industrial and developing countries. Two observations are in order. First, intraregional exports (measured as a percentage of a region's total

Table 20-7 Selected Regional Trade Arrangements of Developing Countries

Name	Objective/Instrument	Implementation Record	Members
Central American Common Market (CACM) Signed: 1960 Effective: June 1961 Revised: June 1991 Population: 25 million GDP: $25 billion	Customs union and joint industrial planning. Elimination of tariffs. QRs within region. Adoption of Common External Tariff (CET).	Initially on schedule; most restrictions lifted by early 1970s, but reintroduced 1980s. CET not effective in all members.	Costa Rica, El Salvador, Guatemala, Honduras, Nicaragua
Andean Pact (AP) Signed: 1969 Population: 88 million GDP: $140 billion	Customs union and joint industrial planning. CET by end–1980. Modified: 1988 Revived: 1989 Establish FTA by 1992, common market by 1993, phase out exceptions by 1995. Harmonize macroeconomic policies.	Postponed several times.	Bolivia, Colombia, Ecuador, Peru, Venezuela
Latin American Integration Association (LAFTA/LAIA) LAFTA signed: 1960 Effective: 1961 Replaced by LAIA: 1980 Population: 375 million GDP: $1,024 billion	Free trade association and industrial planning; common lists of products to be implemented by 1972. Facilitation of bilateral cooperation.	Partial implementation in 1960s. Common lists not liberalized on schedule.	Mexico and all (10) South American countries except Guyana, French Guiana, and Suriname

Table 20-7 Continued

Economic Community of West African States (ECOWAS) Founded: 1975 Population: 180 million GDP: $80 billion	Free trade area and customs union, development and policy harmonization. Original targets for liberalization and CET by 1990. New target to eliminate NTBs by 1995. Enhance labor and capital mobility.	Progress negligible.
		16 countries in West Africa
Association of South East Asian Nations (ASEAN) Founded: 1967 Population: 310 million GDP: $240 billion	Regional industrial cooperation; free trade area (trade policy subordinate to regional import substitution).	FTA repeatedly postponed; industrial cooperation scarcely implemented.
		Brunei, Indonesia, Malaysia, Philippines, Singapore, Thailand

Source: *Source:* Augusto de la Torre and Margaret R. Kelly, *Regional Trade Arrangements*, Occasional Paper 93 (Washington, D.C.: International Monetary Fund, March 1992), pp. 26–27.

Figure 20-7

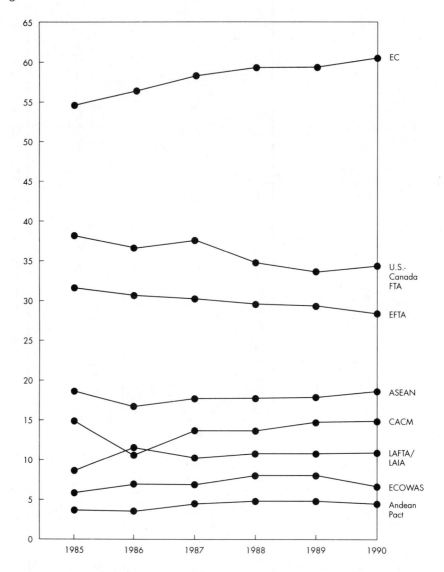

Source: Based on data in Augusto de la Torre and Margaret R. Kelly, *Regional Trade Arrangements,* Occasional Paper 93 (Washington, D.C.: International Monetary Fund, March 1992), Table 5, p. 20 and Table 8, p. 30.

Selected Regional Trade Arrangements of Industrial and Developing Countries: Intraregional Exports (Percent of Region's Total Exports). Intraregional exports among members of LDC regional trade arrangements (expressed as a percentage of a region's total exports) have been low and show no signs of increasing. Hence, the trade creation effects of LDC integration schemes have been small.

exports) are less than 20 percent for all LDC integration schemes, much smaller than the corresponding percentages for OECD schemes. For the EC, intraregional trade was over 60 percent in 1990. Second, intraregional exports have remained at low levels during the period 1985–1990, with no discernible upward trends. In sum, regional trade arrangements among developing countries have created little trade among the members. The static allocation effects of economic integration, discussed in Chapter 10, have been modest indeed.

The immediate trade gains from economic integration among developing countries are small for several reasons. Their export sectors are oriented toward markets in North America, Europe, and Japan rather than toward neighboring countries. Also, a trading infrastructure in transportation, communications, finance, and marketing is notably lacking for intraregional trade. Finally, the factor endowments of developing countries belonging to a region tend to be similar, thus reducing the opportunities for short-term gains from trade.

The special case for economic integration among the developing countries, then, is that the creation of large regional markets will allow the establishments of regional firms that can benefit from the *dynamic* effects of integration (economies of scale, competition, enterprise size, product innovation, and new investment). But to obtain these effects, LDC integration schemes would need to match the EC common market in freedom to move capital and enterprise among the member countries. Dynamic effects are also contingent on a common policy toward foreign investors, something difficult to achieve when member countries compete for scarce investment capital. Another obstacle is an emphasis on *reciprocity* — the effort of each country not to give up more than it receives in return. But the gravest obstacle to economic integration among LDCs is economic nationalism, which favors national industries over regional industries and nationals over foreigners.

EXTERNAL FINANCING AND DEBT OF THE DEVELOPING COUNTRIES

The economic performance of the developing countries in the past three decades would not have been possible without a substantial flow of resources from the advanced industrial countries. By providing compensatory financing of savings and foreign exchange gaps, external assistance has enabled developing countries to increase their rates of capital formation and economic growth. This assistance has paid for imports of equipment and other capital goods for investment in infrastructure, industry, and agriculture. Furthermore, technical assistance has directly enhanced productivity in the developing countries by transferring technology and human skills.

It would be erroneous to view external assistance as the only, or most crucial, factor in the economic performance of the developing countries. Although the correlation between growth and import capacity is high (a finding consistent with the operation of foreign exchange constraints), the correlation between the amounts of external assistance received by a country and its rate of economic growth is low. The explanation is the presence of many other factors that influence economic growth, notably export behavior and LDC policies.

Net Flows of Capital to the Developing Countries

Table 20-8 reveals the net resource flows to developing countries in 1981, 1985, and 1989.

A few words are in order about the major categories of external finance. *Official development finance* involves the transfer of resources by the donor governments with the deliberate intent to promote economic development in the receiving countries. Only official development finance, including grants and concessional (low-interest) loans for development made either bilaterally or through international agencies, fully deserves the designation "foreign aid." *Export credits* are provided to importers by exporters, commercial banks, and government agencies. Although they offer resources to the developing countries, even official export credits are primarily intended to promote donor-country exports rather than economic development.

Table 20-8   Net Resource Flows to Developing Countries, 1981, 1985, and 1989

	Billions of Dollars			*Percent of Total*		
	1981	*1985*	*1989*	*1981*	*1985*	*1989*
Official development finance:	45.5	48.9	69.0	33.1	58.0	62.5
Bilateral	31.9	32.5	49.5	23.2	38.6	44.8
Multilateral[1]	13.6	16.4	19.5	9.9	19.4	17.7
Export credits[2]	17.6	4.0	1.2	12.8	4.7	1.1
Private flows:	74.3	31.4	40.2	54.1	37.2	36.4
Direct investment	17.2	6.6	22.0	12.5	7.8	19.9
Bank lending	52.3	15.2	8.0	38.1	18.0	7.2
Other[3]	4.8	9.6	10.2	3.5	11.4	9.3
Total	137.4	84.3	110.4	100.0	100.0	100.0

[1]Mainly from the United Nations, the European Community, the International Development Association, and regional development banks.

[2]Credits provided to importing countries by exporting firms, commercial banks, and official banks.

[3]Includes bond lending and nongovernmental grants.

Note: Percentage may not add to 100.0 because of rounding.

Source: Based on data in *IMF Survey,* February 18, 1991, p. 62.

By their very nature, *private flows* cannot be directly manipulated by the governments of the industrial countries, although they are commonly subject to regulations of one kind or another. Private flows are the net consequence of decisions by an untold number of entrepreneurs, investors, bankers, and traders. The dominant motivation behind these decisions is the prospect of economic gain (profit, interest, or capital appreciation) for the decision-makers or their organization. Nor do private flows involve grants or concessional loans. Properly speaking, therefore, private flows should not be considered "foreign aid," even though they may provide developing countries with resources that are not obtainable through official assistance, such as technology and industrial management. *Direct investment* occurs when business enterprises in the industrial countries acquire equity interests in affiliates in the developing countries.

Official development finance rose in the 1980s, but export credits and private flows fell from $91.9 billion in 1981 to $41.4 billion in 1989. Why this sudden collapse of export credits and private flows? The answer is the international debt crisis that began with Mexico's announcement of a de facto moratorium on its amortization payments to foreign commercial banks. As the crisis spread to other heavily indebted developing countries, new bank loans almost dried up as banks desperately tried to reduce their loan exposures to LDCs. As shown in Table 20-8, net bank lending dropped to $8 billion in 1989, less than one-sixth the net lending in 1981. Over all, net resource flows to the developing countries in current dollars were lower at the end of the decade ($110.4 billion) than at its start ($137.4 billion). In constant dollars, the deterioration was greater due to inflation in the 1980s. We shall have more to say about the international debt crisis after review of the role of international organizations and the United States in providing external assistance to developing countries.

How much official development assistance *should* the industrial countries provide to the developing countries? Economic analysis cannot answer this question, because it is essentially political in nature. However, the industrial countries have agreed to a target of 0.7 percent of their gross national products (at market prices). How close are they to this target? In 1990, only five of the OECD donor countries reached or exceeded the target: the Netherlands, France, and the three Scandinavian countries.

International Organizations Providing External Assistance

Although the bulk of official assistance to the developing countries has been supplied bilaterally by the industrial countries, substantial resources have also been channeled multilaterally through international organizations.

The most prominent international lending agencies make up the *World Bank Group,* which comprises the *International Bank for Reconstruction and Development* (IBRD or World Bank), the *International Development Association* (IDA), and the

International Finance Corporation (IFC).[15] Each of these agencies has its own resources, lending terms, and policies.

The World Bank finances development projects on long term (ranging up to thirty-five years), for which it charges a market rate of interest. All of its loans must be guaranteed by governments in the borrowing countries and must be repaid in hard, convertible currencies. The World Bank obtains its loan funds from member-country subscriptions to its capital stock by selling its own bonds in international capital markets and by selling off its loan portfolios to private investors. Most World Bank loans are used to finance infrastructure investment in transportation, electric power, agriculture, water supply, and education.

The inability of many developing countries to qualify for World Bank loans and the high interest costs of such loans led to the formation of the IDA. The IDA extends credits to developing countries for up to fifty years. These credits are repayable in easy stages after a ten-year grace period and with no interest except a modest service charge. The IDA is frequently described as a "soft loan" agency while the World Bank is a "hard loan" agency. Unlike the World Bank, IDA does not have its own capital; it is dependent on a continuing replenishment of its funds by the member countries.

The IFC does not make loans to governments, as do the other agencies. Instead, it participates in industrial projects in conjunction with private investors, as either a lender or an investor in equity. The IFC has been able to function as a catalyst by bringing together private investors of the industrial and developing countries. The IFC obtains its investment funds from member country subscriptions to its capital stock, from its right to borrow from the World Bank up to four times its own unimpaired capital and surplus, and from the sale of its own investment portfolio to private investors (thereby "recycling" its investment funds).

The *United Nations Development Program* (UNDP) is the principal international agency in the field of technical assistance and preinvestment aid. It is intended to identify, investigate, and present to financial agencies those projects in developing countries that merit investment. Most of the UNDP assistance is actually carried out by specialized agencies and other bodies of the United Nations.

Several *development banks* have been established to provide multilateral assistance to developing countries in different regions of the world. The *Inter-American Development Bank* was started in 1960 by the United States and all the Latin American countries except Cuba. The bank has three categories of funds: ordinary capital used for loans at market rates ("hard-loan window"); special funds for loans on easy terms ("soft-currency window"); and a Social Program Trust Fund to finance low-income housing, education, and other social projects. The *African Development Bank* started operations in 1964 with a membership limited to independent African countries and an authorized capital of $250 million. The *Asian Development Bank* was established in 1966 with an authorized capital of $1.1 billion

---

[15]The IBRD came into being as a sister organization of the International Monetary Fund and began operations in 1946. The IFC was set up in 1956 and the IDA in 1961; both are affiliates of the IBRD.

by nineteen Asian countries, eleven European countries, Canada, and the United States. The European Community provides assistance to developing countries through the European Development Fund and the *European Investment Bank.*

U.S. Foreign Aid Policy

Foreign aid has been an element in American foreign economic policy since World War II. During the early postwar years, U.S. government assistance was directed mainly toward the rehabilitation and recovery of Western Europe—the Marshall Plan era. At the start of the 1950s, U.S. foreign aid became oriented toward rearmament of the free world, emphasizing military and defense support assistance. It was not until 1957 that U.S. foreign assistance turned toward the developing countries. In that year Congress approved the creation of the Development Loan Fund to finance projects in the developing countries. Formal recognition of this turn in U.S. foreign aid occurred in 1961, when a new agency—the Agency for International Development (AID)—was set up to administer economic and technical assistance programs. Today, U.S. bilateral development assistance relates mainly to food and nutrition, population and health, and education and human resources development.

In the conviction that the most dynamic economic progress in LDCs has been achieved by the "magic of the marketplace," the Reagan administration in 1981 launched a new foreign aid strategy that would strengthen the role of private enterprise in economic development. The principles underlying this strategy are as follows: (1) A growing U.S. economy can do more for LDCs than U.S. foreign aid; (2) the LDCs must put their own economies on a sound footing; (3) U.S. development assistance should continue to concentrate on the least-developed of the LDCs; (4) LDCs can best promote their development by attracting foreign investment, offering incentives to their farmers, and supporting the free flow of trade and capital; (5) more emphasis should be placed on U.S. bilateral aid and less on U.S. multilateral aid channeled through the World Bank and other international agencies; and (6) U.S. security aid to friendly LDCs threatened by hostile forces should take precedence over development aid.

The most ambitious effort to carry out the new U.S. aid strategy is the Caribbean Basin Initiative. Covering some twenty-five small LDCs in Central America, the Caribbean, and northern South America, the centerpiece of the initiative is the removal of U.S. import duties on the products of these countries for a period of twelve years, except for textiles and apparel and a limit on duty-free imports of sugar. Another feature is the extension of the 10 percent domestic investment tax credit to any new investments made by U.S. companies in the Caribbean Basin. A third feature is additional aid to Basin countries.

The new U.S. aid strategy is disappointing to the majority of LDCs that perceives the emphasis on the private sector as simply a way to reduce U.S. development assistance. This suspicion is fed by the secular decline in U.S. foreign assistance from 0.53 percent of U.S. GNP in 1960 to the current 0.21 percent. Although U.S. official development assistance was about one-fifth of total OECD official assistance in 1990, it ranked last among the OECD countries as a percentage of GNP.[16]

The International Debt Crisis

The transfer of financial assistance from the industrial to the developing countries has gone through three phases since World War II. From 1945 to the late 1960s, the main forms of capital were official assistance, direct foreign investment, and trade finance. The current-account deficits of LDCs were mainly financed through international agencies and bilateral government arrangements.

In the second phase, the late 1960s to 1982, the world economy experienced two oil shocks, highly volatile exchange and interest rates, and wide swings in current-account balances. In this new environment, international banks shifted from trade finance to balance of payments finance. Bank loans to the developing countries accelerated, and direct investment flows became less important. During this phase, official flows kept pace with private flows.

The third phase began in August 1982, when Mexico, suffering from a sharp drop in its oil export revenues, announced a de facto moratorium on its amortization payments to foreign commercial banks. This action triggered a loss of confidence in the creditworthiness of LDCs in general. Banks immediately withdrew short-term credit lines and greatly restricted new medium- and long-term lending (see "Bank lending" in Table 20-8). At the same time, budgetary pressures in several industrial countries constrained official development assistance. Also, OPEC's current-account surplus fell along with oil prices, thereby depriving the banks of new loanable funds.[17] The third phase, then, witnessed a massive drop in external financing in response to an international debt crisis. But the origins of this crisis can be traced to the extraordinary rise in the external obligations of the developing countries in the second phase — a time of world inflation and negative real exchange rates. Because most private loans to the LDCs were in dollars with floating interest rates, both the risks of an appreciating dollar and higher interest rates were transferred to the borrowers.

The astounding rise in LDC external debt is suggested by Table 20-9. The external debt of the ten largest debtor countries rose more than twenty-two times between 1970 and 1990 (from $24.4 billion to $550.4 billion), and most of this expansion took place in the 1970s. The ten countries listed in Table 20-9 were responsible for about half of all LDC external debt. External debt was incurred mainly by middle-income countries that (unlike low-income countries) were

---

[16]The World Bank, *World Development Report 1992* (New York: Oxford University Press, 1992), Table 19, p. 254.

[17]OPEC is the Organization of Petroleum Exporting Countries, comprising Saudi Arabia, Kuwait, Iran, Iraq, Libya, United Arab Emirates, Nigeria, Venezuela, Indonesia, Algeria, Qatar, and Gabon. In 1973–1974, OPEC used its monopoly power to quadruple the price of oil, causing an energy crisis. In 1979–1980, a second oil crisis, precipitated by the Iranian revolution, doubled oil prices. In the 1970s the huge current-account surpluses of the OPEC countries were deposited in large commercial banks in the United States and other industrial countries, which then loaned them out to LDCs.

Table 20-9 Total External Debt in 1970 and 1990 and Debt/GNP and Debt/ Service Ratios in 1990 of the Ten Largest LDC Debtors

Country	Total Debt (Billions of Dollars)		Total Debt/ GNP (Percent)	Debt Service Ratio (Percent)
	1970	1990		
Brazil*	5.1	116.2	25.1	20.9
Mexico*	6.0	96.8	42.1	27.8
Argentina*	5.2	61.1	61.7	34.1
Indonesia	2.9	67.9	66.4	30.9
Venezuela*	1.0	33.3	71.0	20.7
Turkey	1.9	49.1	46.1	28.2
Egypt	1.7	39.9	126.5	25.7
Nigeria	0.6	36.1	110.9	20.3
Philippines*	1.5	30.5	69.3	21.2
Malaysia	0.4	19.5	48.0	11.7
Total	26.3	550.4		

Note: The debt service ratio is payments on the debt (interest and amortization) as a percentage of the debtor country's exports of goods and services.

*Classified by the World Bank as "severely indebted" countries in 1989.

Source: Based on data in The World Bank, *World Development Report 1988* (New York: Oxford University Press, 1988), Table 181, pp. 256–57; and The World Bank, *World Development Report 1992* (New York: Oxford University Press, 1992), Table 21, pp. 258–59 and Table 24, pp. 264–65.

judged creditworthy by international lenders. At the start of the international debt crisis in the early 1980s, the three biggest debtor countries in Latin America were Brazil, Mexico, and Argentina.

The key analytical issue is the capacity of LDC countries to make foreign exchange payments to service their external debts. The most commonly used measure of this capacity is the *debt service ratio*: scheduled interest and principal payments as a percentage of exports of goods and services. Except for Malaysia, the debt service ratios of the ten largest LDC debtors were above 20 percent in 1990. These ratios are extraordinarily high compared to historical ratios, which were around 10 percent. The five countries with asterisks (four Latin American countries plus the Philippines) are classified by the World Bank as "severely indebted" countries. The criteria used by the World Bank appear in the note to Figure 20-8.

By the 1990s, the international debt *crisis* had become the international debt *problem*. During the 1980s, the concerted actions of debtor countries, commercial banks, creditor countries, and international agencies (notably the International Monetary Fund and the World Bank) provided new capital to enable debtor countries to overcome immediate cash-flow problems and to give them time to initiate structural economic reforms, such as trade liberalization, disinflation, tax reform, and deregulation. These actions also allowed time for commercial banks to raise new capital and increase reserves against their LDC loans.

At the start of the international debt crisis, the problem was viewed as mainly a lack of liquidity. Remedial action, therefore, focused on debt rescheduling by

Figure 20-8

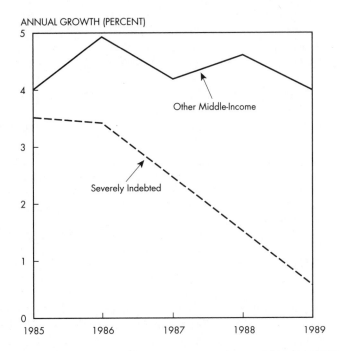

Note: Severely indebted middle-income countries are those in which 1987 GNP per capita was more than $480 and less than $6,000, and in which three of the four key debt ratios are above critical levels. These ratios and their critical levels are debt to GNP (50 percent), debt to exports of goods and all services (275 percent), accrued debt service to exports (30 percent), and accrued interest to exports (20 percent). Other middle-income countries are those in which 1987 GNP per capita was more than $480 and less than $6,000, and in which less than three of the four key debt ratios are above the critical levels described above. This figure covers 19 severely indebted countries and 46 other middle-income countries.

Source: Adapted from Stanley Fischer and Ishrat Husain, "Managing the Debt Crisis in the 1990s," *Finance and Development,* June 1990, p. 25.

GDP Growth and Indebtedness in Middle-Income Countries, 1985–1989. Severely indebted countries experienced a drastic decline in their annual GNP growth rate while other middle-income countries maintained their annual GNP growth rate.

private and official lenders. But toward the end of the 1980s, it was recognized that at least some countries faced insolvency — the inability to service external debt over the long term. Attention then turned to debt reduction. The most common debt reduction techniques are *debt buyback* (the debtor country buys the debt from a bank at a discount), *debt-for-debt swap* (a bank exchanges its loan for bonds issued by the debtor country at a discount or lower interest rate), and *debt-for-equity swap* (a bank exchanges its loan at a discount for local currency, which then finances an equity investment in the debtor country).

By the start of the 1990s, the concerted actions of the previous decade began to pay off for countries that had carried out economic reforms. These countries (Mexico is a notable example) experienced higher rates of growth and once again received capital from foreign investors. Inflows of new capital into Latin America, which were about $8 billion a year in the late 1980s, climbed to a rate of over $40 billion a year in 1992.[18] But the cost of the international debt crisis to the severely indebted countries was staggering, as demonstrated in Figure 20-8. After 1985, the annual GDP growth rate of those countries fell from 3.5 percent to less than 1 percent in 1989. In contrast, the growth rate of the other middle-income countries was the same 4.0 percent in 1989 as in 1985. In effect, the severely indebted countries lost a decade of development.

Although it is no longer a threat to the international financial system, LDC external debt has created a huge "debt overhang" (the contractual value of LDC external liabilities exceeds expected debt-servicing capacity) that persists as an obstacle to economic growth. Some Latin American countries and several countries in Africa have not yet addressed debt problems with structural reforms.[19] Given the strong demand for capital in the world economy, only countries that develop competitive economies will have access to international capital markets as creditworthy borrowers. To build competitive economies, we advocate a "market-friendly" approach to development, a subject to which we now turn.

TOWARD A MARKET-FRIENDLY APPROACH TO ECONOMIC DEVELOPMENT[20]

In the 1980s, a consensus began to form among development theorists and officials in favor of a "market-friendly" approach to economic development. This approach postulates that LDC governments should pursue development strategies that rely on market forces. Hence, government interventions — such as infant-industry protection and subsidies — should be constrained by domestic and international competition, avoid distorting prices, and be openly subject to rules rather than official discretion. But the market-friendly approach is not a policy of *laissez-faire*

---

[18] "Falling in Love Again," *The Economist,* August 22, 1992, p. 63.

[19] As the next chapter relates, countries in Central and Eastern Europe are also burdened by external debt.

[20] This section draws heavily on The World Bank, *World Development Report 1991* (New York: Oxford University Press, 1991), pp. 6–9.

that relies *wholly* on markets. To function properly, markets require a legal and regulatory framework that can be provided only by governments. Also, markets may fail to stimulate sufficient investment in infrastructure, such as education. It follows that both markets and government have indispensable roles in development. The key to development is proper interactions between the two.

Figure 20-9

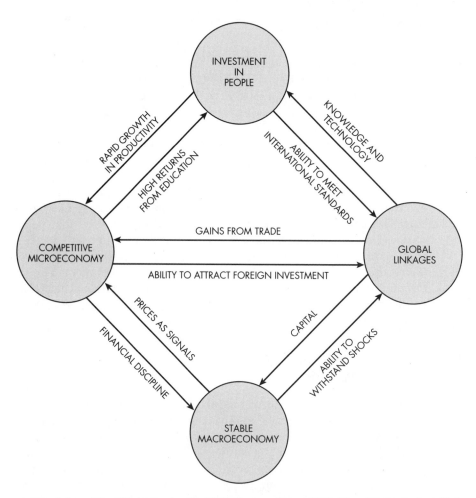

Source: Adapted from The World Bank, *World Development Report 1991* (New York: Oxford University Press, 1991), Figure 4, p. 6.

Interactions in a Market-Friendly Strategy for Development.   A market-friendly development strategy involves interactions among four elements that together determine the relationship between markets and governments. The fundamental thrust of this strategy is a reliance on market forces.

The World Bank perceives the relationship between markets and governments as comprising interactions among four elements: investment in people, competitive microeconomy, stable macroeconomy, and global linkages. The interactions among these elements are depicted in Figure 20-9.

Generally, markets in developing countries cannot be depended on to provide people with satisfactory education, nutrition, health care, and family planning services. Good education can bring about a rapid growth in productivity to help make the domestic economy more productive. Also, good education is needed if a country's people are to meet international standards of economic performance.

A competitive microeconomy is vital to development. Domestic (as well as international) competition spurs innovation, the diffusion of technology, and efficient resource use. In contrast, technological change and productivity gains are held back by government interventions that protect domestic industries, regulate prices, impose state ownership on certain industries, and otherwise weaken competitive forces. Following a market-friendly development strategy, governments create a regulatory framework (including legal and property rights) that stimulates competition and invest in infrastructure that supports private enterprise. A competitive domestic microeconomy provides high returns to an educated workforce and contributes the financial discipline of the marketplace to help maintain a stable macroeconomy.

A key contribution of government to development is a stable macroeconomic foundation for the microeconomic enterprise of firms. Large budgetary deficits and rapid monetary expansion cause inflation, currency overvaluation, a loss of international competitiveness, and demands for import protection. In contrast, a stable macroeconomy makes the microeconomy more competitive by providing prices undistorted by inflation that signal an efficient allocation of resources. It also has a greater capacity to withstand external shocks coming from the global economy.

Openness to international flows of trade, investment, and technology strengthen competitive forces in the domestic microeconomy and offer gains from trade. To survive and prosper, local firms must innovate in both products and production processes and cut costs through higher efficiency. Openness also encourages firms to export to international markets. In sum, global linkages transfer knowledge and technology to raise a country's productivity and capital and buttress its investment in economic development.

It now appears that a market-friendly approach to economic development will dominate development strategies in the 1990s. In many LDCs, international trade is becoming more open while deregulation and the privatization of state enterprises are making their economies more competitive. It is also probable that a market-friendly approach to development will be integrated with an "environment-friendly" approach. Increasingly, economic development is interpreted as "sustainable development" that meets the needs of the present generation without compromising the ability of future generations to meet their own needs.

SUMMARY

1. The drive for economic development shapes the attitudes, policies, and expectations of the developing countries in international trade, external assistance, and international investment.

2. The term *developing countries* generally denotes the countries of Africa (except South Africa), the Middle East, Asia (except Japan), and Latin America.

3. The developing countries (LDCs) can be adequately described only in terms of three subgroups: (1) high-income oil exporters, (2) upper-middle-income economies, and (3) lower-middle-income and low-income economies. The LDCs are also highly diverse in regional economic performance.

4. The inequality of income among countries is enormous. At one extreme, 57.9 percent of the world's population receives only 4.8 percent of the world's income; at the other extreme, 15.4 percent of the world's population receives 72.2 percent of the world's income.

5. The developing countries must overcome many obstacles to achieve a satisfactory rate of economic growth, especially in per capita terms. The situation of the developing countries has been aptly described as interlocking sets of vicious circles that perpetuate economic stagnation and poverty. Major obstacles to economic development include lack of social overhead capital, lack of business managers and administrators, cultural blocks, and the population explosion.

6. The performance of the developing countries over the past three decades compares favorably with the average annual historical growth rate of 2 percent experienced by the industrial countries over the last century.

7. Capital formation is a necessary but not a sufficient condition for economic development. To increase its stock of capital, a country must invest part of its national product. The relationship between new investment and a subsequent increase in real output may be expressed as the *incremental capital-output ratio,* or k. Hence, the growth rate of gross domestic product is r/k, where r is the annual rate of new investment. The per capital growth rate, therefore, is $w = (r/k) - p$, where p is the annual rate of population growth.

8. The rate of domestic investment in a developing country may be constrained by the capacity of the country to absorb additional capital, by the level of its domestic savings, or by the availability of foreign exchange. In the absence of capital-absorption and savings gaps, the growth rate of a developing country may be limited by a *foreign exchange gap*. The most effective way to overcome constraints on investment is through the operation of competitive markets in an open economy.

9. The annual export growth rates of the developing countries showed wide disparities across regions in the 1980s. Over the past quarter century, LDC exports have shifted toward manufactures for all country income groups. LDC

export performance would be better if the European Community, Japan, and the United States lowered their trade barriers.

10. Empirical data demonstrate that the economic performance of developing countries following outward-oriented trade strategies has been superior to that of developing countries following inward-oriented strategies.

11. Developing countries participate in several schemes of regional economic integration. But *intraregional* trade in all these schemes is less than 20 percent of total regional exports. Hence, trade creation effects of these schemes have been modest. Dynamic effects have also been small because the schemes fail to match the EC common market in freedom to move capital and enterprise among the member countries.

12. The impressive economic performance of the developing countries in the past three decades would not have been possible without a substantial flow of resources from the advanced industrial countries. But in the 1980s, the net flow of financial resources from the industrial countries to LDCs fell sharply in real terms, mainly in response to the international debt crisis.

13. Many international agencies provide assistance to the developing countries, including the World Bank Group, the United Nations Development Program, and regional development banks.

14. U.S. official development assistance has become a smaller and smaller percentage of total OECD assistance and of the U.S. GNP. The latest U.S. foreign aid strategy attempts to strengthen the role of private enterprise in economic development.

15. The international debt crisis of the 1980s has become the international debt problem of the 1990s. The cost of the crisis to the severely indebted countries was staggering: They lost a decade of development.

16. In the 1980s, a consensus began to form among development theorists and officials in favor of a "market-friendly" approach to economic development.

QUESTIONS AND APPLICATIONS

1. "The situation of developing countries has been aptly described as interlocking sets of vicious circles." What is meant by this statement?

2. Why do many development experts consider the population explosion as the single greatest obstacle to economic development? Do you agree with them? Why or why not?

3. Suppose a country is investing 20 percent of its gross domestic product on an annual basis and its incremental capital-output ratio is 4. What, then, is the annual rate of growth of its gross domestic product? Suppose further that the annual growth rate of its population is 2.5 percent. What is the per capita annual growth rate of its gross domestic product?

4. Define the three constraints on the rate of domestic investment in a developing country. In the absence of a savings gap, how can a developing country have a foreign exchange gap?
5. (a) Define strongly and moderately outward-oriented trade strategies and moderately and strongly inward-oriented trade strategies.
   (b) Compare the economic performance of countries following outward- and inward-oriented trade strategies over the period 1963–1985.
6. (a) Identify three LDC regional integration schemes.
   (b) Why have these schemes delivered only modest static and dynamic economic effects?
7. (a) Identify the major categories of net resource flows from the industrial countries to the LDCs.
   (b) Why did net resource flows from the industrial countries to the LDCs decline in the 1980s?
8. (a) How can external debt become a "burden" to a developing country?
   (b) What economic factors would you investigate to estimate the debt service capacity of a given developing country?
9. "The international debt crisis of the 1980s has become the international debt problem of the 1990s." Discuss.
10. "A competitive microeconomy is vital to economic development." Do you agree with this statement? Why or why not?

SELECTED READINGS

Bauer, P. T. *Reality and Rhetoric: Studies in the Economics of Development.* Cambridge: Harvard University Press, 1984.

de la Torre, Augusto, and Margaret R. Kelly. *Regional Trade Arrangements,* Occasional Paper 93. Washington, D.C.: International Monetary Fund, March 1992, Chapter V.

Dornbusch, Rudiger. "The Case for Trade Liberalization in Developing Countries." *Journal of Economic Perspectives,* Winter 1992, pp. 69–85.

Dornbusch, Rudiger, and F. Leslie C.H. Helmers, eds. *The Open Economy.* New York: Oxford University Press, 1988.

Guitian, Manuel. "The International Debt Crisis: What Have We Learned?" *Rules and Discretion in International Economic Policy,* Occasional Paper 97. Washington, D.C.: International Monetary Fund, June 1992, Chapter III.

International Monetary Fund. *World Economic Outlook.* Washington, D.C.: International Monetary Fund. Annual.

International Monetary Fund and the World Bank. *Finance and Development.* Quarterly.

Kelley, Allen C. "Economic Consequences of Population Change in the Third World." *Journal of Economic Literature,* December 1988, pp. 1685–1728.

Organization for Economic Cooperation and Development. *Development Assistance.* Paris: Organization for Economic Cooperation and Development. Annual review.

Organization for Economic Cooperation and Development. *Integration of Developing Countries into the International Trading System.* Paris: OECD Publications, 1992.

Rodrik, Dani. "The Limits of Trade Policy Reform in Developing Countries," *Journal of Economic Perspectives,* Winter 1992, pp. 87–105.

Rosenberg, Nathan, and L. E. Birdzell, Jr. *How the West Grew Rich.* New York: Basic Books, 1986.

Stern, Nicholas. "The Economics of Development: A Survey," *The Economic Journal,* September 1989, pp. 597–685.

The World Bank. *Global Economic Prospects and the Developing Countries.* Washington, D.C.: World Bank, April 1992.

The World Bank. *Proceedings of the World Bank Annual Conference on Development Economics.* Washington, D.C.: The World Bank. Annual.

The World Bank. *World Bank Atlas.* Washington, D.C.: The World Bank. Annual.

The World Bank. *World Development Report.* New York: Oxford University Press. Annual.

World Commission on Environment and Development. *Our Common Future.* New York: Oxford University Press, 1987.

EASTERN EUROPE AND CHINA IN THE WORLD ECONOMY: THE TRANSITION FROM CENTRALLY PLANNED TO MARKET ECONOMIES

Over one-quarter of the world's peoples living in China and the countries of Eastern Europe are now engaged in a historical effort to transform their centrally planned economies into market economies that fully participate in the international economy.[1] For decades these countries followed autarkic policies dictated by central-government planning authorities who sought to limit linkages with market economies in the outside world.[2] The transition process launched by these countries will continue over several decades. We can only speculate on the outcome of this process for individual countries, but in one way or another it will affect the world economy profoundly in the years ahead.

This chapter reviews the failure of the centrally planned economies, what needs to be done to transform them into market economies, the reforms undertaken so far in Eastern Europe and China, and the role of the transition countries in the world economy. It is impossible to cover all transition countries in a single chapter; instead, we focus on Poland, the former Czechoslovakia, Hungary, Russia, and China. Even so, we can only highlight certain aspects of their reforms.

Table 21-1 offers some social indicators for the former Soviet Union, other Eastern European countries, China, and the OECD countries of the West. China has about three-fourths of the population of the transition countries, and the former Soviet Union has about one-fifth.[3] The per capita income of the Eastern European countries places them in the upper end of the middle-income economies

---

[1]We define Eastern Europe to include Poland, the Czech and Slovak Republics, Hungary, Romania, Bulgaria, and the fifteen republics of the former Soviet Union. Any departures from this definition in the text, tables, or figures are indicated when they occur.

[2]China began its entry into the world economy in the late 1970s and the Eastern European countries in the early 1990s. Isolation from the world economy lasted about thirty years for China, seventy years for the former Soviet Union, and forty years for the other Eastern European countries.

[3]The former Soviet Union broke apart at the end of 1991 into fifteen independent republics, known as the Commonwealth of Independent States (CIS). The largest republic, Russia, has 51 percent of the CIS population (150 million), and Ukraine has 18 percent.

Table 21-1   Social Indicators for the Former Soviet Union, Eastern European Countries, China, and OECD Countries in 1989

Indicator	Former Soviet Union	Other Eastern European Countries[1]	China	OECD Countries
Population (millions)	288	113	1,114	832
Per capita GNP (U.S. dollars)	1,780	2,465	350	17,606
Life expectancy (1987)				
Male	64	67	69	72
Female	73	74	71	78
Infant mortality (deaths per 1,000 live births)	25	18	30	8

Note: The per capita GNP figures are converted to U.S. dollars at official exchange rates. Since these rates are not market-determined, GNP comparisons derived from them must be regarded as subject to wide margins of error.

[1]Data are for Bulgaria, Czechoslovakia, Hungary, East Germany, Poland, and Romania, except for life expectancy and infant mortality figures, which exclude Hungary.

Source: International Monetary Fund and others, *The Economy of the USSR* (Washington, D.C.: The World Bank, 1990), p. 51; and the World Bank, *World Development Report 1991* (New York: Oxford University Press, 1991) pp. 204, 258, and 266.

as classified by the World Bank. This income level is far below the OECD level. China's per capita income level is below the Eastern European level.[4] The life-expectancy and infant-mortality figures are comparable across the transition countries, but their infant-mortality rates are high compared to those of the OECD countries.

THE FAILURE OF THE CENTRALLY PLANNED ECONOMIES

Every economy must find answers to several fundamental questions: What should it produce? How much should it produce? How should it produce? Where should it produce? When should it produce? For whom should it produce? Centrally planned economies answer these questions through plans laid down by officials in the central government that are carried out by state-owned enterprises.[5] Two key features of socialist economies, therefore, are *state ownership* of the material means

[4]Some experts believe that China's per capita income is on the order of $1,000, because the conversion of China's income into U.S. dollars at the official exchange rate badly underestimates the internal purchasing power of China's currency (the yuan).

[5]Centrally planned economies are also called "communist economies," "socialist economies," and "command economies." These terms are used interchangeably in this chapter.

of production and *central planning* by the political authorities. In contrast, market economies answer these questions through the individual choices of private producers, investors, and consumers who seek to maximize profits and satisfactions in responding to prices determined by the impersonal forces of supply and demand in product and factor markets.

The former Soviet Union is the classic example of a centrally planned economy.[6] Central planning was adopted in the late 1920s, and it remained in place until the early 1990s. The Soviet government nationalized all enterprises and collectivized agriculture, outlawing private ownership of the means of production. The State Planning Commission (Gosplan), assisted by other government agencies, allocated resources to production, investment, and consumption. Prices played little role in this allocation, remaining fixed over long periods of time. State-owned foreign trade organizations (FTOs) conducted all foreign trade. Exports were viewed as a means of obtaining foreign exchange to buy certain imported goods needed to meet targets of the national plan. Domestic prices were insulated from world prices through a system of taxes and subsidies. The foreign exchange rate became merely an accounting device. The financial system was also subordinate to the plan, providing state-owned enterprises with the credits needed to achieve physical plan targets. Hence, interest rates did not influence the allocation of resources.

The Soviet economy generated rapid growth in the 1930s and early post-World War II period, but it experienced a drastic slowdown starting in the late 1960s. Figure 21-1 depicts the decline in the rate of growth of industrial production over the period 1960–1990.

What were the immediate cause or causes of this decline? Why did the decline accelerate after the mid-1970s? Table 21-2 offers an answer. Over the period 1960–1975, the growth of industrial output was sustained by substantial increases in labor and capital inputs and an improvement in labor productivity. But observe that growth was constrained by falling capital productivity. In the following period, 1975–1990, the growth rate of labor and capital inputs dropped sharply, the labor productivity growth rate was less than half of that in the preceding period, and capital productivity continued to fall at a somewhat higher percentage rate than earlier.[7] The deterioration in capital productivity indicated a progressively less efficient use of capital (investment) in industrial production. More generally, *total factor productivity* (labor plus capital) grew at only a 0.3 percent annual rate over the 1960–1990 period, a rate far below rates of the OECD countries.[8] What happened to industrial productivity also happened to productivity in other sectors of the Soviet economy.[9]

---

[6]This and the following paragraph draw heavily on International Monetary Fund and others, *The Economy of the USSR* (Washington, D.C.: The World Bank, 1990), pp. 2–3.

[7]The decline in capital productivity may be designated as a *rise* in the incremental capital-output ratio. See Chapter 20, the section on capital formation, for a discussion of this ratio.

[8]John S. Pitzer and Andrew P. Baukol, "Recent GNP and Productivity Trends," *Soviet Economy,* 1991, 7, I, p. 69.

[9]Ibid., p. 64.

Figure 21-1

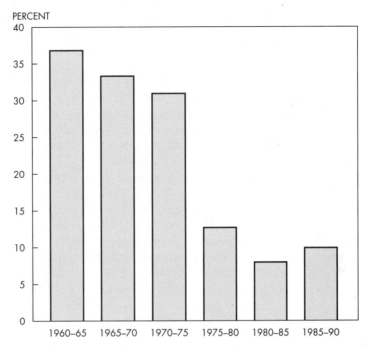

Source: Derived from John S. Pitzer and Andrew P. Baukol, "Recent GNP and Productivity Trends," *Soviet Economy,* 1991, 7, I, Table 5, p. 54.

Five-Year Percentage Growth Rates of Industrial Production in the Former Soviet Union, 1960-1990. During the 1965-1970 period the growth of industrial production in the former Soviet Union began a decline that has continued up to the present.

Table 21-2 Industrial Production in the Former Soviet Union: Growth Rates in Output, Labor and Capital Inputs, and Labor and Capital Productivity, 1960-1990 (Percent)

Period Growth Rates	1960–1975	1975–1990
Industrial production	140.4	34.2
Labor input	44.4	7.2
Capital input	256.1	109.8
Labor productivity	66.5	25.1
Capital productivity	− 33.5	− 36.1
Total factor productivity	21.4	− 1.3

Source: Derived from John S. Pitzer and Andrew P. Baukol, "Recent GNP and Productivity Trends," *Soviet Economy,* 1991, 7, I, Table 5, p. 54.

Summing up, the growth rates of production in the Soviet Union steadily declined because the high growth rates of labor and capital inputs of the early period could not be sustained and the low growth rate of total factor productivity was not enough to offset that decline in inputs. In particular, the deterioration of capital productivity reflected an extraordinary misallocation of investment by the central planners.

This experience of the Soviet Union was duplicated in the other command economies of Eastern Europe (over the same time) and of China (up to the early 1980s). There was no example of a successful centrally planned economy anywhere, and efforts to improve the performance of command economies were counterproductive: Production fell as weaker central controls were not replaced by markets. It became increasingly evident that centrally planned economies were *systemically* inferior to market economies in the creation of wealth and higher living standards.

The failure of the command economies precipitated a breakup of the Soviet Union at the end of 1991 and the collapse of communist regimes in the other Eastern European countries a few years earlier. These regimes were replaced by democratic governments committed to building market economies. Events took a somewhat different turn in China. There the communist regime remained in power, but it started a process of "marketization" of the economy in the late 1970s, more than a decade before reform began in Eastern Europe.

TRANSITION FROM A PLANNED TO A MARKET ECONOMY: WHAT NEEDS TO BE DONE?

There is a consensus among economists about the reform measures needed to transform a centrally planned economy into a market economy. This consensus is based on both economic theory and the experience of market economies in industrial and developing countries. The agreed-upon reform package includes (1) stabilization of the macroeconomy; (2) the establishment of competitive markets through price and wage liberalization, current-account convertibility, and the removal of international trade restrictions; (3) the privatization of state-owned enterprises; and (4) the creation through government of a legal framework (particularly regarding private ownership, property rights, and commercial law) and institutions (fiscal, financial, and others) vital to the functioning of a market economy.[10]

Although economists agree on the areas of reform, they disagree on the *sequence* of reforms. One issue reflects the second-best argument: Can one kind of reform be effective if distortions remain in a transitional economy?

---

[10]The reader may recognize that these reform proposals closely resemble the market-friendly strategy for development taken up in Chapter 20.

Another issue is whether political opposition will thwart reform measures that are scheduled for sometime in the future. A third issue is whether the building of institutions (legal, accounting, and financial systems) will take longer to accomplish than, say, price liberalization. A fourth issue is the degree to which a reform package must be tailored to fit each transitional economy.

One set of reform proposals starts with privatization before or together with stabilization of the macroeconomy and the establishment of competitive markets. Another set begins with macroeconomic stabilization and market-building reforms, leaving privatization of large state enterprises for a later time. Exponents of a radical "big bang" approach argue that partial reforms will not work because a market economy is an indivisible entity: Only a comprehensive reform package implemented all at once can be successful.[11] Other economists support a conservative, "gradualist" approach, arguing that a big bang approach would be too great a shock to economic systems and organizations that cannot change quickly.[12] Some economists propose a middle-of-the-road approach: a "minimum bang" that would begin, for instance, with the creation of a private sector of newly organized firms (in place of privatization of large state enterprises) and the maintenance or restoration of macroeconomic stability.

When we turn from reform proposals to actual reforms, we find that transition countries are using different approaches. China and Hungary are following a gradualist approach, Poland started with a big bang approach, and Russia appears to be abandoning a big bang approach for a gradualist approach in the face of strong political opposition.

Figure 21-2 outlines the phasing of reform advocated by the World Bank, which espouses a radical approach modified by an appreciation that some reforms will take longer than others. At the start, intensive action would focus on macroeconomic stabilization, price deregulation to provide clear price signals for economic decisions and for the valuation of enterprises, the removal of QRs, the privatization of small enterprises, and the revision of regulations to attract foreign investment. In the next phase, the focus would shift to the restructuring and privatization of large state enterprises while reforms continued in all the other areas.

Reform of the transitional economies calls for painful adjustments. Inflation, unemployment, and income inequality are likely to worsen before economic growth and higher productivity bring about an improvement in living standards. But the alternative to reform is far worse: a prolonging of stagnant economies with falling per capita incomes.

---

[11]For this view, see Daniel Gros and Alfred Steinherr, *Economic Reform in the Soviet Union: Pas de Deux Between Disintegration and Macroeconomic Destabilization,* Princeton Studies in International Finance no. 71 (Princeton, N.J.: Princeton University Press, November 1991), p. 67.

[12]See, for example, Ronald McKinnon, "Taxation, Money, and Credit in a Liberalizing Socialist Economy," in Christopher Clague and Gordon C. Rausser, eds., *The Emergence of Market Economies in Eastern Europe* (New York: Basil Blackwell, 1992), pp. 109–128.

Figure 21-2

Note: Dark shading indicates intensive action. QRs are quantitative restrictions.

Source: Adapted from the World Bank, *World Development Report 1991* (New York: Oxford University Press, 1991), p. 146.

The Phasing of Reform in the Transition from a Centrally Planned Economy to a Market Economy. The World Bank advocates a "big bang" reform package to launch the transition to a market economy, but it recognizes that some reforms will take longer than others.

ECONOMIC REFORM
IN EASTERN EUROPE AND CHINA

The process of reform now under way in Eastern Europe and China will go on for decades. It is much too early, therefore, to reach any judgment about its outcome. All we can do at this time is assess the *initiation* of reform in individual countries. Has reform in a transitional economy got off to a strong—or weak—start?

Reform in the Eastern European Countries

The Eastern European countries started their reforms in the early 1990s from different economic situations. To illustrate this observation, Figure 21-3 plots the situations of the former Soviet Union, Hungary, Poland, and Czechoslovakia with respect to their degrees of central planning and macroeconomic stability.[13]

Before reform, the former Soviet Union and the Czech/Slovak Republics were more centralized in their planning than Hungary and Poland. Hungary began significant reforms in the late 1960s, when it gave partial autonomy to state enterprises in choosing the product mix, entering foreign trade, and making investments. Poland never collectivized agriculture, leaving it in the hands of private farmers. As for macroeconomic stability (as measured by the rate of inflation, government budget deficits, and size of external debt), the former Czechoslovakia, at one extreme, maintained tight monetary and fiscal discipline while Poland, at the other extreme, showed little discipline. Macroeconomic stability of the other two countries lay between these extremes, with Hungary leaning toward stability and the former Soviet Union leading toward instability (inflation).

Figure 21-3

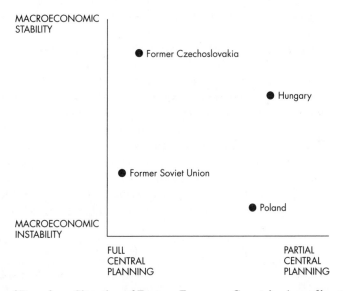

Mapping of Prereform Situation of Eastern European Countries According to Degree of Central Planning and Macroeconomic Stability. The countries of Eastern Europe started their reform programs in different economic situations, as illustrated by their different degrees of central planning and macroeconomic stability.

---

[13]Czechoslovakia split into the Czech Republic and the Slovak Republic in January 1993. Hereafter, we designate them as Czech/Slovak Republics or former Czechoslovakia.

These initial conditions influenced the approach to reform of the Eastern European countries. Macroeconomic disarray persuaded Poland and the former Soviet Union to start with a big bang. Hungary elected a gradualist approach, and the former Czechoslovakia focused its reform on microeconomic issues, such as price deregulation.

Table 21-3 summarizes the reforms started in 1990 by the former Czechoslovakia, Hungary, and Poland. These countries are now well launched on the path of reform: Prices and foreign trade are liberalized, and foreign exchange rates are closer to equilibrium values. However, much remains to be done. The former Czechoslovakia and Hungary need to make their currencies freely convertible, and all three countries have hardly begun the privatization of big state enterprises and the reform of their financial systems.[14] Nonetheless, these countries appear to have turned the corner on reform. By the end of 1992, from two-fifths to one-half of their GDPs were being produced by the private sector.[15] Although the optimism of the early 1990s has been tempered by production slumps, unemployment, and inflation, the governments and peoples of these countries remain committed to market economies. One study concludes that if Eastern Europe (excluding the former Soviet Union) were to accelerate its rate of reform and get more international financial support, it could begin to enjoy positive rates of growth as early as the mid-1990s.[16]

In contrast to this cautious optimism, the prospects for reform in Russia appear poor.[17] Russia began serious reform at the start of 1992 with two objectives: the stabilization of a chaotic, inflationary economy and its opening to private ownership and competition. It was a big bang approach: Price controls were lifted on most goods, companies were allowed to buy foreign exchange at floating rates, and privatization was started with retail shops. Yet one year later, production was dropping, inflation was rising, and the executive branch of government was in a bitter struggle for power with parliament. What went wrong?

By far the most critical failure was the inability of the government to stabilize the economy. The central bank (which is legally responsible to parliament, not the executive) issued trillions of rubles to keep state enterprises in production and thereby maintain employment. In 1992, prices rose more than 2,000 percent, the budget deficit climbed to 15 percent of GDP, the ruble fell sharply against the dollar, output fell at least 20 percent, and real wages fell by over 40 percent. At the

---

[14]In the central-planning system, the main function of the banks was to provide credits to state enterprises. Consequently, the banks are now stuck with enormous bad loans to those enterprises. Retail banking remains primitive by Western standards.

[15]See "Drowning in a Sea of IOUs," *Business Week,* September 28, 1992, pp. 11–13; and "Poland's Economic Reforms," *The Economist,* January 23, 1993, pp. 21–23.

[16]See "Study Advocates Increased Support for Eastern Europe," *IMF Survey,* July 29, 1991, p. 236. The study, titled *Financing Eastern Europe: A Study Group Report,* was published by the Group of Thirty in Washington, D.C.

[17]This and the next paragraph draw heavily on "Russia Reborn, A Survey of Russia," *The Economist,* December 5, 1992, pp. 3–25.

**Table 21-3 Economic Reforms Undertaken by the Former
Czechoslovakia, Hungary, and Poland Through Mid-1991**

Area of Reform	Former Czechoslovakia	Hungary	Poland
Price reform	Prices freed in sectors believed to be competitive.	Domestic pricing freed since 1988. More than 92% now free.	Most price restrictions ended Jan. 1990. 10% of prices now controlled.
Privatization	Started privatizing small businesses. Foreigners can bid only if citizens don't buy.	National Property Agency set up 130 of 3,000 salable firms privatized in 1990.	8,000 firms to be privatized. Eight sold so far. Foreign share limited to 10% without permission.
Foreign trade	As of Feb. 1991, exporters of goods in short supply must have licenses, as must importers of petroleum products and munitions.	90% of imports free from control.	No restrictions on imports. Export restrictions on 15 items accounting for 1% of total exports.
Convertibility	Liberalized in 1991, but local currency not necessarily convertible.	Net export earnings held until year-end in forint accounts with National Bank.	Resident convertibility for current transactions. Profit repatriation limited, use of net hard-currency earnings controlled.
Exchange rate policy	Crown fixed against US$, subject to periodic adjustment. In Dec. 1990, devalued 17% to 28 crowns/ US$1. One rate for all types of transactions.	Forint is fixed against a basket of currencies, subject to periodic adjustments.	In Jan. 1990, zloty devalued from Zl 6,000/US$1 to Zl 9,500/US$1, bringing official rate in line with street rate, legalized at same time. Exchange rate set against US$ for all kinds of transactions.

Source: Adapted from IMF Survey, July 29, 1991, p. 237.

start of 1993, therefore, the reform program was in a shambles as Russia faced the harrowing prospect of hyperinflation.[18] Russia can resume its transition to a market economy only if hyperinflation is avoided with the restoration of macro-economic stability. But that positive outcome is contingent on the establishment of a central government strong enough to make its reforms stick.

Reform in China

China started its transition toward a market economy in the late 1970s, when most prices were freed in the agricultural sector and communes were abolished to be replaced by family farms. Also, China adopted an "open door" policy by eliminating the central government's monopoly over foreign trade and setting up four "special economic zones" in which enterprises were given the right to keep foreign exchange earnings and to hire and fire workers.[19] In the 1980s, reforms were extended to other economic sectors.

China's reform process has been gradual, moving toward "marketization" of the economy through small, step-by-step changes. The government did not announce goals or a timetable. Indeed, some changes first occurred at lower levels (regions, cities, and firms) and were ratified later by the central government. Reform measures were experimental and pragmatic, with a heavy dose of trial-and-error thinking. In this way, reforms minimized economic disruption and political opposition.[20]

To the chagrin of "big bang" proponents, the Chinese reform process has been extraordinarily successful. Since 1978, China's GNP has grown at a real annual rate of 9 percent, doubling about every eight years. Its savings rate of 38 percent of GNP is among the highest in the world. Even the total factor productivity of *state* enterprises rose about 2.5 percent during the 1980s.[21] Exports soared to $85 billion in 1992, making China the eleventh biggest exporter in the world economy.[22] If China's output continues to grow at 9 percent a year, it should become the largest economy in the world by about 2010. Already, it is the fourth largest economy.[23]

The fastest growing economy in the world is Guangdong province, located next to Hong Kong. In 1991, it grew at a rate of 13.5 percent, and over the previous decade it averaged 12 percent a year.[24] Deng Xiaoping, the paramount

---

[18]See "Russia on Verge of Hyperinflation, Premier Says," *The New York Times,* January 31, 1993, p. 12. Hyperinflation begins when the monthly rate of inflation reaches 50 percent, an annual increase in prices of nearly 8,000 percent.

[19]Three zones were situated in Guangdong province, near Hong Kong, and the other zone was situated in Fukien province, across the strait from Taiwan.

[20]Weijan Shan, "The Hybrid System and Continued Marketization of the Chinese Economy," *China Economic Review,* no. 1, 1992, p. 72.

[21]"When China Wakes: A Survey of China," *The Economist,* November 28, 1992, p. 8.

[22]In 1991, Hong Kong was the tenth biggest exporter, with exports of $98 billion. By the time Hong Kong joins China in 1997, China could be the fourth biggest exporter, following the United States, Germany, and Japan.

[23]A conservative estimate of China's GNP in 1992 is $1.4 to $1.5 trillion, about one-quarter of the U.S. GNP. See "When China Wakes," p. 5.

[24]"The Fifth Tiger Is on China's Coast," *Business Week,* April 6, 1992, p. 42.

Chinese leader, hailed the province as a model for the rest of China. Billions of dollars are being invested in new highways, power plants, container ports, and optical fiber telephone lines. An 85-mile superhighway is now under construction by a Hong Kong developer that will connect Guangzhou, the capital of the province, to Hong Kong.

Guangdong has easy access to Hong Kong capital, getting only 3 percent of its capital from the central government in Beijing. Hence, the province demonstrates a considerable degree of independence from central-government bureaucrats. With only sixteen million people, Guangdong manufactures 5 percent of China's total industrial output and 10 percent of its exports.[25] The province has become one of the world's biggest exporters of appliances, watches, garments, and toys. Guangdong is closely linked to Hong Kong, which accounts for over 80 percent of the province's investment and foreign trade. Hong Kong's currency circulates freely in Guangdong.

In turn, the province is a major investor in Hong Kong, second only to Japan. The central government plans to open twelve more free economic zones along China's coast in imitation of the three zones in the Guangdong cities of Shenzhen, Zhuhai, and Shekou.

Why have China's reforms worked so well? In a word, *competition*. The two key features of these reforms are (1) the *decentralization* of economic decision making from the Beijing government to provincial and local governments and to state enterprises, and (2) the formation of nonstate enterprises. The outstanding example of decentralization is Guangdong province. The creation of nonstate firms has been extraordinary. Township and village enterprises in agriculture, industry, construction, transportation, and commerce (as distinct from state-owned enterprises) grew from 1.5 million in 1978 to 18.7 million in 1989. Employment in these enterprises grew from 28 million to 93.7 million over the same years.[26]

Table 21-4 reveals that nonstate enterprises (private and collectives) in 1991 produced 47 percent of China's industrial output.[27] It is estimated that nonstate enterprises will manufacture nearly three-quarters of China's industrial output by the year 2000.

What lessons can we draw from China's reforms? The most important lesson is that reforms will be potent when they unleash the market forces of entry and competition.[28] The removal of entry barriers triggered a proliferation of nonstate firms. Also, the imposition of market-like incentives raised the performance of

---

[25]"Where Capitalism Thrives in China," *Fortune,* March 9, 1992, p. 71.

[26]State Statistical Bureau of the People's Republic of China, *China Statistical Yearbook 1990* (Chicago: The University of Illinois at Chicago, 1990), Table T9.58, p. 386 and Table T9.59, p. 387.

[27]The collective sector is somewhat ambiguous: It is a catch-all category that mainly includes firms owned by private collectives but also includes factories run by township governments.

[28]John McMillan and Barry Naughton, "How to Reform a Planned Economy: Lessons from China," *Oxford Review of Economic Policy,* 1992, no. 1, p. 131.

**Table 21-4   Source of Industrial Output in China: State
Enterprise, Collectives, and Private Enterprise, 1981, 1991,
and Projected 2000 (Percent)**

Source	1981	1991	2000
State enterprise	78	53	27
Collectives	21	36	48
Private enterprise	1	11	25

Source: Derived from data in "Chinese Communism's Secret Aim: Capitalism," *The New York Times,* October 19, 1992, p. A6. The original source of the data is the Chinese National Information Center.

state enterprises.[29] The outcome of these changes has been a dramatic increase in competition among both nonstate and state firms.

The success of China's reforms has also depended on the government's ability to maintain a stable macroeconomy. Bouts of inflation in 1984–1985 and 1987–1988 required a tightening of fiscal and monetary policies. The resulting "stop-and-go" cycles of reform have spawned uncertainties about the durability of reforms.[30] So far, the government has been able to restore macroeconomic stability, enabling China to resume the reform process. But inflation remains a threat to a continuing evolution toward a market economy.[31]

At present, China is best designated as a "hybrid system" that combines elements of both central planning and the market.[32] Although state enterprises have become more market-oriented, they still obtain easy credit from state banks while nonstate enterprises have only limited access to credit. Inadequate laws keep property rights ill-defined, and labor markets remain primitive. Some resources (particularly raw materials and industrial products) are still allocated by state agencies at prices controlled by the state. These resources are sold to nonstate firms that compete in open markets. This state-owned sector is a bottleneck to reform, but most observers believe that marketization of China's economy will continue and eventually displace the centrally planned system.[33]

If the outlook for China's transition to a market economy depended only on economic performance since the late 1970s, then a full transition would be a sure

---

[29]State-owned enterprises are allowed to keep a fraction of their profits (instead of sending all of them to the state), to sell and buy in free markets (instead of only at controlled prices), and to make their own production decisions (instead of getting them from the state). Furthermore, the compensation of managers is based on enterprise performance. These reforms have effected a "commercialization" of state enterprises even though they remain less autonomous than nonstate enterprises.

[30]Mario Blejer and others, *China: Economic Reform and Macroeconomic Management,* Occasional Paper 76 (Washington, D.C.: International Monetary Fund, January 1991), p. 31.

[31]"Overheated About China," *The Economist,* January 23, 1992, p. 18.

[32]Weijan Shan, "The Hybrid System," p. 67.

[33]Ibid., p. 72.

thing by 2010 or so. It appears, then, that only *political* disruption can halt China's economic progress. So far, reformers have operated within the confines of the old communist political and ideological system. Top officials still call on the Chinese to build a "socialist market economy," which appears to mean a market economy with a large public sector.[34] China's government is willing to abandon central economic control but not central political control.

Can this political system survive in the face of all the changes now occurring in China? The examples of Taiwan and South Korea indicate that in the long run (two or three decades) economic growth creates a more open and democratic society. One thing is certain: The government cannot stop the inflow of ideas about political freedom from other countries.

The threat to continuing economic reform is chaotic political change, such as a civil war causing a breakup of China.[35] An optimistic scenario would have China continue to pretend it was a communist country as it became a market economy with a progressive easing of restraints on political freedom. A pessimistic scenario would have the continuing suppression of political freedom instigating growing protests (much like that of Tianamen Square in 1989) that eventually end in social turmoil and even civil war.

SOME CLOSING OBSERVATIONS ON THE ROLE OF EASTERN EUROPE AND CHINA IN THE WORLD ECONOMY

It is too soon to make any empirically based observations about the postreform role of Eastern European countries in the world economy. But such observations can be made about China. After fifteen years of an export-led growth strategy, China has become a major player in the world economy. Its exports have grown almost 15 percent a year since 1978, and it is a major recipient of foreign loans and direct foreign investment by multinational firms. In 1980, China became a member of the World Bank and the International Monetary Fund, symbolizing its entry into the world economy.

Table 21-5 shows the direction of China's trade in 1989. In that year, 41 percent of China's exports went to the Triad (Japan, the United States, and Europe) and 56 percent of its imports came from the Triad. Most of China's remaining trade was with Asia (excluding Japan). In 1989, exports were valued at $52.5 billion. As noted earlier, they reached $85 billion in 1992.

---

[34]"China's Leaders Stress Both Market and Orthodoxy," *The New York Times,* October 13, 1992, p. A3. Chinese intellectuals joke that "under the leadership of the communist party we are advancing from socialism to capitalism." This quotation appears in "Chinese Communism's Secret Aim: Capitalism," *The New York Times,* October 19, 1992, p. 1.

[35]The former prime minister of Singapore, Lee Kuan Yew, stated in 1992: "There is a real danger, if central authority breaks down, that China will break up into the kind of provincialism or warlordism she suffered during the 1920s and 1930s." See "Where Capitalism Thrives in China," *Fortune,* March 9, 1992, pp. 72–74.

Table 21-6 reveals that China's use of foreign capital grew by more than five times from 1983 to 1989. In the latter year, 62 percent of the capital came from loans and the rest from investments by multinational firms.

If the Eastern Europe countries were to evolve toward a market economy as rapidly as China has done since 1978, they would also become important players in the world economy, particularly the big countries of Russia, Poland, and Ukraine. Figure 21-4 maps the shift of the Eastern European countries toward a market economy based on the assumption that they will match the speed of China's reform. For instance, the former Soviet Union would move along the transition axis from 1990 to 2004 as far as China moved from 1978 to 1992 (a 14-year period

Table 21-5 Direction of China's Trade in 1989 (Percent)

Area	Exports	Imports
Asia	70.6	51.9
Japan	*15.9*	*17.8*
Europe	16.7	24.9
North America	9.1	15.1
United States	*8.4*	*13.3*
Latin America	1.0	4.1
Africa	1.4	0.7
Oceania	0.9	3.0
All areas	*100.0*	*100.0*
Value in billions of U.S. dollars	52.5	59.1

Note: Percentages may not add to 100.0 because of rounding.
Source: State Statistical Bureau of the People's Republic of China, *China Statistical Yearbook 1990* (Chicago: The University of Illinois at Chicago, 1990), Table 15.4, pp. 605–607.

Table 21-6 China's Use of Foreign Capital, 1983 and 1989 (Millions of U.S. dollars)

Source of Capital	1983	1989
Foreign loans	1,065	6,286
Direct foreign investment	636	3,392
Other foreign investment[1]	280	381
Total	*1,981*	*10,059*

[1]Value of equipment supplied by foreign firms.
Source: State Statistical Bureau of the People's Republic of China, *China Statistical Yearbook 1990* (Chicago: The University of Illinois at Chicago, 1990), Table 15.8, p. 613.

Figure 21-4

Movement Along the Centrally Planned/Market Economy Transition Axis: China, Russia, Poland, and Hungary. If the Eastern European countries were to match China's pace of reform between 1978 and 1992, they would move on the transition axis to the position indicated for the year 2004.

for both countries). If China were to maintain its reform pace, it would have moved close to a full market economy by 2004. Starting further along the axis and one year earlier, the other Eastern European countries would move closer to a full market economy in 2004 than the former Soviet Union. Based on the writer's perceptions of the complex reform processes in the transition economies, Figure 21-4 is intended to be suggestive only.

How can the industrial countries of the West support the transition process? Three ways come to mind. The first is to open their markets to the transitional countries. By far, this would be the West's most important contribution: The transition economies cannot join the world economy if it is shut to them. Further, the West's exports to the transition economies depend mainly on its imports from them. The second way is for the West to provide the transition countries with debt relief and access to new capital to help in the massive restructuring of their economies. The third way relies on Western firms that can bring capital, technology, and entrepreneurial skills to the transition countries through direct investment, licensing, and other business arrangements. But the West's assistance can be fruitful only if the transition countries make their economies competitive in an environment of macroeconomic stability.

SUMMARY

1. Over one-quarter of the world's peoples living in China and the countries of Eastern Europe are now engaged in a historical effort to transform their centrally planned economies into market economies that fully participate in the world economy.

2. Two key features of socialist economies are *state ownership* of the means of production and *central planning* by the political authorities. The former Soviet Union is a classic example of a centrally planned economy.

3. The Soviet economy generated rapid growth in the 1930s and early post-World War II period, but it experienced a drastic slowdown starting in the late 1960s. The failure of the command economies precipitated a breakup of the Soviet Union at the end of 1991 and the collapse of communist regimes in other Eastern European countries a few years earlier. In China, the government initiated a process of "marketization" of the economy in the late 1970s, more than a decade before reform began in Eastern Europe.

4. Economists agree on a reform package needed to transform a centrally planned economy into a market economy: (1) macroeconomic stabilization, (2) establishment of competitive markets, (3) privatization of state-owned enterprises, and (4) creation of a legal framework and institutions vital to the functioning of a market economy. Economists disagree, however, on the *sequence* of reforms, which can range from a radical "big bang" approach to a conservative, "gradualist" approach.

5. The process of reform now under way in Eastern Europe and China will go on for decades. In Eastern Europe, macroeconomic disarray persuaded Poland and the former Soviet Union (mainly Russia) to start with a big bang, while Hungary and the former Czechoslovakia adopted a gradualist approach.

6. The former Czechoslovakia, Hungary, and Poland appear to have turned the corner on reform. They could enjoy positive rates of growth by the mid-1990s. In contrast, the prospects for reform in Russia appear poor due to political opposition and the failure of the government to stabilize the economy. Russia can resume its transition to a market economy only if it can avoid hyperinflation.

7. China's reform process (which started in the late 1970s) has been gradual, moving toward marketization of the economy through small, step-by-step changes. Nonetheless, it has been extraordinarily successful: Since 1978, China's GNP has grown at a real annual rate of 9 percent, doubling about every eight years. Already, China has the fourth largest economy in the world. Exports have soared, making China a major exporter. If China continues to grow at 9 percent a year, it will become the largest economy in the world by 2010.

8. China's reforms have worked so well because they unleashed the market forces of entry and competition. The removal of entry barriers triggered a proliferation of nonstate firms, and the imposition of market-like incentives raised the performance of state enterprises. Despite bouts of inflation, the government has been able to maintain the macroeconomic stability necessary to reform.

9. At present, China is best designated a "hybrid system" combining elements of both central planning and the market. It appears that only *political* disruption can halt China's economic progress.

10. The industrial countries of the West can support the transition process by opening their markets to the transitional countries; by offering those countries

debt relief and new capital; and by transferring capital, technology, and entrepreneurial skills to them via multinational firms.

QUESTIONS AND APPLICATIONS

1. (a) What questions must every economy answer?
   (b) How does a market economy answer those questions?
   (c) How does a centrally planned economy answer those questions?
2. Why did the Soviet economy experience a drastic slowdown starting in the late 1960s?
3. What do economists agree should be the elements of the reform process needed to transform a centrally planned economy into a market economy?
4. What are the pros and cons of the "big bang" and "gradualist" approaches to economic reform?
5. Discuss: "The former Czechoslovakia, Hungary, and Poland appear to have turned the corner on reform, but the prospects for reform are poor in Russia."
6. Why is macroeconomic stability so critical to the reform process?
7. (a) What approach has China taken to economic reform?
   (b) How successful are China's reforms?
8. What lessons can we draw from China's reforms?
9. (a) What is China's hybrid system?
   (b) Discuss: "It appears that only *political* disruption can halt China's economic progress."
10. What can the industrial countries of the West do to support the transition process?

SELECTED READINGS

Blanchard, Olivier, and others. *Reform in Eastern Europe.* Cambridge: MIT Press, 1991.

Blejer, Mario, and others. *China: Economic Reform and Macroeconomic Management.* IMF Occasional Paper 76. Washington, D.C.: International Monetary Fund, January 1991.

Clague, Christopher, and Gordon C. Rausser, eds. *The Emergence of Market Economies in Eastern Europe.* New York: Blackwell, 1992.

Giustiniani, Alessandro, and others. *Growth and Catch-Up in Central and Eastern Europe: Macroeconomic Effects on Western Countries.* Essays in International Finance, no. 186. Princeton, N.J.: Princeton University Press, April 1992.

Greene, Joshua E., and Peter Isard. *Currency Convertibility and the Transformation of Centrally-Planned Economies.* IMF Occasional Paper no. 81. Washington, D.C.: International Monetary Fund, June 1991.

Gros, Daniel, and Alfred Steinherr. *Economic Reform in the Soviet Union: Pas de Deux Between Disintegration and Macroeconomic Destabilization.* Princeton Studies in International Finance, no. 186. Princeton, N.J.: Princeton University Press, November 1991.

Gur, Ofer. "Soviet Economic Growth: 1928–1985." *Journal of Economic Literature,* December 1987, pp. 1767–1834.

Hamilton, Carl B., and L. Alan Winters. "Trade with Eastern Europe." *Economic Policy,* April 1992, pp. 77–116.

Haus, Leah A. *Globalizing the GATT.* Washington, D.C.: The Brookings Institution, 1992.

Hewett, Ed. A. *Open for Business: Russia's Return to the Global Economy.* Washington, D.C.: The Brookings Institution, 1992.

Kornai, Janos. *The Road to a Free Economy: Shifting from a Socialist System, The Example of Hungary.* New York: W. W. Norton, 1990.

Murrell, Peter. "Symposium on Economic Transition in the Soviet Union and Eastern Europe." *The Journal of Economic Perspectives,* Fall 1991, pp. 3–162.

Peck, Morton J., and Thomas J. Richardson, eds. *What Is to Be Done: Proposals for the Soviet Transition to the Market.* New Haven: Yale University Press, 1991.

Pomfret, Richard. *Investing in China: Ten Years of Open Door Policy.* Ames: Iowa State University Press, 1991.

van Brabant, Jozef M. *Remaking Eastern Europe: On the Political Economy of Transition.* Boston: Kluwer Academic Publishers, 1990.

Williamson, John. *The Economic Opening of Eastern Europe.* Washington, D.C.: Institute for International Economics, May 1991.

INTERNATIONAL INVESTMENT/

part IV

MULTINATIONAL ENTERPRISE

In Parts I, II, and III, a macroscopic, national perspective was assumed in order to describe and analyze international economic relations. Although necessary, this perspective is no longer sufficient to explain the behavior of the world economy. Large multinational business enterprises now possess the financial and market power to make decisions that vitally affect the level, composition, and direction of international trade and investment. Multinational enterprises have become independent actors in the world economy, and there is no area of government policy that escapes their influence. The future evolution of the world economy will depend, therefore, not only on the behavior of national governments but also on the behavior of multinational enterprises as they strive to achieve their goals on a transnational scale. Part IV investigates the nature, scope, and economic role of multinational enterprises; the policies of the United States and other countries toward multinational enterprises; and the tensions that are generated by the complex relations between multinational enterprises and nation-states.

chapter 22

THE NATURE AND SCOPE OF MULTINATIONAL ENTERPRISE

After World War II, U.S. business firms went abroad on a massive scale unprecedented in the history of international enterprise. Today the production and sales of the foreign operations owned and managed by U.S. companies are nearly four times the value of U.S. exports. The prevailing response of big American companies to market opportunities abroad is to establish producing affiliates in foreign countries. The dominant agency in the surge of U.S. business abroad is the multinational enterprise (MNE)—the large industrial or service corporation that possesses plants or other operations in many countries that produce for markets throughout the world. Many industrial firms in Western Europe and Japan have also become MNEs, and they are emerging in newly industrializing countries, such as Mexico and South Korea, as well.

Because of their vast size, the worldwide operations of multinational companies are now a decisive force in shaping the patterns of trade, investment, and technology flows among nations. It has become impossible to understand the world economy without an appreciation of the many roles of multinational enterprises as producers, investors, traders, and innovators on a global scale. National governments must also reckon with this force because of its impact on domestic production, employment, trade, and the balance of payments. In so doing, they are commonly frustrated by the capability of multinational companies to far outrun national jurisdiction in taxation, antitrust, and other policy areas. Moreover, many governments view the multinational enterprise as a *political* threat, representing as it does an intrusion into the national domain by a company whose control is exercised by a headquarters located in another country. Even in the United States, the multinational enterprise has come under attack by labor and protectionist groups who charge it with exporting jobs and technology to the detriment of the U.S. economy.

The expansion of U.S. business into foreign production is not new. Today's multinational enterprises have roots that go deep into the American past. In the decades following the Civil War, the transformation of industrial corporations into national enterprises, together with notable improvements in transportation and communications, encouraged a number of American manufacturers with unique products to make investments in Canada and Europe. One of the pioneers, Singer, licensed a French company in 1855 to manufacture its new sewing machine (the first and last time Singer ever licensed a patent to an independent foreign concern), and in 1867 it established the first plant abroad, in Glasgow.[1] In 1879, Westinghouse started a shop in Paris to manufacture brakes; in 1882, Western Electric and International Bell Telephone Company jointly set up a manufacturing affiliate in Belgium; and by 1889, Eastman had incorporated a company in London to manufacture film for Kodak cameras imported from the United States.[2] In the 1870s and 1880s, then, many American companies with new products (screws, cash registers, elevators, steam pumps, locomotives, locks, and guns) were eagerly seeking export markets and, in some instances, entering into foreign production.[3]

It is noteworthy that this early movement of U.S. manufacturers abroad was based on new products, new methods of production, and new marketing methods that offered strong competitive advantages in foreign markets. From the very beginning, therefore, U.S. business investors appeared primarily as exporters of technology and management rather than exporters of capital. By the turn of the century, the presence of U.S. companies in Europe was sufficient enough to alarm some observers, who spoke of "the American invasion" in much the same terms as J. J. Servan-Schreiber did some seventy years later.[4]

Although its historical roots are deep, the multinational enterprise as we know it today is a recent phenomenon, emerging for the most part only since the mid-1950s. Before that time the inadequacies of the global infrastructure of communications and transportation, as well as the pervasive influence of restrictive government policies, rendered global business strategies nothing more than utopian dreams in the minds of a few entrepreneurs. The emergence of multinational enterprise systems directed and controlled by a single decision center had to await the dramatic postwar improvements in communications and transportation and the massive liberalization of international trade and payments that gathered steam in the late 1950s.

SOME DEFINITIONS
OF THE MULTINATIONAL ENTERPRISE

There is no single agreed-upon definition of the multinational (or transnational) enterprise. This is hardly surprising in view of the fact that "multinationality" has

---

[1]See Mira Wilkins, *The Emergence of Multinational Enterprise* (Cambridge: Harvard University Press, 1970), pp. 38 ff. This book offers a detailed history of U.S. international business up to 1914.

[2]Ibid., pp. 45, 51, and 59.

[3]Ibid., p. 45.

[4]Three publications appeared in London in 1901–1902 titled *The American Invasion, The American Invaders,* and *The Americanization of the World.* See Wilkins, *Multinational Enterprise,* p. 71. Also see J. J. Servan-Schreiber, *The American Challenge* (New York: Atheneum Publishers, 1968).

many dimensions and may be viewed from any of several different perspectives — economic, political, legal, managerial, and others.

Some observers regard *ownership* as the key criterion. In their view an enterprise becomes multinational only when the headquarters or parent company is effectively owned by nationals of at least two countries. Shell and Unilever, which are controlled by British and Dutch interests, are commonly cited as examples. By this ownership test, very few international companies may be called multinational. The dominant ownership interest in the overwhelming majority of big international companies is *uninational,* namely, American, British, French, or Japanese.[5] The ownership criterion has been rejected by most authorities.

A second definition of the MNE relies on the criterion of the *nationality mix* of headquarters management. An international company is seen as multinational only when the managers of the parent company are nationals of several different countries. Here again, very few international companies would qualify as multinational enterprises, because most have headquarters organizations that are entirely or mainly staffed with nationals of the home country. But uninational management may well prove to be a transitional phenomenon. Already it is commonplace for international companies to staff their foreign affiliates with local nationals all the way to the top levels, and some of these nationals are now being promoted to the parent headquarters. Multinational management, then, is more a consequence of the continuing evolution of the MNE than its distinguishing feature.

Most observers of large international companies have been concerned with their economic and business behavior. Accordingly, they have defined the MNE in terms of *organizational structure* or *business strategy.* Vernon sees the multinational enterprise as a "parent company that controls a large cluster of corporations of various nationalities."[6] Finding the essence of the multinational enterprise in its attempt "to treat the various national markets as though they were one," Behrman emphasizes the presence of a single management (strategy) center that guides the actions of foreign affiliates.[7] Perlmutter has distinguished three kinds of international companies by reference to the attitudes held by their top executives. *Ethnocentric* companies follow policies that are home country-oriented, *polycentric* companies follow policies that are host country-oriented, and *geocentric* companies follow policies that are world-oriented. To Perlmutter, a firm's multinationality may be judged by "the pervasiveness with which its executives think geocentrically."[8] More recently, the United Nations defined the essence of multinationalization (which it calls transnationalization) as "the internalization of interna-

---

[5]Of course, the shares of these companies may be held in comparatively small amounts by nationals of many countries. Indeed, several U.S. companies list their shares on stock exchanges in Europe and Japan. But the controlling ownership interest remains in the hands of nationals of the home country, where the parent company is located.

[6]Raymond Vernon, *Sovereignty at Bay* (New York: Basic Books, 1971), p. 4.

[7]Jack N. Behrman, *Some Patterns in the Rise of the Multinational Enterprise* (Chapel Hill: University of North Carolina, 1969), p. 63.

[8]Howard V. Perlmutter, "The Tortuous Evolution of the Multinational Corporation," *Columbia Journal of World Business,* January–February 1969, pp. 9–18.

tional market transactions within an individual decision-making unit, the transnational corporation."[9]

The foregoing conceptions may be covered in a single definition of the multinational enterprise that contains both structural and strategic (attitudinal) elements. A multinational enterprise denotes a headquarters or parent company that

1. engages in foreign production and other activities through its own affiliates located in several different countries
2. exercises direct control over the policies of those affiliates
3. strives to design and implement business strategies in production, marketing, finance, and other functions that transcend national boundaries, becoming thereby progressively more geocentric in outlook

This definition is consistent with the approach taken in this and later chapters.

Unfortunately, organizational structure and business strategy do not lend themselves to direct quantitative measurement. Thus, the definition of the MNE for statistical data-gathering purposes must rely on "proxy variables," such as the percentages of a company's assets, sales, earnings, employment, or production abroad. A company whose foreign sales are 25 percent or more of total sales is certainly heavily involved in international business on both operational and strategic levels, and in most instances it probably qualifies as a multinational enterprise. But there is no magic percentage at which a company is transformed into a multinational enterprise. The MNE is too complex a phenomenon to be captured by a single number. Any statistical definition of the MNE, however useful, is bound to be arbitrary.

THE MULTINATIONAL ENTERPRISE SYSTEM

The multinational enterprise moves products and factor services (capital, technology, and management) among national economies. It performs this role as an international transfer agent through institutional or organizational arrangements that collectively make up the *multinational enterprise system*. This system, as depicted in Figure 22-1, comprises the parent company and its foreign affiliates.

The parent company (denoted by the P circle) is the enterprise decision center that determines the goals and controls the operations of the entire system. The key decisions of the parent company relate to the establishment (or acquisition), country location, size, and "product mix" of its production affiliates; the direction, volume, and composition of transfers among the affiliates; and the national markets to be served by the affiliates. These strategy decisions generate a pattern of factor and product flows among the members of the system. The parent company and its affiliates (denoted by the A circles) are located in different

---

[9]United Nations Center on Transnational Corporations, *Transnational Corporations in World Development* (New York: United Nations, 1988), p. 16.

Figure 22-1

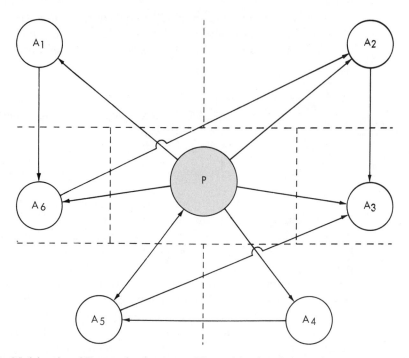

The Multinational Enterprise System. The multinational enterprise system comprises the parent company (P) and its affiliates (the A's) located in different countries, as indicated by the dashed lines. Through ownership of the affiliates, the parent company sets the strategic goals and controls the operations of the enterprise system. The affiliates are tied to the parent company (and in some instances, other affiliates) by cross-national flows of products, capital, technology, and management.

countries, as indicated by the dashed lines. Most of the affiliates perform both production and marketing functions, but some perform only a marketing or financial function.

The affiliates are connected to the parent company and, in some instances, to other affiliates by a variety of cross-national flows of products, capital, technology, and management.[10] Flows of factor services, usually accompanied by product flows, generally move from the parent company to the affiliates. Any of these kinds of flows may also link pairs of affiliates. To illustrate, A_1 may transfer parts or

---

[10]They are also connected by financial flows that represent the financing and payment of the real flows. These include product payments, capital funds, interest and dividend payments, royalties, and management fees. Our interest in this chapter is focused on the real flows of products and factor services rather than on the associated financial flows.

components that it manufactures to A_6, which uses them to manufacture other products. A_4 may transfer certain finished products to A_5, which then resells them in the local market. Idle funds accumulating in A_2 may be transferred to A_3 to finance a capital expansion. A_5 may develop new technology that is transferred to A_3. A manager in A_6 may be transferred to a new position in A_2. Some products and factor services may also be transferred from an affiliate to the parent company, such as from A_5 to P.

One of the distinctive features of the multinational enterprise system is the rapid growth of interaffiliate transfers as managers in the parent company try to improve the performance of the entire system. Managers perceive a worldwide market for the company's products, and they work to build up interaffiliate transfers on regional or global levels to take advantage of similarities among national markets, economies of scale, and international specialization. Hence, the multinational enterprise system becomes progressively more integrated in production, marketing, finance, research and development, and management.

Several *external* constraints may limit the integration of a multinational enterprise system, and a parent company also encounters *internal* constraints, such as the domestic orientation of many managers. External constraints include all of the obstacles to international trade and payments that were examined in Parts I and II. Most prominent are the restrictions imposed by governments on the flows of factor services, products, and current payments. When trade restrictions are severe, they inhibit interaffiliate product transfers. Furthermore, uncertainty about future government actions and unstable political conditions in some host countries may greatly enhance the risks of interdependence among affiliates. In Figure 22-1, for instance, an interruption in the production or shipments of A_1 will halt the production of A_6 unless A_6 has access to another supplier. Or again, the host government may prevent A_5 from importing products from A_4 to fill out its product line.

As a result of external and internal constraints, the parent company will seldom push the integration of its system to a logical extreme. Instead, integration is most likely to be partial, applying to some regions but not to the entire world or to some products but not all products. In particular, many parent companies have been reluctant to integrate the operations of affiliates in the industrial countries with the operations of affiliates in the developing countries because of restrictions and political instability prevalent in developing countries.

To conclude, the multinational enterprise system functions as an international transfer agent for both products and factor services. Although the pattern of these transfers will depend on the parent company's strategy and various constraints, the parent company is the only source of certain factor services (notably, systemwide management) and is usually the principal source of capital and technology. However, as we have seen, the parent company may also initiate factor flows (as well as product flows) among the affiliates in different countries and from them back to itself. Hence, the multinational enterprise system recapitulates in microcosm the international economic system of trade and factor movements among national economies.[11] We now take a closer look at product and factor transfers within the multinational enterprise system.

TRANSFERS OF PRODUCT IN THE MULTINATIONAL ENTERPRISE SYSTEM

As noted earlier, the multinational enterprise system generates many cross-national product transfers within the system itself.[12] These intra-enterprise product transfers are the direct consequence of the decisions made by the parent company managers relating to three strategy questions:

1. Where in the world are the markets for our final products?
2. Where should we locate our production facilities to supply those markets?
3. Where and from whom should we obtain the inputs (raw materials, parts, components, capital equipment) necessary to the manufacture of our final products?

For each country market of the multinational enterprise's final products, parent company managers must decide whether to produce within the market or export into it from a production base located in another country. For each production affiliate, parent company managers must decide whether to make or buy the necessary production inputs. If the decision is to make them, then the managers must decide whether to make them in the same country as the affiliate in question or to obtain them from an affiliate in another country. When the parent company is following a global strategy, these decisions will create some degree of system integration in marketing, production, or both.

Horizontal Integration

Figure 22-2 depicts a pattern of intra-enterprise product transfers resulting from a high degree of integration in the production of *final* products. Instead of having the parent company (P) and each foreign affiliate (the A's) produce full product lines, the parent company managers achieve a pattern of specialization among them, taking into account the scale of operations and the mix of factor services available at each of the country locations (including the home country); the logistical costs of storage, handling, and transportation; and the constraints imposed by import duties, quotas, and other trade restrictions. The transfer of final products among affiliates and between affiliates and the parent company enables the multinational

---

[11]In different language, the MNE *internalizes* cross-national market transactions. The theory of internalization is treated in Chapter 23.

[12]The system also generates cross-national sales to nonsystem customers and cross-national purchases from nonsystem suppliers. Both of these extra-enterprise transactions and the cross-national transfers within the system (intra-enterprise transfers) constitute the international trade created by the system.

Figure 22-2

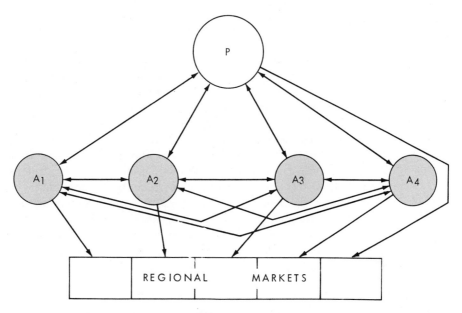

Product Transfers Within the Multinational Enterprise System: Horizontal Integration. This figure depicts the pattern of product flows within the multinational enterprise system when the parent company and its subsidiaries specialize in the production of individual final products rather than the full product line. Also, the parent company and its affiliates are assigned regional markets.

enterprise system to offer full product lines in each country market at lower costs or higher quality levels than would be possible if those lines were entirely produced by each affiliate.

Furthermore, the parent company and each affiliate is assigned a *regional* market that it is best prepared to serve. For example, the French affiliate (A_1) serves all markets in the European Community, the Mexican affiliate (A_2) serves all markets in Latin America, and so on. Hence, the parent company and the affiliates are exporting finished products to multicountry regional markets as well as participating in intra-enterprise trade. This multimarket approach can be the source of advantages separate from economies of specialization and scale derived from production. On the cost side, an international standardization of products in the multinational enterprise system makes possible the application of the same marketing policies to multicountry markets. For instance, the costs of designing an advertising program may now be spread over a hundred country markets. On the demand side, product standardization (involving the same product lines, trademarks, brand names, and packaging offered by all members of the system) helps to create a global product image that can stimulate demand throughout the world. In this way, the multinational enterprise can take advantage of communication links among consumers and industrial buyers in different countries.

Vertical Integration

Vertical integration in production also creates product transfers within the multinational enterprise system. Vertical integration occurs when a producer decides to produce at least some of the intermediate inputs required to make the final products. At the extreme, vertical integration can extend backward into raw material extraction, but for most producers (except for heavy industries, such as steel and other metals, chemicals, and oil refining), it is likely to go no further than the production of certain components and parts that are assembled into final products. Vertical integration becomes international in scope when a multinational enterprise system produces raw materials, components, or other inputs in one or more of its member companies (including the parent company) for use in production by member companies in other countries.

Figure 22-3 depicts one pattern of intra-enterprise product transfers that results from vertical integration in production. The parent company (P) transfers

Figure 22-3

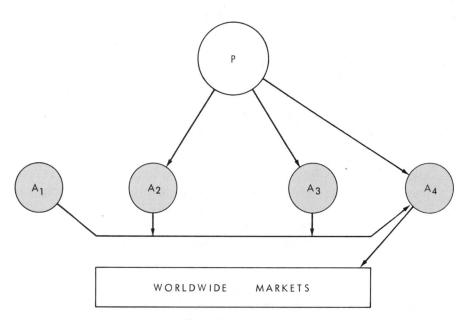

Product Transfers Within the Multinational Enterprise System: Vertical Integration.   This figure depicts the pattern of product flows with the multinational enterprise system when the parent company and some of its foreign affiliates produce intermediate products that are used by other affiliates to produce final products. In this figure, the parent company (P) and three affiliates (A_1, A_2, and A_3) supply intermediate products to a fourth affiliate (A_4), which produces final products for worldwide markets.

intermediate products to affiliates A_2, A_3, and A_4 for use in their production. At the same time, A_1 manufactures a component that is transferred to A_4, while A_2 and A_3 also manufacture inputs for A_4. Subsequently A_4 uses all these inputs to produce the final product, which is then sold to worldwide markets.

Vertical integration enables the multinational enterprise system to reap the advantages of international specialization and increasing returns, as was also true of horizontal integration. The classic example of vertical integration on a global scale is provided by the major petroleum companies, whose affiliates (located in developing countries) ship crude oil to refinery affiliates (mostly located in industrial countries), which in turn ship refined products to marketing affiliates for sale throughout the world.[13]

TRANSFERS OF CAPITAL IN THE MULTINATIONAL ENTERPRISE SYSTEM

The MNE is the dominant vehicle for foreign direct investment. For the most part, decisions to invest directly abroad are made by managers in multinational parent companies. Unlike portfolio investment, which is a pure transfer of capital, foreign direct investment is the transfer of a bundle of factor services that represent in their totality an extension of a business enterprise across national boundaries. In a behavioral sense, therefore, foreign direct investment encompasses everything that MNEs do when they establish and manage their affiliates in different countries.[14]

We have observed that the direct investment activities of MNEs initiate a complex set of product and factor flows within a multinational system, which is an ongoing enterprise with expectations of continuing indefinitely into the future. It follows that no single act of direct investment and, even more so, no single product or factor flow can be fully understood without relating it to the entire system of which it is a part. In particular, any assessment of the economic effects of the MNE should consider the performance of the total system. As long as we avoid mistaking the part for the whole, however, fruitful economic analysis can proceed by investigating the constituent transfer functions of the multinational enterprise system.

The international transfer of *real* capital (plant, equipment, and inventories) commonly (but not always) occurs first as a *financial* transfer of capital funds.[15] In examining the flow of capital in the multinational enterprise system, therefore, we must consider the financial strategy of the parent company. Nonetheless, we should keep in mind that only when capital funds are converted into real capital do they contribute to production in the system.

Upon deciding to undertake new investment abroad, the parent company must then decide on the sources for financing the necessary capital expenditures.

---

[13]In the 1970s, governments in developing countries expropriated the crude-oil operations of the international petroleum companies. Instead of owning their own crude-oil affiliates, the international companies now obtain oil from developing countries under contractual arrangements. Nonetheless, the international petroleum companies retain much of their vertical integration.

[14]For a narrow definition of foreign direct investment as an international capital flow, see Chapter 23.

[15]For a discussion of capital as a factor of production, see Chapter 3.

For a multinational enterprise pursuing a global strategy, the appropriate question is, Where in the world should we obtain financing for our affiliate in country Y? The answer to this question (and others like it) will determine the pattern of capital flows within the enterprise system and between the enterprise system and outside financial sources located in different countries.

Sources of Capital Financing

In deciding on the sources of financing for investment abroad, two questions are prominent in the deliberations of managers in most parent companies: (1) Should funds be obtained at home (the country of the parent) or abroad? (2) Should funds be obtained from sources *within* the system (parent company and affiliates) or from sources *outside* the system (investment banks, security markets, and other financial institutions)? Thus, the enterprise has four basic sourcing options, as depicted in Figure 22-4.

A choice of either option 1 or 2 results in the transfer of capital from the home country to a host country. The transfer may initially take the form of funds (financial transfer) or the form of capital equipment and inventory (real transfer).[16] Again, the transfer may represent an equity contribution, a formal loan, or an informal advance. Under option 1, financing comes from the retained earnings of the parent company. Under option 2, the parent company obtains financing from financial institutions in the home country.

Under options 3 and 4, no net transfer of capital occurs between the home and foreign countries, because the funds are both raised abroad and invested abroad. Alternative 3 is available to the parent company only when it has affiliates with retained earnings.[17] When capital expansion in a given affiliate is financed by the

Figure 22-4

	INTERNAL SOURCES	EXTERNAL SOURCES
HOME COUNTRY	1	2
FOREIGN COUNTRIES	3	4

Basic Capital-Sourcing Options for the Multinational Enterprise. To finance investment abroad, MNEs must decide whether to obtain funds in the home country or in a foreign country and whether to obtain them from internal sources (within the MNE system) or from external sources. Options 1 or 2 result in a transfer of capital from the home country to a host country. Options 3 and 4 do not give rise to such a transfer, because the funds are both raised and invested abroad.

---

[16]Intangibles, such as patent rights, management services, and goodwill may also be capitalized. This practice is more common when the affiliate is a joint venture than when it is wholly owned by the parent company.

[17]The entire cash flow of affiliates (earnings plus depreciation allowances) may be used for capital financing, but we are concerned here only with a *net* expansion of capital.

affiliate's own earnings, no international transfer of capital takes place.[18] When, however, a given affiliate obtains capital funds (or real capital) from another affiliate located in a different country, there does occur an international transfer of capital. If, for example, the parent company directs a transfer of capital from its affiliate in Cologne to its affiliate in Paris, then capital moves from West Germany to France.

Under option 4, the affiliate may obtain capital from local financial institutions with or without the guarantee of the parent company. Or the parent company may raise capital funds under its own name from external sources in the host country of the affiliate. In both instances, the resulting capital flow is domestic, not international.[19] When, however, the parent company (or more rarely, an affiliate) obtains external capital funds from a third country or from an international market (Eurocurrencies), then capital flows to the host country from one or more third countries.[20]

The final choice of a capital-sourcing option depends on the strategy preferences of the parent company and on a variety of constraints. As to the choice between home country versus foreign country sources, apparently the majority of U.S. parent companies favor the use of capital funds generated abroad by their affiliates, including their retained earnings and local loans obtained without the parent's guarantee. Although new affiliates depend much more on parent company funds, established affiliates are almost always compelled to obtain much of their financing from local sources.

Constraints on Capital-Sourcing Policies

Numerous factors both at home and abroad act to constrain the capital-sourcing choices of parent companies. Here we mention only the more prominent ones without going into detail.

Exchange restrictions in the home country may limit the capital a parent company can invest abroad, as did controls in the United States in the late 1960s. Generally controls in the home country compel a parent company to rely more on foreign-source capital than it would otherwise care to do. Exchange restrictions in a *host* country may cause a parent company to rely more on local financing of an affiliate's capital needs because of a reluctance to transfer funds into an inconvertible currency. High rates of *inflation,* high *exchange risks,* or high *political risks* (such as a threat of expropriation) also favor local financing, other things being equal. All too often, however, a parent company encounters these conditions in develop-

---

[18]Since the retained earnings *could* be repatriated to the parent company, one can argue that the use of retained earnings should be considered a capital flow from the parent to the affiliate. However, in their financial decisions most multinational enterprises draw a distinction between repatriated earnings and earnings retained abroad.

[19]The sale of securities abroad by the U.S. parent company is entered in the U.S. balance of payments as a long-term capital inflow, but when the funds are spent on investment abroad an offsetting entry of a long-term capital outflow (direct investment) is also recorded. Hence, the transaction is merely a bookkeeping entry with no net effect on the balance of payments.

[20]Eurocurrencies are described in Chapter 19.

ing countries that cannot provide local financing to meet all of the affiliate's capital requirements. In that event, the parent company has no choice but to transfer capital into the host country unless it is willing to limit the growth (and perhaps endanger the survival) of its affiliate.[21]

Some countries also limit the foreign-owned affiliate in its *access to local capital sources*. Somewhat paradoxically, the same countries may also limit the parent company's *ownership interests* in the local affiliate to a given percentage (commonly 49 percent). This ownership constraint can raise a serious financing problem for the joint-venture affiliate, because the parent company may be unwilling to lend to the affiliate as opposed to making an equity investment.

Taxation in home and host countries may also influence the source of capital financing in a multinational enterprise system as well as the kind of financing used (equity versus loan). To illustrate, the United States does not ordinarily tax foreign earnings until they are repatriated to the parent company, but it may tax capital transfers among foreign affiliates by regarding them as "constructive" loans or investments of the parent company. This tax policy encourages the retention of earnings in the affiliate and thereby encourages local financing. Probably the most important single effect of taxation in host countries on capital-sourcing decisions lies in the differential impact of the diverse tax systems on affiliate earnings and therefore the amounts available for new investment, either in the host country or elsewhere.

Varying *costs of capital* in different countries will also influence the choice of *external* capital sources. As the multinational enterprise becomes more global in its operations, it establishes intimate links with financial institutions in many countries and with international financial centers. Thus, it is in a position to raise capital in low-cost locations for transfer to high-cost locations. Regarding *internal* capital sources, the logical cost to the enterprise is the highest marginal opportunity cost of capital funds anywhere in the entire multinational enterprise system. Nonetheless, parent companies commonly make a decision to invest in a particular country without comparing investment opportunities in other countries (including the home country). Most parent companies do, however, have a desired rate of return on capital, which in effect is their internal cost of capital.

In closing, it should be evident that a U.S. parent company may undertake direct investment abroad without using its own capital resources or even without any transfer of capital from the home country to the host country. An inescapable conclusion is that *international capital transfers are not a necessary element of foreign direct investment*. Rather, the necessary element is an international transfer of management control.

Although not strictly necessary, foreign direct investment almost always involves at least *some* capital transfer from a parent company to its affiliate, especially when the affiliate is new. And, as we have observed, capital-sourcing decisions in

---

[21]Hedging in forward exchange, swap arrangements, and investment guarantees provided by the home government may be used by the parent company to offset some of the risks. For a treatment of the U.S. investment insurance program, see Chapter 24.

the multinational enterprise system may generate many capital transfers between second and third countries.

TRANSFERS OF TECHNOLOGY IN THE MULTINATIONAL ENTERPRISE SYSTEM

The multinational enterprise functions as an *international innovation system* that goes far beyond the traditional mode of international technological diffusion through imitation.[22] Indeed, the comparative advantage of the MNE in world markets centers on its mastery of the innovation process far more than its mere size or financial strength. Multinational enterprises are research-intensive, and their remarkable growth proceeds from their capacity to create and market new products on a global scale.

Technology needs to be distinguished from *technological innovation*. Technology, as such, is a body of knowledge that is applicable to the production of goods and the creation of new goods. Technology, therefore, consists of ideas about products and how to make them rather than the products themselves or production facilities.[23] Today—with only modest exceptions—the source of new technology is scientific research and invention in industrial, government, and university laboratories.

Technological innovation, on the other hand, is the entire process whereby research and invention are converted into technology that is then applied to the production of new products or improvements in the production of older products. Innovation involves many activities performed by different groups of people: technical research, development (the conversion of research into industrial technology through process and product designs, engineering specifications, "scaling-up," and so on), production startup (all activities necessary to begin actual production), marketing startup (all activities necessary to launch a marketing program), and market research (the identification and measurement of market opportunities for new products). Taken together, these activities and their linkages comprise the innovation system. Because of its complexity, the process of innovation is subject to numerous failures. Many research discoveries are not developed into technology, available technology may not be used to transform production functions or create new products, and new products may not succeed in the marketplace for one or more reasons.

International Transfer of Technological Innovation

Technological innovation may spread from one country to another either (1) through the transfer of technical knowledge (via licensing, trade, technical publica-

---

[22]For earlier discussions of technology in the context of international trade theory, see Chapter 5.

[23]Like all words that refer to a wide variety of phenomena, *technology* has no standard definition. In particular, the distinction between technology as knowledge and its embodiment in capital equipment, industrial processes, and products is commonly obscured by writers. The derivation of the word indicates that its essential meaning is that of a kind of knowledge.

tions, official technical assistance programs, and other forms of communication) that is then "imitated" in new production functions and new goods by local business enterprises, or (2) through the transfer of innovation by multinational enterprises that establish operations in the recipient country via direct investment.

The first mode of innovation diffusion is critically dependent on the willingness and capacity of nationals to utilize the imported technology. Nations differ widely in this regard. Japanese entrepreneurs are able to turn imported technology quickly into new products that may even be exported to the country that was the source of the technology. A well-known example was their use of transistor technology to create the transistor radio, which found its biggest market in the United States, the source of the original technology.[24] The United States itself has used European technology to produce new products in advance of the originators. Evidence indicates that imitation works less quickly in Europe than in Japan or the United States. In the developing countries, however, imitation works slowly or not at all, because they lack the industrial and entrepreneurial skills that are necessary for innovation. As the pace of innovation quickens, lags in innovation (to say nothing of complete failure) place a nation at an increasing disadvantage in international competition. The consequences of the failure of a country's nationals to imitate foreign technology (or generate their own) may be alleviated, however, by the transfer of innovation within the multinational enterprise system.

A unique contribution of the multinational enterprise is the *internationalization of the entire innovation process*. The MNE undertakes technical research, development, production startup, marketing startup, and market research on a global scale. In this way the MNE overcomes the entrepreneurial gaps that constrain the spread of innovation through imitation alone.[25]

Multinational manufacturers set up production abroad mainly to gain new markets or to hold on to markets that were first developed through direct exports. International investment strategy, then, is firmly market-oriented; the dominant consideration is the foreign market potential of products in which the company believes it has an advantage. If the investment region is highly developed, such as Western Europe or North America, most opportunities for multinational enterprises are found in new products that have not been imitated by local producers. This is why research-intensive industries are responsible for most of the U.S. direct investment in Western Europe.

When a multinational enterprise establishes operations in a new country, it does not simply duplicate its operations as they exist in the home or third countries. Adaptations to local conditions are usually necessary in production, in marketing, or in the product itself. As a company becomes more international, all the elements of its innovation system are affected by its foreign operations. When a company views itself as a single global entity, a multinational innovation system emerges that ties together research centers, production, and markets located

---

[24]A more recent example is the VCR.

[25]In contrast to entrepreneurial gaps among countries, the international mobility of technical *knowledge* is usually quite high.

throughout the world. Flows of information relating to market research, technical research, production programs, and marketing programs connect the parent company with its affiliates and connect the affiliates with each other to form one system guided by a dominant management center. In this way, each affiliate has access to both the inputs (scientific discoveries, manufacturing engineering specifications, and so on) and the outputs (new products) of the entire multinational enterprise system.

Not all multinational enterprises have fully internationalized their innovation systems. Many American multinationals still try out new products in the United States before producing them abroad, and they concentrate R & D in U.S. laboratories. But as multinational enterprises become more and more global, the innovation function is expanded, since managers perceive the advantages of tapping research brains in several countries and quickly introducing new products in many national markets. We can reasonably expect, therefore, more dispersal of corporate R & D facilities; in effect, laboratories will be taken to the research workers rather than the other way around.[26] Some multinational enterprises economize on research expense by using the small and medium-sized production facilities of their affiliates for trial runs of new products.

The Transfer of Innovation to Developing Countries

Attracted by big, dynamic markets, U.S. industry has moved mainly into Western Europe and other economically advanced areas. Nonetheless, it would be erroneous to infer that the multinational enterprise has contributed little to technological innovation in the developing countries.

As indicated earlier, the capacity of local enterprise in developing countries to imitate imported technology is generally very limited and in some instances virtually nonexistent. Thus, the transfer of technology to these countries is a necessary but insufficient condition for innovation. Unfortunately, the direct transfer of innovation by multinational enterprise is also subject to many constraints in the developing countries. Aside from restrictive government policies, which are taken up in Chapter 24, two factors especially inhibit innovation transfer: (1) small, stagnant, domestic markets, and (2) the absence of an industrial infrastructure consisting of people with technical and management skills, supporting industries, transportation, power, communications, and other services. Apart from the obvious limitations on sales potentials, small markets often require major and costly adaptations in product line and design, manufacturing, and marketing. The absence of an industrial infrastructure makes it very difficult to staff new affiliates with nationals at the technical and management levels. Furthermore, the scarcity of local suppliers of components and other production inputs forces the affiliate either to make many of its required inputs, to buy them

---

[26]The principal arguments for the centralization of R & D in the home country are the ease of coordination and the avoidance of duplication. In view of the remarkable improvements taking place in long-distance communication, these arguments are not convincing when set against the advantages of decentralization.

from abroad (when permitted by the host government), or to develop local sources of supply through technical and financial assistance.

To begin production in a developing country, therefore, multinational enterprises are usually compelled to staff the new affiliate with expatriate technical and management personnel drawn from the parent company or affiliates in other countries. This arrangement not only is costly but may run counter to the nationalistic policies of the host government. Hence, multinationals strive to "nationalize" the affiliate staff as quickly as possible through training programs at the worker, technical, and management levels. The magnitude of this effort is seldom appreciated by host governments or critics of multinational enterprise.

To sum up, the multinational enterprise takes advantage of international technology gaps in producing and marketing new products on a global scale. Although international production is the principal vehicle used by the MNE to transfer technology to host countries, it is by no means the only vehicle. The establishment of local R & D facilities, the training and education of local nationals, the use of local subcontractors and suppliers, and the introduction of advanced management practices also serve to spread technology. Furthermore, the intra-enterprise product transfers (trade) of multinational enterprises and their licensing and cross-licensing arrangements with independent foreign companies transfer technology among countries. Multinational enterprises may also indirectly stimulate innovation in host countries by creating new primary markets (for example, the market for integrated circuits in Europe), by encouraging local companies to emulate them (positive demonstration effect), and by forcing local companies to innovate to withstand competition. The pace of innovation in Western Europe during the 1960s would have been much slower in computers, specialized plastics, electronic test and measuring instruments, numerically controlled machine tools, and many other new products if American companies had not invested there. Because Western Europe has an advanced industrial society, local companies would have eventually imitated these products on their own, but more slowly than the imitation that actually took place because of the direct innovation of U.S. companies in Europe. In the 1980s, European and Japanese multinationals stepped up the pace of innovation in the United States by introducing new products such as the VCR.

TRANSFERS OF ENTREPRENEURIAL SKILLS
IN THE MULTINATIONAL ENTERPRISE SYSTEM

The international transfer of entrepreneurial skills is the distinctive (and unique) function of the multinational enterprise system.[27] Entrepreneurial managers centered in the parent company take the initiative in combining natural resources (land), capital, labor, and technology in different countries to produce goods and services for sale in local and external markets. Ordinarily much of the capital and

---

[27]We distinguish entrepreneurial skills, which innovate, from administrative skills, which direct and otherwise support the routine activities of a program or organizational unit.

all of the technology are brought into a host country by the multinational enterprise, but it is the transfer of entrepreneurial skills that truly distinguishes the MNE from other modes of capital or technology transfer, such as portfolio investment or licensing. In brief, the multinational enterprise, as its name implies, transfers *enterprise* from one country to another.

We have already anticipated the transfer of entrepreneurial skills in our discussion of technology transfer because of our emphasis on technological *innovation*. We noted that the transfer of technical knowledge (technology per se) is a communicative process and that the transfer of technological *innovation* by the MNE requires not only the transfer of technical knowledge but also the transfer of management skills to overcome entrepreneurial gaps.

The international transfer of entrepreneurial skills by the multinational enterprise is not limited to technological innovation; it serves to mobilize all the factors of production for new tasks in new markets. The key decisions that result from the exercise of entrepreneurial skills by the parent company include answers to the strategic questions presented earlier: Where in the world are the best markets? Where in the world should we manufacture our products to supply these markets? Where in the world should we undertake R & D to create new products for future markets? Where in the world should we obtain financing for our capital investments? Where in the world should we recruit the technical and managerial staff for our parent company and affiliates? In short, entrepreneurial decisions determine the structure and evolution of the entire multinational enterprise system.

Two aspects of entrepreneurial management in the multinational enterprise deserve additional comment: (1) the perception of economic opportunity, and (2) the deliberate assumption of risk.

The Perception of Economic Opportunity

Strongly oriented toward corporate growth through innovation, the managers of multinational enterprises continually search for new economic opportunities. Their "opportunity horizons" are far broader than the horizons of domestic managers; they extend into many countries and world regions. What is a dazzling opportunity to a multinational manager may not even be noticed by a domestic manager in the same industry. In general, the managers of a multinational enterprise perceive far more opportunities than managers of uninational enterprises, if only because so many of their opportunities are generated by differences among national economies. For example, a given product is seldom in the same phase of its life cycle in all countries. A product that is experiencing market saturation in the United States may be in a growth stage in, say, Western Europe and not even on the market in some developing countries. Again, local competition may be very strong in one country but moderate in another. Aside from market differences, multinational managers can take advantage of international cost differences, they can alter the patterns of specialization and exchange among affiliate companies, and, in the longer run, they can shift the country locations of production, R & D, and other activities.

The perception of economic opportunity depends not only on the horizons of managers but also on their access to information about markets, competitors, new technology, government policies, and general economic and political conditions. Hence, multinational enterprises organize "strategic intelligence" systems to gather information from sources both inside and outside the enterprise. The intelligence systems of some firms (for example, the large petroleum companies) are superior to those of most national governments. Continuous scanning of the international horizon for new opportunities is a vital entrepreneurial activity of the MNE.

The Deliberate Assumption of Risk

The perception of economic opportunity alone does not make an entrepreneur. The individual must also act to exploit the opportunity in an appropriate way. In so doing, the risks that accompany innovation must also be assumed. Multinational enterprises have demonstrated both a willingness and a capacity to assume risks in countries throughout the world.[28]

Although multinational managers ordinarily perceive far more opportunities than uninational managers, the risks involved tend to be greater. These risks may be broadly classified as *economic* and *political*. Economic risks proceed from uncertainty about demand, competition, costs, and other market conditions. They are the same in kind, if not in degree, for the multinational enterprise as for the domestic enterprise. The same, however, cannot be said of political risks. For the multinational enterprise, political risks emanate from uncertainty about political events of many kinds, such as war, revolution, coup d'état, expropriation, taxation, devaluation or revaluation, exchange controls, and import restrictions. These events are political (as opposed to economic), because they result from government actions or bear on the political authority of a nation, although they may be influenced (or even caused) by economic conditions. In addition to the economic risks of innovation, therefore, multinational enterprises must deliberately assume extraordinary political risks in performing their entrepreneurial role in the world economy.[29] The capacity of multinational enterprises to bear such risks is enormously enhanced by their great size and financial strength, their dispersal of operations in many countries, and the sophistication of their management.

THE CONTRIBUTION OF THE MULTINATIONAL ENTERPRISE TO THE WORLD ECONOMY

Does the multinational enterprise make a positive contribution to the world economy? From the perspective of liberal economic theory, the answer is certainly yes. It is instructive to repeat some statements about international trade and factor movements that were made in Chapter 5.

---

[28]In Chapter 4 we treated the subject of ignorance, uncertainty, and risk in international trade. What we said then is also pertinent to investment and the multinational enterprise.

[29]Some political risks assumed by the multinational enterprise are treated in Chapter 24.

Both trade and factor movements bring about a superior allocation of resources among nations. Trade enables a country to take advantage of international specialization in production by exporting products with low opportunity costs and importing products with high opportunity costs. International factor movements achieve a better allocation of productive agents by transferring relatively abundant factors (such as technology and entrepreneurial skills) in one country to a second country where they are relatively scarce and where they may be combined with relatively abundant factors (such as natural resources and labor) in the production of goods and services. Under conditions of perfect competition, the flow of factors would continue until their marginal productivities (and prices) were the same everywhere. Then the international allocation of factors would be optimal, because any further factor movement would lower production and consumer satisfactions for the world as a whole. Although such an optimal allocation can hardly be achieved in the world as we know it, it follows that the greater the mobility of factors among countries, the better their international allocation and the higher the efficiency of the world economy.

In light of these theoretical considerations, it is evident that the multinational enterprise system is making a major contribution to the allocative efficiency of the world economy in carrying out its role as an international transfer agent. The contribution of the MNE has been compared with the earlier role of the national corporation in building a single national economy by moving capital, technology, and entrepreneurial skills from regions of factor abundance to regions of factor scarcity. In the same way that the activities of national corporations helped to integrate regional economies into national economies, so the activities of multinational enterprises are helping to integrate national economies into a world economy.[30]

But the MNE's contribution to the static, allocative efficiency of the world economy is far less important than its contribution to the rate of innovation within that economy. The multinational enterprise is first and foremost an innovator. Through international production and trade, the MNE quickly spreads new ideas, new products, new production functions, new methods of management and organization, and other innovations on a global scale. *International innovation* defines the special contribution of the multinational enterprise; no other institution or group of institutions can match this contribution. And so, the multinational enterprise has become the preeminent agent of change in the world economy.

The positive contribution of the MNE to the world economy does not necessarily imply a positive economic contribution to each and every country, although the presumption is strong that all countries can share in the benefits of a more

---

[30]Some economists challenge the conclusion that multinational enterprises improve the allocative efficiency of the world economy on grounds that they are oligopolistic rather than purely competitive firms. Although the possible anticompetitive effects of the multinational enterprise should not be ignored, this position surely overstates the case. The national corporations that integrated regional economies into national economies were also, in essence, oligopolists. As we shall see in the next chapter, the MNE is mainly an institutional response to *exogenous* imperfections in the international markets for products (both intermediate and final) and technology.

efficient and more dynamic world economy. The economic benefits and costs of foreign direct investment for both home and host countries are explored in Chapter 24. That chapter also takes up the controversial question of the *political* costs of the multinational enterprise, which may be perceived by some host countries as outweighing any net economic benefits.

SOME EMPIRICAL DATA ON MULTINATIONAL FIRMS

Table 22-1 ranks the world's fifty largest manufacturing companies by their worldwide sales in 1985 and also indicates the percentage of each company's worldwide sales made by its foreign affiliates. This percentage underestimates the *international involvement* of these companies because it excludes any home-country exports. Exports are particularly high for Japanese and West German companies. For instance, in 1985 Toyota Motor exported $12.2 billion of motor vehicles; Matsushita, $5.3 billion of electrical equipment; Volkswagen, $8.2 billion of motor vehicles, and Hoechst, $5.0 billion of chemicals. The sales of foreign affiliates, therefore, are of products manufactured *outside* the home country, and they measure the *international production* of their parent companies, which is a distinctive feature of the multinational enterprise. Japanese and West German companies are now rapidly expanding their international production, following in the footsteps of companies headquartered in the United States, the United Kingdom, the Netherlands, and Switzerland. Not all of the top fifty manufacturing companies are multinational in an organizational or strategic sense, but all of them face competition from both domestic and foreign rivals.

Dutch and Swiss firms show the highest levels of international sales (production) through foreign affiliates (Nestle [98.1 percent] and Philips [93.6 percent]), which reflects the small size of their home-country markets. Nearly half (twenty-four) of the top fifty firms are headquartered in the United States, followed by Japan (nine) and West Germany (six).

Table 22-2 ranks the world's ten largest petroleum companies. Two observations are pertinent. First, most of the petroleum companies depend heavily on the sales (production) of foreign affiliates. With the exception of Pemex, exports of petroleum products from the home countries are comparatively small. Nippon Oil and Pemex are not true multinationals: Nippon Oil's operations are mostly confined to purchasing oil outside Japan for sale inside Japan, and Pemex's operations are mostly limited to the production and sale of oil in Mexico and the export of oil from Mexico. Second, the United States is the dominant home country (six companies), followed by the United Kingdom (two companies).

In the 1980s, many firms in *service* industries—banking, investment services, insurance, retailing, accounting, advertising, market research, law, construction, publishing, air transportation, hotel services, and others—established foreign affiliates (as sole ventures, joint ventures, or franchises) to penetrate world markets. Table 22-3 indicates the international involvement of the world's ten largest fast-food and restaurant chains. U.S. firms are the innovators in this business: *All* of the ten largest chains are headquartered in the United States.

Table 22-1 International Production of the World's Fifty Largest Manufacturing Companies, 1985 (Billions of Dollars)

Rank	Firm	Home Country	Sector	Total Worldwide Sales[1] (A)	Sales of Foreign Affiliates[2] (B)	B/A (Percent)
1.	General Motors	USA	Motor vehicles	96.4	16.2	16.8
2.	Ford Motor	USA	Motor vehicles	52.8	16.0	30.3
3.	IBM	USA	Electrical equipment	50.1	21.5	43.0
4.	E.I. du Pont	USA	Chemicals	29.5	10.4	35.8
5.	General Electric	USA	Electrical equipment	29.3	3.1	10.6
6.	Toyota Motor	JPN	Motor vehicles	28.4	1.4	5.0
7.	ENI	ITA	Chemicals	24.5	—	—
8.	Unilever	NETH-UK	Food, drink	24.2	—	—
9.	Chrysler	USA	Motor vehicles	21.3	2.5	11.7
10.	Matsushita	JPN	Electrical equipment	21.2	1.5	7.0
11.	Hitachi	JPN	Electrical equipment	21.0	2.5	12.1
12.	Siemens	FRG	Electrical equipment	18.6	4.6	24.5
13.	USX	USA	Metals	18.4	1.1	5.8
14.	Philips	NETH	Electrical equipment	18.1	16.9	93.6
15.	Volkswagen	FRG	Motor vehicles	17.8	4.2	23.4
16.	Daimler-Benz	FRG	Motor vehicles	17.8	4.1	23.0
17.	Nestle	SWI	Food, drink	17.2	16.9	98.1
18.	B.A.T.	UK	Food, drink, tobacco	16.5	14.3	86.8
19.	Philip Morris	USA	Food, drink, tobacco	16.0	4.5	28.0
20.	Bayer	FRG	Chemicals	15.6	7.9	50.6
21.	Nissan	JPN	Motor vehicles	15.2	—	—
22.	BASF	FRG	Chemicals	15.1	4.3	28.4
23.	United Technologies	USA	Aerospace	15.0	3.0	20.0
24.	Hoechst	FRG	Chemicals	14.5	5.9	40.6
25.	Mitsubishi	JPN	Industrial equipment	14.5	0.3	1.8
26.	Fiat	ITA	Motor vehicles	14.2	3.9	27.2

Table 22-1 Continued

Rank	Firm	Home Country	Sector	Total Worldwide Sales[1] (A)	Sales of Foreign Affiliates[2] (B)	B/A (Percent)
27. Toshiba	JPN	Electrical equipment		14.0	0.9	6.1
28. Imperial Chemical	UK	Chemicals		13.9	—	—
29. Boeing	USA	Aerospace		13.6	—	—
30. Renault	FRA	Motor vehicles		13.6	4.8	35.1
31. Proctor & Gamble	USA	Chemicals		13.6	3.4	25.1
32. Beatrice	USA	Food, drink		12.6	2.8	21.9
33. RJR Nabisco	USA	Food, drink, tobacco		12.4	2.7	21.4
34. Honda	JPN	Motor vehicles		12.2	1.6	13.2
35. Nippon Steel[3]	JPN	Metals		12.0	—	0.2
36. ITT	USA	Electrical equipment		11.9	6.4	54.0
37. Thyssen	FRG	Metals		11.8	4.5	38.5
38. Dow	USA	Chemicals		11.5	6.3	54.8
39. McDonnell Douglas	USA	Aerospace		11.5	2.7	23.2
40. Rockwell	USA	Aerospace		11.3	0.9	8.4
41. Peugot-Citroen	FRA	Motor vehicles		11.2	4.8	42.6
42. Westinghouse	USA	Electrical equipment		10.7	0.9	8.4
43. Eastman Kodak	USA	Photographic equipment		10.6	3.2	30.5
44. Volvo	SWE	Motor vehicles		10.0	5.0	49.6
45. NEC	JPN	Electrical equipment		9.8	0.6	6.0
46. Goodyear	USA	Rubber		9.6	3.1	32.8
47. Lockheed	USA	Aerospace		9.5	0.2	2.2
48. Allied Signal	USA	Chemicals		9.1	2.0	22.5
49. General Foods	USA	Food, drink		9.0	1.7	19.3
50. Union Carbide	USA	Chemicals		9.0	2.6	29.2

[1]Consolidated sales for the enterprise and its subsidiaries.

[2]Consolidated sales of subsidiaries and affiliates outside the home country.

[3]The sales of Nippon Steel's foreign affiliates totalled less than $100 million.

Key: FRA—France, FRG—Federal Republic of Germany, ITA—Italy, JPN—Japan, NETH—Netherlands, SWE—Sweden, SWI—Switzerland, UK—United Kingdom, and USA—United States.

Source: Derived from United Nations Center on Transnational Corporations, *Transnational Corporations in World Development* (New York: United Nations, 1988), Annex Table B1, pp. 533 ff.

Table 22-2 International Production of the World's Ten Largest Petroleum Companies in 1985 (Billions of Dollars)

Rank	Firm	Home Country	Total Worldwide Sales (A)	Sales of Foreign Affiliates (B)	B/A (Percent)
1.	Exxon	USA	86.7	59.0	68.1
2.	Royal Dutch Shell	NETH-UK	81.8	—	58.0[1]
3.	Mobil	USA	56.0	32.0	57.2
4.	British Petroleum	UK	53.1	29.2	55.4
5.	Texaco	USA	46.3	21.9	47.2
6.	Chevron	USA	43.8	13.6	31.0
7.	Nippon Oil	JPN	27.9	0.1	0.3
8.	Amoco	USA	26.9	6.0	22.2
9.	Atlantic Richfield	USA	21.7	2.1	9.8
10.	Pemex	MEX	20.4	—	—

[1]Percent for 1978.

Source: Derived from United Nations Center on Transnational Corporations, *Transnational Corporations in World Development* (New York: United Nations, 1988), Annex Table B1, pp. 533 ff.

Table 22-3 International Involvement of the World's Ten Largest Fast-Food and Restaurant Chains in 1986

Rank	Firm	Home Country	Total Worldwide Sales (Billions of Dollars)	Total Number of Units (A)	Number of Units Abroad (B)	B/A (Percent)
1.	McDonald's	USA	12.4	9,410	2,138	22.7
2.	Burger King	USA	4.5	5,024	451	8.9
3.	Kentucky Fried Chicken	USA	3.5	6,575	1,855	28.2
4.	Wendy's	USA	2.7	3,727	231	6.2
5.	Pizza Hut	USA	2.6	5,650	633	11.2
6.	Hardee's	USA	2.5	2,711	37	1.4
7.	Dairy Queen	USA	1.6	4,933	580	11.8
8.	Domino's Pizza	USA	1.5	3,608	100	2.8
9.	Taco Bell	USA	1.1	2,470	37	1.5
10.	Denny's	USA	1.1	1,176	56	4.8

Source: Derived from United Nations Center on Transnational Corporations, *Transnational Corporations in World Development* (New York: United Nations, 1988), Annex Table B17, p. 585.

SUMMARY

1. After World War II, U.S. business firms went abroad on a massive scale unprecedented in the history of international enterprise. Many industrial and service companies in Western Europe and Japan have also become multinational enterprises. Because of their vast size, the worldwide operations of multinational companies are now a decisive force in shaping the patterns of trade, investment, and technology flows among nations.

2. There is no single agreed-upon definition of the multinational enterprise. For our purposes, a multinational enterprise denotes a parent company that takes part in foreign production through its own affiliates, exercises direct control over the policies of its affiliates, and seeks to follow a worldwide strategy.

3. The manifold activities of the multinational enterprise may be usefully conceptualized as the performance of international transfer functions. The multinational enterprise becomes an international transfer agent when it moves products and factor services (capital, technology, and management) among national economies.

4. The multinational enterprise performs its role as an international transfer agent through institutional or organizational arrangements that collectively make up the multinational enterprise system. This system comprises the parent company, its foreign affiliates, and the relationships among them. The strategy decisions of the parent company generate a pattern of factor and product flows among the members of the system.

5. Intra-enterprise product transfers are the direct consequence of the strategy of the parent company. When the parent company is following a global strategy, its decisions will create some degree of horizontal and vertical integration.

6. Foreign direct investment is the transfer of a bundle of factor services that represent in their totality an extension of a business enterprise across national boundaries.

7. The international transfer of *real* capital by the MNE commonly (but not always) occurs first as a *financial* transfer of capital funds. The parent company must decide whether to obtain funds at home or abroad and whether to obtain funds from inside the enterprise or outside. The final choice of the capital-sourcing option depends on the strategy preferences of the parent company and on a variety of constraints: exchange restrictions, political risks, access to local capital sources, taxation, and capital costs. International capital transfers are *not* a necessary element of foreign direct investment, although they usually accompany it.

8. The multinational enterprise functions as an international innovation system that goes far beyond the traditional mode of international technological diffusion through local imitation. The MNE undertakes technical research, development, production startup, marketing startup, and market research on a global scale. It would appear that the multinational enterprise transfers more technology (and far more innovation) to the economies of developing countries than all the technical assistance and aid programs of governments and international agencies.

9. The international transfer of entrepreneurial skills is the distinctive (and unique) function of the multinational enterprise. Managers centered in the parent company take the initiative in combining natural resources (land), capital, labor, and technology in different countries to produce goods and services for sale in local and external markets.

10. The multinational enterprise makes a major contribution to the allocative efficiency of the world economy, but its key contribution is innovation.

QUESTIONS AND APPLICATIONS

1. (a) Identify the three elements of the definition of multinational enterprise used in this text.
   (b) Why is an international holding company that owns foreign affiliates but does not exercise active control over affiliate policies excluded from the class of multinational enterprises according to our definition?
2. (a) What are the constituent elements of the multinational enterprise system?
   (b) "The strategy decisions of the parent company generate a pattern of factor and product flows among the members of the system." Explain.
3. Describe five external constraints that may limit the integration of a multinational enterprise system.
4. (a) What is international horizontal integration? International vertical integration?
   (b) Explain the possible advantages of each form of integration to the multinational enterprise. Are there any possible disadvantages?
5. Identify and discuss five constraints on the capital-sourcing policies of MNEs.
6. "International capital transfers are not a necessary element of foreign direct investment." Explain.
7. (a) Distinguish between technology and technological innovation.
   (b) How does technological innovation spread from one country to another?
8. "A unique contribution of the multinational enterprise is the internationalization of the entire innovation process." Explain.
9. (a) What are entrepreneurial skills?
   (b) Why are the political risks assumed by multinational enterprises described as "extraordinary" in the text?
10. Prepare a short report on a multinational enterprise of your choice, indicating its products, worldwide sales, international operations, and current situation.

SELECTED READINGS

See the list of readings at the end of Chapter 23.

chapter 23

THEORIES OF FOREIGN DIRECT INVESTMENT AND THE MULTINATIONAL ENTERPRISE

This chapter examines theories advanced by economists to explain foreign direct investment (FDI) and multinational enterprise (MNE). As a background, we first offer a statistical overview of foreign direct investment.

STATISTICAL OVERVIEW OF FOREIGN DIRECT INVESTMENT

There is a notable scarcity of statistical data on the multifaceted role of the multinational enterprise in the world economy. Conventional statistics are collected by governments and international organizations mainly to measure balance of payments transactions, that is, trade, service, capital, and monetary flows between the reporting country and the rest of the world. National income accounts do not distinguish foreign-owned production from locally owned production, and foreign trade statistics do not distinguish transactions between parent companies and their affiliates or among affiliates (intra-enterprise transactions) from transactions between independent exporters and importers. As a consequence, we lack reliable data on the location, size, and composition of the foreign production carried on by MNEs, as well as on the imports and exports associated with that production. On the financial side, we have only a sketchy knowledge of the aggregate current payments and receipts, sources and uses of capital financing, and size and distribution of earnings of multinational enterprises.

Because of poor statistics, both home and host governments can only guess how the decisions of MNEs affect production, employment, money supply, prices, exports, imports, the balance of payments, and other economic sectors. Thus, they are ill-prepared to devise rational policies toward multinational companies, running the risk that their actual policies will be either ineffective or counterproductive. Better statistics would remove much of the theoretical and policy-level confusion and debate about the economic role of MNEs, although they would hardly quiet debate about the MNEs' political role. Given the economic importance of MNEs, we can expect national governments to improve their statistical coverage. In the end, however, the task will have to be taken on by an international agency, since no one government can hope to cover all the worldwide activities of multinational enterprises.[1]

Before looking at statistical data, it is desirable to define more precisely the meaning of *direct investment* and *book value.* The U.S. Department of Commerce defines foreign direct investment to include all foreign business organizations in which a U.S. person, organization, or affiliated group owns an interest of 10 percent or more.[2] The dollar values of foreign direct investments are the values carried on the books of the U.S. parent companies. The *book value* of an investment is its value at the time the investment was made; thus, it is a "historical" value that is not adjusted to changes in price levels. Since worldwide inflation has been common since the 1960s, the book values of direct investments made some years ago badly understate their current replacement values. The market value of U.S. direct investment abroad is almost certainly substantially higher than the reported book value.

Year-to-year increases in the book value of U.S. foreign direct investment are the net result of (1) the outflow of new capital from the United States, (2) new issues of securities sold abroad by U.S. companies to finance capital expenditures abroad (but not securities issued by their foreign affiliates or short-term borrowing abroad), (3) reinvested earnings of foreign affiliates, and (4) valuation of adjustments (which are mostly associated with liquidations of existing holdings).

Foreign affiliates of parent companies that are organized as foreign corporations are commonly called *subsidiaries;* foreign affiliates may also be organized as *branches* that parent companies use to conduct business in their own names and always have full ownership of. Unless there are special tax advantages for a branch, parent companies generally organize their affiliates as separate corporations. For this reason we shall at times use *subsidiary* as a substitute for *affiliate.*

Rising Importance of Foreign Direct Investment

Foreign direct investment is growing faster than world gross domestic product and world trade. Figure 23-1 depicts the growth relationship between exports and FDI.

Since the early 1980s, FDI outflows have grown three times faster than exports and four times faster than world output. This rising importance of FDI in the international economy reflects several factors, including the adoption of global strategies by more firms, the efforts of countries to attract investment from abroad, and continuing improvements in global communications networks. By the end of

---

[1]The Center on Transnational Corporations at the United Nations now compiles statistics on multinational corporations.

[2]U.S. Department of Commerce, *U.S. Direct Investment Abroad,* 1982 Benchmark Survey Data (Washington, D.C.: U.S. Government Printing Office, December 1985), p. 2. Other industrial countries use a similar definition. See Chapter 14 for an earlier definition of foreign direct investment as investment in enterprises located in one country but effectively controlled by residents of another country.

Figure 23-1

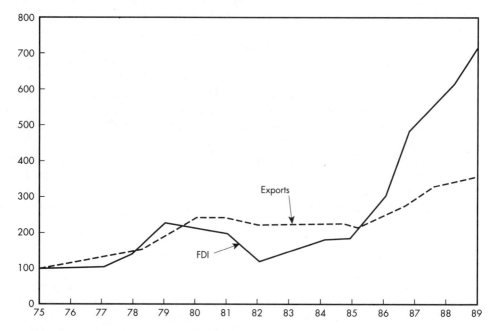

Source: United Nations Center on Transnational Corporations, *World Investment Report: The Triad in Foreign Direct Investment* (New York: United Nations 1991), Figure 1, p. 5.

Index of Foreign Direct Investment Outflows and the Current Value of Exports, 1975–1989 (1975 = 100). Over the 1975–1985 period as a whole, FDI outflows and world exports grew at about the same rate. But since 1985, the growth rate of FDI outflows has spurted ahead of the export growth rate.

the 1980s, the worldwide stock of FDI reached $1.5 trillion, and it was growing at almost $200 billion a year.[3]

Foreign Direct Investment Outflows of Principal Investing Countries

Table 23-1 shows the direct investment outflows of the five biggest investing countries that accounted for 69.1 percent of the world's direct investment over the period 1985–1989. The industrial countries as a group generated most of the world's direct investment. The small share of the developing countries is growing, owing mainly to newly industrializing countries (NICs) such as South Korea, Taiwan, Hong Kong, and Singapore.

---

[3]United Nations Center for Transnational Corporations, *World Investment Report: The Triad in Foreign Direct Investment* (New York: United Nations, 1991), p. 3.

Table 23-1   Average Annual Foreign Direct Investment Outflows by Major Industrial Countries, 1975–1980, 1981–1985, and 1985–1989 (Percentage)

Country	1975–1980	1980–1984	1985–1989
France	4.5	6.0	8.0
Germany	7.7	7.4	7.8
Japan[1]	5.5	8.9	18.8
United Kingdom	17.4	19.4	20.2
United States[2]	42.4	28.1	14.3
Total	*77.5*	*69.8*	*69.1*
All industrial countries	*98.8*	*98.4*	*96.8*
All developing countries	*1.2*	*1.6*	*3.2*
All countries	*100.0*	*100.0*	*100.0*
Total FDI in billions of dollars	$40.3	$45.3[a]	$126.4

[1]Data for Japan do not include reinvested earnings.

[2]Excludes outflows to the finance (except banking), insurance, and real estate sectors of the Netherlands Antilles. Also excludes currency translation adjustments.

[a]1981–1985.

Source: United Nations Center on Transnational Corporations, *Transnational Corporation in World Development: Trends and Prospects* (New York: United Nations, 1988), Table V2, p. 77; and *World Investment Report: The Triad in Foreign Direct Investment* (New York: United Nations, 1991), Table 3, p. 10.

The role of the United States as a direct investor has diminished greatly, dropping from 42.4 percent of the world's average annual outflow of direct investment during the 1975–1980 period to 14.3 percent during the 1985–1989 period. In contrast, Japan's share of the world's direct investment outflows more than tripled between these periods. In the 1985–1989 period, the United States ranked third behind the United Kingdom and Japan in average annual outflows.

The dollar value of annual foreign direct investment outflows grew strongly in the 1980s, rising from an average of $45.3 billion in the first half of that decade to $126.4 billion in the second half.

The Growing Share of Services in Foreign Direct Investment

Table 23-2 depicts a rising share of services in the foreign direct investment outflows of the principal investing countries.

What explains this rising importance of services? Several factors are at work. Services have become the largest sector in the world economy, and many services, such as telecommunications, are undergoing massive transformations through technological innovation. Because many services are not tradable like merchandise, MNEs rely more heavily on foreign direct investment to establish production

Table 23-2   Percentage Shares of Services in the Foreign Direct Investment Outflows of Major Industrial Countries, 1981–1984 and 1985–1989

Country	1981–1985	1985–1989
France	41	49
Germany	55	64[a]
Japan	61	73
United Kingdom	35	38[a]
United States	52	57

[a]1985–1988.

Source: Derived from United Nations Center on Transnational Corporations, *World Investment Report: The Triad in Foreign Direct Investment* (New York: United Nations, 1991), Table 6, p. 16.

of their services in foreign markets. Another factor is the liberalization by countries of their service sectors to attract multinational firms. Finally, the growing prominence of service FDI reflects intense competition among multinationals to exploit foreign market opportunities in financial and business services, wholesaling, retailing, tourism, air transportation, construction, and other services.

The internationalization of services through FDI is at an early stage. The growth in demand for services by business firms and households continues to outpace the growth of merchandise demand. Further liberalization of the service sector (including telecommunications, transportation, and public utilities) will stimulate more investment. Also, the dramatic growth in transborder data transmissions is making it possible to produce some services (such as computer software and data processing) in one location for consumption in another location.

The Triad Countries in Foreign Direct Investment

The global pattern of FDI is *tripolar,* centering on the United States, the European Community, and Japan. Known as the *Triad,* these three countries accounted for more than three-fourths of the world's average annual outward flow of FDI and about two-thirds of its inward flow over the period 1985–1989[4] (see Table 23-3). Moreover, a growing share of FDI is concentrating in the triad. The triad countries also account for about one-half of world *trade.*[5] The combined gross domestic product of the triad in 1987 was $11 trillion (two-thirds of world GDP) allocated as follows: United States — 26 percent, European Community — 25 percent, and Japan — 14 percent.

---

[4]For the sake of convenience we refer to the triad as comprising three "countries." As we know, the EC embraces twelve independent countries forming a common market.

[5]For trade among the three poles more broadly defined as OECD Europe, North America, and East Asia, see Table 1-3 in Chapter 1.

Table 23-3 Average Annual Outward and Inward FDI Flows of the Triad Countries, 1985–1989 (Billions of Dollars)

Country	Outward Flow	Inward Flow
European Community[1]	39	19
United States	18	46
Japan	24	*
Triad	*81*	*65*
World[1]	105	100
Triad as percent of world	*77.1*	*65.0*

[1]Excludes intra-EC foreign direct investment.

*Negligible.

Note: The data for Japan and several European countries do not include reinvested profits. The data for the EC do not include Ireland, Greece, and Luxembourg.

Source: Adapted from United Nations Center on Transnational Corporations, *World Investment Report: The Triad in Foreign Direct Investment* (New York: United Nations, 1991), Table 10, p. 32.

Several shifts occurred within the triad during the 1980s. The United States declined as a home country but became the major host country, receiving $46 billion of the triad's average annual $65 billion inward flow of direct investment during the period 1985–1989. The EC became the leading home country. A third shift relates to Japan. Japan's outward flow of FDI exploded in the 1980s to surpass that of the United States. At the same time, inward flows of FDI to Japan were modest. This imbalance prompted protests from the United States and the EC charging that Japan maintains barriers against foreign multinational firms.

Figure 23-2 illustrates the total FDI stocks in 1988 that each triad member had in the others. Stocks are the cumulative totals of all previous FDI flows. As such, they reveal the structure of international production among the triad countries. Evidently, the most important FDI relationship is between the United States and the EC. As of 1988, the United States had invested $131.1 billion in the EC; the EC had invested $193.9 billion in the United States. The imbalance between Japan as a home country and a host country is striking. By 1988, Japan had invested $53.4 billion in the United States and $12.5 billion in the EC. In contrast, the United States had invested $17.9 billion and the EC only $1.7 billion in Japan.

Linkages Between Foreign Direct Investment and International Trade

The relationship between international production (FDI) and international trade is complex because international production can both *replace* trade (substitution effect) and *create* trade (expansion effect).[6] Which effect predominates depends on

---

[6]International trade and factor movements as both substitutes and complements are discussed in Chapter 5.

Figure 23-2

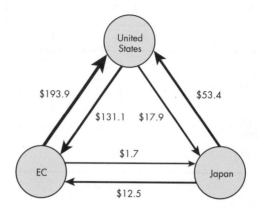

Source: Adapted from United Nations Center on Transnational Corporations, *World Investment Report: The Triad in Foreign Direct Investemnt* (New York: United Nations 1991), Figure II, p. 40.

Intra-Triad Foreign Direct Investment: Outward Stocks in 1988 (Billions of Dollars). This figure shows the stock (book value) of FDI of each member country in the other two in 1988. The most important FDI relationship is between the United States and the European Community. The United States has become the major FDI *host* country and the European Community the major FDI *home* country. Japan is much more important as a home country than a host country.

the specific context of an investment venture. For instance, when an MNE sets up production in a foreign country in response to actual or prospective trade barriers that threaten its exports, then it may replace trade. This may be true of Japanese investments in the United States in automobiles and consumer electronics. But the substitution effect is not certain even in those cases, because if export markets would have been lost anyway, then FDI is *not* replacing them. The expansion effects of FDI occur in nontradable services where local production is the only way to enter a foreign market. Also, multinational enterprises expand trade when they invest abroad to build up horizontally and vertically integrated systems, as described in Chapter 22. Whether or not FDI replaces or creates trade in specific instances, it is indisputable that MNEs are responsible for much of international trade.

Table 23-4 indicates that the U.S. affiliates (subsidiaries) of foreign MNEs and the foreign affiliates of U.S. MNEs account for about half of U.S. exports and imports. Actually, this impressive fraction understates the importance of MNEs in trade. When the exports of the U.S. parent companies (that is, the U.S. companies that own the foreign affiliates) are taken into account, then multinationals undertake at least 80 percent of U.S. trade.[7] It is also noteworthy that over one-third of

---

[7]See United Nations Center for Transnational Corporations, *World Investment Report,* p. 69.

Table 23-4 Percentage of U.S. Merchandise Exports and Imports Attributable to U.S. Affiliates of Foreign MNEs and Foreign Affiliates of U.S. MNEs in 1987

	U.S. Exports	U.S. Imports
U.S. affiliates of foreign MNEs	19.2	35.0
Foreign affiliates of U.S. MNEs	31.5	18.5
All MNEs	50.7	53.5
Intrafirm transactions of all MNEs	*34.4*	*41.2*

Source: Derived from United Nations Center on Transnational Corporations, *World Investment Report, The Triad in Foreign Direct Investment* (New York: United Nations, 1991), Table 12, p. 70.

U.S. exports and imports are intrafirm transactions between parent companies and their affiliates.[8]

To conclude, the impact of FDI on international trade is pervasive. MNEs hold substantial shares of world trade, particularly in technology-intensive products. Massive international flows of trade, technology, and long-term capital are generated by MNE investment in international production, which, in turn, is responsive to MNE strategies. In sum, multinational corporations are becoming ever more dominant in the world economy.

REQUIREMENTS FOR A THEORY OF FOREIGN DIRECT INVESTMENT

Foreign direct investment is the distinctive feature of multinational enterprise. Hence, a theory of foreign direct investment is also a theory of the multinational enterprise as an actor in the world economy.[9] As described in Chapter 22, foreign direct investment is not simply (or even primarily) an international transfer of capital but rather the *extension of an enterprise* from its home country into a foreign host country. The extension of enterprise involves flows of capital, technology, and entrepreneurial skills to the host economy, where they are combined with local factors in the production of goods for local or export markets. This transfer of a "bundle" of factor services remains under the control of the investing (parent) firm, as do the subsequent production and marketing activities of its subsidiary in the host country. Commonly, the transfer of factor services is accompanied by exports from the parent company of *intermediate* goods that are inputs in the subsidiary's production process or by exports of *final* goods channeled through the subsidiary's marketing facilities. In view of the nature of foreign direct investment, therefore, it

---

[8]Intra-industry trade (which includes intrafirm trade) is treated in Chapter 4.

[9]As an *economic* theory, a theory of foreign direct investment would not, of course, seek to explain *all* facets of the multinational enterprise; it would ignore internal management processes as well as political and sociocultural factors.

is evident that a theory of foreign direct investment should be, first and foremost, a theory of international business enterprise.

What are the requirements, then, of a theory of foreign direct investment? Such a theory should answer three fundamental questions:

1. Why do firms go abroad as direct investors?
2. How can direct-investing firms compete successfully with local firms, given the inherent advantage of local firms operating in a familiar business environment?
3. Why do firms choose to enter foreign countries as producers rather than as exporters or licensors?

In answering these questions, a theory of foreign direct investment should also throw light on the following related questions:

4. Why is foreign direct investment dominated by large firms in oligopolistic markets?
5. Why does foreign direct investment occur in some industries and not in others?
6. Why does "reverse investment" occur at both country and industry levels (for example, when U.S. firms make direct investments in European countries and at the same time European firms make direct investments in the United States, usually in the same industries as well)?
7. Why are only a few countries the source of most foreign direct investment in the world?

Unlike trade theory, which stretches back at least to Adam Smith, foreign direct investment theory is a new domain for international economists. This is not surprising, because the contemporary scope of foreign direct investment and multinational enterprise is mainly owing to developments since World War II. Although economists are now busily engaged in theory building, as yet no single dominant theory of foreign direct investment has emerged to match the Heckscher-Ohlin model of international trade.[10] Instead we have several theories, but we shall discover that, for the most part, they are complementary rather than rival explanations of foreign direct investment.

THE THEORY
OF INTERNATIONAL PORTFOLIO INVESTMENT

Conventional economic theory has relied on a model of portfolio investment to explain the international movement of capital as a factor of production. This

---

[10]However, as we saw in Chapter 3, the H-O model has come under attack from new theories of international trade, making its continued dominance highly questionable. Today both trade and investment theory are in intellectual ferment for much the same reason: The multinational enterprise (foreign direct investment) not only calls for explanation but has also undermined the assumptions of conventional trade theory.

theory postulates interest-rate differences among countries as the cause of international capital movements. Capital moves from country A to country B because the long-term interest rate (return on capital) is higher in country B than in country A, reflecting the comparative abundance of capital in the latter. Capital continues to move from country A to country B until interest rates are equal and the marginal product of capital in the two countries is the same.

This theory may be depicted in terms of the simple formula for capitalizing a stream of earnings, $C = Y/i$, where C is the value of a capital asset, Y is the stream of income produced by the asset, and i is the rate of interest.[11] Then capital moves from country A to country B when the value of an asset is higher in country A than in country B for the *same* income stream. Investors in country A will purchase the lower-priced asset in country B. This theory offers a good explanation of international movements of portfolio capital and short-term capital when account is taken of foreign exchange and other risks.[12]

But is a difference in i between two countries a good explanation of foreign direct investment? Do multinational enterprises establish foreign affiliates because they expect to earn higher rates of return on the same assets than at home? Or do they invest abroad because they expect to earn a higher income on the same assets than do local companies in the host country, the cost of capital (i) being the same for both?

Statistical data do not support the hypothesis that rates of return on foreign direct investment are higher than rates of return on home investment, particularly when the higher risks of foreign investment are taken into account. Sometimes they are, sometimes they are not. Nor can the country distribution of U.S. foreign direct investment be explained by yield differences between host countries and the United States.

The second hypothesis, that multinational enterprises expect to earn a higher income (Y) than local competitors, appears to be a better explanation. It is consistent with the observed fact that multinational enterprises must assume many costs of international business that are not assumed by local companies. They must overcome barriers imposed by distance, time, information gaps, nationality, culture, and other aspects of a foreign environment that are not experienced by uninational firms. These higher costs must be offset by higher incomes than are earned by local competitors. To earn a higher income, the multinational enterprise must possess advantages over local competitors that derive from its superior technology, its entrepreneurial and other management skills, and its worldwide organization.[13]

The hypothesis that foreign direct investment occurs because of differences in

---

[11]The more elaborate formula discounts the stream of earnings for futurity to obtain its present value. The simple formula indicates that if an asset *permanently* generates an annual income of, say, $100, then it is worth $2,000 when capitalized at an interest rate of 5 percent.

[12]See the discussion of forward rates of exchange in Chapter 13.

[13]This is not to deny that large multinational enterprises may have better credit ratings than local companies, enabling them to raise capital funds more inexpensively. But local companies do not *necessarily* have lower credit ratings than multinational enterprises.

Y rather than differences in i is also consistent with the acquisition of local companies by multinational enterprises. Why should the MNE be willing to pay more for a company than local investors? The most plausible answer is that the MNE expects to earn higher profits (a higher Y) from the acquired company than do local investors. Furthermore, this hypothesis is consistent with the observed fact that European MNEs invest in the United States at the same time that American MNEs in the same industry are investing in Europe. Both sets of companies believe that they can compete effectively in each other's territory.

To conclude, the theory of international portfolio investment cannot adequately explain foreign direct investment. Indeed, by assuming perfect competition, this theory rules out *any* foreign direct investment. In perfectly competitive markets, local firms could buy the technology and other skills available to nonlocal firms. Hence, international firms possessing no advantages over local firms would have no incentive to produce abroad: They would incur costs of doing business abroad (not incurred by local firms) that would *not* be offset by higher sales revenues. In that kind of world, capital would move through international capital markets rather than through the mediation of the international firm, as occurs with foreign direct investment. It follows that an explanation of foreign direct investment must be found in departures from perfect competition (what the economist calls "market imperfections" or "market failure") that give the direct-investing firm one or more competitive advantages over local firms.

We now turn to three contemporary theories of foreign direct investment that agree on the importance of market imperfections but offer different approaches: the monopolistic advantage theory, the internalization theory, and the eclectic paradigm.

THE MONOPOLISTIC ADVANTAGE THEORY OF FOREIGN DIRECT INVESTMENT

The monopolistic advantage theory postulates that the investing firm possesses monopolistic advantages that enable it to operate subsidiaries abroad more profitably than local competing firms.[14] These advantages are specific to the firm rather than to its production locations. The advantages are owned by the firm and are not available to other firms on the open market. Hence, direct investment belongs more to the theory of industrial organization than to the theory of international capital movements. The monopolistic advantages of the investing firm fall into two broad categories: superior knowledge and economies of scale.

In presenting the monopolistic advantage theory of foreign direct investment, we distinguish between *horizontal foreign investment* and *vertical foreign investment*.

---

[14]The first systematic presentation of this theory was made by Hymer in his doctoral dissertation in 1960. (Stephen H. Hymer, *The International Operations of National Firms* [Cambridge: MIT Press, 1976]). An early statement of the theory appeared in Charles P. Kindleberger, *American Business Abroad* (New Haven, Conn.: Yale University Press, 1969), Chapter 1.

Horizontal foreign investment occurs when the investing company enters foreign countries to produce the same product or products that are produced at home. It represents, therefore, a geographical diversification of the company's product line. In contrast, vertical investment occurs when the investing company enters foreign countries to produce intermediate goods that are intended for use as inputs in its domestic production process (backward vertical integration) or to produce or market its products at later stages closer to the final buyer (forward vertical integration). Backward vertical integration is particularly associated with extractive investment in petroleum and minerals, whereas most forward integration is associated with exporting, such as the establishment of an assembly plant or a sales branch. Product transfers within the multinational enterprise system based on horizontal and vertical investment are depicted in Figures 22-2 and 22-3 in Chapter 22.[15]

Two versions of the monopolistic advantage theory (superior knowledge and product life cycle) focus on horizontal investment, while a third version (oligopoly) focuses on vertical investment.

Superior Knowledge

Superior knowledge includes all *intangible* skills possessed by the firm that give it a competitive advantage wherever it undertakes operations: technology, management and organization skills, marketing skills, and the like. Monopolistic advantage derives from the firm's *control* over the use of its knowledge assets, which are transformed into differentiated products. All knowledge assets have the character of *public goods* in that the marginal cost of exploiting them through foreign direct investment is zero or very small relative to their returns. This is so because at any time the cost to the investing firm of acquiring its knowledge assets has already been incurred sometime in the past (sunk cost) and also because the supply of its knowledge assets is highly elastic (approaching infinity in some instances), since their use in one country does not preclude their use in another country.[16] Although the *marginal* cost of exploiting its knowledge assets in a foreign country is very low for the investing firm, local firms would need to invest the *full cost* to acquire similar assets.

The possession of superior knowledge allows the investing firm to create *differentiated products* with physical differences (deriving from technology skills) or with psychological differences (deriving from marketing skills) that distinguish them from competing products. In this way the firm gains a degree of control over product prices and sales that enables it to obtain an *economic rent* on its knowledge

---

[15] *Conglomerate foreign investment* is investment abroad to manufacture products *not* manufactured by the parent company. It is comparatively rare, occurring mainly as an unintended consequence of foreign acquisitions. For that reason, it will not be discussed here.

[16] Nor in a multiproduct firm does the use of knowledge assets for one product preclude their use for other products. Multinational enterprises engaged in horizontal foreign investment are overwhelmingly multiproduct firms.

assets.[17] In brief, the investing firm with differentiated products controls knowledge that can be transferred to foreign markets at little or no cost.[18]

The monopolistic advantage theory indicates that horizontal foreign direct investment will be undertaken mainly by the more knowledge-intensive industries. This is confirmed by empirical data. Technology-intensive industries (such as petroleum refining, pharmaceuticals, industrial chemicals, farm machinery, office machinery, and transportation equipment) are the biggest source of U.S. direct investment abroad. But industries with high-level marketing skills, such as convenience food and cosmetic industries, are also prominent direct investors abroad. The examples of Coca-Cola and Pepsi-Cola illustrate this point. On the other hand, the U.S. steel and textile industries, which are not knowledge-intensive, are notably absent from horizontal foreign direct investment despite the large size of many companies in those industries.

Product Life Cycle

Vernon's product life cycle model, which was described in Chapter 5, combines both trade and direct investment. Here we offer a few additional comments on this model, highlighting its investment features.[19]

By adding a *time* dimension to the theory of monopolistic advantage, the product life cycle model helps explain why U.S. manufacturers shift from exporting to foreign direct investment. The model asserts that U.S. manufacturers initially gain a monopolistic export advantage from product innovations developed for the U.S. market. In the *product introduction* stage (when production is not yet standardized and changes in design, production processes, and marketing require intimate contacts with research and development specialists, suppliers, and customers), production continues to be concentrated in the United States even though production costs in some foreign countries may be lower. However, when the product becomes standardized in its *product growth* phase, then the U.S. manufacturer has an incentive to invest abroad to exploit lower costs of manufacture and, more important, to prevent the loss of the export market to local producers. The U.S. manufacturer's first investment will be made in another industrial country where export sales are large enough to support economies of scale in local production. According to this model, then, U.S. horizontal foreign investment is essentially *defensive*—to hold on to markets built up through exports.

The monopolistic advantage of the U.S. manufacturer who first introduces a new product erodes over time. First, rival U.S. firms imitate (and sometimes improve on) the product; later, independent foreign firms imitate it. To sustain

---

[17]*Economic rent* is, for any factor, the return over and above its opportunity cost. Because the investing firm cannot control its knowledge assets indefinitely (since they eventually will be matched by competitors), their return is more precisely defined as a *quasi-rent* that will disappear over the long run.

[18]For an elaboration of this point from the perspective of industrial economics, see Richard E. Caves, "International Corporations: The Industrial Economics of Foreign Investment." *Economica,* February 1971, pp. 1-27.

[19]For Vernon's description of his model, see Raymond Vernon, *Sovereignty At Bay* (New York: Basic Books, 1971), pp. 64-112.

the viability of the foreign subsidiary, therefore, the U.S. manufacturer must delay product imitation with patent protection, product improvements, advertising, or new products. Since competition is mainly cost competition in the *product maturity* and *decline* phases, the U.S. manufacturer may also shift production from the country of the initial foreign investment to a lower-cost country, sustaining the old subsidiary with new products.

The product life cycle model was designed to explain U.S. exports and foreign direct investment in differentiated manufactured products. Thus, it cannot explain foreign direct investment by firms in other countries or the phenomenon of cross-investment. In the 1950s and early 1960s, the assumption that product innovations were first developed for the U.S. market and subsequently transferred to foreign markets via exports and foreign direct investment was justified by the overwhelming predominance of U.S. horizontal foreign investment. Over the last quarter-century, however, this assumption has been vitiated by the rise of European and Japanese MNEs. Our statistical overview offered abundant evidence that firms in other industrial countries (and also in newly industrializing countries) are now able to exploit monopolistic advantages through foreign direct investment in the United States and elsewhere.

The life cycle model is most relevant to manufacturers' *initial* entries into foreign markets as direct investors. However, by the same token, it loses relevance to multinational enterprises that have international production and marketing systems already in place. These global corporations are capable of developing new products abroad for subsequent sale in the United States, thereby standing the product life cycle model on its head. Or they can transfer new products from the United States directly to their existing foreign subsidiaries, thereby skipping the export stage. Although the United States remains the principal market and source of new products for U.S.-based multinational enterprises, their worldwide information and logistical systems (described in Chapter 22) create a pattern of investments and product transfers that bear little resemblance to the pattern postulated by the life cycle model. The inability of the model to explain the investment behavior of multinational corporations is recognized by Vernon.[20]

A final observation. In explaining why U.S. manufacturers invest abroad, the product life cycle theory suggests an answer to the question raised previously: Why are only a few countries, notably the triad, the source of most foreign direct investment in the world? Although knowledge assets are firm-specific and, once created, may be transferred easily by a firm to other countries, a firm cannot create knowledge assets out of thin air. In the first instance, it depends on its home-country economy for the inputs necessary for their creation: scientists, engineers, managers, marketing specialists, and other human factors. A firm also needs a high-income, sophisticated domestic market for the early exploitation of its knowledge assets. As we discussed in Chapter 3, the availability of skill-intensive human factors is concentrated in a comparatively few countries, namely, the

---

[20]Raymond Vernon, "The Product Cycle Hypothesis in a New International Environment," *Oxford Bulletin of Economics and Statistics* (November 1979), pp. 255–67.

industrial countries and NICs. The same is true of high-income markets. It follows, therefore, that firms with knowledge assets are also concentrated in a small number of advanced countries and, as the monopolistic advantage theory demonstrates, these firms are the principal source of foreign direct investment.

Oligopoly

Foreign direct investors are, for the most part, big firms in oligopolistic industries characterized by only a few dominant members whose products may be differentiated or the same. Because the dominant members are so few (commonly eight or fewer), each of them is very sensitive to the competitive moves of the others. This *interdependence* among oligopolistic firms in the same industry is the essence of oligopoly; it is the source of distinctive oligopolistic behavior.[21]

When an oligopolistic firm acts to obtain a competitive advantage by introducing a new product, entering a new market, or acquiring a new source of raw materials, then rival firms are forced to respond with counteractions. Not to do so would risk the loss of market position or growth to the advantage of the initiating firm. Indeed, the primary objective of oligopolistic firms appears to be *growth* (subject to a minimum profit constraint) rather than profit maximization. At the very least, each firm wants to grow as rapidly as rival firms; its *relative* rate of growth determines its relative size, which in turn determines its *relative* market power. For that reason, an oligopolistic firm is extremely sensitive to actions of rival firms that threaten its market share. A fall in market share is viewed with alarm even when the total market is expanding so rapidly that the firm's *absolute* profits and sales are rising. Equilibrium in an oligopolistic market exists, therefore, only when there is stability in the market shares of rival firms.[22]

Oligopolistic firms obtain monopoly profits (economic rent) because of entry barriers that keep new firms out of the industry. Common entry barriers are internal economies of scale that require large, lumpy investments of capital to be matched by newcomers; the control over scarce or low-cost raw material supplies through vertical integration; differentiated products; and knowledge assets, such as patents, trademarks, and brand names. In most manufacturing sectors, oligopolies are *heterogeneous,* producing differentiated products, and they derive monopoly profits partly from knowledge assets in the way described and partly from other entry barriers. However, oligopolies in basic manufacturing and natural resource industries (for example, steel, petroleum, and aluminum) are *homogeneous,* with member firms producing the same, nondifferentiated commodity. In the absence of superior knowledge, these industries must rely on other entry barriers to sustain monopoly profits, notably internal economies of scale and vertical integration.

---

[21]For an earlier discussion of oligopoly in the context of international trade theory, see Chapter 4.

[22]Competitive moves and countermoves frequently disrupt market equilibrium. To avoid price wars that hurt all members of the industry, oligopolostic firms try to maintain "market order" by implicit agreement to compete only in product differentiation, advertising, new market entry, and other forms of nonprice competition. Unless prevented by governments, oligopolists are inclined to replace implicit agreements with active collusion, including formal cartels.

What are the implications of oligopolistic behavior for foreign direct investment? We discuss them in terms of oligopolistic reaction, internal economies of scale, and vertical foreign investment.

Oligopolistic Reaction   Assume two firms, A and B, are members of an oligopolistic industry. Both firms are exporting their similar but differentiated products to country Y. Now suppose A establishes a manufacturing subsidiary in country Y. A's aggressive move is threatening to B for one or more reasons: (1) A's subsidiary in country Y could take market share away from B's exports because it can manufacture at a lower cost or mount a stronger marketing effort. If A has entered country Y on the condition that the host government impose import restrictions to create a protected market, then B is threatened with the loss of its entire export market. (2) If A's subsidiary in country Y is intended to be a key element in A's global enterprise system, either through integration in marketing or in production, then A could gain a worldwide competitive advantage over B. (3) Finally, and most threatening, A could obtain through its subsidiary in country Y (which may be an acquired local firm) new capabilities in technology, products, human skills, and knowledge that would enable A to upset the competitive equilibrium of the industry at home and abroad, leaving B and other rivals at a competitive disadvantage.

How should B counter A's investment in country Y? It could pursue any of several strategy options, but its most probable strategy would be to match A's investment in country Y with its own investment in that country. By keeping even with A, B can counter all the threats to its market position. This is a *risk-minimizing* strategy, akin to buying insurance, because the cost of B's investment is far more predictable than the consequences of not matching A's investment. B will, therefore, invest in country Y even if prospective returns are low, because in that event they are presumably also low for A.

The effect of this oligopolistic reaction is a "bunching" or entry concentration of foreign investments in a country by members of an oligopolistic industry. Sometimes called the "bandwagon effect," oligopolistic reaction appears to explain why many U.S. companies in the same industry have made investments in the same foreign country within a short period of time.

In a pioneer study, Knickerbocker investigated the effects of oligopolistic reaction on U.S. foreign direct investment in manufacturing.[23] Using a sample of 187 large U.S. corporations in twelve SIC two-digit industries and in twenty-three foreign countries, he found that almost half of the foreign manufacturing subsidiaries established by the sample corporations during the period 1948–1967 in any given industry and country were established in a three-year peak cluster and that three-fourths were established in a seven-year cluster. He also found that entry concentration was positively related to industry concentration but negatively related to product diversity. Wide-product-line firms were less likely to match a

---

[23]Frederick T. Knickerbocker, *Oligopolistic Reaction and Multinational Enterprise* (Boston: Harvard University Graduate School of Business Administration, 1973).

rival's foreign investment than narrow-product-line firms, because the former had a variety of ways to compete in foreign markets.

To sum up, oligopolistic reaction appears to explain the bunching of foreign investments that causes a rapid proliferation of subsidiaries in a foreign country by members of an oligopolistic industry. However, since it deals only with *defensive* investment behavior, oligopolistic reaction does not explain why a firm makes the *first* investment in a foreign country.

Internal Economies of Scale in Production   Oligopoly is fostered by economies of scale that allow a few companies to supply an entire market. Can the economies of scale enjoyed by an oligopolistic firm become a source of monopolistic advantage over local firms and, therefore, an explanation of foreign direct investment? We have already noted that economies of scale are associated with the exploitation of knowledge assets specific to the firm so that successive foreign investments are less costly than the initial one. But here we are speaking of economies of scale in physical production. Apart from knowledge assets, do internal economies of scale in production help explain foreign direct investment?[24]

In a two-country model, monopolistic advantages from scale economies in production are dependent on the investing firm's having a preferential access to capital in terms of both availability and cost. Although direct investors may indeed have greater access to capital than local firms in the developing countries (especially for large-scale, lumpy investments in natural resource industries), this is not generally true of local firms in foreign industrial countries. After all, large firms in Western Europe and Japan can obtain capital as easily as their counterparts in the United States. Such firms can match the economies of scale in production of a foreign firm that enters their home country. Thus, in a two-country model, internal economies in production do not offer a systemic explanation of foreign direct investment.

When we move from a two-country to a multicountry or world model, internal economies of scale assume a new importance. Through horizontal or vertical integration, the multinational enterprise can benefit from production economies that cannot be matched by local, nonmultinational firms. For example, suppose multinational enterprise A allocates the manufacture of a single product in its product line to its subsidiary in country Y for sale in multicountry markets. If the size of the domestic market in country Y is not sufficient to support optimal-size plants, then local firms will be operating suboptimal-size plants.[25] But A's subsidiary will have an optimal-size plant because it is geared not only to sales in country Y but also to sales in other markets through A's other subsidiaries. As a result, A's subsidiary will have lower unit costs of production than local firms, giving it a competitive advantage in the local market. More generally, economies of scale

---

[24]As we saw in Chapter 4, internal economies of scale in production can serve as a basis for international trade.

[25]This statement deserves some qualification. A local firm in a small domestic market might achieve optimal plant size through exports. But given the risks of exporting and the presence of import restrictions, most firms build plants scaled to the domestic market size.

(and scope) through international specialization of production in many products and in many countries can give the multinational enterprise a competitive advantage in world markets (including the home country), apart from advantages in locating production in the least-cost countries. In effect, the multinational enterprise can escape the limits imposed on economies of scale by country market size more effectively through intra-enterprise product transfers than can the non-multinational enterprise through exports to independent foreign buyers.

Vertical Foreign Investment   Vertical foreign investment is a prominent trait of homogeneous oligopolies in basic manufacturing and natural resources. U.S. companies in steel, aluminum, copper, and petroleum have all invested abroad to acquire sources of raw materials. Why this backward integration into raw material sources? Why not obtain needed raw materials from independent foreign producers? The answers appear to be five: (1) sheer necessity, (2) the avoidance of oligopolistic uncertainty, (3) oligopolistic reaction, (4) the erection of entry barriers to new rivals, and (5) the technical advantages of vertical integration.

When prospective supplies of raw materials are running short and local foreign firms are not capable of discovering and exploiting new sources, an oligopolistic *industry* may be compelled to invest abroad. At the level of the oligopolistic firm, this motive may be accompanied by a desire to gain a competitive advantage over rival firms. Sheer necessity is at least a partial explanation of vertical foreign investments in the developing countries.

When the number of sources of a raw material is small and their exploitation requires large, capital-intensive investment (a common occurrence in minerals), then raw material producers are likely to be oligopolists. An oligopolist who depends on raw material as a critical input in production must, therefore, obtain it from another oligopolist. The first oligopolist can remove the bargaining disadvantages and uncertainties of this bilateral oligopoly most directly by vertical integration that affords control over the first oligopolist's *own* source of supply. Thus, the avoidance of oligopolistic uncertainty is a motive for vertical foreign investment.

As in the case of horizontal investment, oligopolistic reaction explains the proliferation of vertical foreign investments in the same country by members of an oligopolistic industry. Vertical foreign investments may also be intended to build barriers that prevent the entry of new firms into the industry. By denying to potential newcomers access to raw materials, the oligopolist is able to maintain market power. Finally, vertical foreign investment may also generate cost advantages through technical improvements in the coordination of the production and transfer of goods between different stages of production as compared to the coordination of independent producers through external markets. In effect, the oligopolist *internalizes* external economies of scale.[26]

Vertical foreign investment is not confined to raw material extraction. Manufacturing companies may invest abroad to produce parts or components for

---

[26]The technical advantages of backward integration may also extend to forward integration. Petroleum companies have invested abroad not only in crude oil extraction but in marketing outlets as well.

transfer to production units in the home or third countries. This kind of vertical investment is not related to oligopolistic behavior but is rather an effort to minimize production costs.

Summing up, the monopolistic advantage theory asserts that foreign direct investment occurs because *structural* market imperfections enable individual firms to achieve monopoly power in foreign markets. The MNE is an institution embodying market imperfections and would not exist in a world of perfect competition. By definition, therefore, it is a monopolist.

The monopolistic advantage theory also throws light on the phenomenon of reverse investment. Because knowledge assets are firm-specific rather than country-specific, there is no contradiction in a U.S. company's investing in, say, France while at the same time a French company invests in the United States. And because the two firms have differentiated products that appeal to different market segments, they may also belong to the same industry.

This theory also scores well in predicting the *industrial composition* of foreign direct investment. It answers the question, Which kinds of firms and industries are most likely to invest abroad? But the theory does not explain why some knowledge-intensive industries, notably aerospace, are large exporters but only small foreign investors. It would appear that the possession of knowledge and other firm-specific assets is a *necessary* but not a *sufficient* condition for foreign direct investment. A second condition is that a firm with a monopolistic advantage can obtain the highest economic rent for its proprietary assets only by investing abroad in production under its control. That is, the return from foreign investment must be higher than the returns from exporting or licensing.

THE INTERNALIZATION THEORY OF FOREIGN DIRECT INVESTMENT

The theory of internalization (also called transaction cost theory) offers an explanation of why foreign investment may be a more effective way of exploiting foreign resources and markets than exporting or licensing. It is a theory, therefore, of the multinational enterprise, whose hallmark, as observed earlier, is international production.

The internalization theory postulates that (1) markets can fail to allocate factor services and goods efficiently due to natural and government-induced *externalities,* (2) markets and firms are alternative ways to organize the exchange of factor services and goods, (3) exchange is internalized within a firm when its transaction costs are less than market transaction costs, and (4) the MNE is an institution that internalizes cross-national exchanges of factor services and goods (particularly intermediate products) through foreign direct investment (international production).

Markets become less-than-optimal allocators of resources when they fail to capture externalities in market prices. *Natural externalities* may be defined as ownership externalities, technical externalities, and public good externalities.[27] *Owner-ship externalities* occur when a seller is not able to charge users of a product. For instance, a knowledge innovator cannot charge users of that knowledge when the knowledge is disclosed without legal protection (patents and trademarks). *Technical externalities* occur whenever a product experiences increasing returns to scale. *Public good externalities* occur in goods, such as knowledge, whose consumption by one individual does not lower their consumption by another individual.[28] In addition to these natural externalities, government intervention in markets creates *artificial externalities* that cause a divergence between private and social costs and benefits: tariffs, subsidies and other incentives, taxes, price controls, exchange restrictions, investment performance requirements, and so on.[29]

Externalities may be regarded as the costs of organizing exchange — the costs of informing, monitoring, and rewarding buyers and sellers. Markets depend on prices to inform, monitor, and reward participants, and they become inefficient when externalities are not captured in prices. In contrast, firms organize exchange through central direction and control of their operations and employees: Arm's length market transactions give way to intrafirm transfers. In organizing exchange, firms incur the cost of systems to inform, monitor, and reward their employees. Internalization theory asserts that firms will replace external markets with internal flows of factor services and goods when the cost of doing so is less than the cost of organizing markets, that is, when internal transaction costs are less than external transaction costs.

Market failure is most evident in the exchange of knowledge. When a firm creates new knowledge which then becomes disclosed to outsiders, that knowledge becomes a public good. But a public good cannot be priced by a market, because its marginal cost is zero: New users of the good can be supplied at no additional cost. Furthermore, at a zero price, there would be no incentive for firms to create knowledge. This externality can be partly overcome by the assignment of property rights (patents and trademarks) to the innovating firm, enabling it to restrict the use of the knowledge. However, only some of a firm's knowledge can be legally protected; other knowledge must be protected through the firm's own efforts to prevent disclosure to outsiders. The most direct way to prevent disclosure and thereby earn monopoly rent is for the firm to internalize its knowledge. Instead of selling (licensing) its knowledge to outsiders, the firm applies that knowledge only to production under its control. Internalization theory explains *horizontal* foreign

---

[27]Jean-Francois Hennart, *A Theory of Multinational Enterprise* (Ann Arbor: University of Michigan Press, 1980), pp. 32–33. For a more recent statement on internalization theory by Hennart, see "The Transaction Cost Theory of the Multinational Enterprise," in Cristos N. Pitelis and Roger Sugden, eds., *The Nature of the Transnational Firm* (New York: Routledge, 1991). The first book-length presentation of internalization theory is Peter Buckley and Mark Casson, *The Future of the Multinational Enterprise* (London: MacMillan, 1976).

[28]A second feature of a public good is *nonexcludability:* Consumption cannot be restricted to certain consumers but becomes available to all. Public television and military defense are common examples of public goods.

[29]See the discussion of the use of shadow prices to value the benefits and costs of foreign direct investment in Chapter 24.

investment, therefore, as a response to market failure in knowledge. Internalization enables a firm to "appropriate" an economic rent for its knowledge that cannot be obtained in external markets.[30]

Internalization theory also explains *vertical* integration as a replacement of inefficient external markets. *Backward* integration occurs when (1) there are high costs in coordinating successive production stages by market prices when buyers and sellers are few in number, (2) exchange extends over a lengthy period of time, and (3) buyers and sellers experience a high degree of uncertainty. *Forward* integration becomes an efficient way of organizing exchange when there is a high degree of interdependence between the manufacturing firm and marketing channel agencies and it is costly to constrain that interdependence through market prices and market contracts.

In sum, the theory of internalization posits that the multinational enterprise invests abroad in order to capture market externalities: economies of scale in production and marketing, the ownership and public-goods character of knowledge, and government-imposed market constraints. In so doing, the MNE accomplishes an international transfer of factor services and goods more efficiently than external markets. In other words, firm-specific knowledge and other assets lead to foreign direct investment whenever intrafirm transactions become less costly than external market transactions. From the perspective of internalization theory, the MNE is an institution designed to create and exploit internal markets.

THE ECLECTIC PARADIGM
OF FOREIGN DIRECT INVESTMENT

The theories of monopolistic advantage and internalization go a long way toward explaining foreign direct investment—but not all the way. In particular, these theories do not explain why the *pattern* of foreign involvement (the mix of export, licensing, and investment) by MNEs differs across countries. The only plausible explanation of different country patterns is the influence of *country-specific* factors on foreign investment as well as on other forms of international involvement.

The eclectic paradigm of foreign direct investment, associated with Dunning, helps explain cross-country differences in the pattern of international involvement by MNEs.[31] To Dunning, foreign direct investment implies that *location-specific* advantages favor a foreign host country but *ownership-specific* advantages favor the investing firm. International production, therefore, is attributable not only to the firm's monopolistic advantage and its ability to internalize that advantage but also to the presence of a foreign country in which production brings unique benefits to

---

[30]Stephen Magee, "Information and the MNC: An Appropriability Theory of Direct Foreign Investment," in *The New International Economic Order,* ed. Jagdish N. Bhagwati (Cambridge: MIT Press, 1977), pp. 317–40.

[31]John Dunning, *International Production and the Multinational Enterprise* (London: George Allen Unwin, 1981), Chapter 2. For Dunning's recent thoughts on his paradigm, see "The Eclectic Paradigm of International Production: A Personal Perspective," in Christos N. Pitelis and Roger Sugden, eds., *The Nature of the Transnational Firm* (New York: Routledge, 1991), pp. 117–136.

the firm. Because some market imperfections are related to country-specific endowments, the benefits of internalization for the MNE vary across countries. The eclectic paradigm draws, therefore, on the theories of international trade (comparative advantage) and location and also on the theories of monopolistic advantage and internalization.

The principal contribution of the eclectic paradigm is an explanation of the distribution of international production by country. Both firm and country-specific endowments (natural resources, labor, energy, geographical location, markets, government policies, and so on) are necessary for foreign involvement. When it is most profitable for an MNE to internalize its monopolistic advantage in a foreign country, then the MNE favors investment in that country. Otherwise, it exploits the country market through export or licensing.

THE CHOICE AMONG EXPORT, LICENSING, AND FOREIGN DIRECT INVESTMENT

We can bring together the elements of the eclectic theory in a model that demonstrates how these elements influence a firm's choice of the entry mode best suited to a particular foreign country.[32] The variables are interpreted in present value terms because their values relate to a period of time that we take to be the same for the alternative entry modes.[33]

Assume that a knowledge-intensive firm F located in country A wants to service a market located in country B. *Total* production costs over a given period of time (including both fixed and variable costs) of F's product are P_a in country A and P_b in country B.

K represents the cost associated with a *disclosure* of the knowledge possessed by F when it grants a license to a firm in country B. Disclosure weakens F's monopoly advantage, lowering its economic rent in country B and possibly in third countries as well.

The *export marketing cost differential* is designated as M. It is the difference between export and domestic marketing costs and is positive because export marketing costs (communication, shipping, insurance, finance, and so on) are higher than domestic marketing costs.

Transfer costs, designated as T, are the extra costs of operating across national boundaries as compared to operating at home. To operate in country B, firm F must direct, coordinate, and control a subsidiary located in a foreign political, economic, legal, social, and cultural environment. Just as M inhibits exports, so T inhibits direct investment. Since a high proportion of T is fixed, the initial foreign investment by F incurs the total transfer costs, but subsequent investments incur only small incremental expenditures.

---

[32]The model draws on Alan M. Rugman, *Inside the Multinationals* (New York: Columbia University Press, 1981), pp. 54–60. For treatment of the choice of entry mode by international managers, see Franklin R. Root, *Entry Strategies for International Markets* (Lexington, Mass.: Lexington Books, 1987).

[33]We refrain from expressing the model's inequalities in present value terms to keep our presentation simple. For a mathematic expression of present value, see Chapter 24.

We are now prepared to see how these five variables determine F's choice among export, licensing, and investment entry. To start, assume that $K = M = T = 0$. Under these conditions, exporting is the *only* way that F can service the market in country B. Zero knowledge disclosure cost (K) implies that F has no proprietary knowledge that gives it a monopolistic advantage in country B. Hence F can neither license nor invest in that country. F will export to country B if production costs in country A are lower than production costs in country B. If, however, production costs are higher in country A, then F will remain a domestic firm. This is the world of the Heckscher-Ohlin model of international trade presented in Chapter 3. If M is positive while K and T stay at zero, F's exports will be somewhat restricted (assuming lower costs in country A), but exports will remain the only way F can enter country B's market.

Now assume that K, M, and T are all positive. We have the following decision rules:

1. Export if $P_a + M < P_b + K$ (export is more profitable than licensing) *and* $P_a + M < P_b + T$ (export is more profitable than investment).
2. License if $P_b + K < P_a + M$ (licensing is more profitable than export) *and* $P_b + K < P_b + T$ (licensing is more profitable than investment).
3. Invest if $P_b + T < P_a + M$ (investment is more profitable than export) *and* $P_b + T < P_b + K$ (investment is more profitable than licensing).

Clearly, P_b is specific to country B, but M, T, and K are also influenced by country B. The value of M, for instance, is affected by transportation costs between A and B and by B's import duties. The value of T depends in part on F's knowledge and experience concerning country B and in part on B's investment climate. The value of K is influenced by the capability of local firms in B to exploit F's knowledge and by how segmented F's market is from the markets of third countries. It follows, therefore, that F's choice of entry mode for the same product may differ between country B and a third country as P, M, T, and K take on different values.

We can make certain plausible assumptions about the relationships between M, T, and K over time. At the start of F's involvement with country B, $M < T < K$, for F knows little about the country (which raises T) and it wants to protect its knowledge, which is at an early stage of the life cycle. Therefore, the probability is high that F will choose export as the most profitable initial entry mode. As time goes on, however, T falls relative to M because F learns more and more about country B through its export experience. At some point, then, F will invest in country B, particularly if production costs are lower in B. Over a longer period of time, K falls relative to T as F's product knowledge is imitated by other firms. Ultimately, therefore, F may license that knowledge (technology) to a local firm in country B.

This sequence — export, invest, license — is not certain. Government policies, in particular, may distort M, T, and K: Import restrictions increase M, a poor investment climate increases T, and those policies together increase the attractiveness of licensing.

The model is a neat depiction of the trade-offs between export, licensing, and horizontal investment. As do all theoretical models, however, it disregards variables that are deemed of lesser importance. Two missing variables deserve mention. First, by focusing only on costs, the model implicitly assumes that the revenues generated by the different entry modes are the same. But this assumption is unrealistic: Generally, investment generates the highest revenue stream, exporting the next highest, and licensing the lowest. In any event, revenues need to be taken into account in deciding on the most profitable entry mode. Second, the model ignores *risk differentials* among the entry modes. Other things being equal, the higher risk of foreign investment as compared with exporting and licensing (both because a foreign subsidiary is exposed to more kinds of risk and because its risk exposure is greater) makes the trade-off favor them. This is particularly true for smaller firms that have only a limited capacity to bear risk, apart from the question of financing foreign investment. Thus, the greater risk also makes smaller firms less likely than large firms to invest abroad even when they possess knowledge assets.

TOWARD A SYNTHESIS OF INTERNATIONAL TRADE AND INVESTMENT THEORIES

In this closing section, we echo a statement made in Chapter 5 to the effect that the theory of international trade must become part of a broader theory of international enterprise. What is needed is a synthesis of international trade and investment theories to form a single theory of international economic behavior. Traditional theory has explained international trade in terms of a country's factor endowments relative to those of other countries. These endowments are *country-specific*. In contrast, the monopolistic advantage and internalization theories of foreign direct investment emphasize knowledge assets that are *firm-specific* and may be carried by the firm to any country. As the eclectic paradigm postulates, *where* production is located is influenced mainly by country-specific endowments, but the international *control and ownership* of production are mainly owing to firm-specific endowments. A theory of international economic behavior, therefore, would center on the firm operating in imperfect factor and product markets within a world economy of dissimilar factor and market endowments at the country level. Given the recent developments in trade and investment theories, the outlook for a synthesis is favorable: Both sets of theories stress the importance of knowledge assets (technology and human skills), and both abandon the assumptions of perfect competition.

SUMMARY

1. Since the early 1980s, foreign direct investment annual outflows have grown three times faster than world exports and four times faster than world output. By the end of the 1980s, the world FDI stock reached $1.5 trillion, and it was growing at almost $200 billion a year.

2. Services now account for over half the annual outflows of FDI, even though the internationalization of services is at an early stage.

3. The global pattern of FDI is *tripolar,* centering on the United States, the European Community, and Japan. These three countries are the source of more than three-fourths of the world's annual outflow of FDI. In the 1980s, the United States fell behind the other two members as a *home* country, but it became the leading *host* (receiving) country.

4. U.S. affiliates (subsidiaries) of foreign MNEs and the foreign affiliates of U.S. MNEs together account for about half of U.S. exports and imports. When exports of U.S. *parent* companies are included, then MNEs undertake at least 80 percent of U.S. trade.

5. A theory of foreign direct investment should answer three fundamental questions: (1) Why do firms go abroad as direct investors? (2) How can direct-investing firms compete successfully with local firms given the inherent advantage of local firms' operating in a familiar business environment? (3) Why do firms choose to enter foreign countries as producers rather than as exporters or licensors?

6. The theory of international portfolio investment cannot explain foreign direct investment. Indeed, by assuming perfect competition, this theory rules out *any* foreign direct investment.

7. The monopolistic advantage theory postulates that the investing firm possesses monopolistic advantages that enable it to operate subsidiaries abroad more profitably than local competing firms. These advantages fall into two broad categories: superior knowledge and economies of scale. Knowledge assets are specific to the firm, and the marginal cost to the firm of exploiting them in foreign investment is very low because they represent sunk costs. Superior knowledge allows the investing firm to create differentiated products with competitive advantages and thereby earn economic rent.

8. By adding a time dimension to the theory of monopolistic advantage, the product life cycle model helps explain why U.S. manufacturers shift from exporting to foreign direct investment. But the model cannot explain the investment behavior of full-blown multinational corporations.

9. The implications of oligopolistic behavior for foreign direct investment are discussed in terms of oligopolistic reaction, internal economies of scale, and vertical foreign investment.

10. The internalization theory of foreign direct investment postulates that multinational firms will internalize international market transactions when they can capture externalities through internal transfers. The MNE, therefore, is an institution designed to create and exploit internal markets.

11. The eclectic paradigm of foreign direct investment postulates that both firm- and country-specific factors are needed to explain a firm's international behavior. When it is most profitable for an MNE to internalize its monopolistic advantage in a given foreign country, then it will invest in that country.

12. We can bring together the elements of the eclectic paradigm in a model that demonstrates how these elements allow a firm to choose the entry mode (export, licensing, or investment) best suited to a particular country.

13. A synthesis of international trade and investment theory is needed to form a single theory of international economic behavior.

QUESTIONS AND APPLICATIONS

1. Distinguish between *portfolio* and *foreign direct* investment.
2. (a) What is meant by the "book value" of foreign direct investment?
   (b) What are the sources of year-to-year changes in the book value of U.S. foreign direct investment?
3. (a) Explain the growing share of services in FDI.
   (b) Is this share likely to increase in the future? Why or why not?
4. (a) What is the *Triad?*
   (b) What is the Triad's role in FDI?
   (c) What shifts occurred within the Triad during the 1980s?
5. Prepare to discuss: "Massive international flows of trade, technology, and long-term capital are generated by MNE investment in international production, which, in turn, is responsive to MNE strategies."
6. What are the requirements for a theory of foreign direct investment?
7. (a) What is "superior knowledge"?
   (b) Why is superior knowledge specific to the firm?
8. (a) The marginal cost of exploiting knowledge assets in horizontal foreign investment is zero or very low. Why?
   (b) How can the investing firm obtain economic rent on its knowledge assets through horizontal foreign investment?
9. What are the limitations of the product life cycle theory in explaining foreign direct investment?
10. Explain the phenomenon of oligopolistic reaction and its effects on foreign direct investment.
11. Do internal economies of scale in production help to explain foreign direct investment? In what way?
12. How does oligopolistic behavior explain vertical foreign investment?
13. The possession of superior knowledge is a necessary but not a sufficient condition for horizontal foreign investment. Why?
14. (a) What are the postulates of the internalization theory?
   (b) What is the meaning of market failure?
15. What is the contribution of the eclectic paradigm of foreign direct investment?
16. How are *M, T,* and *K* likely to change over time? Why?

SELECTED READINGS

Buckley, Peter J. "The Limits of Explanation: Testing the Internalization Theory of the Multinational Enterprise." *Journal of International Business Studies,* Summer 1988, pp. 181-93.

Casson, Mark. *The Firm and the Market.* Cambridge: MIT Press, 1987. Chapters 1, 2.

Caves, Richard E. *Multinational Enterprise and Economic Analysis.* Cambridge: Cambridge University Press, 1982.

Dunning, John H. *International Production and the Multinational Enterprise.* London: George Allen Unwin, 1981.

Dunning, John H. "The Eclectic Paradigm of International Production: A Restatement and Some Possible Extensions." *Journal of International Business Studies,* Spring 1988, pp. 1-31.

Hennart, Jean-Francois. *A Theory of Multinational Enterprise.* Ann Arbor: University of Michigan Press, 1982.

Hymer, Stephen H. *The International Operations of National Firms.* Cambridge: MIT Press, 1976.

Kindleberger, Charles P., and David B. Andretsch, eds. *The Multinational Corporation in the 1980s.* Cambridge: MIT Press, 1983.

Ohmae, Kenichi. *Triad Power: The Coming Shape of Global Competition.* New York: The Free Press, 1985.

Pitelis, Christos N., and Roger Sugden, eds. *The Nature of the Transnational Firm.* New York: Routledge, 1991.

United Nations. *Multinational Corporations in World Development.* New York: United Nations, 1973. Chapters 1, 2.

United Nations. *Transnational Corporations in World Development: A Re-examination.* New York: United Nations, 1978. Chapters 1, 3.

United Nations. *Transnational Corporations in World Development: Third Survey.* New York: United Nations, 1983. Chapters 1, 2.

United Nations. *Transnational Corporations in World Development: Trends and Prospects.* New York: United Nations, 1988. Overview and Part 1.

United Nations. *Transnational Corporations.* vol. 1, no. 1, February 1992, and later issues. New York: United Nations.

United Nations. *World Investment Report, The Triad in Foreign Direct Investment.* New York: United Nations, 1991. Chapters I, II.

chapter 24

PUBLIC POLICY TOWARD THE MULTINATIONAL ENTERPRISE

To perform its role as an international transfer agent effectively, the multinational enterprise must be able to move capital, technology, entrepreneurial skills, products, and funds freely throughout the world in response to market opportunity, costs, and competition. The contribution of the MNE to the efficiency and growth of the world economy is dependent, therefore, on the willingness of national governments to refrain from restricting its activities in ways that force it to suboptimize international production and trade for the world as a whole. But, as we have frequently observed, national governments are concerned only indirectly, if at all, with the maximization of the world's economic efficiency and growth. Rather, their concern is the protection and advancement of the national interest as they perceive it in any given situation. National governments, therefore, regard the multinational enterprise from the perspective of its political-economic benefits and costs to the nation—not to the world at large.

The activities of multinational enterprises bear directly on the balance of payments, production, trade, employment, growth, and international competitive position of both host and home economies. Furthermore, they raise fundamental political questions relating to external control over the domestic economy, extraterritoriality, and national sovereignty. Consequently, national governments seek to influence, regulate, and otherwise control the behavior of the multinational enterprise so as to promote their own perceived national interests, paying only scant attention to the effects of their policies on the world economy.

In this chapter, we offer a framework for understanding the policies of host governments toward foreign direct investment and the multinational enterprise by looking at the economic benefits and costs of FDI and the challenge of multinational enterprise to national sovereignty. We then examine the FDI policy of the United States, the world's leading home and host country. We close with some thoughts on an accommodation between the interests of nation-states and the multinational enterprise.

THE ECONOMIC BENEFITS AND COSTS
OF FOREIGN DIRECT INVESTMENT
TO HOST COUNTRIES

The multinational enterprise is perceived by policymakers in host countries both as an economic institution that creates benefits for and costs to the local economy and as a quasi-political institution that threatens the power and even the sovereignty of the nation. A lengthy examination of the policy issues generated by this twin role of the multinational enterprise would carry us far beyond the scope of this book and into the realm of political science and international law. Our purpose here is the more modest one of identifying the principal issues and, when possible, offering conceptual approaches to their objective analysis. All of these issues relate in one way or another to the mutuality and conflict of interests between national governments and the multinational enterprise. The crucial question, then, is whether both parties can learn how to expand the mutuality and contract the conflict of their individual interests. The answer to this question will determine the evolution of the world economy.

Foreign direct investment has multiple effects on the economy of a host country in production, employment, income, prices, exports, imports, the balance of payments, economic growth, and general welfare. Some of these effects confer benefits on the host country; some of them incur costs. Some effects occur almost immediately, and some may take a generation. In this section we offer a conceptual approach to the measurement of the net benefit/cost ratio of foreign direct investment that takes into account its many effects and their impact over time.

The fundamental effect of foreign direct investment (representing the sum total of the many individual effects) is its contribution to the national income (net national product) of the host country over time. Closely related to this national income effect but deserving special treatment is the effect of foreign direct investment on the balance of payments of the host country over time.

The National Income Effect

What is the contribution to a host country's net national product of, say, the manufacturing affiliate of a multinational enterprise? Clearly it is less than the value of the affiliate's output, because some of the inputs used to manufacture that output (raw materials, parts, supplies, and so on) were produced by other firms. Our first approximation of the affiliate's contribution, therefore, is to subtract from the value of its output the value of all inputs purchased from other firms (including, of course, the parent company). Algebraically, if O represents the output of the affiliate and I represents the inputs purchased from local and foreign firms, then

$$(1) \text{ Benefits } = O - I.$$

This is the conventional expression of the *net value added* by a firm to national product. When all outside inputs are subtracted from the firm's output, we are left with the contribution of the factors of production directly employed by the firm as measured by the sum total of its factors payments (wages, salaries, interest, rent, and profits). Thus:

$$(2) \ \text{Benefits} = O - I = F + R,$$

where F represents the affiliate's total factor payments to labor, capital, and land, and R represents the return (profit) to entrepreneurial management.

Conventional net value added, however, is not an adequate measure of the contribution of a *new* foreign-owned affiliate to the national product of the host country. It does not take into account the *opportunity cost* of the local factors of production employed by the affiliate, namely, the national product that those factors would have produced if they were *not* employed by the affiliate. Only to the extent that these local factors are used more productively by the affiliate than they would have been in its absence does their employment by the affiliate make a net contribution to national product. When the affiliate uses workers or resources that would otherwise be idle, then the opportunity cost is zero. At the other extreme, if the affiliate takes workers or resources away from other equally productive firms, then the opportunity cost is equal to the payments for their services by the affiliate. Our second approximation of the benefits of the affiliate, therefore, is to deduct the opportunity cost of the *local* factors of production used by the affiliate. Thus,

$$(3) \ \text{Benefits} = (F + R) - N,$$

where N represents the opportunity cost of local factors.

So far we have considered only the direct benefits of the affiliate. To be complete, we must also include the *indirect* benefits, the net sum of its positive and negative external economies.[1] Positive external economies of the affiliate act to raise the productivity of other firms in the host country and thereby increase the national product. To illustrate, the affiliate may enable its local customers to cut costs or enter into more productive lines of activity by selling them established products at lower prices, by assuring them a reliable and adequate supply of products, by selling them new products, by offering technical assistance, and so on. The affiliate may also benefit local suppliers by providing a demand that enables them to achieve economies of scale and by offering them technical assistance to meet the affiliate's requirements. Competitive pressures exerted by the affiliate may force local firms to become more efficient. Training programs of the affiliate to upgrade the skills of its workers benefit other firms when workers leave the affiliate to enter their employ. More generally, the example of a modern,

---

[1]Externalities are the economic effects of a firm's activities that are not reflected in that firm's costs or revenues. Externalities may directly affect the production activities of other firms or consumer welfare (as in the case of pollution). Our present discussion focuses on production externalities. For a treatment of externalities in the context of market failure, see Chapter 23.

progressive enterprise may stimulate innovation by local entrepreneurs (positive demonstration effect). Against these and other positive external economies must be set any negative external economies that decrease the productivity of local firms, such as losses in efficiency because of higher demands placed on them by the affiliate, structural unemployment caused by the competition of the affiliate, and the discouragement of local entrepreneurs (negative demonstration effect). Our third approximation of the affiliate's contribution to the national product of the host country takes into account its net external economies. Thus,

$$(4) \text{ Benefits } = (F + R) - N + L,$$

where L represents *net* external economies (positive *minus* negative externalities).

Our final approximation of benefits explicitly recognizes that the affiliate pays taxes on its net income (R) to the host government. R, therefore, is the sum of the after-tax income of the affiliate (R^*) and the income taxes paid by the affiliate to the host government (T). Thus,

$$(5) \text{ Benefits } = (F + R^* + T) - N + L.$$

The *costs* of foreign direct investment to the host economy are the sum total of all payments to the *foreign* factors of production (including technology) used by the affiliate: profits or dividends, interest, royalties, management fees, and so on. Thus,

$$(6) \text{ Costs } = E,$$

where E represents payments to foreign factors of production.

The net benefit/cost ratio of foreign direct investment to the host economy, therefore, is

$$\frac{(F + R^* + T) - N + L}{E}.$$

If the ratio is greater than 1, then benefits exceed costs to the host economy, and vice versa. Is this ratio likely to be greater than 1 for foreign direct investment in general? Both theoretical and empirical considerations support the assertion that foreign direct investment is generally beneficial to host economies.

Theoretically, it has been shown that under competitive conditions the net addition to the output of the host economy from foreign direct investment must *always* exceed the return to the investor because of the diminishing marginal product of capital. An inflow of foreign investment lowers the marginal product of *all* capital in the host economy and therefore reduces the net income on all previous foreign investments. Even when one drops the assumption of a diminishing marginal product of capital, host-government taxation would appear sufficient in most instances to ensure that the net earnings of foreign investors are less than their contribution to national product, aside from any net external economies.

Empirical verification of the economic benefit/cost ratio of foreign direct investment is difficult to attain.[2] Statistics on the foreign operations of U.S. multinational enterprises offer some basis for estimating factor payments (F), after-tax profits (R^*), and local taxes (T), but none at all for estimating the opportunity cost of local factors (N) or net external economies (L), which would be difficult to quantify in any event. F, R^*, T, and external factor payments (E) for U.S. direct investment in the developing countries are shown in Table 24-1 for the year 1982.

Table 24-1 indicates that U.S. investment in the developing countries made a sizable net contribution to national product in 1982. However, by ignoring opportunity cost, this estimate implicitly assumes that the opportunity cost of the

Table 24-1   Economic Benefits and Costs of U.S. Direct Investment in the Developing Countries in 1982 (Millions of Dollars)

Benefits of Direct Investment		
Factor payments by U.S. majority-owned affiliates (F)		20,236
Employee compensation (F_1)	17,448	
Interest, royalty, and service payments (F_2)	2,788	
Taxes paid to host government (T)		22,696
Net after-tax income (R^*)		11,030
Total benefit to national product $(F + T + R^*)$		53,962

Costs of Direct Investment	
Payments to foreign factors: royalty and service fees (E_1)	3,600
Payments to foreign factors: net interest, dividends, and reinvested earnings (E_2)	6,222
Total cost to national product $(E_1 + E_2 = E)$.	9,822

Benefit/cost ratio before allowance for opportunity cost and net external economies $[(F + T + R^*) / E]$	5.5

Source: U.S. Department of Commerce, *U.S. Direct Investment Abroad: 1982 Benchmark Survey Data* (Washington, D.C.: U.S. Government Printing Office, December 1985), various tables.

---

[2]For a recent empirical verification that found that DFI was "broadly positive" for the host country, see Robert Grosse, "The Economic Impact of Foreign Direct Investment: A Case Study of Venezuela," *MIR*, 1988/4, pp. 63–78.

local factors used by U.S. affiliates was zero. Nonetheless, even if we were to assume that the opportunity costs of labor were equal to one half the compensation received from U.S. affiliates, the contribution would remain positive.

Most probably, opportunity costs are on the low side in developing countries because of high unemployment, the presence of large endowments of unexploited resources, the low level of worker skills, and the frequently unproductive use of local savings. Thus, U.S. affiliates have added to national products by increasing the demand for unemployed or underemployed factors and by improving the allocation of factors. Most observers also conclude that U.S. affiliates have created net external economies that encourage economic growth in developing countries. Certainly the statistical evidence places the burden of proof on those who allege that national product would have been larger in the absence of foreign direct investment.

Our general conclusion that foreign direct investment offers net benefits to host economies should not be taken to mean that *every* foreign-owned affiliate necessarily makes a net contribution. When, for example, a host government exempts an affiliate from taxation, it may be questioned whether the benefits outrun the costs. Also, the foregoing analysis assumes that factor and goods prices in the host economy reflect their true scarcities and that the exchange rate does not seriously depart from the equilibrium rate. If such is not the case, the social contribution of foreign investment may be less than its social costs, although the same is also true of domestic investment. Finally, the benefit/cost ratio may shift over time, a subject we shall explore in a later section.

The Balance of Payments Effect

Foreign direct investment has numerous individual effects on the balance of payments of a host country that change significantly over time. The initial transfer of capital to the host country to establish, say, a manufacturing affiliate contributes a once-for-all benefit to the balance of payments. Once the affiliate starts operations, it may provide continuing benefits to the balance of payments by using some or all of its output for export or for import substitution. On the other hand, the affiliate may import raw materials or other inputs to sustain its operations at a continuing cost to the balance of payments. Repatriation of profits and payments to foreign factors of production by the affiliate also constitute continuing drains on the host country's foreign exchange. Again, higher local income generated by the affiliate may induce more host country imports via the marginal propensity to import. Finally, if the affiliate is liquidated, any capital repatriation is a once-for-all cost to the balance of payments. We can represent these benefits and costs algebraically as follows:

$$\text{(7) Balance of payments benefits} = K + X + S,$$

where K is the initial inflow of investment capital; X, the exports of the affiliate; and S, the replacement of imports by the affiliate's output (import substitution).

(8) Balance of payments costs $= (R^{**} + F^*) + (M + M^*) + D,$

where R^{**} is repatriated earnings; F^*, repatriated payments to other foreign factors of production; M, imports by the affiliate; M^*, imports induced by higher local income via the marginal propensity to import; and D, any disinvestment (liquidation) of the affiliate. The net benefit/cost ratio of direct foreign investment for the balance of payments of the host economy, therefore, is

$$\frac{K + X + S}{(R^{**} + F^*) + (M + M^*) + D}.$$

Over the long run, the balance of payments effect of foreign direct investment cannot be distinguished from its national income effect. We can understand why this is so by returning to equation (17) in Chapter 15, namely, $X - M = GNP - (C + I_d + G)$. This equation indicates that direct foreign investment will *improve* the balance of payments when its national income effect (increase in GNP) is not offset by an equal or greater increase in domestic absorption $(C + I_d + G)$. The most probable outcome over the long run is for domestic absorption to match an increase in gross national product so that the balance of payments effect of foreign direct investment becomes neutral.

Over the shorter run, however, foreign direct investment may cause a balance of payments deficit because factors of production in the host country are not fully mobile. Hence, the economy may not be able to shift quickly out of the production of "home" goods into the production of export or import-substitution goods so as to achieve the net export balance necessary to finance any net foreign-exchange expenditures associated with an affiliate. This condition of lagged adjustment is particularly representative of developing countries that have a structural inability to transform savings into foreign exchange through an increase in exports or a decrease in imports. As a consequence, developing countries commonly experience a foreign exchange constraint on their economic growth that is distinguishable from a savings constraint.[3] Over the shorter run, therefore, a net increase in imports of goods and factor services that are directly or indirectly attributable to the operations of a foreign-owned affiliate may cause a current-account deficit (a decrease in $X - M$) because of structural rigidities in the host economy that prevent an adjustment to the balance of payments. In other words, over the shorter run an affiliate may bring about an increase in domestic absorption that exceeds its own contribution to the national product.

Faced with foreign exchange constraints and heavy debt service burdens, policymakers in host developing countries are highly sensitive to the balance of payments effect of foreign direct investment. They regard with favor those foreign investment projects that will quickly replace imports or create exports so as to provide the foreign exchange necessary to finance the external transfer of earnings and factor payments. Conversely, foreign investment projects that are not import-

---

[3]For a discussion of these constraints, see Chapter 20.

saving or export-creating are likely to be discouraged by policymakers even though the projects in question will contribute significantly to economic growth. Thus, the foreign investment policies of many developing countries seek to maximize short-run balance of payments gains at the cost of sacrificing long-run gains in national income and economic growth.

Ideally, a host country should maintain balance of payments equilibrium by resorting to monetary, fiscal, and exchange rate policies, together with measures to speed up the reallocation of resources. But the fact is that policymakers in the developing countries must deal with immediate, pressing demands for scarce foreign exchange. In that situation, the short-run balance of payments effect of foreign direct investment tends to overwhelm the long-run national income effect in the formulation of policy. It is all the more necessary, therefore, to stress that the fundamental contribution of foreign direct investment to the host economy lies in its positive national income effect achieved through technological innovation, economies of scale, effective use of local factors, and superior management.

Disagreement on the Present Value of Benefits and Costs

So far our conceptual approach to the measurement of the national income and balance of payments effects of foreign direct investment is a static analysis that implicitly assumes that there is time for all the benefits and costs to occur. Since benefits and costs follow different time paths, a more useful approach views benefits as a future stream of annual increments to national income and costs as a future stream of external income and factor payments. To obtain the *present values* of these streams, it is necessary to discount future benefits and costs at an appropriate rate. The present value of benefits (costs), therefore, is the sum of the discounted annual benefits (costs) in the future. We can restate equations (5) and (6) in present value form as follows:

(9) Net present value of benefits =

$$\sum_{t=1}^{t=n} \left(\frac{[F_t + R_t^* + T_t] - N_t + L_t}{[1 + d]^t} \right).$$

(10) Net present value of costs =

$$\sum_{t=1}^{t=n} \left(\frac{E_t}{[1 + d]^t} \right).$$

In these equations, t is the number of years and d is the rate of discount. The higher the value of d, the greater the weight given to benefits and costs in the near future, and vice versa.[4]

---

[4]The net present value of balance of payments benefits is

$$\sum_{t=1}^{t=n} \left(\frac{K_t + X_t + S_t}{[1 + d]^t} \right)$$

and balance of payments costs,

$$\sum_{t=1}^{t=n} \left(\frac{[R_t^{**} + F_t^*] + [M_t + M_t^*] + D_t}{[1 + d]^t} \right).$$

When direct investors implicitly or explicitly discount future benefits and costs at a rate that differs from the rate used by the host government, then the two parties will disagree on the present value of those benefits and costs to the host country. Since it is rational for the multinational enterprise to use the marginal opportunity cost of its capital (the next best alternative use for it elsewhere in the world) to discount its own future benefits and costs, it tends to apply the same rate to discount future benefits and costs to the host country. When the host government seeks to maximize the income effects of foreign investment, the proper discount rate is the marginal productivity of capital in the host economy, a rate that should agree rather closely with the discount rate of the multinational enterprise. In that event, the investor and the host government will reach an easy agreement on the present value of the benefits and costs of a prospective investment. When, however, the multinational enterprise considers *political* risks to be high in the host country, it may add a risk premium to its discount rate so that the combined rate of the multinational enterprise exceeds the host government's rate. Then the enterprise will place a higher value on short-run benefits and costs than the host government.

However, apart from situations of high political risk, it is more common for the host governments of developing countries to discount the future more heavily than the multinational enterprise. Pressed by the need for immediate action to relieve foreign exchange shortages, to slow down inflation, to raise tax revenues, and to curb unemployment, host government officials generally place a much higher value on the early benefits and costs of foreign investment than on its more distant benefits and costs. As we have already noted, this concern with the shorter run frequently makes the balance of payments effects of a prospective foreign investment more critical in the eyes of government officials than its longer run national income effects. The ensuing disagreement between the multinational enterprise and the host government on the present value of a proposed investment is most prominent in negotiations on entry. Once the investment is approved by the host government and the affiliate starts production, then disagreement is more likely to proceed from shifting perceptions of benefits and costs in the *current* period rather than the present value of benefits and costs over the indefinite life of the investment.

Using Shadow Prices to Value Benefits and Costs

Before considering shifting perceptions of benefits and costs over time, we should mention certain adjustments that a host government may make in market prices in order to value the *social* benefits and costs of a proposed foreign investment project. So far our conceptual approach to the national income and balance of payments effects of a direct foreign investment has relied on market prices to value the outputs and inputs of the foreign-owned affiliate with a single exception: the use of opportunity costs to value local labor inputs instead of wage costs. But market prices, particularly in developing countries, may not accurately reflect the relative scarcity of inputs or the relative desirability of outputs because of distortions created by monopoly, import restrictions, overvalued exchange rates, and other market imperfections. Given distortions, market prices will not direct an allocation of national resources that will maximize net social benefits, the objective of the host government. In this second-best world, therefore, a host government may replace actual market prices with social accounting or *shadow prices* to analyze a foreign investment project. Shadow prices are intended to measure accurately the social opportunity costs of inputs and the social utility of outputs.

We do not intend here to explore the often subtle world of social cost/benefit accounting.[5] Instead, we simply indicate the shadow price adjustments that a host government might make in a foreign investor's income statement for a proposed project. These adjustments are shown in Table 24-2.

In preparing the project's income statement for a representative year, the foreign investor uses market prices. The investor's estimates indicate a profit of 2.5 million pesos. Unwilling to accept actual market prices as a valuation basis, the host government adjusts the items in the investor's statement with shadow prices. Shadow prices remove the price distortions caused by import protection (which pushes the local price of widgets above their import value) and by an overvalued exchange rate (which lowers the local currency value of imports). Although the

Table 24-2 Shadow Price Adjustments of the Foreign Investor's Income Statement (Millions of Pesos)

Item	Investor's Income Statement (Market Prices)	Shadow Price Adjustments	Host Country's Social Income Statement (Shadow Prices)
Sales of widgets	20.0	– 9.0	11.0
Costs of goods sold	14.0	– 5.0	9.0
Local labor	6.0	– 6.0	0.0
Imported raw materials	6.0	+ 1.2	7.2
Local raw materials	2.0	– 0.2	1.8
Overhead	2.0	+ 0.4	2.4
Interest	1.5	+ 0.3	1.8
Remitted abroad	1.0	+ 0.2	1.2
Paid locally	0.5	+ 0.1	0.6
Profit	2.5		– 2.2

[5]Readers interested in the application of social cost/benefit analysis to foreign investment projects may consult Anandarup Ray, *Cost-Benefit Analysis: Issues and Methodologies* (Baltimore: Johns Hopkins University Press, 1984). See also Louis T. Wells, Jr., "Social Cost/Benefit Analysis for MNCs," *Harvard Business Review,* March–April 1975, pp. 40 ff; and "Evaluating the Costs and Benefits of Multinational Enterprises to Host Countries: A 'Tool-Kit' Approach," in *International Production and the Multinational Enterprise,* ed. John H. Dunning (London: George Allen & Unwin, 1981), pp. 357–84.

actual exchange rate is $1 = P1.0, the shadow exchange rate is taken to be $1 = P1.2.

First, the host government assesses the social value of widget sales at 11 million pesos because the same quantity of widgets could be imported for that amount at the shadow exchange rate. Second, it prices local labor at a zero shadow wage rate because if the workers were not employed on the foreign investor's project, they would be idle. Third, the preduty value of imported raw materials is calculated at the shadow exchange rate, and local raw materials are valued at their international market prices (removing the price effects of any import protection) converted into peso prices at the shadow exchange rate. Fourth, overhead is adjusted with the shadow exchange rate. Fifth, interest remitted abroad is revalued at the shadow exchange rate while interest paid locally on P3 million in local loans to the project is adjusted to the social opportunity cost of local capital, which is 20 percent. After these adjustments, the social profit of the project becomes negative, calling for rejection by the host government. Alternatively, the social benefit/cost ratio is 0.83.

This illustrative analysis of a proposed foreign investment project has omitted consideration of externalities. If the host government values the project's net externalities at 2.2 million pesos or higher, the project will pass the social benefit/cost test. Although social benefit/cost analysis, with its externalities and shadow prices, appears odd to private foreign investors, host governments in some developing countries are using it to screen foreign investment proposals.

Shifting Perceptions of Benefit/Cost Ratios over Time

As perceived by host country policymakers, the benefit/cost ratio of a foreign-owned affiliate is likely to shift over time and, more often than not, in a negative direction. In the early years of an affiliate's operations, perceived benefits usually substantially exceed perceived costs. On the benefit side, the multinational enterprise brings new capital, technology, and entrepreneurial management to the host economy, and external economies are high as the affiliate trains workers, establishes connections with local suppliers and customers, and begins to compete in local markets. At the same time, perceived costs are usually low in the early years as the affiliate makes only modest profits (or incurs losses) that are mostly reinvested to build up its competitive position. As time goes on, however, host government officials frequently perceive a decline in benefits and a rise in costs. The multinational enterprise may no longer be transferring new capital and technology to the affiliate, and the affiliate may generate fewer external economies as its operations become routine. On the other hand, profit repatriation may become ever larger as the affiliate achieves market success and has only modest needs for new capital. At some point, host government officials may even come to believe that the affiliate's operations could be performed entirely by local managers and workers and that external income and factor payments constitute a continuing cost with no offsetting benefits. Alternatively, they may believe they can negotiate more satisfactory arrangements with another multinational enterprise.

While the host government's perception of the benefit/cost ratio of an affiliate is shifting downward, the parent company's perception may be shifting upward. Managers in the parent company are inclined to interpret the rising production, sales, and local tax payments of the affiliate as evidence of its growing contribution to the host economy. Furthermore, they view repatriated profits as a reward for entrepreneurial efforts that go back to the birth of the affiliate. In effect, the multinational enterprise tells the host government, "Look at all we have done for you since we came to your country!" And the host government replies, "Yes, we appreciate that, but what have you done for us lately?" Figure 24-1 depicts this widening divergence between the benefit/cost perceptions of host government officials and multinational enterprise managers.

Up to point A, the host government is satisfied with the benefit/cost ratio of the affiliate, and it may even believe it has the better of the arrangement with the multinational enterprise. As the zone of disagreement widens beyond point A, however, the host government will undertake measures to reverse the deterioration in its perceived benefit/cost ratio by demanding, for example, that the affiliate establish an R & D center, increase its exports, obtain more materials and components from local suppliers and fewer from abroad, promote nationals to top management positions, pay more taxes, and cease paying royalties to its parent company. If the host government's perception shifts beyond point B, where costs

Figure 24-1

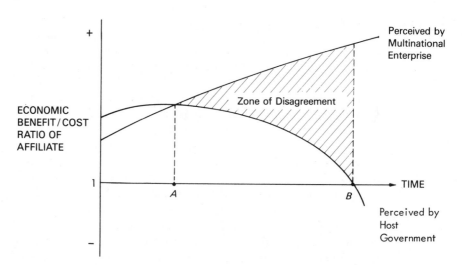

Divergence of Perceived Economic Benefit/Cost Ratios of an Affiliate Between the Host Government and the Multinational Enterprise. Over time, the MNE perceives the economic benefit/cost ratio of its affiliate in a given host country as increasing, while the host government perceives it as decreasing. Up to point A, the host government is satisfied with the benefit/cost ratio, but after A the goverment will take measures to reverse the perceived deterioration in the benefit/cost ratio.

exceed benefits, then it may press the multinational enterprise to sell the affiliate to local investors. The ultimate action of the host government is a unilateral expropriation of the affiliate. Seldom, however, will the host government's perception of the *economic* benefit/cost ratio of an affiliate move beyond point *B* unless that perception is distorted by negative political factors that are unrelated to the economic performance of the affiliate.

These shifting perceptions of economic benefits and costs are closely associated with shifts in the relative power positions of the host country and the multinational enterprise. Before the initial investment is made, the host government is often in a weak bargaining position because the multinational enterprise usually has several options to invest in other countries. To obtain the investment, therefore, the host government may have to offer concessions, such as a tax exemption for the first five years of the affiliate's operations. Once the investment is made, however, the power balance tends to shift in favor of the host government. The multinational enterprise has now committed resources that may be lost if the affiliate does not maintain its viability. As the host country becomes less dependent on the affiliate for capital, technology, management, access to export markets, or external economies, it is in a better position to insist on new conditions to maintain (or increase) its share of economic benefits. As long as the multinational enterprise considers disinvestment more costly than accommodation to the host government's conditions, it will keep its affiliate in operation. On the other hand, it is in the economic interest of the host government to practice some restraint so as not to "kill the golden goose" by forcing the multinational enterprise to abandon local operations. The history of relations between the international petroleum companies and host developing countries is a classic example of the reversal of power positions over time.

The reversal of power positions need not be true of every direct investment; it may be slowed down or even halted when the multinational enterprise is able to keep the host country continually dependent on it for new technology, new products, or access to export markets. The power positions of high-technology multinational enterprises have suffered little, if any, erosion in host countries for this reason.[6]

The Coincidence and Conflict of Economic Interests

Our analysis of the benefits and costs of foreign direct investment points to a coincidence of economic interests between the multinational enterprise and the host country. As is true of other forms of economic specialization and exchange, foreign direct investment is a "positive sum game" that benefits both players. Within this fundamental harmony of interests, however, there is likely to be a

---

[6]In an empirical study, Kobrin found that bargaining shifts in high-technology industries (in contrast to low-technology industries) were outside the host-country's control, responding instead to technological development and degree of global integration. See Stephen J. Kobrin, "Testing the Bargaining Hypothesis in the Manufacturing Sector in Developing Countries," *International Organization*, Autumn 1987, pp. 609–38.

continuing conflict of interests as both the multinational enterprise and the host country strive to maximize their respective shares of the net economic benefits of foreign investment.[7] This conflict may be exacerbated by different perceptions of the benefit/cost ratio of an affiliate held respectively by the parent company and the host government, perceptions that may change radically over time. The resolution of this continuing conflict depends essentially on the current power positions of the two parties. Ordinarily, both sides are constrained in their negotiations and bargaining by the recognition of their own interests regarding the activation and sustained performance of the affiliate in question. By pressing their own interests too hard, both risk the loss of actual or prospective economic gains. Hence, the conflict of economic interests between the foreign investor and the host government tends to be resolved to the satisfaction of both parties by a process of give and take that may be repeated many times over during the life of the affiliate.[8]

THE CHALLENGE OF THE MULTINATIONAL ENTERPRISE TO THE NATIONAL SOVEREIGNTY OF HOST COUNTRIES

Although there is a fundamental harmony of *economic* interests between host countries and the multinational enterprise, there is also a fundamental conflict of *political* interests that poses a challenge to the national sovereignty of host countries. Government officials, intellectuals, labor leaders, business people, and other groups in host countries regard the multinational enterprise as far more than a business institution that raises questions of only *economic* benefits and costs. From their perspective, the multinational enterprise contributes economic benefits, but at the cost of imposing actual or potential constraints on the policy decisions of national authorities as well as threatening the "integrity" of the national community. They see the multinational enterprise as a political institution that can exercise decision-making power over key segments of the national economy from a headquarters located outside the national territory and beyond the jurisdictional reach of their government. They allege, therefore, that the multinational enterprise limits or thwarts the capacity of the host government to achieve economic, social, and other goals in pursuit of the national interest. Furthermore, representatives of host countries perceive the multinational enterprise as an actual or potential instrument for the extraterritorial application of the laws and policies of the parent company's home government. They view a multinational enterprise that is headquartered in the United States as an American enterprise that champions the interests of the United States and, in any event, is fully subject to the authority of the U.S. government. Finally, host country nationals see the multinational enter-

---

[7]The share of the *home* country is also at issue, particularly when a host country attempts to increase its benefit share by imposing performance requirements on the MNE investor.

[8]This statement assumes the absence of any serious *political* conflict between the multinational enterprise and the host government.

prise as an outsider, an intruder into the national community whose loyalty to the host country is questionable at best.

These perceptions of the political role of the multinational enterprise give rise to fears and allegations best described as *issues* that are subject to continuing disagreement, debate, and controversy within host countries (internal conflict of goals), between host countries and multinational enterprises, and between host and home countries. Moreover, these fears and allegations will remain issues in the future unless foreign direct investment and the multinational enterprise can be "depoliticized" by multilateral international agreements that spell out the rights and responsibilities of the multinational enterprise vis-à-vis national governments, together with limitations on the territorial jurisdiction of those governments. In this section we briefly treat the three major political issues of the multinational enterprise: the issue of national interest, the issue of extraterritoriality, and the issue of nationalism.

The Issue of National Interest

The issue of national interest arises on two levels: (1) the divergent policy goals of host governments and the multinational enterprise, and (2) the constraints placed on government policymaking by the independent power of the multinational enterprise to make decisions affecting the host country. It is alleged that the multinational enterprise ignores or opposes national policy goals and renders national policy instruments ineffective.[9]

Apart from the fact that a host government pursues social and national security goals that have no counterparts among the goals of the private multinational enterprise, goal conflicts between the two parties are almost certain to occur because of the profound difference in the perspectives of the respective decision-makers. The host government conceives its economic and other goals in *national* terms; it tries to maximize *national* values in its policies. In contrast, the multinational enterprise conceives its goals in *geocentric* terms; it tries to maximize *enterprise system* values on a global scale. Host government officials ask, "Is this policy good for our country?" Multinational enterprise managers ask, "Is this policy good for our worldwide company?" Clearly the answers to these two questions need not be the same.

The issue of national interest, however, is not simply a matter of a conflict of goals. Rather, the issue is the *power* of the multinational enterprise to act independently of national policies. Even if country and enterprise goals were always harmonious, no government would want to turn its power over to the multinational enterprise. On the other hand, if the multinational enterprise lacked power, then a host government could take measures to ensure that the multinational enterprise always acted in the national interest. The power of the multinational enterprise comes from its possession of scarce capital, technology, and management and its capability to deploy these resources throughout the world. Thus, the

---

[9]For a discussion of national economic goals and policy instruments, see Chapter 1.

multinational enterprise is able to award or deny economic benefits to host countries. This brings us to the second dimension of the national interest issue, namely, the constraints placed on national policymaking by the multinational enterprise, with a consequent loss of "national independence."

Many specific allegations have been made against the multinational enterprise with regard to its power to circumvent national policies. From the perspective of the host government, the multinational enterprise can manipulate intra-enterprise transfer prices to avoid local taxes, minimize import duties, circumvent exchange controls on capital outflows, and accomplish other purposes that are detrimental to the national interest. Other allegations relate to the investment and operating policies of the multinational enterprise. To illustrate, a multinational enterprise may decide that its global logistical system will benefit by shifting production from country A to country B or by lowering exports from country A in favor of more exports from country B. Or again, the multinational enterprise may decide to undertake R & D only in the home country, a policy that makes the affiliates "branch plants" dependent on the parent's technology. Whether or not the multinational enterprise *actually* follows policies that are detrimental to the national interest is not the point; it is the capability of the multinational enterprise to do so that is at issue. No government, jealous sovereign that it is, cares to have a substantial or key element of the national economy controlled by decision centers located in another country.

The Issue of Extraterritoriality

Host countries may also perceive the multinational enterprise as a threat to national sovereignty because of its identification with the policies of the home government. Multinational enterprises headquartered in the United States are particularly suspect because of the extraterritorial claims of the powerful U.S. government. As we shall observe later, the U.S. government may claim jurisdiction not only over the U.S. parent company but over its entire global system as well.

Whereas the issue of national interest arises because the host country perceives the multinational enterprise as being too independent, the issue of extraterritoriality arises because the host country perceives the multinational enterprise as being too dependent on the home country.

In matters of jurisdictional dispute between two sovereign states, the multinational enterprise is caught in the middle. To avoid this unhappy situation, U.S. parent companies have undoubtedly prevented their foreign affiliates from taking actions that would get the parents in trouble with the U.S. government, whether the problem concerns export controls, antitrust policy, or other matters. To host governments, the subjection of U.S.-owned local companies to U.S. government policies constitutes a direct violation of their territorial sovereignty. For that reason, efforts by the United States or any other home country to use parent companies to extend their laws and policies beyond the national domain act to endanger the viability of the multinational enterprise.

Host countries may also be fearful that multinational enterprises will call upon their home governments to support them in disputes with host governments. Particularly sensitive to this possibility, Latin American countries uphold the Calvo Doctrine, which denies the foreign investor any right to obtain support from the home government in a dispute with the host government.

The Issue of Nationalism

In Chapter 1, we pointed out that nationalism injects an emotional energy into international relations, often inciting governments to behavior that undermines the achievement of their own political and economic goals. In no other realm of external economic relations is nationalism more prominent than in foreign direct investment and the multinational enterprise. Economic nationalists are apostles of the closed economy; they regard the multinational enterprise as an enemy that preaches the seditious doctrine of an interdependent world economy. To nationalists, it is essential that the government maintain absolute sovereignty over all business firms within the national domain. Hence, they reject the foreign ownership of local firms on the grounds that it serves as a channel for foreign influence on the economy, the society, and the national culture. The multinational enterprise is the unwelcome guest that establishes permanent residence in "our" country.

All countries experience nationalism to one degree or another. However, the most intense expression of economic nationalism today is found in the developing countries. Nationalists in these countries label foreign direct investment as "neo-colonialism" or "economic imperialism," arguing that its purpose is to perpetuate economic and political dependence on the industrial countries. Governments in some developing countries consciously exploit nationalism to build loyalty to the state; political parties try to ride to power on the horse of antiforeign nationalism that pits "us" against "them." Frustrated by widening gaps between economic expectations and economic performance, governments are eager to use multinational enterprises as scapegoats for their own policy failures.

Nationalism in the developing countries has struck particularly hard at foreign investment in extractive industries. Natural resources are regarded as a national heritage that belongs to all the people. A common allegation against the foreign extractive investor is, "You take away our resources and leave us with an empty hole!" But the real grievance of nationalists is not the economic cost of foreign direct investment but rather the fact of foreign ownership, which sets the local affiliates of multinational enterprises outside the national society and national loyalties. Economic nationalists reject, therefore, the legitimacy of foreign ownership, regardless of the economic benefits it may bring to their country. Economic nationalism is by no means absent in the industrial countries, but it seldom dominates policies toward foreign direct investment.

Ambivalence and Tensions in Host Countries

The coexistence of economic benefits and political costs associated with foreign direct investment makes the attitudes and policies of host countries toward the multinational enterprise highly ambivalent and creates tensions that accompany any "love-hate" relationship. Unfortunately host countries are unable to resolve this ambivalence and relieve their tensions through an objective evaluation of economic benefits and political costs, because there is no way to measure political costs and thereby establish trade-offs between the two. What, after all, is the political cost of foreign ownership? How much is a feeling of national pride that comes from the expropriation of a foreign-owned petroleum or copper company worth to a people? One might answer, It is worth as much as a people are willing to forgo in economic benefits. However, a people can know the economic consequences of these actions only if an objective appraisal of economic benefits and costs is made in advance by responsible authorities.

The most one can reasonably expect, then, is that increasingly host governments will evaluate the full economic benefits and costs of foreign direct investment in formulating their policies toward the multinational enterprise. This will minimize erratic shifts in policy that harm both foreign investors and host countries. But objective economic analysis will not remove ambivalence or cure tensions. These will persist as governments everywhere continue the struggle to maintain national sovereignty in a world economy that is reaching toward ever higher levels of global interdependence.

POLICIES AND ACTIONS OF HOST GOVERNMENTS TO MINIMIZE THE POLITICAL COSTS OF FOREIGN DIRECT INVESTMENT

The concerns in host countries over the political costs of foreign direct investment center on the actual or potential exercise of control over the national economy by foreign companies and by the home governments of those companies. The legal basis of control by a foreign parent company is its ownership of local affiliates. Hence, attempts to prevent, reduce, or eliminate *foreign ownership* constitute many policies and actions of host governments that are taken to minimize the political costs of foreign direct investment. Foreign investment regulations are also intended to maximize the host country's *economic benefits* within ownership constraints.

Restrictions on Foreign Ownership

All countries discriminate against the foreign ownership of local companies in at least some industries. In general, these restrictions are most severe in the developing countries, but they are by no means insignificant in the industrial countries.

Exclusion of Foreigners from Key Industries Both industrial and developing countries exclude foreigners from direct investment in certain "key" industries that are regarded as essential to national security or as having a pervasive influence on the national economy and society. Key industries commonly include public utilities, airlines, shipping lines, communications media (television, radio, and publications), banks, and insurance companies. In developing countries, excluded industries may also encompass agriculture, forestry, fisheries, extraction (mining and petroleum), and basic industries (iron and steel, petrochemicals, and so on), which are sometimes reserved for state enterprise as well.

Requirements for Local Participation in Ownership In addition to excluding foreign ownership from certain sectors of the economy, host governments may also require local ownership participation in some industries.

For many years, Mexico pursued a policy (now reversed) of progressive "Mexicanization" of foreign-owned companies by converting them into joint ventures with local business interests. Another example is India. In 1977, the Indian government demanded that the Coca-Cola Company either transfer its know-how and a majority ownership share of its Indian subsidiary to Indian nationals or else cease to operate in India. Concerned about its trade secrets, Coca-Cola chose to withdraw. About the same time, IBM also pulled out of India, refusing to share its technology with a local partner.

In developing countries where there is no legal requirement for local ownership participation, the host government nonetheless may "persuade" foreign investors to enter into joint ventures with local entrepreneurs.

Prohibition of Acquisitions by Foreign Companies Even the governments of industrial countries that follow liberal policies toward new foreign investment may refuse to approve the acquisition (takeover) of a locally owned company by a foreign investor.

Expropriation

The expropriation of foreign-owned companies is the most dramatic action a host government can take to minimize the political costs of foreign direct investment. Broadly defined, *expropriation* includes any seizure of foreign-owned property by a host government. When foreign owners are not compensated for their seized properties, expropriation becomes *confiscation.* Most expropriation is also *nationalization,* which occurs when the host government assumes permanent ownership of the expropriated property. At a single stroke, then, expropriation deprives the foreign parent company of all ownership rights in its affiliate, including the right to control the affiliate's operations. The economic costs of expropriation to the host country may be extraordinarily severe. Apart from costs associated with the disruption of the affiliate's operations, expropriation commonly deters new foreign investment (which may be desired by the host government) and invites retaliation by the investor's home government.

Expropriation is a direct exercise of national sovereignty. Traditional international law has recognized the right of sovereign states to expropriate the property of foreigners, but it has also upheld an "international standard" that requires "prompt, adequate, and effective" compensation.[10] However, the developing countries (where most expropriations occur) have been loath to enter into bilateral or multilateral treaties that commit them to "just compensation" in the event of expropriation.

INVESTMENT INCENTIVES AND PERFORMANCE REQUIREMENTS OF HOST COUNTRIES

We have now reviewed the policies and actions of host governments to minimize the political costs of foreign investment. For the most part, these are efforts to nationalize control by denying or limiting foreign ownership of domestic economic activities. However, as observed earlier, host governments also seek to maximize their share of the *economic* benefits of foreign investment. Somewhat paradoxically, they pursue this objective by offering incentives to attract foreign investors in the first instance, and then by imposing performance requirements on foreign investors.

Investment Incentives

Investment incentives are host-government policies or actions intended to increase the return to foreign investors above what it would be in the absence of such policies or actions. The most common incentives are tax concessions, tariff concessions, and subsidies.

The effectiveness of incentives in attracting foreign investment is questionable.[11] Because the vast majority of countries offers incentives, the incentives of one country are largely neutralized by the incentives of the others. Apart from matching the incentives of other countries, least-developed countries (LDCs) appear to use investment incentives to offset *dis*incentives, such as small markets, weak infrastructure, and disruptive host-government policies. But foreign investors enter a country only when they anticipate profitable operations, and incentives cannot create profitable operations, although they can make them more profitable.

Not only are incentives generally ineffective in attracting foreign investment, they also are costly, reducing the net social benefits of foreign investment to the host country. The LDCs, therefore, have much to gain from regional or global agreements that would restrain the use of investment incentives. The prospects of

---

[10]"Adequate" compensation is payment of the full market value of the property. "Effective" compensation is payment in a convertible currency.

[11]See Franklin R. Root and Ahmed A. Ahmed, "The Influence of Policy Instruments on Manufacturing Direct Foreign Investment in Developing Countries," *Journal of International Business Studies,* Winter 1978, pp. 81–94.

such agreements, however, are very poor. In any event, LDC governments need to understand that policies aimed at improving the general investment climate can do much more to attract foreign investment than can incentives.

Investment Performance Requirements

Investment performance requirements include any host-government policies or actions that constrain the ownership or operations of a foreign-investment venture in the host country.

Performance requirements of special concern to home countries (as well as third countries) are export, import-limitation, and local-content requirements, for they distort the flows of trade and investment in ways that favor the host country to the detriment of other countries. Export requirements imposed on foreign affiliates not only increase a second country's imports but also may displace a third country's exports to the second country. This occurs without regard to the comparative advantage of the host country. Import-limitation and local-content requirements compel foreign affiliates to use local products regardless of their cost, and they are therefore forms of protection. Their trade-diversion effects have made performance requirements a growing issue between home- and host-country governments. The United States wants GATT to extend its mandate over trade-related investment measures (TRIMs).

TOWARD AN ACCOMMODATION BETWEEN NATION-STATES AND THE MULTINATIONAL ENTERPRISE

Our analysis of the benefits and costs of foreign direct investment demonstrated a coincidence of economic interests between the multinational enterprise and host countries. Within this fundamental harmony of interests, there is, of course, a continuing conflict of interests as both the multinational enterprise and host countries strive to maximize their shares of net economic benefits. But in the absence of political conflict, this conflict over the division of gains can be resolved to the satisfaction of both parties if they mutually recognize that their benefits are dependent on the viability of the foreign investment in question. By pressing their own interests too hard, both risk the loss of actual or prospective economic gains. In principle, conflicts of economic interests are resolvable, because international economic transactions constitute a positive sum game in which both participants can gain from its continuation and both can lose from its cessation. The coincidence of economic interests rests on the contributions that the multinational enterprise makes to the host economy as an international transfer agent of products, capital, technology, and entrepreneurial skills.

In spite of this fundamental harmony of economic interests, MNEs are opposed in many host countries on political grounds. This political conflict centers on control of their behavior within the host country. Host governments want control to maximize national sociopolitical values on a national scale; the multinational enterprise wants control to maximize enterprise economic values on a global scale.

Unlike the conflict of economic interests, the political conflict is a power contest or zero sum game in which one party gains at the expense of the other.

Can governments slay the dragons of multinational enterprise?[12] Certainly no government, acting individually, can do so, because it has jurisdiction over only one national element of the multinational enterprise system.[13] And it is difficult to imagine governments acting collectively to that end. But if many governments were to apply stiff performance requirements on the operations of MNEs within their territories, then they would seriously cripple the economic efficiency of multinational enterprise systems. Can MNEs slay the dragons of national sovereignty? Some scholars, viewing the nation-state as obsolescent, foresee political power passing to the multinational enterprise and other transnational functional institutions. But surely this is a fanciful notion in a world of intense nationalism. If, then, neither party is capable of destroying the other and achieving complete control over its own behavior, each can choose either to reach an accommodation with the other or else to exacerbate the political conflict in pursuit of selfish interests.

Bilateral Accommodation at the National Level

At the bilateral national level, the range of accommodation between a national sovereignty and the multinational enterprise is defined by two extreme postures. For the national sovereignty, the extreme posture is the adoption of a policy of laissez-faire that allows the multinational enterprise to pursue freely its own interests regardless of the benefits and costs to that sovereignty. Laissez-faire policy, therefore, represents a full accommodation by the nation to the multinational enterprise. For the multinational enterprise, the extreme posture is the transfer of all ownership and managerial control of its local operations to the national sovereignty or its representatives while, at the same time, continuing to sustain those operations with loan capital, technology, and management skills. By substituting contractual arrangements for ownership and control, the multinational enterprise becomes a service company that fully accommodates the political interests and nationalism of the host country.

Neither of these extreme postures is probable in the foreseeable future, although they may be assumed by individual nations and multinational enterprises in particular circumstances. The intellectual argument for a laissez-faire market economy has been decisively rejected by nations in the twentieth century for the doctrine of the welfare state, which holds that the state should take on responsibilities for economic growth, employment, and social justice. Furthermore, even during the heyday of laissez-faire policies in the last quarter of the nineteenth century, economic nationalism never disappeared, since nations commonly used

---

[12]Jack N. Behrman, "Can Governments Slay the Dragons of Multinational Enterprise?" *European Business,* Winter 1971, pp. 53–62.

[13]The U.S. government has the power to destroy *U.S.-based* multinational enterprises but not enterprises headquartered in other countries. In any event, U.S. policymakers do not perceive U.S. multinational enterprises as posing a threat to the national sovereignty of the United States.

tariffs to discriminate against foreign business enterprise. Even on purely economic grounds, nations reject a laissez-faire policy that would allow concentrations of private economic power, institutionalized in MNEs and international cartels, to determine the world's pattern of industry and trade and the distribution of the world's income.

As we have discovered, the actual responses of national governments to the political costs of the multinational enterprise range from comparatively mild restrictions on foreign ownership to confiscatory expropriations. By impairing the capacity of MNEs to function as international transfer agents, these responses lower the contribution of MNEs to the world economy and, more often than not, to the host economy, regardless of their political justification. Given the national perspective and nationalistic attitudes of host governments, bilateral policies to minimize the political costs of MNEs are inevitably restrictive, since they are motivated by an intent to prevent, reduce, or eliminate foreign ownership and control. Bilateral accommodation by the nation-state, then, is a question of the degree of restriction on foreign ownership and control: The lower the degree of restriction, the higher the accommodation, but restriction is never entirely absent.

Will MNEs accommodate the political interests and nationalism of host countries by voluntarily abandoning ownership and control over their affiliates? In Chapter 22 we defined the multinational enterprise as a parent company that engages in foreign production through its own affiliates located in several different countries, exercises direct control over the policies of those affiliates, and strives to design and implement business strategies that transcend national boundaries. Hence, a general substitution of contractual service arrangements for the ownership and control of production affiliates would transform the multinational enterprise into an entirely different institution.

Some observers, sensitive to attitudes in developing countries, believe that MNEs will evolve in that direction to eliminate political conflicts with host nations. But what is most probable is that MNEs will generally avoid investing in countries that limit their right to own and control affiliates.[14] Also, if they do invest in such countries, MNEs commonly refrain from integrating their operations in those countries with their global operations. The resulting fragmentation of operations (or lower degree of internalization) makes MNEs less efficient institutions, as suboptimization in individual host countries replaces optimization across national boundaries.

To conclude, bilateral accommodation offers little promise of any general resolution of the political conflict between the multinational enterprise and host nations. Moreover, when individual nations force an accommodation in ownership and control by the multinational enterprise, they limit its economic efficiency to the detriment of both the host and world economies. Is there, then, any way to

---

[14]This does not mean that MNEs avoid contractual business arrangements. In the 1980s, many MNEs entered international cooperative relations with other firms (including MNEs) to support their global strategies. See Farok J. Contractor and Peter Lorange, *Cooperative Strategies in International Business* (Lexington, Mass.: Lexington Books, 1988).

broaden the range of accommodation so as to reduce the political costs of the multinational enterprise as perceived by host nations and, at the same time, preserve the economic efficiency of the multinational enterprise system?

Multilateral Accommodation at the International Level

The range of accommodation between the nation-state and the multinational enterprise would be enormously broadened by multilateral agreements and institutions that conferred both rights and responsibilities on the multinational enterprise vis-à-vis national governments. Indeed, only through international agreements among governments can disputes between multinational enterprises and host countries be transformed from political issues into legal issues to be resolved by impartial international tribunals in accordance with agreed-upon principles of equity.

Today the multinational enterprise has economic power without legitimacy, while many nations have legitimacy without economic power. The multinational enterprise has no transnational legal identity; it is an aggregation of *national* companies. It is dependent on a convention that obligates host governments to extend to foreign enterprise the national treatment they accord to domestic enterprise. Functioning as it does in a legal vacuum, the multinational enterprise has no legal rights or legitimacy as a multinational system, and, accordingly, it has no legal responsibilities toward the world community. George Ball would fill that legal vacuum by an international treaty that would enable a parent company to be incorporated under an international companies law. This law would be administered by a supranational body composed of representatives from various countries that not only would exercise the ordinary domiciliary supervision but also would enforce antitrust laws and administer guarantees with regard to confiscatory expropriation.[15] Under this law, the parent company would trade its national legal identity for legal recognition in all countries. However, Ball's proposal — made over a quarter-century ago — has not struck a responsive chord among national governments.

The multinational enterprise also operates in a *policy* vacuum at the international level. To regulate international trade, governments have created GATT; to regulate international monetary relations, they have established the IMF. But where is the international machinery to regulate foreign direct investment and the multinational enterprise? So far, only a few steps have been taken in that direction. In 1969, the International Center for the Settlement of Investment Disputes was set up under the auspices of the IBRD. Under the convention ratified by the participating governments, the private investor is granted the right for the first time to take direct international legal action against a national state. Once the private investor and the host country have consented to submit a dispute to the center, they come under the conciliation and arbitration provisions of the conven-

---

[15]George W. Ball, "Cosmocorp: The Importance of Being Stateless," *The Columbia Journal of World Business,* November–December 1967, p. 29.

tion. In 1988, the Multilateral Investment Guarantee Agency (MIGA), a World Bank affiliate, came into existence. MIGA supplements political risk insurance facilities of national governments (such as the Overseas Private Investment Corporation [OPIC] in the United States) and private insurers.

To fill the policy vacuum, a much broader approach has been suggested that would be directed toward the formation of a general agreement for the international corporation along the lines of GATT. Apart from a single master agreement, specific international treaties for cooperation, coordination, and harmonization in taxation, antitrust laws, property rights, investment insurance, securities registration, patents, rights of establishments, repatriation of earnings and capital, and other policies would go a long way toward depoliticizing issues between the multinational enterprise and host countries. However, governments are not ready for such an institution, for nothing has been done to bring it into existence. A more likely development is the extension of GATT's jurisdiction to cover trade-related investment measures (TRIMs).

The United Nations, the OECD, and other international organizations have worked on the formulation of codes of conduct for MNEs since the mid-1970s. But only the OECD countries have agreed on guidelines for MNEs.[16] The prospects remain bleak for a code of conduct that would be supported by both the industrial and developing countries. The issue dividing them is fundamental: The industrial countries want a code that places obligations on the host country as well as on the multinational enterprise, but the developing countries reject such a code as an infringement on their national sovereignty.

International regulation of the multinational enterprise will not come quickly or all at once. But as governments come to recognize that uninational efforts to regulate MNEs are ineffective and carry a heavy national cost that is likely to prove unbearable in the long run, we can reasonably look forward to international agreements that will spell out the rights and responsibilities of MNEs in different areas of conduct. MNEs should welcome codes of conduct that spell out the rights and obligations of host countries as well as their own, for they can gain global legitimacy only through an international accommodation of their interests with national interests.

The 1970s were marked by confrontation between developing countries and the multinational enterprise on both bilateral and multilateral levels. But in the 1980s, the relationship between the two parties shifted from confrontation toward accommodation as LDCs liberalized their policies toward foreign direct investment. Expropriations declined drastically, and there was much more acceptance by LDCs of international arbitration to settle investment disputes. Concern over the ownership issue was displaced by concern over the performance criteria to be

---

[16]*International Investment and Multinational Enterprises* (Paris: The Organization for Economic Cooperation and Development, 1976). For a recent proposal to establish an OECD Convention on International Investment, see Donald L. Guertin and John M. Kline, *Building an International Investment Accord,* Occasional Paper (Washington, D.C.: The Atlantic Council of the United States, July 1989). See also C. Fred Bergsten and Edward M. Graham, "Needed: New International Rules for Foreign Direct Investment," *International Trade Journal,* Fall 1992, pp. 15–44.

met by foreign investors. Fewer developing countries saw the MNE as a threat to their national sovereignty.

The liberalization of LDC policies toward the multinational enterprise, which is continuing in the 1990s, is the result of many forces. Prominent among them is the international debt burden. By limiting resources available for domestic capital formation and by drying up imports of new loan capital from banks, the international debt problem has turned LDC governments toward the multinational enterprise as a source of capital and a means to achieve an expansion of industrial exports to earn badly needed foreign exchange. Another force is the widening technology gap between the developing and industrial countries. Increasingly, LDCs perceive the MNE as a source of technological innovation that can overcome the weaknesses of their technological infrastructures.

Although LDC countries have liberalized their policies toward foreign direct investment and the multinational enterprise, they have not given up their belief that the MNE should be subject to some form of control. Their liberalization is a *pragmatic* accommodation to the MNE, not an ideological one. In the absence of international institutions to provide a legal or policy framework for regulating relations between MNEs and host countries, therefore, the accommodation of today can easily revert to the confrontation of the past.

Against this review of FDI benefits and costs, sovereignty issues, host-country policies, and the accommodation of national and MNE interests, we now look at U.S. policy toward foreign direct investment and the multinational enterprise.

U.S. POLICY TOWARD FOREIGN DIRECT INVESTMENT AND THE MULTINATIONAL ENTERPRISE

What is the policy of the U.S. government toward the MNE? The answer to this question is not a simple one. Actually the United States does not have a policy toward the multinational enterprise. The rapid emergence of the multinational enterprise has caught the U.S. government unprepared to deal with it as a distinctive institution. Instead, the United States applies a variety of policies to different facets of the MNE, policies that were mostly formulated at a time when the multinational enterprise was not yet a policy issue, with the result that many of them are based on considerations unrelated to the multinational enterprise as a unique economic organization. Before we examine specific U.S. policies that affect the multinational enterprise, however, a brief review of traditional U.S. policy toward direct investment abroad by U.S. companies is in order.

Traditional U.S. Policy Toward Foreign Direct Investment

The United States became a large recipient of foreign direct investment only in the 1980s. Hence, its traditional policy toward FDI assumed the posture of an investing or *home* country concerned with the treatment of U.S. business abroad by foreign governments.

The fundamental thrust of U.S. foreign economic policy since 1934 has been to extend the freedom of international trade and investment. Before World War II, U.S. foreign investment policy was a mixture of laissez-faire (letting U.S. companies invest abroad when and where they chose to do so) and strong diplomatic protection of U.S. companies in foreign countries. After World War II, U.S. policy shifted to active encouragement of foreign direct investment by American companies, at first as an instrument to help European reconstruction and somewhat later as a means (along with "transitional" foreign aid) to transfer resources to the developing countries. It was also recognized that U.S. foreign investment creates export markets for U.S. products, develops foreign sources of raw materials and fuels needed by U.S. industry, and affords profitable employment of U.S. capital. In the 1950s, the government also supported the foreign investment of U.S. companies as a way of alleviating the "dollar shortage" of foreign countries. Finally, foreign direct investment was viewed as a positive element in the struggle with the communist powers to keep the developing countries in the free world.

The onset of the persistent U.S. balance of payments deficit in 1958 weakened this supportive investment policy. Once promoted as a means of relieving the "dollar shortage," private foreign investment was accused in the 1960s of intensifying the "dollar glut." Capital outflows to Western Europe drew special criticism from government authorities, who asserted that Western Europe was no longer in need of U.S. foreign investment and, indeed, should step up its own foreign assistance and private investment in the developing countries. In 1962 the United States revised its tax code to strike down the use of "tax havens" by U.S. companies abroad and thereby accelerate the repatriation of their foreign earnings to the United States. And in 1965 the government initiated a "voluntary" restraint program (succeeded by a mandatory program in 1968) to curb the outflow of private direct investment to other industrial countries. At the same time, the United States continued to actively support direct investment in the developing countries. Balance of payments controls on FDI were lifted in 1974.

The traditional policy of the United States with respect to private foreign investment has involved treaties of friendship, commerce, and navigation with many countries; diplomatic assistance to American investors abroad; insistence on nondiscriminatory treatment of American investments; and, at times in the past, the military protection of American-owned property abroad, notably in Central American and Caribbean countries.

In recent years the U.S. government has negotiated investment treaties that deal more specifically with the conditions that affect investment abroad. These treaties have included provisions that protect the right of American investors to engage freely in business activities in a foreign country, including freedom from restrictions on the ownership or management of business enterprise. Other provisions may guarantee national or most-favored-nation treatment in taxation and other matters; reasonable requirements regarding the employment of local workers; the unrestricted remittance of earnings and repatriation of capital; and freedom from expropriation or prompt, adequate compensation in the event of expropriation.

In the 1980s, the United States reaffirmed its traditional policy, of which the central feature is a belief that market forces should determine direct investment flows. But the dramatic rise in direct investment in the United States by foreign-based multinationals is now forcing a reconsideration of policy for the 1990s.

U.S. Policy as a Host Country

Supporting the principle of national treatment at home as well as abroad, the United States treats foreign investors the same as domestic investors. There are, however, some exceptions. Federal law does restrict foreign participation in U.S. companies associated with atomic energy, hydroelectric power, communications, air transport, coastal and inland water shipping, fishing, and the development of federally owned lands and mineral resources. Also, under regulations of the Department of Defense, foreigners are generally excluded from participation in, or access to, work covered by classified defense contracts. Furthermore, many states impose additional restrictions on foreign participation in banking, insurance, and land ownership, but these restrictions must be consistent with U.S. treaty obligations. Despite these exceptions, the entry of foreign companies into the United States is freer than entry into any other country in the world.

As the United States does not hinder the entry of foreign companies, neither does it encourage entry with incentives. However, the individual states compete fiercely for the investment of foreign companies by offering inducements such as low-cost financing, the building of infrastructure facilities, and tax concessions. Most states also maintain offices abroad to attract foreign investors.

In the wake of the oil price hike, fears grew in the United States that the oil-rich Arab countries would initiate a massive takeover of American industry. In response to those fears (which proved unwarranted), the U.S. government established a high-level interagency body to ensure that foreign investments in the United States do not injure national interests, and a new office in the Department of Commerce was also created to monitor foreign investments. The interagency advisory committee, the Committee on Foreign Investment in the United States, is charged with reviewing all major inward direct investments. Under the Exon-Florio Amendment to the Omnibus Trade and Competitiveness Act of 1988, the Committee screens all mergers and acquisitions by foreign firms in the United States "affecting national security." National security is not defined, and there is no time limit on presidential action. So far, the Amendment has not been used to restrict the entry of foreign companies, but it has triggered uncertainty in the minds of foreign investors about future U.S. action.

Figure 24-2 depicts foreign direct investment in the United States during the period 1970–1991. Its explosive growth in the 1980s is evident. In 1970, FDI in this country was only $13.3 billion and in 1980, only $68.4 billion. But then it took off, reaching $407.6 billion in 1991. Direct investment in the United States now exceeds U.S. direct investment abroad.

What explains this extraordinary growth? Undoubtedly, several factors—both macroeconomic and structural—are at work. The persistent U.S. deficit on cur-

Figure 24-2

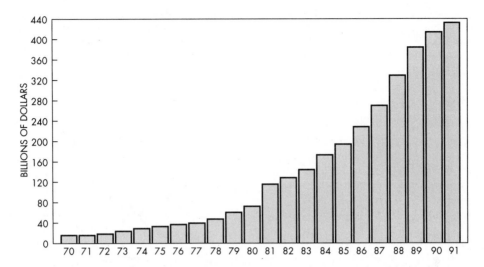

Source: U.S. Department of State, *Foreign Direct Investment in a Global Economy* (Washington, D.C.: U.S. Department of State, March 1989), p. 9; and "Foreign Direct Investment in the United States: Detail for Historical-Cost Position and Balance of Payments Flows," *Survey of Current Business,* various August issues.

Foreign Direct Investment Position in the United States on a Historical Cost Basis, 1970–1991. The stock of FDI in the United States grew slowly in the 1970s, but accelerated in the 1980s, reaching $407.6 billion in 1991.

rent account provides foreign countries with dollar income to finance investments in the United States. Also the trade deficit fans the flames of import protection in the United States, which in turn induces foreign companies to circumvent actual and anticipated import barriers by establishing U.S. plants. Structural factors also promote direct investment in the United States: It is the world's largest single market, its economic growth was rapid in the 1980s, it has a high degree of political stability, and there is a comparatively low level of government interference in the economy. Another structural factor is the emergence of more Japanese and European multinationals with the financial and technological capability to compete directly in the United States. To undertake global strategies, foreign multinationals *must* have a production and marketing presence in the United States.

Figure 24-3 shows the stock of foreign direct investment in the United States by major source country. In 1990, the United Kingdom was still the leading source country ($102.8). But the acceleration of Japan's investment, rising from a mere $200 *million* in 1970 to $81.8 *billion* in 1990, is almost certain to make Japan the most important source of direct investment for the United States in the 1990s.

Foreign multinational enterprises operating through their U.S. subsidiaries now account for a substantial share of the assets of U.S. manufacturing industries.

Figure 24-3

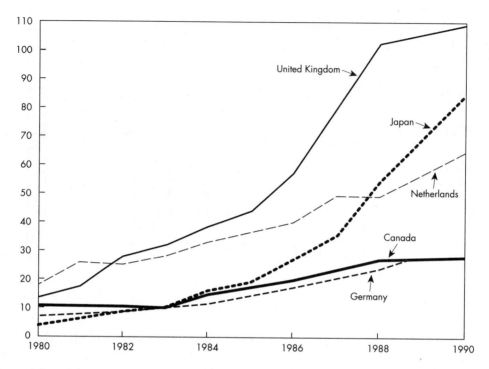

Source: Adapted from Cletus C. Coughlin, "Foreign-owned Companies: Malign or Benign?" *Review,* Federal Reserve Bank of St. Louis, May–June 1992.

Foreign Direct Investment in the United States by Major Country, 1980–1990 (Billions of Dollars). United Kingdom investors still hold the largest share of the FDI stock in the United States. However, the growth rate of Japanese FDI in the United States is far higher than that of the other source countries.

As shown in Table 24-3, the share of U.S. affiliates of foreign MNEs almost tripled from 1977 to 1990, rising from 6.3 percent to 18.6 percent. In 1990, these affiliates held $489.8 billion of assets in the U.S. manufacturing sector. For four industries—chemicals and allied products; stone, clay, and glass products; primary metals; and rubber and plastics products—foreign ownership was more than one-quarter in 1990.

Four of the ten biggest U.S. chemical plants have foreign parents. Many household names, such as Firestone, General Tire, and Armstrong in the rubber industry, are owned by foreign companies (foreign-owned firms make 40 percent of the tires in the United States). There are now eight Japanese automobile assembly plants and more than two hundred foreign suppliers (mostly Japanese) of automobile parts in the United States. In the 1980s, much of the expansion of

Table 24-3 Total Assets of U.S. Affiliates of Foreign-Based Multinational Enterprises as a Percentage of Total Assets of All U.S. Businesses in Manufacturing, 1977, 1986, and 1990

Industry	1977	1986	1990
Chemicals and allied products	15.4	32.5	41.7
Stone, clay, and glass products	7.3	22.8	41.8
Primary metal industries	6.2	20.5	28.7
Petroleum and coal products	12.0	14.9	20.1
Printing and publishing	4.5	11.8	16.8
Electric and electronic equipment	5.1	11.3	20.5
Food, tobacco, and kindred products	4.4	9.5	NA
Paper and allied products	3.8	8.1	8.4
Fabricated metal products	2.8	7.6	21.1
Instruments and related products	3.3	6.4	9.2
Machinery, except electrical	3.7	5.5	12.1
Textile products	3.2	4.4	8.4
Rubber and plastics products	2.6	4.0	27.6
Transportation equipment	0.6	2.9	4.6
Other	2.1	5.6	NA
All industries	*6.3*	*12.1*	*18.6*
Total affiliate assets in billions of dollars	*60.4*	*240.5*	*489.8*
Total assets of all U.S. businesses in billions of dollars	*963.0*	*1,994.1*	*2,629.0*

NA — Not available.

Source: "U.S. Affiliates of Foreign Companies: Operations in (Year)," *Survey of Current Business,* May 1988 and May 1992.

direct investment occurred through the acquisition of U.S. companies by foreign multinationals. Table 24-4 lists the twelve largest foreign acquisitions during the period 1981–1988.

The unprecedented proliferation of foreign direct investments in the United States, often involving takeovers of well-known American companies, has aroused intense opposition by labor unions fearful of anti-union biases of foreign multinationals (particularly Japanese) and by U.S. firms fearful of new competition. These special interest groups promote legislation to curb new direct investments, particularly the acquisition of U.S. companies. In 1989, the Committee on Foreign Investment in the United States recommended for the first time that the president block a proposed acquisition — the acquisition of General Ceramics (a U.S. company engaged in a nuclear weapons program using critical technology) by Tokuyama Soda Company, a Japanese firm. Subsequently, Tokuyama withdrew its offer.

Table 24-4   The Twelve Largest Acquisitions of U.S. Companies by Foreign-Based Multinational Enterprises, 1981–1988

Foreign-Based MNE	U.S. Company	Year	Value (Billions of Dollars)
British Petroleum (United Kingdom)	Standard Oil of Ohio	1987	7.6
Campeau (Canada)	Federated Department Stores	1988	6.5
Grand Metropolitan (United Kingdom)	Pillsbury	1989	5.8
Royal Dutch Shell (Netherlands)	Shell Oil	1985	5.7
B.A.T. Industries (United Kingdom)	Farmers Group	1988	5.2
Campeau (Canada)	Allied Stores	1986	3.6
Unilever (Netherlands)	Chesebrough-Pond	1987	3.1
News Corporation (Australia)	Triangle Publications	1988	3.0
Nestlé (Switzerland)	Carnation	1985	2.9
Elf Aquitaine (France)	Texasgulf	1981	2.7
Hoescht (West Germany)	Celanese	1987	2.7
Bridgestone (Japan)	Firestone	1988	2.7

Source: Adapted from *The New York Times,* May 28, 1989, p. F9.

The massive flows of FDI into the United States are fundamentally an expression of the trend toward the globalization of the international economy that we have noted several times in this text. The policy issue for the 1990s is whether the United States fully participates in the emerging global economy or partly withdraws from it by restraining the entry of foreign multinationals as well as the entry of goods and services.

Specific U.S. Policies Relating to FDI and Multinational Enterprise

This section offers brief comments on three specific U.S. policies that can influence the conduct of MNEs and their direct investment strategies: promotion of direct investment in the developing countries, taxation, and antitrust.

Promotion of Direct Investment in Developing Countries   The United States actively promotes FDI in the developing countries with programs and services administered by the Overseas Private Investment Corporation (OPIC):

1. The *investment insurance program,* under which U.S. investors are provided coverage against the political risks of (a) expropriation and confiscation; (b) war, revolution, insurrection, and civil strife; and (c) inconvertibility of profits and capital.
2. The *investment guaranty program,* under which coverage against both political and commercial risks is provided for financial loans (mostly portfolio investments) by U.S. institutional investors, such as insurance companies.
3. The *direct investment fund program,* which provides dollar loans to help finance foreign direct investment projects.
4. The *investment survey program,* under which OPIC pays half the cost of an investment survey undertaken by a prospective U.S. investor if subsequently the investor decides not to go ahead with the project.
5. *Services* that include the sponsorship of *investment missions* by American business people to foreign countries, the *planning and structuring* of investment projects, and *project brokering* to bring U.S. investors into contact with known opportunities abroad.

These incentives are limited to U.S. nationals. The incentive of most importance to U.S. companies is the investment insurance program. To qualify for this insurance, a U.S. national must demonstrate that the investment is a new project, that it is in a developing country, and that it serves the economic and social needs of the host country.

Has the investment insurance program stimulated U.S. direct investment in the developing countries? No conclusive answer is possible, but the following points are pertinent. First, like other incentives, investment insurance cannot turn an unprofitable investment into a profitable one. A multinational enterprise will not invest in a developing country simply because it can obtain insurance against political risks. If an investment project is judged to be unpromising on economic grounds, the enterprise will not go ahead with it even if investment insurance is available at no cost. Second, there may be situations where a multinational enterprise will not proceed with an economically attractive project in a developing country because political risks are deemed to be too high. Here the availability of insurance may tip the balance in favor of investment, although it is unlikely to do so if political risks are viewed as severe. After all, investment insurance covers only actual asset loss; it does not cover the investor's loss of prospective profits that made the investment desirable in the first place. In light of these considerations, investment insurance has probably encouraged some increase in U.S. direct investment in the developing countries. But investment insurance has not been able to alter the regional pattern of U.S. direct investment, which continues to favor the industrial areas.

Tax Policy Toward the Multinational Enterprise   Operating in many countries, multinational enterprises are subject to multiple tax jurisdictions. National tax systems are exceedingly complex, with many differences among them with respect to forms of taxation (for example, direct and indirect taxes), statutory rates, effective rates (what taxpayers actually pay), and the taxation of foreign-source income and in particular the taxation of the income of multinational enterprises by the U.S. government.

Differences among national income tax systems influence several kinds of decisions made by the managers of multinational parent companies, notably the choice of country in which to locate operations, the method of financing operations (loan or equity, domestic or foreign), and the determination of the prices of products and other assets that are transferred among the many national units of the multinational enterprise system.[17] Because of its potency in influencing business decisions, both home and host governments frequently employ tax policy to promote or deter the investment and other activities of multinational enterprises.

Multiple tax jurisdictions create two sets of problems: (1) "overlapping" jurisdictions, and (2) "underlapping" jurisdictions. When overlapping occurs, two or more governments claim tax jurisdiction over the same income of the same multinational enterprise. Hence, overlapping jurisdictions raise the problem of *double taxation,* a problem of immediate concern to enterprise managers. Conversely, underlapping occurs when some or all of the income of a multinational enterprise falls between tax jurisdictions and thereby escapes any taxation. The result is *tax avoidance,* which is a problem for governments. To understand how overlapping and underlapping can happen, we need to know something about the tax jurisdictions of national governments.

National governments may choose to exercise a *territorial tax jurisdiction,* a *national tax jurisdiction,* or both. Under a territorial tax jurisdiction, a government taxes only business income that is generated by operations located on the national territory. A government following this jurisdictional principle taxes both domestic and foreign-owned business operations taking place *within* its borders but exempts from taxation all foreign-source income that is earned by national companies *outside* its borders.

When a government exercises national tax jurisdiction, both the domestic *and*

---

[17]Differences among national *indirect* tax systems also affect decision making in the multinational enterprise because of their effects on production costs, prices, and the cost of transferring products among countries. The role of indirect taxes as nontariff trade barriers is treated in Chapter 6.

foreign-source incomes of national companies are liable for taxation by that government. Thus, the U.S. government (which follows the national principle, as do the majority of governments) taxes U.S. multinational enterprises on their worldwide incomes. If a government exercised *only* a national tax jurisdiction, it would exempt from taxation the income earned on its territory by nonnational companies owned by foreigners. But this does not happen, because governments that claim a national tax jurisdiction also claim a territorial jurisdiction.

If all national governments were to adopt only a territorial tax jurisdiction, then the problem of double taxation would largely disappear for the multinational enterprise. Its affiliates would pay income taxes to their respective host governments, and dividends paid to the parent company by the affiliates would be exempt from taxation by the home government. Still remaining, however, would be the thorny problem of deciding where the income of a multinational enterprise was "rightfully" earned, a problem that is intensified by the ability of the enterprise to alter the national source of its income through adjustments in transfer prices. Given territorial tax jurisdiction only, a multinational enterprise could minimize its tax liabilities by arranging transfer prices so as to concentrate income in low-tax countries. Hence, governments would have to agree on the proper allocation among countries of the income of multinational enterprises to fully resolve the twin problems of double taxation and tax avoidance.

In general, the U.S. government does not distinguish between income earned at home and income earned abroad. However, to minimize double taxation, the government does allow multinational enterprises headquartered in the United States to credit their U.S. income tax liabilities with income taxes paid to foreign governments.

To get its "fair share" of the income earned by U.S. multinational enterprises, the U.S. Treasury insists that a U.S. parent company use "arm's length" prices in all transactions with its foreign affiliates. Arm's length prices are the prices of the same or similar products and services that are paid or charged by the parent company in transactions with independent sellers and buyers. In the absence of such transactions (a common occurrence), arm's length prices are prices that represent full standard costs and appropriate markups. Section 482 of the Internal Revenue Code gives the Treasury the authority to reallocate the income between a U.S. parent company and its foreign affiliates in accordance with the arm's length standards. The Treasury's interpretation of arm's length pricing has aroused much criticism from managers of multinational enterprises, who consider the Treasury's reallocations as frequently unrealistic and arbitrary. Nonetheless, the Treasury's authority to reallocate income is clearly necessary if U.S. parent companies are to be prevented from shifting income to foreign affiliates at the expense of U.S. tax revenue. It is rational for U.S. parent companies to establish transfer prices that will maximize the posttax consolidated profits of the entire multinational enterprise system, and this behavior could very well involve shifting income from the United States to affiliates in low-tax countries either by charging low prices for the products and services a parent company "sells" to its affiliates or by paying high prices for the products and services it "buys" from them.

Each national government insists that the units of a multinational enterprise operating on its territory make some taxable profits, although no other government has gone as far as the United States in reallocating profits. When the U.S. government reallocates the profits of a multinational enterprise in a way that is unacceptable to a foreign government, then the enterprise may experience double taxation. The U.S. government tries to overcome this problem by negotiating bilateral tax treaties with foreign governments whereby both signatories recognize the same allocation of income between related taxpayers. Bilateral tax treaties also contain provisions designed to eliminate other forms of double taxation and to prevent tax avoidance by nationals of the two countries.

Antitrust Policy   As business firms incorporated in the United States, the U.S. parent companies of multinational enterprises are clearly subject to antitrust laws of the United Sates.[18] But what may surprise many readers is the extent to which these laws also apply to their foreign affiliates, to their licensing arrangements with foreign companies, and to their acquisitions of foreign companies. Even foreign companies operating abroad come under the jurisdictional sweep of U.S. antitrust policy when their behavior has actual or potential anticompetitive effects in the United States.

The application of U.S. antitrust laws to business behavior outside the United States is sure to engender conflicts with the laws and policies of other countries. Indeed, the United States has been accused of "judicial imperialism" in seeking to apply its antitrust laws to the foreign operations of U.S. companies and even to the operations of foreign companies. The probability of conflicts is heightened by the wide diversity of national policies toward anticompetitive business behavior. Most developing countries have no antitrust laws, and the United States is sharply divergent from the other industrial countries in its antitrust philosophy and practice. EC policy, for instance, distinguishes between "good" and "bad" cartels and "good" and "bad" mergers. European governments strongly support mergers between national companies so that they can compete more effectively with the "American and Japanese giants."

The mild enforcement of U.S. policy in the 1980s lessened antitrust conflicts with foreign governments. But as long as the United States claims extraterritorial jurisdiction for its antitrust laws, there remains the potential for future conflict.

Few subjects are as complex, contradictory, and uncertain as U.S. antitrust policy at home and abroad. It is a delight to lawyers, a challenge to economists, a brooding presence to business people, and a profound mystery to laymen. It raises

---

[18]The most important antitrust provisions are Sections 1 and 2 of the Sherman Act and Section 7 of the Clayton Act. Section 1 forbids contracts, combinations, or conspiracies "in restraint of trade or commerce among the several states, or with foreign nations." Section 2 makes illegal the monopolization of or attempt to monopolize "any part of the trade or commerce among the several states or with foreign nations." Section 7 prohibits a corporation from acquiring another corporation "where in any line of commerce in any section of the country, the effect of such acquisition may be substantially to lessen competition, or tend to create a monopoly." In brief, Section 1 is an anticartel provision, Section 2 is an antimonopoly provision, and Section 7 is an antimerger provision.

many political, economic, and social questions that, for lack of space, cannot be treated here.[19] In closing, therefore, we shall simply list the key issues that will continue to make U.S. antitrust policy a subject of controversy.

1. Does U.S. antitrust policy help or hurt the international economic position of the United States?[20] Does it promote or deter the attainment of other goals of U.S. foreign economic policy?
2. Does U.S. antitrust policy weaken the competitive strength of U.S. multinational enterprises vis-à-vis foreign companies that are subject to milder forms of antitrust regulation or to none at all? If so, is this result congruent with the national interest of the United States?
3. Should the United States seek to apply U.S. antitrust standards to the foreign operations of U.S. multinational enterprises? Or should the United States adopt a territorial jurisdiction, leaving the regulation of anticompetitive business behavior to each national government on its own territory?
4. Is the U.S. antitrust policy naive, given the oligopolistic character of U.S. and foreign multinational enterprises? To what extent is U.S. antitrust policy an ideological commitment rather than a realistic policy for the world economy of the 1990s and beyond?
5. Is U.S. antitrust policy alone sufficient to regulate the anticompetitive behavior of U.S. multinational enterprises? Can the United States achieve its antitrust goals by acting unilaterally?
6. What are the prospects for international antitrust regulation? How might it be achieved?

CLOSING OBSERVATIONS ON U.S. POLICY TOWARD THE MULTINATIONAL ENTERPRISE

As observed earlier, the United States does not have a policy toward the multinational enterprise but instead pursues several policies that were formulated either at a time when the multinational enterprise was not a policy issue or for reasons unrelated to its unique characteristics. An examination of traditional policies toward foreign direct investment, the promotion of foreign direct investment in developing countries, tax policy, antitrust policy, and U.S. policy toward foreign investment in the United States substantiates that contention.

---

[19]For a discussion of U.S. antitrust policy in the context of global competition, see the following articles appearing in *The Journal of Economic Perspectives,* Summer 1990: Thomas M. Jorde and David J. Teece, "Innovation and Cooperation: Implications for Competition and Antitrust" (pp. 75–96); Joseph F. Brodley, "Antitrust Law and Innovation Cooperation" (pp. 97–112); and Carl Shapiro and Robert D. Willig, "On the Antitrust Treatment of Production Joint Ventures" (pp. 113–130.

[20]As far back as 1918, the U.S. Congress recognized that antitrust policy might hurt U.S. exports when it passed the Webb-Pomerene Act, which allows American companies to form export cartels. However, Webb-Pomerene Associations are prohibited from restraining trade within the United States or the trade of any U.S. competitor. In practice, these associations have not been important in U.S. exports, and they have been used mainly by primary producers, not manufacturers. The Export Trading Company Act of 1982 allows firms (including banks) to form export consortia, exempting them from current antitrust statutes. Comparatively few firms have taken advantage of this legislation.

Because of their importance to the American economy, new issues relating to U.S. and non-U.S. MNEs will continue to arise in the formulation of U.S. foreign economic policy. One example of an emerging issue is the performance requirements imposed on MNEs by host governments, such as local-content and export requirements. Host-government performance requirements (together with incentives offered to MNEs) distort international trade in ways that can be detrimental to U.S. economic interests. In effect, they are a form of protectionism.[21] The United States is now pressing GATT to address trade-distorting measures applied to foreign investment.

Contemporary U.S. policy toward the multinational enterprise calls to mind the fable of the blind man and the elephant. What is the multinational enterprise? Is it an international trader? An exporter of capital? An exporter of technology? An exporter of management? A possessor of considerable oligopolistic market power? A source of tax revenue? A major source of short-term capital movements? An institution subject to many national jurisdictions but not completely subject to any single jurisdiction? The answer, of course, is that the multinational enterprise is all of these things — and more.

U.S. policymakers need to transcend the traditional distinctions between trade, investment, and balance of payments policies if they are to develop a comprehensive policy toward the multinational enterprise, To design and implement such a policy, U.S. policymakers must obtain the answers to two fundamental questions: (1) What is the national interest of the United States in the multinational enterprise over the long run? (2) What comprehensive policy toward the multinational enterprise will enhance that interest?

The answer to the first question is dependent on the overall goals of U.S. foreign economic policy. The United States can choose to continue a liberal commercial policy or regress to the protectionist policy it espoused before 1934. In the final analysis, it is a choice between a world of economic interdependence and a world of autarkic economic blocs. The multinational enterprise can promote the national interest of the United States only if that interest is defined in terms of an open, competitive world economy. A world of protectionist blocs would doom the multinational enterprise to eventual extinction.

Given a clear perception of the national interest in the multinational enterprise, U.S. policymakers need to design a policy that optimizes the value of that institution to the United States. To a very substantial degree, the instruments of contemporary U.S. foreign economic policy are multinational enterprise systems headquartered in the United States. The success or failure of U.S. policies relating to international trade, global competitiveness, and economic growth depends critically on the behavior of multinational enterprise systems. U.S. policymakers need to learn much more about that behavior and how it can be influenced to serve the national interest. The development of an effective policy, therefore, will require more cooperation than heretofore experienced between the U.S. government and the representatives of multinational enterprises as well as among differ-

---

[21]See Chapter 8.

ent agencies of the U.S. government. But it will also require closer cooperation between the U.S. government and foreign governments, extending even to the harmonization of specific policy areas such as taxation and antitrust. No single government can reasonably expect to regulate the conduct of multinational enterprise systems that operate in multiple national jurisdictions. Attempts by the U.S. government to do so engender extraterritorial disputes with other national governments that embitter international relations.

In the years ahead, many more firms will evolve from U.S. companies that happen to have extensive foreign operations into multinational enterprises that happen to have their headquarters in the United States. And the same evolution will occur elsewhere. The question of U.S. policy toward the multinational enterprise becomes, therefore, part of the larger question of public policy toward the multinational enterprise by the community of nations. The national interests of foreign countries that host the affiliates of U.S. parent companies or have parent companies with affiliates in the United States cannot be ignored in the formation of U.S. international economic policy.

SUMMARY

1. The multinational enterprise is perceived by policymakers in host countries as both an economic institution that creates benefits and costs to the local economy and a quasi-political institution that threatens the power and even the sovereignty of the nation.

2. The fundamental economic effect of foreign direct investment (representing the sum total of many individual effects) is its contribution to the national income (net national product) of the host country over time. Closely related to this national income effect, but deserving special treatment, is the effect of foreign direct investment on the balance of payments of the host country over time.

3. The net benefit/cost ratio of foreign direct investment for the national income of the host economy is

$$\frac{(F + R^* + T) - N + L}{E}.$$

There is both theoretical and empirical evidence that foreign direct investment generally offers net benefits to the host economy.

4. The net benefit/cost ratio of foreign direct investment for the balance of payments of the host economy is

$$\frac{K + X + S}{(R^{**} + F^*) + (M + M^*) + D}.$$

Ideally a host country should maintain balance of payments equilibrium by resorting to monetary, fiscal, and exchange rate policies, together with measures to speed up the reallocation of resources.

5. As is true of other forms of economic specialization and exchange, foreign direct investment is a "positive sum game" that benefits both players. Within its fundamental harmony of interests, however, there is likely to be a continuing conflict of interests as both the multinational enterprise and the host country strive to maximize their respective shares of the net economic benefits of foreign investment.

6. Although there is a fundamental harmony of *economic* interests between host countries and the multinational enterprise, there is also a fundamental conflict of *political* interests inasmuch as the MNE poses a challenge to the national sovereignty of host countries. This political conflict may be treated in terms of three major issues: national interest, extraterritoriality, and nationalism.

7. The coexistence of economic benefits and political costs associated with foreign direct investment makes the attitudes and policies of host countries toward the multinational enterprise highly ambivalent and creates tensions that accompany any "love-hate" relationship.

8. Many policies and actions of host governments intended to minimize the political costs of foreign direct investment are essentially attempts to prevent, reduce, or eliminate *foreign ownership*. Restrictions on foreign ownership include exclusion of foreigners from key industries, requirements for local participation in ownership, and prohibitions against acquisitions by foreign companies.

9. Host countries commonly offer incentives to attract foreign investors and, at the same time, impose performance requirements on them.

10. Bilateral accommodation offers no promise of any general resolution of the political conflict between the multinational enterprise and host nations. But the range of accommodation would be enormously broadened by multilateral agreements and institutions that conferred both rights and responsibilities on the multinational enterprise vis-à-vis national governments.

11. In the 1980s, the United States reaffirmed its traditional policy toward foreign direct investment and the multinational enterprise. The central feature of this policy is a belief that market forces should determine direct investment flows.

12. Foreign direct investment in the United States demonstrated extraordinary growth in the 1980s. Foreign MNEs now control a substantial share of the assets of U.S. manufacturing industries.

13. The United States actively promotes private foreign investment in the developing countries through an investment insurance program that provides coverage against political risks. These and related programs are administered by the Overseas Private Investment Corporation (OPIC).

14. Operating in many countries, multinational enterprises are subject to multiple tax jurisdictions. This situation creates two sets of problems: double taxation and tax avoidance. Following the national rather than the territorial principle of tax jurisdiction, the United States taxes U.S. multinational enterprises on their worldwide income. To limit double taxation, the United States allows credits against foreign taxes; to limit tax avoidance, the United States insists that a U.S. parent company use "arm's length" prices in all transactions with its foreign affiliates.

15. The United States claims antitrust jurisdiction over the behavior of U.S. companies and their foreign affiliates regardless of where that behavior may take place. The rationale for this claim is that business behavior anywhere in the world may restrain U.S. exports or imports or have anticompetitive effects in the United States. As a result of seeking to apply the U.S. antitrust laws to the foreign operations of U.S. companies (and even to the operations of foreign companies), the United States has been accused of "judicial imperialism."

16. U.S. policymakers need to transcend the traditional distinctions between trade, investment, and balance of payments policies if they are to develop a comprehensive policy toward the multinational enterprise.

QUESTIONS AND APPLICATIONS

1. Why is the conventional concept of *net value added* inadequate to measure the contribution of a *new* foreign direct investment to the national product (income) of a host country?

2. Does every foreign-owned affiliate necessarily make a net contribution to the economy of the host country? Be prepared to explain your answer.

3. "Over the long run, the balance of payments effect of foreign direct investment cannot be distinguished from its national income effect." Explain the reasoning behind this statement.

4. What are the coincidence and conflict of economic interests between host countries and the multinational enterprise (foreign direct investment)?

5. Explain the dynamics of shifting perceptions of economic benefit/cost ratios over time.

6. (a) Why do host countries offer incentives to foreign investors?
   (b) Why do host countries impose requirements on foreign investors?
   (c) Evaluate the effects of investment incentives and performance requirements on international trade.

7. Be prepared to discuss the following questions: (1) Can governments slay the dragons of multinational enterprise? (2) Can MNEs slay the dragons of national sovereignty?

8. Explain why you agree or do not agree with the following statement: "Bilateral accommodation offers little promise of any general resolution of the political conflict between the multinational enterprise and host nations."

9. Write a short essay titled "Prospects for the International Regulation of the Multinational Enterprise."

10. (a) Should the United States continue its laissez-faire policy toward investment in the United States by foreign MNEs? Why or why not?
    (b) Should the individual states offer incentives to encourage investment by foreign companies? Why or why not?

11. Has the U.S. investment insurance program stimulated U.S. direct investment in the developing countries? Be prepared to defend your answer.

12. (a) "Multiple tax jurisdictions create two sets of problems." What are they? How do they occur?

(b) Describe the main features of U.S. tax policy toward foreign-source income.

(c) How do the U.S. tax authorities seek to minimize both double taxation and tax avoidance?

13. (a) What is implied by the extraterritorial jurisdiction of U.S. antitrust policy?

(b) Do the lenient antitrust policies of foreign governments place U.S. multinational enterprises at a disadvantage in competing against foreign multinational enterprises in world markets? Why or why not?

SELECTED READINGS

Behrman, Jack N., and Robert E. Grosse. *International Business and Governments.* Columbia, S.C.: University of South Carolina Press, 1990.

Bennett, Douglas, and Kenneth Sharpe. *Transnational Corporations versus the State.* Princeton, N.J. Princeton University Press, 1985.

Coughlin, Cletus C. "Foreign-owned Companies in the United States," *Review.* Federal Reserve Bank of St. Louis, May–June 1992.

Graham, Edward M., and Paul R. Krugman. *Foreign Direct Investment in the United States.* 2nd ed. Washington, D.C.: Institute for International Economics, 1991.

Guisinger, S. E. *Investment Incentives and Performance Requirements: Patterns of International Trade, Production, and Investment.* New York: Praeger Publishing, 1985.

International Center for the Settlement of Investment Disputes. *Annual Report.* Washington, D.C.: ICSID, latest year.

Moran, Theodore, ed. *Multinational Corporations: The Political Economy of Foreign Direct Investment.* Lexington, Mass.: Lexington Books, 1985.

Multilateral Investment Guarantee Agency. *Annual Report.* Washington, D.C.: MIGA, latest year.

Organization for Economic Cooperation and Development. *Trade, Investment, and Technology in the 1990s.* Paris: OECD, 1991.

Overseas Private Investment Corporation. *Annual Report.* Washington, D.C.: OPIC, latest year.

Reich, Robert. *The Work of Nations.* New York: Vintage Books, 1992.

Stopford, John, and Susan Strange. *Rival States, Rival Firms.* New York: Cambridge University Press, 1991.

Tolchin, Martin, and Susan Tolchin. *Buying into America.* New York: Times Books, 1988.

United Nations Center on Transnational Corporations. *Transnational Corporations.* New York: United Nations, February 1992 and later issues.

GLOSSARY OF ABBREVIATIONS AND ACRONYMS

ACP – Africa, the Caribbean, and the Pacific region (Lomé Convention).

ADB – Asian Development Bank.

AFDB – African Development Bank.

ASEAN – Association of South East Asian Nations.

EC – European Community.

ECU – European currency unit.

EFTA – European Free Trade Association.

EMS – European Monetary System.

FDI – Foreign direct investment.

G-5 – France, Germany, Japan, United Kingdom, and United States.

G-7 – G-5 plus Canada and Italy.

GATT – General Agreement on Tariffs and Trade.

GDP – Gross domestic product.

GNP – Gross national product.

H-O model – Heckscher-Ohlin theory of international trade.

IBRD – International Bank for Reconstruction and Development. Also known as the World Bank.

IDA – International Development Association.

IDB – Inter-American Development Bank.

IFC – International Finance Corporation.

IMF – International Monetary Fund.

LAFTA – Latin American Free Trade Association.

LAIA – Latin American Integration Association. LAIA is the successor of LAFTA.

LDC – Less-developed country. Also called developing, nonindustrial, or poor country. LDCs are designated collectively as the South.

MFA – Multifiber arrangement.

MFN – Most-favored nation principle.

MIGA – Multilateral Investment Guarantee Agency.

MNE – Multinational enterprise. Also known as transnational enterprise or multinational company (corporation).

NIC – Newly industrializing (developing) country.

NTB – Nontariff trade barrier.

OECD – Organization for Economic Cooperation and Development. Also used to designate the industrial, advanced, or developed countries and, collectively, the West.

OPEC – Organization of Petroleum Exporting Countries.

OPIC – Overseas Private Investment Corporation.

QR – Quantitative restriction.

RTA – Reciprocal Trade Agreements Act.

SDRs – Special Drawing Rights.

TRIMS – Trade-related investment measures.

TRIPS – Trade-related intellectual property rights.

UNCTAD – United Nations Conference on Trade and Development.

VER – Voluntary export restriction.

INDEX

Abernathy, William J., 94n
absolute advantage, 38
absorption, 421–426, 433; domestic, 378–392
accounting rules, 352, 352t, 366
accounting system, double-entry, 351–352
adjustable-peg system, 408, 408n, 433, 458n
adjustment assistance, 219
adjustment theory, 388, 392–393, 406
administrators, 124–125, 519–520, 590n
Advanced Micro Devices, 247
advertising, 98, 99n
African Development Bank, 542
Agency for International Development (AID), 543
agreements, 24, 187–212, 449–450, 460, 469
agricultural trade, 195–196, 207–209, 262–264
AID. *See* Agency for International Development
Aliber, Robert Z., 463n
Allied Signal, 596t
Allied Stores, 658t
American Selling Price (ASP), 152, 220
Amoco, 597t
Andean Pact (AP), 536t, 538f
Annecy Round, 192t
antidumping regulations, 152–153, 160, 172, 198, 200–202, 238, 240, 242
antitrust policy, 662–663
AP. *See* Andean Pact
Apple Computer, 118n
appreciation, 316n; of currency, 361
arbitragers' schedule, 330–331, 331f
Argentina, 362
arm's length prices, 661
Artus, Jacques R., 420n
ASEAN. *See* Association of South East Asian Nations
Asher, Isaac, 175n
Asian Development Bank, 542–543
ASP. *See* American Selling Price
assets, 352, 358n
Association of South East Asian Nations (ASEAN), 30t, 537t, 538f
Atlantic Richfield, 597t

Australia, 85, 201, 208, 208t, 214f
Austria, 208t, 274n, 275
autarky, 21, 146n, 162
automobiles, 98; trade disputes, 242–245

backward integration, 617, 620
Baily, Martin N., 230n
balance of payments, 22, 23f, 24–25, 34, 321, 350–364, 366, 397–401, 406, 429n, 632–634. *See also* *specific account*; accounting rules, 352t, 366; disequilibrium in, 359, 400, 405; equilibrium in, 359, 405–406; general equilibrium in, 434; world statistical discrepancies, 358n
balance sheets. *See* foreign subsidiary balance sheets
Balassa, Bela, 73n
Baldwin, Robert E., 74, 76, 78, 183n
Ball, George W., 650n, 650
bank draft, 289
banking regulations, 156
bank reserves, 385
banks, 325n, 542, 562n
bank transfers, 289, 293–294, 306t–307t
bargaining-and-retaliation argument, 172–173
bargaining shifts, 639n
barter transaction, 352
BASF, 595t
basic transactions, balance, 359–361, 366
B.A.T., 595t, 658t
Baukol, Andrew P., 556n
Bayer, 595t
beachhead effect, 426
Beatrice, 596t
beggar-my-neighbor policy, 410
Behrman, Jack N., 576, 576n, 648n
Belgium, 4
Belgium-Luxembourg, 28t, 28, 214f
benefit/cost ratios, 637–639, 665
benefits: present value, 634–635; shadow prices value, 635–637
Bergsten, C. Fred, 651n
Bertrand behavior, 183
Bethlehem Steel Corporation, 241
Big Mac index, 338–339
bilateral accommodation, 648–650, 666

bilateral agreements, 199, 449–450
bilateral arbitrage, 299
bilateralism, 448–449
bills of exchange, 291f, 291–292
bills of lading, 290, 290n
Blejer, Mario, 566n
Boeing, 33t, 596t
bonds, 385
book value, definition of, 601
BOP schedule, 402–403, 404f
border tax adjustments, 155
borrower arbitrage, 340–341, 347
borrower arbitrager, 341n
Bosworth, Barry P., 278n
Boward, James, 240n
Bowmar Instrument, 118
box diagram, 61–63
brand competition, 119
Brazil, 201, 205, 362
Brecher, Richard A., 74n
Bretton Woods system, 336n, 456–482
Bridgestone, 658t
British Commonwealth, 189
British Exchange Equalization Account, 316n
British Petroleum, 597t, 658t
British pound sterling, 298, 303, 309–311, 312f, 463n
British pound sterling area, 438
Brodley, Joseph F., 663n
Brunei, 222
Buckley, Peter, 619n
buffer stock financing, IMF facility, 501t
Burger King, 597t
Burma, 222
business residence, 351
Buy American regulations, 154

CACM. *See* Central American Common Market
call option, 296
Campeau, 658t
Canada, 4, 27, 28t, 30t, 74, 156, 194, 201, 208t, 214f, 278, 655, 656f
CAP. *See* common agricultural policy
capital, 68–69; consumption of, 523n; costs of, 586; financial, 69; formation of, 523; human, 68, 73n, 78; long-term, 354; mobility of, 125, 132, 394–396; real, 69, 583;

Page numbers followed by t, f, or n denote tables, figures, or footnotes, respectively.

capital, (*cont.*)
 short-term, 354, 478–480; social, 69; sources of, 584f, 584–585
capital-absorption capacity, 525, 527f
capital account, 354, 357–358, 366, 368–369; adjustments, 406; balance, 368, 405; basic balance, 359, 359t
capital flight, 320–322, 357; destabilizing, 364
capital goods, international mobility of, 125
capital markets: global, 502–506, 509
capital-sourcing policies, 585–587
capital transfers, 583–587
Caribbean Basin Initiative, 543
Carnation, 658t
cartels, 96n
Carter, Jimmy, 220
cash-balance adjustment, 393
cash in advance, 290
Casson, Mark, 619n
Caterpillar, 33t
Caves, Richard E., 612n
Cecchini Report, 266–270, 267f, 268t, 269f
Celanese, 658t
Central American Common Market (CACM), 536t, 538f
central banks, 493–497, 509
centrally planned economies, 6, 555–559, 560f, 562n, 568–570
central planning, 556, 570
Chakrabarti, Alok K., 230n
Chesebrough-Pond, 658t
Chevron, 597t
Chile, 69
China, 30t, 440n, 554–555, 558, 560, 564–570
CHIPS. *See* Clearing House Interbank Payments System
Choudri, Ehsan U., 74n
Chrysler, 33t, 219n, 244–245, 595t
CIS. *See* Commonwealth of Independent States
Clark, Don P., 201n
classical adjustment theory, 392–393, 406
Clayton Act, 662n
clean drafts, 292n
Clearing House Interbank Payments System (CHIPS), 297–298
Cline, William R., 245n
closed economy, 369
Coca Cola, 86, 612, 645
code of fair exchange practices, 457–459
coffee contribution, 448n
cold war, 3
Colombia, 245
command economies. *See* centrally planned economies
commercial drafts, 291–292
commercial policy, 24
Committee on Foreign Investment in the United States, 654

commodity-price ratios, 58
common agricultural policy (CAP), 209, 263–264, 283
common market, 253, 282
Commonwealth of Independent States (CIS), 554
communist countries, 6
Compaq, 246
comparative advantage, 38–39, 73n, 115, 116t, 129–131
comparative investment, 230–233
compensation: adequate, 646, 646n; compensatory, 355; effective, 646, 646n
compensatory and contingency financing facility (CCFF), of IMF, 501t
compensatory financing, 317; by IMF, 459–460
competition, 259, 565; fair, 167; imperfect, 87–90, 88t, 106–107; nonprice, 98–99, 108, 119; perfect, 87, 88t, 88–89, 89f, 130
competitive depreciation, 410
competitiveness, 222; national, 223, 249
Competitiveness Policy Council, 223n, 235–236
confidence, 334n
confiscation, 645
conglomerate foreign investment, 611n
consignment, 292
consumers, 14–15
consumer surplus, 92
consumption inefficiency, 146
contract curve(s), 61, 62f, 64f, 64–65
contraction, 397
Contractor, Farok J., 649n
Convention on the Harmonized System, 222
convergence indicators, 272, 272n
Cook, Victor, 122n
cooperative relations, 649n
cosmopolitanism, 4
costs: long-run average, 93; present value, 634–635; shadow prices value, 635–637
Coughlin, Cletus C., 240n
Council of Ministers, 261–262, 282
countervailing-duty regulations, 153, 197, 200–202, 238, 240
Cournot behavior, 183
Court of Justice, 261–262, 282
Credit-Anstalt bank, 438
credits, 352–353; swing, 449
credit trade balance, 357n
credit tranche, 502
cross-national transfers, 293–294
cross-rates, 299
Cuba, 22
currency, 9, 171n, 298, 303, 361, 448–449, 477–478; cross-rates, 299; domestic price, 305n; foreign price, 305n
currency arbitrage, 298–299, 303

currency areas, 485
current account, 24n, 354, 356–357, 366, 368–369; balance, 359, 366, 368, 405; deficit, 360, 385; net balance, 360, 389; surplus, 360, 385
customs, 7
customs classification, 152, 160
customs duty. *See* tariff(s)
customs union, 253, 281–282; effects, 253–260
customs valuation, 152, 160
customs valuation code, 197–198
Cyprus, 275
Czechoslovakia, 275, 562, 563t, 568, 569f, 570

Daimler-Benz, 595t
Dairy Queen, 597t
deadweight loss, 92, 107, 140f, 141, 157n
debits, 352–353
debit trade balance, 357n
debt buyback, 547
debt crisis, 544–547
debt-for-debt swap, 547
debt-for-equity swap, 547
debt overhand, 547
debt service ratio, 545
decentralization, 565
default risk, 289
defense-essentiality amendment, 216
deficits, 397; disequilibrium, 362, 403
deflation, 362, 366
Del, 246
De La Torre, 122
demand: elasticity of, 135n, 144, 390–391, 416–418; reciprocal, 39
demand bias, 75
demand lag, 117
demand schedule, 309, 322
demonstration effects, 50, 50n
Denison, Edward F., 524n
Denmark, 134n, 272, 274, 274n, 277
Denny's, 597t
depreciation, 316n, 410, 423, 433
deregulation, 297
devaluation, 366, 409–410, 420–421, 427–428
developing countries, 5, 27, 514–523, 524n, 525–531, 531t, 535–547, 550–551, 589–590, 603, 631–632, 659–660
development, 111, 112f
development banks, 542
Dillon Round, 192t
direct investment, 24, 354, 540t, 541, 585n, 586, 601. *See also* foreign direct investment
direct investment fund program, 659
dirty float, 335, 365
disequilibrium, 166, 359, 378, 385–388, 400, 405, 418–419; adjustment, 364–366, 378–396,

disequilibrium, (cont.)
399–400, 405–406, 432–433;
cyclical, 362–363; seasonal and
random, 362; secular, 364;
sources of, 361–364, 366;
structural, 363–364; suppressed,
365; suppression of, 440
disequilibrium deficits, 362, 403
Dispute Settlement Group, 206
dissaving, 232
diversification, 177–178, 178n, 395
documentary draft, 292
Dollar Area, 438
domestic income multiplier, 377–
378, 384
domestic payments, mechanism of,
288
domestic terms of trade (DTT), 41,
45f
Domino's Pizza, 597t
double-entry accounting system,
351–352
double taxation, 660, 666
Dow, 596t
drafts, 290–291
DTT. See domestic terms of trade
dumping, 96–98, 108, 152, 172,
200
Dunning, John, 620, 620n
duopolistic behavior, 183
Du Pont, 33t, 94, 595t
dynamic-random-access memory
(DRAM) chips, 245–247

East Asia, 29
Eastern Europe, 440n, 554–555,
558, 560–564, 568–570
Eastman, 575
Eastman Kodak, 596t
EC. See European Community
Economic and Monetary Union
(EMU), 271, 283
economic development, 17, 22,
528–529; conditions for, 525;
environment-friendly approach,
549; market-friendly approach,
547–549, 548f; obstacles to, 518–
520
economic goals, 26–27
economic growth, 227, 523; cultural
blocks, 520; unbalanced, doctrine
of, 178n
economic integration, 127, 252;
global, 132; international, 129;
regional, 534–539; stages of,
252t; theory of, 253–260
economic interests, 639–640
economic nationalism, 165, 165n,
539
economic opportunity, perception
of, 591–592
economic policy, 18–27, 35
economic profit, 88n
economic reform, 558–567, 570
economic rent, 88n, 611, 612n
economic stability, 21–22
economic union, 253, 282

economic warfare, 22
economic welfare, 21, 163–164
economies of scale, 92–94, 106,
259, 616–617
economies of scope, 95
ECOWAS. See European
Community of West African
States
ECSC. See European Coal and Steel
Community
Edward, John R., 105n
EEA. See European Economic Area
EEC. See European Economic
Community
efficiency loss, 157n
E.I. du Pont, 595t
Eiteman, David K., 343n
elasticity, 144, 413–421, 433
electronic communication(s), 297,
299
Elf Aquitaine, 658t
employment, 17, 21–22, 169–172
ENI, 595t
enterprise, iii
enterprise size, 259
entrepreneurial profits, 100
entrepreneurial skills, 590n, 590–
592
entrepreneurs, lack of, 519–520
environmental protection, 27
environment-friendly approach, 549
equalization-of-costs argument, 167
equilibrium, 359, 378, 399, 405–
406; general, 144–145, 147f, 401–
405, 427, 432–434; immediate-
run, 360–361; long-run, 360,
366; short-run, 361, 366; stock,
427; summary of conditions, 364
equilibrium exchange rates, 44,
311, 312f, 318, 319f, 334–335,
346, 409–410, 429n
equilibrium terms of trade, 53f, 55
Ergas, Henry, 114, 114n
escape clause, 169, 189, 216, 237–
238
Ethyl, 96n
Euratom, 260n
Eurobank, 504
Eurocurrency market, 502n, 502–
505
Eurodollars, 502n, 502–503, 506
Europe, 241
Europe 1992, 265–271, 267f, 268t,
269f, 283
Europe Agreements, 275
European Atomic Energy
Community (Euratom), 260n
European Central Bank, 272, 283
European Coal and Steel
Community (ECSC), 260, 260n
European Commission, 261–262,
265–266, 266t, 282
European Community (EC), 5, 27,
29–30, 124, 127, 155, 181, 194–
195, 196t, 199, 200t, 201, 206–
209, 211, 260–277, 282–283, 529,
531t, 538f, 605, 624

European Community of West
African States (ECOWAS), 537t,
538f
European Council, 261–262, 282
European Currency Units (ECUs),
271n, 271–272
European Development Fund, 543
European Economic Area (EEA),
274–275, 283
European Economic Community
(EEC) See European Community
European Free Trade Association
(EFTA), 261, 274–275, 283, 538f
European Investment Bank, 543
European Monetary Cooperation
Fund, 271
European Monetary Institute, 272
European Monetary System (EMS),
261, 271–272, 283, 484f
European Parliament, 261–262, 282
exchange arbitrage, 298–299, 303
exchange control, 9, 437–454
Exchange Control Area, 438
exchange depreciation, 413–414,
418–420
exchange devaluation, 409
exchange loss, 325
exchange quotas, 445
Exchange Rate Mechanism (ERM),
271n, 272–273, 412n, 483n
exchange rates, 8, 27, 305–308,
310–313, 321–322, 429–431,
447n, 485–490; adjustments,
413–431, 433–434; arrangements,
483–485; base, 307, 322;
controlled, 317–318, 319f, 322;
equilibrium, 44, 318, 319f, 334–
335; fluctuating (flexible or
floating), 308–313, 322, 335–336,
408–409, 429–433; forecasting,
335–339; forward, 324–325, 335,
346; leading indicators, 338;
nominal, 485, 486f–487f, 508;
overshooting, 431, 434; policies,
497–499; real, 485, 487f, 489,
492f, 508; selling, 306t–307t;
stabilization of, 313–317; stable,
313–317, 322, 497; stable system,
497; variable, 9, 171n, 408–413,
433; variations, 346n
exchange restrictions, 9, 585
exchange revaluation, 409
exchange risks, 585
exchange settlement agreements,
450
exchange speculation, 319–320, 322,
346
exchange tax, 442n
Exon-Florio Amendment, 654
expansion, 397
expectations effect, 396, 406
expenditures, 376–377, 421;
switching, 388–390, 421–423
exportables, 388
export balance, 357n
export credits, 540, 540t

export demand, elasticity of, 415
exporters, hedging options, 341, 342t
export financing, letter-of-credit, 290–291
export licenses, 445n
export marketing cost differential, 621
export quotas/restrictions, 148–149; voluntary, 148, 159, 199, 237, 242–244, 249
exports: diversification of, 177; foreign direct investment and, 601, 602f; overinvoicing, 451; underinvoicing, 451
export shares, 225
export subsidy, 182
export supply, elasticity of, 418
Export Trading Company Act, 663n
expropriation, 645–646
external balance, 397f, 397–398, 406
external diseconomies, 163n
external economies, 94n, 163n, 176
external financing, 539–547
externalities, 619, 629n
external trade, 165
extraterritoriality, 642–643
Exxon, 597t

factor endowments, 56–65, 69–73, 80, 102n, 127, 129t, 130, 623
factor inputs, least-cost combination, 59, 60f, 79
factor-intensity reversal, 75–76
factor mobility, 10, 123–127, 131–132
factor payments, 371n
factor-price equalization, 126, 126n, 127
factor-price ratios, 57, 62f, 79
factor prices, 58n
factor proportions, 56n; dissimilar, 58
factor receipts, 371n
factor reversal, 115n
factor reversibility, 44n
fair competition, 167
fair exchange practices code, 457–459
fairness, and protectionism, 167
fair trade, 237, 240
fallacy of composition, 165n
false invoicing, 451
Farmers Group, 658t
FASB. See United States Financial Accounting Standards Board
fast-food chains, 597t
fast-track procedure, 277n
Federal Reserve System, 297, 316, 355, 468–469
Federated Department Stores, 658t
Feldstein, Martin, 497n
Fiat, 595t
financial centers, 299–303
financial transfers, 308, 583–587

financing: compensatory, 317, 459–460; export, 290–291; external, 539–547
Finger, J. Michael, 201n–202n
Finland, 208t, 274n, 275
Firestone, 658t
first-best policy, 281–282
first-difference reciprocity, 237
fixed-rate complex, 411
fixed-rate system, 368–406; French, 171n
floating-rate systems, 433; managed, 408, 412–413; short-term forecasting in, 335–336
footloose industry, 85
Ford Motor Company, 33t, 243–245, 595t
forecasting, 335–339, 347
foreign aid, 540–541
foreign aid policy, 23f, 25
foreign companies, 645
foreign direct investment, 601–607, 623–624, 628–640, 644–646, 652–654, 665–666; eclectic paradigm, 620–621, 624; internalization theory of, 618–620; model of, 621–623, 625; monopolistic advantage theory of, 610–618; as positive sum game, 639–640, 666; statistical overview, 600–607; theory of, requirements for, 607–608, 624
foreign economic policy, 18–27, 35
foreigners, exclusion of, 645
foreign exchange, 289, 294, 303, 305, 308–313, 322, 339–346, 385, 414–418, 443–445, 483–485; futures/options market, 295–296, 303; interbank (wholesale) market, 295–296, 303; retail market, 295–296, 303
foreign exchange gap, 526, 527f, 550
foreign exchange market, 294–298, 303, 335–336, 418–419, 434
foreign investment, 611n, 617–618, 620
foreign investor income statement, 636
foreign-owned companies, 645
foreign ownership, 644–645, 666
foreign repercussion effect, 383–384, 406
foreign retaliation, 183
foreign subsidiary balance sheets, 342–344
foreign trade multiplier, 378, 380–381, 384n, 405
foreign trade organizations (FTOs), 556
forward exchange, 324, 330–335, 346; modern theory, 330–335, 346
forward exchange market, 324–325, 325n; hedging in, 339–340, 344–347
forward exchange rates, 324–325, 335, 346

forward integration, 617, 617n, 620
forward transactions, 296, 303
France, 28t, 171n, 214f, 272, 603, 603t–604t
Frankel, Joseph, 2n
Franklin National Bank of New York, 320
free trade, 21, 26, 162–165, 262–264
free trade area, 253
Fujitsu, 247
full free trade area, 253
full reciprocity, 237, 237n
Functioning of the GATT System Group (FOGS), 206
futures and options markets, 295–296, 303, 325n, 347

Gagnon, Joseph E., 122n
GATT. See General Agreement on Tariffs and Trade
GDP. See gross domestic product
General Agreement on Tariffs and Trade (GATT), 147, 153, 155, 188–195, 198–202, 205–206, 210, 215, 237, 281, 650
General Agreements to Borrow, 460, 460n, 480
General Ceramics, 657
General Electric, 33t, 595t
general equilibrium, 144–145, 147f, 401–405, 427, 432–434
General Foods, 596t
General Motors, 33t, 96n, 244–245, 595t
Geneva Round, 192t, 193n
German mark, 298, 303
Germany, 28, 29n, 35, 131, 214f, 230–233, 234f, 490f, 603, 604t, 655, 656f
global capital market, 502–506, 509
global foreign exchange market, 298–299
global multilateral trading system, 27
global quota, 148; economic effects, 149
GNI. See gross national income
GNP. See gross national product
Gold, Bela, 94n
gold, monetary flows, terminology, 355
Gold Bloc, 438
gold crisis, 470, 470n
gold export point, 315, 315n
gold import point, 315, 315n
gold points, 314
gold standard, 314–315, 322
gold tranche, 460. See also reserve tranche
goods, 83–84; capital, international mobility of, 125; trade in, 205–207
goods-price ratios, 57
goodwill, capitalization of, 584n
Goodyear, 596t
Gosplan, 556

government policy, 19–20
government procurement, 154, 160
government procurement code, 197
government regulation, 9–10
government residence, 351
government revenue, creation of, 442
Graham, Edward M., 651n
Grand Metropolitan, 658t
Great Britain, 9, 134n, 272–273, 274n, 277
Gros, Daniel, 559n
gross domestic product (GDP), 371n, 525–526
Grossman, Gene M., 123
gross national income (GNI), 370, 375–376, 405
gross national product (GNP), 369–376, 405, 525
gross private investment, 230–231
Group of Seven, 488f
Group of Ten, 460n
Group on Negotiations on Goods (GNG), 203, 210
Group on Negotiations on Services (GNS), 203, 210
Grubel, Herbert G., 104
Gruber, William H., 117n, 128
Guangdong, 564n, 564–565
Guertin, Donald L., 651n

Hamilton, Alexander, 175
Hardee's, 597t
Hawley-Smoot Tariff Act, 215n, 215–216
health regulations, 153–154
Heckscher, Eli, 39
Heckscher-Ohlin (H-O) model, 39, 56–81, 113, 123, 127, 163, 528, 608, 608n
hedging, 339–347, 586n
Heller, Peter, 73n
Helpman, Elhanan, 123n
Hennart, Jean-Francois, 619n
Herstatt Bank of West Germany, 320
Hickok, Susan, 157, 157n
high-employment stability, 21–22
highly industrialized countries, 451
high-technology sectors, 117
Himarios, Daniel, 428n
Hirsch, Seev, 79n, 122
Hitachi, 247, 595t
hoarding, 399
Hoechst, 594, 595t, 658t
home market argument, 166–167
H-O model. See Heckscher-Ohlin model
homogeneous products, 105n
Honda, 244, 596t
Hong Kong, 28t–30t, 105, 199, 564n
horizontal integration, 580–582, 581f
host countries, 628–644, 646–647
host economy, 127n
host governments, 644–646

Hufbauer, Gary, 122n, 157, 157n, 242n
Hull, Cordell, 216
human capital, 68, 73n, 78
human factors, 66–68
human-skills theory, 77–79
Hume, David, 392, 392n
Hungary, 275, 562, 563t, 568, 569f, 570
Hymer, Stephen H., 610n
hyperinflation, 564n
hysteresis, 423, 426

IBM, 33t, 246–247, 595t, 645
IBRD. See International Bank for Reconstruction and Development
Iceland, 274n
ignorance, 99–100, 108
IMF. See International Monetary Fund
imitation lag, 117, 131
IMM. See International Monetary Market
immiserizing growth, 72
Imperial Chemical, 596t
importables, 388–389
import balance, 357n
import-competing enterprises, 16
import demand, 135n, 137n, 144, 417–418
import duty: consumption effects, 140–142, 140f; direct effects, 139, 140f; income-redistribution effects, 140f, 141, 160; price effects, 135–138, 139f, 140, 160; protection effects, 140, 142–143, 160; revenue effects, 140, 160; trade effects, 140–141, 160
importers, hedging options, 341, 342t
import licenses, 445–446
import licensing code, 198
import penetration ratios, 226
import quotas/restrictions, 82n, 147–149, 150f, 160, 445–446; outside GATT, 199–200
imports, 14, 376–377; tie-in arrangement, 445
import supply, elasticity of, 418
import supply schedule, 135, 137
import tariff, 134
income: international inequality of, 517, 518f; real, 223n, 379–384
income adjustment, 393; foreign repercussion effect, 383–384; with no savings leakage, 381–382; with savings leakage, 382–383
income equations, 369–371
income injections, 374
income leakages, 374, 375f, 375–376
inconvertibility risk, 289
increasing returns, 90, 92–95, 107, 129t, 130
incremental capital-output ratio, 523, 550, 556n
India, 74, 205

indifference curves, 45, 46n, 55
indifference map, 45
individual allocation, 444
individual residence, 351
industrial countries, 5, 214f, 215, 477–478, 517n, 522t, 538f, 603
industrial free trade area, 253
industrial products, free trade in, 262
industrial property rights, 207, 211
Industrial Revolution, 114
industrial tariffs, 195, 196t
industry, 85–87
infant industry argument, 175–177
inflation, 362, 397, 585; runaway, 362
inflation premium, 396, 430
inflation rates, 338
injury: material, definition of, 238–239; prevention of, 169
innovation, 259, 587, 593
innovation management, 112–113
instability, economic, 17
Intel, 247
intellectual property, 222
intelligence, 112, 592
intelligence systems, 592
Inter-American Development Bank, 542
interbank trading, 299
interest arbitrage, 325, 329–330, 346
interest equalization tax, 468
interest parity, 328
interest parity theory, 325–330, 346
interest rates, short-term, 394–395, 488f
internal balance, 397–398, 406
internal economies of scale, 616–617
internalization theory, 181n, 618–620, 624
internal trade, 165
International Bank for Reconstruction and Development (IBRD), 4, 125, 188, 457n, 541–542, 542n, 549, 559, 560f
International Bell Telephone Company, 575
international business enterprises, 15–16. See also multinational enterprise
International Center for the Settlement of Investment Disputes, 650
International Cotton Textiles Arrangement, 245
international debt crisis, 544–547
international debt problem, 545–546
International Development Association (IDA), 541–542
international diversification theory, 395
international economic policy, 26–27
international economic system, 5–6, 33

international economy, 7
International Finance Corporation (IFC), 542
internationalization, of technological innovation, 588
international monetary crisis of 1971, 471, 481
International Monetary Fund (IMF), 4, 188, 353, 358n, 420n, 451, 452t, 456–461, 457n, 459n, 475t, 476n, 497–502, 509, 650
International Monetary Market (IMM), 296
international monetary system, 506–509
international organizations, 4–5; that provide external assistance, 541–543
international payments, 288–294, 303; adjustments, 368–406, 408–410; centralized system, 300, 301f; decentralized system, 300
international payment system groups, 438
international political system, 2–5, 33
international portfolio investment theory, 608–610, 624
international terms of trade (ITT), 42, 55
international trade, 34; arguments against, 16–17, 34–35; direction of, 1990, 29t; empirical dimensions of, 27–32; features of, 7–10, 34; national gains, 11–13, 34
International Trade Commission (ITC), 217n, 219–220, 239, 241–242
International Trade Organization (ITO), 188, 188n
international trade theory, 623
interregional trade, 29, 34; domestic specialization and, 13–14
interstate trade, 13n
intervention price, 263
intraenterprise transfers, 7, 34
intra-industry trade, 98, 100–101, 104–106
intraregional trade, 29
intra-Triad foreign direct investment, 605, 606f
investment, 259; comparative, 230–233; direct, 24, 354, 354n, 540t, 541, 585n, 586, 601; domestic, 523; foreign, conglomerate, 611n; and national output, 523–525; portfolio, 24, 354; reciprocal, 98n
investment guarantees, 586n
investment guaranty program, 659
investment incentives, 646–647
investment insurance program, 659
investment measures, trade-related, 207, 211
investment missions, 659
investment performance requirements, 646–647

investment policy, 23f, 24
investment projects, 659
investment survey program, 659
invisible trade, 156
invoicing, false, 451
Iraq, 3n, 22
Ireland, 274, 274n, 277
Isaacs, Asher, 215n
iso-cost curve, 59, 60f
isoquant curves, 59–61, 60f
Israel, exports, 29t
IS schedule, 401, 402f
Isuzu, 245
Italy, 28t, 214f, 272–273
ITO. See International Trade Organization
ITT. See international terms of trade
ITT (company), 596t

Jacque, Laurent L., 336n
Japan, 11, 28t, 29, 30t, 35, 57–58, 73n, 74, 116, 118, 122, 131, 148, 154, 156, 195, 196t, 199, 200t, 201, 208t, 214f, 225, 226f, 228–233, 234f, 240–241, 243–244, 246, 302–303, 425–426, 486f–487f, 490f, 529, 531t, 603t–605t, 605, 624, 655, 656f
Japanese yen, 298, 303
Japanese yen area, 438
J-curve, 423, 424f, 433
Jorde, Thomas M., 663n

keep-money-at-home argument, 166
Keesing, Donald B., 78, 78n
Kelly, Allen C., 521n
Kenen, Peter B., 78, 78n
Kennedy Round, 192t, 195–196, 219, 276
Kentucky Fried Chicken, 597t
Kenya, 245
Keynes, John Maynard, 456
Kia, 244
Kindleberger, Charles P., 610n
Kline, John M., 651n
Knickerbocker, Frederick T., 615n
Knight, Malcolm D., 420n
knowledge: superior, 611–612, 624; technical, 588n
knowledge externalities, 181
Kobrin, Stephen J., 639n
Korea, 201
Kravis, Irving B., 78n
Kreinin, Mordechai E., 399n, 427n
Krugman, Paul R., 182n, 184n, 420n
Kuwait, 3n, 29t

labor: backward sloping supply schedule for, 520n;
international mobility of, 124–125
labor force, 66–68
labor productivity, 227
labor theory, 39

LAFTA. See Latin American Integration Association
LAIA. See Latin American Integration Association
laissez-faire, 18
land factors, 65–66
languages, 7
Latin American Integration Association (LAFTA/LAIA), 536t, 538f
law of one price, 428–429
Lawrence, Robert Z., 278n
LDCs. See low-income developing countries
Leamer, Edward E., 74n
learning curve, 94–95
least cost rule, 59n
Leontief, Wassily W., 73, 74n, 75, 75n
Leontief paradox, 73–77, 80
letters of credit, 290–291
level playing field, 237n
liberalization, 247–248
licensing, 198, 445n, 445–446
Liechtenstein, 274n
Linder, Staffan Burenstam, 101, 101n
Linder model, 101–104, 108
liquidity, international, 474–477
liquidity effect, 394, 396
List, Frederick, 175, 175n
Lloyd, P. J., 104, 104n
Lloyds Bank of London, 320
LM schedule, 401–402, 403f
local-content regulations, 155
local participation, 645
local taxes, 86n
location: economics of, 86; effects of transportation costs on, 85–87
Lockheed, 596t
Lomé Convention, 275–276
London (financial center), 300–301, 303–304
long-run average cost (LRAC), 93, 93f
long-term capital, 354
Lorange, Peter, 649n
Louvre Accord, 496, 509
low-income developing countries (LDCs), 529–531, 535–541, 544–545, 546f, 550
Lowinger, Thomas C., 117n
low wage argument, 168–169
LRAC. See long-run average cost
Lustig, Nora, 278n

Maastricht Treaty, 271–272, 283
macroeconomics, iii, 6
Magee, Stephen, 620n
Majundar, Badiul A., 118n
Malta, 275
managed-float system, 408, 412–413, 493, 509
managed trade, 190n, 200, 247–248
management, 68, 132, 584n
managers, 124–125, 519–520

mandatory investment controls, 468
Mansfield, Edwin, 111, 111n
manufacturing, labor productivity
 in, 227
manufacturing companies, 595t–
 596t
maquiladora program, 280, 280n
marginal propensity to consume
 (MPC), 376
marginal propensity to save (MPS),
 376
marginal rate of substitution
 (MRS), 45f, 46, 54
marginal rate of transformation
 (MRT), 41, 54
market adjustment, 365
market economy, 27; transition
 from centrally planned economy
 to, 558–559, 560f, 568–569, 569f,
 570
market efficiency hypothesis, 336,
 347
market extension, 259
market-friendly approach, 547–549,
 548f
marketing start-up/adaptations, 112,
 112f
market intelligence, 112, 112f
market order, 614n
market-oriented industry, 85
market segments, 102; overlapping,
 100–101, 103f
market share, 144
market structures, principal, key
 features, 88t
market transactions, 5
Marshall, 392
Marshall-Lerner condition, 419f,
 419–420, 433
material injury, definition of, 238–
 239
Matsushita, 594, 595t
Mazda, 244, 244n, 245
McDonald's, 597t
McDonnell Douglas, 33t, 596t
McKinnon, Ronald, 559n
McMillan, John, 565n
Meade, J. E., 180n
Mehta, Dileep, 117n, 128
mercantilism, 38
metric system, 222
Mexicanization, 645
Mexico, 30t, 201, 278, 278t
microeconomics, iv, 6
Micron Semiconductor, 247
Micro Technology, 246
middle-income countries, 545, 546f
MIGA. *See* Multilateral Investment
 Guarantee Agency
migration, 124n
Mikesell, Raymond F., 216n,
 449n
Mill, John Stuart, 39, 392
mint parity, 314
MIT, 243–244
Mitsubishi, 244–245, 595t
Mobil, 597t

Mohr, 230n
monetary approach, 398–401, 406,
 427–431, 433–434
monetary authorities, 315–317
monetary base, 386
monetary crises, 470–471, 480
monetary effects, 384–388, 406
monetary gold flows, terminology,
 355
monetary systems: international,
 contemporary, 506–509; national,
 8–9
money, 385–386, 398–399
money incomes, redistribution of,
 450
money market, 340–341;
 equilibrium in, 399
money stock, 385, 385n, 394, 394n
monopolistic advantage theory, 610–
 618, 624
monopolistic competition, 88t, 89
monopoly, 88t, 89–90, 107; trade
 effects, 95–96
monopoly power, 89, 107, 180;
 social cost of, 91–92
monopoly profits, 88n, 90–92
monopsonistic power, 135
Morkre, Morris E., 157, 157n
most-favored-nation (MFN) policy,
 24, 189, 199, 216, 218
Motorola, 247
Mousouris, 122
MPC. *See* marginal propensity to
 consume
MPS. *See* marginal propensity to
 save
MRS. *See* marginal rate of
 substitution
MRT. *See* marginal rate of
 transformation
MultiFiber Arrangement (MFA),
 159, 245
multilateral accommodation, 650–
 652
Multilateral Investment Guarantee
 Agency (MIGA), 651
multilateral trade agreements, 187–
 212
multilateral trade negotiations
 (MTNS), 192
multilateral trading system, global,
 27
multinational corporations, 289n
multinational enterprises, 6–7, 34,
 124, 128–129, 132, 183, 332,
 574–575, 593n, 598–599, 665. *See
 also* foreign direct investment;
 accommodation between nation-
 states and, 647–652; capital-
 sourcing options for, 584f, 584–
 585; challenge to national
 sovereignty of host countries,
 640–644; contribution to world
 economy, 592–593; control of,
 27; cross-country differences,
 620–621; definition of, 575–577;
 economic effects, 628, 629n;

international cooperative
 relations, 649n; international
 regulation, 650–652; international
 trade created by, 580n; location-
 specific advantages, 620; national
 regulation, 648–650; oligopolistic
 reaction of, 615–616; ownership-
 specific advantages, 620; political
 role of, perceptions of, 640–641;
 public policy toward, 627–669;
 tax policy toward, 660–662; U.S.
 policy toward, 652, 663–665
multinational enterprise system,
 577–580, 578f; capital transfers,
 583–587; entrepreneurial skills
 transfers, 590–592; product
 transfers, 580–583, 581f;
 technology transfers, 587–590
multinational firms, empirical data,
 594, 595t–597t
multinationalization, definition of,
 576–577
multiple-rate systems, 446–448, 454
Mun, Thomas, 38n

NAFTA. *See* **North American Free
 Trade Agreement**
National Bureau of Standards, 222
national defense, 16–17
national economies, production
 possibilities of, 39–49
national income: determination of,
 371–376; equilibrium, 405
National Institute of Standards and
 Technology, 222
national interest, 1–2, 11–17, 641–
 642
nationalism, 3–4, 16, 33, 643–644;
 economic, 165, 165n
national output, investment and,
 523–525
national planning, facilitation of,
 440–441
national saving rates, 231f, 231–
 232
national security, and
 protectionism, 174–175
national self-sufficiency, 21
national sovereignty, 2
national tax jurisdiction, 660
national treatment, 24
nation-states, 3; accommodation
 between multinational enterprises
 and, 647–652; external political
 relations, 33
natural externalities, 618–619
natural resources, 65–66, 76–77, 124
Naughton, Barry, 565n
NEC, 596t
negotiating authority, 219, 222
negotiating groups, 206
negotiation groups, 205, 210
NEL, 247
neotechnology approach, 79n
Nestlé, 594, 595t, 658t
Netherlands, 9, 28t, 105, 214f, 655,
 656f

newly industrializing countries
(NICs), 27, 213, 516, 602
new-product phase, 120
new protectionism, 215, 236–237, 249
News Corporation, 658t
New York (financial center), 301–304
New York Clearing House
Association, 297
New Zealand, 12, 85, 208, 208t
Nigeria, 4
Nippon Oil, 594, 597t
Nippon Steel, 596t
Nissan, 244, 595t
nondiscrimination principle, 199
nonexcludability, 619n
nonprice competition, 98–99, 99n, 108, 119
nonresident accounts, control of, 446
nontariff trade barriers (NTBs), 23f, 24, 134, 147–157, 160, 196–198, 202; economic effects, 200t; GATT bargaining, 193; trade coverage, 200–201
nontradables, 388–389
North America, 29, 30t
North American Free Trade
Agreement (NAFTA), 27, 181, 277n, 277–281, 279t–281t, 283
North American Free Trade Area, 30
Norway, 154, 156, 208t, 214f, 274n

OECD. See Organization for
Economic Cooperation and
Development
OECD countries, 28, 29t, 207–208, 229, 517n, 554–555
OECD Europe, 29, 30t
OEEC. See Organization for
European Economic Cooperation
offer curves, 51n, 51–54, 52f–53f
Officer, Lawrence H., 399n, 427n
official development finance, 540, 540t
official reserves account, 355, 358, 366; balance, 359, 361, 366
official reserve transfers, 355, 366
Ohlin, Bertil, 39, 39n
Ohno, Kenichi, 339n
Olechowski, Andrzej, 201n
oligopolistic reaction, 615–616
oligopolists, 96–98, 107–108
oligopoly, 88t, 89, 97–98, 106–107, 614–618, 624; trade effects, 95–96
Omnibus Trade and Competitiveness
Act, 220–223, 249, 654
one price, law of, 428–429
OPEC. See Organization of Petroleum
Exporting Countries
open account, 292
open economy, 369–370; general
equilibrium in, 401–405, 432–433
opportunity costs: constant, 39–44;
increasing, 44–49

opportunity horizons, 591
optimal tariff policy, 179–180
optimal welfare position, 55
orderly marketing agreements
(OMAs), 237, 249
Organization for Economic
Cooperation and Development
(OECD), 208t, 517n, 651
Organization for European
Economic Cooperation (OEEC), 260
Organization of Petroleum
Exporting Countries (OPEC), 31, 180n, 544n
output, investment and, 523–525
Overseas Private Investment
Corporation (OPIC), 659, 666
overshooting, 431, 434
overvaluation, 410, 444
owner arbitrager, 341n
ownership: foreign, 644–645, 666;
state, 555, 570
ownership externalities, 619

Pareto optimality, 126, 162
pass-through effect, 423–426,
424n, 433
patent rights, capitalization of, 584n
patents, 118n
payments adjustment assistance, 499–502
Peace Treaty of Westphalia, 2n
Pemex, 594, 597t
Pepsi Cola, 86, 612
per capita growth rate, 524
per capita income, 102
performance requirements, 155, 160
peril point, 169, 216
Perlmutter, Howard V., 576, 576n
Petersen, Christian E., 202n
petroleum companies, 597t
Peugot-Citroen, 596t
Philadelphia Exchange, 296
Philip Morris, 595t
Philips, 594, 595t
Pillsbury, 658t
Pitzer, John S., 556n
Pizza Hut, 597t
Plaza Agreement, 494, 509
Poland, 275, 562, 563t, 568, 569f, 570
policy, iii
policy coordination, need for, 496–497
policy instrument types, 24
political risks, 585, 592
political union, 282
Polli, Rolando, 122n
population explosion, 515–516, 520–521, 522t
Porter, Michael E., 107n
Porter's model, 106–107
portfolio effect, 395–396, 406
portfolio investment, 24, 354
Portugal, 274n
positioning, 298

Posner, Michael, 117, 117n
Powelson, John P., 176n
power, 2, 33
preferential trade agreements, 275–276, 283
President's Commission on
Industrial Competitiveness, 223, 233
prevention-of-injury argument, 169
price adjustment, obstacles to, 391–392
price competition, 119
price discrimination, by oligopolists, 96–98
price effects, 388–392
price elasticities, 390–391, 406;
short-run, 433
prices: arm's length, 661; factor, 58n; intervention, 263; one, law of, 428–429; shadow, 635–637; strike, 296; target, 263; trigger, 156; world, 146
price-specie flow mechanism, 392–393
price wars, 614n
pricing to market, 425
private firms, 96
private flows, 540t, 541
private interests, 19–20
Proctor & Gamble, 596t
producer subsidy equivalents
(PSEs), 208, 208t
producer surplus, 92
product innovation, 259
production: differentiation in, 129t, 130; functions, 57, 59–61, 114–116; inefficiency, 146; internal
economies of scale in, 616–617;
possibilities, 39–51; product-decline phase, 121, 613; product-growth phase, 120, 612; product-maturity phase, 121, 613; start-up/improvements, 111, 112f; weight gaining, 85; weight losing, 85
production possibilities (or
transformation) curve, 40, 54, 63, 79; derivation of, 58–65
productivity, 227
product life cycle model, 118–123, 130–131, 612–614, 624
products: differentiated, 90, 98–99, 105n, 183, 611–612;
homogeneous or
nondifferentiated, 105n, 183;
intermediate, 105n; introduction
of, 612; new, 116–118; transfers, 580–583, 581f
professional workers, 124
profits: economic, 88n;
entrepreneurial, 100; quota, 149, 150f; windfall, 100
prohibitions, 445
project brokering, 659
protection, 176n; arguments for, 165n, 165–185; costs of, 157–159, 158t; of domestic industries, 441;

dynamic effects, 159; permanent, 176; persistence of, 184-185; temporary, 176; through trade remedies, 237-240
protectionism, 17, 21, 27; versus free trade, 26, 162; new, 215, 236-237, 249
public good, features of, 619, 619n
public good externalities, 619
public policy, 627-669
public subsidy equivalents (PSEs), 208t
purchasing-power parity, 336-339, 338t, 410
pure float policy, 365
put option, 296

Qatar, 29t
Quirk, Peter J., 452n
quota profits, 149, 150f
quotas, 148-151, 160

Radecki, Lawrence J., 505n
rate of exchange. *See* **exchange**
rates
Ray, Anandarup, 636n
reaction lag, 117
recession, 397
reciprocal demand, 39
reciprocal dumping, 98, 108
reciprocal investment, 98n
reciprocal liberalization, 247-248, 248t
Reciprocal Trade Agreements (RTA) Act, 216-217, 249
Reciprocal Trade Agreements (RTA) Program, 215-218
reciprocity, 173-174, 539; full, 237, 237n
regional arrangements, 27
Reinhart, Vincent, 505n
Renault, 596t
research, technical, 111, 112f
research and development, 111n, 589, 589n
reserve assets, 358n
reserve position, 500
reserves, 385
reserve tranche, 500, 500n
residence, 351
resource-oriented industry, 85
resources: international mobility of, 124; natural, 65-66, 76-77, 124
restaurant chains, 597t
revaluation: adjustment through, 409-410
revised antidumping code, 198
Ricardo, David, 38, 38n-39n, 392
risk differentials, 623
risk premium, 395
risks, 100; deliberate assumption of, 592; economic, 592; political, 592
RJR Nabisco, 596t
road taxes, 155
Rockwell, 596t
Roosevelt, Franklin, 216

Root, Franklin R., 621n
Rose, Andrew K., 122n
Royal Dutch Shell, 597t, 658t
Rugman, Alan M., 621n
Russia, 554, 554n, 568, 569f, 570
Rybcznski effect, 72

safeguard provision, 190n
safeguards code, 198
Safeguards Group, 206
Samuelson, Paul A., 126n
sanctions, on trade, 22
Saudi Arabia, 28
saving rates, national, 231f, 231-232
savings, 376-377
savings gap, 525-526, 527f
savings-investment gap, 519
SDRs. *See* Special Drawing Rights
second-best policy, 180n, 180-182, 281
self-sufficiency, national, 21
Semiconductor Industry Association, 246
semiconductors, trade disputes, 245-247
separatist movements, 4
Serbia, 22
Servan-Schreiber, J. J., 575, 575n
services: foreign direct investment in, 603-604, 624; trade in, 82n, 203-205; trade restrictions, 156, 160
shadow prices, 635-637, 636t
Shan, Weijan, 564n, 566n
Shapiro, Carl, 663n
Sharp Corporation, 118, 247
Shell Oil, 576, 658t
Sherman Act, 662n
shipping, 156
short-term capital, disequilibrating movements, 478-480
short-term interest rates: international differentials in, 394-395; real, 488f
Siemens, 247, 595t
sight draft, 290n-291n
Silicon Valley, 92n
Singapore, 105; exports, 29t
Singer, 575
Single European Act (SEA), 265n, 265-266, 283
single-rate systems, 442-446, 454
SITC. *See* Standard Industrial Trade Classification
Smith, Adam, 38, 38n, 174, 174n
Smithsonian Agreement, 471-474, 481
social benefits, 635
social capital, 69, 519
social costs, 107, 635
Somalia, 4
Sony, 247
South Korea, 30t, 199
Soviet Union, 3, 4n, 189n, 554-558, 568-570
Spain, 4

Special Drawing Rights (SDRs), 358n, 460, 476n, 476-477, 480-481, 485n
special interests, 183
specialization, 94; domestic, 13-14
speculation, 298, 319-320, 322, 346; destabilizing, 320, 364; in spot markets, 332; stabilizing, 320
speculators' schedule, 332-334, 333f
spillover effects, 177
spot exchange, 305, 340-341
spot markets, speculation in, 332
spot transactions, 296, 303
stable-rate system. *See* adjustable-peg system
Stackelberg behavior, 183
Standard Industrial Trade Classification (SITC), 105
Standard Oil, 658t
standards, 160; technical, 153-154
standby agreements, 460
state ownership, 555, 570
State Planning Commission (Gosplan), 556
states, external relations of, 2-3
state trading, 96n
statistics, foreign direct investment, 600-607
steel, trade disputes, 241-242
Steinherr, Alfred, 559n
Sterling Area, 438
Stobaugh, Robert B., 122
stock equilibrium, 427
Stonehill, Arthur I., 343n
strategic intelligence, 592
strategic trade policy, 106, 182-184
strike price, 296
Subaru, 244
subsidy, 153, 160, 175n, 197; domestic, 153; export, 182; U.S.-EC dispute, 206-207, 209, 211
superior knowledge, 611-612, 624
supply, price elasticity of, 390-391
supply schedule, 311, 322
surplus, 397
surplus disequilibrium, 403; sources of, 362
Surveillance Body on Standstill and Rollback, 203, 210
Suzuki, 244-245
swap agreements, 469
swap arrangements, 586n
swapping, 325
Sweden, 12n, 156, 208t, 214f, 274n, 275
swing credits, 449
Switzerland, 12n, 66, 208t, 274n

T accounts, 293-294, 303
Taco Bell, 597t
Taiwan, 30t
target price, 263
tariff(s) (customs duty), 22, 23f, 24, 134, 134n, 150n, 160, 446n; ad valorem, 134, 160; compared with quotas, 151, 160; economic

tariff(s) (customs duty) (*cont.*), effects, 134–147; effective versus nominal rates, 142–144; escalation of, 205; export, 182; GATT provisions, 189–190, 192–193; industrial, 195, 196t; net cost (deadweight loss), 140f, 141; optimum, 179–180; protection function, 135, 160; revenue function, 134–135, 160; revenues from, 141–142, 146n, 160; scientific method, 167; social cost, 139–141, 140f, 160; specific, 134, 160

Tariff Commission, 216, 217n

tariff quotas, 147–148, 160

tariff systems: height of duties in, 142, 142n; measurement of, 141–144, 160

Tarr, David G., 157, 157n

Taussig, Frank W., 392–393, 393n

taxation, 586; double, 660, 666

tax avoidance, 660, 666

taxes, 154–155, 160; direct, 155; exchange, 442n; indirect, 155, 660n; interest equalization, 468; local, 86n; road, 155

tax jurisdictions, 660, 666

technical barriers to trade (standards) code, 197

technical externalities, 619

technical knowledge, international mobility of, 588n

technical research, 111, 112f

technical standards, 153–154

technological innovation, 90, 94, 107, 111, 131, 233, 297, 587; antitrade, 114; effects on trade, 113–114; internationalization of, 588; international transfer of, 587–589; neutral, 114; process of, 111–113; protrade, 114; trade effects, 113–114; transfer to developing countries, 589–590

technology, 110, 587; definition of, 587n; international mobility of, 132; transfers, 587–590

technology gaps, 129t, 130–131; international, 114–118, 123n

technology theory, 79, 110–123

Teece, David J., 663n

terms of trade, 390; determination of, 51–54, 53f; domestic, 41, 45f; effect of depreciation on, 433; effect of devaluation on, 420–421; equilibrium, 53f, 55; international, 42, 55; and protectionism, 179–180

territorial tax jurisdiction, 660

Texaco, 597t

Texasgulf, 658t

Texas Instruments, 246–247

textiles, 245n; trade dispute, 245

threshold price, 263

Thyssen, 596t

tie-in import arrangement, 445

time draft, 290n–291n

Tokuyama Soda Company, 657

Tokyo (financial center), 302–304

Tokyo Round, 152, 188, 192t, 195–198, 206, 210, 219, 236, 276

Torquay Round, 192t

Toshiba, 247, 596t

total factor productivity, 227, 227n, 556

Toyota Motor, 243–244, 244n, 594, 595t

TPRM. *See* trade policy review mechanism

tradables, 388–389

trade, basis of, dissimilar factor endowments as, 64–65

trade acceptance, 292

Trade Act of 1930, 238–239

Trade Act of 1974, 219–220, 249

Trade Act of 1979, 220–221, 249

Trade and Tariff Act of 1984, 239

trade barriers, 197, 529, 531t. *See also* nontariff trade barriers; tariff(s)

trade coverage ratios, 200–201

trade creation, 254; consumption effects, 258–259; welfare effects, 255–256

trade deficit, 357n; U.S., 8n, 215, 224t, 224–225, 249

trade disputes, 193–194, 206, 240–247, 250

trade diversion, 254, 254t; consumption effects, 258–259; welfare effects, 257f, 257–258

Trade Expansion Act, 218–219, 219n

trade gap, 526, 527f, 550

trade negotiations, 192, 205–206

Trade Negotiations Committee (TNC), 203

trade policy, 23f, 24; GATT review, 194–195

trade policy review mechanism (TPRM), 194–195

trade-related industrial property rights (TRIPs), 207, 211

trade-related investment measures (TRIMs), 207, 211

trade relief, 221

trade-remedy laws, 237–240, 247, 249–250

trade restrictions, 82n; quantitative, 147–151, 160, 190, 193; in services, 156, 160

traders' schedule, 331–332

trade sanctions, 22

trade strategies: classification of, 532; comparative analysis, 530–535, 533t, 533f–534f

trade surplus, 357n

trade theory, development of, 38–39

transaction cost theory. *See* internalization theory

transaction risks, hedging against, 339–341

transactions, 33, 366; barter, 352; foreign exchange, 303; forward, 296, 303; market, 5

transfer costs, 82–87, 107, 621

transfers, 289; active, 398; autonomous, 398; capital-account, 368; compensatory, 398; cross-national, in ownership of bank deposits, 293–294; current-account, 368; financial, 308; intraenterprise, 7, 34; official reserve, 355, 366; passive, 398; product, 580–583, 581f; real, 308, 366; selling rates, 306t–307t; technology, 587–590; unilateral, 352

transformation curve. *See* production possibilities curve

translation risks, 346n, 347; hedging against, 342–346

translation rules, 342; effects, 342–343, 343t

transnational corporation, 577

transnationalization, definition of, 576–577

transparency, 194n

transportation costs, 82–87, 84f, 107

transportation revolution, 85

treaties, 24

Triad countries, 29n, 604–605, 606f

Triangle Publications, 658t

triangular arbitrage, 299

trigger prices, 156

trigger-pricing mechanism (TPM), 241

Tsurumi, 122

Turkey, 275

uncertainty, in international trade, 100, 108

unemployment, 67n; structural, 171, 171n, 363

unfair practices, 221, 221n

unfair trade statute, 239

unilateral transfers, 352

Unilever, 576, 595t, 658t

Union Bank of Switzerland, 320

Union Carbide, 596t

United Arab Emirates, exports, 29t

United Kingdom, 11, 17, 21, 28t, 126, 214f, 274, 603, 603t–604t, 655, 656f

United Nations, 576–577, 651

United Nations Center on Transnational Corporations, 601n–602n

United Nations Development Program (UNDP), 542

United States, 3, 12–13, 19, 21–22, 27–31, 28t–33t, 35, 57–58, 67n, 68–69, 73–79, 98, 114–119, 122, 124n, 131, 134n, 152, 154, 156–160, 168, 171, 174, 175n, 187–188, 194–195, 196t, 199, 200t, 201, 203, 205–211, 213–237, 238t–239t, 239–250, 263, 276–278, 281, 283, 295f, 302, 342, 358n, 371t, 464n, 467t, 468–470, 486f–488f, 492f, 529, 531t, 543–544, 603, 605–607, 624, 631–632, 647, 648n, 652–667

United States–Canada Free Trade
  Agreement, 277–278, 538f
United States Constitution, 13n
United States deficit, 8n, 215, 224–
  225, 232, 249, 302, 360–361,
  363n, 364, 463–466, 468–469,
  480, 490–493, 508
United States Department of
  Commerce, 354n, 371n
United States dollar, 298, 303, 317,
  461–463, 463n, 480, 494–496,
  509; Big Mac index, 338–339
United States dollar area, 438
United States Federal Reserve
  System, 385
United States Financial Accounting
  Standards Board, 342n
United States Tariff Acts, 167
United States Trade Act, 195
United States Treasury, 316, 355,
  468
United Steelworkers of America, 241
United Technologies, 33t, 595t
unreasonable practices, definition
  of, 239
Uruguay Round, 192t, 203–209,
  204f, 210–211, 276, 281
USX, 595t

Vanek, Jaroslav, 76, 76n
variable import levy, 263
variable-rate system, 171n, 408–
  409, 433

Vernon, Raymond, 117n, 119, 128,
  576, 612, 613n
VERs. *See* voluntary export
  restrictions
vertical integration, 582f, 582–583,
  620
Vietnam, 22
Viner, J., 253n
Volkswagen, 594, 595t
voluntary export restrictions
  (VERs), 148, 159, 199, 237, 242,
  249; automobile, 243–244
voluntary restraint program,
  468
Volvo, 596t

waiting-list method, 445
war. *See* economic warfare
Wayne, Kenneth, 94n
Webb-Pomerene Act, 96n, 663n
welfare, 255–259; economic, 21,
  163–164; optimal position, 55
Wells, Louis T., Jr., 117n, 119n,
  122, 636n
Wendy's, 597t
Western Electric, 575
Western Europe, 27
West Germany, 74, 156, 225, 226f,
  228–229, 486f–487f
Westinghouse, 575, 596t
wheat, price stabilization of,
  314n

Wilkins, 575n
Willig, Robert D., 663n
windfall profits, 100
worker assistance, 221–222
workers, 124
World Bank. *See* International Bank
  for Reconstruction and
  Development (IBRD)
World Bank Group, 541
world economy, 7; contribution of
  multinational enterprise to, 592–
  593; role of Eastern Europe and
  China in, 567–569
world exports, 27–28, 28t;
  origin and destination of, 28–29,
  29t
world imports, 27–28, 28t
world prices, 146
world trade, 28; tripolarization of,
  29–30, 30t, 35
world trade policy, liberalization of,
  202, 202t
World War II, 12n
world welfare, 258

xenophobia, 4
Xiaoping, Deng, 564

Yen Area, 438
Yew, Lee Kuan, 567n
Yugoslavia, 4n, 124n